Georgia

BIBLE RECORDS

Georgia

BIBLE RECORDS

Compiled by

Jeannette Holland Austin

CLEARFIELD

Reprinted for
Clearfield Company, Inc. by
Genealogical Publishing Co., Inc.
Baltimore, Maryland
1998, 2000, 2002

Note to the Reader

his collection of Georgia Bible records contains an itemized list of the births, marriages, and deaths found in approximately 1,000 family Bibles. Included are Bible records of some of Georgia's first settlers and prominent figures, as well as records of ordinary individuals, some of whom migrated to or from other states. Many of the records were sent to me over the past twenty years by the actual owners of the Bibles, while others I copied from Bibles located in the Georgia State Archives and the University of Georgia Library, or from genealogical publications. The collection spans a period stretching from the early 1700s to the 1900s, and because of this range and diversity should be of assistance to the researcher of Georgia families.

Please note that a few Bible records are repeated in the text, sometimes with discrepancies, owing perhaps to two or more readings of the same Bible over the years. All such repetitions are noted by an asterisk, and a cross-reference is provided.

Jeannette Holland Austin

TABLE OF CONTENTS

JOHN M. HEARD BIBLE

Births

John M. Heard 10/26/1830
Rachael E. Heard 1/9/1832
Nancy Mary Emeline Heard
5/21/1855
Susan Elisabeth Heard
10/17/1856
Joseph Curtis Heard 11/20/1858
James Monroe Heard 12/10/1860
Willis Alonzo Heard 12/28/1862
Melissa Ann Heard 9/20/1867
William Franklin Heard
5/22/1870
(faded) - 8/18/1874
Mamie Pauline Taylor 5/24/1886

Deaths

Mary Saturfield 2/15/1858
Curtis Saturfield 8/1853
Susan Elizabeth Heard 8/3/1859
James M. Heard 1/4/1865
Willace A. Heard 1/15/1865
Georgia C. Cline 5/13/1889
William S. Heard 3/28/1881
Rachel Elisabeth Heard 11/14/1895
Mary M. Heard 2/8/1901
John M. Heard 9/15/1904
Nancy M. E. Cline 9/25/1933
Malissa Taylor 1/10/1933
Augustus C. Taylor 1/10/1941

S. E. Heard 12/1/1887
W. D. Heard 2/10/1889
Joseph Roy Heard 12/15/1901
Grady T. Heard 3/8/1903
Annie May? Heard 4/8/1906
John M. Cline 6/26/1852
Georgia C. Cline 2/21/1887
Hirschel E. Cline 3/11/1888

Births

Walter A. Cline 5/15/1893
Ambrazilla E. Cline 6/18/1891
Felix C. Cline 7/18/1928
Lola M. Cline 7/14/1895
Lyda Belle Cline 5/10/1925
Felix L. Cline 1/27/1928
John T. Cline 8/5/1934
Sara Sue Cline 11/1/1939

Marriages

Joseph Heard to Nancy Meaddow 2/12/1826
John M. Heard to Rachael E. Satersfield 1/19/1854
A. C. Taylor to Miss M. A. Heard 9/3/1884?
J. M. Cline to Nannie M. E. Heard 1/24/1886
Job? Heard to N. R. Jackson 11/2/1880
Felix Cline to Millie (faded) 1/13/1924

CALEB MONCRIEF BIBLE

Owner: Michael Kelly, 2508 S. Weaver, Springfield, Mo.

Births

Caleb Moncrief b. Greene Co., Ga. 2/28/1813
Martha B. Vincent, w. of Caleb Moncrief, b. Mecklinburg Co., Va.
4/8/1811

Children of Caleb and Martha Moncrief:

Robert Marshal 12/24/1835
Daniel Washington 12/29/1836
Virginia Martha 4/1/1838
Infant son 4/30/1840
Marion Independence 7/4/1841
William Manoah 4/7/1843
Annie Burchett 8/31/1844
Caleb James 1/12/1846
Infant son 4/21/1847
John Murray 1/16/1849
Drury 7/28/1850
Franklin 6/5/1852
Preston Caleb 10/15/1855

Births

William A. Daniel b. Greene Co., Ga. 12/6/1824
Marion I. Moncrief, w. of W. A. Daniel, b. Lowndes Co., Ala.
7/4/1841

Children of W. A. and M. I. Daniel:

Caleb James Daniel 3/28/1861
William Marion Daniel 8/10/1862
Robert Linton Daniel 2/12/1864
Samuel Sankey Daniel 10/26/1866
Josie Caldwell Daniel 7/11/1869

(Children of W. A. and M. I. Daniel contd.)

Mary Francis Daniel b. McLennan Co., Texas 9/26/1872
Annie Maggie Daniel b. McLennan Co., Texas 9/1/1875
Walter Ivey Moncrief, s. of Robert and Martha Moncrief,
b. 10/26/1866
Martha Amanda Moncrief, dau. of D. W. and A. A. Moncrief,
b. 11/17/1865
India Fleming, dau. of M. M. and H. E. Fleming, b. 7/9/1866
John William Rigler, 1st son of W. S. and W. M. Rigler,
b. 11/2/1880
Jennie Rebecca M. Daniel, 5th dau. of W. A. and M. I. Daniel
b. McLennan Co., Texas 5/26/1882, bapt. 3/17th by Chas. Dobbs 1883
Pattie Daniel, dau. of C. H. Pattie Daniel, b. 1/12/1892
Louise Daniel, dau. of Sam Daniel, b. 8/12/1895
William Hadley b. 6/17/1900
Muriel Grimer Linkenhoger? b. 10/26/1903

Marriages
Caleb Moncrief to Martha B. Vincent 12/22/1834
Marion I. Moncrief to William A. Daniel 12/29/1859
David W. Moncrief to Addie A. Haynie 3/12/1861
Marcus M. Fleming to Virginia E. Moncrief 1/1865
James M. Mims? to Alethia Moncrief 3/28/1865
William M. Moncrief to Julia V. Goodson 10/25/1865
Marie F. Daniel to W. H. Linkanhoger 11/19/1902
Robert M. Moncrief to Martha I. Harrison 12/21/1865
W. S. Rigler to Willie M. Daniel, oldest dau. of W. A. and M. I.
Daniel, 1/7/1880
C. J. Daniel to Pattie Sleeper 10/7/1890
C. J. Daniel to Feby Steinbeck 12/20/1893
S. S. Daniel, son of W. A. and M. I. Daniel, in Brenham, Texas
10/24/1894 to Miss V. V. Lockett
Jennie R. Daniel to David M. Hadley 1/30/1899
Annie Margaret Daniel to J. H. Murphy 12/21/1903

GEORGE W. RUSH BIBLE, Coweta Co., Ga.
Owner: Rosa Lee Newman, 3120 SE 41 Pl., Ocala, Fla. 32671

George W. Rush, s. of William Lassiter Rush and Lucy R. Teagle,
b. 9/3/1829, d. 3/14/1911. Their children:

Births
John Allen Rush b. 3/1/1855	Harris Walter Rush 4/18/1865
d. at 2 yrs. old	Henry Miles Rush 11/3/1867
William Benton Rush 7/2/1856	Tony Parker Rush 6/1/1870
Thomas Levi Rush 4/13/1858	Sim Hilliard Rush 3/10/1872
Rufus Teagle Rush 3/6/1860	Felix Austin Rush 11/7/1874

Deaths
T. L. Rush 2/12/1935	Felix A. Rush 3/2/1936
Sim H. Rush 2/21/1935	Tony P. Rush 9/26/1941
	Henry Miles Rush----

Marriages
John Thomas to July Ann Billingsby 9/1858
John Thomas to Nancy A. Rush 10/31/1871

John Thomas b. 7/28/1795 d. 8/12/1873, aged 78 yrs., 15 days
Nancy A. M. C. Thomas b. 10/29/1836

Births
Henry Thomas 1843	John Thomas 5/7/1848?

2

(Rush Bible contd.)

William L. Rush 3/22/1804	Warren R. Rush 8/14/1834
Lucy Rush 11/31/1806	Nancy A. M. C. Rush 10/29/1836
James F. Rush 12/7/1825	Delila E. Rush 1/16/1839
John O. H. Rush 1/12/1828	William A. Rush 5/4/1841
George W. Rush 9/3/1829	Lucy J. Rush 1/19/1843
	Tabitha A. Rush 12/20/1844

Deaths

William A. Rush 8/3/1843, aged 2 yrs., 3 mos.
T. A. 12/4/1833, aged 3
D. E. 7/2/1871, aged 32 yrs., 16 days.
Lucy Rush 8/28/1878, aged 71 yrs., 8 mos., 28 days
William L. Rush 12/5/1878, aged 74,--mos., 17 days.

James M. Murphy b. 7/31/1857
John W. Murphy b. 9/21/1859
Printis Murphy b. 10/28/1861

DR. JOHN JOSEPH SCOTT BIBLE
Owner: Mrs. Honora Browne, Shreveport, La.

John Joseph Scott b. 10/23/1837 at Scott´s Ferry, Edgefield
Dist., S. C., married Elizabeth Allen of Twiggs Co., Ga.

Births
John Joseph Scott, s. of Sam Calliham and Martha Scott, b.
Edgefield Dist., S. C. 10/23/1837
Elizabeth Allen, dau. of Gideon and Mary Allen b. Twiggs Co.,
Ga., 3/4/1840
Virginia Palmyra Scott, dau. of John Joseph and Elizabeth Scott,
b. Bossier Parish, La., 11/22/1860
Lena Ruana Scott, dau. of John Joseph and Elizabeth Scott, b.
Bossier Parish, La., 4/24/1862
Gideon Allen Scott, son of John Joseph and Elizabeth Scott, b.
Bossier Parish, La. 7/21/1865
Annie Leola Scott, dau. of John Joseph and Honora Cullen Scott b.
8 o´clock a.m., Mon., 5/6/1867 at Red Land, Bossier Parish, La.
Ida Eugenia Scott, dau. of Dr. John Joseph and Honora Cullen
Scott, b. Red Land, Bossier Parish, La., 20 mins. of 5 o´clock
a.m. Tues., 8/31/1869
Lily Parham (Birdie) Scott, dau. of Dr. John Joseph and Honora
Cullen Scott b. at Benton, Bossier Parish, La. 7/19/1873

Marriages
John Joseph Scott, M. D. and Miss Elizabeth Allen, dau. of Gideon
and Mary Allen, by Rev. Robert Martin in Bossier Parish, La.
10/11/1859
Dr. John J. Scott to Miss Honora Cullen of Baton Rouge, La.,
5/13/1866, at res. of Robert E. Wyche at Bossier Parish, La., by
Rev. A. Winham

Deaths
Elizabeth Scott, w. of John Joseph Scott, "departed this life
suddenly in child birth", Bossier Parish, La., Fri. night,
7/21/1865, interred at Salem Baptist Church yard 7/22/1865
Gideon Allen Scott, inf. s. of John Joseph and Elizabeth Scott,
of whooping cough, Bossier Parish, La. 10/31/1865, interred at
Baptist Church yard at Salem, aged 3 mos., 10 days.
Samuel Calliham Scott, father of Dr. John Joseph Scott, of
congestion of the bowels, 12 miles s. of Minden in Brushy River?,
Webster Parish, La., on Natchitoches Rd., 8/3/1873, interred in
graveyard on the ? rd. 1-1/2 miles s. of Brushy River.

ISAAC STEELE BIBLE
From Rev. War Pension, R10094

Births

Isaac Steele 10/23/1732   John Steele 2/27/1780
Grissel Steele 6/10/1750   Ruth Steele 3/13/1782
James Steele 4/4/1771   Isaac Steele 7/18/1786
Michael Steele 4/2/1771   Moses Steele 5/18/1786
Margret Steele 6/28/1775   Jane Steele 9/22/1790
William Steele 1/9/1775

ISAAC STEELE, JR. BIBLE
Owner: Grayum Steele, Ft. Sumner, NM

Births
Isaac Steele 7/18/1786   Rhoda H. Steele 4/1/1823
Cynthia Steele 7/13/1792, nee Cox   Michael A. Steele 3/17/1821
William A. J. Steele 3/26/1815   Ira M. Steele 4/29/1827
Mary I. Steele 5/16/1817   Isaac C. Steele 8/7/1827
John D. Steele 6/7/1819   Moses F. Steele 8/3/1829

Cynthia Steele d. 5/16/1864.   Isaac Steele d. 8/3/1829

WARREN CLARK WATKINS BIBLE
Owner: Sarah Miller Lassiter Watkins

Baker Ewing Watkins and Sallie Sharp Berry m. 4/4/1822
Baker Ewing Watkins and Elizabeth Owens (2d wife) m. 8/2/1860
Their children:-
Baker E. Watkins b. 8/18/1800, Whitley Co., Ky., d. 11/26/1876
Colquitt Co., Ga.
Sallie Sharp Watkins b. 7/6/1805 Whitley Co., Ky., d. Coosa Co.,
Ala.. Baker E. and Sallie's children:-
    Emily Tharsey Ann, b. 2/13/1823, m. William McKay
    Willis Wyckoff, b. 8/9/1824, d. 8/3/1899, m. Sarah C. Fuller
    Nancy Adalina, b. 3/6/1826 m. Jack Sellars.
    J. J. C., b. 1/11/1828 (John J. Crittendon), d. 7/19/1878,
      m. Jane King.
    Frances Matilda, b. 1/8/1830
    Patsa C., b. 9/3/1831, m. Mr. Perkins.
    Jackson Brazil, b. 7/12/1833, d. 12/1/1909, m. Celia A.
      Sherrod
    Warren Clark, b. 3/16/1835, d. 12/27/1890, m. Matilda
      Buchanan and Sallie Elizabeth Miller Lassiter
    Virginia C., b. 2/17/1837, m. William King.
    Gideon G., b. 12/6/1838, d. 11/26/1856.
    Harrison Lee, b. 9/30/1840, d. 8/20/1906, m. Frances Matilda
      Miller.
    Sarah J., b. 11/25/1842, m. Cyrus Graves.
    Harriet M., b. 12/4/1844, m. Spencer Graves of Colquitt Co.
    Rutha S., b. 2/21/1847, died young.

G. W. NUTTING BIBLE
Owner: Mrs. Leora J. Bishop, Okla. City, OK.

Births
G. W. Nutting 10/18/1813   Lafayette 8/25/1844

4

(Nutting Bible contd....)

Mary E. and J. H., twins 1/12/1849
Margaret Nutting 6/20/1816   Margaret C. 8/17/1851
(torn) Nutting 1837   Mary E. and J. H., twins, 1/12/1849
(torn) 1838   Florence J. 11/29/1855
(torn) 11/11/1839   William R. 8/23/1858
Martha J. 11/20/1842   Sirena M. 3/1/1860
J. W. 1/6/1847
(Reverse Page)
Sirena D. Thomas 12/7/1824
Martha A. Thomas 4/1/1848

Deaths

Sarah A. Nutting (torn)   Sirena M. Nutting --/11/1860
Margaret Nutting (torn)   G. W. Nutting 2/9/1862
Mary E. Nutting (torn)   Sirena D. Nutting 3/21/1862

ROBERT RIVERS BIBLE
Fayette Co., Ga., Owner: Adeline Rivers Thornton

John Rivers, Sr. b. 8/25/1775, d. 1/5/1826
Sarah Hunt, b. 12/3/1777, d. 1/30/1859 Their children:-
Mary Rivers b. 9/28/1797   William Judkins Rivers b. 8/21/1813
Joel Rivers b. 2/13/1804   Nancy Couls Rivers b. 12/9/1815
John Rivers b. 8/26/1806   Sarah Rivers b. 11/30/1817
Robert Rivers b. 1/15/1809   James Hunt Rivers b. 12/13/1819
  d. 6/20/1891   Caroline Turner Rivers b. 1/22/1822
Betsy Green Rivers 3/12/1811
Betsy Ann Franklin Rivers, b. 9/7/1823

WILLIAM HARDMAN BIBLE, Oglethorpe Co., Ga.

William Hardman b. 10/1/1745   William Hardman b.1/13/1779
Zillah Hardman b. 7/18/1755   Nancy Hardman b. 5/23/1781
John   Hardman b. 9/20/1773   Salley Hardman b. 8/3/1787
Elizabeth Hardman b. 11/16/1784 Martin Hardman b. 11/1/1789
Martha Hardman b. 9/2/1775   Sarah Hardman b. 9/9/1796
Fanny Hardman b. 3/20/1777

William Hardman b. 5/15/1824
Zillah Hardman, the wife of the above, d. 10/18/1838
R. (Robert) Floyd d. 1/5/1855
Nancy (Hardman) Floyd b. 2/17/1867

Robert D. Floyd m. Nancy Hardman 12/27/1799 Oglethorpe Co.

HENRY MORRIS BUCKNER BIBLE
Owner: Mrs. L. E. Lee Baggarley, Culloden, Ga.

Deaths
Rebecca Buckner, beloved wife of Henry M. Buckner, d. 10/26/1888
James A. Buckner, son of Henry M. Buckner and Rebecca Buckner,
his wife, d.---
John H. Buckner, son of Henry Buckner and Mary Buckner, his wife,
d. 10/14/1841
John H. Fallen d. 6/8/1852

(Buckner Bible contd....)
Births
John H. Fallen 4/10/1778
Elizabeth Fallin, w. of John H. Fallin, b.---
Willace Fallin, son of John H. Fallin, b. 12/9/1804
Jesse Fallin, b. 12/25/1806
Mary Fallin, b. 12/25/1808
Lucy Fallin, b. 6/22/1811
    Note: Much of this Bible torn away.

                    FATIO-BALLINGER BIBLE

Owner: Mrs. Buhl Moore, nee Katherine Fatio Ballinger, dau. of
Phillip Fatio Ballinger, b. 11/7/1912 Charlotte, N. C.,
d. 5/16/1978 Augusta, Ga.

Marriages
Louis Charles Frances Fatio and Glorvina Emmeline America Burch
    m. Washington 6/29/1841
John Carder Pedrick and Mrs. Glorvina A. E. Fatio m. in
    Washington 8/3/1854
Frank Morehead Balinger of Iowa to Florence M. A. Fatio, oldest
    dau. of Louis C. and America G. Fatio, by Rev. Dr. Pinkney, in
    City of Washington, 10/3/1865
Brevet Major John Hartwell Butler, U. S. Army, to Ida de
    Mariateque Fatio, second dau. of Louis C. and America G. Fatio,
    5/30/1867, in City of Washington, by Rev. Dr. Pinkney
Madison Adams Ballinger of Gallatin, Mo. to Frances Marion Fatio,
    youngest dau. of Louis and America Fatio, at res. of Frank M.
    Ballinger in Lee Co., Iowa by Rev. James Woodward, 2/19/1873

Births
Louis Charles Francis Fatio, son of Philip Michael and Theresa
    Fatio, b. City of Philadelphia 11/2/1803
Glorvina Emmeline America Burch, dau. of Samuel and Susan Maria
    Burch, b. City of Washington 3/9/1813
Florence America Maria Fatio, dau. of Louis and America G. Fatio,
    b. at Ellerslie, the res. of her grandfather, Samuel Burch, in
    City of Washington, 4/13/1842.
Ida de Mariateque Fatio, second dau. of Louis and America Fatio,
    b. Ellerslie, the res. of Samuel Burch, her grandfather, in City
    of Washington, 1/18/1844
Frances Marion Fatio, third dau. of Louis and America Fatio, b.
    Ellerslie, the res. of her grandfather, Samuel Burch, in City of
    Washington, 8/21/1847
John Carder Pedrick, son of John Pedrick, b. Marblehead, Mass.,
    11/3/1804
John Carder Pedrick, Jr., son of John Carder and America Pedrick,
    b. in Washington, 5/23/1855
Henry Martyn Pedrick, second son of John C. and America G.
    Pedrick, b. in Washington, 1/9/1857
Frank Fatio Ballinger, first child of Frank and Florence
    Ballinger, b. 5/2/1867 at res. of his grandfather, Judge
    Ballinger, near Sandusky, Lee Co., Iowa.
Ida Fatio Butler, called "Dimple", first child of Major J. H. and
    Ida F. Butler, b. Madison Barracks, Sacketts Harbor, N. Y.,
    3/18/1868
Miriam Pedrick Ballinger, dau. of Frank and Florence Ballinger,
    b. Lee Co., Iowa, 6/29/1869
John Hartwell Butler, son of Major J. H. and Ida F. Butler, b. at
    res. of his great grandmother in City of Washington, 1/21/1870
Ida Fatio Ballinger, second dau. of Frank and Florence Ballinger,
    b. Lee Co., Iowa, 12/6/1870

                              6

(Fatio-Ballinger Bible contd....)
Louis Pedrick Butler, second son of Major J. H. and Ida F.
Butler, b. Hartford, Conn., 7/1871
Jane Adams Ballinger, third dau. of Frank and Florence Ballinger,
b. Lee Co., Iowa, 2/19/1872
Miriam Butler, second dau. of Major J. H. and Ida F. Butler, b.
at North Manchester, Conn., 2/14/1873
Webster Ballinger, second son of Frank and Florence Ballinger, b.
Lee Co., Iowa, 4/22/1873

Deaths
Louis Charles Fatio d. of dropsy, City of Boston, 8/13/1850, aged
46 yrs., 9 mos.
Henry Martyn Pedrick, inf. son of John C. and America G. Pedrick,
d. 9/14/1857 in City of Washington, lived only eight mos.
John Carder Pedrick d. City of Washington, D. C. 2/18/1871, aged
66 yrs., 3 mos.
Jane Adams Ballinger, inf. dau. of Frank and Florence Ballinger,
d. at her father's res. in Iowa, 8/7/1872, lived only 5 mos., 16
days.
Ida Fatio Butler, wife of Major J. H. Butler, d. at her
grandmother's res. in City of Washington, D. C., 11/30/1873,
aged 29 yrs., 10 mos.

Little Mad (Madison) Ballinger, first child of Madison and Mannie
Ballinger, b. in Gallatin, Mo., 4/7/1874, d. 8/14th same yr.,
lived 4 mos.
Little Maddie was b. 4/7/1874
(Ascension Parish, Washington, D. C. 6/29/1875 written on reverse
side.)

                    BENJAMIN F. UNDERWOOD BIBLE
          Owner: Mrs. J. V. Underwood, Siloam, Ga.

                              Births
Benjamin F. Underwood b. 4/12/1819, killed by one of his company,
accidentally, in Dec. 1864
Elizabeth L. Underwood, b. 4/29/1825, d. 12/22/1901.
Their children:
Sarah Carter Underwood 12/28/1845
Margarett Ann Underwood 7/8/1848
George Daniel Underwood 11/10/1850
John Vinson Underwood 11/28/1852
Jessey Hill Underwood 12/27/1854
Benjamin Cowdry Underwood 5/15/1857
William Judson Underwood 10/24/1859
Cornelia F. Underwood 3/14/1862

                           Marriages

Benjamin F. Underwood and Elizabeth L. Veazey m. 1/14/1845
John V. Underwood and Dora V. Holmes 10/11/1857
(Married at E. A. Holmes, by T. J. Pilcher, minister)

John V. Underwood, b. 11/28/1852, d. 8/19/1925

Parents
Edward A. Holmes b. 10/8/1850, d. 1914
Sarah H. Holmes b. 12/26/1837, d. 4/1917

Children of J. V. and D. V. Underwood

Procyon D. b. 9/29/1879   Sarah N. E. b. 9/4/1998
Holmes F. b. 10/6/1881   Bertha L. b. 8/14/1889

                               7

(Underwood Bible contd....)

Ona E. b. 5/5/1883   Cattie F. b. 4/19/1891
Connie Lou b. 9/28/1884   John G. b. 4/7/1893
Roy P. b. 3/24/1886   Ira Lee b. 2/7/1895

ELISHA DAVID STRONG BIBLE
Owner: Gene Strong, Rt A, Box 52, Franklin, La. 70538

Robert Strong d. 5/25/1841
Elizabeth Strong d. 10/30/1844. Their Children:

Births

Marsh Strong 5/14/1806   Frances Strong 5/19/1820
John Strong 12/15/1807 d. 4/20/1892   Sarah Strong 3/9/1822
Creed J. Strong 12/30/1809   Tabitha Strong 6/5/1824
Elizabeth Strong 2/17/1812   Susanah Strong 6/13/--
Magan Strong 11/24/1813   Simmeyan Strong 10/14/1828
Nathan Strong 3/14/18--

John Strong m. Mary Allen 3/10/1844. Mary Allen was b. 4/16/1826,
d. 1/10/1909. Children of John and Mary Strong:-
John R. Strong b. 11/5/1845   Mary Strong b. 1/30/1860
Charles A. Strong--   Parthena Strong b. 4/28/1862
Creed J. (Bud) Strong b. 4/3/1847   Martha J. Strong b. 2/2/1868
Mandy   Strong   b.   9/23/1851 George Monroe Strong b.10/5/1865
Lewis W. Strong b. 10/18/1853
Allen J. Strong b. 1/14/1855
Elisha David Strong b. 5/16/1858, d. 12/2/1956

Elisha David Strong m. Allison Missouri Watson 10/12/1882
    Mother's Family
John Andrew Watson b. 8/20/1833, d. 11/10/1878 m. Martha Ann
Mosby, b. 3/31/1837, d. 8/1/1916
    Children of John Andrew and Martha Ann Watson:
Andrew Hulme Watson, b. 9/20/1868, d. 9/5/1920
Julian Watson b. 11/10/1872, d. 7/14/1947
Allison Missouri Watson, b. 11/7/1866, d. 2/13/1946
Bettie Watson
    Children of Elisha David Strong and Allison Missouri Watson
    Strong:
Albert Mosby Strong b. 7/29/1883, d. 10/1/1936
Infant son b. and d. 5/16/1885
Columbus Allen Strong b. 7/25/1886, d. 1/3/1966
Walter Strong b. 11/29/1889, d. 1/26/1976
Lunie Shrred Strong b. 7/13/1892, d. 1/8/1960
Francis Olney Strong b. 1/11/1895, d. 4/1918
Elisha Hugh Strong b. 7/25/1897, d. 6/21/1975
Lena May Strong b. 5/26/1901
Herman Edwin Strong b. 5/26/1901
Floy Ruth Strong b. 7/18/1906, d. 8/25/1918
John Heflin Strong b. 3/17/1909, d. 6/10/1909

JOHN BEVERLEY SULLINS BIBLE
Owner: Ella Segars Sullins, Murrayville, Ga. 30564

Births

John Beverley Sullins 3/8/1824   Mary Arminda Sullins 2/19/1852
J. P. Childers 3/21/1859   Mariah Roxana Sullins 12/9/1856
Lucindia Childers 3/29/1855   Josiah Sullins 9/9/1858

(Sullins Bible contd....)

Sarah Jane Childers 11/14/1857   Lieuvenia Sullins 6/27/1870
Marien Emanuel Sullins 2/17/1850?
Macey Sullins 2/17/1873
Nancey Ann Lucinda Sullins 2/13/1851

S. T. WHEELUS BIBLE
Owner: John M. Wheelus, 2805 Zane Grey Dr., S. E.
Atlanta, Ga. 30316

Births

S. T. Wheelus 4/28/1859   Hardy L. Wheelus 10/19/1890
Hattie M. Wheelus 1/13/1862   Bufford P. Wheelus 6/21/1898
Nona Wheelus 12/15/1880   Sheron Thomas Wheelus 11/16/1914
Johnnie T. Wheelus 7/15/1886

Marriages

S. T. Wheelus to Hattie Wheelus
Edward Murray to Miss Mary Leonona Wheelus, 1901

Susie M. Murray b. 2/3/1902   Virgie E. Murray b. 10/17/1907
Mary L. Murray b. 9/5/1904   Altie Ellen Murray b. 12/25/1910
Ethel Lee Murray b. 2/17/1906
Addie Glory Murray b. 11/19/1912
Lula Helene Murray b. 1/25/1916

H. L. Wheelus and Emmie Tucker m. 1/4/1914

Deaths

S. T. Wheelus 9/16/1899   Bufford P. Wheelus 10/31/1899
Hattie Wheelus 3/14/1926

THOMAS L. BLITCH BIBLE
Owner: Mrs. Annie Mirian Hearn, Box 367, Riceboro, Ga.

Thomas L. Blitch and Georgia Ann Wilson m. 1/27/1853, moved to
this place 4/2/1853 Their Children:-
Larrah Francis Blitch b. 2/20/1854
Lidia Ann Lavinia Blitch b. 11/19/1855
Georgia Ann Blitch b. 11/19/1855
Virgil Agustus Blitch b. 11/5/1857
William Thomas Blitch b. 7/29/1861
Marthar Rebecker Blitch b. 6/10/1864
Georgia Ann Blitch, wife of Thomas L. Blitch, b. 7/31/1831
James E. Wilson, father of Georgia Ann Blitch, d. 10/29/1864
Georgia Ann Blitch, wife of Thomas L.Blitch, d. 8/8/1869

JAMES STEPHENS' BIBLE
Owner: Mrs. Annie Mirian Hearn, Box 367, Riceboro, Ga. 31323

Marriages
James Stephens and Elizabeth W.-----m. 12/28/1820
Caroline Stephens m. 12/25/1844
Mary Stephens m. 1/12/1845
James Stephens and Rebekah m. 5/--/1790

(Stephens Bible contd....)

James Stephens and Mary, his 2d wife, m. 1/-----

Births
Isaac Stephens, son of James Stephens and Rebekah his wife, b.
4/10/1791
A child, a dau. has died, b. 1/4/1792?
William Smith?, son of youngest S Smith?, b. 1/12--
John Stephens, son of James Stephens and Mary his wife b.
11/11/1795
James Stephens, son of James Stephens and Mary his wife b.
9/8/1798
Hiram Stephens, son of James Stephens and Mary his wife b.
10/11/1806

Births-Deaths
Caroline Stephens, dau. of James Stephens and Elizabeth, his
wife, b. __/14/1821
James Stephens, son of James Stephens and Elizabeth, his wife, b.
1/15/1823
Mary Stephens, dau. of James Stephens and Elizabeth, his wife, b.
3/6/1825
Robert?, b. 4/15/1835?
Rebekah Stephens, wife of James Stephens, d. 1/11/1794
Second child, a dau. of James Stephens and Rebekah, his wife, d.
1/22/--
James Thomas Stephens
James--1835?

Deaths
James Stephens, the father of Isaac Stephens, d. 4/13/1826
James Stephens
James Stephens d. 10/7/1875

JOSEPH DEASON BIBLE
Owner: Miss Mozelle Kerss, Rt 5, Box 202, Nacogdoches, Tx

Births
Joseph Deason b. 6/8/1784   Malinda Deason b. 1/11/1819
Jellico Deason b. 6/2/1795   Milessa Deason b. 5/30/1822
William Deason b. 9/25/1810   Jeremiah Deason b. 10/26/1829
Williard J. Deason b. 11/27/1812 Joseph Collingsworth Deason
Elizabeth Deason b. 12/14/1814   b. 11/11/1827
John Deason b. 8/25/1816   Frances C. M. Deason
                                   b. 3/14/1833
                               Sarah C. M. Deason b. 11/30/1851

Marriages
Joseph Deason to Jellico Deason 8/2/1809
Jeremiah Deason to Frances C. M. Deason 10/3/1871

The following Obituary was pasted in Bible:

DEASON. Joseph C. Deason was born in Pike County, Georgia Nov.
1., 1827; professed religion and joined the M. E. Church, South
in 1851; moved to Texas in 1859, and departed this life at his
home in Rusk County, Texas May 14, 1883. Bro. Deason was very
suddenly called from time into that great eternity to which we
are all tending. On Sabbath he attended church, which was his
usual custom; returned home and at night ate his supper and
retired, as usual, and rose Monday morning at his accustomed
time; and ere he was dressed he fell helpless on the floor,

(Deason obit. contd....)

unconscious and speechless, and in this condition he lingered til 3 o'clock p.m., and, at peace with God and all men, he passed from labor to his reward in heaven. His body was buried by the Masonic order, in the cemetery at Minden Church, where he held his membership so long. He was a good and faithful officer in the Church; hence his place will be difficult to fill. His home was the resting place of the wayworn itinerant minister. He leaves a wife and two sons, and a young lady they have raised, to mourn their loss; but they have the assurance that he now rests in peace with God. Bro. Deason was truly a peace-maker in the community and in the church. `There remaineth, therefore, a rest to the people of God.´"

T. P. TUCKER BIBLE
Owner: Curtis Tucker, Forsyth, Ga.

William Tucker, b. 1810, m. Elizabeth---in the year 1830.
Children:-
Thomas P. Tucker b. 10/2/1833, d. 3/14/1926
William L. b. 8/23/1840   Elonzo B. b. 9/17/1847
Miream E. b. 5/3/1842   Elizaier Amanda b. 12/2/1849
Emerial L. b. 2/2/1844   Charles W. b. 9/23/1851
Addeline L. b. 1/10/1846   Edward J. b. 6/13/1855

Thomas P. Tucker, b. 10/2/1833, m. Georgianna F. Jarvis, dau. of James Jarvis and Louisa Massey, on 4/2/1854. Their children:

Mary Francis b. 10/2/1855   Fanny Elizabeth b. 2/4/1867
Thomas James b. 1/15/1857   Elizor Buler b. 8/24/1869
  d. 1896
Louisa Elizabeth b. 2/4/1859 Ellen Lee b. 4/15/1872
George D. b. 2/4/1861   Sally R. b. 1/2/1875
  d. 4/15/1939
Anna b. 3/11/1864   Ellen Violet b. 4/29/1878

Marriages
Thomas James Tucker to Mattie Etheridge 10/28/1890
George D. Tucker to Sally Hardison
Anna Tucker to Tom Akins
Fanny Elizabeth Tucker to John Wesley Newell of Peach Co.
Elizor Buler Tucker to Tom Akins.

Thomas James Tucker m. Mattie Etheridge 10/28/1890. Children:-
Mary Emmie Tucker b. 10/8/1891 m. Hardy L. Wheelus of Wellston, Ga., 1/4/1914
Esselee Tucker, b. 5/1895 m. Lester Bartlett of Macon, Ga.

SAMUEL H. STEPHENS BIBLE
Owner: Mrs. A. L. Stephens, Rt. 1, Box 126, Decatur, MS 39327

Marriages
Samuel H. Stephens and Sarah Kelly 7/1/1832
Samuel H. Stephens and Susannah Blackburn 2/26/1852
Samuel H. Stephens and Emilh Roberson 1/31/1858
Albert B. Stephens and P. A. Roberson 12/24/1879

Births
Ruthy Stephens b. Va. 9/24/1795
Samuel H. Stephens b. Madison Co., Ga. 7/10/1814 and moved to

11

(Stephens Bible contd.....)

Miss. in 11/1838
Sarah Kelly b. Elbert Co., Ga. 4/3/1813
George Washington Stephens b. Ga. 9/7/1834
Hamilton Capers Stephens b. Ga. 9/5/1836
Caroline Stephens b. Ga. 2/20/1838
Micajah Taply Stephens b. Miss. 6/1/1840
Neisiseia Ann Stephens b. Newton, Miss. 2/2/1842
Thomas Stephens b. Newton, Miss. 12/2/1843
Henry Robert Stephens b. Newton, Miss. 1/28/1846
Sarah Susan Stephens b. Newton, Miss. 4/6/1845
Louisa Blanch Stephens b. Newton, Miss. 3/2/1850
Marittah Stephens b. Newton, Miss. 4/28/1853
Elizabeth Stephens b. Newton, Miss. 11/21/1855

Deaths
Ruthy Stephens 8/1/1839   Thomas Stephens   7/30/1844
Sarah Stephens 12/6/1851   Micajah Taply Stephens 11/12/1850
George Washington Stephens 3/19/1847

GANAWAY DURDEN BIBLE
Owner: Mrs. Beatrice Durden Hanson, Atlanta, Ga.

Births
Ganaway Durden, son of Elisha Durden and Nancy, his wife, was b.
4/6/1826 and Mahaly, his wife, was b. 1/3/1826. Their children:

Mary Frances 3/24/1850   Abijah T. 7/4/1859
Martha 4/28/1851   Katharine 4/21/1861
Nancy Ann 9/22/1852   Warren J. 8/17/1862
Reubin S. 3/22/1854   James J. 8/15/1864
John G. 9/20/1855   George M. 6/6/1866
David G. 10/25/1859   Mahaly Ebalelah? 9/5/1868
                            Andrew Jackson 11/7/1870

Marriages
Ganaway Durden to Mahaly---4/29/1849
G. P. Sawyer to Mattie Durden 5/15/1893

Deaths
Mary Frances 3/17/1854, age 3 yrs, 11 mos., 23 days
Abijah T. 11/5/1860, age 1 yr, 4 mos., 1 day
Mahaly Ebalelah 5/13/1869, age 8 mos., 8 days
Mahala, wife of Ganaway Durden, 1/4/1889
Ganaway Durden 4/21/1902, age 76 yrs.
Katharine 8/4/1862, age 1 yr, 3 mos., 13 days.
Warren J. 6/7/1864, age one year, 9 mos., 21 days
Andrew J. 6/27/1873, age 2 years, 7 mos., 20 days
James J. 8/21/1893, age 29 years, 15 days
Nancy Ann, 10/21/1894, age 41 years, 1 mo., 1 day
Mattie Durden Sawyer d. 2/28/1931, age 79 years, 10 mos.
George Washington Durden d. 11/26/1950

GEORGE W. CHAMLEE BIBLE
Owner: Mrs. John R. Doyle, Jr., Huntsville, Ala.

This is to certify that George W. Chamlee and Sallie K. Palmer
were united by me in Holy Matrimony at Charleston, Tennessee on
the second day of November in the year of our Lord One Thousand
Eight Hundred and Ninety Eight in the presence of witnesses.

(Chamlee Bible contd....)

Signed M. W. Edgerton, Minister. Witnesses: W. S. Palmer; Miss
Sallie Barret; Miss Allie Bryant; R. L. Chamlee; Joseph C.
Palmer; Mrs. Mary E. Carmack-Browder; R. A. Palmer; Tilman P.
Chamlee.

Children
G. W. Chamlee, Jr., b. 8/5/1901 Chattanooga, m. 1931 Mary Bruce
Grandchild Mary Bruce Chamlee b. 10/31/1937 at Chattanooga, Tenn.
Sallie Katherine Chamlee b. 9/9/1944 at Chattanooga, Tenn.

Names, Nationality, Where Educated, Occupation or Profession
George W. Chamlee, AM, Mercer College, Atty. at Law.
George W. Chamlee, 3rd, Vanderbilt College, Atty.
Graduated with First Honor at the Chattanooga College of Law.
Elected to the Tenn. Legislature 4 times from Hamilton County.
District Attorney General 1918-1926; G. W. Chamlee, City Atty
1903-1909.

Great Grand Parents
Father's Father, Tilmon Chamlee, b. 1807 Ga., d. 1887 Canton, Ga.
Father's Mother, Kindress Light Chamlee, b. 1807 Ga., d. 1892
  Canton, Ga.
Mother's Father, John Robertson, b. 1810 S. C., d. 1885 Dawson,
  Ga.
Mother's Mother, Eliza Robertson, b. 1812, d. 1889 Dawson, Ga.

Grand Parents
Father's Father, G. W. CHamlee, b. 1840 Canton, Ga., d. 1923
  Atlanta, Ga.
Father's Mother, Malinda Robertson Chamlee, b. 1844 Canton, Ga.,
  d. 1927 Atlanta, Ga.
Mother's Father, W. P. Palmer, b. 1826 Danville, Va., d. 1909,
  Charleston, Tenn.
Mother's Mother, Eliza Palmer, b. 1830 Athens, Tenn., d. 1899
  Charleston, Tenn.

Parents
G. W. Chamlee, Jr., b. 1872 Canton, Ga., d.---
Sallie K. Chamlee b. 1873 Cleveland, Tenn., d. 8/21/1951
Knoxville, Tenn.

Great Great Grandfather	Wife
William Chamlee b. 1776	
Tilmon Chamlee b. 1807	Kindres Light
George W. Chamlee b. 1840	Malinda Robertson
George W. Chamblee, Jr. b. 1872	Sallie Palmer
George W. Chamlee, Jr., 3rd, b. 1901	Mary Bruce

Names, Cause of Death, Where Buried, Vault, Monument or Headstone
Tilmon Chamlee, Dropsy, Canton, Ga., family grave
George W. Chamlee, old age, Atlanta, Ga., 1923
Malinda Chamlee, old age, Atlanta, Ga., 1927
Victory Chamlee Keith?, 85, Selma, Cal.
John B. Chamlee, 84, Atlanta, Ga.
Tilmon Perkins Chamlee, 36, Chattanooga, Forest Hill
Mrs. J. H. Johnston, old age, 82, Atlanta, Ga.
Allen K. Chamlee, Sparts, Ga.
Alx. S. Chamlee, Bartow, Ga.
Jerry W. Chamlee, Canton, Ga.
Emery Chamlee, baby 6 mos., Canton, Ga., family grave

13

E. H. WHITE BIBLE
Owner: Mrs. John Sewell, Hartwell, Ga.

Parents
Father- E. H. White b. 6/15/1856 Hart Co., Ga., d. 12/9/1910 Hart
Co., Ga. Mother- Mary A. Duncan, b. 4/1/1856 Hart Co., Ga., d.
7/6/1913, Hart Co., Ga. They were married 11/27/1879 at O. M.
Duncan's by L. W. Stephens.

Children
James Walton White b. 10/19/1880 Hart Co., Ga. m. 10/17/1917
Hattie Ophelia Patterson, d. 4/19/1927
Annie Gertrude White, b. 4/15/1882 Hart Co., Ga., m. 11/15/1906
J. N. Mayes, d. 10/30/1938
Oliver C. White, b. 1/18/1885 Hart Co., Ga., d. 1/24/1888
Neal J. White, b. 9/27/1886 Hart Co., Ga., d. 9/27/1891
John A. White, b. 2/11/1889 Hart Co., Ga., m. 12/28/1922
Indianapolis Mary Lee Dinwiddie.
W. Sanford White, b. 2/9/1891 Hart Co., Ga. m. Gene Sims
Sarah K. White, b. 10/2/1895 Hart Co., Ga. m. Vane G. Hawkins
3/2/1927

Miscellaneous
James F. White and Martha J. Cobb m. 9/15/1870
Eppy H. White and Fannie E. Crawford m. 5/5/1904
Rolland B. Johnson d. 6/28/1857, age 22 yrs., 4 mos., 24 days.
Neal Johnson Father M. R. White d. 6/13/1864, age 62
Mildred E. Jones sister of J. F. White d. 9/5/1865, age 45 yrs.
James Cobb d. 2/24/1876
Mary Cobb d. 2/22/1886
Martha J. White, wife of J. F. White, d. 1/29/1901

Grandparents
Father's Father, James F. (Franklin) White b. 9/15/1826 Hart Co.,
Ga., d. 5/1/1898 Hart Co., Ga.
Father's Mother, Martha R. White, b. 3/16/1833 Hart Co., Ga., d.
5/23/1870 Hart Co., Ga.
Children
Eppy H. White b. 6/15/1856 Hart Co., Ga. m. 11/27/1870 Mary A.
Duncan, d. 12/9/1910
Neal J. White, b. 4/17/1858 Hart Co., Ga., m. 12/17/1885 Nora K.
Duncan
John M. White, b. 2/21/1885 Hart Co,, Ga., d. 12/3/1856
Martin White, b. 2/21/1855, d. 12/3/1856
Sarah K. White, b. 1/10/1860 Hart Co., Ga. m. 12/13/1888 L. H.
Cobb, d. 12/17/1895
Ann H. White, b. 7/24/1861 Hart Co., Ga. m. 3/19/1891 Lucinda F.
Moss
Thomas E. V. White, b. 3/7/1866 Hart Co., Ga. m. 10/9/1898 Clara
M. Myers
Mary M. White, b. 3/16/1869 Hart Co., Ga., d. 7/7/1870
Malissa M. White, b. 11/26/1871 Hart Co., Ga., GJames Rayford Gilmer
Orris E. Edge and Alma Louise Mahaffey 9/19/1941
Robert L. Edge and Clifford Patterson 6/1943
James P. Edge and Anita (Reurich) 7/1950
Albert R. Edge and Daniel F. Mann 7/6/1940

Deaths
Carry Lela Edge 1/19/1887   Robert Louis Edge 6/2/1962
Dora Etta Edge 8/15/1912   James Pomeroy Edge 8/31/1965
Henry Tipton Edge 12/23/1913   Isabella E

(White Bible contd....)

Births, John Eppy Mayes Family
James Edward Mayes 4/8/1941   Billy Frank Mayes 5/20/1943

Grandparents
Mother´s Father, E. H. White, b. 6/15/1856 Hart Co., Ga., d.
12/9/1910 Hart Co., Ga.
Mother´s Mother, Mary A. Duncan, b. 4/4/1856 Hart Co., Ga., d.
7/6/1883 Hart Co., Ga.

Parents
Father, J. N. Mayes, b. 6/23/1859 Banks Co., Ga.
Mother, Gertrude White, b. 4/15/1882 Hart Co., Ga., d. 10/30/1938
They were married 11/15/1906 at E. H. White´s by Rev. T. M.
Galphin.

Children
John Eppy Mayes, b. 11/26/1907 Banks Co., Ga. m. 11/19/1938
Lizzie Mae Campbell, d. 5/20/1963.
Mary E. Mayes, b. 12/31/1909 Banks Co., Ga., m. 3/10/1932 John
Payne Sewell.

Miscellaneous
Mary Mayes and John P. Sewell Family births:
Sarah Ann Sewell b. 1/20/1933   Peggy Mae Sewell b. 12/31/1943
Barbara Jean Sewell 6/12/1935   James Charles Sewell 4/12/1946

Grandparents
Father´s Father, E. H. White, b. 6/15/1856 Hart Co., Ga., d.
12/9/1910 Hart Co., Ga.
Father´s Mother, Mary A. Duncan, b. 4/4/1845 Hart Co., Ga., d.
7/6/1903 Hart Co., Ga.
Mother´s Father, G. M. Patterson, b. 8/15/1862 Banks Co., Ga., d.
1/21/1924 Banks Co., Ga.
Mother´s Mother, Elizabeth Mayes, b. 5/9/1863 Banks Co., Ga., d.
4/17/1952 Hart Co., Ga.

Parents
Father, James Walton White, b. 10/19/1880 Hart Co., Ga., d.
4/19/1927 Hart Co., Ga.
Mother, Hattie Ophelia Patterson, b. 12/10/1890 Banks Co., Ga.,
d. 12/28/1919 Hart Co., Ga.
They were married 10/17/1917 at G. M. Patterson´s by Rev. T. M.
Galphin.

Children:
Mary E. White, b. 10/21/1918 Hart Co., Ga. m. Gene Albrecht.
Ruth P. White, b. 2/6/1920 Hart Co. m. Francis Bulrice.
Reba Johnson White, b. 2/6/1920 Hart Co. d. 2/6/1920
Ruby Duncan White, b. 2/6/1920 Hart Co., d. 5/1/1920
John Walton White, b. 12/5/1922 Hart Co., Ga.
Helen Ophelia White, b. 4/23/1924 Hart Co., Ga. m. Walton Osborn.
William Mayes White, b. 11/10/1926 Hart Co., Ga., d. 11/29/1926.

JOHN E. CHISOLM BIBLE
Owner: Charles Clay Grace, 113 E. Park Ave.
Greenwood, Ms 38930

Births
John E. Chisolm 11/17/1828   Grace F. Chisolm 9/28/1873
Mary N. Chisolm 6/6/1835?   Munsen M. Chisolm 9/2/1876
Ann L. Chisolm 11/30/1851   Sarah Chisolm 1/5/1881

15

(Chisolm Bible contd....)

William J. M. Chisolm 1/17/1853
Benjamin B. Chisolm 2/25/1855
Harvey C. Chisolm 10/26/1856
Mary T. Chisolm 12/24/1858
Emerson E. Chisolm 2/6/1861
Julia J. Chisolm 1/29/1865
John T. Chisolm 1/29/1865
Emily M. Chisolm 10/2/1867

Marvin Stanley Chisolm 12/5/1882
Walter Lee Chisolm 3/15/188--
Rosco Ervin Chisolm 12/15/1886
Rufus Chisolm 5/1/188-
Carie Lilla Chisolm 2/10/1895?
Grace Willard Chisolm 7/18/1899
Mary Eileene Chisolm 9/25/1900

Deaths
Mary T. Chisolm 6/13/1861
Ann T. Chisolm 10/17/1867
John E. Chisolm 9/29/1886
Munson M. Chisolm 8/26/1905
William J. M. Chisolm 8/26/1905

Julia Chisolm Perry 3/17/1919
Mary N. Chisolm 4/2/1919
Grace T. Chisolm 9/10/1927
Henry Clay Chisolm 12/14/1936
Sarah Victoria Chisolm 1/4/1924

Memoranda
William J. M. Chisolm b. 10/12/1797
J. T. CHisolm b. 7/19/1803
William J. M. Chisolm d. 3/21/1851
J. T. CHisolm d. 6/26/1883

Children of H. C. Chisolm and Sara V. Moore:-
Sarah Chisolm Lockard d. 7/25/1958   Carrie Chisolm Benton
Roscoe Chisolm d. 2/15/1952   Grace Williard Chisolm Duke
Narvub Chisolm d. 3/1952   Eileen Mary Chisolm Grace

Marriages
B. B. Chisolm and Emma H. Thompson 12/13/1877
H. C. Chisolm and S. V. Moore 2/26/1880
W. J. M. Chisolm and L. A. Thompson 12/19/1881
Sarah Chisolm to Albert Lockard 4/1/1900
Marvin Chisolm to Dora Belle Bozeman 1/1/1910
Roscoe Chisolm to Myrtle Carter 6/22/1912
Carrie Chisolm to Thomas Gaston Benton 6/2/1914
Roscoe C. Chisolm to Betty F. Baker 12/12/1920
Eileene Chisolm to Frank Grace 11/26/1924
Grace Williard Chisolm to Dr. W. M. Duke 8/22/1927

G. W. RAY BIBLE
Owner: Mrs. Harvey L. Seymour
2875 Dellinger Dr., N. E., Marietta, Ga. 30062

Elizabeth Ann Brown b. 5/11/1840
G. W. Ray and Elizabeth A. Brown m. 1/5/1857
Excelion Ray b. 8/3/1859
Jan J. Ray b. 9/21/1861
Ida Isabell Ray b. 9/21/1861
John Elmer Ray b. 12/27/1863
George Washington Ray b. 8/9/1835, d. 5/31/1865, age 29 years, 8
mos., 22 days.
Elizabeth Ray m. N. A. Painter 3/25/1867.

I. D. McCORMICK BIBLE
Owner: Mrs. Harvey L. Seymour, Marietta, Ga. 30062

I. D. McCormick b. Jefferson Co., Ill. 10/9/1854
Miss Ida I. Ray, his wife, b. Clark Co., Ind. 9/21/1861
Lulu R. McCormack,, b. 10/6/1876 (sp. of surname changes now)

16

(I. D. McCormick Bible contd...)

Susie L. McCormack b. 11/20/1879
Johney R. McCormack b. 4/14/1885   Inf. dau. b. 12/28/1890
Harry J. McCormack b. 3/24/1887   Ruby M. McCormack b. 5/7/1892
Margaret T. McCormack b. 3/18/1889 Elmer L.McCormack b.7/14/1894

Deaths
Inf. dau. 12/29/1890   Lulu R. Bellville 11/3/1955
Harry   J. McCormack 7/12/1910   Mrs. Susie L. Madden 2/2/1975
Isaac D. McCormack 1/30/1940   Wenatchee, Washington
Ida   I. McCormack 7/16/1942   Maxine McC. Bishop 9/18/1979
Johney McCormack 4/6/--   Jonesboro, Ark.
Ruby May Martin 2/25/1953   Margaret T. McCormack
Elmer Lewis McCormack 5/20/1955   10/30/1970
                                   Lillie Grady McCormack
                                     9/13/1936, Brookland, Ark.

ELDRIDGE H. WHITEHEAD BIBLE
Owner: Ms. Elizabeth Shelton
853 Iveywood Drive, Athens, Ga.

Births
Eldridge H. Whitehead 12/14/1809   Mary A. E. Whitehead 3/16/1840
Sarah Mathews 4/7/1813   John C. Whitehead 1/25/1842
Eliza C. Whitehead 11/22/1830   Marcus J. Whitehead 4/8/1843
William J. Whitehead 4/1/1834   Francis R. Whitehead 2/25/1845
Charles T. Whitehead 9/7/1835   Sarah M. Whitehead 2/11/1847
George W. M. Whitehead 9/7/1835   Eldridge M. Whitehead
                                     11/26/1848
                                   Asbury P. Whitehead 9/23/1950

J. N. Ross 11/7/1855
Lucy Whitehead Ross 3/13/1866

Tommie Bascomb Ross b. 2/7/1885

Marriages
E. H. Whitehead and Sarah Mathews 2/9/1830
J. N. Ross and Lucy Whitehead 9/30/1883
At the res. of C. T. Whitehead by H. C. Appleby, Jackson Co. Ga.

Deaths
Sarah Mathews Whitehead 1/15/1871, consumption
Asbury Parks Whitehead 3/1881, chronic disb/
E. H. Whitehead 8/15/1889 of paralysis
Marcus J. Whitehead dropped dead 3/31/1890
Charles T. Whitehead 2/28/1906 of acute?
John C. Whitehead 3/24/1910 pneumonia
Mrs. E. C. Ross 5/31/1904
Mr. T. L. Ross 9/10/1910
Lucy Whitehead Ross 5/15/1921
Mr. J. N. Ross 4/9/1928 at his home on Sycamore St. in Jefferson,
72 yrs., 5 mos., 2 days.
Tommie Bascomb Ross 7/4/1885

MRS. HOMER ENGLAND BIBLE
Gainesville, Ga.

W. C. England b. 2/15/1908
B. M. England b. 10/9/1911

(England Bible contd....)

M. L. England b. 12/12/1912
Mattie L. England b. 7/1913, d. 7/16/1954
W. A. England (Gus) b. 4/4/1885, d. 11/1/1914
E. J. England b. 1/4/1894, d. 5/23/1921
V. H. England b. 11/19/1890, d. 7/24/1922
V. X. England b. 3/12/1856
Eliza (Akins) England b. 4/13/1866
J. F. -James Fernando England b. 11/12/1889, d. 7/17/1954
A. R. ENgland b. 3/19/1892
R. J.-J. R. England b. 4/20/1896
M. R. England b. 8/23/1898
Arnie England b. 6/12/1900
J. Homer England b. 4/19/1908
Pat England b. 1/20/1906
Ages up to date: 1905
W. A. England, age 23   A. R. England, age 16
J. F. England, age 19   E. J. England, age 14
V. L. England, age 18   J. R. England, age ?

William J. Hunter b. 4/26/1854, d. 12/25/1909
Nancy L. Hunter b. 3/25/1857
Margarett E. Hunter b. 1/20/1879 m. Virge Hunter
Frances M. Hunter b. 4/22/1881
Nellie Adder Hunter b. 10/21/1883, d. 8/22/1968, m. Andrew T.
  England
Jasper A. Hunter b. 3/1/1886, d. 6/4/1887
James W. Hunter b. 5/10/1888, d. 6/5/1888
Marvin C. Hunter b. 12/14/1889
Emma L. Hunter b. 3/19/1892
Grady J. Hunter b. 7/16/1895
Burion W. Hunter b. 9/2/1879
Andrew Thompson England b. 11/1887 m. 7/30/1903, d. 3/13/1954
Nellie (Hunter) England b. 10/21/1883, d. 8/22/1968
Ernest Mado England b. 6/27/1907, d. 2/22/1962
Waco Francis England b. 4/7/1912, d. 6/22/1977
Burie William England b. 7/3/1904, d. 2/3/1977
Thelma Cannie England b. 7/27/1909, living, Gainesville, Ga.

Mado England Family:
Margarett Elizabeth England m. B. L. Lipscombe 5/26/1955, b.
  7/31/1931
William Ralph England b. 6/27/1933 m. Betty Carter
James Andrew England m. Mildred---
Ernest Willie England b. 5/12/1939 m. Lorene---
Clearnce Lenard England b. 10/26/1941
Brenda
Guy
Lawrence Stanley m.---Marchbanks
Richard Dwight m. Ruth---
Thelma England m. Robert Motes 6/1935
dau. Lurline Muzette Motes b. 6/27/1935, d. 8/3/1935

Burie England Family:
Jennette b. 3/9/1936 m. Royce Collins on 1/8/1955
Mildred b. 12/22/1939
Janie Nell b. 2/22/1941
Johnny
Linda

LAWRENCE TONDEE ELKINS BIBLE
Owner: Mrs. Mary E. Amason Newton, Savannah, Ga.

Births
Lawrence Tondee Elkins, son of Selina Ann and Harmon Elkins,
b, 2/5/1827
Margaret Frances Wilson, dau. of Eliza Ann and Francis Wilson,
b. 7/22/1831. Their children:

James Wilson Elkins b. 12/4/1851   Georgia Bartow Elkins
Anna Alberta Elkins 3/11/1854   b. 12/14/1861
Selina Maria Elkins b. 9/20/1856   Lawrence Edward Elkins
Almer Eliza Elkins b. 1/5/1859   b. 8/13/1864
William Franklin Elkins b. 5/7/1867   Ward Habersham Elkins
                                            b. 11/2/1872
Veleta Newton, dau. of Alma Eliza and William Newton, b.
  1/25/1879
Eliet Elkins, son of James Wilson and Martha Ann Elkins, b.
  9/16/1879
James Albert Elkins b. 5/7/1882
Rufus Newton b. 2/25/1881
Angus Emin Newton b. 1/25/1884
Laura Alberta Defoor b. 12/2/1882
Frances Caroline Defoor b. 12/28/1884
Herman Shearouse
William Newton b. 12/30/1854
Prat Leroy Elkins b. 5/19/1888
Fannie Alma Newton b. 3/8/1891
Vetta Gertrude Futrell b. 9/12/1899
Hugh Preston Futrell b. 9/22/1901
Robert Ira Futrell b. 9/20/1903

Marriages
Lawrence Tondee Elkins to Margaret Frances Wilson 10/2/1850
James Wilson Elkins to Martha Ann Newton 1/18/1877
William Newton to Alma Eliza Elkins 9/22/1977
Barnard Nesbiet Shearouse to Selina Marie Elkins 4/15/1880
David I. Defoor to Georgia Bartow Elkins 2/8/1882
Lawrence E. Elkins to Ida F. hunter 2/16/1887
William Franklin Elkins to Tallulah F. Taylor 4/2/--
Hugh Preston Futrell to Jessie May Long 6/10/1922

Deaths
Anna Alberta Elkins 7/7/1867   James W. Elkins 11/31/1881
Selina Ann Guyton 8/25/1856   James Wilson 4/15/1876
Eliza Ann Wilson 10/3/1865   David I. DeFoor 7/19/1886
Georgia Ann Barnett 1/4/1848   Ira D. Futrell 6/6/1903
Charles Tondee 1/4/--   Margaret Frances Elkins 7/25/1912
Eliet Elkins 5/11/1880   William Newton 6/12/1922
Lawrence T. Elkins 3/9/1881

                    LARKIN STRICKLAND BIBLE
              Owner: Mrs. Harrison Latimer Anderson
              163 Hope St., N. W., Marietta, Ga. 30064

Births
Larkin Strickland 5/1/1799   James Larkin Strickland 12/30/1842
Margarett Strickland 7/3/1799   Mary Elisabeth Strickland 6/14/1845
James D. Strickland 2/8/1822   Sarah M. Strickland 11/3/1855
Julius A. Strickland 5/14/1823   W. C. Strickland 4/4/1857
Mary Strickland 12/29/1824   J. L. Strickland 1/7/1859
Sarah Ann Strickland 8/31/1826   M. J. Strickland 6/30/1868

(Strickland Bible contd....)

Elizabeth Strickland 4/3/1828   C. D. Strickland 1/19/1871
John Carliss Strickland 1/1/1830   Stephen Bishop 6/28/1825
Nancy Strickland 8/3/1831   Enoch D. Bishop 10/27/1848
David Loyd Strickland 3/20/1833   William L. Bishop 10/21/1849
William F. Strickland 10/29/1834   Mary Jane Bishop 8/30/1851
Larkin M. Strickland 1/1/1837   Sarah Marget Bishop 4/8/1853
Leroy Strickland 8/7/1822   John E. Bishop 7/23/1855
George Washington Strickland 6/1/1838
Florance Virgia Strickland 11/3/1850
Margery E. Bishop 8/19/1858
David L. Bishop 5/2/1861
Stephen M. Bishop 8/29/1862
Lanorah and Derah Strickland 7/4/1869
Ollie Strickland 3/17/1873

Marriages
Larkin Strick,and and Margarett 3/13/1821
James P. Strickland and Margarett C. Lawrence 3/27/1842
Sarah Ann Strickland and William Belcher 5/9/1844
Stephen Bishop and Elizabeth Strickland 12/16/1847
Charley J. T. Cambell and Nancy Strickland 8/22/1850
J. C. Strickland and A. S. Hudson 12/21/1854

Deaths
Leroy Strickland 9/10/1839
Larkin Strickland 5/11/1848
Julius A. Strickland, in Camden Co., Ga., 2/6/1851
George Washington Strickland 7/7/1860
Jefferson Strickland 1/2/1862
Madison Strickland 1/19/1862
Margrett Strickland 5/21/1869 near Hickory Flat, bur. Standing
    Rock Church, Chambers Co., Ala.
David L. Strickland 4/31/1893, bur. Bethel Church, Chambers Co.,
    Ala.
Elizabeth Bishop 12/17/1906 (overwritten 1904)
William Cicero Strickland, son of John C. and Ann S., 9/21/1876.

DANIEL BARTLETT BIBLE
Owner: Mrs. Helen Womack
3461 Manana Drive, Dallas, Tx 75520

Births
Daniel Bartlett 12/17/1813   J. R. Bartlett 10/29/1846
N. D. Bartlett 11/20/1820   W. N. Bartlett 3/1/1849
J. M. Barlett 12/17/1837   J. F. Bartlett 12/30/1850
E. A. Bartlett 9/19/1939   A. L. Bartlett 3/17/1853
F. N. Bartlett 4/6/1844   M. A. Bartlett 11/19/1841

Deaths
Daniel Bartlett 12/1880   Clide Bartlett 4/22/1898
N. D. Bartlett 9/11/1890   Claude Bartlett 8/21/1898
E. A. Bartlett 6/1/1852   J. F. Bartlett 6/26/1906
F. N. Bartlett 6/5/1899   M. A. Crane 7/1919
M. M. Bartlett 3/2/1892

Marriages
Lee and Hannah Ring 9/23/1900

ROBERTSON BIBLE

Births
Vincent Franklin Robertson 5/27/1867   Avery Robertson 10/6/1869
Thomas William Robertson 3/6/1874
Ezekiel Wagner Robertson 10/9/1877
Henry Clay Robertson 2/15/1880
William Robertson 1/6/1771
His wife, Anna Mercer Robertson, 12/10/1774
Their son, Gilbert Robertson, 8/15/1794
His wife, Matilda Robertson, 1801
Their son, Silas Mercer Robertson, 12/13/1833
His wife, Prudence Ann Robertson, 6/29/1837
Winnie Ann Thornton Robertson, dau. of Gilbert and Matilda
  Robertson, 12/6/1835
Matilda Robertson 12/6/1835
Vincent Franklin Robertson, son of Silas Mercer Robertson and his
  wife, Prudence Ann Robertson, b. Lincoln Co., Tenn. 5/27/1867
Addie Lenora Robertson, wife of V. F. Robertson, b. 9/19/1885
  Sevier Co., Tenn.

Marriages
William Robertson and Anna Mercer m. in Ga. 6/28/1792
Gilbert Robertson and Matilda Andrews m. in Ga. 1817
Silas Mercer Robertson and Prudence Ann Robertson m. in Tenn.
  8/1865
V. F. Robertson and Addie Cunnington m. 12/18/1912

Deaths
Winnie T. Robertson 7/39/1896
Prudence Ann Robertson 8/3/1898
Silas Mercer Robertson 10/18/1910

FELTS BIBLE
Owner: Lula Bell Felts, Musella, Ga.

Births
Ewell Webb 7/10/1807
Isabelle Crowell Webb 8/2/1843
William Bryant, son of Ewell and Gabriella A. E. Webb 6/19/1848
William Allen Felts, husband of Lizzie Webb Felts, 5/4/1866, son
  of Matilda and Marion Felts
Sidney Ewell, son of Ewell and Isabella Webb, 3/31/1872
Lizzie Lou, dau. of Ewell and Isabella Webb, 2/7/1875
Joseph Allen, son of William and Lizzie Felts, 9/20/1893
Joseph Allen Felts, son of Mr. and Mrs. W. A. Felts, b. 9/20/1893
William Wesley Felts, son of above, b. 8/20/1895
Fred, son of above, b. 10/8/1910
Robert Lee Felts, son of above, b. 5/29/1913
Barney T. Ware, Jr., son of Mr. and Mrs. Barney Ware, b.
  3/6/1919, son of Mattie Ruth and Barney Ware
Wesley Allen Felts, Jr., son of Mr. and Mrs. W. W. Felts, b.
  4/25/1924
Mattie Ruth, dau. of above, b. 6/6/1898
Lulabelle Felts, dau. of above, b. 4/27/1902
Annie Pearl Felts, dau. of above, b. 11/21/1904
Lois Felts, dau. of above, b. 12/10/1906
Doris Ruth Ware, dau. of Mr. and Mrs. Barney T. Ware, b.

21

(Felts Bible contd....)

2/27/1922, dau. of Mattie Ruth and Barney Ware
Elizabeth Gwendolyn Felts, dau. of Flora A. and Robert Lee Felts,
   b. 12/8/1945
Robyn Felts, dau. of above, b. 10/31/--

Marriages
Ewell Webb and Gabriella A. E. Sanders m. 6/3/1847
Ewell Webb and Isabella Crowell m. 5/3/1871
William A. Felts and Lizzie Lou Webb m. 11/30/1892
Barney T. Ware and Mattie Ruth Felts m. 6/7/1919
William Wesley Felts and Ruth Cockreham m. 7/2/1823
Lois Felts and Virgil W. Mathews m. 10/29/1939
Flora Aiken and Robert Lee Felts m. 2/1945
Lois Felts Mathews and Samuel J. Mercer m. 4/15/1956

Deaths
William Bryant, son of Ewell and Gabriella A. E. Webb d.
   9/23/1848, aged 3 mos, 3 days
Mrs. Elizabeth Sanders, wife of William Sanders, d. 8/14/1837,
   aged 44 yrs, 4 mos, 6 days
Elinora Catharine Sanders, dau. of William and Elizabeth
   Sanders, d. 8/26/1844, aged 15 yrs, 7 mos., 16 days
Henry F. Sanders, son of William and Elizabeth Sanders, d.
   10/20/1844, aged 18 yrs, 7 mos.
William Sanders d. 8/25/1854, aged 64 yrs., 10 mos., 10 days
Mark W. Sanders, son of William and Elizabeth Sanders,
   d. 10/21/1855, aged 36 yrs., 11 mos., 15 days
Mrs. Alie L. Sanders, 2nd wife of Ewell Webb, d. 1/6/1871, age 52
Mrs. Gabriela A. E. Sanders, wife of Ewell Webb, d. 1/6/1871,
   aged 52 yrs.
Sidney Ewell, son of Ewell and Isabella Webb, d. 3/24/1873,
   aged 11 mos., 24 days
Ewell Webb d. 8/23/1879, aged 72 yrs., 1 mo., 13 days
Joe A. Felts, son of William and Elizabeth Felts, d. 2/8/1923,
   age 29 yrs, 3 mos., 17 days
Isabelle Crowell Webb, wife of Ewell Webb, d. 2/18/1930, aged
   86 yrs., 6 mos., 16 days
Larry Keith Felts, son of Wesley W. Felts and Ruth Cocraham
   Felts, d. 7/29/1940, bur. Johnson, Kansas 8/4/1940, age 10 yrs.
Lizzie Lou Webb Felts, dau. of Ewell and Isabella Crowell Webb,
   d. 1/5/1942, aged 66 yrs., 10 mos., 28 days
William Allen Felts, Husband of Lizzie Lou Webb Felts, d.
   6/12/1952, age 86 yrs., 1 mo., 21 days, son of Matilda and Marion
   Felts.
Mrs. Mattie Ruth Felts Ware, wife of Barney T. Ware, dau. of
   William Allen and Lizzie Webb Felts, d. 7/10/1971, age 73 yrs.,
   1 mo., 4 days.
Mrs. Lois Felts Mathews Mercer, dau. of William Allen Felts and
   Lizzie Webb Felts, d. 5/7/1975, age 63 yrs., 6 mos., 27 days.
William Wesley Felts, son of William Allen Felts and Lizzie Webb
   Felts, d. 7/10/1976, age 80 yrs., 10 mos., 10 days., bur.
   Johnson, Kansas 7/13/1976

RUSH BIBLE
Owner: Mary Rush Adams, Columbus, Ga.

Marriages
Mary Ann Jane Rush and Ezekiel M. Wall m. 1/18/1854
Martha A. D. Rush and John R. Short m. 10/28/1858

(Rush Bible, Marriages, contd....)

Telefaro Rush and Dicy Green m. 3/1/1835 (Talbot Co., Ga.)

Births
George G. J. Rush, son of Telefaro and Dicy Rush, b. 12/9/1835
Second son b. & d. 4/10/1837
C. A. Short b. & d. 6/19/1860
John P. Short b. 6/1869?
Mary Ann J. Rush b. 12/22/1832
Henry Smith Rush b. 12/30/1836
Martha Anner Caroline Rush b. 4/25/1838
John Wesley Rush b. 4/12/1842
Abbi Rush b. 2/12/1844
Nancy Matilda Rush b. 4/14/1846
Elizabeth F. Rush b. 12/18/1848
Richmond C. Rush b. 1/27/1850?
Harriet Ivins Rush b. 11/12/1856
Elizabeth Rush b. 6/23/1814 Newberry Dist., S. C.

Deaths
John Rush 2/19/1864   Abbie Rush 12/13/1864
Harriet Ivins Rush Goodroe 3/19/1910   John B. Rush d. 5/10/1897
Martha A. C. Short, wife of John P. Short, d. 6/29/18--
Emmer Adelle Rush, wife of R. C. Rush, d. 9/19/1885
Frances Elizabeth Rush d. 10/23/1898
Richmond Carroll Rush d. 3/8/1917
Laura Lee Rush, wife of Richmond C. Rush d. 3/7/1941

Births
Henry Adelle Rush 10/15/1884   Mazie Bell Rush 11/1/1899
Frances Elizabeth Rush 9/7/1892   Loomis R. Rush 12/21/1901
Monie Eva Rush 4/19/1896   Ruby D. Rush 6/22/1904
Lenard C. Rush 11/6/1897   Willie Weaver Rush 9/11/1907

                    WILLIAM HENRY KINARD BIBLE
              Owner: Mattie Kate Kinard, Griffin, Ga.

George Washington Kinard b. 3/7/1822, d. 3/8/1904
Edna Waldrop Kinard b. 2/14/1828, d. 3/30/1919
Mary E. b. 2/15/1847, d. 8/5/1887
Martha Ann, b. 3/17/1856, d. 3/28/1940
Martin J., b. 12/27/1857
Delpha Lula, b. 9/11/1860, d. 3/24/1930
John L. T., b. 6/28/1863, d. 11/21/1864
Francis Marion, b. 4/23/1866, d. 4/28/1939
William Henry, b. 2/13/1869, d. 6/14/1956
Sarah Leamon b. 9/4/1872, d. 2/7/1925
George Washington, Jr. b. 3/8/1875
Earl Dean b. 12/4/1877
Joshua Hammond b. 7/9/1836
Cyrena Ann (Wise) Hammond b. 4/1/1843
Walter D. Hammond b. 11/20/1866, d. 6/1/1937
Charles Marion Hammond. b. 5/15/1868, d. 6/6/1917
William Clayton Hammond, b. 5/20/1870. d. 5/15/1923
Georgia Luvenia Hammond, b. 11/26/1871, d. 1918
Thomas Taylor Hammond, b. 5/1/1874, d. 1958
Martha Viola Hammond, b. 8/17/1876, d. 8/6/1946
Nancy Christenor Hammond, b. 4/21/1878, d. 5/21/1878
Mary Izada Hammond, b. 11/17/1879, d. 12/13/1879
Sarah Rosannah Hammond, b. 3/10/1881, d. 10/27/1883

(Kinard Bible contd....)

Cora Elizabeth Hammond, b. 10/24/1884, d. 10/24/1884

JAMES ANDREW HOLLON BIBLE
Owner: Mrs. John Futral, Franklin, Ga.

Births

J. A. Hollon 12/7/1859	Bessie Ophelia Hollon 6/3/1900
Alice Hollon 11/18/1870	Annie Lee Hollon 11/3/1901
William Hollon 4/26/1894	James Hollon 7/12/1903
Clifford Hollon 4/12/1895	Mary Eunice Hollon 9/11/1906
Lily Mae Hollon 10/3/1897	Myrtice Mann Hollon 7/9/1909
W. H. Turner 9/14/1826	T. W. Turner 2/1/1853
Frances A. Turner 6/5/1838	Mary M. Turner 8/31/1855
D. B. Hollon 8/2/1862	Ora Kate Morgan 1/10/1900
W. S. Turner 5/24/1865	Bessie Lorrine Morgan 8/18/1901
L. M. Turner 11/5/1877	Frances Irene Turner 9/15/1903
A. L. Turner 10/2/1881	

Deaths

Mary Frances 11/20/1871	Willie's twin 4/21/1924
W. H. Turner 12/25/1899	Annie Lee 4/21/1924
J. H. Hollon 3/1/1904	J. C. Emery 2/13/1919
C. B. Hollon 8/17/1912	David J. Emery 9/12/1924

LARKIN JOHNSTON BIBLE

Larkin Johnston, oldest child of William and Ann Chew Johnston,
b. 5/1/1727 Spotsylvania Co., Va., d. 3/16/1816 Jasper Co., Ga.
m. 5/2/1745 to Mary Rogers, b. 1/2/1727 Stratton Parish, Va., d.
10/25/1800 at Hico, Person Co., N. C. Children:
William Johnston b. 10/14 oald stile 10/25, new stile 1746, d.
   11/29/1759
Ann Johnston b. 6/22/1749 oald stile, 7/3 new stile, m. 8/26/1772
   to Samuel Cush.
Larkin Johnston b. 7/11/1752, oald stile, d. 3/9/1757
Lucy Johnston, b. 5/15/1755, d. 10/9/1832 in DeKalb Co., Ga., m.
   11/30/1783 to John Landers.
Sarah Johnston b. 5/18/1758, m. 1/25/1778 to Francis Howard and
   since to Henry Finlless.
Littleton Johnston b. 2/18/1761, d. 7/7/1842, Jasper Co., Ga., m.
   (1) 1/4/1781 to Lucy Childs (2) 2/12/1828 to Sarah Dirbin, wid.
John Johnston b. 12/22/1763, d. 11/14/1817 Elbert Co., Ga., First
   wife was Sarah Long, second wife was Mary Wansen, wid.
John Johnston, son of Larkin and Mary, d. 7/7/1842 in Jasper Co.,
   Ga., age 81 yrs., 4 mos., 18 days.
Theodorick Johnston, b. 8/20/1766, m. Elizabeth Stuard.
Sophia Johnston, b. 12/15/1769, m. 8/20/1802 to Larkin Herndon
Richard Johnston b. 3/14/1778, in 52nd year of his mother's age,
   d. 1/17/1837 in Walton Co., Ga., m. 3/1802 to Elizabeth
   Hemphill.

"My wife Mary Johnston departed this life 10/25/1800...was bur. by
her bro., John, at his place on Hico on Tues. after she died,
being kept out of the ground four days according to her request.
We lived together upward of 55 years in which time she brought me
ten children and eight of which is alive now - 1802."

24

(Larkin Johnston Bible Contd....)

William Johnston, father, b. 12/19/1697, d. 8/16/1756,
Spotsylvania Co., Va., m. 10/12/1723 to Ann Chew who d.
11/2/1742, dau. of Hannah Roy and Larkin Chew.

JAMES HAIL BIBLE
Owner: William E. Wooten, Quitman, Ga.

Births
James Hail 1/6/1790   Sarah Hail 10/2/1826
Nancy Hail 12/28/1797   James C. Hail 7/31/1828
Rebecca Hail 8/21/1813   Judethan Hail 4/29/1831
Louisa Hail 12/25/1814   Thomas C. Hail 1/3/1836
Elizabeth Hail 8/26/1816   Jonas Hail 8/3/1837
Livina Hail 1/15/1819   Joseph John Chappel Hail 6/25/1839
Mary Ann Hail 8/10/1820   William A. Miller 4/21/1852
Susannah Hail 3/4/1822   James M. Miller---
Matilda Hail 10/19/1824
Reubin G. Miller and Soucyann? Marshall m. 6/19/1856

James Y. Marshall 7/12/1854   Nora Marine Wooten 10/18/1897
James H. Miller 8/8/1854   Enoch Vann Wooten 7/24/1899
B. R. Wooten 4/5/1854   Anthy Lee Wooten 5/14/1901
Elizabeth Rebecca Wooten 6/11/1866   Iver Alon 10/24/1904
Nannie Lee Wooten 9/22/1886   J. B. Wooten 8/7/1906
Ruben Byrd 5/9/1888   William Carl Wooten 1/14/1930
Jesse Gordon Wooten 11/18/1889   Linda Wooten 10/8/1954
-----3/25/1891 b. dead   Wm. Michael Wooten 5/27/1956
Ilah Mai Wooten 8/12/1894   Joan Wooten---

Marriages
Rebecca Hail m. 12/24/1829
Louisa Hail m. 8/26/1830
Levina Hail m. 12/9/1834
Elizabeth Hail m. 4/13/1836
Mary A. Hail and William Hodges m. 10/8/1832
Susannah Hail and L.? Lingo m. --/15/1840
Matilda Hail m. William Roberson 2/7/1845?
Sarah Humes? Hail m. Robert Johnson 11/1844
Sarah? Hail m. H. Butler? 12/1846
Juda A. Hail and A. G. R. Porter m. 1851
T. C. Hail m. 2/11/1855
J. J. Hail and M. Roberson m. 1/1856?
Enoch V. Wooten and Erma Crystell Simpson m. 1/1/1928

Deaths
Livinia Foutrel 12/23/1831   Rebecca Elizabeth Wooten 2/8/1948
Mary Stallings 7/26/1953, age 33   Iver Leon Wooten 9/1945
Louisa Braswell 8/30/1857,age 40   James Hail 10/25/1847, age 58
Thomas Hail 1864, age 28   Nancy H. Hail 10/6/1816, age 59
Rebecca Marshall 1877   Jonas M. Hail 9/22/1857, age 21
Nancy Miller 8/1910   James C. Hail 9/15/1858, age 3-
Anthony Lee Wooten 3/2/1902   B. R. Wooten 1/2/1928
J. B. Wooten 5/2/1907   Nannie Leola Wooten 7/10/1910
Reuben Byrd Wooten 7/7/1910

R. Y. Miller and Nancy? m. last day of Aug. 1865
Lizzie R. Miller b. 6/11/1866
Tolbert Simen Miller b. 10/4/1870

(James Hail Bible contd....)

Sally V. Miller b. 2/15/1872   J. A. Miller 11/24/1874
Fannie Lee b. 7/31/1877
Charley Edward b. 4/6/1880, d. 12/13/1880

HENDON BIBLE
Owner: Sarah Francis Hill, Gadsden, Ala.

Marriages
William C. L. Hendon to Susan F. Colley 12/17/1865
Robert A. Wright and Amanda J. Hendon 7/11/1889
A. B. Purcell and Mary M. Hendon 10/31/1889
E. G. and M. B. (Belle) Smothers 11/18/1896?

Births
William Cincinnatus Lykergus Hendon 10/26/1841
Susan Francis Hendon 1/19/1845
William Asa Hendon 9/12/1866
Mary Margaret Hendon 4/18/1868
Amanda Jane Hendon 1/8/1870
Andrew Newell Hendon 1/4/1872
May Belle Hendon 4/21/1874
George Henry Hendon 5/24/1876
Martha Elizabeth Hendon 12/9/1878
John Edward Hendon 2/4/1881
Cora Tulula Francis Hendon 7/18/1883

Deaths
William A. Hendon 11/19/1869   Henry T. Hendon 1/4/1874
Andrew N. Hendon 9/6/1873   Martha E. Hendon 8/29/1880
Margaret Hendon 1/4/1874   Cora T. F. Hendon 11/7/1885

Marriages
G. H. and T. B. Hendon (Tinie Cole) m. 12/16/1897
J. E. Hendon and L. P. Cole (Lona) m. 12/22/1901

Births
Jessie Cullman Hendon 10/10/1898   Claud William Hendon 8/27/1903
Vera Pauline Hendon 11/14/1900   Curton McCoy Hendon 10/14/1904

Deaths   Deaths
Jessie Culman Hendon 7/7/1900   S. F. Hendon 10/29/1914
W. C. L. Hendon 8/14/1908   Amanda Jane (Hendon) Wright
G. H. Hendon 7/19/1910   1/29/1940
                                     John Edwin Hendon 9/18/1942
Births of J. E. Hendon's FamilyTinnie B. Hendon 3/30/1809
J. E. Hendon b. 2/5/1881   Robert A. Wright 8/23/1921
Lonar P. Hendon b. 2/27/1881
William Luther Hendon b. 10/29/1902

Births of Family of Andrew Hendon:
Andrew Hendon 5/27/1800   Sarah Elizabeth Hendon 1/9/1831
Margaret Hendon 5/6/1802   Francis Robinson Hendon 11/2/1833
Josiah Newton Hendon 10/29/1826 Henry Thomas Hendon 12/19/1836
Lucy Jane Hendon 2/24/1829   Flemmon Asa Hendon 2/3/1838
                                Wiley Hartsfield Hendon 2/7/1840

Marriages of Family of Andrew Hendon
Andrew and Margaret Hendon 1/20/1826
Robert W. Hamrick and Sarah E. Hendon 10/14/1847

26

(Hendon Bible contd....)

Francis R. and Elizabeth D. Hendon 2/10/1853
Henry T. and Cytha E. Hendon 12/15/1853

Deaths of Family of Andrew Hendon
Josiah Newton Hendon 1/1/1828   Andrew Hendon 9/14/1847
Wiley Hartsfield Hendon 4/7/1840   Flemmon Asa Hendon 1/13/1848
Lucy Jane Hendon 10/4/1841

Births of Family of Sebern Newell Colley
Sebern Newell Colley 2/13/1822   Susan Francis Colley 1/19/1845
Mary Colley 5/2/1823   William Franklin Colley
John Thomas Colley 11/23/1841   4/11/1846
Mary Ann Elizabeth Colley 8/31/1843
Zachariah Colley 6/7/1847
George Colley 1/29/1849

Charles William Newell Pollard b. 12/31/1864

Marriages
Sebern N. and Mary Colley 11/29/1840
Charles S. and Mary Ann Pollard 12/6/1863
William W. and Mary Ann E. Wielder 10/24/1867

Deaths
John Thomas Colley 5/18/1864   Charles Smith Pollard 6/15/1864
William Franklin Colley 7/6/1864

JAMES L. ALDRIDGE BIBLE
Owner: Mrs. E. B. Dill, West Point, Miss.

James L. Aldridge b. 8/15/1833, d. 2/5/1861
Sara Frances Hayes b. 2/21/1839, d. 3/8/1904 Grandparents
Ruben Marion Aldridge b. 3/2/1855, d. 5/8/1922
Willie Pearl Williams b. 9/12/1861, d. 1/26/1939 Parents
  Children:
Fannie Vera Aldridge b. 2/23/1883
Willia Maud Aldridge b. 5/14/1885, d. 4/25/1960
James Ruben Aldridge b. 5/3/1887, d. 9/1/1952
Hubert Leon Aldridge b. 8/24/1888
Burt Marshall Aldridge b. 12/28/1889
Euella Lee Aldridge b. 1/11/1892
Lewis Hayes Aldridge b. 5/5/1894
Dewey Atwell Aldridge b. 12/12/1896
Rosie Mildred Aldridge b. 6/20/1898
Constance Aldridge b. 8/19/1901
Charles Edward Aldridge b. 5/17/1903, d. 4/20/1960
J. D. Aldridge b. 9/8/1908
Ruben M. Aldridge and Willie Pearl Williams were m. 11/6/1881
W. R. Evans b. 1891
Rosie Mildred Evans b. 1898
Papa d. 5/8/1922
Mamma d. 1/26/1939
Bill d. 2/5/1955
Ernest, Jr. d. 7/29/1957
Charley d. 4/20/1960
Maud d. 4/25/1960
James L. Aldridge and Sarah F. Hayes m. 10/2/1856
William H. Hoskins and Connie A. Aldridge m. 11/1/1860
William K. Aldridge and Lucinda House m. 2/27/1823

27

(James L. Aldridge Bible contd....)

William K. Aldridge and M. R. Motley m. 11/11/1841
Willie P. Williams and Ruben M. Aldridge m. 11/6/1881

LITTLETON JOHNSTON BIBLE
Owner: Mrs. Myrtle Andrew Roberts, Taylors, S. C.

Littleton Johnston b. Granville Co., N. C. 2/18/1761, d. in
Jasper Co., Ga. 7/7/1843, m. (1) 1/4/1781 Lucy Childs, (2)
1/12/1828 Mrs. Sarah Durbin. Lucy Childs b. 1/30/1756, d.
6/9/1826.

Children of Littleton and Lucy Childs Johnston:

John Chew Johnston b. Orange Co., N. C. 3/17/1782, d. Granville
  Co., N. C. 7/18/1792, bur. at "my father Larkin Johnston´s at his
  old place."
Larkin Johnston b. 9/13/1783 Orange Co., N. C., d. 5/12/1834
  Monroe Co., Ga., m. 6/29/1803 Sally Underwood.
Elizabeth Johnson b. 4/26/1795 Caswell Co., N. C., m. 5/7/1803 to
  Wiley Thornton.
William Johnston b. 1/19/1787 Granville Co., N. C., m. 11/17/1805
  in Elbert Co., Ga. Sarah Grizel of that co.
Thomas Johnston b. 2/5/1789 in N. C., d. 9/17/1848 in Ga., m.
  1/18/1816 Peggy C. Gaines.
Margaret C. Gaines, wife of Thomas Johnston, b. 12/22/1798,
  d. 12/8/1847.
Nathan Johnston b. 6/27/1790 in Person Co., N. C., d. 8/10/1843
  in Jasper Co., Ga., m. 3/19/1812 Biddy Thornton.
Bridget Thornton, wife of Nathan Johnson, d. 6/9/1837.
Frankey Johnston b. 3/18/1792 Person Co., N. C., d. 7/14/1844 in
  Jasper Co., Ga.
James Johnston b. 12/13/1795 Person Co., N. C., d. 12/1/1863, m.
  in Elbert Co., Ga. 12/12/1816 Jane Gaines.
Lucy Johnston b. 5/24/1800 Elbert Co., Ga., d. 4/18/1801.
Richard Johnston b. 12/16/1802 Elbert Co., Ga., d. 2/1859 in
  Jasper Co., Ga. at William S. Lanis.
Ann Wilson Childs b. 11/11/1804, dau. of Nathan Childs, Sr. and
  wife, Jane.
Margaret C. Gaines, dau. of Hiram and Ann Gaines, b. 12/22/1798,
  d. 12/8/1847, wife of Thomas Johnston.

Children of William Johnston and wife, Sarah:
Toil Johnston, son, b. 8/4/1813, d. 11/10/1817
Elizabeth Johnston b. 10/24/1809
Patsey Usolom Johnston b. 8/6/1811.

WALDEN-BOYD BIBLE
Owner: Mrs. R. S. Heard, West Point, Ga.

"A Free Gift of Dismukes in the year 1757 to Mary Walden for the
love of her mother, Mary Ellis. God be close to all!"
"Samuel Walden, his Book"
Fannie Waldin b. 2/8/1757   Sarah Walding b. 12/10/1758
Richard Walding b. 10/10/1760   Owen Walden b. 12/26/1762
William Walden b. 11/24/1768   Lewis Walden b. 1/13/1771
Anne Walden b. 10/20/1773   Elijah Walden b. 4/10/1775

(Walden-Boyd Bible contd....)

Anderson Fambrough b. 1/24/1782   Byrd Fambrough b. 5/4/1778
Samuel Boyd b. 10/8/1782   Clayburn Inroughtee b. 3/10/1777
Nancy Inroughtee b. 12/10/1780   Mary Boyd b. 2/24/1784
Fanny Boyd b. 1/28/1787   ---Boyd b. 2/11/1789
---Boyd b. 1/30/1791   ---Boyd b. 2/12/1793

Robert Dismukes Thompson, son of Sarah Thompson, dau. of John
  Thompson, b. 8/22/1791

Richard Boyd, Jr. son of Richard Boyd, b. 9/4/1795
Henry Boyd, son of Richard Boyd and Fanny, his wife, b. 5/20/1797
John Coleman Boyd, son of Richard Boyd and Fanny, his wife, b.
  3/16/1802
Averilla? Boyd b. 1/11/1805

James M. Trammell? b. 10/11/1762
John Boyd b. 3/16/1802
Richard Boyd d. 9/28/1823

RICHARD HEAD BIBLE
Owner: W. M. Bowers, Jr., Elberton, Ga.

Births
John R. Head 8/5/1816   Susannah Head 12/25/1835
James A. Head 9/5/1817   Elizabeth Head 1/29/1827
Andrew J. Head 12/5/1820   Christopher Head 10/24/1823
Malissa Head 10/8/1829   Cinthia? Head 12/5/1832
Charles P. Mannon Head -/26/1830

Richard H. Head 7/16/1840   Margaret M. Head 11/22/1838
Richard A. Head 12/29/1858   Frances M. Beauregard Head
Susannah Manda Head 5/28/1862   9/21/1860

Malinda Ann Head 3/23/1839   Sarah Elizabeth Head 1/28/1862
Mary Ann S. Head 6/19/1819   Misourie Viola Head 5/9/1865
Sherman   Head 11/13/1866   Georgia Ann Louisa Head
                           4/6/1868
Marriages
Richard H. Head and Margaret M. Head 3/22/1858
Richard Head and Susannah B. Head 9/22/1815

Deaths
Charles P. Mannon Head 6/13/1849   Susannah Head 6/4/1858
Susannah B. Head 4/22/1860   John H. Head 8/1866
F. M. Beauregard Head 9/12/1863   Shearman Head 1/19/1867

Births
A. J. Head 12/4/1820   Christer Amanuel Head 11/6/1845
Susan Amanda Head 10/24/1841   Mary Ann Malissa Head 7/31/1852
Adline Persiler Head 2/24/1844   Joseph Henry Head 7/27/1859
Elizabeth Catherine Head 8/8/1848
Flourida Josephine Head 7/30/1854

Mary Jane Allen 3/7/1858   Martha Ann Allen 9/10/1860
Sarah Adline Allen 3/16/1863   Cordelia Allen 4/20/1867
Flourida Josephine Allen 5/17/1867   Thomas Allen 11/7/1869
Andrew J. Stone 9/26/1834   Thomas J. Allen 3/5/1831
A. J. Head 12/4/1821   Maran Head 2/16/1826

(Richard Head Bible, Births, Contd....)

Susan Amandrill Head 10/24/1841   Adline P. Head 2/24/1844

Joseph H. Head m. Savannah Dykes 8/22/1878 by Rev. Taliaferro,
Pastor of their church. Children:

James A. Head b. 7/22/1879   Charles C. W. Head b.
                                    1/11/1881
William Layfett Head b. 8/4/1883   Laura Eleanor Head b.
                                    10/26/1893

MAJ. MATTHEW M. DEAS BIBLE
Owner: Mrs. Milton I. Hudson
Jacksonville, Fla.

Births
These are the ages of Matthew M. Deas Sr. and Jane, his wife's
   children:
Lewis M. Deas b. 2/8/1815   Elizabeth Deas b. 3/10/1825
John M. Deas b. 9/26/1816   Mary Deas b. 6/28/1828
Matthew M. Deas b. 8/11/1818   Louisa Deas b. 9/18/1830
Aaron M. Deas b. 10/29/1820   Samuel M. Deas b. 9/18/1832
                                    Maria Deas b. 4/20/1834

SAMUEL F. FLOOD BIBLE
Owner: Mrs. Carolyn Flood Durden
Fernandina Beach, Fla.

Marriages
Samuel and Rebecca (Grovenstein) Flood m. 3/27/1827 (St. Marys, Ga.)

Births
James Vincent b. Manoroneck, N. Y. 11/13/1784
Ann Vincent Flood 1/14/1830   Rebecca Grovenstein Flood
Elizabeth Cooper Flood 10/14/1833   10/3/1839
John Hebbard Flood 4/17/1837   Susan Stafford Flood 4/17/1842
                              ·   Isaac Secor Flood 12/1/1845

Samuel F. Flood b. Morrich, N. Y. 8/17/1780
Mrs. Rebecca Flood b. Jefferston (Camden Co.) 6/30/1805
Samuel F. Flood, the 4th, b. St. Marys, Ga. 7/6/1876
Samuel F. Flood, 5th, b. Jacksonville, Fla. 5/3/1901

Deaths
Samuel F. Flood 2/10/1848, age 68 yrs.
Mrs. Elizabeth Grovenstine 12/14/1866, age 84 yrs.
Rebecca Flood, wife of S. F. Flood, 1/11/1871, age 66 yrs.
Mrs. A. V. Sterling 8/6/1893

Charles Sterling 6/22/95
Samuel F. Sterling 8/7/1900, son of Charles G. and A. V. Sterling

NATHANIEL VARNEDOE BIBLE
Of Liberty Co., Ga.
Owner: Capt. Zach Varnedoe, Jr.

Marriages

Nathaniel Varnedoe and Ann T. Jones m. 5/5/1814
Samuel McW. Varnedoe and Caroline B. Law m. 12/13/1837
Nathaniel Varnedoe and Hannah M. Cosby m. 7/14/1840
William Winn and Louisa Varnedoe m. 8/30/1843
W. Q. Baker and Sarah J. Varnedoe m. 4/24/1844
Leander Varnedoe and Ann Eliza Mallard m. 12/11/1849
Nathaniel J. Varnedoe and Mary A. Ladson m. 3/26/1850
Joseph H. Ladson and Anne C. Varnedoe m. 12/9/1856
William W. Winn and Claudia Varnedoe m. 10/26/1859
Rufus A. Varnedoe and Anna M. Rockenbaugh m. 11/18/1857
John A. Crawford and Matilda Varnedoe m. 11/8/1858

Births

Ann Caroline Varnedoe, dau. of Nathaniel and Ann T. Varnedoe,
  8/14/1816
Samuel McWhir Varnedoe, son of Nathaniel and Ann T. Varnedoe,
  8/3/1817
Mary Bethanah Varnedoe, dau. of Nathaniel and Ann Varnedoe,
  5/10/1819
Sarah Jones Varnedoe 8/28/1820
Claudia Rebecca Varnedoe 12/31/1821
Louisa Varnedoe 8/30/1824
Nathaniel J. Varnedoe 5/26/1826
Leander Varnedoe 5/16/1829
Matilda Varnedoe 2/13/1831
Claudia Varnedoe 9/29/1832
Rufus Alonzo Varnedoe 9/14/1834
Ann Caroline Varnedoe 3/13/1838
(By second marriage)
Mary Ellen, child of Hannah M. and Nathaniel Varnedoe, 9/23/1846
Charles Stockton 5/29/1848, child of Hannah M. and Nathaniel
  Varnedoe
Frances Elizabeth, child of Hannah M. and Nathaniel Varnedoe,
  12/6/1847
James S. Cosby, child of Hannah M. and J. C. Cosby, 9/1/1837

Deaths

Mary B. Varnedoe 5/28/1820
Claudia R. Varnedoe 6/2/1823
William Baker 1/6/1827
Ann Caroline Varnedoe --/27/1837
Ann J. Varnedoe, wife of Nathaniel Varnedoe, 2/8/1839
Sarah Jones, dau. of Nathaniel and Ann Varnedoe, wife of W. Q.
  Baker, 3/21/1852
Frances Elizabeth Varnedoe 7/6/1848
Charles Stockton Varnedoe 8/1/1853
Nathaniel Varnedoe (son) 2/12/1856
Hannah M. Varnedoe, wife of Nathaniel Varnedoe, 8/1858
Louisa Winn, dau. of Nathaniel and A. Varnedoe and wife of W. W.
  Winn, 12/2/1857
Joseph H. Ladson, husband of Ann C. Varnedoe, 2/11/1862
Samuel McWhir Varnedoe 4/23/1870
M. J. Varnedoe 1886
Claudia Winn, dau. of Nathaniel and Ann Varnedoe, wife of W. W.
  Winn, 5/21/1890
Matilda, wife of Mr. Crawford, supposedly d. Texas 1870, found to
  be living in 1912 in New Mexico at age of 80, now a Mrs. Hines.

Marriages
Benjamin S. Caswell and Elizabeth P. Chapman 5/24/1857
Thomas C. Sherman and Katie S. Caswell--
Warren Lyman Hunt and Elizabeth Evans Caswell 7/20/1905

Births
Katie S. Caswell 7/8/1858
Lizzie E. Caswell 7/27/1861

Deaths
Benjamin S. C<swell 2/8/1903   F. W. Hunt 6/4/1908
Elizabeth P. Caswell 10/12/1902   Warren Lyman Hunt 11/4/1920
Thomas C. Sherman 11/30/1908

RICHARD WASHINGTON HEETH BIBLE
Of Thomas Co., Ga.
Owner: May B. Heeth, Jacksonville, Fla.

Marriages
Richard Washington Heeth and Susan M. Sheffield 12/28/1843
Richard Washington Heeth, Jr. and Hattie Pauline Gilbert at res.
of her father 12/15/1881, Rev. J. H. Battles officiating,
Jefferson Co., Fla.

Births
Richard Washington Heeth 4/17/1817
Susan Mitchell Sheffield, dau. of Pliny Sheffield and Mary H.
Sheffield, his wife, b. 1/30/1825
Pliny Sheffield Heeth, son of R. W. Heeth and Susan M. Heeth, his
wife, b. 9/22/1845 (m. Florida Mallard)
Henry Mance Heeth, son f R. W. Heeth and Susan M. Heeth, his
wife, b. 2/26/1848, d. 9/10/1849
Nathaniel Reines Mitchell, son f R. W. Heeth and Susan M. Heeth,
his wife, b. 1/10/1850 (m. 12/20/1877 Louisa Jones Varnedoe)
Julia Elizabeth, dau. of R. W. Heeth and Susan M. Heeth, his
wife, b. 10/18/1851 (m. 3/14/1872 Lewis Clinton Varnedoe)
Chapel Marion Heeth, son of R. W. Heeth and Susan M. heeth, his
wife, b. 7/27/1856
Mary Susan Heeth, dau. of R. W. Heeth and Susan M. Heeth, his
wife, b. 1*/1/1859, 3. 7/31/1860
Robert S. Heeth, son of R. W. Heeth and Susan M. Heeth, b.
5/15/1861 (m. Rosa Alexander)
Lee Heeth, son of R. W. Heeth and Susan M. Heeth, b. 12/19/1863,
d. 6/19/1888
Clarence M. Heeth, son of R. W. Heeth and Susan M. Heeth, his
wife, b. 2/17/1867, d. 5/20/1867
Susan Bertha Heeth, dau. of Richard Heeth and his wife, b.
11/11/1882
Hattie Gilbert Heeth b. 4/27/1885
Richard W. Heeth, Jr., son of Richard W. Heeth and Hattie Pauline
Heeth, b. 1/25/1888
May Agnes Heeth b. 3/26/1891
Virgil Hunter Heeth b. 9/1/1893
Births of L. C. and Julia E. Varnedoe's children:
Susan Annie Varnedoe b. 3/2/1873
Ida May Varnedoe b. 5/9/1875

(Richard Washington Heeth Bible, contd....)

Deaths
Susan M. Heeth, wife of R. W. Heeth, d. 2/28/1867

DOWNS BIBLE
Owner: Mrs. C. D. Weddington
2929 Shahan Ave., Gadsden, Ala. 35901

W. M. F. Downs and M. E. Downs m. 3/9/1871
W. M. F. Downs b. 7/5/1853   Elizabeth E. Downs b. 3/26/1881
M. E. Downs b. 6/10/1854   Tinsy Ann Downs b. 1/18/1884
Lula Loretta Downs b. 2/19/1872   Talmage L. Downs b. 7/20/1886
Cora F. Downs b. 12/23/1873   Leroy and David Downs b.
Willis Shelly Downs b. 2/7/1876   11/7/1888
Rhoda E. Downs b. 12/16/1877   Martha A. Downs b. 4/24/1892
Infant b. & d. 3/3/1880   Exa Cleo Downs b. 10/22/1896

Deaths
W. M. F. Downs 7/20/1915   Rhoda Evie G. 5/23/1964
Willis Shelly Downs 7/25/1929   Lee Roy 5/22/1966
Martha E. Downs 5/8/1944   Talmadge L. Sr. 6/24/1966
Lula Loretta 8/1/1949   David 2/11/67
Cora Florence O. 10/10/1951   Martha Agnes 9/30/69
Tinsy Ann 12/7/1956   Elizabeth Ellen 10/66

NEWEL TULLIS BIBLE
Of Troup Co., Ga., later Texas
Owner: Mrs. Estelle Ray Walker, Beaumont, Tx.

Marriages
Charles L. Price and Rebecca W. Tullis 11/16/1848
Robert Ray and Rebecca W. Price 6/1/1856

Births
Newel Tullis 3/5/1799   Jonathan D. Tullis 5/19/1833
Elizabeth W. Rainey 3/13/1801   Gilbert G. Tullis 3/14/1835
John B. Tullis 8/8/1825   Newel Tullis 3/13/1837
William L. Tullis 9/19/1827   James M. Tullis 1/27/1839
Rebecca W. Tullis 10/10/1829   Sarah A. E. Tullis 11/27/1841
Moses Tullis 8/31/1831

John W. Price 11/20/1849   Charles C. Price 12/21/1853
Mary A. E. Price 9/4/1851
Robert Ray 11/1/1814   Martha Latitia Ray 1/18/1862
William C. Ray 3/22/1857   Wiley Wilson Ray 5/23/1865
James C. Ray 10/14/1858   Newel Tullis Ray 9/10/1870
Robert Jonathan Ray 12/24/1860   Jesse Monroe Ray 9/15/1872

Deaths
Charles L. Price 7/16/1853   William C. Ray 10/13/1925
Robert Jonathan Ray 6/23/1866   Jesse Monroe Ray 11/25/1935
Martha Latitia Ray 10/1/1866   Wiley Wilson Ray 9/4/1938
Rebecca W. Ray 1/20/1877   James C. Ray 7/20/1940
Robert Ray 9/2/1878   Newel Tullis Ray 4/26/1950
John W. Price 12/3/1896   Chas. C. Price 1/23/1923

HOYLE-BLOUNT BIBLE
Owner: Mrs. W. L. Crawford, Memphis, Tenn.

William S. Hoyle b. 1/10/1796
W. B. Hoyle b. 9/25/1816
John S. Hoyle b. 12/21/1817
James M. Hoyle b. 2/15/1819
Nancy Hoyle b. 7/27/1821
Martha Ann Hoyle b. 6/14/1823

W. O. Hoyle b. 4/24/1825
Lafayette W. Hoyle b. 2/3/1827
B. F. Hoyle b. 8/16/1829
F. M. Hoyle b. 3/27/1832
Frances Ann T. Hoyle
b. 1/25/1852

William Blount b. 9/13/1823
Martha Ann Blount b. 6/14/1823
Sarah F. Blount b. 12/11/1845
Emit F. Blount b. 9/30/1847

William J. Blount b. 9/13/1823
James Wesley Blount
b. 9/23/1853
Mary Elizabeth Blount
b. 5/23/1855

O. Marshall Blount b. 11/9/1857
John Andrew Blount b. 5/22/1860
Lefelia Blount b. 5/30/1863
William A. Findley b. 8/31/1864
Emma Langley b. 11/17/1865

W. G. Blount b. 11/20/1885
J. F. Blount b. 12/11/1888
O. D. Blount b. 3/26/1891

C. R. Blount b. 8/29/1893
Dewey Blount b. 5/16/1898

Marriages
William Blount to Martha Ann Blount 11/10/1844
A. J. Findley and Sarah F. Blount 4/16/1863
E. F. Blount and Eadey Johnson 12/25/1866
W. B. Landers and W. E. Blount 2/23/1871
W. J. Blount and Julia Wyatt 12/8/1873
O. M. Blount and Emma Langley 2/5/1885
J. A. Blount and Aner Guthery 12/30/1885
O. M. Blount and Genie Stuckey 1/24/1901

Deaths
William S. Hoyle 5/22/1853   Martha A. Blount 1/8/1878
Lefelia Blount 6/13/1863   William Blount 5/16/1884

THOMAS ARDEN BIBLE
Of Beaufort, S. C. and Effingham Co., Ga.
Owner: Irene Arden, Decatur, Ga.

Marriages
Bonnier Peterson Thomas Arden and Eve Mickler 11/20/1823
Daniel D. Arden and Margaret? E. Garvin 7/8/1851
S. C. Catherwood and Lydia Arden 4/28/1853
Sarah E. Arden and James W. LaMotte 4/23/1856
Thomas M. Williams, son of Matthew and Charity Williams, by Rev.
St. Lee to Frances Eve, dau. of John and Catherine Blewer
7/6/1820 on Wassamasaw (Swamp, Berkley Co., S. C.)

Births
Thomas Arden 5/31/1794
Eve Mickler 8/17/1803
Daniel Douglas, son of Thomas and Eve Arden, 10/11/1824
Lydia Ann Caroline, dau. of Thomas and Eve Arden, 2/7/1828
Sarah Elizabeth, dau. of Thomas and Eve Arden, 1/20/1831
Caroline Matilda, dau. of Thomas and Eve Arden, 11/2/1834

(Thomas Arden Bible, Births, contd....

Mahala Arden Williams, the adopted dau. of Thomas M. and Frances
  E. Williams, b. in Beaufort, 4/23/1836
Franklin Benjamin Arden, son of Daniel and Margaret Arden,
  3/17/1853
Frances Benjamin Arden, Jr., 4/28/1893
Frances Benjamin Arden III, 10/5/1923
Thomas M. Williams, b. on Santee Canal, S. C., 9/20/1798
Frances Eve Blewer, b. on Wassamasaw, 8/11/1800

Deaths
Eve Arden, wife of Thomas Arden and dau. of Peter and Lydia
  Mickler, d. 11/10/1836 in Town of Beaufort, S. C.
Thomas Williams 12/26/1851
Arden M. Williams 10/11/1854, age 18 yrs., 5 mos.
Lydia Ann Catherwood 7/26/1882, age 54 yrs., 5 mos., 20 days
Sarah E. LaMotte 4/4/1887, age 56 yrs., 2 mos., 14 days

                   ROBERT MICKLER BIBLE
             Owner: Irene Arden, Decatur, Ga.

Births
Robert Mickler, son of Robert and Ann Mickler, 12/12/1825
James Arden Mickler, son of Robert and Ann Mickler, 12/12/1827
Daniel Jencks? Mickler, son of Robert and Ann Mickler, 7/12/1833
Mary Frances, dau. of Archibald and Elizabeth Seals, b. at
  Laways?. 2/26/1849
Next six births were those of slaves:
Fannie, dau. of Hannah, b. St. Marys, Ga. 4/5/1852
Washington, son of our servant, Lydia, b. 4/17/1852, St. Marys.
Rose, dau. of Andrew and Hannah, b. 12/9/1838 at St. Marys.
Fannie, dau. of Hannah, b. at St. Marys, 4/5/1852
Mary Martha,---------, b. 5/185-

Sarah Louisa, dau. of Archibald and Elizabeth Seals, b. 10/9/1849
  at St. Marys.
John Hebbard Seals, son of Archibald and Elizabeth Seals, b.
  4/14/1852, at St. Marys.
John Henry Helveston, son of James and Louisa, b. at St. Marys,
  Ga., 10/11/1852.

Deaths
Daniel Mickler 10/31/1866   Robert Seals 10/13/1867
William W. Seals 9/29/1867   Allie? A. Seals 8/22/1873
  at Palatka, Fla.   ----Hebbard----at Bagdad, Fla.,---
Margaret Seals 10/3/1867

Births
Lydia Allen Mickler 12/29/1774
Thomas Arden, son of John and Sarah Arden, 5/31/1794
William Mickler, son of Jacob Mickler, 7/14/1800
John H. Mickler----
Robert Mickler, son of Robert and Ann Mickler, 12/12/1825
James Arden Mickler, son of Robert and Ann Mickler, 12/12/1827
Mahala Mickler, dau. of Thomas and Eve Arden, 4/23/1836

Deaths
Eve Arden 11/10/1836   Peter Mickler 11/23/1839
William Arden Seals 7/23/1838

(Robert Mickler Bible contd.....)

Marriages

John Hebbard to Elizabeth Allen Mickler 12/19/1824, by Hon.
William Gibson
Robert Mickler to Ann Ortega 3/14/1825, by E. B. Gould
Isabella Hebbard to Cyrus H. Stedwell 4/5/1855 by Rev. J. Turner
Elizabeth A. Hebbard to Archibald W. Seals 6/18/1846
Louisa S. Hebbard to James H. Helveston 10/1/1848
J. W. Hebbard to R. E.--Stark 4/19/1888, by Rev. J. H. James
Euphemia T. Hebbard to Edward F. Gates 12/8/1856 by Rev. Gardner
Amanda M. Hebbard to John Peel 9/7/1854

Births

John Hebbard b. at St. Marys, Ga. 3/19/1802
Elizabeth Allen Mickler b. at St. Marys, Ga. 8/1/1803
Samuel Flood Hebbard, son of John and Elizabeth Hebbard, b. at
St. Marys, Ga., 12/10/1825
Elizabeth Ann Hebbard, dau. of John and Elizabeth Hebbard, b.
at. St. Marys, 6/2/1828
Mary Catherine, dau. of John and Elizabeth Hebbard, b. 11/6/1829
Mahala Amanda Hebbard, dau. of John and Elizabeth Hebbard, b.
at St. Marys, 12/8/1831
Louisa Satira Hebbard, dau. of John and Elizabeth Hebbard, b. at
St. Marys, 2/19/1833
Isabella Matilda Hebbard, dau. of John and Elizabeth Hebbard, b.
at St. Marys, 10/1835
Euphemia Thuriza Hebbard, dau. of John and Elizabeth Hebbard,
b. at St. Marys, 1/10/1839
Laura Eliza Hebbard, dau. of John and Elizabeth Hebbard, b. at
St. Marys, 1/25/1841

DANIEL D. ARDEN BIBLE
Owner: Irene Arden, Decatur, Ga.

Francis Benjamin, son of Margaret E. and Daniel D. Arden, b. in
Savannah 3/17/1853
William Willey Arden b. 10/1/1854 at Beaufort, S. C.
Peter Hawkins, b. 10/1854 (servant of Margaret E. G. Arden many
years.)
Thomas Milton Arden b. 8/29/1856   Mary Eve Arden b. 1/23/1863
James Edward Arden b. 6/28/1858   Laurence Edward Arden b.
James Read Arden b. 7/10/1859   10/24/1871
Daniel Douglas Arden b. 6/18/1861   Mary Osgood Arden b.
                                       1/12/1873
Daniel D. Arden, Jr., b. 6/18/1861
Irene Maria Rawls b. 11/23/1863
Inez Rawls Arden, their 1st child, b. at Guyton, Ga., 6/9/1888
Irene Arden, their 2d child, b. at Guyton, Ga., 5/1/1891
Daniel D. Arden, Jr., their 3rd child, b. at Guyton, Ga.,
10/25/1892
Morgan Rawls Arden, their 4th child, b. at Guyton, Ga., 7/20/1898
Daniel D. Arden b. 10/11/1824
Margaret E. Garven b. 10/13/1828. They were married 7/8/1851,
in Savannah, Ga.
Frank Benjamin Arden m. 11/12/1878?
William Wylly Arden m. 11/30/1875
Thomas Milton Arden m. 2/25/1885
James Read Arden m. 8/1878
Daniel Douglas Arden m. 10/20/1886

(Daniel D. Arden Bible, Marriages, contd....

Mary Eva Arden m. 11/18/1886
E. E. Arden to Susie Footman 6/25/1890
Daniel D. Arden, Jr. to Irene M. Rawls 10/20/1886, Guyton, Ga.
Mary Osgood Arden to Robert K. King of Atlanta, at Guyton, Ga.,
   9/6/1896
Daniel D. Arden III m. 11/16/1921 Caroline Battle at Bainbridge,
   Ga. He was son of Daniel D. Arden and Irene Rawls.
Morgan Rawls Arden, son of D. D. and Irene Arden, m. Sarah
   Frances Fullerton at Hillsboro, Ga., 4/27/1927
Irene Arden to Brook G. Ellison 8/16/1936, 9 W. Grady St.,
   Statesboro, Ga.
Carrie Matilda Arden b. in Beaufort, S. C., 11/2/1834, dau. of
   Thomas (Milton) Arden

Deaths
James Edward Arden 7/8/1858   W. W. Arden 4/27/1890 Guyton, Ga.
Thomas M. Arden, Sr. 11/15/1872 Inez Rawls Arden 3/20/1891
Mary D. Lippsy 8/20/1882 in   at Guyton, Ga., bur. Guyton
   Scarboro.   cem., dau. of Daniel & Irene

Frank Benjamin Arden d. 7/10/1926 Brimingham, at home of Martha,
   his dau. by his 1st wife. Bur. in Bonaventure Cemetery, 7/12th
Margaret E. Arden, wife of D. D. Arden, Sr., d. at Guyton, Ga.,
   4/21/1892, bur. at Laurel Grove Cemetery, Savannah, Ga.
Daniel D. Arden, Sr., husband of M. E. Arden, d. at Guyton, Ga.,
   10/11/1896, 72 yrs., bur. at Laurel Grove Cemetery, Savannah,
   Ga.
James Read Arden b. 7/10/1893 at Savannah, Ga., bur. in Laurel
   Grove Cemetery, Savannah, Ga., leaving wife and 5 children.
Daniel D. Arden, 2nd son of Daniel D. and Margaret E. Arden,
   d. 2/18/1936 in Statesboro, Ga., bur. Guyton, Ga. Cemetery,
   2/19th.

               WILLIAM BULLOCK BIBLE Of Franklin Co., Ga.
               Owner: Mrs. Joe Erickson, Nacogdoches, Texas

Marriages
William Bullock and Elizabeth Oliphant 9/30/1784
William Bullock and Spicey Bowman 8/23/1796

Deaths
Elizabeth Oliphant Bullock 6/24/1796

Births
William Bullock 3/1/1764   Edward Bullock 8/27/1797
Elizabeth Oliphant 10/29/1764   David Bullock 2/20/1799
Winifred Bullock 10/14/1785   Elizabeth Bullock 8/22/1803
Sally Bullock 7/1/1787   William O. Bullock 9/22/1805
James Bullock 11/30/1789   John Bullock 3/8/1807
Susannah Bullock 1/17/1792   Zachariah Bullock 5/3/1809

                        W. WHITTING BIBLE
               Owner: Mrs. Merlyn H. Whiting
          103-B Westcliff Center, Warner Robins, Ga. 31093

Betty Whitting b. 2/17/1846   Robert Whitting b. 5/27/1855
W. Whitting b. 9/17/1842   Besty Whitting b. 4/7/1858

(Whitting Bible, Births, contd....)

W. Whitting b. 5/26/1849   Lizer Jane b. 5/17/1860
George Whitting b. 9/27/1851   Mairthey Ann b. 8/1/1862
Betsy Whitting b. 3/9/1854   John T. Whitting b. 6/11/1865

Family Record of John and Clara Whiting:
John Whiting b. 6/11/1865   George Aurthur Whiting
Clara Felty Whiting --   b. 4/1/1893
Homer Floyd Whiting b. 11/15/1890   Raney Whiting b. 6/23/1895
                                    Laura Whiting b. 7/20/1897
Paper in Bible:
"Whiting Home in England was Mayne Eng. their Grandfather Edgely
Home was in Chatters Eng. in Camereashire County near London.
Their G. F. name was Frances or Frank. Their G. M. name was Mary
Edgelly. John Thomas Edgely an uncle md. in Dodkin Eng. Thomas
Felty son of Michael and Alpha b. 1821 d. 1851. Ellen G. Felty
wife of T. N. Felty d. 7/5/1902 age 69 yrs., 6 mos., 21 days.
Robert W. Felty son of T. N. and Ellen G. Felty b. 1822? d. 1888
Alpha Felty wife of Michael Felty b. 1803 d. 1866."

LORENZO IRVIN HANSFORD
Of Putnam Co., Ga.
Owner: Mrs. W. P. Garrett, Chester Heights, Pa.

Lorenzo Irvin Hansford b. 11/19/1809, d. 9/21/1868
Matilda b. 3/1/1818, d. 9/25/1869
Luisa Jane b. 12/31/1835
Rhoda Elender b. 4/14/1837
James Jones b. 6/24/1839
Sarah Elizabeth b. 6/28/1841
Milly Adaline b. 5/11/1844
John William Jasper b. 1/16/1849
-----b. 1852

Mary Ann Matilda d. 1863   Benjamin Irvin d. 1864

JOHN ANDERSON BIBLE
Owner: Melton Anderson, RFD, Claxton, Ga.

John Anderson b. 2/2/1794, m. 11/27/1817, d. 12/2/1876
Children:
Harriet, b. 3/12/1818   David C. b. 3/13/1827
James b. 10/12/1819   Moses b. 11/23/1829
Martha b. 3/20/1821   Edmond W. b. 10/30/1831
John F. b. 11/1/1822   Josiah Eldridge b. 1/1/1834
William C. b. 9/14/1824   Jasper V. b. 6/1/1836
                               Elizabeth b. 3/13/1838

David C. Anderson b. 3/13/1827 d. 11/11/1899
Jincy W. Anderson b. 5/14/1831 d. 9/27/1900

JAMES MONROE CULPEPPER BIBLE
Owner: Barbara Lockard
6305 Greencastle Ct., Ft. Worth, Tx. 76118

Births
James Monroe Culpepper b. 6/28/1823
Nancy Culpepper b. 5/1/1816
E. A. R. Culpepper b. 11/8/1843   William Culpepper b. 11/14/1845
John H. Culpepper b. 3/13/1847   Cordealia A. Culpepper
Martha A. R. Culpepper b. 2/8/1849   b. 2/20/1865
Early G. H. Culpepper b. 12/16/1850   Francis Monroe Culpepper
Sarah Jane Culpepper b. 8/30/1853   b. 6/22/1865
Samuel Bartley Culpepper   Columbus C. Culpepper
  b. 6/17/1856   b. 11/18/1866
James Culpepper b. 11/26/1859   Absalom Culpepper b. 3/6/1868
Mary A. Culpepper b. 9/5/1861   George W.Culpepper b. 11/29/-
                                       Charlie T. Culpepper b.
                                         10/15/1871
                                       Henry H. Culpepper b.
                                         9/28/1873
                                       Mercer Culpepper b. 7/6/1876

Marriages
James M. Culpepper and Nancy Collins 12/22/1842
James M. Culpepper and M. F. DeLoach 11/1/1870?
William Culpepper and M. E. F. Huff 11/20/1866

Deaths
Levin Collins 4/15/1855   James M. Culpepper 6/8/1894
Ann Collins 4/29/1860?   Mary F. Culpepper 1/24/1897
Nancy Culpepper 5/21/1866?   Cordilia A. Koon 6/29/1902
Columbus C. Culpepper 4/13/1867   S. B. Culpepper 10/15/1941

JOSIAH PATTERSON BIBLE
Owner: W. L. Templeton, McCormick, S. C.

Josiah Patterson, son of Samuel Patterson and Abegail Blair, dau.
  of Samuel Blair, m. by Rev. Francis Cummins 2/6/1794

R. B. Cater, son of Thomas W. Cater and Jane L. Patterson, dau.
  of Josiah Patterson, m. by Rev. Dr. Waddel 8/23/1832

Josiah Patterson was again m. to Mrs. Sarah Terry, wid. of Dr.
  Jeremiah S. Terry by Rev. Dr. Barr 9/16/1824

Josiah Patterson again m. wid. Phelps (Eleanor Phelps 11/27/1832)

Births
Sarah Cowan, 1st born of J. & A. Patterson, b. 1/24/1795, m. Sqr.
  Andrew Giles (3/5/1812)
Mary Adams b. 1/17/1797 m. Rev. Robert Campbell
Samuel b. 1/27/1799, d. young
John Adams b. 3/10/1801 m. Miss Breazel
James Cowan b. 10/6/1803 m. Laura Evan Winn
Elizabeth Pleasant b. 9/1/1807 d. young
Louisia Abigail b. 10/15/1810, m. Twining Hamilton
Jane Lovely b. 1/11/1813 m. Richard Bohun Cater
Josiah Blair b. 7/9/1815 m. Mary McNeal

JAMES BARNARD BIBLE
Owner: Mrs. John B. Mills, Ocala, Fla.

Marriages
James Barnard to Catherine Guerard 1/23/1811
James Barnard to Margaret C. Williams 4/23/1819
A. F. Barnard to Fannie E. Turner 10/18/1877
L. Demere to Virginia Barnard 7/19/1842
G. W. Hardee to Margaret L. Barnard 8/13/1844
Campbell J. Barnard to Helen Williams 3/19/1859
James L. hines to Vernon Barnard 12/12/1860
L. S. Quarterman to Julia Barnard 9/30/1862

Births
James S. Barnard 12/9/1811   Mary Henrietta Barnard 5/2/1816
Catherine C. Barnard 10/17/1813   Bradley G. Barnard 2/2/1818
Godin G. Barnard 12/24/1815

Ann Catherine Barnard b. 4/1/1820   James Campbell Barnard b.
Virginia Clancy Barnard b. 11/7/1821   5/1/1830
Williams B. Barnard b. 5/30/1823   Isabella Lenobia Barnard
Vernon Rosa Barnard b. 11/21/1824   b. 1/9/1835
Margaret Louisa Barnard b. 8/23/1826 Clifford Victoria Barnard
b. 4/29/1828, a son   b. 1/15/1837
                                     Andrew Fuller Barnard
                                         b. 4.6.1839
                                     Florence Augusta Barnard
                                         b. 1/27/1841

Deaths
James S. Barnard 10/25/1817   Mrs. Margaret L. Hardee 11/1885
Godin G. Barnard 4/18/1816   C. J. Barnard 7/1889
Catherine G. Barnard 2/18/1818 Mrs. Virginia Demere 10/1900
Mary Henrietta Barnard---   Mrs. L. S. Quarterman 7/22/1906
Dr. Williams Barnard 7/26/1854 Miss Clifford Barnard 3/30/1907
  age 30 at Fancy Bluff, Ga.   Mrs. V. R. Hines 12/29/1907
Dr. James Barnard 2/1859   Dr. A. F. Barnard 1/11/1908
  age 73 yrs.   Mrs. F. E. Barnard 11/25/1911
Margaret C. Barnard 11/1877   at Savannah, Ga.
  age 76 yrs.   Mrs. Florence Fulton 4/25/1925
Isabel B. Barnard 7/1879   at Tampa
Ann C. Barnard 12/1882

JOHN PRIAR ANDERSON BIBLE
Owner: Mrs. A. G. Richardson, Bowden, Ga.

"Mr. Albert Garner d. at his home 7/21/1921. He lived a good life
and is supping in glory! He just lacked 20 days being 72 yrs. old
at time of his death."
John Priar Anderson b. 12/17/1826
Martha Malysa Anderson b. 6/6/1830. They were m. 1/18/1849
                        Children:
Cyntheann Josephine Anderson b. 2/8/1850
Thomas Wesley Anderson b. 6/7/1852
Lucinda Elizabeth Anderson b. 6/29/1854
Jeptha Manson Anderson b. 5/2/1856
Marion Jefferson Anderson b. 5/15/1858
Frances Cyndonia Anderson b. 2/17/1860
James Henry Anderson b. 12/28/1861

(John Priar Anderson Bible contd....)
John Priar Anderson b. 8/31/1864
Zachariah Harris Anderson b. 10/12/1866
William Gardner Anderson b. 2/13/1870
Lydia Mae Doner Anderson b. 2/17/1876

                BENJAMIN W. MADDUX BIBLE of Jasper Co., Ga.
                Owner: Rev. Silas Emmett Lucas, Jr., Vidalia, Ga.

Benjamin Wills Maddux b. 1/29/1786 m. 2/14/1815 Kathrine Powell,
    b. 6/22/1793.
Civility J. Maddux m. Alfred Poe 9/16/1840
James M. Maddux m. Sarah H.---11/1/184-
B. F. (Benjamin Fletcher) Maddux b. 1/26/1823
Elizabeth Powell b. 4/22/--
B. F. Maddux m. Elizabeth Powell 1/4/1844
Evan Powell Maddux b. 12/1/1815
James Monroe Maddux b. 2/16/1818
Zachariah Maddux b. 12/8/1819
George W. Maddux b. 2/21/1821
Sarah Ann Jane Gaines b. 5/12/1816
Sivility Jane Maddux b. 1/14/1825
Maria Ann Maddux b. 11/28/1826
Moses Maddux b. 3/1829

Zachariah Maddux d. 4/23/1825, age 80
Zachariah Maddux, son of Zachariah Maddux, d. 5/18/1825, aged 40?
    Was Preacher of the Gospel....
B. F. Maddux d. 1/7/1890
Audie Cantey Dale 9/30/1859
Sarah H. Powell, consort of Moses Powell and dau. of William
    Maddux, d. 4/24/1841
Mary Maddux d.---

Oliver Maddux b. 5/5/1831
Sarah Elizabeth Maddux b. 3/16/1833
Harvey Maddux b. 8/28/1835
Mary J. (Jane) Gladen b. 3/5/1845
Sarah N. (Naomi) Harris b. 6/24/1824, consort of James M.
    (Monroe) Maddux
Samuel T. Poe b. 1841
Tom Drummer b. 11/18/1834
Claud Maddux d. 12/22/1839
Myrtle Crabtree m. J. C. White 12/24/1937
John Calvin Crabtree b. 6/20/1878 d. 1/3/1943

                        JOHN MORGAN DAVIS BIBLE
                Owner: Thomas A. Valentine, Atlanta, Ga.

John Morgan Davis b. 10/21/1822, d. 12/16/1893 (son of George
    Cook Davis and Jane Montgomery Davis)
Mary M. Malcom b. 4/5/1825, d. 11/17/1903 (dau. of George W.
    Malcom and Susannah Allen Malcom)
                Children of John M. and Mary M. Davis:
Susan Ann Davis b. 9/27/1843, d. 8/8/1844
Eliza Jane Davis b. 2/14/1845, d. 2/5/1847

(John Morgan Davis Bible contd....)

Joel Colley Davis b. 9/11/1847, d. 12/10/1914
George W. Davis b. 11/8/1849, d. 7/16/1924
Laura Ann Davis b. 11/18/1851, d. 12/6/1927
Elizabeth America Davis b. 3/8/1854, d. 1/15/1926
Eugenia F. Davis b. 10/9/1856, d. 3/14/1905
Mary Fletta Davis b. 1/31/1859, d. 1945
James Montgomery Davis b. 3/13/1861, d. 3/17/1954
John Morgan Davis Jr. b. 1/7/1863, d. 12/1896
Twin dau. b. 1/7/1863, d. 1/8/1863

Marriages of Children:
Joel C. Davis to Emma Johnson Day 12/5/1867
George W. Davis to Emma Hurst 11/17/1870
Laura A. Davis to Thomas F. Hollis 1872
Elizabeth A. Davis to James F. Almond 1875 (1st)
Elizabeth A. Davis to James Estes (2d)
Eugenia F. Davis to W. F. Robertson
James M. Davis to Nealie E. Thomas 10/16/1882
James M. Davis to Minerva Hurst 4/19/1936
Mary Fleeta Davis to Eugene E. Ozburn
John M. Davis, Jr. to Mattie Hill

NATHANIEL DAY BIBLE
Owner: Mrs. Florence Day Ellis, Monroe, Ga.

Nathaniel Day, son of David and Mary Day, b. 3/5/1775, d.
1/11/1855, m. 5/21/1807 to Hannah Mendenhall, dau. of Markaduke
and Alice Mendenhall, b. 2/20/1785, d. 4/3/1848.
Children:

Mary Day b. 12/16/1810
Lucinda Day b. 1812 d. 6/1813
Lucinda Day II b. 2/18/1814 d. 9/22/1891
John Day d. 1/20/1835
David Day b. 9/12/1818 d. 10/13/1838
Benson Day b. 10/5/1819 d. 1/17/1874
Elizabeth Day b. 1/3/1822
Frances Day b. 3/27/1824
Nathaniel James Day b. 9/12/1826
Martha Day b. 1828

Marriages
Mary Day to John Miller 8/26/1830
Lucinda Day II to William Phillips
David Day to Amanda Daniel 11/18/1836
Benson Day to Narcisa F. Henderson 3/5/1840
Elizabeth Day to David Studdard 12/22/18--
Frances Day to---Smith
Nathaniel J. Day to Martha E. Tucker 7/3/1855
Martha Day to lewis A. Mayo

WILLIAM J. EVANS BIBLE
Owner: Mrs. Joseph A. Ross, Henderson, Texas

Births
--H. Evans, -- of William J. Evans and Elizabeth Evans, b.
12/29/1832
Charles H. Evans, son of William J. Evans and Sarah Elizabeth
Evans b. 7/7/1836
Edmund L. Nicholus Evans, son of William J. and Sarah Elizabeth
Evans, b. 9/11/1838
Sarah Ann Elizabeth Fox, dau. of Charles and Lucinda Fox, b.
3/14/1839
William O'Neal, son of G. W. and S. A. E. Hampton, b. 9/21/1865
George Walker, son of G. W. and S. A. E. Hampton, b. 2/15/1868
Susan Bonner, dau. of G. W. and S. A. E. Hampton, b. 2/11/1875
Edmund Fox, son of G. W. and S. A. E. Hampton, b. 2/28/1877
John Randolph, son of G. W. and S. A. E. Hampton, b. 11/17/1870
Ruth Ella, dau. of G. W. and S. A. E. Hampton, b. 1/3/1873
Jesse, dau. of G. W. and S. A. E. Hampton, b. 3/3/1880
Enock Marvin, son of G. W. and S. A. E. Hampton, b. 11/17/1882
Elliott, dau. of E. and Lula G. Hampton, b. 10/29/1890

Deaths
John Fox, son of Nicholas and Susan, d. 10/27/1817, age 2 yrs.,
4 mos., 15 days
Frances Agniss Fox, dau. of Nicholas and Susan,, d. 6/24/1820,
age 2 yrs., 6 mos., 21 days
Sarah Elizabeth Evans d. 3/23/1839, age 26 yrs., 3 mos., 2 days
Edmond Fox, son of G. W. and S. A. E. Hampton, d. 9/1884
Robert Wal- Fox d. 2/6/18--
Nicholas Fox, son of James and Sarah Fox, d. 9/15/1847, age 72
Edmond B. Fox d. 3/22/1858, age 54
Susannah Fox d. 9/19/1852
Susan Ann Kizzah Hampton d. 3/3/1868

WILLIAM F. TARPLEY BIBLE
Owner: Luther R. Underwood, Macon, Ga.

Marriages
William F. Tarpley and Elvenia M. Metts m. 10/23/1876

Births
William F. Tarpley 10/18/1852   Charlie Otis Tarpley 11/3/1889
Elvenia M. Metts 9/18/1860   Clarence Gordon Tarpley 4/16/1892?
Annie Lee Tarpley 7/14/1878   Marshall Jones Tarpley 4/11/1894
William Benjamin Tarpley   Horace Edward Tarpley 3/1/1898
2/8/1881   Mattie Alina Tarpley 2/13/1901
Mary Evelyn Tarpley 2/12/1884   Bernice Carolyn Tarpley 5/16/1936
Nora Virginia Tarpley 10/21/1886

Deaths
Charlie Otis Tarpley 5/19/1892   Bernice Carolyn Tarpley 7/6/1938
Nora Virginia Tarpley 3/18/1903   Mary Evelyn Tarpley 5/14/1954
Horace Edward Tarpley 5/1/1909   (wife of Luther R. Underwood Sr.)
Willie Tarpley 10/18/1922   Annie L. Tarpley 7/1/1962
Elvenia Tarpley 7/19/1932   (wife of James Fordham)
William F. Tarpley 11/9/1938   Marshall Jonas Tarpley 1/3/1963
Clarence G. Tarpley 3/31/1977

NATHANIEL HARBIN GOSS BIBLE of Hall Co., Ga.
Owner: George Sampson Goss, Conroe, Texas

Nathaniel H. Goss b. 9/3/1805 Pendleton Dist., S. C., d. 9/5/1888
in Phelps, Lawrence Co., Mo., m. 1/10/1828 in Hall Co., Ga.,
Melicent Whitten, b. 1/1/1814 Spartanburg Dist., S. C., dau. of
Rev. James Whitten and Elizabeth Ann Thompson; she d. 4/27/1900
in Phelps, Mo. Their children:

Benjamin Franklin Goss b. 3/30/1829 m. Louisa Perry 1/23/1851,
d. 12/7/1894 in Arkansas, killed by falling tree.
Martha Elizabeth Goss b. 2/3/1831 m. Jackson Ayres 2/2/1847,
d. 9/3/1864
Malinda E. Goss b. 8/21/1832 m. Evan P. Perry 8/21/1851, d.
12/12/1907 in Phelps, Lawrence Co., Mo.

James Whitten Goss b. 1/29/1834 m. 1st to Eunice West, 3/3/1853,
2nd, Malinda Caroline Pain (Payne) 12/23/1870, d. 9/1914, in
Dallas, Texas, bur. in Old Soldiers Cemetery.
Louisa Caroline Goss b. 2/5/1836 m. Rev. James M. West 7/30/1854,
d. 4/26/1864

Calvin Benson Goss b. 12/9/1847 m. Mary Ann Densmore 10/10/1858,
d. 2/28/1863 at Vicksburg, Miss., a Confederate Soldier, bur. in
Confederate Cemetery there.

Melicent Elvira Goss b. 7/14/1840 m. Samuel Mercer Densmore
7/25/1858, d. 3/14/1912, Bluff Dale, Erath Co., Texas.
Nathaniel Jackson Goss b. 7/15/1842 m. Mary Elizabeth Roe
2/14/1865, d. 1/31/1918, bur. Goss Cemetery, Phelps, Mo.
Alfred Webb Goss b. 9/26/1844, d. 3/5/1845
Robert Lewis Goss b. 12/11/1845 m. Hannah Mancennella Roe
12/28/1873, d. 3/19/1923, at Rodgers, Benton Co., Ark.
Silas Washington Goss b. 2/2/1848 m. Catherine Ellen Shelton
11/26/1872, d. 11/18/1920, bur. Springfield, Mo.
Wilson Lumpkin Goss b. 7/8/1850 m. Huldah Jane Wilkins 9/19/1867,
d. 10/22/--, Humble, Texas.
Mary Irene Goss b. 8/20/1852, d. 4/1/1893 in Phelps, Mo.
Baby girl Goss b. 8/20/1854, d. 9/3/1854.
Orpha Louisa Goss b. 2/18/1856, d. 9/21/1880 Phelps, Mo.
Juliann Melissa Goss b. 6/21/1858 m. John Franklin Morgan
12/30/1877 at Phelps, Mo. She d. 6/18/1934, bur. Colfax, Whitman
Co., State of Washington.

JACOB DICUS BIBLE

Jacob B. Dicus b. 3/25/--   Harrison B. Dicus b. 10/4/1837
Haner Dicus b. 6/--   Rebecca Ann Dicus b. 11/11/1839
William C. Dicus b. 12/27/1828   Kayziah Dicus b. 5/17/1842
James E. Dicus b. 2/14/1830   Milton Dicus b. 8/26/1844
Elisey Jain Dicus b. 2/14/1833   Winfield Dicus b. 9/2/1847
America Dicus b. 8/27/1835

James E. Dicus and Rhoda L. Hicks m. 2/24/1853

JONATHAN WRIGHT NOLES BIBLE
Owner: Mrs. C. F. Noles, Eastman, Ga.

Births
Jonathan Wright Noles 5/31/1852   Winaford Endora Noles 8/14/1881
Columbia Jane Noles 8/22/1861   Mattie Viola Noles Anderson
Wright Noles 4/26/1828   10/5/1883
Mary Frances Noles 10/29/1879   Bessie Vienna Noles Hull
                     8/14/1887
                     Charles Parker Noles 8/14/1887

JOAB RASAN TISON BIBLE
Owner: Mrs. Willie Gibson, Dawson, Ga.

Children of Joab Ragan Tison and Mary Elizabeth Green:

Tallulah Mattie b. 8/4/1866   Leonora Augusta b. 12/25/1871
Mary Rebecca b. 12/28/1868   George Eason b. 1/8/1874
                     Willie Elector 8/4/1876

MRS. EMMA M. BUSH BIBLE
322 Sidney St., Atlanta, Ga.

Deaths
Jones Howard Bush 7/14/1900

MRS. W. N. LEITCH BIBLE
Eastman, Ga.

Marriages
William N. Leitch m. Elizabeth Braswell 3/14/1869 near Cross
  Keys Post Office, DeKalb Co., Ga.
William N. Leitch m. Jane F. Woodruff 12/16/1874
William N. Leitch m. Addie Louise Heaner 11/19/1902 by Rev. T. M.
  Galphin at John C. Hearner's res., Orangeburg Co., S. C.

WILLIAM N. LEITCH BIBLE
Owner: Mrs. W. N. Leitch, Eastman, Ga.

Births
William N. Leitch, DeKalb Co. 11/17/1846
Jane F. Woodruff, DeKalb Co. 5/13/1840
William J. Leitch, Hall Co., 1872
William R. Leitch, Dodge Co., 8/21/1876
Arthur Mr. Leitch, Dodge Co., 2/5/1879

(William N. Leitch Bible contd....)

Mary E. Leitch, Dodge Co., 8/2/1882
Addie Louise Leitch, Orangeburg Co., S. C. 11/5/1872
Bertha Doyle Leitch, Orangeburg Co., S. C. 3/9/1904
Marie Louise, Orangeburg Co., S. C. 4/15/1909
Eliza Leitch nee Braswell b. 3/11/1852 Cross Keys, DeKalb Co.

JOHN B. NEWMAN
Owner: Mrs. Mattie H. Wright

John B. Newman, Ga. and Harriet Whittaker, S. C., m. 2/17/1843
Edgefield, S. C. by Rev. N. Holmes. Wit: David Hofman and H. C.
Davis.

John B. Newman b. 11/17/1820
Harriett Whittaker b. 1/9/1826   Their Children:

Martha E. b. 2/11/1844   Fannie A. b. 1/29/1856
Harriett F. b. 8/31/1849   John C. b. 3/26/1862
Albert H. b. 8/25/1852

Martha E. m. 7/22/1866
Hattie F. m. 12/28/1870
Fannie A. m. 12/28/1870

GIBSON-BIVINS BIBLE
Owner: Mrs. Homer Bivins
Milledgeville, Ga.

Annie Jones Gibson m. Homer Bivins 10/28/1909
Children:
Thomas Ellsworth Bivins b. 8/25/1910
Hazel Bivins b. 5/25/1912 m. 10/5/1933 to James H. Craig, Jr.

ADAMS BIBLE

James Adams b. 6/2/1816 d. 11/26/1818
Sarah Adams b. 4/11/1819
Jane Adams b. 9/28/1820 m. James Grimes
Jefferson Adams b. 10/22/1823 d. 5/21/1864 m. Susan Meriwether
Robert Adams b. 3/22/1825 m. Rebecca Bass
Frances Adams b. 1/5/1828 m. Gen. Brantley of Savannah
Robert Adams m. Frances Hudson 9/9/1815 by Rev. Daniel Duffie.
Both d. 1828

CHARLES ABERCROMBIE BIBLE
Owner: Mrs. Robert S. Lovett
Locust Valley, Long Isl, N. Y.

Abner Abercrombie b. 1/10/1771   Jane Abercrombie b. 12/25/1781
Edmund Abercrombie b. 1/12/1773   John Abercrombie b. 8/12/1785
Sallie Abercrombie b. 1/29/1775   Anderson Abercrombie
Wiley Abercrombie b. 2/17/1777   b. 8/28/1786
Leonard Abercrombie b. 2/17/1779   Nancy Abercrombie b. 6/3/1788
                                 Charles Abercrombie
                                   b. 4/8/1792
                                James Abercrombie b. 2/18/1792

JAMES HENRY BONNER BIBLE
Owner: Mrs. Sarah Hearn Garrard
Milledgeville, Ga.

Mrs. Sarah E. Bonner, Putnam Co., Ga.
James Henry Bonner b. 7/11/1849 Putnam Co., d. 1918
Sarah E. b. 10/28/1851
William Melrose Gregory b. 7/8/1849 d. 6/8/1856
Mattie W. Gregory b. 6/8/1856

HUGH PERCIVAL BRANNEN BIBLE
Owner: Mrs. D. W. Brannen

Hugh Percival Brannen b. 7/7/1906
Wife, Mary Katherine Read b. 7/22/1904

BRANNEN BIBLE
Owner: Mrs. D. W. Brannen

James Beatty Griffith b. 7/18/1890
Wife, Sarah Florence Brannen b. 11/17/1897

47

DENTON WILLIAMS BRANNEN BIBLE
Owner: Mrs. D. W. Brannen

Denton Williams Brannen b. 9/25/1870
Wife, Eliza Neyle Thomas b. 5/2/1874   Their Children:

Births
Denton Williams Jr. 10/18/1896   Eleanor 11/15/1907
Sarah Florence 11/17/1897   Neyle Thomas 11/23/1910
Hugh Percival 7/7/1900   Eugene Bryan 8/27/1913
Walter Campbell 2/11/1902   Lewis Alexander 5/22/1916

CASE-MILLER BIBLE Of Milledgeville
Owner: Mrs. L. S. Fowler, Milledgeville, Ga.

Charles Lane Case b. 5/1/1859
Otelia Miller b. 7/5/1861   Their Children:

Henrietta Louise Case b. 3/24/1883
Annie Otelia Case b. 5/3/1885
Twins - Charles Weiderman Case & George Joseph Case b. 10/8/1890

JOSEPH FLETCHER COMER BIBLE *

Joseph Fletcher Comer, son of Reuben Tally Comer, b. 3/23/1844
Martha Hannah Comer b. 11/9/1840
Henry Tally David Comer b. 3/21/1870
Joseph Fletcher Comer b. 10/13/1871
Thomas Fletcher Johnson Comer b. 10/13/1871
Joseph Fletcher Comer and Martha Hannah Johnson m. 5/13/1839
Henry T. D. Comer m. Minnie Baugh abt. 1892
Thomas Fletcher Comer m. ida Pauline Howard 6/12/1896

Joseph Fletcher Comer d. 8/5/1918, age 74 yrs., 4 mos., 22 days
Martha H. Comer d. 1/14/1895, 54 yrs., 2 mos., 5 days

LEWIS J. DEUPREE BIBLE
Owner: Miss Mary Deupree Hunnicutt, Athens, Ga.

Marriages
Lewis J. Deupree and Martha J. Adams 12/9/1849
Lewis J. Deupree and Lucy Y. Peelbes 5/24/1864 by Rev. William
  Parks
Mary L. Deupree to J. A. Hunnicutt 2/22/1870
John W. McCalla and Francina Deupree 5/16/1871 by Rev. F. H. Ivey
Goodloe H. Yancey and Lucy G. Deupree 9/26/1872 by Rev.Dr.Skinner

*See also p. 438.   48

(Lewis J. Deupree Bible contd....)

Births
Lewis J. Deupree 7/31/1793   Mary Lewis Deupree 10/12/1852
Martha J. Deupree 5/15/1829   Lucy Gratton Deupree 12/5/1854
Francina Deupree 12/19/1850   Martha Mourning Deupree 9/24/1856

Deaths
Martha J. Deupree 10/14/1856, age 28 yrs.
Martha Mourning Deupree 8/8/1854
Lewis J. Deupree 4/17/1870, age 77 yrs.
Francina McCalla, formerly Francina Deupree, 9/2/1872, at res.
in Athens, age 22 yrs.

                CAMILLA OLIVER PHARR BIBLE Of Washington, Ga.
                     Owner: Mrs. Andrew C. Erwin, Athens, Ga.

Alexander Pharr b. 3/4/1792 d. Newton Co. 11/9/1865
Permelia A. Pharr, his wife, b. Oglethorpe C., 2/1/1800
d. Newton Co. 5/17/1865
Shelton Oliver b. Elbert Co. 7/9/1801, d. Oglethorpe Co.
9/17/1870
Martha W. Oliver b. Elbert Co. 8/24/1811, d. Oglethorpe Co.
1/1/1881
Marcus A. Pharr b. 3/22/1823
Camilla Oliver, his wife, b. 7/19/1834

They were m. 12/21/1852

Fannie Williams, their 1st dau., b. 5/17/1855
Emma Pharr Willingham
Sallie Pharr McWhorter
Marcus Aurelius
Lizzie Pharr Dyson

Deaths
Marcus A. Pharr 1897   Emma Pharr Willingham---
Camilla Oliver Pharr 1914   Sallie Pharr McWhorter 11/12/1923

                          JOSEPH RUCKER BIBLE
                  Owner: Mrs. T. W. Rucker, Athens, Ga.

Joseph Rucker and Margaret W. Speer m. at Cherokee Ford,
    Abbeville Dist., S. C. by Rev. Moses Waddell, 3/5/1812
Jeptha V. Harris and Sally Hunt m. at Apple Hill, Elbert Co.,
    Ga., by Hon. Charles Tait, 10/4/1804
Tinsley W. Rucker and Sarah E. harris m. at Farm Hill, Elbert
    Co., Ga., by Rev. Moses Waddell, 12/23/1834

Births
Tinsley W. Rucker b. Elbert Co., Ga. 4/24/1813
Sarah E. Harris b. Elbert Co., Ga. 8/18/1814

                                49

(Joseph Rucker Bible contd.....)

Sarah Margaret, eldest dau. of Tinsley W. and Sarah E. Rucker,
  b. at Farm Hill, Elbert Co., Ga., 9/15/1835

Deaths
Tinsley W. Rucker 1/8/1864, age 50 yrs., 8 mos., 14 days at
  Savannah, Ga. at Angus McAlpin's.
Sarah E. Rucker 4/13/1895 Athens, Ga.
James M. Hull 2/8/1864 at res. in Athens, Ga.
Joseph Rucker 9/17/1864 Ruckersville, Ga.

JOSEPH FLETCHER COMER, SR. BIBLE
Owner: Elizabeth Fletcher Comer Chapman

Joseph F. Comer b. 11/17/1788
Mary Comer b. 1/14/1795   Their Children:

Asbury Fletcher Comer b. 5.26.1810
William Jenkins Comer b. 9/28/1811
Elizabeth Fletcher Comer b. 11/21/1813
Reuben Tally Comer b. 2/8/1817

Joseph Fletcher Comer d. 2/1845
Mary Comer (his wife) d. 8/15/1817
William Jenkins d. 4/15/1894
Elizabeth Fletcher Comer Chapman d. 6/29/1894
Asbury Fletcher Comer d. 5/1839
Reuben Tally Comer d. 9/6/1893

JOHN MORRIS BIBLE
Owner: Mrs. L. L. Hendren, Athens, Ga.

John Morris b. 4/25/1763, d. 4/9/1833
Richard Morris b. 8/2/1765
James Morris b. 7/20/1767
  Ages of Youngest Sons:
John Morris and Elisabeth m. 8/19/1790
Joseph Cantrell b. 12/20/1813
William Cantrell b. 8/1816
Rebeckah Morris b. 2/22/1794?
Nathan B.? Cantrell b. 6/9/1818
Philip Cantrell, son of N. Cantrell and Nancy, b. -/31/1806
Mark Cantrell b. 2/26/1808
Elizabeth Cantrell b. 1/25/1810
David Cantrell b. 2/14/1812
William Cantrell b. 2/1816
Alexander Cantrell b. 4/22/1821
Elizabeth Morris, wife of John Morris, b. 9/1772

Wiley Morris b. 3/12/1812
John Morris m. Elizabeth Briscoe 8/19/1790. Their Children:
Nancy Morris b. 3/7/1791   Jemima Morris b. 3/18/1796
Mary Morris b. 8/31/1792   William Morris b. 3/6/1798
Rebecah Morris b. 2/22/1794   Joseph Morris b. 3/26/1800

50

WILLIAM MORGAN BIBLE

Marriages
William Morgan and Orra Gathright 8/4/1825
William M. Wilhite and Esther Caroline Morgan 1/7/1841
Hosea A. Bennett and Armelia A. Morgan 3/1845
Dilmus L. Jarrett and Joice Josephine Morgan 11/15/1845
William W. Morgan and Martha A. Pollard 1/30/1851
Blake B. Morgan and Nancy E. Nunn 10/9/1851

Births

William Morgan 7/30/1797	Jesse Cleveland Morgan 7/6/1837
Orra Gathright 2/13/1808	Daniel Moseley Morgan 3/5/1841
Easther Caroline Morgan 7/16/1826	Sarah Lucinda Morgan 8/18/1842
William Kesley Morgan 3/14/1827	James Polk Morgan 5/25/1844
Amelia Ann Morgan 3/14/1827	George Dales Morgan 1/15/1846
Joyce Josephine Morgan 11/11/1830	Louisa Cass Morgan 8/16/1848
Blake Brantley Morgan 2/22/1832	Benjamin Franklin Morgan
Andrew Jackson Morgan 10/29/1833	12/19/1849
Thos. Jefferson Morgan 10/29/1833	William Marcellus Morgan
Christopher Columbus Morgan 11/8/1835	12/21/1851
Dilmus Marshall Jarrett 5/25/1859	

Deaths
Thomas Jefferson Morgan 8/13/1835
Easther Caroline Wilhite 3/13/1852
William Wesley Morgan 7/12/1853
Louisa Cass Morgan 4/8/1856
Lucy Ann Wilhite 4/11/1856
George Dales Morgan 12/13/1862 in battle of Fredericksburg
William Morgan, Sr. 10/18/1863
Amelia Ann Bennett 10/16/1858
Daniel M. Morgan 1/1864
Sarah Lucinda Bennett 7/19/1874
James Polk Morgan 11/29/1873
George D. Lester 7/25/1843
Priscilla Lester 10/29/1843
Mahala Wilhite 10/26/1850
Ora Morgan 2/13/1891

ARCHIBALD MOON BIBLE Of Clarke Co.
Owner: Mrs. E. A. Lampkin, Athens, Ga.

Archibald Moon b. 1/12/1803
Nicy Moon b. 4/11/1811

Susan C. Moon b. 10/13/1828	John E. Moon b. 4/15/1840
William M. Moon b. 7/18/1830	Joseph A. A. Moon b. 4/30/1843
Philip W. Moon b. 3/6/1832	Almon R. Moon b. 8/4/1848
Maryann Elizabeth Moon b. 7/6/1837	Camila Moon b. 10/29/1850

A. Moon m. 12/13/1827
P. W. Moon m. 7/30/1851
Mary A. E. Moon m. 8/30/1852

William M. Moon d. 7/2/1893	Mrs. Nicy Moon d. 1/31/1893
John E. Moon d. 1/29/1842	Camila d. 6/13/1852

51

Marriages
Mmckleberry Merritt and Jane Brown 1/1/1824
William R. Murphey and Lucy Ann Floyd 12/21/1837
Erastus J. Murphey and Laura Ida Merritt 4/15/1866

Births

Mickleberry Merritt 12/30/1802   M. Thomas Merritt 1/28/1836
Jane Brown Merritt 10/12/1808   Juhn R. Merritt 4/16/1838
William D. Merritt 11/27/1824   James R. Merritt 7/28/1840
Mary E. Merritt 4/5/1827   Angus C. Merritt 1/11/1843
H. Wade Merritt 8/31/1829   Sarah R. merritt 1/7/1845
Eliza Ann Meritt 7/24/1831   Laura Ida Merritt 8/3/1847
Elizabeth Janie Merritt 12/30/1833   Warren A. Merritt 11/12/1849

William Reid Murphey 11/17/1819   Erasmus Milledge Murphey
Lucy Ann Floyd Murphey 12/13/1818   3/8/1848
John T. Murphey 3/15/1840   Asmon A. Murphey 9/9/1850
Erastus J. Murphey 8/10/1842   Phinchas A. Murphey 11/1852
Willie M. Murphey 5/9/1844   Artemus A. Murphey 11/6/1855
Elizabeth Murphey 5/16/1846   Melatish S. Murphey 4/20/1858
                                      Priscilla A. Murphey 11/7/1860

WILLIAM F. MATTHEWS BIBLE
The Elms, Clarke Co.

William F. Matthews and Nicy C. Matthews 6/16/1860
William F. Matthews and Martha E. Bell 2/11/1868
Robert J. hancock and Hattie L. Matthews 11/21/1897
Willie Matthews and George H. Hulme ---
Paul B. Matthews and Leta Pucket ---
Edgar Matthews and Hannah Malcy ---

Births

William F. Matthews 12/25/1824   Edgar Morton Matthews 8/23/1869
Nicy C. Matthews 8/12/1840   Lena Octavia Matthews 9/14/1871
Callie D. Matthews 6/18/1861   Paul Bell Matthews 4/29/1876
Mattie N. Matthews 3/15/1863   Hattie Louise Matthews
Willie Leona Matthews 5/4/1864   4/19/1878

Deaths

Callie D. Matthews 10/22/1862   Lena O. Matthews 7/4/1872
Mattie N. Matthews 1/6/1864   William F. Matthews 2/17/1879
Nicy C. Matthews 10/17/1865   Martha E. Bell Matthews
                                         5/6/1881

```
                    W. B. LANGFORD BIBLE
              Owner: Mrs. Cleo Langford Hodges
                        Watkinsville, Ga.
```

Births
William Bedford Langford 4/14/1848
Nellie Irene Langford 11/6/1868
George William Langofrd 10/1/1870
Cleo Estelle Langford 3/29/1872
Susan Malinda Langford 4/14/1875
Florine Cassandra Langford 9/16/1878
Fannie Barton Langford 3/7/1880
Mable Lee Langford 7/27/1888

Marriages
Cleo Estelle to Dr. William Henry Hodges 6/9/1892
Susan Malinda Langford to C. P. Hutchings 3/7/1893
Florine Cassandra Langford to A. W. Meaders 7/16/1895
Fannie Barton to E. F. Shellnutt 2/3/1904
Mable Lee Langford to Charles Mathis 6/3/1914
William Bedford Langford to Nancy Eleanor Elder 11/29/1867

Deaths
William Bedford Langford 11/27/1915
Nancy Elder Langford 3/25/1926
Nellie Irene Langford 7/12/1890
George William Langford 10/8/1871
Susan M. Hutchings (Langford) 8/3/1911
Fannie B. Langford 6/9/1912


```
                    JEREMIAH GARTRELL BIBLE
              Owner: Homer K. Nicholson, Athens, Ga.
```

Marriages
Jeremiah Gartrell to Julia Ann Eliza Thompson 12/23/1824
Jeremiah Gartrell to Margaret Rebecca Mangum 7/5/1842

Births
Jeremiah Gartrell 6/12/1801
Julia Ann Eliza Thompson 8/29/1808
Margaret Rebecca Mangum 2/11/1825
Henry Alexander Gartrell 12/6/1826
Homer Lycurgus Gartrell 11/22/1828
Ann Eliza Gartrell 1/23/1831
James Madison Gartrell 4/28/1832
Thomas Minor Gartrell 2/23/1834
Martha Matilda Gartrell 1/19/1836
John Leonard Gartrell 11/23/1825

Deaths
Julia Ann Eliza Gartrell 12/29/1837
Margaret Rebecca Gartrell 4/21/1846
John Leonard Gartrell 1/13/1826
Jeremiah Gartrell 1/11/1853
Homer Lycurgus Gartrell 2/5/1853
Thomas Minor Gartrell 7/3/1861

LEWIS JACKSON LAMPKIN BIBLE
Owner: Mrs. Henry Reid, Athens, Ga.

L. J. Lampkin and Lucy P. Haynes m. 5/27/1844

Births
Lewis Jackson Lampkin 1816
Lucy Phelps Haynes 1/15/1821

Lucas H. Lampkin 5/7/1845   J. T. C. Lampkin 7/27/1855
W. W. Lampkin 8/28/1848   Lucy Isabella Lampkin 3/12/1858
Robert H. Lampkin 12/11/1850   Lucy Marion Lampkin 9/29/1862
Leila Lampkin 2/13/1853

Deaths
Lucas H. Lampkin 10/5/1866   L. J. Lampkin 6/19/1885
Robert Henry Lampkin 1/20/1869   Lucy P. Lampkin 12/6/1892
Leila Lampkin 9/13/1854   W. W. Lampkin 3/28/1902
Lucy Isabella Lampkin 7/11/1859 Marion Lampkin West 5/21/1916

REV. W. W. LAMPKIN BIBLE
Owner: Miss Carrie Lampkin, Atlanta, Ga.

Memoranda
W. W. Lampkin entered the North Ga. Methodist Conference 1872.
He served Athens Circuit, Culloden Circuit, Little River Circuit,
LaFayette, Walker Co., Norcross, Franklin, Heard Co., Morgan
Circuit, Rome Circuit, Clarksville, 3 yrs., Commerce, East Point,
2 yrs., Hancock Circuit.

W. W. Lampkin, son of Lewis Jackson Lampkin
Lewis Jackson Lampkin b. 1816, d. 6/9/1885 Athens, Ga. m. Lucy
   Phelps Haynes
Lewis J. lampkin belonged to Home Guards, Athens, Ga., organized
for purpose of protecting property and lives of citizens during
War Between the States 1861-65

W. W. Lampkin and Fannie M. Booker m. 11/25/1875
Annie Myrick Lampkin and James Edward Porter m. 9/28/1910

Births
W. W. Lampkin 8/28/1848   Annie Myrick Lampkin 9/20/1884
Fannie M. Booker 9/24/1857   Frank Harris Lampkin 1/20/1889
Lucy Carrie Lampkin 10/3/1876   Marion Edward Porter 7/9/1911
Lewis J. Lampkin Jr. 11/9/1878   Macon, Ga.
Addie Marion Lampkin 1/26/1880

Caroline Lampkin Porter 9/17/1917 Macon, Ga.
Frank Lampkin Porter 7/15/1920 Atlanta, Ga.

Deaths
Lewis J. Lampkin 6/27/1897   Frank Lampkin Porter 4/9/1924
W. W. Lampkin 3/28/1902   Fannie M. Booker Lampkin 4/5/1930

54

THOMAS LAMAR BIBLE

Thomas Lamar I. from Wicre, Flanders (Anjou) France (a Hugenot) b. 16--, d. 1714, m. 1st Mary Pottinger, 2d Ann Pottinger

Thomas Lamar II his son, b. 16--, d. 1747, m. Martha Urquart (sister of Rev. John Urquart, Rector of All Faith parish, St. Mary Co., Md.)

Capt. John Lamar, his son, b. 1740, d. 1799, m. 1st Elizabeth Bugg, 2d Priscilla Bugg, which d. 1765 (niece of Elizabeth), 3rd Lucy Appling.

Basil Lamar (son of Capt. John Lamar and Priscilla Bugg) b. 1764 d. 11/5/1827, m. 1794 Rebecca Kelly b. 1762, d. 8/27/1829

George Washington Lamar (son of Basil Lamar and Rebecca Kelly) b. 1/27/1801 d. 12/21/1872, m. Sarah Walker Harlow, b. 2/11/1811, d. 5/13/1876, dau. of Dr. Southworth Harlow of Plymouth, Mass. and Rebecca Walker, m. at Barh near Augusta, Ga. 7/8/1835.

Rebecca Louisa Lamar (dau. of George Washington and Sarah Harlow Lamar) b. Augusta, Ga. 4/10/1841, d. 7/28/1878, m. Antoine Poullain II 2/25/1868 at Savannah, Ga. by Dr. J. S. K. Axon (father-in-law of Woodrow Wilson, while Dr. Joseph R. Wilson of Augusta was their pastor - he was Woodrow Wilson's father).

BASIL LAMAR BIBLE

Births
Priscilla Lamar, dau. of Basil and Rebecca, 12/2/1795
John Thomas Lamar, son of above, 3/13/1797
Gazzaway Bugg Lamar, son of above, 10/2/1798
James Jackson lamar, son of above, 5/9/1800
George Washington Lamar, son of above, 1/27/1802
Oswald Lamar, son of above, 1/7/1804
Basil Lamar, son of above, 12/30/1805
Sarah Ann Lamar, dau. of above, 11/26/1807
Zachariah lamar, son of above, 11/22/1809
Rebecca Johnson Lamar, dau. of above, 12/22/1811
Thomas Jefferson Lamar, son of above, 3/8/1814

Eliza Lamar, 2d dau. of John Thomas Lamar, 9/22/1830 at Macon
Allen Lamar, eldest son of above, 10/22/1827 at Augusta

(N. B. Eliza and Ellen were granddaus. of Basil and Rebecca Lamar)

Deaths
Basil Lamar Sr. 11/5/1827, age 53 yrs.
Rebecca Kelly lamar Sr. 8/22/1829, aged 58 yrs.
Priscilla Lamar 12/3/1797, 2 yrs., 1 day
James Jackson lamar 7/10/1820, 20 yrs., 20 mos., 1 day
Rebecca Johnson Lamar, wife of Hugh McLeod, 1/19/1891 at Richmond, Va., age 80, bur. Hollywood Cemetery, Richmond, Va.

55

DAVID HILL JOHNSON BIBLE
Owner: O. H. Arnold, Jr., Athens, Ga.

Births
David H. Johnson 1/9/1808
Sarah A. Johnson 10/2/1818

Children:

Thomas R. Johnson 1/9/1835   Katherine J. Johnson 11/1843
Mary A. S. Johnson 6/9/1836   Robert G. Johnson 1/9/1845
N. E. Johnson 10/11/1838   Sarah J. Johnson 12/31/1848
Martha H. Johnson 1841   Nathan D. Johnson 8/28/1852

Death
Sarah A. Johnson 8/22/1853   Katherine J. Christian 7/25/1881
Nathan D. Johnson 1/1853   Mary A. S. Arnold 8/20/1884
Robert G. Johnson 7/25/1862   David H. Johnson 7/5/1886
Sarah J. Thompson 12/1873   Martha H. Comer 1/18/1897

Children of David Hill Johnson and Sarah Ann Dowdy (m.
   12/10/1833)
Thomas Johnson d. when child
Mary Susan Ann Johnson m. Moses Henderson Arnold 1/5/1854
Nancy Elizabeth Johnson m. Oliver Hazzard Perry Arnold 4/10/1856
Martha H. Johnson m. Joseph Comer
Katherine J. Johnson m. James Christian
Robert G. Johnson d. Richmond Battle 7/25/1862
Sarah Jane Johnson m. Elisha Thompson
Nathan D. Johnson d. when child

JEPTHA V. HARRIS BIBLE
Owner: Mrs. T. W. Rucker, Athens, Ga.

Jeptha V. Harris b. 4/27/1782
Sallie Hunt, wife, b. 6/15/1789   Their Children:

James W. Harris 8/1/1805   Ann R. Harris 5/17/1811
William L. Harris 7/6/1807   Sarah E. harris 8/18/1814
George H. harris 3/4/1809

Marriages
Jeptha V. Harris and Sallie Hunt 10/11/1804
James W. Harris to Martha Watkins 12/28/1830
William L. Harris to Francis Semmes 5/13/1830
George H. Harris to May W. Dowse 5/22/1833
Ann R. Harris to George R. Clayton 10/7/1830
Sarah E. Harris to Tinsley W. Rucker 12/23/1834

Deaths
Sallie Harris, wife of Jeptha, d. Madison Ga. 12/18/1871
Jeptha V. Harris d. at home near Marietta, Ga. 1856
Lola B. Gresham, only child of Susan and J. A. Billups, d. Macon,
   Ga. 9/29/1871

HENRY GRADY BIBLE
Owner: Mrs. John C. West, Atlanta, Ga.

Births
Henry Grady 5/1/1788
Leah King 3/27/1796

John W. Grady 12/6/1813   William S. Grady 6/10/1821
Harriet S. Grady 5/26/1815   Elizabeth Ann Grady 10/31/1823
Sarah M. Grady 12/1/1818

Marriages
John W. Grady 12/31/1840

Births
Louisa W. Grady 2/11/1821
Harriet Matilda Grady 11/19/1841

Charles M. Neblo 11/19/1843   Henry C. Grady 6/18/1844
John W. Neblo 2/3/184-   Wm. G. S. Grady 2/24/1848
Henry G. Neblo 3/30/184-   Lillia D. Grady 2/20/1855
Sarrah L. Neblo 9/5/1849   Jesse B. Grady 2/9/1857
Henry Woodfin Grady 5/24/1850   John W. Walker 8/1823
Martha   Nicholson   Grady   9/30/1855   Caroline Walker 12/13/1850
Annie King Grady 3/10/1857   Jesse Walker 6/9/1853
Agnes Louisa Grady 3/7/1843   Helen Louisa Walker
Harriett Virginia Walker 2/3/1859   2/18/1852

ISAAC P. GAY BIBLE *
Owner: Mrs. W. W. Redwine
Fayetteville, Ga.

Marriages
Isaac P. Gay to Elizabeth Shepard 12/19/1824
Zorada Gay to Benjamin W. North 7/2/1850
Thomas G. Gay to Harriett Lynch 2/14/1856
Winston W. Gay to Martha Glass 3/7/1855
Sandford Gay to Caroline P. Cole 10/18/1860
William J. Gay to Georgia Jones 2/6/1861

Births
Isaac P. Gay 12/14/1804   Edwin Gay 12/8/1833
Elizabeth Gay 11/1/1805   Zorada Gay 12/16/1835
Winston W. Gay 9/30/1825   John Henry Gay 7/10/1838
Thomas G. Gay 10/23/1827   Sarah Frances Gay 8/18/1840
Robert Gay 11/21/1829   Sanford Gay 8/18/1840
Mary Elizabeth Gay 10/27/1831   Wm. Judson Gay 5/6/1843

Deaths
Edwin Gay 8/13/1836   John H. Gay 10/18/1862
Sarah Frances Gay 7/13/1843   Zorada North 3/12/1876
Robert Gay 1/5/1854   Isaac P. Gay 3/20/1877
Elizabeth Gay 4/17/1857   Carrie P. Gay 10/22/1924

*See also p. 420.   57

NATHANIEL ESTES BIBLE
Owner: Mr. Roy Bowden, Athens, Ga.

Nathaniel Estes b. 5/15/1777 d. 11/14/1841
Nancy Estes, Sr. b. 10/26/1771 d. 7/31/1856
Thomas Estes b. 3/4/1803 d. 5/21/1841
Nancy Estes Richardson b. 7/8/1806 d. 3/4/1856
Elizabeth Estes Brown b. 7/1/1808 d. 12/1/1856

Micajah Estes and Nancy Owen m. 12/24/1829

Micajah Estes 11/4/1804 d. 5/1883
Nancy Owen Estes b. 10/22/1802 d. 1/28/1853
Martha Ann Summerfield Estes b. 3/15/1832
Martha Ann Summerfield Estes Bray d. 4/15/1864
John B. Estes b. 6/4/1835 d. 9/15/1902
Obediah N. Estes b. 7/7/1837 d. 9/15/1861
Fredric B. Estes b. 12/1839 d. 1/15/1844
Joshua F. Estes b. 7/24/1841 d. 2/8/1843
M. Van Estes b. 8/9/1843 d. --
Eliza K. Estes b. 1/20/1845 d. 12/1909

Micajah Estes and Julia F. Headen m. 12/31/1854

JOHN ASKEW ERWIN BIBLE
Owner: Mrs. Julius Y. Talmadge
Athens, Ga.

John Askew Erwin b. Habersham Co., Ga. 11/13/1824, His First
wife: Jane Elizabeth Hooper, b. in DeKalb Co., Ga. 9/22/1829.
Their Children:

Ella Erwin b. Cassville, Ga. 7/24/1850
Hugh Banks Erwin b. Cassville, Ga. 11/28/1852
Harry Johnson Erwin b. Cartersville, Ga. 5/18/1856
Harriette Miller Erwin b. Cartersville, Ga. 8/24/1858
    Second wife of John Askew Erwin:
Mary Isa Beall b. Campbell Co., Ga. 7/25/1839. Their Children:
Fanny Cordelia Erwin, b. Cartersville, Ga. 8/28/1862
Grace Erwin b. Athens, Ga. 9/16/1865
Sam Beall Erwin b. Cartersville, Ga. 5/15/1867
Justinia Elizabeth Erwin b. Cartersville, Ga. 10/26/1869
Allie Evans Erwin b. Cartersville, Ga. 7/27/1872

Mollie Eliza Mills b. 2/28/1859 (wife of Harry J. Erwin). Their
    children:
Charles Henry Erwin b. 6/10/1882 Rhea Co., Tenn.
John Hooper Erwin b. 10/24/1883 Rhea Co., Tenn.
Sara May Erwin, 1st dau. of Harry and Mollie Erwin, b. 2/26/1885
    Rhea Co., Tenn.
Willie Howard Erwin, son of Harry and Mollie Erwin, b. 4/13/1887
    Rhea Co., Tenn.
Julius Young Talmadge, husband of Sara May Erwin, b. Athens, Ga.
    4/14/1880
Harry Erwin Talmadge, son of Julius and Sara May Talmadge, b.
    in Athens, Ga. 2/18/1907

(John Askew Erwin Bible contd....)

Marriages
John Askew Erwin and Jane Hooper 12/13/1848 Cassville, Ga.
John Askew Erwin and Isa Bealle 12/6/1860 Tishamingo Co., Miss.
Oliver E. Mitchell and Ella Erwin 11/3/1870 Cartersville, Ga.
Luke L. Peak and Hattie Erwin 10/14/1880 near Pin Hook Landing,
   Rhea Co., Tenn.
Harry J. Erwin and Mollie Mills 8/31/1881 Spring City, Rhea Co.
Julius Young Talmadge and Sara May Erwin 10/18/1905 Chattanooga

Deaths
Jane Elizabeth Erwin 9/16/1859 Cartersville, Ga.
John Askew Erwin 10/31/1883 Lebanon, Ohio
Charles Henry Erwin 3/22/1884 Rhea Co., Tenn.
Willie Howard Erwin 11/8/1906 Chattanooga, Tenn.
Harry Johnson Erwin 3/13/1930 Athens, Ga., bur. Forest Hill
Cemetery, Chattanooga, Tenn., aged 73 yrs.

REV. WILLIAM ESTON EPPES BIBLE
Owner: William E. Eppes, Jr.
Athens, Ga.

(Episcopal Minister of Ga., great grandson of Thomas Jefferson)

Marriages
Rev. William Eston Eppes and Emily Bancroft 7/27/1854 in Immanuel
   Church, Athens, Ga. by Rev. I. H. Linebaugh
Rev. William E. Eppes and Augusta Johnston Kollock 1/15/1878 at
   Woodlands, Ga. by Rev. S. E. Barnwell
William Eston Eppes Jr. and Irene Ada Bancroft 1/2/1889 Athens,
   Ga. by Rev. W. E. Eppes
Edward Bancroft to Lucy Randolph Eppes 8/18/1881 in Chapel of the
   Holy Cross, habersham Co., Ga., by Rev. W. E. Eppes
Francis Eppes and Mary Margaret Bancroft 11/17/1881 at Sunny
   Side, Habersham Co., Ga. by Rev. W. E. Eppes
Edward Bancroft Eppes and Jennie Kendall 3/3/1908 Spartanburg,
   S. C. at her sister's home by Rev. Trusdale

Births
Matilda Eppes 8/9/1855 Athens, Ga., baptised in Immanuel Church
   by Rev. I. H. Linebaugh 9/1855. Sponsors: Mrs. Matilda
   R. Bancroft, Miss Elizabeth Bancroft. Dr. James Camak, Augusta
Jones K. Eppes d. 4/25/1918
Elizabeth Cleland Eppes b. 8/25/1857 Athens, Ga., baptised in
   Christ Church Monticello by her Father, Rev. W. E. Eppes,
   11/3/1857. Sponsors: Francis Eppes, jane Carey Eppes and Mary E.
   C. Eppes
Frances Eppes b. Camden, Ark. 6/20/1859, baptised in private.
   Sponsors: Dr. John Seay, Mrs. Selina W. Seay
James Bancroft Eppes b. Athens, Ga. 7/17/1860, baptised Christ
   Church, Monticello.
Lucy Randolph Eppes b. Sunnyside, Habersham Co. 7/31/1861
Jane Carey Eppes b. Sunnyside, Habersham Co. 11/19/1863
William Eston Eppes b. at farm near Monticello 12/24/1864
John Wayles Eppes b. at farm near Monticello 8/11/1866
Emily Bancroft Eppes b. Jacksonville, Fla. 2/18/1868
Edward Bancroft Eppes b. Marietta, Ga. 10/23/1869
Maria Jefferson Eppes b. Marietta, Ga. 1/9/1871

(Rev. William Eston Eppes Bible contd....)

Deaths

James Bancroft Eppes 6/2/1861, 10 mos., 15 days
Maria Jefferson Eppes 8/1/1916
Jane Cary Eppes 2/11/1864, 2 mos., 23 days
Edward Bancroft Eppes 7/1/1918
Mrs. Emily Eppes 5/8/1873, 41 yrs., 3 mos., 22 days
Francis Eppes 1/12/1921, bur. Athens, Ga.
Emily Bancroft Eppes 12/19/1874, age 6 yrs., 10 mos., 1 day
Emily Bancroft Eppes b. 1/16/1832
John Wayles Eppes 2/11/1875, 8 yrs, 7 mos.
Elizabeth Cleland Eppes 5/17/1881, 23 yrs., 8 mos., 22 days
Rev. William Eston Eppes 4/25/1896 at Woodlands, Habersham Co.
   age 65 yrs., 9 mos., 20 days., b. 7/5/1830
Lucy Randolph Bancroft 6/16/1896 at Athens, Ga., 34 yrs., 10
   mos., 16 days

EBENEZER ELIASON BIBLE

Births

Ebenezer Eliason, son of John and Lydia Eliason, 9/26/1772
Ann Hersey, dau. of Isaac and Jane Hersey, 12/1/1776

Rebecca C. Eliason 1/30/1800   Jane Mary Eliason 3/7/1804
John H. Eliason 12/28/1801   William P. Eliason 1/26/1807
Ebenezer Eliason 10/3/1809   Ann Eliza Eliason 10/3/1814
George Pannill Eliason, son of William P. and Susan G.
   Eliason 1/30/1841
Ann Hersey Eliason 9/5/1843   Fanny Pannill Eliason 12/11/1848
John Blackwell Eliason 5/9/1846
William Ebenezer Eliason 11/11/1851
Susan Blackwell Eliason 10/27/185

Marriages

Ebenezer Eliason and Rebecca Carnan 6/11/1798
Ebenezer Eliason and Ann Hersey 2/24/1801
Rebecca C. Eliason, dau. of E. & R. Eliason, and William Winnard
   6/6/1821
Jane Mary Eliason, dau. of E. & A. Eliason, to William D. Clark,
   3/16/1825
William P. Eliason, son f above, to Susan G. Pannill 2/25/1840
Ann Eliza Eliason, dau. of above, to James M. Walker 8/18/1840
G. P. Eliason, son of W. P. and S. G. Eliason, to Z. P.
   Sutherland of Franklin Co., Va., 12/7/1882
E. B. Sisson, son of William and S. J. Sisson, to H. Eliason, all
   of Orange Co., Va., 1/31/1867

JOHN P. ELDER BIBLE
Owner: Robert Elder, Framington, Ga.

Births

John P. Elder 12/10/1800	Nancy A. Elder 4/28/1836
Susan G. Elder 1/31/1806	Christian B. Elder 9/20/1838
Nathan T. Elder 10/8/1824	Susan J. Elder 1/3/1841
Aveann Elder 8/19/1827	Martha J. Elder 11/10/1842
Mary E. Elder 9/24/1829	John H. Elder 5/22/1845
David G. Elder 12/18/1831	Almeda M. Elder 7/22/1848
Lucy J.? Elder 3/31/1834	W. G. Elder 5/13/1865

Marriages

John P. Elder to Susan G. Barnett 11/26/1823
Nathan T. Elder to Lucy G. Brown 12/15/1847
David G. Elder to Martha C. Henry 9/14/1854
John H. Elder to E. L. Cox 3/24/1864
Mary E. Elder to R. B. McRee 3/14/1847
Aveann Elder to William H. Marshall 10/19/1848
Nancy A. Elder to George E. Griffith 3/2/1854
Christian B. Elder to S. E. F. Jackson 4/28/1859
Susan J. Elder to Drew Jackson 2/3/1863

Deaths

Ave G. Barnett 7/6/1851	Mrs. Lucy ? Elder 5/15/1870
N. Barnett 4/4/1818	Mary E. McRee 2/28/1860
David Elder 8/7/1853	Almeda M. Elder 5/6/1863
John P. Elder 8/9/1862 in Augusta Hospital	
Susan G. Elder 4/1/1877	
Ave Marshall 8/25/1908	

JOHN WOODS EBERHART BIBLE
Owner: Mrs. J. W. Eberhart, Athens, Ga.

R. J. H. Dottery b. Pickens, S. C. 8/18/1822 m. 9/9/1847,
   d. 5/28/1898
Susan C. Stone b. Jasper Co., Ga. 11/29/1827 m. 9/9/1847,
   d. 12/6/1900
J. W. Dottery b. Hall Co., Ga. 6/19/1848 m. 8/6/1874
M. E. Dottery b. Princeton, Ga. 12/24/1849 m. 11/7/1867
W. G. Dottery b. Princeton, Ga. 1/27/1852 d. 8/28/1853
S. P. Eberhart b. Madison, Ga. 10/12/1814 d. 1/20/1895
Mahala Eberhart b. Jackson Co., Ga. 10/17/1815 d. 5/21/1891
W. J. Eberhart b. Hall Co., Ga. 2/27/1841 d. 12/12/1868
R. G. Eberhart b. Hall Co., Ga. 5/12/1842 d. 8/12/1866
M. E. J. Eberhart b. Hall Co., Ga. 10/12/1844 d. 8/10/1867
N. M. K. Eberhart b. Hall Co., Ga. 4/3/1836
R. P. Eberhart b. Hall Co., Ga. 11/27/1847 m. 11/28/1868
   d. 6/20/1899
J. M. A. Eberhart b. Hall Co., Ga. 11/9/1849 m. 12/26/1875
J. T. Eberhart b. Hall Co., Ga. 4/5/1852 m. 5/10/1873 & 9/16/1880
S. F. S. Eberhart b. Hall Co., Ga. 12/5/1853 d. 9/29/1877
E. A. S. Eberhart b. Hall Co., Ga. 5/8/1856 d. 10/7/1880
R. P. Eberhart d. 6/20/1899
John W. Eberhart b. Hall Co., Ga. 6/25/1839 m. 11/7/1867
   d. 5/12/1912

61

(John Woods Eberhart Bible contd....)

M. E. Dottery b. Princeton, Ga. 12/24/1839 m. 11/7/1867
   d. 5/12/1912
J. W. Eberhart b. Athens, Ga. 5/27/1871
Minia F. Eberhart b. Athens, Ga. 9/12/1868 d. 10/17/1868
R. J. P. Eberhart b. Athens, Ga. 10/13/1874 d. 6/17/1883

ROBERT JACKSON HANCOCK BIBLE
Jackson Co., Jefferson, Ga.

Robert J. Hancock and Sallie S. Pendergrass 1/15/1868
Sam Kelly and Jennie May Hancock 12/30/1894
Robert J. hancock and Hattie Louise Matthews 11/21/1897
Benjamin F. Carr and Lucy Bryant 12/20/1897
William Lane Hancock and Ethel N. Swafford 4/19/1916 at
   Chattanooga, Tenn.
Robert Judson Kelly and Blondine Hardy ---
Earl Dunbar Harrison and Mary Bell Hancock 6/17/1926

Births
Robert J. Hancock 2/9/1839   William L. Hancock 12/7/1870
Sallie S. Pendergrass 9/22/1858   Robert J. Hancock 2/14/1872
Myrtice Hancock 12/26/1868   Jennie May Hancock 5/5/1875
                                    Lucy Bryant Hancock 1/4/1877

Wilmont Holingsworth Pendergrass 12/6/1887
Edwin Leary Kelly 12/3/1896
Robert Judson Kelly 9/5/1899
Mary Bell Hancock 9/14/1905
Sarah Pendergrass Hancock 8/13/1907
Benjamin Franklin Carr Jr. 12/30/1906
Sarah Bess Kelly 2/11/1913

Deaths
Myrtice Hancock 4/12/1870
Sallie Pendergass Hancock 10/9/1927
Robert J. Hancock 7/6/1877
Benjamin F. Carr Sr. 12/24/1938
Robert Jackson Hancock 5/3/1929

WILLIAM H. HALE BIBLE
Owner: Mrs. Nancy E. Hale, Athens, Ga.

Marriages
William H. Hale and Nancy Emma Porterfield 9/29/1870
William Henry hale and Maggie E. Beavers 4/5/1890
Rufus L. M. Hale and Devona D. Puckett 6/15/1892
Peter H. Culp and Mary Lou Hale 12/23/1894
William P. Reynolds and Laura Ann Hall 9/23/1900
William J. Allen and Sarah Isaettie Hale 6/2/1901
Charles E. Marshall and Emma Jane Hale 9/4/1901
Patrick Holman Fulcher and Margaret Marcella Hale 4/8/1906
Homer G. Hale and Effie E. Bramblett 10/24/1909
Howard Thomas Hale and Hattie Fulcher 12/25/1910

(William J. Hale Bible contd...

Births
William J. Hale 12/17/1846   Laura Ann Hale 7/10/1881
Nancy Emma Porterfield 10/12/1850 Sarah Isaetta Hale 8/25/1883
William Henry Hale 6/16/1871   Margaret Marcella Hale
                          7/1/1885
Martha E. Hale 6/5/1873   Homer Griffeth Hale 9/26/1887
Rufus L. M. Hale 3/7/1875   Howard Thomas Hale 9/9/1890
Mary Lou Hale 7/22/1877
Emma Jane Hale 7/19/1879

Deaths
Martha E. Hale 11/6/1874   Mary Lou Hale Culp 10/14/1919
William J. Hale 7/20/1909   Howard Thomas Hale 11/9*1924
                        Rufus L. M. Hale 12/30/1927

BURRELL LEVERETT BIBLE Of Jasper Co.
Owner: Miss Jennie Leverett
Capitol Ave., Atlanta, Ga.

Burrell Leverett b. 1/14/1793 d. 12/20/1883 m. 1814 Nancy Goode
Children:

Births
William Goode 3/18/1815   Nancy Jane 3/28/1829
Sealy Ann 12/28/1816   Clayton Moseley1/2/1831
Emilizer 12/1/1819   Martha Caroline 2/12/1833
Edward 10/11/1822   Mariah Elizabeth 11/10/1834
Many Martin 1/31/1825   Katherine 11/6/1833
Frank Marion 9/6/826   Thomas Madison 2/1/1841

GEORGE LOYD BIBLE
Owner: Mrs. Estelle Loyd Stone
Monticello, Ga.

George Loyd d. 2/19/1872, age 92 m. Polly Tawkesley 9/28/1805 who
d. 9/29/1855. Children:

Births
Alford 6/20/1806   Thomas 7/30/1818
Green 2/28/1808   Naomi 9/3/1820
Washington 2/5/1810   Mary Ann 11/6/1822
John Emory 7/30/1813   Martha Folds 11/20/1825
James 8/2/1815

BUCKNER LEVERETT BIBLE
Owner: Miss Jennie Leverett
Capitol Ave., Atlanta, Ga.

Marriages
Buckner Leverett b. 1/23/1801 (prob. Wilkes Co., Ga.) d.
8/21/1882 m. Frances Stamper b. 3/18/1799 d. 8/19/1869
Katherine Leverett m. Ben Wallace
Elizabeth Jane Leverett, dau. of Buckner and Frances, b.
9/18/1832 m. 9/3/1848 S. Burton Miller
Sarah Ann Frances Leverett b. 7/4/1837 m.------Cook

Births
         Children of Buckner Leverett and Frances Stamper:
Martin W. 5/8/1819   Elizabeth Jane 9/18/1832
Littleton H. 1/3/1821   Matthew 4/12/1834
William J. 3/30/1825   Sarah Ann Frances 7/4/1837
Simeon 3/14/1830   Martin S. V.---
Thomas J. 8/17/1828

                    JOHN J. GUNTER BIBLE

John J. Gunter b. 10/22/1814
Lucretia Ann Adams Gunter, his wife, b. 2/26/1817 Their
   Children:
James J. Gunter b. 12/9/1839   Sarah Frances b. 3/18/1850
Mary Ann Gunter b. 10/22/1841   Theophilus H. b.4/12/1852
William Henry b. 7/13/1843   Susan Sophia b. 8/9/1855
Jerusha Caroline b. 7/5/1846   Martha Bush b. 6/15/1858
Mahala Emeline b. 3/24/1848   Dr. Weyman T. b. 9/12/1860
                                  James Weyman Gunter Jr. b.
                                     10/9/1898

Marriages
John J. Gunter and Lucretia Ann Adams 10/8/1837 Their Children:
J. J. Gunter and M. E. Cook 11/12/1867
J. B. Cook and S. F. Gunter 12/22/1870
J. M. Breedlove and M. E. Gunter 9/24/1874
W. H. Gunter and Mattie L. Barrett 1/14/1875
J. W. Bradberry and J. C. Gunter 3/2/1876
Theophilus H. Gunter and F. L. Breedlove 3/18/1877
B. F. Camp and Mary A. Gunter 1/29/1882
R. H. Wier and Martha B. Gunter 4/15/1883
Dr. Park and Mary A. Camp 9/14/1893
Dr. Weyman T. Gunter and Mary E. Park 12/26/1897

Deaths
John G. Gunter (father) 3/7/1889   Dr.Weyman Gunter 2/18/1926
Lucretia Ann Gunter (mother) 6/13/1899 Wm. Henry Gunter 4/23/1900
B. F. Camp 9/1/1887
Jerusha C. Bradberry 1/13/1894
Mary Ann Park 6/22/1897
Sophia S. Sheppard 3/9/1899
Mahala E. Breedlove 6/21/1899
J. B. Cook 6/2/1928
Lucy Josephine Cook 1/23/1930

CHARLES WESLEY TUCKER BIBLE
Owner: Ann Tucker Garrington Wright

Charles Wesley Tucker b. 9/23/1851 Bibb Co., Ga. d. 1909 Dooly
Co., m. 3/1/1874 by Meredith McCoy, J. P. to Finney C. Thompson
b. 12/18/1854 d. 1925, d. Andalusia, Ala. Both are bur. Pinehurst
Cemetery, Pinehurst, Ga. (Dooly Co.) Their Children:

Henry Albert Tucker b. 4/28/1875 d. 1/22/1944
Mattie Lena Tucker b. 6/22/1877 d. 1968
Dorah Lee Tucker b. 2/26/1879 d. 10/16/1957
M. Carlton Tucker b. 12/19/1880 d. 8/6/1938
Charlie D. Tucker b. 12/30/1883
Willie Tucker b. 2/3/1885
Virgil Tucker b. 10/5/1886
Buford Daniel Tucker (twin) b. 9/25/1888 d. 1/21/1961
Chevy Tucker (twin) b.9/25/1888 d. birth 1888
Paul Tucker b. 10/24/1890 d. 7/11/1920
Perry Green Tucker b. 9/24/1892 d. 5/30/1964
Cliff Tucker b. 8/24/1894
Mamie Lizzie Tucker b. 6/7/1896

THOMAS PHILLIP TUCKER BIBLE
Owner: Curtis L. Tucker, Forsyth, Ga.

Bible presented to Thomas Phillip Tucker by his Father-in-Law,
James Harvis, in 1855.

George D. Tucker b. 2/4/1861 d. 4/15/1939 bur. Byron Baptist
Church Cemetery. Wife, Sallie Hardison b. 4/4/1867 d. 4/17/1946
  Children:
Curtis Linwood Tucker b. 8/*16/1897 m. Nancy Moore 12/11/1925. He
  d. 1981.
Ainia Pearl Tucker b. 10/19/1887 d. 5/26/1889
Allen phillip Tucker b. 10/9/1890 d. 12/1979
Elma Sanford Tucker b. 7/23/1889 d. 12/20/1930
Mineola Tucker b. 10/5/1893 d. 5/25/1894

James Jarvis m. Louise Massey2/7/1833
Anna Tucker b. 3/11/1864
Fanny Elizabeth Tucker b. 2/4/1867
Elizor Buler Tucker b. 8/24/1869
Ellen Lee Tucker b. 4/15/1872
Thomas Phillip Tucker m. Georgiana F. Jarvis 4/2/1854
Sally R. N. Tucker b. 4/15/1872
Etta Viola Tucker b. 4/29/1878
Georgiana Francis Jarvis b. 3/2/1834
William Daniel Jarvis b. 2/20/1838
Mary Jimerison Jarvis b. 8/12/1838
T. P. Tucker b. 10/2/1833
Mary Francis Tucker b. 2/4/1855
Elmer Curneles Tucker b. 1/2/1855
Thomas Jarvis b. 10/15/1810
Louise Massey b. 11/26/1810
James Thomas Tucker b. 1/15/1857

(Thomas Phillip Tucker Bible, contd....)

Louise E. Elizabeth Tucker b. 2/4/1859
George D. Tucker b. 2/4/1861

Mrs. Lucy Massey, mother of Mrs. Jarvis, d. 8/28/1840
Mary Jimerson Jarvis 10/1/1840
Frances Gillilon d. 9/27/1841
Daniel Massey d. 1/9/1847
Mrs. Louise Jarvis d. 6/2/1853, age 43 yrs.
James Jarvis d. 8/24/1853, age 43 yrs.
Thomas J. Tucker d. 6/15/1896
Mrs. Mattie Tucker d. 2/22/1895

Marriages (Date shown is birth date)
Anna Tucker to Tom Akin 1864
Fronez (safraia) Tucker to Dan Thompson 1867
Sally R. Tucker to Ed Rape 1875
Viola Tucker to E. Garvin 1878
Mary Francis Tucker to John W. Newell 1855
James Thomas Tucker to Mattie Etheridge 1857
   His children Essie Lee Barlett and Emmie Wheelus

               W. A. BURCKHALTER BIBLE Of Oglethorpe Co.
               Owner: George W. Eberhart, Athens, Ga.

"This certifies that the rite of Holy Matrimony was celebrated
between W. A. Burckhalter of Aiken, S. C. and Mary E. Butler of
Augusta, Ga. on 4/4/1854, by Daniel S. Bush. Wit: Edwin Hill,
Eliz. Stevens."

Births
Mary Eliza Butler 8/2/1833   Minia Arozer Burckhalter 4/4/1864
Wm. A. Burckhalter 2/5/1830   Hattey Lular Burckhalter 12/21/1865
John W. W. Burckhalter   Thomas Edgar Burckhalter
   12/6/1855   10/19/1867
Nary Idarlizer Burckhalter   Walter Marshal Burckhalter 3/2/1870
   2/10/1858
David Lane Burckhalter   Susan Emer Burckhalter 12/19/1873
   6/3/1859
Wm. Wiley Burckhalter 2/3/1861

Deaths
John W. W. Burckhalter 9/18/1857   Mary Elizabeth 5/31/1907
Thomas Edgar Burckhalter 10/30/1868 Walter Marshall Burckhalter
William Andrew Burckhalter 12/22/1902   3/21/1930

               JOHN MILTON BURNS BIBLE
               Owner: A. H. Burns, Athens, Ga.

Births
John Milton Burns 12/12/1833   David Lenoa Milford 12/28/1859
Sarah Harriette Long 10/7/1837   Sarah Harriette Milford
Julia Caroline Telford 1/17/1846   4/7/1887
Lula Samuel Burns 4/19/1857   Lee Milton Milford 4/15/1889
Alice Isabella Burns 5/13/1859   William Brantley Milford

(John Milton Burns Bible, Births, contd....)

Joseph Brantley Burns 5/26/1865   7/23/1891
Willie Jones Burns 10/25/1866   Roy Burns Milford 12/14/1893
Egbert Telford Burns 6/10/1880   D. L. Milford, Jr. 5/3/1895
Alonzo Hay Burns 3/3/1883   John Milton Burns 10/21/1909
                                     James Elmer Burns 9/21/1913
                                     Alonzo Merrett Burns 1/3/1927

Marriages
John M. Burns to Sarah H. Long 7/3/1856
John M. Burns to Julia C. Telford 1/16/1879
David L. Milford to Lula S. Burns 12/15/1885
Willie J. Burns to Bessie Blanche Jackson 1/2/1894
Lucas Newton Turk to Alice J. Burns 1/17/1895
Alonzo H. Burns to Mary Frances Mill 12/23/1908
Lee Milton Milford to Maude Langston 12/10/1911
Egbert Telford Burns to Cora L. Wilhite 12/17/1913

Deaths
Joseph Brantley Burns 10/25/1865, 4 mos., 29 days
Sarah H. Burns 9/27/1877, 39 yrs., 11 mos., 20 days
Ann W. Long 2/13/1893, 77 yrs., 1 mo., 16 days
Roy Burns Milford 6/6/1894, 5 mos., 20 days
D. L. Milford 7/5/1906
John M. Burns 11/21/1908
Julia C. Telford Burns 3/1/1920, 74 yrs., 1 mo., 14 days

                        R. P. CARTER BIBLE
            Owner: Miss Fannie Carter, Elberton, Ga.

R. P. Carter b. 3/14/1858 m. Lucy E. Beasley 1/3/1878, said Lucy
Teasley b. 11/1/1859 (Lucy Teasley was gr. dau. of E. B. Norman,
Sr.)

Births
Fannie B. Carter 11/18/1878   James Martin Carter 10/27/1887
Infant 7/9/1880   McAlphin Calvin Carter 8/14/1892
Infant 11/18/1881   Clyde Swift Carter 3/24/1898
Thomas H. Carter 10/17/1883   Riley Benson Carter 1/14/1901
Mary E. Carter 3/18/1885

Marriages
R. C. Carter and Azalee Johnson 11/29/1914, T. J. Rucker
    officating
J. M. Carter and Mearle Eavenson 12/10/1918, J. C. Adams
    officiating
Thomas Henry Carter and Aurice Christian 1/26/1923, Clark Edwards
    officiating
M. C. Carter and Mae Shiflet 9/6/1932, J. E. Holbrooks officating

Deaths
Reuben P. Carter 12/10/1922
Lucy Ellen Carter 10/13/1905
Clyde Swift Carter 8/4/1901

                              67

JOHN ADDISON COBB BIBLE

John Addison Cobb and Lucy Pope Barrow 7/29/1863 in Athens, by
   Rev. Joseph S. Key
John A. Cobb b. 10/20/1838
Lucy Barrow Cobb b. 2/2/1845, d. Athens, Ga. 6/2/1880
Wilson Lumpkin Cobb, first-born son of John A. and Lucy B. Cobb,
   b. 12/12/1865, fifth generation from his living grandfather,
   Wilson Lumpkin, Ex-Gov. of Ga., d. Athens, Ga. 5/28/1871
Howell Cobb, second son of John A. and Lucy B. b. 5/29/1868,
   named for his grandfather.
Sarah Pope, first dau. of John A. and Lucy B. Cobb,
   b. 10/31/1870, named for her grandmother, Sarah Pope Barrow.
John Addison, third son of John and Lucy B. Cobb, b. Athens, Ga.,
   2/11/1873
Lucy Middleton Cobb, second dau. of John A. and Lucy Cobb, b. at
   Athens, Ga., 8/8/1875, named for her great grandfather and
   mother on the maternal side - Middleton Pope and Lucy Pope
Mary Ann Lamar Cobb, third dau. of John and Lucy B. Cobb b. on
   the Domine Plantation, Sumter Co., Ga. 5/10/1877, named for
   ber grandmother, Mary Ann Cobb, d. at Syllsfork, Oglethorpe
   Co., Ga. 10/26/1880
John A. Cobb and Miss Mattie Bivins m. in M. E. Church in
   Americus, Ga. by Rev. Lewis 9/13/1881
George Calhoun, son of J. A. and M. B. Cobb, b. 8/31/1882
   Americus, Ga.
Lamar and Eldridge, twin sons of J. A. and M. B. Cobb, b.
   1/9/1884, Americus.
Harper Bivins Cobb b. --
Elizabeth Craig Cobb b. 4/28/1887 Americus, Ga.

WARREN JAMES CONOLLY BIBLE
Owner: Mrs. W. J. Conolly, Athens, Ga.

Warren James Conolly and Sarah Ida Wingfield m. 4/3/1889

Births
Warren James Conolly 10/16/1857 Fayetteville, N. C.
Sarah Ida Wingfield 2/26/1868 Wilkes Co., Ga.
Paul Hybart Conolly, son of Warren J. and Sarah I. Conolly,
   b. 1/12/1890
Marion Wingfield Conolly, son of Warren J. and Sarah I.,
   7/23/1892
W. J. Conolly, Jr., son of W. J. and Ida W. Conolly, 4/14/1903
Ralph N. Conolly, son of W. J. and Ida W. Conolly, 10/13/1905

Deaths
Infant son of W. J. and Ida W. Conolly 6/13/1900

Clipping from Banner-Herald, Athens, Ga., 1/30/1913, in Bible:

"Judge Samuel B. Wingfeld, married Miss Callaway, daughter of
William R. Callaway of Wilkes Co., Ga.

Samuel B. Wingfield, b. Washington, Wilkes Co., Ga. 1838, d.
Athens, Ga. 1/29/1913

(Warren James Conolly Bible newspaper clipping, contd....)

Samuel B. Wingfield, father of Mrs. Warren J. Conolly, A. S., W. C., S. B., Jr. and George T. Wingfield, Mrs. E. P. Short, Mrs. Annie O'Farrell, Mrs. J. N. Williamson, and four children (not named in article) who preceded him."

JAMES C. COVINGTON BIBLE
Owner: Mrs. J. S. Bayless
Watkinsville, Ga.

Births
James C. Covington 2/20/1820
Mary M. Orton 2/26/1820
Dick Oscar, son of J. C. & M. Covington 3/17/1847
Mary Louise James, dau. of above, b. 11/19/1848
Anna L. Barry 2/10/1854
John H. Barry 8/13/1855
Augusta Lee Barry 10/25/1857
Ida O. H. Barry 11/20/1861
Basil Earle Overby 5/5/1848

Marriages
James C. Covington and Mary M. Orton 12/21/1843
Andrew L. Barry and Mary M. Covington (wid. of James C.) 7/23/1851
Basil Earle Overby and Mary (L. J.) Covington 11/29/1875
Anna L. Barry and Samuel David Igou 10/5/1874
Anna L. Barry Igou (wid. of S. D. Igou) and John Samuel Bayless 20/24/1889

Deaths
James Covington 10/31/1850
Dick Oscar Covington 8/4/1850
Lutie B. (Augusta Lee) Barry 3/2/1863
Ida O. Barry 3/7/1863
John H. Barry 2/7/1873, Atlanta, Ga.
Mary M., wife of James Covington, 9/2/1866, DeSoto Co., Miss.
Dr. A. L. Barry ---

WILLIAM CREIGHTON BIBLE
Owner: Miss Mattie Creighton
Athens, Ga.

William Creighton m. Sarah W. Born 4/30/1854

Births
William Creighton 11/17/1828
Sarah Ward Creighton, his wife, 4/23/1829
William Alonzo Creighton 3/23/1855
Mary A. T. Creighton 3/16/1857
John Hiram Creighton 6/6/1858
Mattie King Creighton 8/12/1860
Sarah Jane Creighton 3/19/1862
Georgia A. D. Creighton 11/25/1863
Daniel Arthur Creighton 1/7/1865
Ida Philippa Creighton 1/11/1871

69

(William Creighton Bible contd....)

Deaths

William Alonzo Creighton 7/24/1855	Georgia Ann Dorcas Creighton
Mary Ann Talula Creighton 8/22/1857	4/17/1864
John Hiram Creighton 1/17/1859	Daniel Arthur Creighton
Sarah Jane Creighton 6/4/1863	8/26/1865
William Creighton 12/10/1902	Sarah Creighton 8/25/1911

Miss Dorcas Bone, sister of Mrs. Sarah Creighton, d. 8/22/1911,
    was b. 7/20/1830

MILUS A. OLIVER BIBLE Of Greene Co.
Owner: Mrs. Heard Oliver, Atlanta, Ga.

Milus A. Oliver m. Margaret Delaney Heard 12/3/1874
Annia Oliver m. W. G. Tarvis 4/10/1900
James Heard Oliver m. Birdie Marchman 1/1/1906

Births
Milus Oliver 5/4/1844
Margaret Delaney Heard 2/5/1847
Annie Oliver 9/23/1875
James Heard Oliver 12/10/1877
Willis Heard, son of Heard and Birdie Oliver, 9/3/1906

Deaths
Milus Oliver 10/15/1911
Margaret Delaney Heard Oliver 2/5/1917
Annie Oliver Tarvis 8/12/1901
James Heard Oliver 12/24/1909

GOODWIN MYRICK BIBLE
Owner: Mrs. Charles Wynn
Meriwether, Ga.

John Myrick b. 1751 m. 1778 to Amy Goodwin. Died 8/29/1835
    Issue:
Goodwin Myrick b. 10/23/1779 d. 3/5/1831
John Myrick
Polly T. Myrick (Jones)
Martha Myrick (Horton)
Elizabeth Myrick (Green)
Lucy Myrick (Rev. Jackson Gorry)

Goodwin Myrick b. 10/23/1779 m. 5/9/1809 Martha Parham b.
    12/19/1790 d. 5/13/1862. Issue:
Elizabeth Ingram Myrick (Clements) b. 1810
Nancy S. Murick b. 1811 d. 1812
John F. Myrick b. 8/1813 d. 8/27/1824
Stith Parham Myrick b. 3/7/1815 d. 1/20/1885
Mary Ann Parham Myrick b. 2/21/1817 d. 1/20/1825
Sara Myrick b. 1819 d. 1835

Ben Harvey Myrick	William Myrick
Goodwin Myrick	John Myrick

MRS. ELIZABETH DOWDELL MYRICK BIBLE
Owner: Miss Elizabeth Jones, Milledgeville, Ga.

Stith Parham Myrick b. 3/7/1815 m. 5/7/1834 to Mary Eliza
Peebles. Issue:

Mary Elizabeth Myrick (Daniel) b. 5/18/1835

CHARLES MALONE BIBLE
Owner: Miss Elizabeth Jones, Milledgeville, Ga.

Stith P. Myrick and Mary E. Peeples m. 5/7/1834
Elizabeth Myrick, dau. of S. P. and Mary E. Myrick, b. 5/18/1835
Mary E. Myrick d. 12/22/1836

JOSEPH L. LANE BIBLE
Hapeville, Ga.

Frances Ann Heard and Joseph L. Lane m. 1/5/1871 Greene Co., Ga.

Births
Joseph L. Lane 2/16/1848
Frances Ann, dau. of Thomas and Ann Heard, 3/14/1849
Walter Lane, son of J. L. and Frances Lane, 4/25/1874
Margaret Lane, dau. of above, 2/14/1876
Arthur Lane, son of above, 11/1/1877
Frank Lane, son of above, 8/22/1879
Fannie Bell Lane, dau. of above, 8/26/1882
Ann Heard Lane, dau. of above, 9/16/1885

Marriages
Arthur Lane and Nancy Powell 8/18/1889
Walter Lane and Florella Rebecca Franklin of Baltimore, Md.,
   10/22/1897
Margaret Lane and William Baker 12/23/1897
Frank Lane and Hattie Cook 8/1/1903

Deaths
Frances Ann Heard Lane, wife of J. L. Lane, 8/30/1913 at
   Hapeville, Ga.

MARSHALL BIBLE
Owner: Mrs. W. R. Respess
Atlanta, Ga.

Births Children:
Katie 2/18/1756   James 8/30/1762   Mary 4/17/1770
Lucy 9/4/1758   Ann 5/7/1765   Jane 4/26/1772
William 10/3/1760   Stephens 8/27/1767   Sueky 2/26/1774

(Marshall Bible, Births, contd....)

Elizabeth 2/26/1776   Sarah 2/14/1778   Martha 11/21/1780

STEPHEN MARSHALL BIBLE

Family Record of Stephen Marshall:
Elizabeth Burt b. 1/20/1774
Children:

Nancy b. 7/4/1794 m. Thomas Mahone
William B. 5/6/1796 m. Miss Turner, first wife, Miss Flourney,
    second wife
Stephens B. 3/14/1798 m. Martha Reese
Elizabeth H. b. 3/8/1800 m. Flournoy Mahone
Harriet b. 3/6/1802 m. James D. Lester
Mary Jane b. 4/12/1804
Lucy B. b. 12/1/1805 m. Bushrod Johnson
Margaret Ellen b. 10/4/1809 d. 12/1/1885 m. Allen little 1828
Martha b. 2/14/1812 m. Robert Dixon
Caroline M. b. 11/15/1816 m. Joel Reese
James Franklin b. 6/18/1820 m. Virginia Leonard first wife,
    Clifford Weaver, second wife

JAMES FRANKLIN LITTLE BIBLE
Owner: Mrs. J. C. Lumsden, Talbotton, Ga.

James F. Little b. 1/1/1830 d. 12/19/1897
Mattie Jane Seals b. 3/27/1841 d. 12/11/1895
    Their Children:

Mary Birdsong b. 9/11/1861 d. 5/15/1893
Margaret Elizabeth b. 5/13/1862 d. 8/19/1931
Henry Wort b. 6/29/1865
Ansel Blake b. 7/16/1867
Lulu Trippe b. 8/25/1869
Alice Phelps b. 4/6/1872 d. 5/1920
Thomas Allen b. 10/3/1874
James Millard b. 2/10/1877 d. 3/22/1935

James Franklin Little m. Mattie Jane Seals 1860
Mary Birdsong Little m. Thomas Albert Kimbrough 1883
Margaret Elizabeth Little m. Simeon Dutch Maxwell 12/1/1886
Henry Wort Little m. Katherine Belvin 1898
Lulu Trippe Little m. Dr. D. R. Lide 1896
Alice Phelps Little m. Thomas Finley Matthews 1895
Thomas Allen little m. Janie Brawner 1808
James Franklin Little m. Mabel Bowen 12/15/1909

ALLEN LITTLE BIBLE Of Baldwin Co.
Owner: Mrs. J. C. Lumsden, Talbotton, Ga.

Allen Little b. 3/6/1784 d. 12/24/1853
Margaret Marshall b. 10/4/1807 d. 12/1/1885 Their Children:

James Franklin Little b. 1/1/1830 d. 12/19/1897
Mary Virginia b. 1/20/1847 d. 2/2/1867
Other children died in infancy

Allen Little m. Margaret Marshall 1828
James Franklin Little m. Mattie Jane Seals 1860
Mary Virginia Little m. B. B. Adams 1866

THOMAS HUDSON BIBLE
Owner: Thomas Hudson Little
Sparta, Ga.

Thomas Hudson and Elizabeth Little m. 12/10/1801
Thomas Little b. 3/19/1774
Elizabeth, his wife, b. 6/3/1784
John C. Gregory and Sarah H. Little, dau. of Thomas Little m.
   12/23/1824
J. G. Coleman and Elizabeth F. Little m. 1/28/1830
Barnaby Shivers and Sarah H. Gregory, Relict of J. G. Gregory
   m. 9/5/1832

Births
William Featherston, son of Thomas Little and Elizabeth, his
wife,
   b. 10/26/1802
Sarah Hudson, their first dau., b. 9/3/1804
Thomas Hudson, their second son, b. 8/24/1806
Eliza Featherston, their second dau. b. 12/5/1808
Margaret Forrester, their third dau., b. 8/22/1811
The next dau. prematurely born
Henry Hudson, their third son, b. 6/2/1813
William Sydney, their fourth son, b. 9/12/1814
Phoebe, their fifth dau., b. 9/8/1817
Mary Frances, their sixth dau. and John henry, their sixth son,
   b. 7/19/1820
Caroline Elizabeth, dau. of J. C. Gregory and Sarah, his wife,
   b. 10/27/1825
John Cary b. 2/20/1827
Ann Elizabeth, dau. of J. C. Coleman and Elizabeth, his wife,
   b. 11/27/1830
Sarah Jane, second dau. of J. C. Coleman and Elizabeth, his wife,
   b. 2/19/1832

Deaths
Capt. John C. Gregory 9/23/1825
Thomas Little 1852
Jane Ware Little, wife of Thomas Irby Little, 7/25/1881
Thomas Irby Little 11/2/1881

ELIJAH W. CARR BIBLE

Marriages
12/19/1860 by Rev. W. M. Crawford, Elijah Walker, son of William
    A. Carr and Cynthia Walker, to Anna, dau. of Dr. Edwin H. Macon
    and Lilias Amanda Grimes.
William A. Carr and Cynthia M. Walker 7/13/1817
Edwin Hunt Mason and Lilias Amanda Grimes by Rev. Lovick Pierce--
7/15/1890 by Rev. J. C. Davis at Emmanuel Episcopal Church,
    Athens, Ga., Robert C. Orr, son of William C. Orr and Ann
    Montgomery, to Florida Agnes Carr, dau. of Elijah and Anna Carr.
10/29/1919 Julia Walden Orr, dau. of Robert C. Orr and Florida
    Carr Orr to Evan Worth Hadley, at First Presbyterian Church,
    Athens, Ga., Rev. E. L. Hill officating
12/28/1920 Robert Craig Orr (Jr.) to Sarah Wylly Treanor at
    Ridgeville, mcIntosh Co., Ga., Rev. E. L. Hill of First
    Presbyterian Church, Athens, Ga., officating.

Births
Elijah Walker, son of William A. Carr and Cynthia, his wife,
    3/28/1829
Anna E. Carr, dau. of Edwin H. Macon and Lilian Amanda, his wife,
    12/27/1836
Florida Agnes, dau. of Elijah W. and Anna E., Carr, 8/20/1866 -
    son, stillborn, at same time
Susan Crawford Carr, dau. of Elijah W. and Anna E. Carr,
    11/27/1867
Robert Craig Carr, son of Robert C. and Florida A. C. Orr,
    6/3/1891 (named for his father)
Julia Walden Orr, dau. of Robert C. and Florida A. C. Orr,
    11/4/1896 (Named for Dr. Julius Walden, Pastor, Presby. Church)
Joan Orr, dau. of Robert C. Orr, Jr. and Sarah Wylly (Treanor)
    Orr, St. Mary´s Hospital, Athens, Ga., 10/20/1921 (Named for
    Joan Treanor, Mother´s sister.)
Ann Montgomery Orr, 2nd child of Robert C. Orr, Jr. and Sarah W.
    Treanor Orr, his wife, 8/5/1924 at St. Mary´s Hospital, Athens,
    Ga. (Named for Ann (Montgomery) Orr - Grandmother of Robert C.
    Orr, Jr.

Deaths
Anna E. Carr, wife of Elijah W., Carr, dau. of Dr. Edwin E. Macon
    and Lilias Amanda, his wife, 2/27/1868
Lilias Amanda, eldest child of E. W. Carr, 1/1869 (Jan. 15th)
Elijah Walker Carr, son of William A. Carr, 12/24/1872
Susan Crawford Carr, youngest child of E. W. Carr, 1/24/1879

WILLIAM A. CARR Of Athens, Ga.

Marriages
William A. Carr to Cynthia M. Walker of Burke Co. 7/31/1817
William A. Carr to Jane Aiken of Tallahassee, Fla., his second
    wife, 2/18/1835
John Thomas and Susan A. Carr 11/12/1856

Births
William A. Carr 8/13/1796
Cynthia Marie Carr, 1st wife of William A. Carr, 12/7/1799

(William A. Carr Bible, Births, contd.....)

Jane Carr, 2nd wife of William A. Carr, 11/6/1801, Baltimore, Md.
Frances Selina Carr, 1st dau. of William and Cynthia, 12/4/1818
Mary Eliza Carr, 2d dau. of above, 10/27/1820
Thomas Walker, son of above, 9/17/1822, Athens, Ga.
William Walter Carr, son of above, 8/8/1824, near Athens, Ga.
Charles Nelson Carr, son of above, 10/38/1826 Burke Co., Ga.
Elijah Walker Carr, son of above, 3/28/1829 Athens, Ga.
Florida Cynthia Carr, dau. of above, 7/11/1831, Athens, Ga.
John, last child of above, 7/12/1833, d. with mother same day
Susan Agnes Carr, first dau. of William and Jane, his 2nd wife,
    12/16/1835, Athens, Ga.
Mary Bryan Thomas, 1st dau. of John and Susan Thomas, 11/8/1857
Susan Agnes Thomas, 2d dau. of John & Susan Thomas 2/11/1860 Fla.

Deaths
Frances Selina Carr 12/16/1822, 4 yrs., 12 days.
Charles Nelson Car 10/25/1831, lacking 3 days of 5 yrs.
Mary Eliza Carr 11/6/1831, age 11 yrs., 10 days
Cynthia Maria Carr, wife of Wm. A. Carr, 7/12/1833, in great pain
    of child birth, funeral preached 8/25 by Rev. Elijah Sinclair.
Susan A. Thomas, wife of John G., dau. of William A. and Jane
    Carr, d. Fla. of childbed fever 1/13, remains deposited at
    Oconee Cemetery at Athens on 22nd---, service by Rev. C. Coley,
    age 25, 1 mo., 2 days
Jane Carr, 2d wife of William A. Carr, 11/11/1869, age 68, 5 days
Anthony Carr 4/20/1873, age 76, at his home at Athens, Ga.
Elijah Walker Carr 12/24/1872, age 42.
Thomas Walker Carr, 3/28/1895, at Lake Jackson, Fla., bur.
    Bradford Cemetery, Bradford, Leon Co., Fa.
Florida Cynthia Carr 2/1/1905 Athens, Ga., age 73 yrs.

                    DAVID COOK BIBLE Of Oconee Co.

Zadock Cook b. 2/18/1769 d. 8/3/1863, bur. at Jackson Cemetery,
    Oconee Co., also Betsie Cook, his wife, b. 12/10/1773.
    Their Children:

Nancy Cook the 1st b. 8/9/1790   Zadock Cook 5/12/1808
Rebecca Cook 9/29/1794   William Cook 6/24/1810
Mary Cook 11/20/1798   David Cook 12/24/1812
Purnal Cook 6/4/1801   Nancy Cook the 2d 8/30/1815
Nathan Cook 10/1/1803   John Cook 2/18/1818

David Cook and Elmira Browning m. 12/20/1838. Their Children:

William Francis Cook b. 1/7/1840   Josiah Browning b. 8/13/1850
Sarah jane Cook b. 11/18/1841   James Griffeth b. 2/11/1853
Mary Frances b. 12/24/1843   Granby Darius b. 7/19/1855
Missoura Eveline b. 2/27/1846   Lucy Josephine b. 7/13/1859
David J. b. 5/26/1848

Deaths
William Francis Cook 7/17/1862 in Va.   Josiah Browning Cook
Sarah Jane 3/16/1917   6/2/1928
James Griffeth Cook 7/14/1911   Lucy Josephine Cook
Missoura E. Cook Gunter 7/3/1920   1/23/1930
Fannie Cook Camp 11/14/1929

NICHOLAS POWERS BIBLE
Owner: Mrs. Louise Powers Underwood
Carrs Sta., Ga.

Births
Nicholas Powers 1/1/1783
Mary Meriwether Gilmer, dau. of Thomas Meriwether Gilmer
  (Rev. Soldier) and Elizabeth Lewis, b. 6/23/1786
Their son, George Powers, b. 5/18/1821
Tabitha Jane Williams, dau. of John and Lilly Williams, b.
  6/5/1824 Their Children:
Mary Harriet Sophia Powers b. 11/27/1842
Eliza George Powers b. 12/16/1844
Lilly Ann Lynn Powers b. 5/15/1847
Nicholas Fanning Powers b. 6/18/1849
George Thomas Powers b. 5/3/1851
Jane Elizabeth Caroline Powers b. 12/5/1852
Rebecca Mildred Powers b. 11/27/1854
William Benjamin Strawther Gilmer Powers b. 4/1/1857
Stella Marks Powers (twins) b. 4/1/1857
Charles Boutwell Taliaferro Powers b. 5/22/1859
Florida May Powers b. 5/3/1861
Lorena Morgan Powers b. 8/25/1862

Deaths
Nicholas Powers 6/3/1843   William B. Strawther Powers
                                        4/11/1871
Mildred Rebecca Powers 11/7/1855 Lorena Morgan Powers
                                        10/4/1876
Mary M. Gilmer Powers 7/12/1856   Stella Marks Powers Shannon
Florida May Powers 5/3/1861   10/3/1881
George Powers 5/24/1871   Nicholas Fanning Powers
                                        7/9/1908
Marriages   George Thomas Powers
George Powers and Tabitha   2/27/1929
Powers 11/1/1841 by Rev. Nicholas Glenn

BENSON MAXWELL BIBLE
Owner: Mrs. W. Baker
Baldwin, Junction City, Ga.

Benson Maxwell b. 12/11/1799
Elizabeth B. Johnston Maxwell b. 10/12/1802   Children:

John W. b. 10/7/1827 d. 8/20/1892 m. Martha Stephens Greer
Simeon b. 12/14/1829 d. 12/14/1896 m. Sara Elizabeth Stinson
  10/3/1854

L. F. Maxwell b. 11/14/1831
Mary b. 1/25/1837 m. John Robbins
Richard b. 8/26/1839 m. Melissa Ann Williams 1865

Sara Elizabeth b. 11/25/1841
L. B. Maxwell b. 8/9/1845
M. M. Maxwell b. 7/14/1848 d. 1/8/1904 m. William Sarcy 1877

EDWARD THOMAS McJUNKIN BIBLE Of Greene Co.
Owner: Mrs. Lucy Soles, Mobile, Ala.

Edward Thomas McJunkin and Jessie Frances Dolvin m. 5/9/1886 at
Union Point, Ga. by Rev. M. W. Lewis

Births
Edward Thomas McJunkin 7/21/1847 Greene Co., Ga.
Jessie Frances Dolvin 6/9/1862 Greene Co., Ga., near Union Point

Lucy Bagby McJunkin 1/10/1889
Robert Edward McJunkin 3/31/1891
James Dolvin McJunkin 4/11/1893
Mabel Mitchell McJunkin 8/29/1897
Walter Moss McJunkin 7/15/1894

Marriages
William Henry Soles and Lucy Bagby McJunkin 8/15/1910, Union
Point, Ga. Their Children:

Anna Soles 9/29/1911   Albert Shelton Soles 4/9/1917
William Edward Soles 3/2/1915   Harold Eugene Soles 9/12/1919
Lucy McJunkin Soles 2/13/1922

Deaths
Robert Edward McJunkin 6/8/1892
James Dolvin McJunkin 5/20/1893
Mable Mitchel McJunkin 9/3/1898
Jessie Frances Dolvin McJunkin 8/16/1898, bur. Union Point, Ga.
Edward Thomas McJunkin 9/5/1919, bur. Rutledge, Ga.

LUCIUS JAMES LAMAR BIBLE
Owner: Mrs. Leila Lamar Sibley
Milledgeville, Ga.

Lucius James Lamar b. 5/10/1847 d. 6/11/1924 m. 10/27/1868 Helen
Jones Robinson b. 7/14/1849, d. 11/13/1886. Their Children:

William Robinson lamar b. 4/21/1870 d. 1/15/1927
James Nichols Lamar b. 5/6/1872 d. 10/12/1899
Lucius Lamar b. 5/9/1872
Thomas Windsor Lamar b. 3/8/1876 d. 2/21/1922
Legare Jones Lamar b. 2/12/1879 d. 7/5/1926
Hugh McCaw Lamar b. 8/29/1881 d. 7/15/1933
Richard Vanderhorst Lamar b. 4/8/1883
Leon Lamar b. 5/3/1885 d. 7/14/1885

Marriages
William Robinson Lamar to Alice Younglof
James Nicholas Lamar to Mattie Ryan 2/22/1897
Lucius Lamar to Maria Teresa Perez Chaumont 9/19/1922
Thomas Windsor Lamar to Edith Walker 6/9/1898
Legare J. Lamar to Lucie Calloway
Hugh McCaw Lamar to Lillian Johnson 1/10/1898
Richard Vanderhorst Lamar to Delores Faglia 10/8/1912

LUCIUS JAMES LAMAR BIBLE
Owner: Mrs. Leila Lamar Sibley
Milledgeville, Ga.

Lucius James Lamar b. 5/10/1847 d. 6/11/1924 m. 2nd 5/10/1887 to
Mrs. Leila Belle Horne Nall b. 7/28/1850. Children:

Mark O'Daniel Lamar b. 4/3/1889 m. 1st 10/8/1913 to Jessie McCarr
who d. 7/8/1933, m. 2nd Leah Sessions 3/8/1924. She was b.
11/15/1891. Their child:
Richard Mirabeau Lamar b. 7/20/1927
Leila Rebecca Lamar b. 8/4/1891 m. 8/3/1933 to James Longstreet
  Sibley b. 8/4/1863

JAMES EDWARD KIDD BIBLE
Owner: Mrs. J. E. Kidd
Milledgeville, Ga.

Grandparents:
S. J. Kidd b. Baltimore, Md.
Annie Edwards b. 9/25/1843 Milledgeville, Ga.
John L. Culver b. 12/26/1829 Hancock Co., Ga.
Mary Lewis Cheeley b. 45/1829 Glascock Co., Ga.

Parents:
James Edward Kidd b. 1/28/1829 d. Milledgeville, Ga. 3/31/1929
Bell Louwill Culver b. 8/26/1871 Culverton, Ga.

Children:
J. E. Kidd, Jr. b. 5/1/1891 Milledgeville, Ga.
Edwards Culver Kidd b. 7/31/1892 Milledgeville, Ga.
Henry Owens Kidd b. 8/26/1895 Milledgeville, Ga.
Anne Kidd b. 7/16/1901 Milledgeville, Ga.
John Warren Kidd b. 9/17/1913

Marriages
James Edwards Kidd and Bell Louwill Culver 6/26/1890
Edwards Culver Kidd and Tilly Freeman Smith 9/23/1913
Anne Kidd and Harold Shepherd Day 4/26/1927

DR. PETERSON W. HARPER BIBLE
Owner: Mrs. R. S. Alford
Milledgeville, Ga.

Peterson W. Harper and Emily Ann, dau. of Kennon Harper and Ann
Harper m. 9/12/1821

Births
Peterson W. Harper, son of James T. Harper and Elizabeth, his
wife, b. 10/25/1791
Emily Ann, wife of Peterson W. harper and dau. of Kennon Harper
and Ann, his wife, b. 2/1807
Ann Elizabeth, dau. of P. W. Harper and Emily Ann, b. 7/15/1822,
  d. 8/1823

(Dr. Peterson W. Harper Bible, Births, contd....)

John James, son of above, 12/13/1823, d. 11/4/1824
Robert Goodloe, son of above, 11/15/1825
Henry Quincy, son of above, 3/14/1829
Ann Missouri, dau. of above, 6/22/1833
Elizabeth Winfield, dau. of above, 6/15/1836
Indianna Treat, dau. of above, 2/14/1838, d. 8/12/1838
Charles Drayton, son of above, 7/19/1839 d. 8/22/1841

Mrs. Emily Ann Carper d. 4/1/1842 and next day her funeral
preached by Rev. Asa Crenshaw....

                    WILLIAM FRANKLIN JENKINS BIBLE
                    Owner: Miss Caroline V. Jenkins
                           Eatonton, Ga.

Births
William Franklin Jenkins b. 3/26/1845 Sumter Co., Ga.
Leila Ulrica (Willow) Head b. 12/12/1849 Madison Parish, La.

Children:

Joseph Robert Jenkins b. 5/4/1871 Eatonton, Ga.
Caroline Virginia Jenkins b. 4/15/1874 Eatonton, Ga.
William Franklin Jenkins, Jr. b. 9/7/1876 at Woodlawn,
  Webster Co., Ga.

Deaths
Joseph Wood d. Woodlawn, his res., Webster Co., Ga. 9/21/1879,
  aged 70 yrs.
William Franklin Jenkins d. at his res. Eatonton, Ga. 12/17/1909,
  aged 64 yrs.
Leila Ulrica Head Jenkins, wife of William Franklin Jenkins, Sr.,
  d. Eatonton, Ga. 9/15/1933

                    ROBERT CARTER JENKINS BIBLE
                Owner: Miss Caroline Virginia Jenkins
                           Eatonton, Ga.

(Father, Mother, Brothers and Sisters of W. F. Jenkins, Sr.)

Robert Carter Jenkins b. 11/15/1818 d. 5/2/1888
Caroline Frances Hudson b. 3/5/1821 d. 2/10/1884. Children:
James Frances Jenkins b. -/7/1842 d. 8/14/1842
Robert Hudson Jenkins b. 1/11/1843 d. 5/1907
Birwell Wynn Jenkins b. 3/23/1847
Wilbur Gibson Jenkins b. 5/30/1848
Caroline Virginia Jenkins b. 10/19/1849
Georgia Eliza Jenkins b. 10/21/1851 d. 1/1908
David Henry Jenkins b. 1/1/1853
Hudson Augustus Jenkins b. 3/21/1855
Robert Carter Jenkins and Caroline Frances Hudson 3/4/1841

                              79

DANIEL POPE BIBLE *

Daniel Pope b. 11/21/1805
Rebecca Pope b. 2/13/1805
Mary Ann Pope and Martha Ann Pope, daus. of Daniel and Rebecca
Pope were b. 1/10.1827, and the residue of their children as
follows:
Comforte Eliza Pope b. 2/10/1829
William Wiley Pope b. 10/7/1830
John Allen Pope b. 6/9/1832
Simon Daniel Pope b. 1/23/1834
Andrew Jackson Pope b. 6/26/1836
Alston B. Pope b. 4/10/1839
Sarah D. Rebecca Pope b. 11/19/1840
Henry G. W. Funderburke b. 12/1/1844
Zachariah Daniel Booth b. 7/27/1845
Sarah Elizabeth Booth b. 2//17/1847
Laura Booth b. 9/29/1848
James H. Funderburke b. 6/17/1846
Mary E. Funderburke b. 7/27/1848
Rufus H. Jenkins b. 11/6/1858
L. S. Jenkins b. 4/25/1862

Mary Allice Pope b. 7/3/1862 (dau. of A. J. & F. M. Pope)
Lewis Alston Pope b. 10/16/1864
Martha Susan Funderburk b. 3/28/1850
Sarah Rebecca b. 4/12/1852
William Daniel Funderburk b. 6/23/1856
John A. J. Funderburk b. 4/12/1859
Thomas Austin Funderburk b. 12/9/1861
Julie Funderburk b. 9/29/1864

Deaths
Comforte Eliza Pope 8/13/1835, aged 6 yrs., 6 mos., 3 days
Daniel Pope 11/13/1840, aged 45 yrs., 11 mos., 22 days
L. S. Jenkins 5/3/1862
Lewis S. Jenkins, the dau. of Lewis S. and Sarah H. Jenkins, d.
   5/17/1863, aged 1 yr., 22 days
Rebecca Pope 1/3/1895, aged 89 yrs., 10 mos., 20 days
Simon Daniel Pope 5/3/1907
Minerva Pope 3/22/1911

Marriages
Daniel Pope and Rebecca Pope m. 4/9/1826
Martha Ann Pope and David H. Funderburke m. 3/7/1844
Mary Ann Pope and James A. Booth m. 10/14/1844
Sarah R. Pope and Louis S. Jenkins m. 2/4/1858
Simon D. Pope and Minerva A. Davy m. 7/25/1860

Fannie M. Cason m. 2/11/1861 Andrew J. Pope
Mary Alice Pope, dau. of A. J. and F. M. Pope, b. 7/3/1862

*See also p. 377.

JOHN BERRIEN WHITEHEAD BIBLE
Owner: Mrs. Eleanor Whitehead Simms, Jr.
Gatlinburg, Tenn.

John Berrien Whitehead b. 2/24/1820, d. 7/13/1879
Catherine Matilda Whitehead b. 1/20/1824, d. 12/11/1897
  Both buried at Richmond Bath. Children:
Ruth Berrien Whitehead, b. 10/27/1843
William Harper Whitehead, b. 1/16/1846, d. 9/19/1915,
buried Rose Hill Cemetery, Macon.
Mary Ann Whitehead, b. 11/13/1847, bur. Bath.
Virginia Whitehead, b. 11/4/1849.
Margaret Whitehead, b. 7/20/1851, bur. Bath.
Addie Harper Whitehead, b. 12/8/1855.
Catherine Matilda Whitehead, b. 10/7/1862

John Berrien Whitehead and Catherine Matilda Harper m. 10/13/1842
in Augusta, Ga.

William Harper Whitehead, b. 1/16/1846, d. 9/19/1915
and Mary Eunice Thomson, b. 9/26/1851, d. 6/27/1922 m. 6/11/1874
in Macon, Ga. Their Children:
William Harper Whitehead b. 6/1875, d. 8/29/1875
Eunice Thomson Whitehead, b. 7/28/1876
Henry Whitehead b. 5/24/1878, d. 1/29/1938
John Berrien Whitehead b. 7/31/1881, d. 11/21/1939
Mary Catherine Whitehead, b. 11/30/1881, d. 9/4/1919
Kittie Freeman Whitehead, b. 8/22/1884, d. 6/9/1899

John Berrien Whitehead (1881-1939) m. 1/23/1907 in Montezuma,
Ga., Stella Louise Taylor, b. 12/15/1882. Their children:
Eleanor Eunice Whitehead b. 12/14/1909
John Berrien Whitehead b. 11/24/1911

Mary Catherine Whitehead (1882-1919) m. 10/25/1911 in Macon, Ga.,
John Harris Mathis, b. 5/24/1876, d. 9/22/1918. Their Child:
Mary Thomson Mathis, b. 8/22/1915, d. 9/4/1919

Children of John Berrien and Stella Taylor Whitehead:
Eleanor Whitehead, b. 12/14/1909, m. at Greenville, S. C. on
    6/23/1938 Charles Sumner Simms, Jr., b. 4/3/1907. Their
    children:
        Charles Sumner Simms III b. 2/3/1939
        Stella and Norma Taylor Sims, twin daus., b. & d. 5/31/193-
John Berrien Whitehead, b. 11/24/1911 m. at Macon 12/24/1936
Regina Pritchard, b. 12/28/1910. Their Children:
        John Berrien Whitehead III, b. 4/28/1942
        Jane Pritchard Whitehead, b. 7/5/1944
        Charles Pritchard Whitehead, b. 9/13/1953
Charles Sumner Simms III m. 3/20/1960 at Jacksonville, Fla.,
Martha Ann Gay. Their child: Susan Gay Simms, b. 1/9/1963

Deaths
Margaret Whitehead, dau. of John Berrien and Catherine Matilda
Whitehead, d. in Augusta 5/1/1852, 9 mos. 11 days.
Mary Ann Whitehead, dau. of John Berrien and Catherine Matilda
Whitehead, d. in Daughterty Co. 1/13/1863.
William Harper Whitehead, Jr., son of William Harper and Mary
Eunice Whitehead, d. in Macon, 8/29/1875.
John Berrien Whitehead d. in Baker Co., Ga. 7/13/1879, 59 yrs., 4
mos., 23 days.
Maude Glover, dau. of Virginia and Louis B. Glover d. in

(Whitehead Bible contd....)

Savannah, 4/23/1887.
Louis B. Glover d. in Savannah, 1/13/1897.
L. B. Glover d. 10/13/1897 iN Savannah.
Mrs. C. M. Whitehead d. in Macon 12/11/1897.
James Whitehead d. in Warrenton, Ga. 1/1/1899.
James Troup Whitehead d. 3/15/1890 in Warrenton.

Marriages
John Berrien Whitehead and Catherine Matilda Harper m. in
  Augusta, Ga. 10/13/1842.
William Harper Whitehead, son of above, m. Mary Eunice Thomson,
  6/11/1874.
Virginia Whitehead, dau. of J. B. and C. M. Whitehead, m. Lewis
  Bee Glover 10/30/1878.
Addie Harper Whiteheard, dau. of J. B. and C. M. Whitehead, m.
  William Wert Williams, 12/20/1882.
Ruth Berrien Whitehead, dau. of J. B. and C. M. Whitehead, m.
  Christopher J. Wilson, 4/3/1883.
Kate Whitehead, dau. of J. B. and C. M. Whitehead, m. Henry
  Phillip Jones, 6/17/1896.
Catherine Matilda Glover, dau. of Virginia and L. B. Glover, b.
  Isle of Hope, 1/13/1879.
John Berrien Glover, son of above, b. Isle of Hope, 2/12/1880.
William Berrien Williams, son of Addie Harper and William Wirt
  Williams, b. in Newton, Ga. 11/5/1883.

THOMAS NESBITT BIBLE
Owners: Virginia and Mary Holt
Richmond Bath, Ga.

Births
Thomas Nesbitt b. Augusta, Ga. 12/24/1821
Virginia Louise, dau. of James and Ruth Lowndes Whitehead, b. at
  Richmond Bath 8/2/1825
Ruth Lowndes, dau. of Thomas and Virginia Louisa Nesbitt, b. at
  Richmond Bath 6/12/1845
James Whitehead, son of Thomas and Virginia Louisa Nesbitt, b.
  at Richmond Bath 8/24/1847
At the plantation in Baker Co., Ga. on 9/4/1872 Virginia
  Whitehead, dau. of James Whitehead and Mary Eliza Nesbitt.
At residence of Anderson M. Watson in Augusta, Ga., Thomas
  Nesbitt, son of Alfred Charles and Ruth Lowndes Holt, 4/20/1873

Marriages
Thomas Nesbitt, son of Hugh Nesbitt and Eleanor Lucinda Nesbitt,
  m. Virginia Louisa, dau. of James Whitehead and Ruth Lowndes
  Whitehead by Rev. Francis Goulding 5/23/1844 at Richmond Bath.
At the Union Church in Newton 11/8/1871 by Rev. J. T. Auysworth,
  James W. Nesbitt to Mary Eliza McGregor, dau. of Capt. John A.
  McGregor of Baker Co., Ga.
At the Presbyterian Church in Augusta, Ga. 4/30/1872 by Rev. Dr.
  Robert Irvine, Alfred Charles Holt of Augusta, Ga. to Ruth
  Lowndes Nesbitt, dau. of Thomas Nesbitt.

Deaths
Virginia Louisa, wife of Thomas Nesbitt, d. at Richmond Bath
  4/2/1850. Her remains interred in Summerville Cemetery on the
  Hill, Augusta, Ga.
In Augusta, Ga. 6/27/1873, Thomas Nesbitt, son of Alfred Charles

(Thomas Nesbitt Bible contd....)

and Ruth Lowndes Holt.

AMOS WHITEHEAD BIBLE
Owner: Mrs. James Miller Byne

Amos Whitehead b. 8/11/1744
Mary Whitehead, wife of Amos.Whitehead, b. 12/31/1747
Elizebeth Whitehead b. 12/1/1768
Martha Whitehead b. 1/22/1770
Bithiah Whitehead b. 11/13/1771
William Whitehead b. 11/29/1773
David Whitehead b. 2/14/1776
Alcey Whitehead b. 2/27/1778
Amos Whitehead, Jr., b. 1/31/1781
John Whitehead, b. 12/14/1783, d. 5/31/1857
James Whitehead, b. 4/7/1786, d. 10/11/1847
Amaninthia Whitehead, b. 10/7/1789
Mary Whitehead, b. 5/2/1794
Ruth Lowndes Whitehead, wife of James Whitehead, b. 6/9/1798
Mary Susan Whitehead, b. 9/24/1817
John Berrien Whitehead, b. 2/24/1820
Williamina Whitehead, b. 11/22/1821
Eliza Matilda Whitehead, b. 9/24/1823
Virginia Louisa Whitehead, b. 8/2/1825
James Troup Whitehead, b. 10/13/1827
William Harlow Whitehead, b. 12/19/1830
Thomas and Julia Whitehead, twins, b. 1/20/1833
Richard MacPherson Whitehead b. 4/17/1835, d. 8/16/1864
Amos Whitehead, b. 6/13/1837, d. 1875
Catherina Matilda Whitehead, w. of John B. Whitehead, b.1/20/1824
Ruth Berrien Whitehead, b. 10/27/1843
William Harper Whitehead, b. 1/11/1846
Thomas Nesbit m. Virginia L. Whitehead 5/23/1844
Ruth Lowndes Nesbit b. 2/12/1868, d. 2/18/1894
Amos Whitehead, Jr., b. 3/8/1870
Sarah Donalson Whitehead, b. 7/11/1871
John Berrien Whitehead, b. 8/1/1874
James Edward Whitehead m. Charlotte Arthur Croucher 2/3/1888
Charlotte Arthur Crougher, wife of James Edward Whitehead, b. in
    Liverpool, England, 7/14/1863
Alice Whitehead, b. 2/2/1889
Amos Whitehead, b. 2/7/1891, d. 5/5/1893
George Arthur Whitehead, b. 11/10/1895
Edward Bradford Whitehead, b. 7/22/1893
Margaret Maria Whitehead, b. 12/31/1897
James Edward Whitehead, b. 3/1/1903
Ruth Louise Whitehead, b. 7/10/1906

ROBERT GRIER BIBLE
Owner: Calvin Grier, Charlotte, N. C.

Robert Grier m. Margaret Livingston 9/9/1775
Mary Grier m. John Johnson 11/13/1800
Aron Grier m. Polly Grier 12/25/1804
Elizabeth Grier m. Robert Grier 4/2/1805
Isaac Grier m. Isabel Harris 10/7/18--

(Robert Grier Bible, Marriages, Contd.....)

Robert Grier, Jr. m. 2/9/1809 Mary Heard
His dau., Judith, the first fruit of this marriage, b. 7/1/1810
His son, Isaac Grier, b. 8/29/1811
Margaret Grier m. Jose--10/-/-

Births
Isaac Grier 10/7/1776
Aron Grier 5/1/1778
Mary Grier 8/19/1780
--eth Grier 11/26/1783
--obert Grier --/4/1786
Eliza Grier 12/8/1805, dau. of Aron and Polly
M. P. Grier, dau. of I. H. and M. S. Grier, 1/22/1860
Judith Grier 7/1/1810
Isaac Grier 8/29/1811
Margaret Grier 3/2/1813
Melvina B. Grier 4/12/1814
Jesse H. Grier 10/22/1815
Judith Grier 1/7/1816
Adeline Grier 11/10/1818
Eliza Grier 3/9/1820
Aaron Grier 5/12/1821
Robert Grier 10/28/1822
Robert Alexr. Grier 12/20/1823

Deaths
Robert Grier, my Father, d. 2/8/1801
Elizabeth, my Mother, d. 10/27/1776
Polly Grier, my dau.-in-law, 4/30/1807
Eliza Grier 8/15/1806, dau. of Aaron.
Demaris Key 4/7/1814, dau. of Peggy G.
Judith Grier 9/28/1814, aged 4 yrs., 2 mos., 28 days, dau. of
   Robert
Aaron Grier, my 2nd son, d. 11/20/1815, age 37
The above Judith Grier was bur. in Ga. on Gap Creek.
Eliza, the dau. of Robert and Mary Grier d. 7/26/1822, bur. on W.
   1/4 of Sec. 23 T 14 R. G.
My father-in-law, Robert Grier, d. 8/6/1822 and was buried where
   Eliza was.
Jane Grier, my sister, was murdered 2/12/1819
Robert, son of Robert and Mary Grier, d. 11/1822, bur. on S. W.
   1/4 of Sec. 23 T 14 R. G.
Robert Grier, spouse of Mary Grier, d. 11/8/1823, bur. on S. W.
   1/4 of Sec. 23 T. 14 R. G.

Mary Grier, wife of Robert Grier, d. 8/2/1827, bur. by side of
   her husband.
Aaron Grier d. 11/1/1827
Rev. Isaac Grier d. 11/2/1843, bur. at Sardis Church, N. C.,
   Mecklenburg Co.

Marriages
Hugh McCauley m. Mary Black 9/19/1850, his own niece.
Isaac Grier and Isabella Robinson m. 3/1/1831

Births
Robert L. Grier b. 6/18/1832   William P. Grier b. 7/24/1840
Isaac H. Grier b. 7/21/1834   James M. Grier b. 9/1/--
James R. Grier b. 7/23/1838   John Owen b. 6/21/1846
Aaron Grier b. 6/4/1839

(Robert Grier Bible contd....)

An Eliza Isabell Canon b. 10/24/1852
M. A. Grier, wife of R. L. Grier, b. 2/13/1836
I. D. Grier, son of R. L. and M. A. Grier, b. 3/1/1857
L. I. Grier, dau. of R. L. and M. A. Grier, b. 3/22/1859
H. K. Grier, son of R. L. and M. A. Grier, b. 9/28/1861

Deaths
James R. Grier 9/19/1838, bur. at Coddle Creek Church, Iredell
  Co., N. C.
Aaron Grier 7/27/1837, bur. at Sardis, Mecklenburg Co., N.C.
Eliza I. Canon 11/10/1852
Eleanor Robinson 6/8/1854
Martha Ann Grier, wife of R. L. Grier, 6/22/1874 or 1894, bur. at
  Mt. Carmel Church, Marshel Co., Miss.
R. L. Grier 2/16/1881, bur. at Salem Church, Tenn.
H. H. Roberson d. 5/19/1881, bur. at Ebenezer Church, ? Co.,
  Miss.
W. B. Grier 11/17/1859

The decd graduated at Erskine College and was bur. at Sardis,
  Mecklenburg, N. C.
Isaac Grier 5/9/1862, bur. at Sardis Church, N. C.
William B. Grier 10/14/1875, son of I. M. and A. M. Grier.
I. O. Grier 5/29/1881, bur. at Ebenezer Church, Mecklenburg, N.C.
H. K. Grier 12/5/1881, bur. at Ebenezer Church, Mecklenburg
  Co., N. C.
Isabella Grier 7/28/1889, bur. Sardis Church, Mecklenburg Co.,
  N.C.

Marriages
Neel McCauley m. Melvina B. Grier 1/12/1832
Hugh McCauley m. Adaline Grier 4/29/1840
Judith E. Grier m. Samuel N. Black 6/3/1840
R. L. Grier m. Martha Ann Kirkpatrick 4/24/1856
I. H. Grier m. Mag. S. Parks 10/21/1856 by Rev. J. E. Pressly
J. N. Grier m. A. M. McLaughlin 3/1/1866

HEARD BIBLE
Owner: Willard Colvin, Dubach, Lincoln Par., La.

Births
Stephen B. Heard 12/20/1811   Martha Heard 9/7/1823
William M. Heard 10/10/1814   Sarah Heard 8/13/1826
Charles Heard 10/17/1817   Elizabeth Heard 7/31/1829
Jesse W. Heard 1/5/1820
John G. Wright, son of John Wright, 9/7/1807
Martha Jane Heard 9/27/1851
Sarah or Dorah Ann Francis 3/26/1856
William Charles Heard 11/6/1860
Joseph Stephen Heard 8/14/1867
Jesse Anderson Heard 11/15/1845   Parthena C. Davis 8/31/1827
Cintha Elizabeth Heard 7/30/1848   Sarah Ann Davis 1/20/1812

Deaths
Stephen B. Heard 5/27/1835   Elizabeth Heard 8/15/1847
Jesse A. Heard 12/20/1845   William M. Heard 8/29/1847
Jesse Heard 10/17/1840   John C. Wright 8/10/1864
Jesse W. Heard 7/22/1846   Amanda D. Autrey 2/26/1868

85

(Heard Bible contd....)   Deaths

                    Cintha K. Autrey 7/26/1884

Marriages
William T. Edwards and Martha A. Heard m. 1/12/1848
Charles F. Heard and Parthenia C. Davis m. 9/19/1844
L. P. B.? and Deleny Heard m. 2/7/1845
John G. Wright and S. A. Davis m. 8/10/1862
Thomas A. Wright and Martha J. Heard m. 3/26/1868
Richard C. Colvin and Dorah A. Heard m. 12/25/1870
Thomas J. Autrey and Cinthia E. Heard m. 11/19/18-9

Births
John Wright 2/14/1775   Stephen Wright 7/9/1779
Arthur Wright 8/7/1760   Elizabeth Wright 8/27/1787
Owen Mitchel Wright 7/26/1863
Jesse Heard, son of William Heard, 2/14/1780
Liveller Jane Autrey 11/3/1866
Dorah Telephone Wright 8/4/1800
Amanda Dorathe Autrey 1/30/1868
Charles A. Autrey 1/25/1869

                    JAMES W. HEARD BIBLE*
            Owner: Mrs. J. L. Holloway, Indian Springs, Ga.

James W. Heard of Indian Springs and Adalaide Barkley of Monroe
Co., Ga. m. 12/20/1866 at Monroe Co. by Rev. Millins, Baptist
Church. Wit: Midlton Wise, Jane H. Moore.

Births
James W. Heard 11/14/1834, Indian Springs, Ga.
Adalaide Gertrude Barkley 10/18/1846, Monroe Co., Ga.
Lilliam Lee Heard 1/6/1870
Ada Gertrude Heard 11/14/1871
Claudine Heard 9/14/1873

                    STEPHEN HEARD BIBLE

Stephen and Betsy Heard m. 8/25/1785
Barnard Carol b. 3/12/1787   Jane Lanier b. 3/23/1797
Patsy Burch b. 10/10/1788   Permelia Darden b. 2/23/1799
George Washington b. 6/17/1791 Thomas Jefferson b. 8/21/1801
John Adams b. 3/17/1793   Sarah Hammond b. 12/24/1804
Bridge Carol b. 6/17/1795

Deaths
Col. Stephen Heard 11/13/1815   Bridge Carol--
Permelia Darden Heard 2/13/1816   John Lanier--
Patsy Burch 12/7/1824   Thomas Jefferson 5/4/1876
Sarah Hammond 8/16/1825
Maj. Barnard Carol Heard---
Gen. John Adams Heard 1/6/1829
George Washington 10/17/1838
Elizabeth, wife of Stephen, 6/5/1848

    *See also p. 197.
                    86

HUGH H. HEARD BIBLE
Owner: Mrs. J. L. Holloway, Indian Springs, Ga.

Hugh H. Heard b. 2/3/1796
Jane H. Gilmore b. 6/15/1809
Hugh H. Heard and Jane H. Gilmore m. 12/23/1827

Births
William G. Heard 10/12/1828   Isabella I. Heard 9/3/1838
Eleanor E. Heard 4/11/1830   (d. 1840)
George W. Heard 7/6/1831   Mary Ann Heard 7/30/1840
Charles L. Heard 3/4/1833   (d. 1844)
James W. Heard 11/14/1834   Hugh H. Heard 4/8/1842
Catherine M. Heard 12/16/1836   (d. 1/7/1845)
Eleanor S. Heard m. Charles C. Heard 12/28/1848
Julyann Heard m. Richard R. Osborne 8/24/1845
Louisa Amanda Heard m. Reuben Boyett 11/18/1849 (Reuben d. 1858)
Louisa Amanda Heard Boyett m. James M. Pittman 1/28/1860

Births
John Jasper Heard 3/16/1798 (son of Charles and Elinor)
Amanda Malvina Heard 5/9/1806
Martha Nobles Heard 11/27/1826
Eleanor Silverster Heard 8/31/1828
Julyann Heard 10/20/1830
Louisa Amanda Heard 7/8/1833
Caroline M. Heard 8/30/1835
Susannah Heard 11/23/1837
Elizabeth E. Heard 1/18/1840
Charles Jackson Heard 7/3/1842
John Washington Columbus Heard 11/28/1845
Eleanor's son, Lewis Washington, b. 12/10/1849.
Eleanor's son, Joseph Sanford Heard, b. 11/11/1851
Louisa Amanda's son, John Jasper Boyett, b. 1/18/1853, d. 1862
Erwin Newton Boyett b. 11/19/1854, d. 3/1930
George Washington Boyett b. 11/28/1856, d. 5/21/1945
Reuben Charles Boyett b. 10/30/1858, d. infancy
dau., Lucinda Elama Pittman, b. 5/1/1861

Julyann's dau., Georgia A. Osborne, b. 12/23/1848.
Son, Sammie Y. V. Osborne, b. 5/23/1851

Deaths
Susannah Heard d. 9/23/1842   Eleanor S. Heard d. 11/1/1842
Caroline M. Heard d. 9/25/1842   Louise Amanda Boyette 7/1/1862
Julyann Osborne d. 7/23/1851

Charles J. Heard, a Confederate Soldier, vol. under Capt. Brown
on 5/21/1861. He was in 1st battle of Manassas, Va., after which
he was appointed Corpl. of Color Guards. He stood gallantly by
the flag of his country, and at the battle of Malvin Hill, he
received a mortal wound on July 1st and d. 7/5/1862.

John W. C. Heard vol. in Confederate Army at age 18, acted the
part of a brave soldier for the space of 12 mos. He was taken
sick and died of a short illness 3/10/1865.

John J. (John Jasper) Heard d. 7/4/1867
Amanda Malvina Heard d. 7/29/1873

(Info. from Mrs. George Boyett, Moss Point, Miss.)

87

JOHN HEARD BIBLE
From Rev. War Pension R4822

Appl. dtd 11/18/1845 of John Germany Heard, aged 81 on 11/12th
last from Walton Co., Ga., states was b. Columbia Co., Ga.
11/12/1763. Affidavit of Charles M. Heard, Jackson Co., Ga. dtd
8/10/1852, aged 64, son of John G. Heard.

John Heard m. Elizabeth 1/15/1787. Their children:
Margrett Forgason Heard b. 10/30/1787
Barnard Heard b. 10/16/1787
William Brady Heard b. 3/3/1797
John Heard b. 12/1795
John Germany Heard
Elizabeth Heard b. 8/1803

WOODSON HEARD BIBLE
Owner: Mrs. Fannie Weathers

Births
Woodson Heard 3/4/1782
Polly Heard 3/30/1792
Marshall Peeples Heard, son of Woodson and Polly Heard,
   9/14/1806
Sophronia Massy Heard 11/1807
Almira Ann Heard 6/21/1810
Joseph Collumbus Heard 10/17/1812
Cordelia Elizabeth Heard 4/17/1815
Thomas Amiruns Heard 11/29/1817
Gustavus Peeples Heard 3/31/1820
Patton Alanson Heard 3/16/1822
Mary Frances 9/4/1824
Sabrina Catherine Heard 11/19/1826
David Woodson Heard 6/15/1829
Caleenah America Heard 5/18/1831
Abraham Faulkner Heard 12/17/1837
Joseph Collumbus Sanders 8/17/1839

John D. Sanders b. 12/3/1841, aged 42.

Deaths
Elizabeth Heard 9/24/1790, aged 40.
Thomas Heard 1/17/1808, aged 10 yrs.
Marshall Peeples Heard 117/1806, aged 9 wks., 1 day.
Gustavus Peeples Heard 11/23/1834, aged 14.

Joseph Collumbus Heard, grandson of Woodson and Polly Heard,
   b. 10/23/1837
Abraham Faulkner Heard d. 1/7/1838, aged 21 days.
Nathan Peeples, d. 10/1/1797, aged 41 yrs.
Frances peeples, d. 1/21/1799, aged 49 yrs.
Leenah Peeples d. 7/25/1799, aged 14 yrs.
Elizabeth Peeples d. 5/14/1806.
David Peeples, Jr. d. 9/25/1807, aged 20 yrs.
Elizabeth Lee d. 8/12/1809, aged 27 yrs.
Woodson Heard d. 1/1829, aged 66 yrs., 10 mos., 10 days.
Mary Heard d. -/5/1863 or 1865, aged 42 yrs, 22 mos., 5 days.

W. A. HUNTER BIBLE
Owner: John Richard Hunter, Lafayette, Ala.

Sophrona Massy Hunter b. 11/20/1807, d. 2/14/1839
W. A. Hunter and Sophrona M. Heard m. 4/13/1826
Cornelius Peeples Hunter b. 4/24/1827
Eleazer Elisha Hunter b. 10/19/1828, d. 11/25/1869
Columbus Vespacuius Hunter b. 8/4/1830
Mary Ann Sophrona Hunter b. 2/22/1836
William Gustavus Hunter b. 5/11/1838
Cornelius P. Hunter b. 4/24/1827
Malissa S. Hunter b. 2/24/1835

Cornelius P. Hunter and Melissa S. Boyd m. 11/28/1850
Cornelius Peeples and Malissa Susan Hunter united with Baptist
   Church 8/16/1852

JOHN H. NEELY BIBLE Of Coweta Co.

John H. Neely b. 2/4/1796. Rebecca P. Neely b. 12/16/1803.
John H. Neely and Rebecca P. Whitten m. 11/12/1822

Births
William A. B. Neely 9/2/1823   Robert L. Neely 3/9/1838
Craten Alonzo Neely 7/6/1825   Betsy A. Neely 8/18/1841
Jonathan P. Neely 5/24/1827   Nancy Caroline Neely 11/8/1843
Adaline D. Neely 4/5/1832   John H. Neely 11/15/1847

Deaths
Robert L. Neely 11/8/1842   Rebecca P. Neely 12/8/1880
William A. B. Neely 2/7/1863   John Hubbard Neely 7/12/1934
John H. Neely, Sr. 3/8/1864   age 86 yrs., 7 mos., 27 days

Rebecca Whitten Neely was the dau. of Philip and Delilah Whitten.

Births
Phillip Whitten 9/13/1776   Johnathan Whitten 12/6/1805
Delilah Whitten 2/9/1777   Rachel A. Whitten 9/4/1808
Robert Whitten 10/1/1800   Lucinda H. Whitten 6/4/1814
Littleton Whitten 3/7/1802   Elizabeth E. M. Whitten
Rebecca Whitten 12/16/1803   12/31/1816

Deaths
Delilah Whitten 1/19/1835   Augustus R. Graves 5/25/1863
Rachel Alman 10/20/1834   Elizabeth A. Graves 3/21/1902
Philip Whitten 11/3/1858

WILLIAM B. DANIELL
Owner: Sidney M. Johnson, Bogart, Ga.

"This is to certify that William B. Daniell of Clarke Co. in the
State of Ga. and Julia Burnett of Clarke Co. in State of Ga. were
united together in Holy Matrimony 7/26/1831. William Stroud, JP."

(William B. Daniell Bible contd....)

Marriages
Josiah Daniell to Sarah Burrough 7/16/1811, and marriages of
their children as follows:
Elizabeth Daniell to L. B. Burnett 5/28/1829
William B. Daniell to Julia Burnett 7/26/1831
Eleanor Daniell to James Lester 8/1/1839
Sarah Daniell to Hardy Strickland 10/4/1831
Jesse Daniell to Martha Smith 10/19/1841
Nathaniel Daniell to Eliza Harper 11/17/1844
Josiah Daniell to Susan Lester 1/16/1845
Susan Daniell to Patman Lester 8/5/1847
William B. Daniell to Julia Burnett 7/26/1831

Deaths
Josiah William Daniell 8/5/1833, aged 10 mos., 24 days
John B. Daniell, killed at Chancellorsville fight 5/2/1865,
    aged 26 yrs, 4 mos, 30 days
Nathaniel J. Daniell killed near Gawlsoury in N. C. by the
    car running off 4/17/1865, aged 30 yrs., 1 mo., 29 days
Mother d. 7/24/1838 (Sarah Ann Owens Burroughs Daniell)
Father d. 6/22/1845, aged 53 yrs., 3 mos., 26 days (Josiah
    Daniell)
William B. Daniell d. 9/10/1886
Sarah Ann Daniell Bradberry d. 8/13/1918
Julia F. Bradberry d. 10/23/1862, aged 7 mos., 28 days.

                    JOHN ABERCROMBIE BIBLE *
             Owner: Edith Barlow, Gainesville, Ga.

Marriages
John Abercrombie to Catharine Peck 10/8/1846

Births
John Abercrombie 12/22/1822
Catharine Abercrombie 1/14/1827
Eliza and Fanny Abercrombie 7/17/1847
Elizabeth Abercrombie 6/13/1849
Joseph Abercrombie 3/6/1851
John Abercrombie 6/5/1853
Rebecca J. Abercrombie 6/23/1855
James Abercrombie 5/29/1857
Isabel Caroline Abercrombie 7/11/1859
Harriett Lovey Abercrombie 11/13/1861

Deaths
John Abercrombie 8/9/1854   John Abercrombie 9/30/1864
Catharine Abercrombie 5/25/1864 Martha Elizabeth Abercrombie
                                     5/18/1896

*See also p. 364.   90

JOHN MARTIN DANIEL STALLINGS BIBLE

Josiah Stallings d. 3/1/1857
Mary Alberta Callista Stallings d. 1874

Rev. John D. Stallings b. Heard Co. 2/20/1842, d. Carroll Co.,
3/13/1921, m. Elizabeth Moor, b. Newberry Co., S. C. 7/14/1841,
d. Carroll Co. 3/23/1885, dau. of Robert and Sarah Moore, bur.
New Lebanon Church, Carroll Co.

John M. D. Stallings m. 2d Emily Huckaby.
His sisters, Sally Richards; Martha C. Huckaby
Josiah Robert b. 11/13/1867 m. Letha Wrenn 10/7/1885
John William Benson Stallings b. 2/5/1870
Idella Wootson Stallings b. 9/21/1871 m. J. N. Webb 12/27/1888
Cora Gertrude b. 6/10/1875 m. Charles C. Williams
James Thomas b. 8/12/1877, d. 11/1/1918
Palasman Franklin Stallings b. 1/4/1881
Luther b. 12/29/1882, d. 8/9/1888
Louise Whitaker Stallings b. 2/22/1885
Lucious M.
Minnie Lou b. 8/1840, wife of James Thomas
James L. Bartlett b. 12/27/1862
Mary Jane Bartlett b. 7/1/1886
Sarah Janneh Stallings m. James Leroy Bartlett 9/24/1882

JOHN SEE BIBLE

John See b. 7/1/1812   Laurenia S. See b. 9/3/1814
Mary Ann See b. 12/11/1831   Joshua F. See b. 11/15/1834
John Washington See b. 11/27/1836 Lavina Bell b. 6/3/1829
Hartmell Harris See b. 6/6/1838 George Winkfeld See
Sarah Barthella See b. 1/1/1842   b. 10/24/1839
Emeline Elizabeth See b. 2/23/1843 David Tillman See b. 2/12/1849
Levi P.? See b. 12/9/1845
Barbary Virginia See b. 7/29/1847

Mosses W. See b. 2/24/1861
David T. See b. 2/-/1809, d. 1863

ISAAC SMITH BIBLE
From Rev. War Pension W4338

Isaac Smith's appl. dtd 10/22/1832, Monroe Co., Ga., states he
was b. New Kent Co., Va. Wid., Ann R. Smith, in 1840, aged 67,
states husband d. 7/12/1834, and she m. him 1/1/1794.
Children of Isaac and Ann Rebecca Smith:

Births
Nancy Smith 4/20/1793   George G. Smith 12/19/1804
Elizabeth Smith 10/9/1796, d. 10/13/1804
Jane Smith 11/4/1798   Margaret Smith 3/23/1809
Ann Smith 1/18/1800, d. 8/21/1802   d. 4/18/1816
Isaac G. Smith, jr. 12/23/1802

(Isaac Smith Bible contd....)

James Rambert Smith 7/17/1811
Elizabeth Ann 1813, d. 11/3/1820
William Joseph Smith 9/6/1817, d. 5/11/1819

Marriages
Isaac Smith to Ann Rebecca Gilman 2/2/1792
Mark R. Smith to Hope H. Lenoir 12/20/1810
Jane P. Smith to Wutman C. Hill 1/11/1816

ELIJAH FRANKS BLACKSHEAR BIBLE
Owner: Miss A. Laura Eve Blackshear, Athens, Ga.

The Bible is a gift from Mother of Mary LaFayette Hamilton
Blackshear, who was the dau. of Gen. John Floyd (Mary Floyd
Hamilton) 10/16/1845.

Marriages
Elijah F. Blackshear m. Mary L. Hamilton 10/16/1845 Savannah, Ga.
by Rev. C. W. Key
James E. Blackshear m. Katherine M. Baker 7/16/1873 Floral
College, N. C.

Births
Elijah Franks Blackshear b. Springfield, Laurens Co., Ga.
9/26/1822
Mary L. Hamilton b. Milledgeville, Ga. 7/30/1824
Children:
James Everard Blackshear b. Marianna, Laurens Co., Ga. 1/12/1847
Mary Hamilton Blackshear b. 12/25/1847 Marianna, Laurens Co., Ga.
Elijah Franks Blackshear b. 6/7/1849 Marianna, Laurens Co., Ga.
Joseph William Blackshear b. 7/25/1851 Marianna, Laurens Co., Ga.
Zoe Frances Blackshear b. 7/21/1853 Marianna, Laurens Co., Ga.
Charles Jefferson Blackshear b. 2/26/1855 Laurens Co., Ga.
Clarence Hamilton Blackshear b. 11/16/1856 Laurens Co., Ga.
Marmaduke David Blackshear b. 8/15/1858 Laurens Co., Ga.
Isabella Powell Blackshear b. 10/26/1862 Marianna, Laurens Co.
Walter Floyd Blackshear b. 8/17/1864 Laurens Co., Ga.
    Children of James Everard and Katherine Baker Blackshear:
Annie Laura Eve Blackshear b. 10/30/1876 Augusta, Ga.
Archie Baker Blackshear b. 8/27/1877 Augusta, Ga.
James Everard Blackshear b. 8/26/1878 Augusta, Ga.
Marion Floyd Blackshear b. 1/30/1880, d. same day, Atlanta, Ga.
Sterling Hamilton Blackshear b. 9/8/1881 Augusta, Ga.
Mary Floyd Hamilton Blackshear b. 1/3/1886 Augusta, Ga.

Deaths
E. F. Blackshear, Sr. d. 7/26/1879 Marianna, Laurens Co., Ga.
E. F. Blackshear, Jr. d. 8/25/1888 Waycross, Ga.
M. L. Blackshear d. 3/30/1890 Waycross, Ga.
Joseph W. Blackshear d. 7/29/1891 Waycross, Ga.
Walter F. Blackshear d. 8/2/1891 Waycross, Ga.
Mary H. Blackshear d. 2/29/1892 Savannah, Ga.
J. E. Blackshear d. 2/9/1896 Guyton, Ga.
Isabella Powell Blackshear d. 4/17/1929 Waycross, Ga.
Zoe Frances Blackshear d. 7/28/1933 Waycross, Ga.
Archibald B. Blackshear d. 3/27/1919 Waycross, Ga.
Sterling Hamilton Blackshear d. 10/10/1917 Washington, D. C.

(Blackshear Bible contd....)

Lt. Col. James Everard Blackshear, Jr. d. 7/21/1946 Charleston,
    S. C.

WILLIAM LYLE BIBLE
Owner: Elizabeth Shelton, Athens, Ga.

Marriages
William Lyle to Elizabeth Boring 3/25/1803
Dilmus J. Lyle to Sarah Green 2/21/1828
Elizabeth G. Lyle to Ishum Dalton 3/1/1832
James B. Lyle to Nancy Dalton 2/29/1833
Rebecka A. Lyle to John Hancock 12/30/1834
Charles B. Lyle to Julia E. Carlton 12/4/1837

Births
Mahershallal Hashbaz Lyle 3/14/1737	Isaac Boring 3/8/1762
Betty Lyle 2/13/1741	Phebe Boring 9/19/1762
William Lyle Sr. 12/21/1770	slaves? follow:
Elizabeth Lyle Sr. 10/29/1784?	Black Polly 8/4/1790
Dilmas Johnston Lyle 1/4/1804	Caster 5/6/1829
Zachariah? D. Lyle 10/1805	Margreet 6/15/1833
Charles Lyle 6/4/1807	George Morgin 11/16/1832
James B. Lyle 11/6/1810	Blackeys Mary 10/19/1821
John E. F. Lyle 10/29/1813	Black Jack 7/27/1823
Elizabeth G. Lyle 1/19/1816	Black H. Judge 3/24/1825
Rebecca A. Lyle 1/28/1818	George Morgan Lyle (col.)
William C. Lyle 11/29/1819	d. 4/30/1929
David Smith Lyle 9/19/1821	Martha D. Lyle 9/28/1825
Aseneth Ann Lyle 1/8/1824	
Francis Marion Lyle 2/1827	
J. Westly b. 6/26/1820	

Deaths
Mahershallal Hashbaz Lyle 1/30/1814, aged 76 yrs., 9 mos., 2 wks.
Susannah Lyle 4/16/1806, aged 1 yr., 5 mos., 25 days.
Isaac Boring 5/18/1831, aged 67 yrs., 7 mos., 29 days.
Elizabeth Lyle 1/1/1831, aged 89 yrs., 10 mos., 17 days.
William Lyle 10/24/1860, aged 89 yrs., 10 mos., 25 days.
David Smith Lyle 7/7/1844, aged 22 yrs.
Phebe Boring 7/30/1857, aged 95 yrs.
Elizabeth Lyle 9/17/1863, aged 79 yrs.

EVERARD HAMILTON BIBLE
Owner: Miss A. Laura Blackshear, Athens, Ga.

Births
Everard Hamilton, youngest son of John and Tabitha Hamilton, b.
    Hancock Co. (near Sparta) Ga., 12/4/1791
Mary Hazzard Floyd, sau. of John and Isabella Maria Floyd, b.
    near Darien, McIntosh Co., Ga., 10/1/1793
Everard Hamilton and Mary Hazzard Floyd m. at Fairfield Place,
    Camden Co., Ga., ceremony performed by Rev. Matthews 10/31/1816

93

(Hamilton Bible contd...)

Their Children:

Charles Floyd Hamilton b. Fairfield, Camden Co., Ga. 8/24/1817
John Floyd Caesar Hamilton b. Ft. Creek near Sparta, Hancock Co.,
    Ga., 11/14/1819
Isabella Maria Caroline Hamilton b. Darien, McIntosh Co., Ga.,
    11/21/1821
Mary Anne LaFayette Hamilton b. at Milledgeville, Ga. 7/30/1824
John Floyd Hamilton b. Twiggs Co., Ga. 9/20/1826
Sarah Frances Charlessina Hamilton b. Milledgeville, Ga.
    11/7/1828
Everard Hamilton b. Milledgeville, Ga. 9/22/1830, twin
Marmaduke Hamilton b. Milledgeville, Ga. 9/22/1830, twin
Richard William Hamilton b. Milledgeville, Ga. 11/3/1832
Zoe Decima Hamilton b. Macon, Ga. 1/8/1836
James Thweatt Hamilton b. Macon, Ga. 8/15/1838

Marriages
Isabella Maria Caroline Hamilton to Everard Hamilton Blackshear
    by Rev. Josiah Lewis 10/10/1844 Savannah, Ga.
Mary Ann LaFayette Hamilton to Elijah Franks Blackshear by Rev.
    Caleb W. Key 10/16/1845 Savannah, Ga.
Charles Floyd Hamilton to Isabella Caroline DeLarocheaulion by
    Rev. Washington Baird at Bluck Point, Camden Co., Ga.
    11/11/1847

Deaths
John Floyd Caesar Hamilton d. at Fairfield, Camden Co., Ga.
    6/29/1821
Sarah Frances Charlessina d. Bellevue, Camden Co., Ga., 5/6/1830
Col. Everard Hamilton d. Savannah, Ga. 1/12/1847
Sarah Catherine Hamilton d. at Bluck Point, Camden Co., Ga.,
    7/5/1848, aged 12 days

Births of Grandchildren:-

Everard Hamilton Blackshear, son of Evd. H. and Isabella
    Blackshear b. at Mairanna, Laurens Co., Ga. 1/12/1847
James Everard Blackshear, son of Elijah F. and Mary Anne L.
    Blackshear b. Marianna, laurens Co., Ga. 1/12/1847
Mary Hamilton, dau. of Elijah F. and Mary L. Blackshear, b. at
    Marianna, Laurens Co., Ga. 12/25/1847
Sarah Catherine, dau. of Isabell and C. F. Hamilton, b. at Bluck
    Pont, Camden Co., Ga. 6/24/1848
David, son of Isabell and Everard H. Blackshear, b. at DoLittle,
    Laurens Co., Ga., 6/30/1848
Elijah Franks Blackshear b. 6/7/1849 of M. L. and Elijah F.
    Blackshear at Marianna, Laurens Co., Ga.
Joseph William, son of M. L. and E. F. Blackshear, b. 8/25/1851
    at Marianna, Laurens Co., Ga.
Zoe Frances, dau. of M. L. and E. F. Blackshear, b. 7/21/1853 at
    Marianna, laurens Co., Ga.
Charles Jefferson, son of M. L. and E. F. Blackshear, b.
    11/16/1856 in Laurens Co., Ga.
Clarence Hamilton, son of M. L. and E. F. Blackshear, b.
    11/16/1856 Laurens Co., Ga.
Marmaduke David, son of E. F. and M. L. Blackshear, b. 10/26/1862
    at Marianna, Laurens Co., Ga.
Isabella Powell, dau. of E. F. and M. L. Blackshear, b.
    10/26/1862 at Marianna, Laurens Co., Ga.

Young Stokes b. 3/21/1773, d. 8/27/1843, aged 70 yrs., 5 mos., 6
days.
Martha Stokes b. 2/28/1777, d. 5/30/1846, aged 69 yrs., 2 mos.,
28 days.
Augustus Henry Stokes b. 7/28/1802, d. Atlanta, 10/21/1859, aged
58 yrs.
William Charles Young Stokes b. 5/7/1821, d. 7/10/1853, aged 32
yrs., 2 mos., 3 days.
William Young Stokes, Jr., son of William Y. and Mary J. Stokes,
b. 11/11/1852, d. 3/4/1854, aged 1 yr., 3 mos., 21 days.
James W. McHenry b. 9/28/1852, d. 2/28/1854, aged 1 yr., 5 mos.
William S. Stokes d. 8/8/1879
Thomas Stokes---
Archibald Stokes---
Augustus Stokes---
---Stokes
William Sanders Stokes b. 3/6/1798, d. 8/8/1870
Eliza Stokes, his wife, b. 12/6/1800, and killed instantly by
falling down steps at Eden Museum in N. Y. C. 7/3/1888

William S. Stokes and Eliza Smith m. 7/19/1820

William S. Stokes united himself with Baptist Church at Sugar
Creek, Morgan Co., Ga., baptised 10/25/1831
Judge William Sanders Stokes Mother d.---was Miss---Lamar of
Beach Island, Edgefield Dist., S. C. Thomas Lamar came from Md.
10 yrs. before Revolution. Had 5 sons. james settled in N. C.
Alex and John in Georgia near Steels Creek. Thomas and Robert in
Edgefield, S. C.
Thomas Pinckard, Sr., Capt. in Revolution, was father of Thomas
Pinckard, Jr. who was father of Jane Pinckard, wife of Charles
Smith.
Peyton Randolph Smith of Va. was father of Charles Smith who m.
Jane Pinckard. Their dau., Eliza Smith, was wife of Judge
William Sanders Stokes, m. 7/19/1820
John Grieve of Edinburgh, Kinlock and Forres, Scotland, m. Miss
Marion Miller, dau. of Daniel Miller f Edinburgh.
Issue:-John Grieve, Jr., d. single
Marion Grier m. James Hall McHenry, he was partner in Andrew Lowe
& Co. in Savannah, Ga. Both died and bur. Lexington, Ga. in
granite wall plot near Gov. Gilmer´s home. Three children:
James Hall McHenry m. Sarah Poullain, dau. of Dr. Poullain of
Greensboro, Ga. Marion and Noel McHenry. Marion m. John B.
Moore. C. Noel Moore m. Miss Chaffee.
John G. McHenry m. Miss Harriott C. S. Stokes, dau. of Judge
William S. Stokes, Madison, Ga.
C. William S. McHenry m. Miss Mamie Brown, Madison, Ga.
John Griefe McHenry m. Miss Zoe E. Blackshear (granddau. of Dr.
Richard Banks of Gainesville, Ga.)
C. Zoe Harriott and Marion Louise McHenry. Louise M. Daniel
Hicky (New Orleans) 12/19/1916. C. Dan McHenry Hicky b.
9/16/1917
Miller Grieve, U. S. Minister to Austria, m. Sarah Grantland C.
Miller, Jr. Marion IV Fleming Eliza J. John Joseph Henry
Lumpkin, Marion Miller, George Gilmer, Sarah Calendar.
Calendar McGregor Grieve m. Joseph Henry Lumpkin, Chief Justice,
Supreme Court of Ga., Athens, Ga. C. james Troupe-Marion
McHenry IV

JOHN ROSS CRANE BIBLE
Owner: George S. Crane, 897 Prince Ave., Athens, Ga.

John Ross Crane m. Fannie Thweatt Moore by Rev. Mr. Ivey, Pastor
  of Baptist Church, Athens, Ga.
John R. Crane, son of Ross Crane and Martha W. Elliott, who were
  parents of 9 children. Seven raised to age of maturity, two
  died while infants. James R. Crane was killed while in army of
  Southern Confederacy in 1865.
Fannie T. Moore, dau. of Thomas Moore and Martha Hicks Jackson,
  who were parents of three children raised to maturity.
James Ross Crane and Daisey Davis m. 11/24/1896 by Rev. M. Foot,
  Pastor of First Methodist Church, Athens, Ga.
George Shaw Crane m. Hallie Watkins in Athens, Ga. 6/15/1898
William Moore Craine m. Irmine Missouri Sims 10/18/1899
Benjamin Albert Crane m. Blanche Crawford 6/1905
Rufus S. Crane m. Esther Patterson 6/15/1911
James Ross Crane m. Ulah Maxine Dobbs 4/14/1921
George Shaw Crane m. Mamie Davis 7/9/1919 at Emanuel Episcopal
  Church, Athens, Ga. by Dr. A. G. Richards, Rector

Births
John R. Crane 12/17/1842   Benjamin Albert Crane 3/1/1877
Fannie T. Moore, wife of   Frank Grady Crane 12/20/1879
  John R. Crane 2/13/1843   Rufus Samuel Crane 6/13/1881
William Moore Crane 4/10/1870   James Ross Crane 9/7/1871
George Shaw Crane 5/5/1875
          The six sons of John Ross and Fannie Moore Crane:
James Ross, son of James Ross and Daisy Davis Crane b. 12/23/1897
William Moore Crane, son of William Moore Crane and Irmine Sims
  Crane b. 9/19/1900
Sarah Frances, dau. of W. M. and I. S. Crane, b. 1/2/1903
Frances Watkins Crane, dau. of George S. and Hallie W. Crane, b.
  3*30/1907
Benjamin Albert Crane, son of Benjamin A. Crane and Blanche C.
  Crane, b. 5/10/1912
Vinita Tate Crane, b. 7/3/1912, dau. of Rufus S. and Esther P.
  Crane
Esther P. Crane
Baxter Crawford Crane, son of B. A. and Blanche Crane, b.
  3/30/1914
Rufus Samuel Crane, son of R. S. and E. P. Crane, b. 12/30/1914
George Shaw Crane, son of B. A. and B. C. Crane, b. 2/21/1916
Frank Forbes Crane, son of B. A. and B. C. Crane, b. 10/5/1917

Deaths
John Ross Crane 6/30/1887
Frank Grady Crane, 5th son of J. R. and Fannie Crane, d. Clayton,
  Ga., 9/8/1900
Sarah Frances Crane, dau. of W. M. and I. S. Crane, 1/4/1903
James Ross Crane, 2nd son of J. R. and Fannie M. Crane,
  11/14/1912
Benjamin Albert Crane, son of Benjamin A. and Blanche C. Crane,
  d. Athens, Ga., 4/14/1913
Daisy Davis, wife of James Ross Crane, d. 12/8/1916
Miss George Whitley Shaw, b. 5/19/1836, d. 127/1920
Hallie Watkins Crane, wife of George Shaw Crane, 10/24/1918
Benjamin A. Crane, son of J. R. and F. T. Crane, 2/9/1926
Mrs. Fannie T. Crane, wife of John Ross Crane, 3/16/1927
George Moore, bro. of Frances Moore Crane, 3/13/1930 (his birth-
  day), age 85.

(Crane Bible contd....)

William Moore Crane, son of John Ross and Fannie Moore Crane, d.
in Athens, Ga. 10/14/1938
James Ross Crane, Jr., son of James Ross and Daisy Davis Crane,
d. in Athens, Ga. 12/13/1941

Loose Sheets in Bible:

William Moore Crane and Irmine S. Crane, b. Clarke Co., now
Oconeem Co., 6/25/1984. 2-Sarah Frances Crane b. 1/2/1903,
d. 1/4/1903. Their Children:-
William Moore Crane, Jr. m. 10/17/1931 in First Congregational
Church, W. Newton, Mass. to Elenor Elizabeth Bowen, b. in
Newton, Mass., 11/11/1907. Their Children:
    Boy stillborn.
    William Bowen Crane, b. 6/26/1934
    Eleanor Thayer Crane b. 10/1/1936
    Richard Albert Sims Crane b. 5/31/1940
All born in Newton Hospital, Newton, Mass. Returned to Athens,
Ga., as their home in 1938.

James Ross Crane and Daisy Davis Crane b. in Oglethorpe Co.,
1/28/1873. Their child: James Ross Crane, Jr. m. Ilah Maxine
Dobbs, b. in Marietta, Ga. 12/10/1898. Their children:
    James Ross Crane III b. Athens, Ga. 8/25/1922
    Elizabeth Springer Crane b. Athens, Ga. 9/25/1928
George Shaw Crane and Hallie Watkins Crane, b. Otterwah, Tenn.
11/3/1876. Their child: Frances Watkins Crane m. 6/28/1932 in
Emanuel Episcopal Church, Athens, Ga. by Rt. Rev. H. J. Mikell,
Bishop of Diocese of Atlanta, to The Rev. Benjamin Scott Eppes,
b. in Athens, Ga., 8/15/1906. Their children:
Frances Crane Eppes b. 897 Prince Ave., Athens, Ga. 12/21/1933
Amalia Scott Eppes, b. in Gen. Hospital, Athens, Ga. 1/29/1937
Benjamin Scott Eppes, Jr. b. in Baptist Hospital, 4/17/1943
Benjamin Albert Crane and Blanche Crawford Crane, b. Vandalia,
Mo., 11/21/1879. Their children:
Benjamin Albert Crane, Jr., b. 9/17/1909, d. 4/14/1913
Rebecca Jane Crane m. 6/8/1935 at home, 763 Cobb St., Athens,
Ga., to Robert Lee Cauthen, b. 1/22/1908 in Elberton, Ga. Their
children: Robert Lee Cauthen, Jr. b. Cincinnati, Ohio,
/13/1937, Blanche Crawford Cauthen, b. Cincinnati, Ohio
7/13/1941
Baxter Crawford Crane m. 1/27/1940 in Christ Church of Frederica,
St. Sims, Ga. to Norma Frances Guerard, b. Baltimore, Md.,
5/4/1919. Their children: Baxger Crawford Crane, Jr. b. Atlanta,
Ga. 2/18/1941. Norma Jane Crane, b. Athens, Ga., St. Mary's
Hospital, 1/10/1947

George Shaw Crane II m. 6/26/1938 in LaFayette, Ala. Elizabeth
Jane Adams, b. LaGrange, Ga. 2/1916. Their child: Eloise Heard
Crane, b. LaGrange, Ga. 2/16/1943
Frank Forbes Crane m. 2/26/1943 at First Presbyterian Church,
Athens, Ga. by Dr. E. L. Smith to Mary Cornelia Martin, b. in
Valdosta, Ga. 10/1918. Their child: Frank Forbes Crane, Jr., b.
in Valdosta, Ga. 7/19/1946

Rufus Samuel Crane and Esther Patterson Crane b. 1/23/1891. Their
children: Vinita Tate Crane m. George Chrisfield. 2nd, marriage
to Robert Bogartus Schall. Rufus Samuel Crane, Jr.

97

SAMUEL WORTHAM BIBLE
Owner: John Thomas, Newnan, Ga.

Entry made by Samuel Wortham's grandson, John D. Pearson:
"This book is 78 years old. It was the property of my Grandfather
Samuel I. Wortham. I like very much to read this good old book
because it was once the book of my dear old Grand Daddy. He
wanted all of his children to call him Daddy and his
grandchildren to say Granddaddy. He was a Primitive Baptist and
as a man of the 'old' school, a patriot and agentleman. His last
words on earth Nov. 2nd, 1867 were that he wanted to see a free
and independent country. A government of the people - an old
Democrat - a detestor of Whigs. A Great and Good Old Man."

Thomas Wortham b. 1731. His wife, Elizabeth Taliaferro Wortham,
b. 11/2/1741. Their son, Samuel Wortham, was b. 9/6/1784. His
wife, jane Powell Wortham, was b. 11/6/1795. Samuel and Jane
Wortham m. 11/19/1812. The ages of children of Samuel Wortham and
Jane, his wife.

Births
Elizabeth Taliaferro Wortham 11/30/1813
Mary Ormond Wortham 3/6/1816
Behetheland Frances Wortham 11/6/1817
Sarah Ann Whitehead Wortham 4/23/1819
Leucy Warner Wortham 1/7/1821
Christopher Columbus Wortham 5/19/1822
Martha Jane Wortham 3/31/1824
Caroline Rose Wortham 11/3/1827
Andrew Doria Wortham 8/13/1829
Petrarch Wortham 3/20/1832
Joseph Chilton Wortham 10/29/1833
Sophia Ursula Wortham 2/27/1837
Georgia A. F. Wortham 4/16/1837 (dau.-in-law)
John Doria Pearson 7/3/1858
Benjamin Hope Pearson 7/28/1859
L. J. Bevis 2/2/1829
Ider Bevis 6/1/1867
Rosa Frances Pearson 10/25/1886
Benjamin Wortham Pearson 6/23/1892

Marriages
Elizabeth T. Wortham to George C. Heard 12/6/1832
Mary O. Wortham to Achibod Phillips 12/6/1832
Lucy W. Wortham to Robert C. Pullen 4/4/1839
Sarah Ann W. Wortham to Thomas C. Thomas 12/4/1839
Christopher C. Wortham to Palatiah Darden 4/14/1845
Martha Jane Wortham to John W. Nall 9/4/1845
A. D. Wortham to Georgeann F. Stamps 7/17/1855
Caroline Rose Wortham to John Pearson 9/9/1857
Sophia U. Wortham to Levi J. Bevis 11/1/1863
Joseph C. Wortham to Mary A. Braswell 12/-/1866

Deaths
Elizabeth Heard 4/5/1855   John E. Pearson 9/30/1862
Petrarch Wortham 9/27/1856   Samuel Wortham 11/2/1867
Jane Wortham, wife of Samuel   Sophia Ursula Bevis 12/18/1898
   Wortham, 8/28/1862   Caroline Rose Wortham d. at home
                                  4th Dist., Coweta Co., 1/21/1894

98

```
                    JONES SEABORN WHATLEY BIBLE
                    Owner: Frederick S. Mulder
                 1482 York Ave., N. Y., N. Y. 10021


Jones Seaborn Whatley b. 5/7/1813    Deaths
Sarah Hill Whatley b. 1/5/1826       Dau. twin 4/25/1858
William Jesse 9/23/1842              Seaborn J. 10/8/1860
Tabitha Elizabeth --/22/1844         William Jesse, killed with a
Mary Jane 8/17/184-                   shell at Suffolk 5/3/1863
Sarah Frances 12/19/1848             Etta? Caroline 1/4/1844
Thomas A. 2/11/1851                  Ida Antonet 6/4/1868
Susan Catharine---                   Lola? Jones 3/24/1871
Lydia Ann 7/--/1855
Jingree 4/27/1857
dau., twin, --/27/1857
Seaborn 4/20/1860
Louisa Bonner 12/27/--
```

SAMUEL WHATLEY BIBLE

```
Samuel Whatley b. 3/2/1762, d. 10/3/1826
Catherine Whatley b. 5/2/1762, d. 8/7/1857  Children:
James Whatley d. 7/31/1856
Wilson Whatley d. 2/20/1875
William Whatley d. 2/22/1876
```

Births

Seaborn J. Whatley, b. Wilkes Co., Ga. 10/18/1798, son of Samuel
  and Catherine Whatley.
Martha E. Whatley, dau. of John and Elizabeth Livingston, b. in
  Edgefield Dist., S. C. 7/17/1808
     And their children in following order:
William Henry b. 2/2/1833 Wilkes Co., Ga.
Samuel John b. 10/31/1834 Harris Co., Ga.
Elizabeth Anna b. 3/4/1836 Harris Co., Ga.
Katherine Savannah b. 11/28/1837 Harris Co., Ga.
Sarah Jane b. 7/12/1839 Harris Co., Ga.
Mary Frances b. 2/28/1841 Harris Co., Ga.
Susan Wilson b. 12/23/1842 Harris Co., Ga.
James Lewis b. 11/2/1844 Harris Co., Ga.
Martha Milford b. 9/10/1849 Harris Co., Ga.
Laura Cassandra b. 10/25/1849 Harris Co., Ga.

Marriages

Seaborn J. Whatley of Wilkes Co. to Martha Elizabeth Livingston
  of Harris Co., Ga. 1/15/1832
William H. Whatley to Ann C. Sutton 12/20/1855
Sarah Jane Whatley to John A. Partridge 3/20/1856
Elizabeth A. Whatley to James M. young 8/25/1857
Katherine S. Whatley to Warren A. Clark 1/14/1868
Laura C. Whatley to William Moses Jones 1/13/1869
James L. Whatley to Mary E. Keyes 4/30/1879

Deaths

Martha E. Whatley, wife of S. J. Whatley and mother of all these
  children d. 7/18/1868, aged 60 yrs.

                              99

(Whatley Bible contd....)

Seaborn J. Whatley d. 2/9/1886, aged 87 yrs., 3 mos., 21 days.
Samuel John Whatley d. 9/12/1843
Martha Milford Whatley d. 11/11/1862
Susan Wilson Whatley d. 10/1/1879
Mary Frances Whatley d. 5/7/1881
Katherine Savanna Clark d. 10/1/1881

William Alford, son of S. J. and I. T. Whatley b. 6/28/1858
James Wilson, son of S. J. and I. T. Whatley, b. 12/7/1859
Samuel Willis, son of S. J. and I. T. Whatley b. 4/17/1861
Thomas Columbus, son of S. J. and I. T. Whatley b. 9/18/1862
Henry Taylor, son of S. J. and I. T. Whatley b. 5/9/1864
Lucy Cena, dau. of S. J. and I. T. Whatley b. 3/13/1866
Sarah Catherine, dau. of S. J. and I. T. Whatley b. 4/6/1867
Emily Albino, dau. of S. J. and I. T. Whatley b. 8/6/1868
Lilly Lee, dau. of S. J. and I. T. Whatley b. 5/1/1873
Melissa Ann, dau. of S. J. and I. T. Whatley b. 5/31/1874
Pearly Abscilla, dau. of S. J. and I. T. Whatley b. 7/16/1876
Alma Mater, dau. of S. J. and I. T. Whatley b. 2/2/1878
Anna Miles, dau. of S. J. and I. T. Whatley b. 2/5/1880.

Deaths
Samuel Willis, son of S. J. and I. T. Whatley d. 11/12/1862
Anna Miles, dau. of S. J. and I. T. Whatley d. 7/26/1880
Billie d. 11/4/1894
Mother d. 10/23/1910
Father d. 11/24/1911
Sallie d. 5/27/1913
Lucy d. 12/12/1921
L. W. P. b. 11/9/1860, d. 10/6/1907
W. J. S. b. 1/--/--, d. --/1914

Samuel J. Whatley, son of Willis and Lucy Whatley, b. 6/22/1831,
    Washington, Wilkes Co., Ga.
Isabella T. Harp, dau. of Wm. & Cena Harp b. 6/16/1841 Pike Co.
Samuel J. Whatley m. Isabella Harp 10/27/1857

Lucy Whatley, mother of S. J. Whatley and four of their children
    d. at home of her dau., Jane Collier, 6/21st, age 70.

Cena Harp, mother of I. T. Harp and ten other children, d.
    3/21st. aged 46.

Wilson Whatley, son of Samuel and Catherine Whatley d. at res. of
    his nephew, Samuel J. Whatley 2/21/1875, aged 84 yrs.

Zachariah T. Harp, son of William and Cena Harp, d. 1/19/1864,
    aged 18 yrs.

                    WILLIAM HARRISON COMBS BIBLE
                 Owner: Lewis Combs, Carrollton, Ga.

William H. Combs, son of William F. Combs, b. 2/9/1825
Martha Jane Woodard, wife of William H. Combs, b. 9/30/1827
William H. Combs and Martha Woodard m. 12/15/1850
George Ann Combs, dau. of William H. Combs and Martha J. Combs,
    b. 10/18/1851

(William Harrison Combs Bible contd....)

John Monroe Combs b. 11/17/1852
William Lewis Combs b. 8/19/1854

Teseas Orleans Combs b. 10/9/1855
James Buchanon Combs b. 12/10/1856
Arkansas Combs b. 11/28/1858
Evaline Virginia Combs b. 11/14/1861
Apelonia Jagitia Combs b. 3/5/1863

William Lewis Combs d. 8/16/1856
James Buchanon Combs d. 11/4/1857
Martha J. Combs d. 3/31/1865

Andrew Combs b. 11/10/1866
James A. Combs b. 12/5/1867
Reuben W. Combs b. 3/27/1870
Marthaette Combs b. 3/9/1872

JAMES F. EDGE BIBLE
Owner: Mrs. Robert Sanders, Stephens, Ga.

Births
James F. Edge 12/24/1858
Dora Etta Edge 11/16/1870
Henry Tipton Edge 5/1/1882
Carry Lela Edge 1/29/1884
James Pomeroy Edge 7/4/1889
William Alonzo Edge 4/18/1892

Stella L. Edge 5/17/1900
Nellie Edge 4/27/1902
Orris? Elbert Edge 2/19/1904
Dora Isabella Edge 8/15/1906
Alberta Rosalyn Edge 11/5/1910

Marriages
Henry Tipton Edge and Manely Evans? 3/9/1910
Artha Lee Della Edge and W. C. Cutts 9/12/1915
Stella L. Edge and W. W. Washburj 4/2/1921
Albert Edge and Mamie Lee Rutledge 10/8/1923
Dora Isabella Edge and W. M. Mason 7/1925
Robert Louis Edge and Bessie Maud Wilson Schumacher 1/7/1929
Dora Isabella Edge Mason and R. Martin Henderson 10/4/1931
Nellie Edge and Jack Howard Riddle 10/15/1934
Nellie Edge and James Rayford Gilmer 4/15/1939
Orris E. Edge and Alma Louise Mahaffey 9/19/1941
Robert L. Edge and Clifford Patterson 6/1943
James P. Edge and Anita (Reurich) 7/1950
Albert R. Edge and Daniel F. Mann 7/6/1940

Deaths
Carry Lela Edge 1/19/1887
Dora Etta Edge 8/15/1912
Henry Tipton Edge 12/23/1913
James Filmore Edge 3/4/1930

Robert Louis Edge 6/2/1962
James Pomeroy Edge 8/31/1965
Isabella Edge Henderson 12/1973

```
                    HOLSTIN BIBLE
                 Owner: Mrs. Fred Mangham
                    Jackson, Georgia


Records from Swenfka Pfalm Baken ef hunungen gillad eeh fedfehad
er 1819 falon Carl Rebin
Stikepers Eni Olifen Tedd 1848
den 5 fibnen gift 1848
Hufbana Cherftin Hans Dateni Todd
1826 den 5 Heberson
Son obf Enfen Fedd 1848 den 6, November
Son Ader Enfen Fedd 1852 den 15, October
Dotter Karene Fedd 1856,  2 November
Son Erri Fedd 1861, den 12 Janiare
Son Hans Fedd 1864, den 24
Dotter Christina Holsten Oct. 2, 1869
Son Olaf Oscar Born
```

```
                   MICHAEL D. GARR BIBLE
                 Owner: Mrs. W. T. Scarbrough
                    Barnesville, Georgia
```

Births

Michael D. Garr 3/10/1849	Robert H. Garr 10/26/1884
Mary J. Garr 5/2/1857	Zadie J. Garr 10/17/1886
Willis G. Garr 1/11/1878	Nina B. Garr 4/19/1890
Martha Alberta Garr 8/4/1879	Maurice A. Garr 4/10/1892
Ella May Garr 7/2/1881	Esta L. Garr 6/45/1895
E. D. Garr 12/24/1882	John omar Garr 11/11/1898

Deaths
William A. Garr 9/16/1903
Mary Jane Garr 8/30/1921
Michael D. Garr 5/13/1929

Marriages
William T. Scarbrough to Willie Gertude Garr 2/22/1899
William H. Phinazoe to Martha Albert Garr 11/4/1902
Kennith H. Hines to Ella May Garr 9/12/1914
Charles S. Wyatt to Zadie Jane Garr 6/4/1910
William Gordon Barnes to Nina B. Garr 5/7/1912
Samuel D. Johnson to Esta L. Garr 11/25/1915


```
                 NATHAN BUSSEY SR. BIBLE
```

Births

David Bussey 9/14/1822	Peter Bussey 7/7/1835-8/1835
William Daniel Bussey 6/6/1825	Lucy Ann Bussey 5/5/1837
Nathan Bussey 10/10/1830	Hezekiah Bussey 4/18/1840
Susanna Bussey 7/1/1833	

ABNER WEBSTER BIBLE*
Owner: Mrs. L. M. Kelley
Thomaston, Georgia

Births
Abner Webster 12/25/1761   Mariah Webster 1/20/1793
Elizabeth Webster 2/14/1766   Martin Webster 11/10/1794
William Webster 9/21/1784   Seborn Webster 8/10/1796
Ann Webster 1/13/1786   Reuben Webster 12/17/1800
Pherebea Webster 12/24/1788   Samuel Webster 6/24/1802
John Webster 12/15/1790   Labon & Elbom Webster 7/25/1798

JAMES N. LYNCH BIBLE of Putnam Co.
Owner: Emmett Lynch, Machen, Ga.

Marriages
James N. Lynch b. 11/12/1820 d. 12/18/1868 m. 10/19/1840 A. A.
   Lynch b. 6/26/1824 d. 4/19/1865
I. B. Lynch m. 12/18/1855 E. B. Hardeman
C. N. Lynch m. 12/2/1869 E. Cowan

Births
Iantha D. Lynch 9/17/1840   Epsie Amanda Lynch 12/9/1853
James H. Lynch 2/27/1843   Mary L. Lynch 9/17/1856
Olive A. Lynch 6/5/1847   Amanda Lucy Lynch 4/1/1859
Charles E. Lynch 2/22/1849   Emmett Lynch 9/8/1862

Deaths
Charles E. Lynch 11/18/1867

JARRAT LYNCH BIBLE
Owner: W. W. Williams
Monticello, Georgia

Jarrat Lynch 6/6/1781-1/26/1864 m. Mary H. Lynch 11/12/1782-
   6/8/1861. Their Children:

Births
Ephraim Lynch 3/16/1808   Zaccheus Lynch 2/6/1817
Mary Lynch 9/27/1809   Sackville Lynch 7/19/1819
Grief Lynch 6/2/1822   Melvina Lynch 1/31/1822
Rinza Lynch 8/2/1813   Nancy Lynch 6/26/1826
Fleet Lynch 9/18/1815   Martha Lynch 5/8/1828

Deaths
Ephraim Lynch 9/16/1857   Olive A. Lynch 1/10/1870
Sarah Martha Lynch 4/26/1852   Epsie A. Lynch 12/30/1871
Elizabeth Lynch 7/14/1857, wife of Ephraim Lynch
James H. Lynch 11/9/1868
Amanda Lucy Lynch Pearson 5/5/1930

*See also p. 352.

WILLIAM HARRISS BIBLE
Owner: Robert S. Harris
Madison, Georgia

William Harriss b. Northampton Co., N. C. 1772, d. Morgan Co.,
Ga., m. Lucy Brown, m. 2nd Nancy.

Births of Children of William and Lucy Harriss:

Mary Harriss 8/2/1802   William Harriss 10/9/1807
Thomas Harriss 11/10/1803   Sarah Harriss 10/3/1809
Benjamin Harriss 8/29/1805   Henry Harriss 9/19/1812

FRANCIS MALONE BIBLE
Owner: Walker Malone
Monticello, Georgia

Marriages
Francis Malone to Martha Chafin 1/5/1802
Samuel H. Blackwell 1/11/1827 to Katherine Malone 8/5/1808-
   2/6/1834
John Malone b. 8/29/1805 to Nancy Hammock 1/20/1828
Cader Malone b. 1/3/1812 to Sarah Banks 3/9/1837
Floyd Malone b. 3/12/1815 to Elizabeth Compton 2/22/1838
William Malone b. 2/21/1826 to Miss C. Phillips 1/11/1849
W. W. Walker to Nancy J. Malone 1/12/1842 (Nancy b. 7/4/1827)
W. F. Malone to H. O. Walker 12/21/1876

Births
Jared Malone 11/14/1803   Jeptha Malone 3/8/1820
Elizabeth Malone 5/29/1810   Franklin Malone 4/26/1822
Isam Malone 1/18/1818   Martha Malone 2/21/1824
Martha Blackwell 1/2/1828   Emma Katie Malone 7/23/1880
William F. Blackwell 1/24/1834   Eula Clide Malone 2/17/1883
Martha C. Malone 7/17/1844   Andrew B. Malone 12/16/1888
Wm. Fleetwood Walker Malone 1/10/1878
Weyman Malone 11/14/1894

BROOKS Of Houston Co.
Owner: Mrs. J. T. Dudley
Athens, Georgia

Noah P. Brooks m. Lula C. Joyner 12/20/1876

GEORGE WASHINGTON JORDAN BIBLE
Owner: Virginia Jelks
Hawkinsville, Georgia

George Washington Jordan, son of Briton Jordan and his wife,
Margaret J. Bell, b. 2/11/1826 Washington Co., Ga. m. 3/26/1850
Rebecca Walker, dau. of George Walker and Martha Spann Childers
b. 10/29/1830 Pulaski Co., Ga., d. 4/30/1864. Their Children:

Inf. son (stillborn) 3/5/1851   Albert Augustus Jordan 7/24/1857
Ann Bell Jordan 8/31/1852   Martha Spann Jordan 9/3/1862
George Walker Jordan 9/24/1855   Richard Childers Jordan
                                       4/28/1764

JOSEPH H. YOUNG BIBLE
Owner: C. W. Renew, Americus, Ga.

Joseph H. Young b. 1820 in England d. Sumter Co., Ga. 1890
Macy Jones Young b. 1819 in Wales d. Sumter Co., Ga. 1906

Children:

William Young b. 1856 Liverpool, Lancastershire, England,
    d. Sumter Co., Ga., m. Lula Renew 1890.
John Harrison Young b. 1863 Liverpool, Lancastershire, England,
    m. 1899 Lula Renew d. Leslie, Sumter Co, Ga. 1904.
James Young b. 1853 Liverpool, Lancastershire, England,
    d. 11/17/1949 Leslie, Ga. (emigrated in 1875 to Canada)
Edward David Young b. 1871 Bolton, Lancastershire, England,
    d. 2/6/1853 Leslie, Ga.
James William Young b. 1879 in Canada, d. 1931 Sumter Co., Ga.
Elizabeth Young b. 1874 on the way to Canada. d. 1887 Sumter Co.
Joseph Harrison Young, jr. b. 1863 Liverpool, Lancastershire,
    England, d. 1904 Sumter Co., Ga.

WILLIAM E. COOK BIBLE
Owner: Jim McGhee
Monticello, Ga.

Mrs. Mary A. L. Cook d. 8/1/1897   William E. Cook d. 1/17/1882

WILLIAM JEFFERSON GREER BIBLE
Owner: Olin Greer, Flovilla, Ga.

Births
William Jefferson Greer 9/29/1869   James Nathl. Greer 4/23/1902
Lula Matilda Greer 5/5/1872   Alvin Eugene Greer 8/29/1904
Olin Legree Greer 12/17/1894   Howard Jackson Greer 8/1907
Rubie Lee Greer 9/13/1896
Ernest Willie Greer 5/23/1899

Deaths
William Jefferson Greer 10/17/1937

Marriages
W. O. Greer to Leila Niblett 1/11/1894
Forest Washington to Rubie Greer 2/13/1916
Olin Greer to Nell Morton 12/19/1917
Olin Greer to Nena Morton 6/1/1919
Ernest Greer to Margaret Gillard 1/17/1920
James Greer to Violet Ann Nesteaux 7/7/1925
Alvin Eugenia Greer to Jewel Beatrice Greer 7/9/1927
Howard Jackson Greer to Martha Ruth Bilews 10/14/1928

JOSIAH CARTER BIBLE
Owner: Olin Greer
Flovilla, Georgia

Marriages
Josiah W. Carter to Mary R. Askew 9/19/1867
Nena Violata Carter to Robert Franklin Cook 11/23/1897
Dixie Winfield Carter to Thomas Marten 3/1/1898
Simeon Josiah Carter to Frances Campbell 8/23/1899
Simeon Josiah Carter to Alma McLain 2/19/1924

Births
Josiah W. Carter 9/25/1845   Henry James Carter 8/16/1873
Mary R. Askew 2/6/1850   Clarence Eugene Carter 6/30/1876
Simeon Josiah Carter 11/25/1868   Dixie Winfield Carter 8/7/1878
Mena OViela Carter 7/24/1871

Deaths
Dr. Josiah Winfield Carter 8/25/1878, aged 32 yrs., 11 mos.
Clarence Eugene Carter 3/1/1893, aged 16 yrs., 8 mos., 1 day
Henry James Carter 3/4/1894, aged 20 yrs., 18 days
Mary Rebecca Askew Carter 8/23/1900, aged 50 yrs., 8 mos.
Simeon Josiah Carter 5/24/1936, aged 67 yrs., 6 mos., 1 day

WILLIAM STADDEN BIBLE
Owner: Mrs. M. N. Dieffenderfer
Brunswick, Georgia

William Stadden 1760-3/20/1838 m. mary White 1764-1845, had one
son, John Stadden 1/1791-10/1874 m. Jean Sample 1791-1828, had
one William Stadden 2/28/1815-11/7/1889 m. Sarah Irland 8/3/1815-
1887, one dau: Martha Ann Stadden b. 1846 m. Z. Taylor Martz
1846-10/1879--Three children:

William Stadden Martz b. 12/26/1872
Elizabeth M. Martz b. 8/6/1874
Eleanor Taylor Martz b. 3/3/1879

ASA MARTIN BIBLE
Owner: Doc Martin
Shady Dale, Georgia

Marriages
Asa Martin b. 5/31/1791 m. 10/27/1819 Nancy K. Whitfield
    11/12/1798-10/22/1862
William J. Martin 3/18/1824-5/22/1886 m. 10/1/1850 Mary Ann Lynch
    d. 5/17/1908

Births

Children of Asa Martin and Nancy Whitfield:

John Clark Martin 11/15/1820   Sarah Elizabeth Martin 1/17/1831
Mary Louisa Martin 10/26/1822   Joshua Franklin Martin 3/18/1833
Wm. Jackson Martin 3/18/1824   Asa LaFayette Martin 8/28/1835
Elizabeth Ann Martin 12/23/1825   Susan Mildred Martin 2/28/1838
Martha Ann Martin 2/15/1827   Mary Ann Martin 7/6/1830

Martha Sophia Martin, dau. of William J. Martin and Mary Ann
    Lynch 10/16/1851
William Benjamin Franklin Martin 4/9/1854
Mary King Martin 11/23/1857
John B. Wardlaw Martin 10/24/1859
Sarah Frances Martin 11/14/1861
Alexander Sevens Martin 2/25/1864
Robert E. lee Martin 4/22/1866
Carrie Lou Martin 2/22/1868
Nathaniel Walker Martin, son of William J. and Mary A.
    Martin, 9/26/1874

PETER PERRY BIBLE
Owner: Mrs. William H. Smith

Peter Perry of Fairfield, Conn. 1/24/1739-9/16/1804 m. 11/6/1763
Sarah Bradley by Mr. Buckingham.

CURTIS ADAMS BIBLE
Owner: Martha Lou Houston
Washington, D. C.

Marriages
Curtis Adams (son of Benjamin Adams d. 3/26/1863 and Emily d.
3/15/1863), killed 7/9/1864 on James Island, S. C. iN Civil War.
He m. Elizabeth Revier.

Albert Benjamin Adams, son of Curtis Adams, m. 4/14/1856 Nancy
Emma Watson in Upson Co., Ga., they have five children who live
in Columbus, Ga.

JAMES ANDREW DUNBAR BIBLE Of Pike Co.
Owner: Mrs. Mamie Milner, Lamar Co.

Marriages
Daniel Engles Dunbar 1/29/1846-9/5/1898 m. 11/28/1865 Margaret
    Ann Powell 2/12/1845-9/1/1927
Charley F. Foster to Carrie Leola Dunbar on 12/23/1883 b. 9/4/1866
Jennie S. Milner to Mamie Dunbar 11/26/1890

Births
Carrie Leola Dunbar 9/4/1866   Lizzie Ella Dunbar 6/16/1878
James Andrew Dunbar 23/27/1869   Maggie Dunbar 10/24/1881
Mary Hannah Lake Dunbar 6/21/1872   Opal May Dunbar 5/29/1886
Nettie Dunbar 3/18/1875   Daniel Edgar Dunbar 10/5/1888

ARTHUR; CLARK BIBLE Of Monroe Co.
Owner: Mrs. Mittie Clark Dumas, Lamar Co., Ga.

Marriages
Arthur Clark b. Ireland abt 1770, came to America and settled in
    S. C., then moved to Ga. in 1823 m. Elizabeth Wilson
Wilson Clark 9/3/1806-2/1897 m. Elizabeth Milner in 1830
Elizabeth Clark m. Mr. Pepper
Arthur Simeon Clark b. 10/27/1833 m. 1867 Artimisia Fizer of
    Bedford, Va. who d. 1827 m. 2nd Nannie Cauthen.
Mittie Clark m. 5/27/1888 B. Dumas
Elmer Clifford Clark b. 11/23/1883 m. Opal Wilson in 1906

Births

Elizabeth Wilson, dau. of Arthur Clark and Elizabeth Wilson Clark
Wilson, dau. of Arthur Clark and Elizabeth Wilson Clark
Mittie Fizer, dau. of Arthur Simeon and Artimisia Fizer Clark
Elmer Clifford, son of Arthur Simeon and Nannie Cauthen Clark
Wilson, son of Elmer Clifford and Opal Wilson Clark
Eugene, son of Elmer Clifford and Opal Wilson Clark
Jeff, son of Elmer Clifford and Opal Wilson Clark

ALEXANDER DUDLEY HAMMOND BIBLE
Owner: Mrs. Mary Swatts, Barnesville, Ga.

Marriages
Alexander Dudley Hammond 12/5/1833-3/8/1892 in Forsyth, Ga. m.
1st 6/3/1856 Marie Antionette Hammond 1/9/1836-6/22/1868 Forsyth,
Ga., m. 2nd 2/4/1869 Mary Holland 9/12/1850-9/12/1895 in Forsyth
Co., Ga.
Mary Hammond b. 1/14/1870 Forsyth, Ga. m. 12/18/1889 Robt. Swatts
Maud Hammond b. 4/3/1875 Forsyth, Ga. d. 3/8/1901 Stone Mtn, Ga.,
   m. 10/4/1893 C. S. Johnson
Pierce Hammond b. 9/16/1886 m. 6/1/1904 Annie Edwin Lambdin
Rosa Hammond to Clarence Irvin 10/12/1909 Barnesville, Ga.

Births
Georgia Hammond 5/8/1857 Forsyth, Ga.
Alice Hammond 11/4/1858 Forsyth, Ga.
Augusta Hammond 8/7/1860 Forsyth, Ga. d. 9/2/1862
Dudley Wright Hammond 9/11/1864 Forsyth, Ga.
Holland Hammond 8/14/1890 Forsyth, Ga.

SAMUEL SMITH BIBLE
Owner: Mrs. Alexander MacNeill
Cumberland Co., N. C.

Marriages
Samuel Smith Sr. 5/27/1709-1783 m. Edith 9/7/1717-9/3/1785
David Smith 9/10/1746-3/10/1795 m. 12/31/-- Charity 4/6/1756-
8/21/1818

Births
Edith Smith 12/26/1772-3/1842
Samuel Smith 9/30/1774-5/20/1842
Mary Smith 12/10/1779-2/1/1797
David Smith, Jr. 9/18/1781-6/11/1847
Jonathan Smith 6/20/1783-9/2/1805
Whitfield Smith 9/7/1785-3/25/1817
Charity Smith 1/8/1788-10/15/1843
Elizabeth Smith 1/27/1790-11/24/1790
Needham Smith 10/22/1795-9/1/17--
Sarah Smith, wife of Needham Smith, 12/13/1794 m. 4/20/1815

EPHRAIM GREGORY BIBLE
Owner: Edwina Holt, Columbus, Ga.

Ephraim Gregory m. Emeline Perry 6/20/1826, dau. of Job
and Sarah Perry

Deaths
Job Perry 8/18/1821, and his wid. d. at Danbury 1/20/1852

109

JUDGE JAMES DANIEL WOODALL BIBLE Of Talbot Co.
Owner: Mrs. Jennie White Woodall, Barnesville, Ga.

James Daniel Woodall b. 3/13/1852 m. 11/28/1878 Jennie White of
Lebanon, Tenn. Their Children:

Births
Benjamin Tarver Woodall 6/1880   Henry Grady Woodall 1/16/1889
James Daniel Woodall 11/16/1881   Mary Cornelia Woodall 2/18/1892
David Stewart Woodall 12/13/1883   Jennie Napier Woodall 2/18/1892
Frank Hamilton Woodall 8/10/1885   Sallie Olivia Woodall 4/9/1893
Nellie Sue Camille Woodall 8/10/1885
Fannie Virginia Woodall 9/14/1887-6/15/1888

JOHN HENRY MOSELEY BIBLE
Owner: Mrs. Janie Moseley Betts, Ocilla, Ga.

Marriages
John Henry Moseley b. 2/9/1847 Polk Co., Ga. d. 6/5/1928 m.
9/7/1871 Mary Pauline Kirby Spear b. 1/14/1852 Morgan Co., Ga.,
d. 1/5/1909. Their Children:

Births
John Wm. Moseley 6/15/1872   Robert Smith Moseley 2/6/1885
Thomas Alphonse Moseley 3/2/1874   Wade Pauline Moseley 11/2/1887
Sarah Jane Moseley 1/2/1876   Malcolm Jos. Moseley 11/4/1890
Amy Augusta Moseley 1/2/1878   Mary Ethel Moseley 8/16/1892
Benjamine Richard Moseley   Arthur Jefferson Moseley
  3/6/1880   12/14/1894

Deaths
Mary Ethel Moseley 10/23/1896   Amy Augusta Moseley 10/14/1929
Wade Pauline Moseley 8/10/1900
Benjamine Richard Moseley ---

CHARLES AUGUSTUS DIEFFENDERFER BIBLE
Owner: Mrs. M. N. Dieffenderfer, Brunswick, Ga.

Charles Augustus Dieffenderfer b. 12/12/1827 Whitedeer Township,
Union Co., Pa., d. 10/13/1887 m. 5/9/1854 Margaret Showers b.
4/18/1834 McCollistersville, Pa., d. 1/19/1891. Had Five Children:

Henrietta Frances Dieffenderfer 1/12/1855-2/27/1900 m. 5/20/1880
    P.W. Rauch (had three children: Charles, Nellie and Russell Rauch)
Barbara Ellen Dieffenderfer 5/31/1857 m. James H. Smith (had 4
    children: Maggie, Etta, Oliver and Charles Smith)
Thomas Elmer Dieffenderfer 1/14/1860-2/22/1864
Maurice Newton Dieffenderfer b. 1/15/1863 m. 9/1886 Carrie
    Stadden d. 2/20/1905, (had dau., Arlene Stadden b. 2/20/1899, m. 2r
    6/23/1909 Elizabeth Martz)
Dora Alma Dieffenderfer b. 7/16/1868 m. Ernest Blind (had dau.,
    Ellen Blind b. 2/19/1893)

ROBERT DANIELL BIBLE

Sarah b. 5/22/1762, a twin   John b. 5/22/1762, a twin
Thomas b. 1765   William Jr. b. 9/22/1767
James--   Elizabeth b. 3/16/1769
Mary b. 2/22/1772   Nathaniel b. 3/18/1774
Rebecca b. 7/7/1779   Isaac b. 10/13/1781
George b. 9/17/1783

Births
William Daniell 11/25/1743   Beaton Daniell 3/8/1801
Mary Daniell 3/11/1770   Masters H. Daniell 12/27/1802
Rachael Daniell 7/31/1789   Clarissa Daniell 12/29/1804
Josiah Daniell 2/26/1792   Alfred Daniell 2/17/1807
Susannah Daniell 6/8/1794   Stephen Daniell 2/4/1809
Jeremiah M. Daniell 1/18/1797   Moses Daniell 5/4/1811
Eleanor Daniell 2/19/1799   Robert Daniell 2/28/1813

Ollive Daniell 2/15/1815
Marian Fuller 4/29/1821
Rachel Crow 2/10/1779

The ages of children of William and Rachael Daniell:

William Daniell 9/22/1767   Nathaniell Daniell 3/18/1774
Elisabeth Daniell 3/16/1769   Rebecca Daniell 7/7/1779
Mary Daniell 2/22/1772   Isaac Daniell 10/13/1781
                                   George Daniell 9/17/1783

JOSIAH DANIELL BIBLE

The property of Josiah Daniell. Feb. 2, 1819 Josiah Daniell his
Book given by his Father William Daniell.

W. B. Burnett b. 10/13/1869 Watkinsville, Oconee Co., Ga.

Georgia, Clarke Co., the Record of Josiah and Sarah Daniell´s
   children:
William Daniell b. 5/2/1812
Elizabeth Daniell b. 12/22/1813
Mary Daniell b. 9/22/1815, d. 1/1/1817
Sarah Daniell b. 8/22/1816
Nathaniel Daniell b. 7/15/1818
Jessa Daniell b. 4/15/1820
Senor? Daniell b. 10/19/1822
Sarah Ann Burrow b. 6/25/1824
Josiah Daniell b. 9/24/1826
Susannah Daniell b. 6/10/1828
Mary Ann Susan Burnett b. 9/5/1830
Sarah Anzaline Burnett b. 1/20/1833
John William Burnett b. 8/1/1836

LEONIDAS FRANKLIN DANIELL BIBLE
Owner: Forrest Daniell
3611 Sunset Blvd., Houston, Texas 77005

"Hoping that brother Frank and Estelle may study daily this----
Lovingly Sister Pearl, Beaumont, Texas October 18th 1894 married
1 yr ago today."
Leonidas Franklin Daniell b. Clarke Co., Ga. 4/24/1857, d.
7/28/1938 Beaumont, Texas
Estelle Wilson Daniell b. Bonham, Texas 2/3/1866, m. 10/18/1893,
d. 12/7/1929 Beaumont
Born to them in Beaumont, Texas:
Leonidas Franklin Daniell, Jr. 9/13/1900, d. 10/26/1957 Beaumont,
Texas
Wilson Bedford Forrest Daniell 8/19/1902
Charles Edward Daniell 2/8/1905, d. 2/17/1957 San Antonio, Texas

FORREST DANIELL BIBLE
Owner: Forrest Daniell
3611 Sunset Blvd., Houston, Texas 77005

"Prater Genealogy taken from DAR application 502306 of Alice
Prater Daniell, dated Dec. 9, 1963, Houston, Texas. `I am the
daughter of James Preston Prater born on 6-17-1859 Edgefield Co.,
S. C., died at Beaumont, Texas (actually on Prater Farm 9 miles
or so west of Beaumont) 6-7-1917 and his wife Mary Angie Dearing,
born on April 5, 1875 at Hart Co., Ky., died at Houston, Texas on
Oct. 7, 1952, married on 3-3-1903 (both buried Magnolia Cemetery,
Beaumont, Texas).

#2. The said James Preston Prater was the child of Larkin
Christwell Prater (Chris) born on 2-8-1832 at Lexington (Co.), S.
C. died at Atlanta, Ga. on 7-22-1864 (Battle of Atlanta) and his
only wife Emaline Rhoden born on 11-7-1822 (10 years his senior)
at Edgefield Co., S. C., died at Louise, Wharton Co., Texas 2-5-
1899, married on 11-1-1853.

#3. The said Larkin Christwell Prater was the child of Hezekiah
Prater born in 1784 at Edgefield Co., S. C., died at Lexington
(Co.), S. C. on May 1850 and his wife Ellen Hartley (daughter of
Lewis Hartley, the son of Revolutionary soldier Daniel Hartley
who died in Crawford Co., Ga. in 1850 age 107) born in 1790 at
Lexington (Co.), S. C., died at Lexington (Co.), S. C.

#4. The said Hezekiah Prater was the child of Zachariah Prater
born ca. 1752 at Maryland, died at Newberry Co., S. C., ca. 1814
(a Revolutionary War Soldier) and his wife Ruth Allison, born ca.
1755 at Montgomery Co., Md., died at Newberry Dist., S. C. after
1825, married Aug. 25, 1788.

#5. The said Zachariah Prater was the child of Aaron Prater born
ca. 1710 at Prince George Co., Md., died at Montgomery Co., Md.
ca. 1777, and his wife Jane Prather, a cousin, b. 1710 Maryland,
died Maryland, married 10-10-1738.

I was born on April 3, 1905 at Beaumont, Texas, married Oct. 14,
1925, First Baptist Church, Beaumont, Texas by Dr. Julian H.
Pace, pastor to Wilson Forrest Daniell, who was born on August

(Forrest Daniel Bible contd....)

19, 1902 Beaumont, Texas. He was County Surveyor, Jefferson Co.,
from 1928 through Oct. 1942. We moved to 3611 Sunset Houston on
Nov. 14, 1942 through Aug. 31, 1967. (dated) Jan. 10, 1972."

DAVID GLAZE BIBLE
Owner: Dr. Lois L. Norman
400 N. Crockett, Sherman, Tx. 75090

David Glaze and wife Susanna Norman m. 11/13/1798
Henry H. Glaze and wife m. 4/18/1835
David Glaze, son of Benjamin Glaze, b. 2/5/1769, his wife,
Susannah Norman, b. 3/9/1780
Thomas G. Glaze, son of David Glaze and his wife Susanna b.
6/24/1799
William Glaze, son of above, b. 9/25/1800?
Joseph W. Glaze, son o f above, b. 4/10/1802
Sidney N. Glaze, dau. of above, b. 1/1/1804
Euphony H. Glaze, dau. of above, b. 9/11/1805
Delia Seward Glaze, dau. of above, b. 8/10/1807
Julia Maria Glaze, dau. of above, b. 1/15/1809
Henry Harvey Glaze, son of above, b. 8/26/1810
Eleanor Mercer Glaze, dau. of above, b. 7/29/1812
Sarah katharine Glaze, dau. of above, b. 6/8/1814
Elizabeth Matilda Glaze, dau. of above, b. 2/25/1817
John Milton Glaze, son f above, b. 10/17/1818
Susanna Harriet Glaze, dau. of above, b. 11/26/1820

Departed this life Twin of Thomas G. Glaze a few hours after his
birth
Died 9/12 Euphony Harris Glaze
Julia Maria Glaze d. 8/29/1811
David Glaze d. 12/16/1820
George W. Glaze b. 4/26/1837

DANIEL H. STANDARD BIBLE
Owner: Mrs. Louise Poole Norman, Washington, Ga.

Deaths
Daniel H. Standard 2/13/1873   Daniel H. Standard Jr. 5/23/1918
William L. Standard 7/13/1887   Jane E. Standard, wife of W. L.
Prudence Blalock 7/8/18--   Standard, 12/16/1906
James B. Snelson baby 2/8/18--   John R. Standard, son of William
                                   and Jane Standard, 8/27/1920

Births
Daniel H. Standard, son of William and Jane E. Standard,
b. 10/27/1853
Emma Jane, dau. of above, b. 7/11/1858
Mary L. Standard, dau. of above, b. 2/21/1861
John L. Blalock, son of David and Margaret Blalock,b. 8/14/1797
Prudence Guise, wife of John L. Blalock, b. 7/8/1799
Thomas J. Blalock, son of J. L. and Prudence Blalock,
b. 5/22/1838
Annie J. Standard b. 7/20/186-

113

(Daniel H. Standard Bible contd....)

William Lamkin Standard, son of Kimbro and Elisabeth Standard,
  b. 7/26/1815
Jane Elisabeth Blalock, wife of William L. Standard, b. 6/4/1822
Francis Elisabeth Standard, dau. of William and Jane Standard,
  b. 7/14/1846
Sallie P. Standard, dau. of William and Jane Standard,
  b. 6/1/1849
John H. Standard, son of William and Jane Standard, b. 6/16/1851

Marriages
William L. Standard and Jane Elisabeth Blalock m. 7/31/18--
Danniel H. Standard and---Huguley m. 2/18/1873
Lou M. Standard and William P. Stone m. 10/25/1887
Emma J. Standard and James Bellows m. 4/---
Annie T. Standard and Osborn Snelson m. 12/16/1888
Velma Snelson Poole b. 6/13/1895?, d. 8/3/1966

WILLIAM THOMAS STANDARD BIBLE
Owner: Mrs. Angie Standard Warren, Tignall, Ga.

Husband's Father - Daniel Harvey Standard
Husband's Mother - Celestia Angeline Cullers
Wife's Father -   Charles Stewart Heard
Wife's Mother -   Elizabeth Ann Jackson (later Mrs. House)
Husband -   William Thomas Standard
Birthplace -   Wilkes Co., Ga., 12/13/1858
Wife -   Mary Elizabeth Heard
Birthplace -   Wilkes Co., Ga., 10/26/1859
Place of Marriage -Wilkes Co., Ga.
Date of Marriage - Dec. 19, 1880
Officiating Clergyman - Rev. J. H. Fortson
Witnesses: T. J. Mulligan, W. S. Kendall, J. W. Ware

Names of Children:

Samuel J. Standard b. 5/30/1882   Daniel H. Standard b. 4/7/1892
Lizzie H. Standard b. 12/17/1883   Mary Elizabeth Standard
Aelise M. Standard b. 12/11/1886   b. 4/4/1894
Celestia Angeline (Angie)   Lucy Zellars Standard
Standard b. 11/26/1889   b. 1/3/1897
William T. Standard (Jr.) b. 11/28/1900

Grandchildren:

Francis Joseph Warren, Jr. b. 9/1/1918
Mary Will Warren b. 5/14/1920
James Randolph Warren b. 6/6/1927

Great Grandchildren:

Lucy Angieline Dunson b. 7/17/1952 Amy Moss Warren b. 12/21/1957
Eve Bondurant Warren b. 6/26/1954   Mary Lou Dunson b. 10/28/1954
Mark Standard Warren b. 9/1/1955
Stuart Heard Warren b. 10/9/1959
Lisa Brannon Warren b. 10/2/1960

114

(William Thomas Standard Bible contd....)

Marriages
Samuel J. Standard to Nannie Kate Fortson, Wilkes Co., Ga.,
    1/12/1902
Aelise M. Standard to Thomas Emmett Granade, Wilkes Co., Ga.,
    6/30/1914
C. Angie Standard to Francis Joseph Warren, Tignall, Wilkes
    Co., Ga., 12/26/1917
Daniel Haynes Standard to Marie Diffee, Cordele, Ga.
Mary Elizabeth Standard to Dr. C. F. Cooper, Cordele, Ga.,
    6/1931
Lucy Zellars Standard to J. P. Doster, Jr., Wilkes Co., Ga., 1919
William Thomas Standard, Jr. to Pauline Doster, Rochelle, Ga.

Deaths
Lizzie H. Standard 8/19/1889   Samuel Johns Standard 12/21/1942
W. T. Standard 3/25/1928   Lucy S. Doster 6/9/1953
Mrs. W. T. Standard 7/13/1933   W. T. Standard Jr. 6/9/1953
(Aelise M. Standard Granade)

(Celestia Angeline (Angie) Standard Warren, (Mrs. F. J.), d.
10/18/1974 at Toccoa, Stephens Co., Ga., buried Oct. 20, Baptist
Cemetery, Tignall, Ga.)

DR. WILLIAM DAVENPORT BIBLE
Owner: Fred P. Davenport
1669 23rd St., Wyandotte, Mich. 48192

Marriages
Dr. W. W. Davenport and S. E. Tiller (Sidney) 1/31/1865 (2d wife)
Jesse Davenport and Susannah Thompson 6/22/1802
William W. Davenport and Mary Ann Glen 1/8/1852 (1st wife)
Mary F. Davenport and Tunis W. Powell 12/23/1875 (Mary Frances
    Davenport's dau., Miss Florence Powell, is res. of the Heritage
    Nursing Home, Athens, Ga. 9/74)
Mrs. S. E. Davenport and J. G. Eberhart 12/14/1880

Jesse Davenport b. 1/12/1767, d. 9/28/1822
Susannah Davenport b. 7/2/1772, d. 8/19/1859
James W. Davenport b. 5/13/1803, d. 10/1/1841
William W. Davenport b.7/7/1805, d. 6/23/1878
John L. Davenport b. 5/18/1807
Charles W. Davenport b. 7/2/1809, d. 3/11/1860
Mary Frances b. 9/7/1812, d. 1/21/1836
Susan Thompson b. 3/5/1815
Sidney E. b. 12/1/1839
William J. b. 10/21/1853
Mary Frances b. 8/19/1855
John Louis b. 12/28/1857, d. 6/13/1860
Mary Anne d. 2/4/1860
Martha Ann Susan b. 12/7/1859, d. 10/21/1860

```
                  JOHN C. DUNCAN BIBLE
                Owner: Mrs. William H. Booth
                  Rt. 2, Commerce, Ga. 30529


John Charles Duncan and Jane M. Roberts m. 10/13?/1851

John Charles Duncan b. 4/17/1829
Jane M. Duncan b. 3/24/1836

Matilda Adaline Duncan b. 10/14/1853
Elizabeth Caroline Duncan b. 10/22/1855
George Alexander Duncan b. 10/3/1857
Mary Ann Duncan b. 1/10/1860
Thomas Johnson Duncan b. 3/16/1862
Sarah Mananr? Duncan b. 3/1/1865
Alice Sophronia Duncan b. 7/2/1867
Louisa Oleva Duncan b. 6/14/1869


                   ISAAC K. BALDREE BIBLE
           Rev. Pension Appl. dtd 1833 Tattnall Co., Ga.



Isaac K.  Baldree d. 12/1/1836 Tattnall Co., Ga., b. Pitt Co.,
N. C. 1758 m. Elizabeth Sapp (dau. of Levi Sapp, b. 1751),
3/1828 Tattnall Co., Ga., by Joseph Collins, J. P. and had
four children:

Isaac Baldree b. 3/11/1833 Tattnall Co., Ga.
Celia Baldree b. 10/9/1831 Tattnall Co., Ga.
William Baldree b. 5/4/1834 Tattnall Co., Ga.
Catherine Baldree b. 6/1/1836 Tattnall Co., Ga.


                   RICHARD HEARD BIBLE
                   From Rev. War Pension


Application of Capt. Richard Heard's son, Charles M. Heard of
Jackson Co., Ga., dtd 5/18/1844.

Daniel Coleman Heard, son of Richard and Elizabeth, b. 2/21/1785
Charles McHolton Heard b. 6/8/1786
Ezerbelan? Heard b. 8/20/1791
----Coleman Heard b. 12/3/1794
Mary Heard b. 4/17/1797
```

JONATHAN MILNER BIBLE
Owner: Mrs. William H. Booth
Rt. 2, Commerce, Ga. 30529

Birth of slave children:
Jacob Netty, first son, b. -/30/1841   Betsy Jan & Jess dau.
Peter b. 11/1842   b. 9/27/1844
Eliza b. 8/10/1840
Joseph b. 4/1841

Marriages
Jonathan Milner and Rebecca Dunn 12/11/1805
Samuel Glenn and Sophia D. Miler 10/21/1830
Robert C. Daniel and Emily G. Miler 6/23/1831
George W. Calaway and Elizabeth B. Milner---
John D. Milner and Matilda P. Lumpkin 9/11/1833
William Howard and Rebecca W. Milner 9/12/1833
Thomas H. Hawkins and Amoretta F. Milner 1/17/1840

Births
Jonathan Milner, son of John Milner, b. 1/26/1778
Rebecca Dunn, dau. of Drury and Martha Dunn, b. 4/26/1783
Martha W. Milner, dau. of Jonathan and Rebecca Milner,
    b. 1/14/1807
John D. Milner, son of Jonathan and Rebecca, b. 5/6/1808
Sophia D. Milner, dau. of above, b. 1/3/1810
Emily G. Milner, dau. of above, b. 7/27/1812
Rebecca W. Milner, dau. of above, b. 3/10/1814
Elizabeth B. Milner, dau. of above, b. 8/10/1815
Sarah Ann Milner, dau. of above, b. 11/24/1816
Jonathan G. Milner, son of above, b. 12/8/1818
Mary A. Milner, dau. of above, b. 3/2/1821
Amoretta F. Milner, dau. of above, b. 8/21/1823

Thomas H. Hawkins b. 6/4/1814

Charles Alexander Hawkins, second son o f Thomas H. and Amoretta
    F. Hawkins, b. 12/7/1844
John Milner Hawkins b. 9/1/1843
Emily Sophia Ann Hawkins b. 9/15/1846
Amoretta F. Hawkins, dau. of Thomas H. and Amoretta F. Hawkins,
    b. 2/7/1854
Thomas I. (Ira) Hawkins b. 9/27/1870
Charles A. (Alexander) Hawkins b. 4/30/1875
Annie G. (Glorianna) Hawkins b. 2/19/1881

Deaths
Mary A. Milner, dau. of Jonathan and Rebecca, d. 10/15/1821,
    aged 7 mos., 13 days
Martha Dunn, mother of Rebecca Milner, d. 3/21/1825, aged 72
    yrs., 11 mos., 21 days
Martha W. Milner, dau. of Jonathan and Rebecca, d. 10/7/1827,
    aged 20 yrs., 8 mos., 23 days
Rebecca Milner, wife of Jonathan Milner, d. 9/29/1829, aged 46
    yrs., 5 mos., 5 days
Jonathan Milner d. 12/24/1844, aged 66 yrs., 10 mos., 29 days
Thomas H. Hawkins d. 4/24/1877
Emily S. Brawner, dau. of Thomas H. and Amoretta Hawkins,
    d. 6/25/1877

117

JAMES L. BRASINGTON BIBLE
Owner: Mrs. J. W. Bray
Rt. 4, Box 621, Ocala, Fla. 32670

Henrietta Helen Hunley b. 2/7/1844
James L. Brasington and Henrietta Helen Hunley m. 3/21/1864
Marion Helen Brasington b. 10/10/1873
Willie Shepperd Bray and Marion Helen Brasington m. 11/17/1899
Henrietta Helen Brasington d. 4/7/1901
James L. Brasington d. 2/27/1883
Marion Helen (Emma) Bray d. 4/16/1901

OBEDIAH STEVENS BIBLE *
Owner: Claude Stevens, Carlton, Ga.

This certifies that the Rite of Holy Matrimony was celebrated between Obadiah Stevens of Oglethorpe and Martha Watkins of Oglethorpe on 26th July 1832 at Rese Watkins' by Rev. Sylvanus Gibson.

Births
Joseph Stevens 3/9/1787
Martha Stevens 4/22/1787
Obediah Stevens 5/7/1809
Haley Stevens 3/30/1811
Allen Stevens 6/16/1812
Jasper Stevens 9/27/1813
Thomas Stevens 10/22/1818
Elizabeth Stevens 2/8/1822
Martha Stevens 2/22/1824
Newton Stevens 12/19/1825
Walton Stevens 3/11/1829
W. C. Stevens 2/21/1831
J. R. Stevens 4/30/1834
W. W. Stevens 3/29/1837
C. A. Stevens 6/26/1844

Rese Watkins Sr. 8/20/1779
Milly Watkins 9/26/1779
Ben Watkins 10/12/1801
Elizabeth Watkins 12/5/1803
Nancy Watkins 10/12/1807
Charly Watkins 9/1/1809
Olive Watkins 9/25/1811
Martha Watkins 9/5/1814
William Watkins 3/22/1818
Rese Watkins 7/22/1822

James Appling 3/16/1825

WILLIAM D. HEDLESTON BIBLE
Owner: Mrs. A. K. Register, Norfolk, Va.

Births
Jane P. Hedelston 9/15/1818
John James Hedelston 7/17/1820
William Davis Hedleston 2/22/1822

Ann Susannah Ulmer 8/3/1825
Mary Agnes Hedleston 7/15/1849
John Presley Hedleston
    8/10/1851

Sarah Jane Hedleston 8/6/1853
--Elizabeth Hedleston 5/6/1889?
Jefferson Davis Hedleston 11/-/18--
William Davis Hedleston 10/5/1879
Ernestine Sutton Hedleston, dau. of William C. and Allis
Hedleston b. 10/8/1881
Samuel Barlow Hedleston 8/24/1883

*See also p. 179.   118

(William D. Hedleston Bible contd....)

Annie Gertrude Hedleston 1/12/18--
Maggie Lou Hedleston 6/18/1890

Marriages
William Davis Hedleston and Ann Susannah Ulmer 4/9/1846
William Charles Hedleston and Allie Gertrude Brannen 9/7/1878
Samuel Barlow Hedleston and Susie Edna Hodges 1/24/1904
Glendine Elizabeth Hedleston and Mooney Alphonso Strouse
    10/12/1921
William Barlow Hedleston and Debbie Iona Durrance 5/7/1932
Edna Mae Hedleston and Redic L. DeLoach 7/4/1936

Deaths
John James Hedleston 9/11/1851, age 31 yrs., 1 mo., 24 days
Mary Agnes Hedleston 6/11/1854, age 4 yrs., 10 mos., 26 days
John Presley Hedleston 6/13/1854, age 2 yrs., 10 mos., 3 days
William Davis Hedleston 11/10/1879, age 57 yrs., 7 mos., 18 days
Ann Susannah Hedleston 1/11/1880, age 54 yrs., 5 mos., 8 days
William Davis Hedleston, son of William C. and Allie Hedleston,
    d. 5/26/1880, age 7 mos., 21 days
Willie C. Hedleston 3/8/1890
Maggie Lou Hedleston 6/28/1890
Infant baby of Samuel Barlow Hedleston and Susie Edna Hedleston,
    b. 8/6/1912, d. 8/8/1912
Mattie Lou Hedleston, dau. of Samuel and Susie Hedleston
    5/13/1925
Herbert Nathaniel Hedleston 12/8/1926

Births
Glendine Elizabeth Hedleston 2/16/1905
Willie Barlow Hedleston 7/13/1906
Mattie Lou Hedleston 12/17/1908
Herbert Nathaniel Hedleston 9/19/1910
Edna Mae Hedleston 9/23/1915

SIMEON AUGUSTUS BEAUCHAMP BIBLE

Simeon Augustus Beauchamp b. Coffee Co., Ga. 12/19/1823,
    d. 7/9/1897, m. Elizabeth Cook 2/24/1850 Jackson Co., Fla.
Elizabeth Cook Beauchamp d. 11/25/1860
Simeon Augustus Beauchamp m. Martha Ellen Cook, sister of
    Elizabeth, his first wife, 3/17/1862, Jackson Co., Fla.

Children of Simeon and Elizabeth Cook Beauchamp:

Augustus Carey Beauchamp b. 5/11/1851 d. 9/19/1924
James Labron Beauchamp b. 6/26/1854 d. 11/11/1940
Nancy Jane Beauchamp b. 5/31/1857 d. 1898
Elizabeth Beauchamp b. 1859
        Children of Simeon and Martha Cook Beauchamp:
John Beauchamp b. 1863
William Hardie b. 3/31/1866 d. 8/5/1950
Henry Green 1868
Martha Ellen b. 5/31/1869 d. 10/1/1938
Erastus White b. 8/23/1871 d. 11/9/1923
Thomas Jefferson b. 3/24/1874 d. 12/25/1955
George Lee b. 8/8/1876 d. 1/14/1949

(Simeon Augustus Beauchamp Bible contd....)

Charles Wright b. 2/20/1880 d. 6/11/1943
Francis Arthur b. 12/27/1880 d. 5/31/1934
Sarah Amanda b. 4/23/1884 d. 1/14/1960
Perry b. 1886 d. 7/9/1893
Andrew Jackson b. 3/18/1888
Elijah Curry b. 1870 d. 12/28/1928
Augustus Carey Beauchamp m. Mollie Ann Stephens, dau. of Dick
  Stephens 1/14/1869. Children:
Sarah Elizabeth b. 12/25/1869   Annie Eliza b. 10/2/1879
Laura b. 8/5/1871   Martha Alma b. 7/27/1885
James Riley b. 5/17/1873   Richard Simeon b. 10/25/1887
John Hudson b. 3/11/1875   Edward Augustus b. 10/6/1889
Lucy Ellen b. 5/9/1877

JEREMIAH WHITE BIBLE
Owner: Va. Historical Society
Richmond, Va.

Jeremiah White, His Book May 11, 1722

Jere White b. 10/11/1728   Mary White b. 1/27/1735
Lettice White b. 4/9/1732   Millie White b. 3/20/1740
Mary White b. 1/27/1735   John Martin White b. 6/27/1743
Daniell, Ann and Reuben White b. at one birth on Thursday the 19
  June 1746
Betty White b. 1749

"I hereby promis to clear and pay all cost charges as Clarks
Sherifs and Aloyers fees belonging to ye estate of Robert Martin
and James Holl Hollway as witnessed my hand, this 25 day of March
1727. /s/ James G. Holloway"

"966 weight of tobacco coming to John Holt These to Mr. John
  White"

John Martin White b. 6/27/1743
Milly (Martin) White b. 10/23/1756
Reuben White, son of John and Milly White, b. 3/3/1776
Sarah F. White b. 4/10/1777
Mary M. White b. 11/16/1778
John White b. 7/5/1780 d. 12/13/1789
Nancy Kidd White b. 2/23/1787
Patsy Gaines White b. 12/25/1788
Eppy White b. 3/16/1792
Betsy Johnston White b. 2/7/1793
Franky White b. 7/14/1795

"March 23, 1811. I do hereby certify that my daughter Franky
(White) Robuck has recd of my estate the underwritten articles--
        To 1 Negro girl Rachel $250.00 cts
        To Bed & furniture   32.50
        To 1 saddle   16.00
        To 1 cow & calf   10.00
        To 1 chest   5.50
        To 1 Ewe & lamb   3.00
                                  $317.00
        To 1 Mare

120

(Jeremiah White Bible contd....)

```
To 1 cow                    7.00
                         $397.00
$404
 167  To Cash
$571  amount        (signed) John White
```

"He leaves a similar list of articles to: daughter Betsey Mann;
son Eppy White, son John White, daughter Lucy Thornton, daughter
Patsey White, daughter Nancy Mann, daughter Polley Tonyhay,
daughter Salley Morris, son Reuben White to whom he gives besides
articles named 'To Land in Franklin - $428.00'"
Jeremiah White ye son of Jeremiah and Mary White he was born
October ye 11 in ye yare of our Lord God 1729
John White was born March ye 22 1703 Deceased September ye 15,
  1732
Lettituce White was born April ye 9, 1732
Rachel White was born August ye 28, 1733
     Note: Other articles listed. This Bible also a Diary.

                 JOHN M. WHITE, SR. BIBLE
                 Owner: Albert Crayton White

Jeremiah White b. 10/8/1695
John White b. 3/22/1703
Jeremiah White, son of Jeremiah White and wife, Mary Martin
  White, b. 10/11/1728
John White, son of Jeremiah and Mary White, b. 3/2/1730, d. 1732
Lettie, dau. of Jeremiah and Mary White, b. 4/9/1733
Rachel, dau. of above, b. 8/2/1735
Lettice, dau. of above, 1/27/1737
Mildred, dau. of above, b. 3/20/1740
John Martin White, son of above, 6/27/1743
Daniel, Ruben and Ann White b. at one birth, Thursday, 6/17/1746

Ethan Ballenger, son of Joseph and Sarah Ballenger b. 4/21/1754
Milly Ballenger, dau. of above, b. 10/23/1767
Betsy Ballender, dau. of above, b. 2/14/1758
Peggy H. Ballenger, dau. of above, b. 3/16/1762
Charity C. Ballenger, dau. of above, b. 6/14/1764
Achilles Ballenger, son of above, b. 9/20/1766
Richard Ballenger, son of above, b. 1/18/1769
James Ballenger, son of above, b. 4/21/1771
Phoebe Ballenger, dau. of above, b. 7/14/1774
Joseph Ballenger, Jr., son of above, b. 12/5/1776

John White and Milly, dau. of Joseph and Sarah Ballenger, were
  m. 5/29/1775
Ruben, son of John and Milley White, b. 3/3/1776
Sarah White, dau. of above, b. 4/10/1777
Mary Martin, dau. of above, b. 11/16/1778
John, son of above, b. 7/5/1780
Elizabeth Johnson White, dau. of John and Milley White, b.
  2/18/1782
Betsy White, dau. of above, b.---
Nancy Kidd White, dau. of above, b. 1/22/1785
Lucy Thornton White, dau. of above, b. 2/23/1787
Patsey Gaines White, dau. of above, b. 12/25/1788
```
```

(John M. White, Sr. Bible contd....)

Eppe White, son of above, b. 3/16/1793
Elizabeth Johnson, 2d dau. of John and Milley White, b. 2/17/1794
Franky, dau. of above, b. 7/14/1795
John Martin, Jr., son of John White, Sr., and Milley White, b. 2/23/1798
Elizabeth Johnson White, dau. of John & Milley White, d. 1/9/1789
Ruben White and Betsy Heard m. 11/12/1798
Sally White, dau. of Ruben White and Betsy, b. 10/25/1802
James Franklin White b. 9/13/1804
John Martin White b. 9/28/1806
Elizabeth Amelia White b. 5/2/1810
Sabrina Lucinda Aseneth White b. 5/23/1802
Andrew Jackson White b. 4/25/1815
Ruben Harrison White b. 2/2/1818

Eppe White and Catherine Herndon m. 5/11/1815. Ages of their children:

Thomas Herndon b. 2/20/1816	Ann Herndon b. 1/9/1829
John Martin b. 7/28/1817	Rachel E. b. 4/10/1831
Mildred Elizabeth b. 10/15/1819	Sarah Catherine b. 11/13/1833
Dillard Herndon b. 1/13/1822	Mary F. b. 5/7/1836
Edward Rucker b. 4/8/1824	Malissa Frances b. 11/14/1839
James Franklin b. 9/15/1826	

Marriages
John White and Milly Ballenger, dau. of Joseph and Sarah Ballenger m. 5/29/1775
John Morris and Sarah White 10/30/1793
William Morris and Mary White 12/8/1796
Jesse Mann and Nancy Kidd White 2/2/1801
Martin White and Patsy White 2/2/1807
John White Jr. and Elizabeth Harper 12/26/1810
Ruben White and Betsy Heard 11/12/1798
Thomas Thornton and Lucy White 12/25/1805
Eppy White and Catherine Herndon 5/11/1815
Asa Mann and Betsy White 1/25/1810
Edmund Murry and Patsy Mann, granddau. of John White, 1/19/1819
William Jackson and Lucy Morris, granddau. of John White, 11/11/1811
Elijah Moore and Sally White, grandau. of John White, 1811
Richard Rice and Elizabeth J. White 1/1/1822
Robert Roebuck and Franky White 5/27/1810
Littleton Meeks and Milly Morris 3/16/1823
Jeremiah Warren and Elizabeth Thornton 10/14/1823
James Morris and Harriet Beall 5/18/1823
John Morris and Polly Harrison 9/28/1824
Elzy B. Thornton and Nancy C. Harper 4/13/1826
Thomas Johnson and Mildred F. Roebuck 5/4/1826
Elizabeth Mann, dau. of Jeptha Mann and nancy Mann his wife, and Kinnon Vanderpoole 1/27/1824
Elisha Coffee and Mary Morris 3/1825
John M. White, son of Eppy and Catherine White, and Mary L. Jordan 12/5/1844
Thomas Hernon White and Martha Cheeke McMillan 3/19/1840
Masling Y. Keith and Eliza Jones 2/14/1834
Memorable Thornton and Parmelia A. Higginbotham 2/9/1832
Edward Rucker White and Elizabeth Roberts 7/8/1846
James F. White and Martha J. Cobb 9/18/1870
Charles W. Christian, Jr. and Sarah C. White 3/31/1853
James E. Strickland and Rachel E. White 5/15/1857
Dillard Herndon White and Mary Ann Duncan 11/9/1854

(John M. White, Sr. Bible, Marriages, contd....)

John L. Christian and Malissa F. White 11/13/1856
Joseph B. Chambers and Malissa F. White Christian   /18/1803
James Jones and Mildred E. White 10/25/1842
Jones Stonecypher and ---Morris 1/1/1821
Nathan Meeks and----12/24/1822
Jeptha Jones and Rebecca Ramsey 7/4/1895
Thomas Hernon White and Malissa C. Walters 2/1/1866
Charles White and Lucinda Moss 11/19/1891

Deaths
John White 1733, age 30
Jeremiah White, father of John Martin White, 10/25/1776, age 81
Mary White, mother of John White, Sr., 9/23/1796, age 91 yrs.
Joseph Ballenger, Sr., father of Milly Thornton White, 2/1802,
   age 66 yrs.
John Martin White, son of John M. White and Milly, 3/31/1840
John White, son of John Martin White and Milly his wife, 6/9/1781
Elizabeth Johnson White, dau. of John M. White and Milly White,
   12/13/1789
Elizabeth Mann 11/14/1834
Sarah Ballenger, mother of Milly White 1/8/1777, age 40 yrs.
John M. White, Sr., the 1st owner of this book, 2/6/1833, age 90.
Milly White, wife of John M. White, 9/2/1840, age 84 yrs.
Joseph Ballenger 8/9/1777
Esthan Ballenger, son of Joseph Ballenger, 8/12/1777
Ruben White, son of Jeremiah White, 8/11/1811, age 65 yrs.
Daniel White, son f Jeremiah White, 11/7/1806, age 40 yrs.
Jacob Cleveland, Sr. 6/13/1799 or 1791
Milly Cleveland 11/5/1805
Webb Kidd 4/1805
Elizabeth Kidd 8/1804
Robert Roebuck 4/28/1829
Mary White, wife of Daniel White, 9/28/1804
Elizabeth Jones, dau. of William and Mary Jones, 9/25/1871
   (1817?) age 11 mos.
Lewis Jones 6/15/1818 age 10 yrs.
Ruben White, son of John M. White, 2/22/1820, age 44 yrs.
John D. White 8/9/1821
Patsy, wife of Martin White, 11/16/1821
John Roebuck 5/1822
Elizabeth Rice 1/8/1830
Betsy Mann 11/14/1831
Lucy Thornton 1/25/1837
William Jones, Sr. 1/6/1838
William Asa White, son of John White, 4/23/1825
Elizabeth White, wife of Edward Rucker White, 11/5/1863
Martha Cheeke White, wife of Thomas Herndon White 12/11/1864
Martha R. White, wife of James F. White, d. of consumption
   5/23/1870
James F. White 5/1/1898
Mary Mildred White, dau. of James F. White & Martha R., 7/7/1890
Ann Herndon White 5/15/1863 of consumption
Thomas Herndon White 1/2/1892
Lucy T. Thornton 1/25/1837
William Jones Sr. 1/6/1837
William Asa, son of John White, 4/23/1825
Robert Roebuck 10/1822
Franky Roebuck 10/1822
Mary Francis, dau. of Eppy and Catherine White, 12/31/1838, age 3
Sarah Morris 10/1856

(John M. White, Sr. Bible, Deaths, contd....)

Eppy W. Morris, son of John and Sarah Morris 10/1857
Polly Coffee 1861
Eppy White 9/19/1854
John W. Morris 10/27/1854, age 57 yrs., 8 mos., 8 days
Malissa F. Gaines, dau. of Eppy and Catherine White, 9/9/1896
Ann H. Cobb, dau. of James F. White, 12/17/1895
John M. White 12/31/1866
Martha M. White 5/23/1870

THOMAS THORNTON BIBLE

(Children of Thomas Thornton and Lucy Thornton White)

Elzabad Thornton, son of Thomas and Lucy Thornton, b. 9/28/1806
Betsy White Thornton, b. 12/29/1807
Memorable Thornton b. 1/7/1810
Eppy White Thornton b. 5/22/1811
John Martin Thornton b. 10/10/1814
Sally Thornton b. 5/30/1816
Mark Thornton b. 10/31/1819

JAMES MORRIS BIBLE

James Morris b. 10/28/1794
John Morris and Patsy W. Moris (twins) b. 12/15/1798
Lucy W. Morris b. 12/18/1800
Milly White Morris b. 4/5/1804
Bolley Morris and Eppy White Morris (twins) b. at one birth
  4/13/1810
Elizabeth Heard Morris b. 11/6/1812
Susannah Morris b. 3/17/1815
Franklin Ballenger Morris b. 12/9/1816

JOHN JONES BIBLE

John Jones b. 9/26/1799   Lewis Jones b. 5/11/1808
Sally C. Jones b. 1/22/1801   Allen Ballenger Jones
Stephen Jones b. 1/1/1802   b. 4/17/1810
Mary Ballenger Jones b. 3/7/1805 Polly Simpson Jones
William Jones b. 5/11/1806   b. 1/10/1812
Elizabeth Jackson Jones b. 11/18/1814

JAMES M. WHITE BIBLE

Children of James M. White and Patsy White:

Polly Wade White b. 1/31/1808   Asa Jackson White b. 1/17/1815
Ruben Ballenger White b. 4/18/1809 Eliza Amelia White b.9/26/1816

Jeremiah Franklin White b. 9/1/1810
Eppy Warren White b. 1/30/1813
John Daniel White b. 10/1/1818
Patsey E. White b. 10/1/1821
Nancy Kidd Mann b. 3/29/1807   Sintha Eliza Mann b. 4/5/1816
Jesse Martin Mann b. 2/22/1809 James Jackson Mann b. 10/10/1818
Milly White Mann b. 10/15/1810 John Washington b. 7/1/1820
Eppy White Mann b. 8/22/1812   Naisai Mann b. 12/27/1822
Judah John Mann b. 4/14/1814   Elbert Mann b. 7/12/1825
                                Elbert Mann b. 2/20/1828

RICHARD RICE BIBLE

Children of Richard Rice and Elizabeth, his wife. Richard Rice and
   Eliza J. White were m. 1/1/1822:
Milly Ann Rice b. 2/28/1825   Charles Rice b. 1/5/1830
Richard M. Rice b. 10/11/1826   Eliza Rice d. 1/8/1830
Asa Rice b. 9/4/1828

JAMES WASHINGTON WHITE BIBLE

James Washington White, son of John & Elizabeth, b. 2/20/1817
Eliza Harriot White b. 2/10/1817
Ruben White b. 8/28/1820
William Asa White b. 3/16/1822
Elizabeth Francis White b. 1/29/1824
Thomas M. White b. 10/23/1825
Nancy Kidd White b. 1/7/1828
Lucy Ann White and Richard Livey White (twins) b. 8/6/1830
John Martin White b. 2/1837
Polly M. White b. 12/25/1839

ROBERT ROEBUCK BIBLE

Milly Harriet Roebuck, dau. of Robert & Franky, b.2/23/1822
Eppy White Roebuck b. 1/7/1813
Sally C. W. Roebuck 2/26/1815
William T. Roebuck 4/24/1817
Robert Morris Roebuck 2/2/1819 or 1811
John T. Roebuck 1/19/1821
Polly Meeks, dau. of Littleton Meeks and Milley, his wife, b.
   1/13/1824

JEREMIAH WARREN BIBLE

Children of Jeremiah and Elizabeth Warren. Jeremiah (Stanfield)
  Warren and Elizabeth Thornton m. 10/24/1823 (Elbert Co., Ga.)
Lucy Emily Warren b. 9/30/1824
Mary Elizabeth Warren b. 6/6/1826
Sarah Francis Warren b. 10/27/1828
William H. Warren b. 9/26/1830
Thomas I. Warren b. 6/1/1832
Mary A. Warren b. 7/1834
Thomas M. Warren b. 12/4/1836

ELISHA COFFEE BIBLE

Elisha Coffee b. 7/27/1801. Children of Elisha Coffee and Mary,
  his wife:
Elisha Coffee b. 7/27/1801. Elisha Coffee and Mary Morris m.
  3/1825
John Morris Coffee b. 6/26/1826
Milly Coffee b. 12/15/1827
John Alvin Coffee b. 8/24/1829
Sarah Ann Coffee b. 11/12/1827 or 1831?
Elizabeth Francis Coffee b. 7/12/1833
Eppy F. Coffee b. 4/22/1835

Frances Elizabeth Johnson, dau. of Thomas and Mildred F. Johnson
  b. 10/1828

Bethena and Telena Vanderpool (twin) children of Kinnon and
Elizabeth Vanderpool were b. 10/4/1825
Leonard Vanderpool b. 8/24/1828
Martha J. Cobb b. 5/1833
Martha R. White, wife of James F. White b. 3/16/1833
Mary A. L., wife of John M. White, b. 12/25/1827

JOHN MARTIN WHITE BIBLE

John M. White, son of Eppy and Catherine White, and Mary L.
  Jordan m. 12/5/1844
Mary A. L. White, wife of John M. White, b. 12/25/1827
Thomas Lowndes White, son of John M. and Mary A. L. White,
  b. 2/13/1846
Emma Lauretta White b. 6/17/1847
George Walton White, son of above, b. 3/12/1849
Mary Ella Catherine White, dau. of above, b. 6/15/1850
John Martin White b. 12/18/1851
Eugenia Herndon White b. 9/25/1853
Walter Tillman White, son of above, b. 2/15/1853
Adolphus Herndon White, son of above, b. 1/26/1857

126

```
                        THOMAS H. WHITE BIBLE*
                      Owner: Albert Crayton White


Martha C. McMillian b. 3/15/1819
Thomas H. White and Martha C. McMillan m. 3/15/1840

Children of Thomas H. White and Martha C. White, his wife:

Mildred M. White b. 6/1841        Eppie White b. 5/27/1843
Sarah C. White b. 12/20/1841      Martha Ann White b. 1/29/1846
                                  Mary E. White b. 10/2/1852

Melissa C. Walters b. 4/9/1837
M. C. Walters and Thomas H. White m. 2/1/1866
Asa Salmon White b. 8/20/1873
Albert Crayton White b. 5/12/1876

William, son of Merling Keith and Eliza Jones, his wife,  b.
  9/3/1836

Ruben Henry Jackson Garland b. 3/25/1836
Sarah Ann Elizabeth Garland b. 11/11/1837

John Martin Vincent Harris b. 12/9/1831
Elizabeth Jane Harris b. 5/20/1834
Martha Emily Harris b. 4/13/1836?
Ruben Thomas Harris b. 1/18/1839



                    EDWARD CLAUDIUS JONES BIBLE


Edward Claudius Jones, son of James Jones and Mildred Jones, his
  wife, b. 2/1844
Lambert Lucius Jones, dau. of above, b. 8/7/1849
Ella Catherine Jones, dau. of above, b. 12/1852



              MEMORABLE AND PARMELIA A. THORNTON BIBLE


Children of Memorable Thornton and Parmelia A., his wife:

James A. Thornton b. 11/28/1832
William M. Thornton b. 3/20/1834
Thomas B. Thornton b. 3/20/1836

Ages of Eppy Thornton children:

Lucinda K. Thornton b. 10/4/1833
Tabitha E. Thornton b. 7/22/1836
```

THOMAS EAVENSON BIBLE

Ages of Children:
John M. Eavenson b. 8/29/1831
William Allen Eavenson b. 9/22/1833
Thomas M. Eavenson b. 10/2/1835

ALLEN BIBLE

Augustus Lafayette Allen b. 7/3/1828   Larat Ann Allen b. 1/20/1834
James F. Allen b. 6/14/1830   Lucinda Adaline Allen
Elizabeth Caroline Allen b. 3/8/1832   b. 8/9/1835
Reuben Thomas Allen b. 11/15/1837   John Wesley Allen
                                                              b. 6/6/1839

JAMES STONECYPHER BIBLE

James Stonecypher and-----Morris m. 1/1/1821. Children:
James F. Stonecypher b. 9/4/1822   Sarah Stonecypher b. 9/21/1824
Benjamin Stonecypher b. 3/21/1824   William Stonecypher b.
                                                       8/30/1830

WILLIAM JACKSON BIBLE

Ages of William Jackson's children:
Sally F. Jackson b. 8/5/1820   John M. Jackson b. -/7/1824
Pacy Jackson b. 3/26/1822   John M. Jackson b. 11/1/1820
Joseph B. F. Jackson b. 1/31/1829

JAMES F. WHITE BIBLE

James F. White b. 9/15/1826
Martha R. White b. 3/16/1833
J. F. White and M. R. Johnson m. 4/27/1854. Their children:

John M. White b. 2/21/1855   Ann H. White b. 7/4/1861
Eppy White b. 6/15/1856   d. 10/17/1895
Neal J. White b. 4/17/1858   Charles E. White b. 8/24/1863
Sarah C. White b. 6/10/1860   Thomas E. White b. 3/7/1863?

Mary M. White b. 3/16/1870   John M. White d. 12/3/1856

(James F. White Bible contd....)

Martha M. White d. 5/23/1870   Martha W. Cobb b. 5/6/1833
James F. White and Martha J. Cobb m. 9/15/1870
Malissa E. White b. 11/26/1871
Charles E. White and Lucinda Moss m. 11/19/1891

EPPY WHITE BIBLE

From a letter dated Jasper Co., Ga. 8/7/1836 contained inside
Bible, in response to a request from Catherine Herndon, wife of
Eppy White, who owned White Bible in 1836:

George M. Adams, 15 yrs. old 8/16 (1836)
Edward H. Adams, 12 yrs. old 2/7
Sarah Ann Adams, 10 yrs. old 2/2
Catherine Adams age 9 yrs. 3/20
Elizabeth A. Adams age 8 7/10
William Adams age 6 2/2
Rachel Lane age 4 3/19
Martha W. age 1 12/15
Dillard 4 mos. old 4th of this mo. (Aug.)
Sarah E. Baker b. 8/3/1838
Betsy White, wife of Ruben, b. 2/23/1783

Marriages
James Sheeflett and Mildred M. White 9/28/1865
Eppy White and Catherine Duncan 11/12/1865
Elbert McDaniel and Martha Ann White 3/12/1866
James W. hicks and Sarah Catherine White 4/5/1869
Charles E. White and Lucinda Moss 11/19/1891

CHARLES STRONG BIBLE
Owner: Mrs. Henry Harris

Marriages
Charles Strong to Jane Winfrey 4/12/1832
Charles Strong to Adeline Brooks 3/28/1844
John Hill Echols to Sarah Jane Strong 12/19/1854
Thomas H. C. Strong to Susan Jane Strong 12/19/1854
Thomas H. C. Strong to Susan A. Strong 4/16/1867
William Goldsmith Turner to Addie May Echols 1/19/1881
William Conyers Clark to Sarah Strong Echols 1/22/1885
George Pinckney Shingler to Adele Strong Turner 12/23/1908
John St. Claire Brooks to May Belle Clark 11/26/1917
Leila Pope Strong to Rufus L. Moss, Jr. 2/7/1898 Columbus, Miss.
Charles Strong to Susie Meriwether 11/2/1905 Montgomery, Ala.
Elisha Strong to Ann Scott Hill 7/24/1823

Births
First Strong known of in America was William and wife Frances.
Their only child was John. His two children were Sarah, who
married John Thompson and Charles who married Sarah Thompson.
Charles Strong 12/20/1802   Ella Strong 4/4/1845
Jane Strong 10/21/1810   Susie Ada Strong 10/13/1846
Sarah Jane Strong 11/4/1832   Adline Kennon 5/10/1818

129

(Bible of Charles Strong, Births contd....)

Charles Strong 1/8/1764
Elisabeth Strong, dau. of Charles and Sarah Strong 1/1/1787
William Strong, son of above, 9/1788
Elisha Strong, son of above, 2/11/1792
Sarah Key Strong 7/15/1795
Ann Thompson Strong 12/1/1797
Susan Strong 10/16/1799
Charles Strong 12/20/1802 (same child listed above)
Martha Strong 11.7/1805
Nancy Strong 7/7/1814

Leila Pope Echols, dau. of John H. and Sarah J. Echols
    b. 3/5/1857
Anne Hill Echols, dau. of above, b. 3/30/1855
Addie May Echols b. 12/23/1859
John Hill Echols b. 8/28/1861
Sallie Strong Echols b. 3/8/1863
Charles Henry Echols b. 2/8/1865

Ella Strong, dau. of T. H. C. and S. A. Strong b. 1/6/1870
Addie Hill Strong, dau. of Thos. H. C. and Susan A. Strong
    b. 3/31/1871
Adele Strong Turner, dau. of W. Y. and A. M. Turner,
    b.12/20/1881
Sarah Turner, dau. of above, b. 8/3/1883

William White Clark, son of William C. and Sarah S. Clark
    b. 5/30/1886
Watton Conyers Clark, son of above, b. 3/22/1889
May Belle Clark, dau. of above, b. 7/26/1894

Children of Elisha Strong and Ann Scott Hill Strong:

Elisha m. Rebecca Harris
Martin Luther m. Georgia Hill
Sarah d. unmd.
Celeste m. Burwell A. Duncan
Gustavus Adolphus d. unmd
Charles killed in Pickett's charge at Gettysburg
Thomas Hill Charles m. Susan A., dau. of Charles (Strong), the
    bro. of Elisha (Strong).
Georgia m. Richard L. Sykes
Pope d. unmd.

Children of Rufus L. Moss and Leila Strong Moss:

Elizabeth Luckie b. 11/23/1898 m. Henry Harris 4/18/1925. Their
    children:
Mary Emily b. 9/23/1926, d. unmd. 1967
Henry Moss b. 8/13/1929
Elizabeth Strong b. 2/27/1932 (m. William Gettys Carter)

Thomas Strong b. 10/19/1900 m. 1st Sarah Leslie 11/25/1924,
    div., child: Sarah Jane b. 7/16/1926
Thomas Strong b. 10/19/1900 m. 2d Ruby McMahan (Mrs. Wesley) b.
    6/2/1905 m. 12/16/1937. Their children: Patsy Anne b.
    9/24/1938, Thomas Strong b. 4/10/1941

(Rufus Lafayette IV b. 12/24/1902, decd, m. Blanche ----, had one
son: Rufus Lafayette VI m. Sallye Jo---, two daus., Susan and
Sarah)

130

(Charles Strong Bible contd....)

Susan Strong (b. 12/3/1904 m. 1st Harry T. Daniel, Jr., 2d, Julian Deen Clement (no children)

Deaths
Ella Strong, dau. of Charles and Adline Strong, 1/23/1864
William Henry Strong, son of Charles and Jane Strong, 4/29/1864
John Hill Echols, son of Wattro? and Ann Echols 1/10/1866
Ella Strong, dau. of Thomas and Susie Strong, 8/24/1870
Charles, son of Charles and Sarah Strong, 12/10/1870
Addie Hill Sgrong, dau. of T.M.C. and S. A. Strong 7/8/1872
Leila Pope Echols 6/8/1885
Sarah Jane Echols 7/9/1913
John Hills Echols 9/9/1913
William Goldsmith Turner 10/22/1902
Sarah Claude Turner---
Adele Turner Shingler 9/17/1914
May Belle Clark Brookes 10/12/1918
Addie M. Turner 4/20/1920

JOHN S. LINTON BIBLE

John S. Linton b. 2/21/1813, d. 9/10/1891 m. on 5/14/1840,
Cordelia Ann Golding b. 12/20/1818 d. 3/21/1848
John S. Linton and Lucy Ann Hull m. 12/18/1849

Cordelia Ann Linton, wife of John S. Linton and dau. of Thomas
   W. and Susan Golding, d. 3/21/1848, aged 29 yrs., 8 mos., 29
   days
Lucy Ann Linton, wife of John S. Linton and dau. of Dr. Henry and
   Mary A. Hull, d. 6/24/1880

John Sankey Linton, the darling son of John S. and Anne Linton,
   d. 10/1/1857, aged 3 yrs., 5 mos., 2 days
Dau. Julia d. 8/16/1887
John S. Linton d. 9/10/1895
Henry Hull Linton d. 8/13/1926
Annie Linton d. 7/23/1942?
Mary Cordelia Linton (Mamie), dau. of John S. and Cordelia A.
   Linton b. 7/20/1842, d. 11/20/1930
Henry Hull Linton (Hal), son of John S. and Lucy Ann Linton b.
   10/29/1850, d. 8/13/1926
John Sankey, son f John S. and Ann Linton b. 4/29/1854
Julia, dau. of J. S. and L. A. Linton b. 5/2/1861, d. 8/16/1887
Annie Linton b. 5/10/1863
Lucy Linton b. 6/14/1865

JOSEPH BRACKINRIDGE BIBLE
Owner: Milton Page Barr, Marengo Co., Ala.

Marriages
Married 12/23/1804 to Maryann Bigham
Married the second time to Margaret Isebell Gibson 3/30/1814
   Signed--Joseph Brackinridge
Married 8/21/1828 Jane Brackinridge to John Mathers

(Joseph Brackinridge Bible, Marriages contd....)

Married 5/12/1831 Sarah Brackinridge to Merit Morgan
Samuel Brackinridge m. Caroline Mathers wife 6/1/1837
Married 4/30/1845 Lydia Ann Garrard to R. J. Brackenridge
Tabitha Victoria Breckenridge,   dau. of R.J. and L. A.
Brackinridge to D. W. Thompson 9/28/1865
Married 12/22/1881 to S. A. Ward to E. S. Breckenbridge

Death
Mary Ann Brackinridge 1/13/1813
Mary Emanda 2/19/1824
William John Brackinridge 10/2/1835
Margaret Isebell Brackinridge 12/8/1835
Joseph Brackenridge 3/14/1837
William Robert Brackinridge 2/9/1840
Samuel Brackenridge 6/24/1840
Mary Margret 8/19/1840
Joseph L. Brackenridge 5/20/1840
Amtheana Vermela Breckenridge 9/3/1856
Gayns Lewis Garrard Breckenridge 9/5/1846
Babe not named -/15/1857 R. J. B. and L. A. Brackenridge's baby
Polina Breckenridge 4/15/1860
R. J. Breckenridge 5/23/1872

Births
Joseph Brackinridge Sr. 5/31/1777
Mary Ann, first wife, 12/19/1784
Margaret Isabell, second wife, 3/26/1794
James Brackinridge 4/24/1805
Jane Brackinridge 9/25/1808
Sarah Brackinridge 10/20/1811
Samuel Brackinridge 6/1/1815
Joseph Lowry Brackinridge 2/16/1817
Elizabeth Ann Brackinridge 3/3/1819
William John Brackinridge 5/25/1822
Mary Emanda Brackinridge 4/4/1823
Robert Jackson Brackinridge 1/30/1825
Thomas Glenn Brackinridge 12/17/1826
Jefferson Brackinridge 10/14/1828
Mary Margaret Brackinridge 10/23/1830
Josiah Newton Brackinridge 8/29/1832
Ebenezer Brackinridge 12/11/1834
William Robert Brackinridge 11/11/1839
R. J. Brackenridge child - Elvira Blanch b. 7/9/1858
Tabitha Victoria Brackenridge 1/10/1847
Benjamin Franklin Brackenridge 8/12/1848
---Brackenridge 2/3/1850
Gains Lewis Garrard Brackenridge 1/16/1855
The baby not named 1857

ROBERT PRESTON BROOKS BIBLE

Births
Joseph Daniel Brooks, son of Isham Brooks & Serena, b. 5/21/1814
James Henry Brooks, son of Joseph Daniel Brooks and Teresa
   b. Maria Brooks, his wife, 1/12/1850
Teresa Maria Sikes, dau. of John Sikes & Elizabeth, b. 10/12/1811

(Robert Preston Brooks Bible, Births, contd....)

William Sidney Brooks, son of Joseph Daniel Brooks and Teresa
   Maria, his wife, b. 6/11/1852
Robert Augustus Brooks, son of Joseph Daniel Brooks and Teresa
   Maria, his wife, b. 9/26/1842
James Henry Brooks, son of above, b. 9/27/1844
Joseph Wiley Brooks, son of above, b. 4/23/1847

Marriages
Mr. J. H. Brooks, son of Dr. J. D. Brooks and T. M. Brooks, his
   wife, m. Miss Anna M. Moore, dau. of L. M. & M. G. Moore,
   1/7/1873

Deaths
Joseph Daniel Brooks, son of Isham Brooks & Serena, d. 12/25/1868
Robert Augustus Brooks, son of Joseph Daniel Brooks and Teresa
   Maria, his wife, d. 12/23/1862
Joseph Wiley Brooks, son of Joseph Daniel Brooks and Teresa
   Maria, his wife, d. 9/5/1866

Memorandum

James Henry Brooks, son of Dr. J. D. and Mrs. T. M. Brooks, his
   wife, b. 1/12/1850, d. 4/29/1886
Anna M. Brooks, dau. of L. M. and M. G. Moore, wife,
   b. 9/15/1854, d. 1907
Edgar Roland Brooks, son of James Henry and Anna M. Brooks, his
   wife, b. 2/14/1874, d. 1936
Rosa Clifford Brooks, dau. of James Henry and Anna M. Brooks,
   his wife, b. 9/5/1876, d. infancy.
Roland Edgar and Rosa Clifford Brooks were christened by Rev.
   W. R. Foote 6/30/1877
Robert Preston Brooks b. 7/23/1881
Carlton Parks b. 1883, d. 1939
Henry Candler b. 1885, d. 1921

JOHN A. BRADLEY BIBLE

"Mrs. Martha Jameson Meriwether gave me this book in 1816. Mary
Ardis Bradley Weaver."

Births
John A. Bradley 9/4/1773
Margaret Jameson Meriwether, wife of John A. Bradley, 9/1/1776,
   called Peggy. Children of John A. Bradley and Margaret J.:
Mary Ardis Bradley 6/21/1799   Martha J. Bradley 9/9/1805
James I. Bradley 12/26/1800   Francis Meriwether Bradley 5/2/1802
John A. Bradley 12/20/1803   Thomas Lutius Bradley 8/10/1812
                               Ann Marks Bradley 8/171815
Nicholas Meriwether Bradley and Elizabeth Mildred Bradley (twins)
   6/13/1807

Marriages
John A. Bradley and Margaret Jameson Meriwether 6/24/1798.
Childrens Marriages
Mary Ardis Bradley and Isham Weaver 4/5/1820
Ann Marks to Penny---
Elizabeth Mildred to ------Smith (Larkin Smith, Jr.)

133

(John A. Bradley Bible, Marriages contd....)

Martha J. to ---Ward (Robert P. Ward)

Deaths
Francis Meriwether, father of Margaret (Peggy) J. Meriwether
    d. 1/2/1803
Martha J. Meriwether, mother of Peggy J. Meriwether Bradley
    d. 5/29/.1818
Margaret Jamison Bradley, wife of John A. Bradley, d. 3/14/1819
Mary Noil, mother of E. H. Bradley, d. 11/5/1827
John A. Bradley d. 8/2/1828
Elizabeth M. Bradley Smith d. 12/29/1846
Martha Margaret Bradley, consort of Thomas L. Bradley,
    d. 3/23/1844
Thomas L. Bradley d. 10/30/1857
Nicholas Meriwether Bradley d. 12/20/1860
Mary Ardis Bradley Weaver d. 8/22/1867

JAMES BAIRD BIBLE

"Amy Bradley's Bible Bought at the sale of her dearest Brother.
She is to give it to who she pleases at her death. Wrote by
William D. Bradley. The 3rd of May 1828."

Marriages
James Baird and Rebeckah Jackson 1/28/1819
William D. Bradley and Amy Baird 12/24/1818
William Drury Bradley and Clary McLendon 3/2/1843
Toliver Jones and Lucy W. Bradley 6/26/1839
Frances E. Smith and Sarah Bradley 11/28/1842
B. Franklin Bradley and Martha Roberson 11/13/1855 Elbert Co.

Births
James Baird 9/17/1796
Rebecca (Jackson) Baird 8/8/--
William Wyche Baird, son of James and Rebecca, 2/22/1820
Mary Wyneford 6/22/1821
Sophia Amanda Baird 8/28/1822
George Washington Baird 8/28/1824
Benjamin Jackson Baird 9/8/1826

William D. Bradley 1/11/1794
Amy Baird, his wife, 4/7/1794
Lucy Winnefred Bradley 11/15/1821
William Drury Bradley 11/15/1821
Sally Bradley 1/23/1827
Benjamin Franklin Bradley 11/14/1830
Terend Frances Jones, the first of Toliver and L. W. Jones, his
    wife 9/28/1840
Julia Emer Jones 2/1843
William R. Bradley 8/29/1858
Benjamin Franklin Bradley 6/6/1860
William Drury Smith, first child of F. E. and Sarah Smith,
    10/21/1843
William Drury Bradley and Clary Bradley, his wife, first child,
    George Moss Bradley, 12/17/1843
Francis Wyet Smith, second child of F. E. and Sarah Smith,
    9/26/1845

(James Baird Bible, Births, contd....)

Sarah Winefred, 2nd child of W. D. Bradley & Clary, 6/29/1845
Lucy Christian Bradley, third child, 7/11/1846
Amy Frances Bradley 3/2/1848
Sarah W. Smith 5/13/1848

Deaths

William Baird Sr. 8/2/1839	James Baird 10/9/1827,
Mrs. Winefred Baird 8/17/1844	age 31
William D. Bradley Sr. 9/12/1848	Rebecah Baird 10/11/1827
Amy Frances Bradley 6/1/1849	Sally Baird 10/17/1826,
Amy Bradley 4/5/1855	age 21
B. F. Bradley 6/22/1861	George W. Baird 8/8/1844
Mary Wineford Baird 7/16/1826, age 5	Benjamin J. Baird 8/12/1844

FRANCIS MERIWETHER BIBLE*
Owner: J. B. Jenkins, Albany, Ga.

Marriages
Francis Meriwether, son of Col. Nichlas Meriwether of Virginia
came to Ga. in 1784. Francis was b. 10/31/1737, d. 1/2/1803, m.
abt 1765 to Martha Jameson who d. 5/29/1818.

Births (Children)
Thomas b. 1766 m. Rebecca Matthews
Valentine b. 1768 m. Barbara Crosby
Mary b. 1770 m. William Barnett
Elizabeth b. 1772 m. William Matthews
Mildred b. 1774 m. Joel Barnett
Margaret b. 1776 d. 3/14/1819 m. Dr. John A. Bradley
D. Nancy b. 1778 m. William Glenn
Lucy b. 1780 m. Grover Howard
Sarah b. 1782 m. James Olive
Nicholas b. 1784 lived in Montgomery, Ala.

Deaths
Francis Meriwether 1/2/1803
Martha Jameson Meriwether Bradley, wife of Dr. John A. Bradley,
    3/14/1819
Martha Jameson Meriwether, wife of Francis Meriwether, 5/29/1818
    Francis Meriwether was educated at William and Mary College
                    (Williamsburg, Va.)

SAMUEL FLEMING BIBLE
Owner: Mrs. Phillips Seebach, Louisville, Ga.

Deaths
Samuel Fleming Jr. 8/29/1847, age 24 yrs., 6 mos., 4 days
James Fleming 2/9/1858, age 32 yrs., 2 mos., 9 days
Samuel Fleming, Sr. 9/27/1860, age 78 yrs.
Elvirah Fleming 10/15/1869, age 86 yrs.
Laird Fleming 12/17/1873
Mary Ann Green 11/16/1882
Oliver Fleming 10/9/1885

*See also p. 391.   135

(Samuel Fleming Bible, Deaths, contd....)

Martha Jane Fleming 11/5/1887
Allen Fleming 5/5/1889
Benjamin Franklin Fleming 5/19/1888

Marriages
Oliver Fleming 11/30/1829
Allen Fleming 11/1841
Mary Ann Fleming 11/5/1855
Laird Fleming 2/11/1844
James Fleming 1/18/1855
Benjamin Franklin Fleming 4/8/1856

Births
Oliver Fleming 3/23/1808   Mary Ann Fleming 4/30/1810
Allen Fleming 7/2/1812   Martha Jane Fleming 3/16/1815
William Fleming 7/22/1817   Laird Fleming 2/21/1820
Samuel Fleming 2/25/1823   James Fleming 12/1/1825

T. M. FLORENCE BIBLE
Owner: Mrs. Emaline Carpenter
Box 34, Madison, Fla. 32340

John L. Blalock b. 8/14/1797 d. 1/6/1849, age 51 yrs., 4 mos.,
    22 days
Prudence Blalock b. 7/8/1799
Tolivar Florence, son of Thomas Florence, b. 1/9/1827
Margaret Florence b. 10/29/1829, d. 6/14/1904
Mary L. Blalock b. 8/10/1856 Watkinsville, Ga., d. 1/4/--, age 91
James Blalock b. & d. Lee Co., Ga., 21 yrs. old.
Mrs. jane Standard, sister of T. J. Blalock, d. 12/4/1907, age 85
Tolivar Florence d. 1/2/1887
Sara A. Simmons d. 4/7/1886
Mamie L. Caloway nee Blalock d. 1/7/--, age 91
Thomas J. Blalock, son of John L. Blalock, b. 5/22/1838,
    d. 11/7/1915
Alonzo L. Blalock, son of Thomas J. Blalock, b. 3/17/1862,
    d. 7/17/1946

ISAAC CUTHBERT COLLIER BIBLE

Marriages
Robert M. Collier to Amanda Greene who d. 11/22/1864, 12/24/1835
Robert T. Collier d. 6/29/1862 Savannah, Ga. m. 5/6/1856 Sarah
    E. Stafford, d. 7/14/1854
Isaac C. Collier 6/24/1844-7/11/1908 m. 12/21/1865 Sallie
    Elizabeth Means b. 6/10/1844
Jena Cuthbert Collier, son of Sallie E. and Isaac C. Collier
    was b. 11/11/1866

Deaths
William V. Collier 5/9/1849   Obediah G. Collier 11/16/1853

ZADOCK COOK BIBLE Of Clarke Co. (now Oconee Co.)
Owner: Mrs. J. E. Cook, Athens, Ga.

Children of Mark and Rachel Cook:

Mary Cook b. 1/14/1764   Elizabeth Cook b. 11/1/1771
Zadock Cook b. 2/18/1769

Zadock Cook b. 2/18/1769, his wife, Betsy, b. 12/1/1773
Rebeckah, their dau., b. 9/29/1794
Mary b. 11/20/1798
Pernal b. 6/4/1801
Nathan b. 10/1/1803
Betsy b. 4/16/1806
Nancy, dau. of Zadock and Betsy, b. 8/9/1792
Zadock Jr. b. 5/12/1808
William b. 6/24/1810

MOSES TULLIS BIBLE
Owner: Mrs. Zola S. Hardy
1217 Rice Ranch Rd.
Santa Maria, Ca. 93454

Moses Tullis Sr. b. 2/8/1777 m. 12/24/1800 d. 1/5/1844
Polley Blalock, his wife, b. 10/25/1783
John Blalock Tullis b. 10/27/1801

Moses Tullis Sr. b. 2/8/1777 m. 12/24/1800 d. 11/11/1846
Moses Tullis (Jr.) b. 6/9/1801 m. 8/10/1826 d. 10/27/1869
Elizabeth Tullis b. 10/22/1808 m. 11/17/1825 d. 8/27/1830
Elijah Tullis b. 8/25/1810
Gipson Tullis b. 3/10/1813 m. 11/8/1835 Penelopy Mayo
Catherine Tullis b. 11/8/1815 m. 12/10/1835 Benjamin Langford
Thomas Jefferson Tullis b. 8/3/1818 d. 9/24/1818
James Monroe Tullis b. 6/22/1822
Martha Tullis b. 3/8/1824 m. 12/23/1841 Alfred Cook
Newel Hill Tullis b. 3/4/1828

COOPER BIBLE
Owner: Mrs. J. Tom White
Dublin, Ga.

Maria Cooper b. 2/21/1816 m. Zachariah Haynes 6/9/1831
Thomas W. Cooper m. Frances I. S. Falligant 3/2/1837
Peter Goodwin Cooper m. Sarah I. Maher 7/4/1837
Aaron C. Fitts m. Lydia Ann Hood 2/19/1835
Peter G. Cooper m. Anna Maira Brownjohn 3/13/1840
James B. Norris m. Mrs. Lydia Ann Fitts 5/1/1839

THOMAS FLORENCE BIBLE

Great grandmother Florence was Jane Lashbrook
Grandfather Thomas Florence b. 3/5/1789 d. 6/3/1863, m. twice,
1st Lucy Blalock - eleven children, 2nd Ann Blalock - six
children

JESSE CRENSHAW BIBLE

Jesse Crenshaw b. 9/11/1755
Precious Cain Crenshaw b. 2/6/1758
Patience Crenshaw b. 5/15/1779
Miles Crenshaw b. 2/14/1784 d. 10/26/1817
Maryan Nancy Crenshaw b. 12/26/1787
William Henry Crenshaw b. 6/4/1790

William Clinton, son of Miles and Patience Crenshaw, b. 11/8/1811

JAMES DANIELL BIBLE

Children of James Daniell:

Jesse Daniell b. 12/2/1754
Sarah Daniell b. 5/4/1756
Jose. Daniel b. 12/6/1757
Levi Daniell b. 12/21/1754

Mary Daniell b. 2/20/1775
Jesse Daniell Austin b. 9/9/1794
James Daniell b. 7/11/1797
Caty Daniell b. 3/4/1799

ISAAC CHIDSEY BIBLE

Children of Isaac and Sarah Bradley Chidsey:

Births
Sarah Chidsey 1/28/1753 m. Levi Pardee
Samuel Chidsey 8/28/1754 d. 1/22/1761
Abigail Chidsey 10/5/1758 m. John Goodsell
Lydia Chidsey 5/8/1761 m. 1781 Edmund Bradley
Caleb Chidsey m. Rebecca Page
Annorah Chidsey 7/3/1771 m. William Smith, son of Isaac and Mabel
     Smith b. 5/25/1765
Deborah Chidsey 1/3/1768 m. Nathan Godard
Samuel Chidsey 4/24/1773 m. Betsy Holt
Isaac Chidsey 1776-10/23/1779
Isaac Chidsey 1731-1814 was Rev. Soldier in Lt. Bradley's Co. of
Matrosses, Conn. He enlisted 4/13/1778, and served 8 mos. and 23
days. (Report of Adj. Gen.)

138

T. D. DISMUKE BIBLE
Owner: Mrs. J. Tom White, Dublin, Ga.

Anna Sophia Haynes m. T. D. Dismuke 1/25/1859
Anna Sophia Haynes, dau. of Zachariah and Maria Haynes, b.
   7/24/1838
Minnie Lee Dismuke b. 10/13/1860
Susan Maria Dismuke b. 1/23/1856
William Haynes Dismuke ---
Rosamond Cooper Dismuke ---
Amanda Pearl Dismuke ---
Minnie Lee Dismuke d. 9/13/1861, age 11 mos.

JAMES DOTTERY BIBLE
Of Hall Co. and S. C.
Owner: Mrs. J. W. Eberhart, Athens, Ga.

James Dottery b. 8/18/1822
Susan C. Stone b. 11/29/1827 m. 9/9/1847
John Eberhart m. Mary Dottery 11/7/1867
John Dottery m. Sally Royal 8/6/1874

John M. Dottery b. 6/19/1848
Mary Elizabeth Dottery b. 12/24/1849
William Green Dottery b. 1/27/1852
John W. Dottery b. 6/25/1859
Minia F. Dottery b. 9/12/1868
John W. Dottery b. 5/27/1871
Robert J. P. Dottery b. 10/13/1874
Faney C. Dottery b. 7/31/1876

Deaths
William Green Dottery 8/28/1853, age 19 mos.
Minia F. Eberhart 10/17/1868
Infant babe of John and Sally Dottery b. 8/6 d. 8/10/1875

DAVID EBERHART BIBLE Of Hall Co.
Owner: Mrs. J. W. Eberhart, Athens, Ga.

John, son of David and Susannah Eberhart, b. 9/7/1783
Jacob, son of above, b. 10/26/1786
Joseph, son of above, b. 7/3/1788
Ann Woods Griffeth b. 8/29/1793

JAMES K. EIDSON BIBLE Of Clarke Co.
Owner: Mrs. W. G. Yarbrough, Athens, Ga.

James K. Eidson b. 3/8/1848
Martha M. Wise b. 12/6/1852 Their children:

Minnie R. Eidson b. 12/6/1875   John Deward Eidson b. 9/14/1883
Mary Blanche Eidson b. 6/3/1876   Hattie L. Eidson b. 2/13/1885
Arthur W. Eidson b. 3/11/1878   Maudie Eidson b. 3/11/1887
James Ernest Eidson b. 9/17/1881 Wilmot K. Eidson b. 5/11/1889
                                  George P. Eidson b. 10/19/1892

James K. Eidson of Oglethorpe Co. m. Martha M. Wise of Clarke Co.
  2/20/1872 at Sherwood Wise's, by Franklin McCroy
Mary Blanche Eidson m. Robert J. Trible 2/9/1893
Minnie R. Eidson m. Wiley Godfrey 10/4/1899

               WILLIAM JOSEPH ELDER BIBLE
         Owner: Mrs. Alice Elder, Watkinsville, Ga.

Births
William Joseph Elder 7/18/1844   Martha Pearl Elder 9/11/1872
Elizabeth Ann Elder 7/20/1848   Lilly May Elder 8/3/1880
Clara Lee Elder 8/5/1867   Omer Franklin Elder 9/2/1886
William Shannon Elder 3/30/1869   Martha Belle Elder 3/16/1912

Marriages
William Joseph Elder to Elizabeth Ann Osborn 5/28/1864
William Joseph Elder to Cora L. Anderson 8/7/1890
William Joseph Elder to Alice Shelnutt 12/2/1902

Deaths
Lilly May Elder 11/24/1884   Clara Lee Elder 7/30/1889
Mrs. Elizabeth Ann Elder 8/6/1889 Mrs. Cora L. Elder 11/10/1896
                                  William Joseph Elder 4/12/1920

               JOSEPH ESPEY Of Clarke Co.
         Owner: Mrs. John Carlton, Athens, Ga.

Joseph Espey b. 12/7/1771 d. 11/13/1848
Mary Epsey b. 3/26/1774 d. 3/25/1849
Joseph Espey and Mary Barnett m. 9/26/1799 Their children:

Martha Espey b. 9/27/1800
Elizabeth Ann Espey b. 2/19/1802 d. 5/13/1865
Tirzah Espey b. 11/16/1803
Martha Espey b. 10/20/1803
Tirzah Mitchell d. 5/6/1839
Elizabeth A. Carlton d. 5/13/1865

                        140

SILAS FLOYD BIBLE

Silas Floyd, son of Urian and Elizabeth Floyd, b 3/22/1790
Martha Dorsey, wife, b. 1786. Their Children:

Eliza Ann b. 6/4/1814   Cherry Margaret b. 2/9/1827
Nancy Smith b. 11/16/1815   Susan Isabella L. Young b. 12/10/1828
James Uriah b. 11/4/1817   Silas Dorsey Jr. b. 11/23/1830
Elizabeth b. 8/12/1819   Caroline b. 12/9/1832
Sarah Crowel b. 4/18/1821   Louise Virginia b. 4/25/1834
Mary Dorsey b. 3/22/1823   Thomas LaFatte b. 3/23/1836
Martha b. 1/12/1825   Amanda Cornelia Flourney
                                   b. 11/18/1837

ISAAC J. GILES BIBLE
Owner: J. W. Giles, Athens, Ga.

Births
Isaac J. Giles 3/5/1833 d. 7/25/1889
Mary E. 2/7/1828

Roxey A. Giles 7/16/1858   Isaac J. 9/20/1862
James W. Giles 4/27/1861   Mary E. 7/6/1869

Deaths
Roxey A. Giles 12/17/1887   Mary E. Giles 8/1896
Mary E. Giles 6/18/1890   Isaac J. Giles 7/20/1914

WILLIAM GLENN Of Oglethorpe Co.*
Owner: George H. Howard, Comer, Ga.

William Glenn m. Elizabeth 9/3/1798
Asa J. Howard m. Elizabeth Gilmer Glenn 11/21/1822
Robert Howard m. Polly Glenn 12/19/1822
John A. Glenn m. Matilda Graham 1/22/1829
Minor U. Stephens m. Mildred L. Gleen 8/3/1852
William Glenn b. 3/8/1766
John Allen Glenn, son of William and Elizabeth, b. 12/19/1800
Elizabeth Gilmer Glenn b. 8/2/1802
Polly Glenn b. 6/22/1805
Mildred Louisa Glenn b. 9/3/1807
Rebecca Glenn b. 12/3/1810
William Hamilton Glenn, son of John and Matilda Glenn,
   b. 10/22/1829

Deaths
Polly Howard 7/24/1827, 22 yrs., 22 days
Mary Elizabeth Howard 7/18/1827, 5 mos., 6 days
John A. Glenn 10/2/1853, 53 yrs., 10 mos., 11 days
Mildred L. Stephens 10/11/1855, 48 yrs., 1 mo., 8 days
Rebecca Glenn Butter 1/25/1894
Elizabeth Gilmer Howard 1/6/1883

*See also p. 429.   141

(William Glenn Bible, Deaths, contd....)

Elizabeth Glenn, wife of William, 12/22/1850, 83 yrs.
William Glenn Sr. 9/2/1857, 91 yrs., 5 mos., 24 days

BERRY AND SYNTHA GORDON BIBLE
Of Banks Co., Ga.
Owner: W. B. Cash, Bogart, Ga.

Marriages
A. D. Wilbanks to Martha C. Gorden 1/1/1868
Berry Gorden to Sarah J. Bradley 3/19/1843

Births
Berry Gorden 11/24/1820   Henry W. 6/17/1854
Sarah J. 9/23/1824   Josiah F. 8/16/1852
George W. 4/30/1845   James M. 3/14/1856
Lewis J. 5/24/1846   Sarah J. 1/16/1858
Martha C. 10/23/1847   Asbury B. 1/27/1860
William T. 1/29/1849   Crawford Davis 2/9/1862
Syntha A. 5/13/1850   Robert Lee 7/19/1867?

JEREMIAH G. GRAY Of Clarke Co.
Owner: C. D. Booth, Athens, Ga.

Jeremiah G. Gray b. 7/28/1801
Naomi Gray, his wife, b. 3/8/1799, m. 12/1822 Their Children:

Elizabeth Gray b. 7/11/1825   Jeremiah Griffin Gray b. 12/20/1838
Evaline Gray b. 7/13/1827   Frances Ann Gray b. 10/3/1842
William Gray b. 10/16/1829
Susannah Caroline Gray b. 12/2/1830
Evaline Gray d. 7/28/1834
Frances Ann Gray d. 7/20/1865

George Gray, husband of Anna, d. 12/15/1806 at his plantation in
   Clarke Co., Ga.
Ann Gray, wife of George, d. 12/26/1821, age 73, at her plantation
   in Clarke Co., Ga.

MARION WATSON BIBLE
Owner: A. J. Watson
127 Springdale St., Athens, Ga.

Births
Janes W. Watson 5/8/1850   Martha T. Watson 4/23/1862
Millard F. Watson 10/17/1852 Marion C. Watson 11/4/1862
Mary T. Watson 10/22/1854   Adoniram Jackson (Jud written over)
Susan G. Watson 3/22/1857   Watson 2/16/1869
Nancy A. Watson 9/15/1859

(Marion Watson Bible contd....)

Grandchild:

Gracie G. Watson b. Watkinsville the 28, 1885
Marrian Watson b. 1/12/1823 near Greenville
E. A. Watson nee Norton b. Oglethorpe Co., Ga. 8/26/1823

Deaths
E. A. Watson 6/3/1902
Marrian Watson 6/1/1903
  Buried at Winterville, Ga.

JOHN PINKNEY HANDCOCK & SUSAN PEELER HANDCOCK BIBLE
Of Clarke Co., Ga.
Owner: Mrs. J. H. Elder, Athens, Ga.

Marriages
Fances Cynthia Handcock to James Howard Elder 3/12/1882

Births
John P. Handcock 3/15/1812   Benjamin A. Handcock 5/1/1855
Susan Handcock 7/2/1821   Cynthia F. Handcock 2/1/1857
Edward Linsy Handcock 7/11/1851   Cathanna Handcock 1/19/1859
Mary D. Handcock 8/24/1853   Sallie J. Handcock 10/23/1860
                                                  d. 9/8/1863
                                    Emily J. Handcock 2/10/1863

"Edmund L. Handcock, his hand and pen"

WILLIAM HARDWICK BIBLE

(Father of Nancy who was 2d wife of James Barrow of
Milledgeville, Ga.)

William Hardwick b. 6/27/1727 d. 2/24/1803
Keziah, his wife, b. 1727, d. 8/18/1787
James Hardwick b. 12/16/1750, d. in War Furgeson´s defeat
Martha Hardwick b. 12/13/1752
Hancy Hardwick b. 4/4/1755
Nancy Hardwick b. 1/6/1758, d. 1/18/1814
William Hardwick b. 3/17/1760
Molley Hardwick b. 3/5/1762, d. infant
Molley Hardwick b. 7/12/1763
George Hardwick b. 1/31/1766
Garland Hardwick b. 5/22/1768
Peggy Hardwick b. 6/7/1773

143

Marriages

Thomas Y. (Young) Brent and Jennie Clements, dau. of Davis Smith, 5/1/1867 Monroe Co., Ga.
Taylor Y. Brent, 1st son of above, to Annie Tindall 1/29/1893, in Macon, Ga.
Jack Innis Brent, son of above, b. 5/1/1893
Harry Tindall Brent, 1st son of Taylor Y. and Annie T. Brent, to Ruth Helen Newman 11/29/1917
Jane Kate Brent, dau. of Taylor Y. and Annie T. Brent, to Wilmer C. Haynes 2/19/1921 in Atlanta, Ga.

Davis Smith to Hannah Tuttle 7/23/1816 (Laurens Co.)
Davis Smith to Elizabeth D. (Dixon) Jordan 1/6/1820 (Laurens Co.)
Mary W. Smith to Urbane Billingsley 8/13/1840
James Richard Rollins to Jennie Ruth Newman (Wookie) Brent, dau. of Harry Tindall Brent and Helen Newman, 11/30/1939 Conyers, Ga.
William Madison Linnes? to Jacquelyn Brent, dau. of Harry Tindall Brent and Helen Newman, 12/18/1948, in Camden Co.

Births

Davis Smith 9/5/1791 - His children:

William Frankling Smith 1/29/1817	James Smith 2/14/1830
Martha Franklin Smith 12/29/1820	Davis Smith Jr. 5/20/1826
Miranda Smith 3/23/1822	Judson Smith 7/26/1833
Mary Warren Smith 4/11/1823	Jane Smith 3/21/1836
Tyrus Thomas Smith 7/25/1824	
John Dickson Smith 5/10/1824	
Elizabeth Smith 6/14/1832	

Taylor Y. Brent, son of Thomas Y. and Jennie Brent 2/11/1869 Brent, Ga.
Jack Innis Brent, son of Thomas Y. and Jennie Brent, 12/18/1871
Lucy Palmer Brent, dau. of Taylor Y. and Annie Brent, 5/9/1894 Brent, Ga.
Harry Tindall Brent, son of Taylor Y. and Annie Brent, 7/29/1876
Minnie Lee Brent, dau. of Taylor Y. and Annie Brent, 1/11/1897
Howard Crumbley Brent, son of Taylor Y. and Annie Brent, 12/25/1899
Jennie Kate Brent, dau. of Taylor Y. and Annie Brent, 1/29/1903

Deaths

Hannah, wife of Davis Smith 2/15/1818
Martha Franklin Smith 10/5/1821
John Dixon Smith 8/30/1829
Mary W. Billingsley 6/4/1841
William H. Smith 6/30/1842
Elizabeth D., wife of Davis Smith, 3/26/1867
Judson Smith 8/6/1864
Davis Smith 5/14/1868, age 76 yrs.
Jennie Brent, wife of Thomas Y. Brent, d. Ft. McPherson, Ga., 10/12/1903
Jack Innis Brent 6/5/1908 New York City

(Thomas Young Brent Bible, Deaths, contd....)

Taylor Young Brent, son of Thomas Y. and Jennie Brent, Forsyth,
Ga., 3/20/1934
Lucy Palmer Brent, dau. of Taylor Y. and Annie Brent, 5/3/1896
Minnie Sue, dau. of Taylor Y. and Annie Brent, 2/1/1897
Howard C. Brent, son of Taylor Y. and Annie Brent, 5/11/1959
Tonzoulez, Texas

ALLEY BIBLE
Owner: Shade Alley
Clarkesville, Ga.

Births

Mary Augustia Alley 5/15/1844   Howell L. Alley 6/26/1779
Onie Alley 1/29/1774   Polly Alley 12/20/1781
Winefred Alley 1/25/1776   James P. Alley 12/1/1783
John H. Allen 12/28/1778
Georgia Ann Habersham Alley 3/28/1843

SHEPARD GRIFFIN BIBLE

Births
Shepard Griffin 11/22/1814   Wiley F. Griffin 12/29/1845
Mary Ann Griffin 2/20/1812   Fanny R. T. Griffin 9/22/1848
William E. Griffin 4/16/1836   Waldon W. Griffin 12/28/1850
John H. M. Griffin 10/30/1833   Amanda Gordon Griffin 4/11/1853
Mary H. Griffin 1/6/1840   Laura Armstrong Griffin 9/8/1855
Burten B. Griffin 12/13/1841   Gordon B. Griffin 7/29/1864
Margaret A. E. Griffin 1/3/1844   William E. Griffin 5/23/1864

Shepard Griffin m. Mary Armstrong 5/12/1835

C. E. GROOVER BIBLE
Owner: C. T. Tillman
Quitman, Ga.

Births
Sarah R. Groover 9/13/1813   Agnes A. Groover 7/1820
Julia E. Groover 4/17/1818   Charles E. Groover 3/13/1821
Saphina R. Groover 12/16/1811   Samuel E. Groover 9/22/1823
Amanda R. Groover 5/12/1816   Daniel R. Groover 5/12/1825

Sarah R., mother of C. E. Groover, d. 4/30/1858, age 70 yrs.
Charles E. Groover d. 7/5/1877, age 56 yrs.
C. E. Groover and Eliza E. Tillman m. 11/11/1852

145

JOHN R. GRUBBS BIBLE
Owner: Mrs. C. B. Sewell
Lavonia, Ga.

John R. Grubbs and Francis E. Grubbs m. 11/1/1860

Births
John R. Grubbs 7/13/1834   Francis E. Grubbs 4/2/1845
Florence Matilda Grubbs 7/31/1862

Deaths
John R. Grubbs 5/1/1863   Florence Matilda Grubbs 9/14/1865

LEVI HARRELL BIBLE
Owner: Mrs. J. D. Humphreys

Births
Levi Harrell 9/16/1777   Samuel Harrell 4/13/1821
Elizabeth Harrell 10/16/1794   Elizabeth Harrell 9/28/1823
    Their Children: Levi H. Harrell 12/20/1825
Isaac Harrell 1/13/1809   John W. Harrell 3/11/1827
William Harrell 7/27/1811   Nancy Harrell 1/13/1830
Polley Harrell 4/5/1813   Catharine Harrell 11/6/1832
Lovett L. Harrell 3/6/1815   Needham M. Harrell 12/27/1833
Sarah Harrell 3/4/1817   Joanna Harrell 12/24/1835
Wright W. Harrell 2/11/1819   Elvey Harrell 2/19/1838

WILLIAM H. HARRIS BIBLE
Owner: Mrs. Thomas Arrington
Quitman, Ga.

William H. Harris b. 9/24/1823 m. Sarah A. King 9/25/1857
Sarah A. King b. 3/5/1829 Talbotton, Ga.
William Harris d. 5/13/1864 Columbus, Ga.
Sarah A. Harris d. 6/6/1869 Columbus, Ga.

ISAAC HOLLAND BIBLE
Owner: Mrs. Evelyn Gilbert
Columbus, Ga.

Births
Isaac Holland 4/13/1770-9/1/1790
Samuel Holland 6/21/1791   Amelia (nee Brewington)
John Holland 5/12/1792   Holland 9/10/1772

146

William Holland 8/3/1802   Hetty Cale Holland 5/28/1793
James Holland 12/27/1804   Hannah Holland 8/16/1794
Orlando Holland 9/30/1806   Nancy Holland 3/20/1799
Arestus Holland 4/9/1813   Amelia Brewington Holland
                                       11/7/1800
                                  Elmina Holland 1/9/1809
                                  Julia Ann Holland 3/22/1811
                                  Cynthia Holland 5/6/1816

Maria Louisa Holland b. 3/16/1839 in Chambers Co., Ala. m. John
Wesley Cargill, Jr., b. 11/19/1833 Laurens Dist., S. C.

                WILLIAM JENKINS BIBLE Of Harris Co.
                Owner: B. F. Lancaster, Atlanta, Ga.

William Jenkins b. 2/1802, joined Church abt 1828 and m. (abt
1825), d. 2/12/1878
Jane Jenkins d. 2/3/1891
(rest of Bible torn out)

                        STERLING JENKINS

Births   Deaths
Willis Jenkins 2/24/1809   Sterling Jenkins 2/4/1812
Sterling L. Jenkins 9/29/1810   Willis C.Jenkins 12/4/1860
William T. Jenkins 5/8/1822
Sterling Jenkins, Jr. 5/6/1781
Martha G. Jenkins 4/5/1789

                JOHN AND ALICE MOORE LAWSON BIBLE

Births
Col. John Lawson 1731
Alice Moore --
                        Their Children:

Roger Lawson 1757   Marry Barry Lawson 1789
Maj. Roger Lawson 1786   Violet Lawson 1796
Andrew Lawson 1785   John Gamble Lawson 1799
Hannah Lawson 1787

Col. John Lawson m. Alice Moore
Hannah Lawson m. Archie McIntyre
Marry Barry Lawson m. Frank Kirby

                              147

ELIJAH AMOS, JR. BIBLE

Elijah M. Amos, Jr. b. 11/27/1817 m. Lucinda Ansley 12/21/1841
Lucinda Ansley b. 11/1/1818

Births of Children:
Charles Joseph Amos 12/19/1842   Eugenia A. Amos 2/3/1853
John Elijah Amos 3/13/1845   Helena Amos 7/4/1855
Wm. Baxter Amos 8/21/1847   Emma Amos 10/30/1857
Edgar Amos 3/12/1850   Marianne Amos 1/14/1860

RICHARD FRETWELL BIBLE
Owner: Mrs. E. C. McDowell
Social Circle, Ga.

Births
Richard Fretwell 12/24/1752. His Children:
Leonard Fretwell 1/11/1789   Nancy Fretwell 6/24/1822
Mary Fretwell 5/4/1791   Elizabeth Fretwell 5/13/1824
Richard Fretwell 11/11/1811   William Fretwell 3/13/1826
Martha Fretwell 2/16/1814   Phillip Fretwell 9/27/1826
Frances Fretwell 9/25/1816   Mary Rebecca Whiterspoon
Leonard Fretwell, Jr. 3/4/1819   Fretwell 10/2/1831

REUBEN GARLAND BIBLE

Reuben Henry Garland 3/25/1836-11/17/1909
Elizabeth Varner Head b. 1/8/1833   Their Children:

Births
Sara Ann Elizabeth 10/9/1857   Reuben Pitt 12/9/1867
Henry Jackson 4/19/1861   James J. 6/22/1869
Fannie Lloyd 7/19/1864   John White 8/29/1871

GILBERT GAY BIBLE Of Fayette Co.

Gilbert Gay b. 2/20/1771
Levise, his wife, b. 12/27/1769   Their Children:

Births
Nancy 9/5/1794   Levise 8/12/1802   Gilbert 11/26/1809
Thomas B. 5/15/1797   Isaac P. 12/14/1804   Henry M. 3/9/1812
Elizabeth 1/22/1800   Dicey 3/22/1807   Sophia 7/31/1814

Gilbert Devane d. 7/3/1823

SAMUEL BECKHAM BIBLE *
Owner: Mrs. Pensacola Musgrove
Atlanta, Georgia

Marriages
Samuel Beckham, son of Simon and Susan Beckham, b. 11/24/1760
m. 2/18/1790 Elizabeth Houghton, dau. of Joshua and Nancy
Hougton, 12/18/1769-1/31/1805. He d. 11/2/1825
Nancy F. Beckham b. 6/18/1792 m. Mr. Mitchell, dau., Elizabeth m.
William Rogers 12/24/1829
Susan C. Beckham m. Mr. Burch. Two daus., Susan m. Benjamin F.
Malone in Columbus, Ga. and Addie m. Mr. Musgrove and had four
children: Emma, Susan, Pensacola, and Ed.

Births

Children of Samuel and Elizabeth H. Beckham:

Nancy F. Beckham 6/18/1792   Erasmus G. Beckham 4/3/1798
Mary B. Beckham 10/11/1794   Susan C. Beckham 4/13/1800
Elizabeth H. Beckham 11/24/1796   Albert G. Beckham 6/18/1802

Deaths
Samuel D. B. Mitchell 7/25/1807   Andrew A. E. Mitchell
8/14/1825
Erasmus G. Beckham 1/11/1820

DR. & MRS. JAMES MCFADDEN GASTON BIBLE

Marriages
Joseph Gaston to Jinney Brown 4/20/1790
John Brown Gaston to Polly Buford McFadden 3/4/1824

Births
John Brown Gaston 1/22/1791   Richard Trapier Brunby 8/7/1804
James McFadden Gaston 12/24/1824   Mary Martha Brevard 5/27/1806

Deaths
John Brown Gaston, M. D. 1863   Prof. R. T. Brunby 10/6/1875
Polly Buford Gaston 8/7/1886   Mrs. Mary Brevard Brunby
                                       10/5/1875

HARDY DURHAM BIBLE
Owner: Mrs. Frederick Davis Wimberly

Hardy Durham b. 9/8/1786
Caroline b. 7/22/1817
Samuel, father of Hardy Durham, d. 1794

*See also p. 397. 149

(Hardy Durham Bible contd....)

Mary Durham d. 6/15/1794
Caroline Wimberly, wife of H. S. Wimberly and dau. of H. & S.
Durham, d. 3/1864
Laura Lawson Wimberly, dau. of Henry S. and Caroline Wimberly,
b. 10/19/1846

GEORGE W. AND DORA A. EDMONDSON BIBLE
Owner: Mrs. E. T. Hines, Bainbridge, Ga.

Ella N., dau. of George W. and Dora A. Edmondson, b. 12/15/1855
Ella, inf. dau. of above, d. 8/9/1856
George W. Edmondson d. 6/2/1888
Dora N. Edmondson d. 9/4/1900

WILLIAM STANHOPE ERWIN BIBLE
Clarkesville, Ga.

William S. Erwin m. Ruth Sevier Clark 11/27/1867

Births
Joseph A. Erwin 10/30/1868
George Phillip Erwin 11/9/1870
William Stanhope Erwin 3/12/1873

ABEL FARRAR BIBLE Of Jasper Co.*
Owner: Mrs. Mary Farrar Blackwell
Monticello, Ga.

Abel Farrar b. 11/13/1850
Mary Jane Turk Farrar b. 12/16/1849
Otis Farrar b. 10/30/1877
Mary Farrar b. 3/4/1880
Abel Farrar m. M. J. Turk 11/22/1876
M. J. Farrar d. 5/4/1915, age 65 yrs., 4 mos.

MAJOR WILLIAM POWELL FARRAR BIBLE
Owner: Miss Lilla Odom, Putnam, Ga.

Major William Powell Farrar 1801-1861 was from Mecklenburg Co.,
Va. to Putnam Co., Ga. in 1832. He was b. Mecklenburg Co., Va.,
d. Atlanta, Ga.
Thomas Mathis b. 1756 S. C. d. 1829 Hancock Co. Had dau., Nancy
Mathis

*See also p. 226.

WILLIAM FARRIS BIBLE
Owner: Mrs. H. B. Herrin
Dalton, Ga.

William Farris m. Martha 10/11/1810

Births
William Farris 12/23/1782   Nancy C. Farris 5/30/1820
Martha 6/16/1794   Samuel K. Farris 9/25/1822
Agnes Farris 11/6/1811   Mary T. Farris 1/13/1825
Richard C. Farris 4/11/1814   Harvy W. Farris 2/14/1827
Abram S. Farris 7/1/1816   Edward B. Farris 1/11/1829
Samuel C. Farris 6/15/1819   Martha Farris -/11/1831

JOHN THRASHER BIBLE

John Thrasher b. 1761 m. Susan Barton, had ten children:

An infant d. 1788   David Thrasher b. 1796
Barton Thrasher b. 1790   John Thrasher b. 1800
Ruth Thrasher b. 1792   Frances Thrasher b. 1801
Elizabeth Thrasher b. 1793   Susan Thrasher b. 1802
Isaac Thrasher b. 1794   Mary Thrasher b. 1804

Susan Barton Thrasher d. 4/21/1837
John Thrasher d. 6/5/1844

JOHN FOSTER BIBLE

John Foster b. 12/23/1770
Margaret Foster b. 5/7/1775   Their Children:

Births
Mary Foster 9/27/1796   James Kirkwood Foster 8/18/1809
William Foster 12/1798   Samuel M. Foster 1/15/1812
Maleny Foster 5/14/1801   Robert & Margaret Foster 6/2/1815
John Fletcher Foster 1/20/1804   George W. Foster 2/24/1818
Nancy Foster 11/5/1806   John Steven Foster 11/5/1833
                                  Julia Ann Hester 7/7/1836
                                  Martha Foster Hester 12/7/1837

Frances Thrasher, wife of John Fletcher Foster, b. 2/19/1801 m.
4/28/1829. Children:
John Cloud Foster b. 2/17/1830
Susan Margaret Foster b. 5/18/1836
John Fletcher Foster m. Margaret Furlow 3/12/1795
William Beall m. Mary Foster 10/3/1814
John Fletcher Foster m. Frances Thrasher 4/28/1829
Steven Cloud Hester m. Margaret Furlow Foster 12/27/1832

151

BARTLEY GREER BIBLE
Owner: Mrs. Courtney Leevis
Thomaston, Ga.

Bartley Greer and Ann, his wife, m. 12/12/1775
Thomas Archer and Ann, his wife, m. 12/11/1768

Births
Thomas Gill Greer 9/13/1776   Jerry Greer -/29/1826
Sarah Greer 8/6/1778   Susan Greer 9/15/1828
Sam Greer 12/24/1809
Sally Greer 6/7/1811
Ben Greer 4/15/1813

Joseph Glenn, son of Simeon and Elizabeth Glenn, b. 4/30/1775
Simeon Glenn, son of Simeon and Elizabeth Glenn, b. 12/2/1789
James Glenn, son of Simeon and Elizabeth Glenn, b. 7/15/1761
Glizts.? Glenn b. 2/1778

Deaths
William Glenn 9/27/1825
Simeon Glenn 10/10/18--

P. D. CULLER BIBLE

P. D. Culler d. at res. of his son-in-law, Dr. Culler in Perry,
Ga. 6/15/1861, Mrs. Rebecca Cobb, wife of Col. Howell Cobb, age
75 yrs.

From newspaper clippings inserted in Bible:

"Col. Howell Cobb died at his residence near Perry, Ga. Feb. 15,
1864, in the 69th year of his age."

"Mrs. Mary S. Culler, dau. of Hon. Howell Cobb, formerly of
Houston Co., and wife of Dr. P. B. Culler of Perry, Ga., died in
Macon, Ga. on 28th day of Nov. 1871 in the 48th year of her age.
She died t the residence of her son-in-law, Major J. B. Cobb in
Macon."

Mrs. Mary S. Culler, dau. of Hon. Howell Cobb, and wife of Dr. P.
B. D. H. Culler, was b. 11/17/1823 and d. 11/27/1871, 48 yrs., 10
days.

Mrs. E. C. White d. Macon 4/5/1895

152

DARWIN BIBLE
Owner: Mrs. Mary Darwin Hope
623 Grant St., S. E.
Atlanta, Ga.

Marriages
Jeptha Harrington to Nancy Darwin 1/17/1800
John Kindrick to Mary Darwin 1/28/1803
William Darwin to Elizabeth Powell 1/17/1818
John Powell to Rachel Darwin 1/17/1819
John Darwin to Gilly Sandlin 11/15/1818
William Berry to Matilda Darwin 1/17/1819
John Smarr to Jane Darwin 1/27/1825
Isaac Summerford to Pamela Darwin 1/27/1822

JOHN ARCHER BIBLE
Owner: Mrs. Courtney Lewis
Thomaston, Ga.

Births

Mary Archer 9/22/1769	Charles L. Smith 2/16/1795
Aley Archer 10/11/1770 (Elexander)	Martha T. Smith 12/31/1801
Nancy Archber 12/1/1771	Avery M. Smith 6/9/1831
Martha, dau. of John Archber, 9/1773	Elizabeth M. Smith 6/2/1823
Thomas Archer 9/26/1776	Asberry Fletcher Smith 3/23/1825
	Permely Frances Smith 7/23/1827

Miscellaneous
Bartley Greer bought this Book at Mr. John Archer's sale, decd.,
6/8/1780, price thereof 15#, 5S, 0D.
Armeli Gill, her hand and ---
John Archer 1771
Lewis Archer
Daniel Chandler began his ---
John Archer 1749-1822   11/24/1822   11/19/1779
Juler Cesar Moncrow

ROBERT MARSHALL DIXON BIBLE Of Richland, Ga.
Owner: R. T. Dixon

Births
R. M. Dixon 12/26/1826
Elizabeth Clements Dixon, wife, 12/26/1826

J. J. Dixon 5/14/1847	Robert T. Dixon 2/1856
W. N. Dixon 3/11/1849	Marshall Lafayette Dixon 10/5/1859
Georgia Ann Dixon 8/21/1850	R. J. Dixon 12/30/1869
Thomas S. Dixon 1/17/1854	Cora L. Dixon 12/20/1871

(Robert Marshall Dixon Bible contd....)

Marriages
R. M. Dixon to E. C. Dixon 7/2/1846
J. J. Dixon to G. A. Nicholson 11/1/1866
J. J. Dixon to L. A. Dixon 12/10/1868

Deaths
Thomas S. Dixon 7/20/1854   E. C. Dixon 2/14/1869
R. M. Dixon 9/22/1882

WALTER DOCKINS BIBLE
Owner: Mrs. M. A. Dockins
Turnersville, Ga.

Births
Walter Dockins 4/7/1852   Lillie V. Dockins 7/10/1871
Hepsy Ann Ellard Dockins 11/2/1850 Grovs Dockins 2/28/1873

THOMAS DOUGLAS BIBLE

Thomas Douglas m. Susan H. Pearman 11/28/1830
Isabel Elizabeth Douglas b. 11/5/1831
Susan Weakley Douglas b. 11/14/1833

Thomas Douglas Sr. d. 8/9*1862
Isabel E. Amos (Douglas that was) d. 8/6/1866
Susan Douglas Gunn d. 11/22/1904

JASON A. DOVER BIBLE
Owner: Mrs. P. C. Humphries
Habersham, Ga.

Jason A. Dover m. 12/9/1841

Births
Jason A. Dover 2/7/1823   Martha Dover 9/1/1846
Hillary J. Dover 10/23/1843   Mary Caroline Dover 2/9/1851
Emly Malinda Dover 3/10/1844 Clearsa E. Scroggs 7/30/1850

```
                    JOSHUA DRISKELL BIBLE
              Owner: James Thomas Driskell
                    Monticello, Ga.


Joshua  Driskell  b.  6/5/1799 Worcester Co.,  eastern  shore  of
Maryland, and emigrated to Ga. 11/1820.

Julia E. Mathis Driskell, wife, b.  12/12/1812
Joshua Driskell m. Julia E. Mathis 10/15/1829


              JAMES DUNCAN BIBLE Of Jasper Co.
                   Owner: Mrs. Buleah Price
                     Monticello, Ga.



Births
James Duncan 5/20/1785            Rebecca 1/5/1816
Sarah Lumsden Duncan 4/20/1785    James L. 9/25/1817
Elizabeth D. 12/25/1806          Phebie A. 11/29/1819
Robert L. 10/21/1808             Thomas M. 9/21/1821
Maria S. 7/7/1810                Mary Ann 9/20/1823
Jessey . 9/2/1812                Robert 5/4/1827
Elminia L. 1/13/1814             John 7/23/1831

James Duncan m. Sarah Lumsden 7/21/1808

Deaths
James Duncan 12/21/1851
Sarah Lumsden Duncan 2/11/1860


                   MARGARET BUTCHER BIBLE
              Owner: Mrs. Mae Morgan Atkinson
                     Madison Co., Ga.



Births
Mary Butcher, dau. of Thomas and Sara, 2/20/1756
Margaret Butcher 5/11/1758
John Butcher 1/5/1761
Edward Butcher 2/28/1763-6/16/1772
Benjamin Butcher 12/9/1764
Thomas Butcher 1/16/1767
Kathrine Butcher 10/18/1769-3/30/1772
Martha Butcher 2/18/1772-3/30/1772
Sarah Butcher 6/1/1773-9/10/1775
Bathsheba Butcher 10/7/1775
Ephraira Butcher 7/37/1778

Margaret, wife of John Butcher, d. 3/3/1758


                          155
```

```
                      MILES CANNON BIBLE
                      Owner: John F. Cannon
                      Bulloch Co., Ga.


Miles Cannon 10/2/1797-10/16/1853
Mary Isler, dau. of Nathan and Lishy (or Licia) Isler, wife of
  Miles Cannon, b. 12/28/1803

Their Children:

Wylie Lewis Cannon 11/3/1827-3/14/1863

Millie Ann Green m. Wylie Lewis Cannon 5/25/1848
Millie Ann Green, wife of Wylie Lewis Cannon, 10/30/1826-6/1/1905
Nancy Alice Cannon, dau. of Wylie Lewis Cannon, b. 9/23/1862
Nancy Alice Cannon m. Richard Randolph Carr 1/19/1879

Eason Green 1/23/1806-3/15/1879
Eliza (Weaver) Green, wife of Eason Green, 8/16/1802-2/16/1881



                   CHARLES FREEMAN CARDEN BIBLE



Charles Freeman Carden b. 7/26/1828
Mary Taylor, wife of Charles Freeman Carden, b. 11/12/1830
Georgia Ellis Carden 6/1849-1875
Catherine Carden b. 1/23/1823
Charles F. Carden Jr. 3/16/1857-1875
Catherine Carden d. 1917
Charles Carden m. Mary Taylor 4/12/1847
George Hill 1847-1917 m. Catherine Carden 1874
Macon Warthen m. George Carden 12/22/1874



                   JOHN CAUDELL BIBLE Of Baldwin Co.



John M. Caudell m. Rebecca Minerva Maxwell 10/11/1888 by Robert
Winn

Births
John M. Caudell 7/12/1866          Mattie Caudell 9/22/1889
Rebecca M. Caudell 1/21/1868       William W. Caudell 3/21/1892
```

JOHN JAMES PENFIELD BOIFEUILLET BIBLE

John James Penfield Boifeuillet b. 6/1/1794 on the island of
Jamaica, came to U. S. in 1819

Elizabeth Cecil Virginia Arnaud b. 9/30/1801 Savannah, Ga.

John P. Arnaud, father of Cecil Arnaud Boifeuillet was b. in
France 1758, came to U. S. in 1776 and fought for Independence
under Lafayette.

John T. Boifeuillet b. 6/16/1821
Anne Lydia McKennon b. 10/16/1825

Marriages
John James Penfield Boifeuillet and Elizabeth Cecil Virginia
    Arnold 4/13/1820 Savannah, Ga.
John P. Arnaud and wife m. in Norfolk, Va.

Deaths
John James Penfield Boifeuillet 1863, Savannah, Ga.
Elizabeth Cecil Virginia Arnaud 8/1839, Savannah, Ga.
The wife of J. P. Arnaud b. Norfolk, Va.
John T. Boifeuillet 4/18/1878
Anne Lydia McKennon Boifeuillet 5/26/1901

LEVI CHENEY BIBLE

Levi Cheney m. Mehitable Morse 1752. Their Children:

Births
Asa Cheney 9/29/1752	Priscilla Cheney d. 1/30/1764
Abigail Cheney 3/4/1754	Priscilla Cheney 1/8/1764
Mary Cheney 10/9/1755	Levi Cheney 10/11/1765
Mehitable Cheney 4/25/1757	Levina Cheney 10/11/1765
Tamar Cheney 2/25/1759	Olive Cheney 6/9/1770
Aquilla Cheney 9/12/1761	Tryphena Cheney 8/10/1773

BENAJAH BIRDSONG

Benajah, son of John and Elizabeth Birdsong, b. 6/3/1792 m.
4/6/1820 Aera Ann Reese Clark, b. 8/23/1789, dau. of George and
Mary Clarke. Their Children:

George Lawrence Forsyth Birdsong b. 2/25/1821
Parthenope Hamilton Birdsong b. 6/26/1822
Benajah, father of George L. F. Birdsong, d. 12/24/1824 Jasper
    Co., abt. 6 miles south of Roundoak, Ga.
Aera Ann Reese Birdsong, wife of Benajah Birdsong, d. 7/23/1843
Parthenope Hamilton Birdsong, only dau. of Benajah and Aera,
    d. 7/26/1825

THOMAS H. COOPER BIBLE
Owner: Mrs. J. Tom White
Dublin, Ga.

Marriages
Maria Cooper b. 2/21/1816 to Zachariah Haynes 6/9/1831
Thomas W. Cooper to Frances I. S. Falligant 3/2/1837
Peter Goodwin Cooper to Sarah I. Maher 7/4/1837
Aaron C. Fitts to Lydia Ann Hood 2/19/1835
Peter C. Cooper to Anna Maria Brownjohn 3/13/184
James B. Norris to Mrs. Lydia Ann Fitts 5/1/1839

JOSIAH COTTON BIBLE
Owner: Mrs. L. O. Hooper

Josiah Cotton d. 6/8/1781 m. Elizebeth Skinner 4/23/1777
   Children:
Penelope Cotton 2/7/1778   Dolly Cotton 12/11/1780
Nancy Cotton 8/8/1779

WILLIAM H. AND SALLIE CRAWFORD BIBLE
Of Lowndes Co.

William H. Crawford 10/17/1834-2/7/1884
Sallie M. Bates 12/15/1836-10/3/1888

William H. Crawford m. Sallie M. Bates 11/16/1858

GRAY CROWE BIBLE
Owner: Mrs. T. E. Stribling

Marriages
Gray Crowe to Myry Henson 9/30/1827

Births
Gray Crowe 3/18/1793   John Green Crowe 8/26/1833
Myry Henson Crowe 1/1/1798   Marion Josephine Crowe 1/2/1836
Augustus Haywood Crowe 8/8/1828   Saraugh Elebeth Crowe
11/15/1838
Alphonzo Mason Crowe 11/17/1830

WILLIAM LEE GARY BIBLE Of Hancock Co.

William Lee Gary m. Elizabeth N. Rutherford 11/11/1813
Jarrett Ward m. E. N. Gary 11/2/1828

Births
William Lee Gary Sr. 11/5/1790   Abner Mitchell Gary 2/4/1818
Elizabeth N. Rutherford 12/31/1796   Patrick Gary 5/11/1821
James Gary 12/13/1814   Roderick Gary 7/27/1822
Robert Franklin Gary 7/1/1816   William Lee Gary 2/21/1824

Deaths
William Lee Gary Sr. 10/7/1825
Robert Franklin Gary 12/10/1817

B. F. BURSON BIBLE Of Oconee Co.

B. F. Burson b. 2/20/1797
Synthia, his wife, b. 9/12/1799, married on 12/23/1819

Births
Lucinda Aline Burson 10/2/1820   George David Burson 12/12/1835
Isaac Ethreldred Burson 9/24/1821   Joseph Green Burson 8/28/1837
James Crossley Burson 5/4/1825   Sarah Eveline Burson 11/5/1840
Nancy Emeline Burson 11/5/1833   Julian Frances Burson
                                        7/28/1842

ISAAC ETHRELDRED BURSON & MARTHA ANN ELIZABETH BIBLE
Of Oconee Co.

Births
Dickie Angeline Wood Burson 8/8/1846
William Brookfield Newton Burson 11/18/1847
Mary Caroline and Cynthia Emaline Burson 8/4/1849
James Francis Marion Burson 11/22/1851
Martha Anne America Burson 5/27/1833
Susan Arline Burson 5/5/1855
Julie Jane Burson 11/22/1857
Isaac E. Burson 9/15/1821-5/16/1864
Martha Anne Elizabeth Burson 11/7/1822-9/6/1886

Rev. George Franklin, son of Rev. William Franklin and his wife,
Sarah Boone, b. Va. 1741. Rev. William Franklin with his family
moved to N. C., Currituck Co. in 1760. George Franklin and Vashti
Mercer were m. in 1770.

George Franklin d. 1/1816
George Franklin and wife, Vashti Mercer, had three children:
Vashti Franklin m. Daniel Harris 12/28/1826
William Franklin m. Eliza Floyd
George Franklin

Rev. Thomas Marcus Harris, son of Daniel Harris and wife, Vashti
Franklin, b. 7/6/1829 m. Mary Sarah Smith, dau. of Jordan Richard
Smith and his wife, Sarah Butts, 10/1/1851., d. 10/19/1893

Sarah Smith Harris d. 7/10/1900

ARCHIBALD PERKINS & FRANCES WARE BIBLE

Marriages
Archibald Perkins to Frances Ware 11/26/1818 Morgan Co.
Pleasant P. Coleman to Frances Ware Perkins 7/17/1828 Jasper Co.
Solon L. Coleman to Rosa Scott 6/13/1866

Births
William Columbus Perkins, their 1st son, 9/18/1819
Bennett Hamilton Perkins, their 2d son, 12/16/1820
Mary Elizabeth Perkins, their 1st dau., 3/11/1822
Abram Newton, their 3rd son, 12/7/1823
Emily Frances Perkins, their 2d dau., 12/7/1824
Archibald Nicholas Perkins, their 4th son, 10/17/1826 Jasper Co.

Pleasant P. Coleman 6/21/1796
Frances Ware Coleman 5/25/1797 Morgan Co.

Herbert Henry Coleman, their 1st son, 5/20/1829
Asbury Richardson Coleman, their 2d son, 1/19/1831
Ann Eliza Coleman, their 1st dau., 5/26/1832
Martha Jane Coleman, their 2d dau., 1/13/1834
Thomas Kennew Coleman, their 3rd son, 5/19/1836
Solon Lychurgus Coleman, their 4th son, 1/26/1838

Deaths
Dr. Archibald Perkins 8/21/1826
Bennet Hamilton Perkins 11/7/1856
William Columbus Perkins 10/20/1862
Ann Elizabeth Coleman 4/5/1855   S. L. Coleman 1/20/1874
Pleasant P. Coleman 12/17/1859   Frances Ware Perkins
Thomas K. Coleman 10/3/1861   Coleman 9/24/1884

W. W. BERRY BIBLE
Owner: Edward Berry
Clarkesville, Ga.

W. W. Perry m. Elizabeth King 1/18/---by Rev. William C. Brown

Births

W. W. Berry 2/22/1819   Florence Berry 3/14/1861
Elizabeth King Berry 12/17/1833   Emma Augustia Berry 12/8/1865
Sarah Colona Berry 5/4/1855   William W. berry 1/10/1870

Their first baby was b. 6/26/1853 d. 1/1/1854

HOPEWELL ADAMS BIBLE

Births

Hopewell Adams, son of Hopewell Adams and Elizabeth, 7/22/1769
Nancy Manning, dau. of Benjamin Manning and Pharaby, 4/10/1783
Pharaby Adams, dau. of Hopewell Adams and Nancy, 7/21/1799
James Adams, son of Hopewell Adams and Nancy, 12/18/1801
Elizabeth Adams, dau. of Hopewell Adams and Nancy, 10/10/1803
John W. Adams, son of Hopewell Adams and Nancy, 7/30/1807
Levy A. Adams, son of Hopewell Adams and Nancy, 3/26/1810
Benjamin Adams, son of Hopewell Adams and Nancy, 5/16/1812
Alsy Adams, dau. of Hopewell Adams and Nancy, 8/3/1814
Nancy Adams, dau. of Hopewell Adams and Nancy, 5/17/1816
Hopewell Adams, son of Hopewell Adams and Nancy, 8/14/1818
Jordan Adams, son of Hopewell Adams and Nancy, 1/4/1821
Rebecca Adams, dau. of Hopewell Adams and Nancy, 1/31/1824

Nancy Adams, wife of Hopewell, d. 6/15/1842
Hopewell Adams, husband of Nancy Adams, d. 6/14/1847

ELBERT B. ADAMS
Owner: J. H. Land, Jr.
Hartwell, Ga.

Births

Elbert B. Adams 1/19/1823
Miriam E. Adams 2/4/1825

Children:

Dunston L. Adams 8/16/1845   Sarah C. Adams 12/8/1853
William A. Adams 11/19/1847   Martha B. Adams 12/8/1853
Mary T. Adams 3/31/1850   Simmeon H. D. Adams 3/3/1856
Cincinatta Adams 2/11/1852   Joseph S. Adams 11/15/1858

161

(Elbert B. Adams Bible contd....)

Deaths

Elbert B. Adams 9/7/1860	Cincinatta A. Adams 8/6/1852
Miriam E. Adams 3/10/1873	Martha E. Adams 12/10/1853
Dunston L. Adams 5/5/1884	Mary T. Adams Land 1/5/1916

L T. ADAMS BIBLE
Owner: L. P. Adams
Hartwell, Ga.

L. T. Adams b. 2.2.1859   W. T. R. Adams b. 1/17/1854
            They were married 10/25/1880

MRS. JOHN HURST ADAMS BIBLE
Social Circle, Ga.

Births
John Hurst Adams 1/19/1853
Mary E. Whatley 2/20/1869   Their Children:

John Coleman Adams 6/18/1894	Rachel Adams 9/15/1907
Georgia Ann Adams 3/4/1897	Sara Rebecca Adams 1/7/1912
Martha Frances Adams 1/2/1900	

John Daniel Bateman 1/2/1929

Marriages
Mary E. Whatley to John Hurst Adams 6/9/1891
John Coleman Adams to Lois Aiken 3/2/1921
Georgia Ann Adams to H. O. Godwin 7/29/1916
Martha Frances Adams to W. D. Partee 3/4/1922
Rachel Adams to L. H. Bateman 10/26/1927
Sara Rebecca Adams to A. P. Malcom 8/4/1934

ISAAC DAVIS ADERHOLD BIBLE*
Owner: Mrs. Carlton Thomas
Lavonia, Ga.

Isaac Davis Aderhold, C. N., b. 6/26/1834
Elizabeth Jacobs b. 3/12/1837
Isaac Davis Aderhold m. Elizabeth Jacobs of Ga., Gwinnett Co., on
9/23/1858 at Joseph Jacobs by Jack Nunley, J. P.
Isaac Aderhold d. 5/26/1880, age 45 yrs., 11 mos.
Elizabeth Aderhold d. 6/5/1915

*See also p. 338.   162

W. V. ALMAND BIBLE
Owner: Mrs. E. C. McDowell
Social Circle, Ga.

W. V. Almand b. 3/31/1850
L. E. Almand, wife of W. V. Almand, b. 6/29/1855
William M. Almand, son of W. V. and L. E. Almand, b. 9/22/1872
E. T. Almand, dau. of W. V. and L. E. Almand, b. 1/4/1874
Mary Frances Eloise Almand b. 10/22/1875
Edward L. Almand b. 9/17/1877
Henry Lafayette Almand b. 10/28/1879
Arrie L. Almand b. 11/4/1881

Marriages
W. V. Almand and Leonora E. Kennon 12/23/1871
F. G. Dunn and Emma I. Almand 7/12/1891
A. L. Dabney to Fannie May Almand 11/9/1893
(W. V. Almand Bible, Marriages, contd.....)

Edward L. Almand and Willie D. Peek 3/30/1897

Deaths
William M. Almand, son of W. V. and L. E. Almand, 11/19/1872
Henry Lafayette Almand 10/19/1881
Arrie L. Almand 7/27/1882
F. G. Dunn 3/13/1922
Mrs. W. V. Almand 12/5/1926
W. V. Almand 4/16/1929

COKE BLALOCK BIBLE

Coke Blalock and Mattie T. Tyler m. 12/20/1870 Barnesville, Ga.

Births
Coke Blalock 9/1/1847   Mattie Alberta Blalock 7/29/1874
Mattie Talula Blalock 8/26/1849 Hessie Belle Blalock 11/29/1876
Wm. H. Blalock, Jr. 10/14/1871 Nellie Coke Blalock 2/16/1878

ARVA ALLEN BIBLE

Arva Allen m. Polly Clarke in Mecklenburg Co., Va. 8/1/1786
with Bolling Clarke as second.

Births
John Showell Allen 9/19/1787 Mecklenburg Co., Va.
Bannister Allen 10/13/1788 Petersburg, Va.
Charlotte Allen 2/2/1794 S. C.
Nancy Allen 3/17/1797 S. C.

163

(Arva Allen Bible contd....)

Thompson Allen 12/22/1802 S. C.
LeRoy Allen 7/20/1806 Abbeville Co., S. C.
Three children d. when infants - two sons, one dau.

EPHRAIM BARNES BIBLE
Owner: Mrs. E. J. Dudley
Swainesboro, Ga.

Ephraim Barnes b. 12/20/1866
Nancy Barnes b. 6/21/1809   Their Children:

Sarah Frances Barnes b. 5/7/1835
Elizabeth Francina Barnes b. 4/17/1837
Elmirah Jane Barnes b. 10/17/1853
Ephraim Barnes m. Nancy Barnes 7/11/1833

GEORGE H. ALLEN
Owner: Mrs. Lillie Allen Harrison

Births
George H. Allen 4/10/1734
Mary Ballard (wife) 11/22/1737, m. 12/28/1756
                    Children:
Mary 12/8/1760-3/11/1803 m. Glover
Elizabeth 3/3/1758-1808 m. Cottrell
Martha 6/22/1763 m. Chambers
Anne 4/6/1765
John 3/26/1767-1793 m. Elizabeth Bugg 1791
Sarah 5/1/1769-1788
William 4/3/1771-1824
Judith 11/5/1773-1810 m. Winfrey
Lucy H. 12/31/1776

JULIA ALLEN BIBLE

Births
Sarah M. Allen 12/20/1841
Harris Heard Allen 4/6/1847
Bryant Hubard Allen 7/26/1849

Deaths
Ann Allen 2/1/1842   Mary Allen 4/8/1850
Emilla Barns 2/6/1845   George W. Allen 11/18/1863
Malinda H. Brinkley 7/18/1843   John M. Allen 6/27/1900
Harris Allen 5/19/1854   Mrs. A. G. Roberts 9/13/1891

164

(Julia Allen Bible contd.....)

Marriages
Harris Allen to Ann Buchanon 3/6/1833
Harris Allen to mary Bechwith 1/7/1845
Harris Allen to Lucy C. Mann 11/15/1853

Harris Allen b. 12/11/1810   Elizabeth J. Allen b. 4/30/1836
Ann Allen b. 4/24/1815   John M. Allen b. 11/18/1838
Lucy C. Allen b. 2/7/1812   Julia Allen b. 10/29/1839
George W. Allen b. 6/17/1834

SIMEON BISHOP BIBLE
Owner: Helen Bishop, Eastman, Ga.

Simeon Bishop m. Nancy J. Bishop 12/12/1827 Pulaski Co., Ga.
Simeon Bishop 3/21/1795-10/15/1836
Nancy J. Bishop 3/10/1801-3/16/1874
John Bishop, eldest son of Simeon and Nancy J. Bishop,
    9/20/1828-9/3/1832
James Bishop b. 12/1/1829
James Bishop, Jr. d. 2/20/1908, age 51 yrs., 11 mos., 20 days

WILLIAM ROBERT BARRY BIBLE
Owner: John Forrester
Cornelia, Ga.

Births
Oliver Vaughn 9/18/1848   Bartly Barry 4/2/1845
William Robert Barry 5/8/1830   Catherine Elizabeth Barry
Benj. Franklin Barry 6/30/183   9/11/1847
Mary Pendleton Barry 12/31/1839   H. F. Blair 4/12/1857
Rebecca Sloan Barry 9/4/1842   A. J. Blair 1/21/1860

FRANKLIN ASKIN BIBLE

Franklin Askin b. Monroe Co. 8/28/1829 m. 12/23/1853,
    d. 3/11/1899
Rebecca Reeves Askin b. Monroe Co. 8/24/1834 m. 12/22/1853,
    d. 11/15/1914
Freddie Askin 10/19/1854-9/29/1855
Isaac W. Askin 7/2/1856-11/13/1887 m. 11/27/1879
Mary Askin 12/12/1858-1/1/1865
Addie A. Askin 9/24/1863-12/2/1881 m. 2d time 4/1895

165

(Franklin Askin Bible contd....)

Sarah D. Askin b. 12/25/1865 m. 11/25/1884
Samantha R. Askin b. 4/24/1868 m. 10/27/1887
Lou Askin b. 9/28/1870 m. 11/18/1890
J. Holland Askin b. 10/15/1872 m. 12/23/1897
Franklin Askin Jr. 7/20/1877-10/23/1930 m. 1/11/1899

Sarah D. Askin m. H. Everitt Bankston 11/25/1884

BASIL EARL OVERBY BIBLE

Births
Ann Elizabeth Overby 1/12/1816 m. B. Allen 6/3/1845

Children:

Bannister Bowling Allen 12/13/1847
Basil Barrian Allen 5/11/1849
Mary Asenath Allen 10/1/1850
E. S. Haralson Allen, dau. of B. Allen and wife, Ann Elizabeth,
    11/21/1852 in Abbeville, S. C.

Richard A. Rapley Hallum 5/24/1809
Gilford B. Reid 5/10/1832
Mary Ann Reid 10/17/1833
Caroline Gilmore 4/30/1835
Ginnie Talburn 8/2/1859
Nicholas Overby, Father of Ann Elizabeth Allen 1784-1841
Mary Hallum Overby, Mother of Ann Elizabeth Allen, 2/3/1783-
    11/4/1862
Nicholas Overby m. Mary Hallum 1/10/1814

JOHN BALE BIBLE
Owner: Judge John Bale
Rome, Ga.

John Bale b. London, England 12/15/1795 d. 1/4/1864 in Floyd
    Co., Ga.
Malinda Mason b. S. C.
William Mason b. S. C. (father of Malinda Mason)

John Bale m. Malinda Mason Greenville, S. C. 1822
                    Children:
Caroline Emeline b. 1824 Greenville, S. C. m. J. T. Stewart,
    d. 8/20/1893
Matilda Moore Bale b. 1826 Greenville, S. C.
James Alfred Bale b. 1828 d. 12/15/1900 m. Naomi Shropshire
    4/12/1866
Amanda Bale b. 1830 Greenville, S. C.

166

JACOB BRASELTON BIBLE

Births
Jacob Braselton 6/27/1749
Hannah Braselton 4/8/1757   Their Children:

John Braselton 2/27/1774   Green Braselton 12/5/1786
Elizabeth Braselton 11/5/1775   Ruben Braselton 12/30/1788
Henry Braselton 4/5/1777   Daniel Braselton 11/5/1790
William Braselton 3/26/1779   Job Braselton 12/30/1792
Hannah Braselton 6/24/1781   Rebeccah Braselton 2/3/1795
Mary Braselton 2/21/1783   Amos Braselton 5/15/1797
Jacob Braselton 3/17/1785   Sarah Braselton 10/29/1799

MARTIN AYRES BIBLE

Martin Ayres b. 1800
Sarah Simmons ---

Children:

Austin Ayres b. 5/18/1822 d. 1905
Julia Ann m. William Lassiter
Sarah m. William Bradley
Olivia m.---Perryman
William m.---
Mary m. William Johnson
Austin m. Susan Gann 9/28/1843, d. 1910
Susan Gann b. 4/30/1825   Their Children:

Harriet b. 7/14/1844   Lugenia b. 8/30/1854
Mary b. 6/23/1846   William Solomon b. 2/7/1856
Jane b. 6/11/1851   d. 1859
Nancy Letitia b. 2/4/1853   Alfred b. 7/8/1857
Isaac b. 4/22/1859 d. 3/21/1864
Berry Reuben 3/16/1861-1930
Hiram 5/12/1866-10/31/1896
Sarah Frances 1/9/1864

Marriages
Harriett to Thomas Worthey   Alfred to Sarah Frances Baker
Mary to William Wilson   Berry Reuben to Lou Bradley
Jane to George Fincher   Sarrah Frances to Jack Brown
Nancy Letitia to James Bailey
Lugenia to Duke Chandler

```
                    JESSE M. BLAIR BIBLE
                   Owner W. H. Nichols
                    Clarkesville, Ga.


Births
Jesse M. Blair 5/16/1819          Mary Etta Blair 10/20/1844
Falba N. Blair  5/5/18-           Georgia Caroline Blair
William Wesley Blair 12/17/1842      10/16/1846
Martha Blair 12/7/1848



                    JONATHAN BAKER BIBLE



Jonathan Baker 1/1/1790-3/9/1873
Mary W. Baker, his wife, 1/14/1796-3/15/1881

Their Children:

James R. Baker b. 8/18/1817
Eliza Baker b. 10/19/1820
Silas Baker b. 10/21/1822
Seletha Baker b. 12/9/1824
Mary G. Baker 5/17/1826-3/15/1881
Elizabeth Baker 9/14/1828-5/2/1901
Emily Baker 11/25/1830
Amanda Baker 4/23/1833
Lydia Linea Baker 12/25/1835-9/13/1899
Sarah Frances Baker 10/27/1838
John Green Duke Baker 12/25/1839-6/28/1920 (He had a leg shot
   off during the Civil War)
Lydia Baker m. Willingham
Elizabeth Baker m. Anderson
Frances Baker m. M. D. Stone 1/2/1879 d. 1/10/1929
Eliza Young, dau. of N. W. Baker, d. 4/1857



                 ALBERT BENTON BARRON BIBLE
                 Owner: Willie Joseph Barron
                    Clarkesville, Ga.


Nancy Caroline Free m. Albert Benton Barron 7/14/1858, signed
   Jim Jarrard.  Their Children:
Albert Barron b. 8/18/1860 Habersham Co., Fairplay
Frances Barron b. 6/13/1866 Habersham Co., Fairplay
Etna Benjamin Barron b. 2/14/1869 Habersham Co., Batesville
Jeams Barron b. 4/4/1874 Habersham Co., Batesville
Lodelia Barron b. 3/12/1877 Habersham Co., Batesville
Alice Angeline Barron b. 1/24/1880 Habersham Co., Batesville
Willie Joseph Barron b. 10/30/1883 Habersham Co.,Batesville

Marriages
Albert Barron 8/9/1878          Willie Joseph Barron 4/4/1915
```

WILLIAM GREEN BENTLEY BIBLE
Owner: Mrs. J. E. McMullen
Selma, Ala.

Births
William Green Bentley 4/2/1830 Lincoln Co., Ga.
Mary Frances Brightwell 10/25/1837 Clarke Co., Ga.
Benjamin William Bentley, son of William G. and Mary F. Bentley,
  12/19/1856 Clarke Co., Ga.
Mary Lula Bentley, dau. of above, 0/21/1858 Brooks Co., Ga.
Cynthia Ann Bentley, dau. of above, 7/26/1861 Brooks Co., Ga.
Annie Kate Bentley, dau. of above, 10/31/1864 Brooks Co., Ga.
Ada Legette Bentley, dau. of above, 9/22/1868 Brooks Co., Ga.
Mary T. Bentley 10/30/1872 Brooks Co., Ga.

Marriages
William G. Bentley and Mary Frances Brightwell 10/25/1855 Clarke
  Co., Ga.

Deaths
William G. Bentley 10/6/1888
Mary F. Bentley, wife of William G. Bentley, 2/25/1904
Cynthia Ann Bentley 9/1861
John Andrew Bentley, son of W. G. and Mary F. Bentley, 8/19/1873,
  age 9 mos., 20 days
Mary Lula Bentley Owens, dau. of W. G. and Mary F. Bentley,
  6/20/1903, Thomas Co., Ga.
Benjamin William Bentley 1825, Lowndes Co., Ga.

WILLIAM BEMBRY BIBLE

Births
William Bemby 8/23/1795   Catharine Bemby 4/6/1824
Marina Mayo, his wife, 11/14/1799 Miles Bemby 1/28/1826
Eliza Bemby 7/27/1819   Nancy Bemby 4/17/1829
Mary Bemby 8/8/1821   Martha W. Bemby 11/14/1832
Margaret Bemby 8/11/1822   William Bemby 12/9/1834
Sarah Louise Bemby 1/13/1838

Deaths
Catharine Bemby 5/23/1834
William Bemby 4/22/1839

OWEN J. BOWEN BIBLE
Owner: Mrs. J. H. McWhorter
36 Clay St., Atlanta, Ga.

Births
Owen J. Bowen 9/1764   Lavina Bowen 11/13/1825
Thomas Jones Bowen 10/19/1788   Caleb Perry Bowen 12/4/1827

(Owen J. Bowen Bible contd....)

Horatio Yarbrough Bowen 11/6/1819   Jonathan Jones Bowen
Clemantine Bowen 1/25/1824   10/18/1829
Elmina Bowen 11/13/1825   Andrew Jackson Bowen
                           10/25/1831

Deaths
Owen J. Bowen 2/6/1828
Thomas Jones Bowen 11/23/1854

POWELL BLAIR BIBLE
Owner: Mrs. J. A. Blair
Mt. Airy, Ga.

Powell Blair m. 2/27/1825

Births
Powell Blair 9/3/1800   Elizabeth Blair 5/9/1829
Sarah Blair 2/9/1804   William D. Blair 6/6/1831
James Blair 3/6/1763   George H. Blair 11/7/1833
Elizabeth Blair 4/16/1765   Sarah F. Blair 8/12/1835
James M. Blair 1/22/1826   Edley Blair 9/6/1837
Catherine Blair 8/11/1827   Benjamin C. Blair 7/11/1839
                        Lucy Blair 9/11/1841
                        Manda Shurley 10/7/1856

Deaths
Powell Blair 4/7/1844   Lucy Weatherford 1/22/1880
Sarah Blair 4/6/1880   Manda Shurley 2/1/1877
Benjamin C. Blair 2/20/1863

ROBERT BULLOCK BIBLE

Robert Bullock m. Amanda L. Waterman 5/7/1852

Births
Sumter Aden Bullock, 1st son of Robert and Amanda L. Bullock
   2/14/1853
Robert Albert Bullock, 2d child of above, 3/7/1855
Willie Simon Bullock, 3rd son of above, 5/16/1856
Charles Bullock, 4th son of above, 12/3/1858
Marie Eliza Bullock, 5th child of above, 9/7/1860
Josephine Amelia Bullock, 2d dau. of above, 4/22/1862
Raymond Bramhill Bullock, 7th child of above, 9/16/1866
Robert Bullock Sr. 12/8/1828
Amanda Bullock, wife of Robert Bullock, 9/22/1835
Burton T.? Bullock, 11th child of R. and A. L. Bullock, 8/16/1872
Amanda Loretta Bullock, 13th child of above, 3/20/1877
Francis Henrietta Bullock, 8th child of above, 9/14/1868,
   d. 8/8/1959

(Robert Bullock Bible contd.....)

R. Freeland, Bullock, 9th child of above, 3/14/1870
Burton Finly Bullock, 10th child of above, 8/15/1872
Shelbey Simwood Bullock, 12th child of above, 9/4/1875

Deaths
Robert Albert Bullock, 2nd son of Robert and Amanda L. Bullock,
  4/25/1855, of whooping cough, age 7 wks.
Charles Bullock, 4th son of above, 12/18/1861
Josephine Amelia Bullock, 2d dau. of above, 10/1/1868, age 6
  yrs., 6 mos.
Robert Freeland Bullock, child of above, 10/18/1874
Shelbey Linwood Bullock, son of above, 5/11/--
Amanda L. Bullock, wife of Robert Bullock, 7/10/1904, age 68 yrs.
Robert Bullock, husband of Amanda L., 7/27/1905, age 78 yrs.

JAMES MADISON HUDSON BIBLE

James Madison Hudson and Sarah A. Davenport Wilkins m. 1859

Births
James Thomas Hudson, son of above, 5/19/1860
Mary Eliza Hudson, dau. of above, 9/26/1862
Cora Lu Hudson, dau. of above, 2/28/1866
Francis Tallulah Hudson, dau. of above, 4/11/1868
Eva May Hudson, dau. of above, 3/10/1870
Sarah Clementine Hudson, dau. of above, 12/15/1871
Alice Hudson, dau. of above, 4/8/1873
Adelaide Hudson, dau. of above, 7/1/1875
Emma Salonia Hudson, dau. of above, 7/13/1877
Rosa or Viola? Hudson, dau. of above, --/31/1879
Kate Estelle Hudson, dau. of above, 8/30/1881

MARY WRIGHT SHELL BIBLE
Owner: Mrs. Lucius Arnold, Jr.
Hogansville, Ga.

Marriages
James Wright to Lucy 1/23/1774
William Wright to Lucy Tucker 9/1/1803
William Dugan to Elizabeth L. Wright 12/17/1807
Zacheus Wright to Mary Glasgow 12/7/1809
Edmond Shell to Lucy 11/9/1815
Isham M. Shell to Mary Wright 4/16/1818

Births
James Wright 11/27/1745
Lucy Wright, his wife, 11/27/1756
William Wright, son of James Wright & Lucy, his wife, 1/29/1775

(Mary Wright Shell Bible contd....)

Milly Wright, dau. of above, 1/13/1777
Joseph Wright, son of above, 1/7/1779
Zacheus Wright, son of above, 1/9/1783
Elizabeth L. Wright, dau. of above, 2/12/1787
Mary Wright, dau. of above, 12/18/1788
Lucy Wright, dau. of above, 11/9/1792
James Wright, son of above, 6/29/1797
James (L. or T.) Wright, son of William Wright and Lucy,
    8/24/1804
Nancy R. Wright, dau. of William Wright and Lucy, 1/6/1806
Mary W. Wright, dau. of William Wright and Lucy, 4/14/1807
Elizabeth A. Wright, dau. of William Wright and Lucy, 6/10/1809
Lucy B. Wright 3/21/1811
Lucinda Dugan, dau. of William Dugan and Elizabeth L., 2/14/1809
Martha Ann Wright, dau. of Zacheus Wright and Mary, 10/25/1810
Laura Ann L. Shell, dau. of Isum M. Shell and Mary, 6/15/1819,
    baptized 9/19/1819
James G. C. Shell, son of I. M. Shell and Mary, 9/18/1820,
    baptized 10/22/1820 by G. Christopher.
Isham Abner Fletcher, son of Isham M. Shell and Mary, 8/11/1822
Lucy Elizabeth Malviney Shell, dau. of Isham and Mary Shell,
    8/11/1822
Ivery Isham Malone, son of Isham M. Shell and Mary, 11/5/1826
John Abner Zaccheus Shell, son of Isham M. Shell and Mary,
    1/10/1829

Deaths
Lucy Wright, wife of James Wright, 9/27/1824, 67 yrs., 10 mos.
James Wright 1/3/1825, 79 yrs., one mo., 6 days
Emily E. Shell, wife of Z. A. Z. Shell, 4/6/1867
Milly Wright 8/22/1785
Joseph Wright 1/9/1779
James Wright 9/17/1797
Lucy Wright, wife of William Wright, 6/28/1811
Lucy Shell, wife of Edmond Shell, 10/21/1819
Edmond Shell 9/1832
Isham M. Shell 10/5/1871
Mary Shell, wife of Isham M. Shell, 5/21/1880, 91 yrs., 6 mos.,
    3 days
John Abner Fletcher, son of Isham M. Shell and Mary, 8/5/1827,
    age 5 yrs.
William Rufus Dugan 8/10/--, age 17 mos.
Rufus Shell, son of Isham and Mary Shell, 6/10/1886, 54 yrs.

On flyleaf dated 1817:

Black Names
Lucy b. 6/4/1793   Peter Harvey b. 10/15/1819
Hager b. 10/18/1811   Benj. Allen 1/25/1820
Moses Andrew b. 7/29/1813   Rebecca Antonett 11/3/1830
Esther Jane b. 10/7/1815
             Found on loose paper inside Bible:
Ruffus Shell and Hariett Shell m.3/22/1866
Mary Lee Shell b. 7/9/1869
Martha Ann Elizabeth Shell b. 4/21/1871
John Isom Columbus Shell b. 12/-/--
Martha ---
Mary L. E. Shell, dau. of R. H. Shell and Harriet P. S. Shell,
    b. 7/9/1869

172

WILLIAM HOPSON BIBLE
Owner: Mrs. T. F. Depourcq
Hogansville, Ga.

Marriages
William Hopson to Hannah Wicker 2/11/1821
William Hopson to Permelia A. Bird 5/16/1833

Births

William Hopson 12/7/1800	William B. Hopson 3/10/1834
Hannah Hopson 3/6/1806	Francis M. Hopson 12/26/1836?
Permelia A. Hopson 11/30/1812	Permelia A. Hopson 1/27/1838
Angeline B. Hopson 8/18/1822	Rasmus L. Hopson 9/11/1840
Nathaniel W. Hopson 8/13/1824	Cassandra E. Hopson 10/20/1842
James A. Hopson 6/30/1826	Lucy T. Hopson 11/6/1844
Virgil L. Hopson 9/5/1828	Texannah P. Hopson 5/10/1848
John S. Hopson 11/24/1830	Almira Bill Hopson 3/23/1854

Deaths

Hannah Hopson 1/4/1831	Sabra Hopson 4/7/1858
Lucy T. Hopson 7/13/1847	Nancy Bird 2/22/1837
Francis M. Hopson 9/15/1853	Singleton L. Trawick 4/12/1860
Cassandra E. Hopson 4/3/1859	John S. Hopson 8/1892
James A. Hopson 9/19/1862	Permelia A. Hopson 10/30/1886
Hardy Hopson 1/21/1832	Rasmus L. Hopson 12/31/1904
Lucy Hopson 9/1/1844	Texannah P. Hopson 5/9/1906
Warren Hopson 11/7/1848	Permelia A. Hopson 2/20/1911

Remarks
William Hopson's gift to his wife, Permelia A. Hopson, 8/6/1852
William Hopson d. 8/8/1875, bur. at Emmaus Church, Troup Co.
Permelia A. Hopson d. 10/30/1886

JOSIAH JACKSON BIBLE Of Corinth, Ga.
Owner: Mrs. W. L. Martin, Jr.
Hogansville, Ga.

This certifies that the rite of Holy Matrimony was celebrated
between Josiah Jackson of Greene Co., Ga. and Sarah A. Cook of
Heard Co., Ga. on 3/25/1858, at Mr. H. H. Cook's by David L.
Grimes

Marriages
Josiah Jackson and Sarah A. Cook 3/25/1858
W. C. Matthews and Josie D. jackson 12/18/1878
W. C. matthews and Jeanie Ettie Jackson 6/24/1894
J. Enoch Jackson and Lena Rawlins 12/21/1893
J. Hope Jackson and Eula Strong 12/23/1890
L. B. Webb, M. D. and Jeroline Heard Jackson 12/28/1893
Josiah S. Jackson and nancy F. Miller 11/1/1893
Flur Matthews and Jessie N. jackson ---
James L. Webb and Alma Odelle Formy 2/6/1943

173

(Josiah Jackson Bible contd.....)

Births
Josiah Jackaon 1/15/1837   Dr. L. B. Webb 4/10/1866
Sarah A. Jackson 8/1/1841   L. B. Webb, Jr. 5/13/1896
Josie D. Jackson 7/17/1859   Louis Clifford Webb 5/15/1898
Jessie N. Jackson 3/19/1862   Roy Lee Webb 1/28/1901
James E. Jackson 1/31/1865   James Lowe Webb 1/3/1904
Jeremiah H. jackson 9/19/1866   Josiah J. Matthews 8/8/1880
Jeroline H. jackson 9/2/1869   Leta Matthews 10/20/1881
Josiah Jackson "Junior" 2/6/1871 William Henry Matthews 8/3/1885
Jeannie E. Jackson 5/10/1873   Hubert F. Matthews 5/17/1892
Justin Lowe Jackson 4/10/1875   Maidee Matthews 9/13/--
Jimmie Stell Jackson 4/13/1881

Deaths
Josiah Jackson 7/3/1895   L. B. Webb, Jr. 6/30/1897
Sarah Jackson 5/20/1912   Louis Clifford Webb 5/12/1899
Josie Matthews 7/12/1893   Dr. L. B. Webb 1/1/1922
Jeanie Matthews 1/13/1908   Mrs. L. B. Webb 8/3/1942

CHRISTOPHER ORR BIBLE
Owner: Mrs. Oscar Cole, Jackson, Ga.

Christopher Orr and Martha, his wife, joined in affinity
    8/27/1778
Henry J. Nise and Elizabeth, his wife, m. 1/5/1825
Christopher Orr b. 10/1/1754
Martha Orr b. 3/16/1761

Births (Children of Christopher and Martha Orr)

Sarah Orr 9/25/1779   Jacob Orr 12/11/1790
Philip Orr 1/7/1781   Margaret Orr 12/26/1791
Ann Orr 12/11/1782   Walker Orr 12/20/1793
Mary Orr 3/17/1785   Martha Orr 1/1/1799
John Orr 4/16/1787   Elizabeth Orr 10/1/1801
                             Olive Orr 1/1803

Deaths
Christopher Orr 10/5/1830   Robert Barber 9/14/1851
Martha Orr 10/1/1830

Christopher W. Orr m. Mary Emily Simms 11/1/1853
William D. Orr m. Susan R. Herring 8/25/1853

174

PHILIP ORR BIBLE
Owner: Mrs. Jonathan Orr, Newnan, Ga.

Marriages
Philip Orr and Niah Rucker 12/12/1820
Joseph T. Brown and Amanda F. orr 10/25/1832
Robert Orr and Almira E. Simms 12/3/1835
Robert W. Simms and Araminta Jane Orr 11/29/1838
Joseph T. Brown and Camilla Ann Orr 11/13/1839
Watkins Orr and Susan F. Simms 12/17/1846
Andrew J. Stallings and Martha Elizabeth Orr 1/13/1853
Christopher W. Orr and Mary Emily Simms 11/1/1853
William D. Orr and Susan R. Herring 8/25/1853

Births
Philip Orr Sr. 1/7/1781   John Pope Orr 5/3/1825
Niah W. Orr-wife of Philip 4/5/1800 Henry Orr 1/4/1827
Robert Orr 10/19/1813   Martha Eliza Orr 12/16/1828
Amanda M. F. Orr 5/20/1815   Christopher Willis Orr
William D. Orr 11/17/1816   11/3/1830
Christopher Orr 8/25/1818   James Philip Orr 11/10/1833
Watkins Orr 9/7/1821   Jonathan Leonidas Orr
Camilla Ann Orr 11/30/1822   9/30/1835
Araminta Jane Orr 11/30/1822   Nicholas Tompkins Orr
                                      9/16/1837
Joseph Orr Brown, son of Joseph and Amanda Brown, 8/18/1835
Walter Gibson Orr 12/14/1840

Deaths
Evaline Orr 4/8/1855
Elnorah Orr 4/8/1855
Franklin W. Orr 9/8/1863, killed in defense of Confederate cause
James H. Orr 3/3/1864
Martha E. Stallings 7/13/1872
Tuminus S. Orr, son of Robert and Almira E. Orr, 10/23/1872

Births
John Simms 6/8/1782   Comfort M. Simms 2/26/1798

Deaths
John Simms, son of Robert and Sarah Simms, 12/7/186-
Briton Simms, son of John and Mary Simms, 9/1871
Robert Orr 9/26/1880
Comfort Simms, wife of John Simms, 7/1880
Mary Dallis Orr, wife of W. Or, 5/29/1881
Sallie F. Willcoxon, wife of J. W. Willcoxon, 4/7/1900
Amanda M. F. Brown 8/21/1835, 20 yrs., 13 mos., 1 day
Philip Orr Sr. 4/4/1841, 60 yrs., 2 mos., 27 days
Martha E. Stallings, wife of A. J. Stallings, 7/13/1872, 43 yrs.,
   6 mos., 27 days
Jonathan L. Orr 3/25/1859, 23 yrs., 5 mos., 25 days
Niah W. Orr 8/29/1861, 61 yrs., 4 mos., 24 days
Susan R. Orr, wife of W. D. Orr, 6/18/1871

Marriages
Robert Orr and Almira Elizabeth Simms 12/3/1835
John Philip Orr and Martha Ann Simms 3/4/1858
William Benjamin Orr and Mary Dalls Brewster 9/7/1865
Isaac Newton Davis Orr and Aldorar Johnson 1/28/1867

(Philip Orr Bible contd....)

Tuminus Silvanus Orr and Sarah J. Edwards 2/25/1868
Nathan David Mattox and Elizabeth Amanda Orr 9/12/1869
Robert Simms Orr and Sarah Emma Brewster 1/24/1871

MICHAEL F. HAMMER BIBLE

Michiael F. Hammer of Schellsburg, Bedford Co., Pa. m. Eliza A.
Maken of Schellsburg, Bedford Co., Pa. at Pleasantville, Bedford
Co., 1/27/1856, by Jacob Wright, J. P.

Births
Lovina Jane Hammer 3/7/1857   Sarah Irene Hammer 6/30/1871
Elizabeth Ann Hammer 12/5/1858   Michael Francis Hammer
Matilda Lucartha Hammer 7/26/1868   11/30/1861
George Washington Hammer 6/23/1863   Baby 8/9/1874

Michael Francis Hammer, Sr. 6/3/1832 Eliza Ann Hammer 5/11/1835

Marriages
Elizabeth A. Hammer and James C. Shaw
Lovina J. Hammer and Norbert W. Woodard
Michael F. Hammer and Emma Hess 9/22/1885
Matilda L. Hammer and William E. Woodard 10/7/1886
Sarah Irene Hammer and George W. Jones 7/26/1893 by P. McGough
Michael Frances Hammer and Eliza Ann Maken 1/27/1856

Deaths
George W. Hammer 9/4/1867   Sarah Irene Jones 4/27/1900
Lovina J. Hammer 5/16/1890

DR. B. J. DISMUKES BIBLE

This certifies that the Rite of Holy Matrimony was celebrated
between Dr. B. J. Dismukes of Mt. Hilliard and Mary E. Brundage
of Mt. Hilliard 11/22/1865, at Mt. Hilliard

Marriages
Fannie E. Dismukes to R. J. Sims 2/15/1887
Sallie L. Dismukes to R. J. Sims 1/16/1894
Bennie D. Dismukes to Ella L. Casing 9/30/1896
(Dr. B. J. Dismukes Bible, Marriages, contd....)

Bennie David Dismukes to Bessie Ellison
Jimmie H. Dismukes to James Wilson Beasley 4/1897
Ida Josephine Dismukes to John Sanford Branscomb 10/26/1899
Louis Leon Dismukes to Annie Gertrude Justice
Lula Virginia Dismukes to James William Beasley 10/18/1905

176

(Dr. B. J. Dismukes contd.....)

Births

Dr. B. J. Dismukes 4/28/1833	Henry M. Dismukes 1/19/1881
M. E. Brundage 2/10/1848	Lula V. Dismukes 1/20/1883
Finnie D. Dismukes 11/6/1867	John C. Dismukes 10/12/1885
David B. Dismukes 1/27/1869	Mary C. Dismukes 12/22/1886
Louis L. Dismukes 12/31/1871	Finnie Estelle Sims 3/4/1888
Sallie L. Dismukes 4/9/1872	Mabe Ruth Sims 2/4/1895
Jimmie H. Dismukes 1/16/1874	Ida Leona Sims 12/25/1896
Ida J. Dismukes 12/14/1875	Benj. Akious Beasley 6/1898
Regina A. Dismukes 12/16/1876	Mary Estelle Dismukes 8/1897
Jackey Dismukes 1/3/1879	Mary Louis Sims 9/1898

Deaths

Regina A. Dismukes 9/11/1879	Dr. B. J. Dismukes 9/16/1908
Finnie E. Dismukes 11/27/1888	Ida Dismukes 12/18/1914
Jackey Dismukes 1/3/1879	Sallie Sims ---
Jimmie Beasley 9/26/1904	

Births

Benjamin Beasley	Mary Gertrude Dismukes 10/1908
James Benjamin Sims 4/1899	Lucile Elizabeth Branscomb
William Cecil Beasley 12/12/1900	4/4/1907
Albert Leon Branscomb 9/1900	------Sims 8/1908
Lewis Leon Dismukes ---	Byron Eugene Beasley 8/25/1908
Alma Erline Beasley 10/1901	Annie Laurie Sims 1908
Clayton Sanford Branscomb	Camillus Dismukes --
4/21/1902	Horace Clifford Sims 1910
Richard Leon Sims ---	Jackson Ernest Branscomb
Jackson Bernard Sims ---	8/1910
Benjamin Ellison Dismukes ---	Joseph Wm. Beasley 10/1912
Janie Lillian Sims 4/1904	Martha Elizabeth Dismukes
Leon Dismukes 8/19/1904	10/1912
John Warren Branscomb 5/1905	Lewis Lightfoot Branscomb
William Moseley Sims 8/1906	12/1912
James Moseley Beasley 10/1906	Robert Dismukes Beasley
	3/3/1917

Deaths

Benjamin Akious Beasley 1899	James Leonard Beasley 1903,
William Cecil Beasley 10/7/1903	Aged a few hrs.
Alma Erline Beasley 5/12/1902	Joseph Leon Dismukes 4/4/1908

ANDREW M. WARE BIBLE

This book was purchased of the Rev. Samuel Rudd by Andrew M. Ware
in 1806 Debtford Township, Gloucester Co., N. J.

John F. Ware, son of Andrew Ware and Abigail
His wife b. 3/1/1814
James M. Ware, son of Andrew Ware and Abigail
His wife b. 8/6/1816
Abigail Ware, dau. of Andrew Ware and Abigail, b. 4/1/1819
Anna Maria Ware, dau. of Andrew Ware and Abigail, b. 4/17/1823

(Andrew M. Ware Bible contd....)

Marriages
Andrew Ware, son of John Ware and Sarah, his wife to Abigail
Whitacar, dau. of Samuel Whitacar and Ruth Whitacar, his wife,
10/21/1800
Samuel W. Ware, son of Andrew and Abigail Ware, to Charlotte
Martin ---
Priscilla Rige Ware to Washington Mason 1825
Ruth Ann Ware, dau. of Andrew and Abigail Ware, to Joseph Bates,
son of Clark and Rachel Bates ---
Abigail Ware, dau. of Andrew and Abigail Ware to Andrew Roan
Foote, son of Thomas and Mary Tweed Foote 9/12/1837
Anna Mariah Ware, dau. of Andrew and Abigail Ware, to Abram
Morrell ---

NAPOLEON H. CHESHIRE BIBLE
Owner: Mrs. Homer M. Cheshire
Atlanta, Ga.

Marriages
Napoleon H. Chesire to Carrie E. Mayson 12/19/1867
Homer Mayson Sheshire to Clara Annie Fritz 11/22/1899

Births
Napoleon H. Cheshire 4/9/1843, Guess Farm, DeKalb Co., Ga.
Carrie E. May 9/19/1845, Benj. Plaster´s Farm, Fulton Co.
Sarah Cora Cheshire, dau. of N. H. and C. E. Chieshire,
12/29/1869 at Mrs. Sarah Mayson´s Farm, Fulton Co., Ga.
Walter H. Cheshire, 2d child of above, 10/31/1871, at Mrs. Sarah
Mayson´s Farm
Ellie Glover Cheshire, 3rd child of above, 1/28/1874, at Mrs.
Sarah Mayson´s Farm
Homer M. Cheshire, 4th child of above, 3/15/1876 at Cheshire
Farm, Fulton Co., Ga.
Edna Belle Cheshire, 5th child of above, 7/21/1878, Cheshire Farm
Estelle Susan Cheshire, 6th child of above, 1/15/1881, Cheshire
Farm
Carrie Mae Chesire, 7th child of above, 12/24/1886, Cheshire Farm

JOHN COLLEY BIBLE *

Marriages
Elizabeth Tindall to John Peetett 2/12/1811
Nancy Colley to Kirby Goolsbe 7/25/1813
Mary Colley to James V. Brown 9/26/1816
Francis Colley to F. L. Owens 12/24/1818
Louisa Colley to Welcome Fanning 3/23/1820

Births
Gabriel Colley 6/17/1809   Lieusinday E. Tindall 4/26/1809

*See also p. 448.

(John Colley Bible, Births, contd....)

Elizabeth Colley 5/1/1808
John Colley 9/14/1752
Gabriel Colley 2/23/1782
Frances Colley 2/20/1785
Eliza Colley 5/12/1788
Mary Colley 5/26/1790
Nancy Colley 1/3/1792
Spain Colley 1/22/1794
Louisa Colley 9/23/1801

Demaris Goolsbe 4/25/1814
Sarah Colley 6/4/1763, dau. of
    Hen T. Fran, Jr.
John C. Fanning 1/19/1821
Sarah F. Fanning 9/11/1822
Mary Fanning 7/5/1824
Nancy Fanning 3/9/1827
Martha Fanning 2/1/1829

Deaths
Parks Fanning 8/4/1835
Frances Fanning 10/1/1846
Abina Victoria Fanning 12/24/1846
Charles Ann Fanning 12/28/1850
Mrs. Louisa Fanning 10/1/1853
Welcome Fanning 7/14/1799-10/3/1873

William S. Brown 1/16/1855
Rev. A. J. Orr 7/12/1860
John C. Fanning 4/19/1870
Sarah F. Fanning 11/30/1869
Webster Fanning 4/24/1903
J. A. Brown 1/10/1903
Mary P. Johnson 3/29/1904
Sabrina Ellen Fanning Brown
    6/23/1905

Births
Webster Fanning 3/25/1831
Parks Fanning 3/9/1833
Sabrina Ellen Fanning 7/13/1835
Charles Ann Fanning 9/23/1838
Victoria A. Fanning 11/16/1840

Bryan Fanning 10/18/1842
Frances Fanning 1/6/1845
Samuel D. Fanning 7/4/1862
Alace Estelle Fanning
    4/23/1864

Deaths
Nimrod Colley
Lieusenday Colley
Lewis Colley

John Colley 6/9/1815
Sarah Colley 12/21/1833
Thomas B. Tindall 11/20/1809
    (or 11/27/1809)

OBEDIAH STEVENS BIBLE *

Births
Joseph Stevens 3/9/1787
Martha Stevens 4/22/1787
Obediah Stevens 5/7/1809
Haley Stevens 3/30/1811
Allen Stevens 6/16/1812
Jasper Stevens 9/27/1813
Thomas Stevens 10/22/1818
Elizabeth Stevens 2/8/1822
Martha Stevens 2/22/1824
Newton Stevens 12/19/1825
Walton Stevens 3/11/1829
W. C. Stevens 2/21/1831
J. R. Stevens 4/20/1824

W. W. Stevens 3/24/1837
C. A. Stevens 6/26/1844
Rese Watkins Sr. 8/20/1779
Milly Watkins 9/26/1779
Ben Watkins 10/12/1801
Elizabeth Watkins 12/5/1803
Nancy Watkins 10/12/1807
Charly Watkins 9/1/1809
Olive Watkins 9/25/1811
Martha Watkins 9/5/1814
William Watkins 3/22/1818
Rese Watkins 7/22/1822
James Appling 3/16/1825

*See also p. 118.   179

C. V. FURLOW BIBLE
Owner: Irma Ragsdale Hart

This certifies that I performed the marriage ceremony for C. V.
Furlow of Heard Co., Ga. and Amanda Peddy of Heard Co., Ga. on
31st day of October 1849 at the Bride's mothers. /s/ Rev. T. E.
Reece."

Births

C. W. Furlow 1818	Catherine Furlow 3/4/1854
Amanda Peddy 12/15/1830	Parrie Furlow 2/16/1856
Queenie Furlow 10/17/1850	Eliza Furlow 7/17/1865
G. W. Furlow 4/8/1852	V. F. Furlow 11/2/1867

Marriages
Parrie Furlow to A. R. Lester 11/10/1880
Eliza Furlow to S. W. Howard 4/6/1884

Deaths

Catherine Furlow 3/4/1862	Parrie Lester 9/22/1889
Charles V. Furlos 9/8/1882	Infant was burned 8/29/1889
Eliza Howard 5/26/1888	

GEORGE CHANCE BIBLE
Owner: Pearl Raburn
Carrollton, Ga. 30117

George Chance, son of Cannon and Nancy Chance m. Eliza Briant
1/15/1835
Sarah Elen d. 3/27/1855

Births
George W. Chance, son of Cannon and Nancy Chance, 11/30/1813
Eliza Chance, dau. of Edward Briant and Nancy, 7/15/1818
William H. Chance, son of George W. and Eliza Chance, 12/30/1835
Caccon B. Chance, son of George W. and Eliza Chance, 4/25/1837
Nancy A. Chance, dau. of George W. and Eliza Chance, 3/9/1839
Mary J. T. Chance 3/8/1841
Lucy Ann W. Chance, dau. of George W. and Eliza Chance, 5/15/1843
James W. Chance, son of George W. and Eliza Chance, 8/22/1845
-------9/2/1921 ?
Nathan T. Chance, son of George W. and Eliza Chance, 6/22/1848
Elizabeth E. Chance 10/15/1850
Sarah Ellen C. Chance 10/15/1850
Josifeen 8/22/1856
Pink Riler Brice 10/15/1859
Elizar Brice 4/14/1861
Gr Chance 10/15/1856

JAMES W. CHANCE BIBLE
Owner: Pearl Raburn
Carrollton, Ga.

This certifies that the rite of Holy Matrimony was celebrated
between James W. Chance of Carroll Co., Ga. and Martha T. Cochran
of Carroll Co., Ga. 19th of Oct. 1865

Births
William T. Chance 9/5/1866   Talula V. Chance 9/9/1876
Charles C. Chance 3/20/186-   Thomas W. Chance 11/28/1878
Noel E. Chance 5/9/1870   Bishop M. Chance 11/2/1881
Preston Chance 8/12/1872   Mary M. Chance 10/21/1884
Lizzie T. Chance 7/2/1874   James W. Chance 5/6/1890

Deaths
Preston Chance 9/18/1872
Martha T. Chance 11/6/1915
Martha T. Chance 3/10/1847
James W. Chance 8/22/1845-9/22/1921

OWENS GAMBLES McCOY BIBLE

Births
Owens Gambles McCoy 10/27/1804   Martha Jane McCoy 2/12/1836
Martha Mason Coker McCoy 1/18/1809 Wm. Thomas McCoy 12/26/1837
Warren Sanders McCoy 10/26/1828   Frederick Davis McCoy
Sarah Elizabeth McCoy 11/16/1830   2/20/1847
Isabella Ann LaCastle McCoy 4/26/1833
Frances L. P. E. McCoy 8/20/1849

JOHN M. SWINNEY BIBLE

John M. Swinney m. Augusta Swinney 12/19/1888 by A. P. Adamson

Births
John M. Swinney 11/30/1851   Tommie Grady Swinney 4/29/1890
Lavinnia A. Swinney 3/27/1858   Jesse Watson Swinney 10/1/1892
Lonnie Phillip Swinney 10/12/1881 Ossie Mae Swinney 12/27/1894
Melissa Francis Swinney 4/28/1883 Lottie Gladys Swinney 4/10/1897
Maggie Odell Swinney 5/23/1885   Grace Corine Swinney 10/1/1900
Fred Lee Swinney 5/2/1887

Marriages
Lonnie Swinney 7/2/1905   Grace C. Swinney 6/26/1921/4
Melissa F. Swinney 1/17/1909   Lottie G. Swinney 4/2/1927 in
Fred L. Swinney 12/19/1914   Fulton Co., Ga.

(John M. Swinney Bible, Marriages, contd....)

Deaths
Tommie G. Swinney 5/7/1892   Fred L. Swinney 4/6/1970
Ossie May Swinney 2/18/1896   Melissia F. Swinney Stewart

Lavinnia Augusta Swinney 7/16/1930   11/29/1971
J. M. Swinney 12/29/1950   Jess W. Swinney 1/5/1973
Lonnie P. Swinney 1/4/1968   Maggie Odelle Swinney
                                       8/22/1974

WILLIAM PENNINGTON BIBLE Of Campbell Co.
Owner: Mrs. Emma Skeen
Palmetto, Ga.

Marriages
William Pennington to Matilda Ann Davenport 12/9/1845
Thomas E. Pennington to Alice Wilkerson 11/26/1876
William J. Stipe to Lucy E. Pennington 3/13/1878
John H. Pennington to Roxien L. Barfield 11/2/1881

Births
John Henry Pennington 9/18/1847
Mary Caroline Pennington 7/25/1849
Margaret Susan Pennington 8/22/1851
Lucy Elizabeth Pennington 8/14/1853
Thomas Ephraim Pennington 2/28/1855
Sarah Eveline Pennington 2/15/1857
James Edward Pennington 3/18/1859
William Overton Pennington 3/1/1861
Sarah Emily Pennington 8/2/1879
William Hanley Pennington 4/2/1881
Benjamin Hill Pennington 10/20/1882 (son of J. H. P.)
Louis Agnes Pennington 9/9/1884
Mary Witt (Daisey) Pennington 12/22/1884
Tom Pierce Pennington 2/2/1890
Lucy Pennington 11/12/1892

Deaths
Margaret Susan Pennington 3/8/1885
William Brown Pennington 7/11/1863   Alice Pennington 5/9/1929
Sarah Evaline Pennington 10/23/1864
Matilda Ann Pennington 1/3/1866   Daisy Pennington 1/4/1934
Benjamin Hill Pennington, son of J. S. and R. L. Pennington,
   12/12/1883
N. O. Skeen 4/7/1949
Lucy Elizabeth Stipe 9/16/1889
Dr. T. E. Pennington 5/9/1929

JAMES WILSON EDWARDS BIBLE

James Wilson Edwards of Macon, Ga., Bibb Co., m. Miss Pennie
Bryan of near Visina, Dooly Co., Ga., 12/17/1874. Wit: Martha W.
Bryan

Births
Ellen Findley Edwards 1/16/1876   Richard S. Edwards 5/22/1883
Bryan Edwards 12/24/1878   Elizabeth Winifred Edwards
James Wilson Edwards 3/31/1881   11/30/1886
Elizabeth Corning Edwards 3/10/1893

Name- Ellen changed to Nellie 1876
Name- Elizabeth changed to Susan 1887
Deaths
Elizabeth Corning Edwards 8/24/1896, age 3 yrs., 4 mos., 20 days
James Wilson Edwards Sr. 4/1903

JACOB KELLY BIBLE
Owner: Mrs. Emily Brown Edwards, Sr.
Macon, Ga.

Marriages
Jacob Kelly to Julia F. Darwin 6/23/1842
Jacob Kelly Sr. to Ada Locke 1/15/1885
J. R. Crawford to Mary C. Kelly 2/23/1870
Martha Emily Crawford to T. H. Brown 8/1/1893, Dayton, Tenn.
W. B. Kelly to Ada Morrison 11/28/1883
Vesta Ann Kelly to Robert L. Allen 6/20/1877 Washington, Tenn.

Births
Mary Catharine Kelly 9/21/1843   Jacob Kelly 2/28/1811
Bethiah White Kelly 2/2/1845   Julia Franklin Darwin 2/4/1824
Jane Adams Kelly 3/25/1847   Virginia Tennessee Kelly
Thomas Darwin Kelly 6/19/1849   12/15/1858
James Elmore Kelly 10/24/1851   William Brown Kelly 2/29/1860
Robert Peyton Kelly 10/16/1854   Jacob Kelly Sr. 2/8/1862
Vesta Ann Kelly 6/19/1856   Martha Emily Crawford
                                     12/14/1872

Deaths
Jane Adams Kelly 2/13/1849
James Elmore & Peyton Kelly 7/5/1855
William B. Kelly 2/29/1860
Virginia Tennessee Kelly 3/3/1859
Bethiah White Kelly 11/17/1859
Jacob Kelly Jr. 6/21/1886
Jacob Kelly Sr. 7/6/1862
Julia F. Kelly 11/5/1905

Births
Mary Ellen Brown 1/28/1895, Dayton, Tenn.
Jefferson Crawford Brown 5/2/1896, Dayton, Tenn.
Emily Louise Brown, 3/6/1905, Macon, Ga.

ANDREW CHAMBLESS BIBLE
Owner: Mrs. C. W. Harris
Columbus, Ga.

Andrew Chambless b. 7/4/1821 m. 1844
Lovenia Sullivan b. 1820, dau. of Sara Russell and Isaac Sullivan
   of N. C.
Aurelius Chambless 1845-1848
Mary Lovenia Chambless 2/3/1848-
Lovenia Sullivan Chambless d. 1854

Andrew Chambless m. 2nd Harriet Athon 1855

COL. WILLIAM JONES MORTON BIBLE

William M. Morton m. Caroline Matilda Jones 1/24/1826.   Their
children:

Henry Clay Morton b. 9/30/1842
Josephine Isabel Morton b. 12/20/1844
John S. A. Morton b. 9/14/1846

5/6/1851 Lou Morton, dau. of William M. Morton m. J. Sinclair
   Wiggins of Waynesville, Ga. by Rev. J. M. Bonnell at res. of
   her father

Mrs. Mary Jones d. 8/28/1843, age 76 yrs.
Henry Clay Morton d. 9/10/1843, age 1 yr., 11 mos., 10 days
Mrs. Carolina Matilda Morton d. 3/21/1851

MARY LOVENIA CHAMBLESS WEATHERS BIBLE
Owner: Mrs. C. W. Harris, Columbus, Ga.

Mary Lovenia Chambless b. 2/3/1848 m. Jesse Lee Weathers
Fannie Weathers b. 8/13/1867 m. Charles Newton Humber 1/28/1886
Andrew Fletcher Weathers b. 3/28/1871 m. Mattie Mae Watson
   4/20/1896
Gladys Lovenia Weathers b. 7/31/1876
Jesse Seabron Weathers b. 1/22/1877 m. Nannie
Carlton Kitchens b. 12/31/1909
Henry Edgar Weathers b. 12/21/1879 m. Madge Norman 6/12/1913
Hattie Mae Weathers 2/18/1886-5/24/1902

Mary Lovenia Chambless Weathers d. 12/9/1921
Jesse Lee Weathers d. 8/23/1926
Andrew Fletcher Weathers d. 10/12/1938
Charles Newton Humber 6/7/1862-7/17/1927

THOMAS KENDRICK BIBLE
Owner: Mrs. Edna D. Kendrick

Thomas Kendrick b. 8/26/1908 m. 7/12/1936 Edna Delamar
  b. 3/30/1911
Edna Rebecca Kendrick b. 2/24/1938
Barbra Jane Kendrick b. 9/22/1939

WILLIAM CROW BIBLE
Owner: G. G. Strange, Toccoa, Ga.

William Crow d. 6/6/1878   Judith Worsham Crow
8/5/1796-1882
Jesse Crow 3/9/1826-6/19/1863
Nancy Crow 9/8/1822-7/27/1896
Elizabeth Crow 3/13/1834-2/2/1919

JAMES DANIEL BAILEY BIBLE
Owner: Mrs. W. A. Bailey, Toccoa, Ga.

Births
James Daniel Bailey 1843   William Asbury Bailey 4/28/1873
Amanda Vickery Bailey 1848   Lou Emma Cray Bailey 3/17/1859
John Johnson Kimsey 5/23/1849

F. L. JOLLEY BIBLE
Owner: Mrs. W. R. Beasley
Toccoa, Ga.

F. L. Jolley b. 1/15/1845
Mary M. Hamilton Jolley b. 1/20/1834

MRS. GEORGE F. EVERETT BIBLE
Owner: Mrs. Marvin Hall, Irwinton, Ga.

Eva P. Wilson m. George F. Everett 11/7/1895.
  Births of Their Children:
Eva Madeline Everett 1/10/1898   Eula Everett 9/23/1901
Elizabeth Virginia Everett 3/27/1909   Dorothy Judson 8/25/1917
Ruth Everett ---

185

MRS. ROBERT WALTERS BIBLE
Toccoa, Georgia

<u>Births</u>
Robert Lee Walters 10/2/1882   Harold Lee Walters 7/11/1906
George T. Walters 5/15/1884   Garver Edward Walters 11/3/1909
Winnie Lucille Walters 7/21/1904   Robert Sewell 5/12/1919

JULIUS J. PRUITT BIBLE Of Homer, Ga.

<u>Births</u>
Julius J. Pruitt 12/31/1857   Clara V. Pruitt 2/14/1884
Mary Lee Strange Pruitt 9/21/1862
Robert Adolphus Pruitt 12/11/1879

TYRA H. STRANGE BIBLE
Owner: Mrs. T. H. Strange
Eatonton, Ga.

<u>Births</u>
Tyra H. Strange 4/20/1870-10/1/1933
Francis Leolian Neal Strange 8/12/1872
Hubert Strange 4/26/1872
Jesse Neal Strange 11/17/1895
Buie Garnett Strange 4/10/1898

ELISHA M. POOL, JR. BIBLE
Owner: Mrs. E. M. Poole, Jr.
Homer, Ga.

<u>Births</u>
Elisha M. Poole, Jr. 3/21/1863-12/1/1931   Minnie Poole 2/4/1889
Lucy Coffee Poole 8/22/1865   Emma Poole 4/24/1892
Everag T. Poole 10/25/1885   Lila Poole 5/6/1898

J. J. STRANGE BIBLE Of Winder, Ga.

Jesse Jackson Strange b. 3/29/1877
Arra Gene Purcell Strange b. 8/1/1883

186

FLETCHER ALLISON GARRISON BIBLE Of Cornelia, Ga.

<u>Births</u>
Fletcher Allison Garrison 5/20/1901
Laura Brawner Martin Garrison 8/27/1902
Fletcher Orland Garrison 10/3/1924
Myra Jacqueline Garrison 11/8/1928

THOMAS HORNE
Owner: Mrs. W. B. Schaefer
Toccoa, Ga.

Thomas Horne 2/25/1785-9/21/1858
Wife, Christian Horne 8/1/1795-8/26/1869
James Monroe Horne 1/26/1839-7/11/1899, his wife, Isabel Dumas
   Horne 7/30/1845-4/14/1915
Zada Horne 9/29/1869-11/28/1936

WILLIAM HARRISON STRANGE BIBLE Of Cornelia, Ga.

William Harrison Strange b. 11/26/1868
Ruth Fennell Strange 4/5/1874-5/12/1927
His 2nd wife, Samantha R. Fowler Strange b. 2/16/1893
William Aiken Strange b. 4/18/1898
John Fennell Strange b. 2/4/1900

DAVID WASHINGTON GARRISON BIBLE
Owner: Mrs. Joseph Ariail
Maysville, Ga.

<u>Births</u>
David Washington Garrison 12/16/1856-9/27/1923
Mary Heney Kesler Garrison 12/8/1862-9/1/1930
William Garrison 11/23/1883
Mallie Ophelia Garrison 11/7/1881

WILLIAM H. KESLER BIBLE
Owner: G. G. Strange, Toccoa, Ga.

William H. Kesler 4/2/1840-7/2/1863
Judah Elizabeth Pool Kesler 2/7/1843-3/14/1918
Mary Honey Kesler 12/8/1862-9/14/1930

JOHN WILMOT, SR. BIBLE
Owner: G. G. Strange, Toccoa, Ga.

Births
John Wilmot Sr. 1862-1/8/1914   Mary Jane Wilmot 3/16/1861
Mary Strange Wilmot 6/2/1833   John E. Wilmot 1/27/1863-
                                            2/15/1907

JAMES H. STRANGE BIBLE
Owner: G. G. Strange, Toccoa, Ga.

James H. Strange b. 4/4/1827
Nancy Gordon Strange d. 12/7/1889
Mary R. Strange 8/4/1853-9/24/1862
Seth Marion Strange 4/21/1857-5/3/1930
John Erwin Strange 4/13/1862-9/22/1876

WILLIAM STRANGE BIBLE
Owner: G. G. Strange, Toccoa, Ga.

William Strange 10/27/1797-1/18/1874
Mary (Polly) (White) Strange 6/2/1803-5/17/1829
James H. Strange b. 4/4/1827
Seth M. Strange Jr. 1/5/1829-4/19/1851
John Erwin Strange 1/25/1832-12/4/1904
Jesse D. Strange 5/22/1834-3/7/1909
William Strange Jr. 10/27/1837-8/18/1862
Mary Strange 6/2/1833-1/8/1914
Polly Strange b. 2/20/1839

188

SETH M. STRANGE, SR. BIBLE
Owner: G. G. Strange, Toccoa, Ga.

Seth M. Strange 1772-4/15/1851   Seth Strange 1804-
Mary Dobbs Strange 6/14/1771-1/31/1838   Elizabeth Strange 1806-
William Strange 10/27/1797-1/18/1874
Jesse Strange 7/7/1808-1/5/1837
Harrison Strange 12/1/1813-
John Strange 1/1/1802-11/22/1833

MRS. C. A. MERCK BIBLE Of Toccoa, Ga.

Births
Clarence Allen Merck 5/28/1904   Mildred F. Merck 5/25/1926
Eula Foster Merck 5/25/1906   Clarence Allen Merck, Jr.
Edna Jeanette Merck 9/26/1924   6/6/1929

HORACE MILTON WILLIAMS BIBLE
Owner: Mrs. Richard Addison, Toccoa, Ga.

Births
Horace Milton Williams 2/1/1851   Stanford Williams 7/30/1857
Corinthia Cordelia Halcomb 3/15/1854   Marcus Robert Williams
Virgil Sutton Williams 6/3/1854   1/19/1860
William Irwin Jefferson Williams 12/19/1862

HENRY MITCHELL BIBLE
Owner: Mrs. J. B. McMurry
Toccoa, Ga.

Births
Henry Mitchell 5/14/1832   Elizabeth J. Mitchell 8/3/1868
Rhoda E. Mitchell 9/29/1832   Wm. A. Landrum 1845
William B. Mitchell 4/8/1858   Ida Landrum 1852

JOHN GRESHAM BIBLE

John Gresham b. 3/14/1761 m. 11/13/1788 Martha, b. 3/17/1772

HUGH CRAWFORD VERNER BIBLE
Owner: Mrs. E. F. Chaffin
Toccoa, Ga.

Hugh Crawford Verner b. 6/30/1852
Mary Scott Verner b. 6/1/1852

EPP M. WILLIAMS BIBLE
Owner: Mrs. E. A. Williams
Toccoa, Ga.

Births
Epp M. Williams b. 8/18/1853   Eliza Williams 12/27/1874
Essie Ayers Williams 3/10/1857

T. R. YOW BIBLE
Owner: Cynthia Williams
Martin, Ga.

T. R. Yow b. 8/5/1855 m. 10/17/1878
Cynthia Elizabeth Dean Yow b. 10/13/1851

ELBERT JACKSON BROWN BIBLE
Owner: Mrs. Loyd Brown, Martin, Ga.

Births
Elbert Jackson Brown 8/17/1817   John Dozier Brown 1/14/1846
Sarah Presley Brown 10/11/1824   John Dozier 1/14/1846
John Harber Aderhold 5/9/1812
Sarah Aderhold 12/25/1808
Winnie Rebecca Brown 4/21/1848

NEWTON RUFUS HERRON BIBLE
Owner: Albert Burton Herron
Martin, Ga.

Newton Rufus Herron b. 4/23/1852
Sarah Jane Pitts Herron b. 3/19/1854

190

JAMES WALLACE PRATHER BIBLE
Owner: Mrs. J. D. Prather, Toccoa, Ga.

James Wallace Prather 4/28/1782-3/15/1869 m. 12/9/1806
Sarah Bell Prather 7/27/1790-

GEORGE E. McCALL BIBLE
Owner: Miss Eunice McCall
Martin, Ga.

George E. McCall b. 12/3/1866
Mattie Fulgham McCall b. 5/22/1872

WILLIAM PICKEN BRADLEY BIBLE
Owner: Mrs. Dave Farmer
Townsville, S. C.

Births
William Picken Bradley 2/12/1888   Joe E. Bradley 11/1/1849
Mary Ann Hilley Bradley 2/24/1866   Isaac N. Bradley 12/16/1845

IRA BENA CALHOUN BIBLE
Owner: Mrs. Ira Calhoun
Columbus, Ga.

Ira Bena Calhoun b. 5/18/1904 m. 2/2/1934 Germaine Doucet
  b. 9/2/1908 Lafayette, La.
Germaine Pauline Calhoun b. 6/26/1940

MARY NELL PERRY GRADDY BIBLE
Of Columbus, Ga.

Mary Nell Perry b. 6/20/1891
William Mercer Graddy 10/13/1888-6/6/1930
Mary N. Perry m. W. M. Graddy 9/1/1926
Ida Nell Graddy b. 12/12/1927

MRS. JAMES H. CRAIG, JR. BIBLE
Of Columbus, Ga.

James H. Craig Jr. b. 10/31/1909 m. 10/5/1925
Hzel Bivins b. 5/25/1912
Jeane Marie Craig b. 9/21/1940

HOWARD LEON MULLIN BIBLE
Of Columbus, Ga.

Howard Leon Mullin b. 9/19/1906
Margaret McCutchen, wife, b. 4/24/1909
Peggie Mullin b. 12/1/1934

FREDERICK K. NORRIS BIBLE
Owner: Frederick K. Norris
Eatawville, S. C.

Gladys Eudell Duggan b. 10/27/1898 m. 1/12/1927 Frederick Keating
   Norris b. 10/5/1881
Frederick Keating Norris Jr. b. 2/25/1927
Caroline Gladys Norris b. 3/23/1932

W. J. McMICHAEL BIBLE
Owner: Mrs. Jim McMichael
Monticello, Ga.

Births
W. J. McMichael 8/29/1870   Paul Griffin McMichael 1/21/1900
Lizzie McMichael 12/3/1871   Henry Hulyn McMichael 8/1/1902
Annie Irene McMichael 10/1/1893 Seaborn laurence McMichael
Jame Troy McMichael 10/13/1893   5/2/1905
L. Berta McMichael 9/12/1897   Lizzie Alena McMichael 7/21/1908
                                   Minnie Lou McMichael 2/28/1911

W. J. McMichael m. Lizzie 11/20/1892

JOSEPH MORELAND BIBLE
Owner: Fel Phillips, Monticello, Ga.

Births
Joseph F. Moreland 11/4/1824   Mary R. Moreland 10/14/1834
Sarah H. Moreland 8/6/1830   Mildred A. Moreland 6/5/1838
Hannah R. Moreland 8/16/1832   Susan T. Moreland 1/15/1841

Thomas Moreland d. 3/14/1847, age 57 yrs., b. 4/28/1790
Minnor Phillips b. 10/8/1884

Slaves
Major 6/29/1857   Harriet 6/5/1859   Letta 8/4/1861

S. W. TURNER BIBLE
Owner: Susie Alexander
Hillsboro, Ga.

S. W. Turner d. 3/21/1901
Mrs. S. W. Turner d. 6/26/1912
S. W. Turner, Jr., husband of Adie Alexander, d. 1/26/1926

COL. BENJAMIN HAWKINS BIBLE

Col. Benjamin Hawkins, Agent for Creek Indians, d. 6/6/1816, age
    63. "He has served as a Publick in various departments and
    always discharged his trust faithfully for 35 years."

Elinor Hawkins m. Sherwood Haywood
Delia, Mother of Philemon Hawkins of Pleasant Hill, d. 8/20/1794
N. C., where her husband, Philemon, owned a mill...lived to be 73
yrs.

Philemon, father of Philemon of Pleasant Hill, b. in Va., d.
9/10/1801, nearly 84.

DR. CECIL G. MOYE BIBLE
Owner: Mrs. Moye, Brewton, Ga.

Clara Lou Duggan b. 12/27/1897 m. 6/5/1921 Dr. Cecil G. Moye
    b. 4/21/1888 Ga.
Duggan Moye b. 4/10/1922   Victor Moye b. 10/10/1923
Agnes Moye b. 6/8/1926

193

PHILEMON HAWKINS II BIBLE
Son of Philemon Hawkins of N. C.

Births
Philemon Hawkins, II 12/3/1752 m. 8/31/1775 Lucy, wife,
   b. 7/9/1759
Eleanor Hawkins 6/23/1776   Benjamin F. Hawkins 10/28/1787
William Hawkins 10/20/1777   Philemon Hawkins 6/5/1789
Ann Hawkins 9/3/1779   Frank Hawkins 3/29/1791
Delia Hawkins 10/16/1782   Geo. Washington Hawkins 10/20/1793
Sarah Hawkins 3/5/1784   Lucinda David Ruffin Hawkins
Joseph Hawkins 9/15/1785   6/26/1795
                                   Mildred Hawkins 12/13/1801
                                   Thomas P. Hawkins 8/29/1808

Lucy Hawkins d. 9/29/1807

LAWRENCE SHIELDS BIBLE
Owner: Mrs. I. L. Shields
St. Elmo, Columbus, Ga.

Lawrence Shields b. 7/1/1894 m. 9/8/1931 Reba Meadows
   b. 8/31/1909
Reba Jane Shields b. 9/13/1934

JOHN LAVENDER BIBLE
Owner: Mrs. E. C. Alford
Columbus, Ga.

John Lavender m. Sarah Eliza Moore
Frank Gillard Lavender b. 10/25/1880 m. Mary Eva Gentry
   b. 1/18/1881 Martha on 10/13/1910

ARTHUR HAYNES DUGGAN BIBLE
Owner: A. H. Duggan, Atlanta, Ga.

Arthur Haynes Duggan b. 1/6/1891 m. 8/10/1919 Thelma Beasley
   b. 1/3/1900
Josee Lou Duggan Pruitt b. 7/28/1920
Robert Clay Duggan b. 7/8/1923
Miriam Duggan b. 2/14/1933

```
                    JOHN WALLER BIBLE
            Owner: Mrs. Emily Waller Olive
                    Lisbon, Arkansas


John Waller b. 1749 m. Elizabeth Rhodes b. 9/17/1746

Births
John Waller Sr. 3/13/1749      Charles R. Waller 9/14/1780
Hardy Waller 12/1768           Elizabeth Waller 2/26/1783
Daniel Waller 8/10/1772
John Waller 6/8/1775
William Waller 1/9/1777
Nathaniel E. Waller 10/12/1787 m. Elizabeth 2/29/1833



                    G. M. CLEMENTS BIBLE
                  Owner: Mrs. G. M. Clements
                       Eastman, Ga.



Gabriel McArrol Clements m. Aleph Thomas Sikes, Lumber City,
    Ga., 5/7/1884

Births
Gabriel McArrol Clements 10/27/1859
Aleph Sikes Clements 10/21/1861
Infant 5/4/1885-5/4/1885
Ben Harvey Clements 6/21/1886-6/19/1887
Collier Leon Clements 4/6/1888-9/21/1901
Fred Julian Clements 5/4/1890
Henrietta Clements 11/1/1892
Leroy Hamilton Clements 12/15/1894
Mamie Gertrude Clements 4/5/1898
Alva Edison Clements 10/16/1901



                       HILEY BIBLE
                  Owner: Dr. Hollinshead
                    Nashville, Tenn.



Births
Anna Sophia Hiley 4/17/1787      Mary Magdaline Hiley 10/4/1795
Barbary Hiley 4/20/1789          Thomas Hiley 3/20/1797
Elizabeth Hiley 1/8/1792         Cathrina Hiley 3/9/1819
John Hiley 7/27/1794
```

WILLIAM C. LOWERY BIBLE
Owner: Mrs. Mattie Lowery
Eastman, Ga.

Births
William C. Lowery 12/15/1815
Daniel Lowery 2/5/1846
Angeline E. Lowery 3/1848
Margret J. Lowery 4/1/1850
Haras R. Lowery 2/6/1855
William J. Lowery 4/5/1857

William A. Lowery 3/8/1859
Isabella S. Lowery 3/8/1861
Hugh B. Lowery 2/25/1863
George W. Lowery 2/5/1865
Jeremiah W. Lowery 3/5/1865
Nancy H. Lowery 11/1/1870

MICHAEL LONG BIBLE

Michael Long 1782-1824 m. Mary Waddell, 1785-1846

Harriet Rebecca Long d. 1/17/1898
John Long d. 8/30/1813
Zachariah Long d. 4/25/1813

Thos. Edward Long 6/23/1815
Henry Long d. 11/15/1837

WILLIAM MOSS CAPPS BIBLE
Owner: Mrs. Moss Harrison
Columbus, Ga.

William Moss Capps 2/6/1826-6/11/1897
Sarah Jane Sikes 12/31/1833-7/3/1920
Martha Jane Capps b. 1/1/1852 m. Thomas Wesley Harrison 1874

ALFRED HARRISON BIBLE
Owner: Mrs. Moss Harrison
Columbus, Ga.

Alfred Harrison 1/31/1816-9/10/1884 m. Letitia Harrison
    b. 4/20/1816
Thomas Wesley Harrison 11/28/1851-8/2/1908 m. Martha Jane Capps
    1/1/1852-3/10/1909
Wesley Moss Harrison b. 9/18/1876

196

```
                    WESLEY MOSS HARRISON BIBLE
                    Owner: Mrs. Moss Harrison
                         Columbus, Ga.
```

Wesley Moss Harrison b. 9/18/1876 m. Lille May Clark 1/1/1904
Eva Elsie Harrison b. 5/14/1905
Evelyn Margaret Harrison 2/8/1910-3/27/1941


```
                      JAMES W. HEARD BIBLE *
                      Owner: Mrs. J. L. Holloway
                         Indian Springs, Ga.
```

James W. Heard of Indian Springs m. Adalaide Barkley of Monroe
Co. 12/20/1866 by Rev. Mullins, Monroe Co., Baptist Church, wit:
Midlton Wise, Jane H. Moore

Births
James W. Heard 11/14/1834 Indian Springs, Ga.
Adalaide Gertrude Barkley 10/18/1846 Monroe Co., Ga.
Lillian lee Heard 1/6/1870
Ada Gertrude Heard 11/14/1871
Claudine Heard 9/14/1873


```
                      THOMAS M. HARKNESS BIBLE
                      Owner: Miss Hattie Butrill
                           Jackson, Ga.
```

Thomas M. Harkness b. 5/8/1814 m. 12/19/1839
Harriet Caroline, dau. of David and Martha Berry, b. 5/6/1815

Births
John B. Harkness 3/11/1841
Martha Rosannah Harkness 11/7/1843
John B. Harkness d. 1/7/1843
John James David Berry b. 6/1/1838 and killed t Battle of
Sharpsburg 9/17/1862


```
                         VAUGHN BIBLE
```

Births
Broxton B. Vaughn 9/13/1888   Troy Vaughn 1/14/1882
George Clifford Vaughn 5/26/1890   Thernellar Vaughn 4/13/1885
Taylor W. Vaughn 10/21/1883   Henry M. Vaughn 1/26/1891
Sarah A. Vaughn 1/20/1879

*See also p. 86.   197

EUEL WRIGHT McMICHAEL BIBLE
Owner: Elby Wright McMichael
Linden, Texas

Evel Wright McMichael, son of Griffin C. McMichael, b. and m. in
Butts Co., moved to Cusseta, Texas in 1852

Griffin C. McMichael 1/6/1814-2/14/1904
Evel Wright McMichael 12/8/1846-
Elizabeth lee McMichael 7/17/1848-7/12/1883

Children by first wife:

William L. McMichael 9/17/1868-2/8/1921
Flora McMichael 12/24/1870
Griffin McMichael 1/20/1873
James R. McMichael 2/14/1875
Sallie Lee McMichael 6/16/1877
Elby Wright McMichael 10/14/1879
                    Children by second wife:
Nannie, Marvin, and Minnie

STERLING JENKINS BIBLE
Owner. Mrs. Leon W. Cunningham, Sr.
Columbus, Georgia

Sterling Jenkins b. 3/30/1813 m. 11/24/1839 Lucinda McClendon,
    b. 7/28/1817

Births
Stephen Francis Jenkins 5/18/1840
Thomas Washington Jenkins 3/15/1843
Jane Elizabeth Jenkins 8/22/1840
Sarah Cornelia Jenkins 12/22/1851
Sterling Jenkins 2/9/1854
Martha Lucinda Jenkins 2/21/1857
Willie Leon Jenkins 12/15/1861

T. W. Jenkins started to Virginia to war on 8/14/1861

Stephen McClendon b. 9/19/1783
Elizabeth Collens (Collins) b. 1/31/1786
Stephen McClendon d. 6/5/1836
Elizabeth McClendon d. 12/20/1845

Stephen Francis Jenkins d. 12/18/1846
Edmond W. Jenkins d. 7/23/1856
Thomas W. Jenkins d. 6/24/1862
Edmon Jenkins Jackson b. 3/26/1871
Albert Cunningham 8/14/1883-6/6/1885
Sterling Jenkins Jr. d. 8/24/1879
Sterling Jenkins Sr. d. 9/2/1881
Lucinda Jenkins d. 1/24/1891
Leon W. Jenkins 12/15/1861-3/22/1900

ARCHIBALD L. POLK BIBLE
Owner: Mrs. M. C. Johnson
Jackson, Ga.

Archibald L. Polk b. 5/26/1799 m. 11/9/1824
Kizziah (Morgan) Polk b. 8/19/1806

Births
Elizabeth Malinda Polk 3/4/1826   Sarah Ann Polk 4/30/1839
Charley Ellison Polk 9/13/1828   James Knox Polk 9/3/1845
John Edmuns Polk 12/19/1830   Frances Jane Polk 12/11/1848
Jemima Catherine Polk 12/27/1832   Berry Franklin Polk 3/20/1850
Leah Ellender Polk 9/30/1834
Georgia Ann Elizur Manerva Polk 12/13/1842
Joshua Alexander Polk 2/24/1852

JUDGE BENJAMIN WALLER BIBLE
Owner: Miss Juliet Fauntleroy
Alta Vista, Virginia

Judge Benjamin Waller m. 1/2/1746 Martha Hall b. 7/2/1728 on
8/9/1780. Judge Waller b. Spotsylvania Co., Va. 10/1/1716

Martha Waller b. 11/28/1747 m. 1767 William Tayloe
Robert Waller 7/16/1749-10/4/1749
Benjamin Waller 12/3/1750-8/31/1751
Mary Waller b. 7/14/1752 m. 2/16/1772 John Taylo Corbin
John Waller b. 7/25/1753 m. 9/1774 Judith Page
Dorothy Elizabeth Waller b. 9/2/1754 m. 1/13/1774 Henry Tazewell
Benjamin Carter Waller b. 12/24/1757 m. 2/1778 Catharine Page
Anne Waller b. 2/29/1756 m. 4/18/1773 John Boush
Clara Waller b. 9/2/1759 m. 1st 2/20/1779 Edward Travis, 2nd,
   Mordecai Boots
William Waller b. 2/16/1762 m. 11/30/1786 Elizabeth Macon of
   Hanover Co.
Robert Hall Waller b. 1/7/1764 m. 3/5/1789---
dau. (Mrs. Smith)
Frances Waller 4/6/1766-1767

JANET NEEL BIBLE
Owner: Miss Jeannette Wilhoite
LaGrange, Ga.

Janet Neel, Her Bible, 4/4/1803

Births
Daniel Boozer 9/27/1788   John Neel 712/1793
Janet Neel 10/21/1787   Robert Neel 4/22/1794
Margaret Neel 5/16/1789   Elizabeth Boozer 5/13/1809

199

ROBERT A. HARDY BIBLE
Owner: Mrs. Robert Teat
600 22 St., N. W.
St. Petersburg, Fla.

Robert A. Hardy of Troup Co. m. Martha L. Freeman of Troup
  Co. 1/23/1868
H. O. Teat of Bartow Co. m. Annie Lee Hardy of Troup Co.
  10/21/1888

Births
R. A. Hardy 5/19/1844   Maggie May Hardy 4/30/1872
Martha Hardy 9/1/1847   Martha Hardy 7/9/1882
Anna Lee Hardy 4/23/1869   R. A. Hardy 7/28/1910

ELIJAH J. HERRING BIBLE
Owner: Mrs. J. A. Herring
Athens, Ga.

Births
Elijah E. Herring 6/6/1834   Henry Bradley Herring 7/21/1858
Mary Ann Herring 7/14/1836   Milton Thomas Herring 2/19/1860
John Newton Herring 10/27/1856 Elijah Jefferson Herring 1/9/1862
Elijah J. Herring m. Mary A. 11/21/1855

WILLIAM J. TOMLINSON BIBLE
Owner: Mrs. J. A. Minter
Cairo, Georgia

William M. Tomlinson 7/2/1844-4/16/1930
Nancy Emily McMichael 2/2/1844-2/9/1909
John Lee McMichael 2/1/1820-1880
Sarah Laurence 3/2/1823-1890
John D. Tomlinson 4/2/1812-

JOHN ELLIS POPE BIBLE*
Owner: Mrs. John Pope
Jackson, Ga.

John Ellis Pope b. 2/13/1916 m. 8/29/1936 Dorothy Alexander Pope
b. 7/10/1919
John Ronald Pope b. 11/1/1938   John Ellis Pope (Jr.)10/7/1944
Dorothy Marilyn Pope b. 11/5/1940

*See also p. 214.   200

```
                    BENJAMIN WHEELER FOSSETT BIBLE
                    Owner: B. W. Fossett, Jackson, Ga.
```

Benjamin Wheeler Fossett b. Gwinnett Co. 3/7/1865
Laura Cornelia Hobbs b. Dodge Co. 5/16/1873


```
                         MRS. J. L. COOK BIBLE
                            Molena, Georgia
```

Jesse Linton Cook b. 10/11/1922 m. 10/13/1943 Betty Anne Willis
   4/9/1924
Charles Linton Cook b. 8/1/1944


```
                         SAMUEL A. HARRIS BIBLE
```

Samuel A. Harris m. Mary A. Page 3/5/1867

Births
Lula Alberta Harris 3/3/1868   James Arthur Harris 2/1873
John Emory Harris 1870   Earnest Blake Harris 2/1879


```
                         BENJAMIN A. SMITH BIBLE
                           Owner: W. D. Harvey
                           Americus, Ga. 31709
```

Benjamin A. Smith 1724-7/29/1799 m. (abt 1753) Mary Smith
   1734-12/2/1794

Births
Brittain Smith 1754   Simon Smith 1768
Mary Smith 1756   Samuel Smith 1774
Sion Smith 1759   Jordan Smith 1777
Elizabeth Smith 1764   Bennett Smith 1779

Births
Leroy Hinton, son of James and Sophia, 8/10/1801
Jesse Hinton 9/3/1802   Eliza Ritter Hinton 7/18/1810
Fielder Lewis Hinton 2/26/1806   Melissa Hinton 9/25/1812
James Whitfield Hinton 9/12/1806   Norman H. Pope 11/11/1771
Polly Ann Hinton 7/10/1808   Amelia Hinton 3/27/1815

CHARLES H. CROMWELL BIBLE Of Macon
Owner: Mrs. Lehman E. Huey
2104 Ocean Road
St. Simons Island, Ga. 315201

Charles Hardeman Cromwell b. 10/6/1851 Milledgeville, Ga.
Mary Moultrie Quarterman b. 9/15/1856 Walthourville, Ga.
Marion Moultrie Cromwell b. 12/12/1876 Macon, Ga.
Charles H. Cromwell Jr. d. 9/6/1875, 16 days old

Charles Cromwell m. Mary Moultrie Quarterman 10/21/1874, by
Rev. A. W. Clisby

JOSHUA HUTCHERSON BIBLE Of Elbert Co.
Owner: Mrs. R. A. Wilbanks, Lavonia, Ga.

Births
Joshua Hutcherson 2/16/1808   Sarah M. Hutcherson 3/24/1845
Flora Hutcherson 1/26/1813   Olivia A. Hutcherson 11/6/1847
Mary E. Hutcherson 10/14/1835   Amanda E. Hutcherson 7/17/1850
Martha J. Hutcherson 1/23/1838   James M. Hutcherson 4/4/1840
John M. D. Hutcherson 9/14/1842
Thomas S. Hutcherson 8/23/1852-3/14/1853
Donald W. Hutcherson 12/15/1853

ALEXANDER JONES BIBLE
Owner: Mrs. Mary Morris
Hartwell, Ga.

Births
Alexander Jones 1/7/1811   George M. Jones 1/31/182-
Rachel Jones 11/30/1812   Elizabeth Ann Jones 3/22/1830
Lavinia Jones 6/11/1815   Polly Jane Jones 8/29/1832
Wilson Jones 3/1/1817-12/17/1819

WILLIAM NEWTON KAY BIBLE

William Newton Kay 1/27/1833-12/2/1862
Emma Manerva Kay 6/9/1857-10/5/1898

William Newton Kay m. 11/29/1835 Mary Caroline Parker (4/25/1837-
5/7/1864)

JOHN B. MAXWELL BIBLE

John B. Maxwell 12/1/1811-11/5/1906
Martha W. Maxwell 5/30/1820-2/6/1863
George W. Maxwell 12/31/1846-4/23/1864
Mildred J. Maxwell 8/8/1833-10/23/1916
Mary A. Maxwell 3/17/1867-8/8/1916
Martha A. Maxwell 1/5/1869-5/19/1928
Richard L. Gaines 4/1855
William R. maxwell 7/17/1871

JOSEPH McCONNELL BIBLE
Owner: Mrs. R. P. Robertson
Airline, Ga. (Hart Co.)

Nancy Richardson d. 11/28/1855   Joseph McConnell d. 1/1857
Margaret Clark d. 11/28/1853   ---Wilson d. 7/13/185-
Drucilla Crosen McConnell 3/14/185- C. P. Striblin d. 7/9/-

THOMAS H. WHITE BIBLE *
Owner: Mr. Hays, Hart Co., Ga.

Births
Thomas H. White 2/2/1816   Eppie White 5/27/1843
Martha C. White 3/15/1819   Asa Salmon White 8/20/1878
M. M. White 1/6/1841   Albert Crayton White 5/12/1876
Sarah C. White 12/20/1841   Martha Ann White 1/29/1846

Thomas H. White m. Martha McMillen 3/15/1840

*See also p. 127.   203

VINING A. WILSON BIBLE
Owner: Mrs. Jesse Clay
Monticello, Ga.

Births
Elizabeth G. Vining 2/8/1882   Joseph Benton Wilson 12/1/1887
Sarah A. Vining 9/16/1884   Rachel Lowery 12/22/1801
Elizabeth M. A. Holland 2/12/1827
Eugenia Kate Wilson 10/16/1891

Deaths
William T. Wilson 9/18/1871   V. A. Wilson 12/16/1898
John R. Wilson 12/26/1876   G. M. Wilson 4/12/1907
George J. Wilson 12/22/1871   Martha Wilson 8/18/1907
Elizabeth M. A. Wilson 8/2/1875   Willie Dora Wilson 12/17/1912

CHERRY LANDSLOT BUNTZ BIBLE
Owner: Mrs. Elizabeth Buntz
Savannah, Georgia

Cherry Landslot Buntz b. 10/8/1876 (never married)

CRISSON BIBLE Of Lumpkin Co.

Bolling W. Field b. 5/1/1807   Nevada Field b. 7/4/1810
Miss Stevens ---

JOHN FLETCHER FOSTER BIBLE

John Fletcher Foster m. Margaret Furlow 3/12/1795
John Fletcher Foster m. Frances Thrasher 11/28/1799
William Beall m. Mary Foster 10/3/1814
Steven Cloud Hester m. Margaret Fujrlow Foster 12/27/1832

MICAJAH McGEHEE BIBLE Of Broad River
Owner: Mrs. Lamar Smith, Como, Miss.

Births

James McGehee 11/26/1770	Sarah McGehee 7/11/1784
Thomas McGehee 12/1/1771	Edward McGehee 11/12/1786
Elizabeth McGehee 10/21/1773	John McGehee 1/15/1789
Francis McGehee 1/19/1777	Abraham McGehee 1/1/1791
Abner McGehee 2/17/1779	Hugh McGehee 1/4/1793
William McGehee 3/9/1782	Lucinda McGehee 1/1/1795

"Cousin Hugh gave me this."

L. C. ECHOLS BIBLE

L. C. Echols b. Tallahassee, Ala. 8/31/1868 m. 11/12/1898
   d. 11/16/1944 Atlanta, Ga.
Katherine V. Brand b. Maplesville, Ala. 1/21/1873 m. 11/12/1898
   d. 11/30/1959
James Lee Echols b. Randolph, Ala. 9/21/1891 m. 5/8/1917
Oliver C. Echols b. Randolph, Ala. 9/16/1892 m. 12/9/1916
Annie E. Echols b. Randolph, Ala. 8/7/1895 m. 9/10/1913
Willie A. Echols b. Chepultapec, Ala. 10/28/1897 m. 8/9/1916
Katherine V. Echols b. Birmingham, Ala. 6/12/1900 m. 5/5/1929
Hattie L. Echols b. Birmingham, Ala. 4/12/1903 m. 7/20/1919
Maggie M. Echols b. Birmingham, Ala. 12/9/1905 m. 7/16/1926
Gaston T. Echols b. Birmingham, Ala. 12/9/1905 d. 11/11/1906
Mattie L. Echols b. Birmingham, Ala. 6/16/1908 m. 3/1/1930

Grandchildren of Mr. and Mrs. L. C. Echols:

William H. Giles b. Montgomery, Ala. 7/5/1914
Geraldine Echols b. Montgomery, Ala. 7/28/1917
Cathleen C. Echols b. 5/23/1918 Atlanta, Ga.
Catherine L. Echols b. 5/23/1918 Atlanta, Ga.
Milton A. Mensinger, Jr. b. Atlanta, Ga. 6/11/1920 d. 1/17/1936
Charles Lee Mensinger b. Atlanta, Ga. 8/12/1921 m. 2/2/1940

THOMAS M. COLLINS BIBLE
Owner: Mrs. Florence Foster
2520 Sylvan Road, E. Point, Ga.

Thomas M. Collins b. 7/25/1856 Paulding Co., Ga. d. 3/3/1903
Ben Hill, Fulton Co., Ga. (son of Humphrey Collins), m. Nancy
Carrie Lane b. 5/4/1851 Paulding Co., Ga., d. 10/15/1940
Paulding Co., Ga. (dau. of James C. Lane and Nancy Williams)
                        Their Children:
Ida Genette Collins 11/5/1876-8/27/1961 m. 1st 8/20/1899 Radford
   L. Johns m. 2nd Marshall Oscar Wiley

(Thomas M. Collins Bible contd....)

John Thomas Collins 12/17/1881-10/31/1936 m. Laura Rebecca
Jeffries
Willie Florence Collins 9/1/1884-7/8/1914 m. 12/2/1900 James Tom
Holland

CHARLES CRAWFORD EVANS BIBLE
Owner: Mrs. Pearl Howard
904 Ponce de Leon Ave.
Atlanta, Ga. (decd)

Charles Crawford Evans b. 3/7/1861 Stone Mountain, Ga., m.
1884 (Dekalb Co. marr. record says 1879) Martha Josephine
Perkins, b. 1/6/1863.

Charles Crawford Evans d. 3/29/1943 Atlanta, Ga.
Martha Josephine Perkins Evans d. 1/19/1944 Atlanta, Ga.

Births of Their Children:

Laura Annie Evans 9/25/1883 Atlanta, Ga., d. 10/26/1964 m.
1899 William Edward Sealock
Homer James Evans 8/17/1885 DeKalb Co., m. 9/26/1909 Mary
Brent Chambless. He d. 7/16/1943 Atlanta, Ga.
Pearl Evans 1/4/1895 Rockmart, Ga., m. 1st 7/4/1909 Jesse Roy
Jackson, Sr., m. 2d 7/13/1936, m. 3rd 12/25/1947 Roy Howard

MARY A. SAPP BIBLE
Owner: Mrs. Bunyan Webb
99 Cherokee Drive
Memphis, Tenn.

Benjamin Sapp b. 10/26/1799
Nancy Sapp b. 1/1/1799 or 1797   Their Children:

Births
Jane Sapp 2/4/1822   Hannah C. Sapp 2/22/1828
Thomas A.? Sapp 1/11/1823   William S. Sapp 5/1/1831
Mary B. Sapp 8/28/1824   Elizabeth Sapp 8/10/1833
Martha E. Sapp 5/21/1826   Benjamin F. Sapp 6/14/1836
                                  Nancy A. Sapp 5/13/1838
                                  Arkansas Sapp 10/1/1840
Deaths
Benjamin F. Sapp 11/13/1874   Nancy Sapp 10/26/1853 or 8

THOMAS WALTON DURHAM BIBLE
Owner: Vera Durham, Dallas, Ga.

Births
Thomas Walton Durham 4/27/1876 Paulding Co., Ga., son of Lindsey
  Durham
Mary Elizabeth Holland 12/26/1871 Paulding Co., Ga., dau. of
  George Washington Holland and his wife, Lydia Camp Holland

Their Children:

Lillie Mae Durham 8/2/1901 Dallas, Ga. m. Frank Cochran
Ben Young Durham 2/16/1904 Dallas, Ga. m. Lula Ledbetter
Tommie Irene Durham 3/28/1907 Dallas, Ga.-10/14/1962, m. Jave
  Mitchell
Vera Durham 3/6/1909 Dallas, Ga.
Willie Ora Durham 1/20/1913 Dallas, Ga. m. Frank Carruth

Deaths
Thomas Walton Durham 5/24/1946 Dallas, Ga.
Mary Elizabeth Durham 5/20/1928 Gadsden, Etowah Co., Ala.

LAUREL BENJAMIN HOLLAND BIBLE
Owner: Marguerite Evans Holland
Atlanta, Georgia

Laurel Benjamin Holland b. 2/15/1903 Paulding Co., Ga., son of
James Tom Holland and his wife, Willie Florence Collins Holland, m.
10/18/1930 Atlanta, Ga., Marguerite Elizabeth Evans, dau. of
Homer James Evans and Mary Brent Chambliss Evans, b. 5/26/1910
Atlanta, Ga.
                    Their Children:

Births
Marianne Holland 11/4/1931 Atlanta, Ga.
Inf. son b. dead Georgetown, S. C. 8/1932
Laurel Benjamin Holland 4/8/1934 Georgetown, S. C.
Willie Jeannette Holland 7/28/1936 Atlanta, Ga.
Dorothy Elizabeth Holland 7/24/1937 Abbeville, S. C.
Marie Eleanor Holland 2/17/1941 Atlanta, Ga.

Deaths
Laurel Benjamin Holland (Sr.) 7/28/1955 Charlotte, N. C.

Marriages
Marianne Holland 1st to Haig Daniel Keishian 4/29/1950, 2nd
  to Robert Tobin
Laurel Benjamin Holland to Barbara Cowan, 1955, Charlotte, N. C.
Willie Jeannette Holland 1st 4/25/1953 to Edwin Gerald Stucki,
  2nd to Kenneth Milton McCall, 3rd 5/13/1977 Jerry Franklin
  Austin, Jekyll Island, Ga.
Dorothy Elizabeth Holland 9/14/1953 to Billie Frank Herring
Marie Eleanor Holland 1st 10/25/1957 to Harry Bing Robinson,
  2nd to Derwood Johnson, 3rd to Don Roach, Charlotte, N. C.

207

GEORGE WASHINGTON HOLLAND BIBLE
Owner: Mrs. Lula Holland Keaten (decd)
1540 Olympian Circle, Atlanta, Ga.

George Washington Holland 7/15/1839-6/10/1896 Paulding Co., Ga.
(son of Archibald Holland and wife, Sarah Elizabeth Hagin) m.
Lydia Camp, 12/26/1849-8/27/1883, dau. of Burrell M. Camp and
wife, Mary E. Stegall Camp, all of Paulding Co., Ga.
Their Children:

Births
Johnny Holland 1866-1866
Silas Casey Holland 1/13/1868-7/15/1933
Mary Elizabeth Holland 12/26/1871-5/20/1938
Samuel Marion Holland 1872-1908
Charles Hartwell Holland 5/22/1874-7/1/1934
James Tom Holland 10/11/1876-2/26/1939
William Holland 1879-1886
Lula Ann Holland 3/31/1881-

Marriages
Silas Casey Holland 1st to Vicki Moon, 2nd to Susie Elizabeth
   Keaten
Mary Elizabeth Holland to Thomas Walton Durham
Charles Hartwell Holland to Alice V. Howell 10/1900
James Tom Holland to Willie Florence Collins 12/2/1900
Lula Ann Holland to William Robert Keaten 5/8/1898

WILLIAM ROBERT KEATEN BIBLE
Owner: Mrs. Lula Keaten (decd)
1540 Olympian Circle, Atlanta, Ga.

William Robert Keaten 10/31/1875 Carrollton, Ga.-11/1961 Atlanta,
Ga. m. 5/8/1898 Dallas, Ga.
Lula Ann Holland 3/31/1881 Paulding Co. Their Children:

Births
Willie Audrey Keaten 5/18/1899 Douglasville, Ga.-2/11/1904
Clarice Lorraine Keaten 6/15/1901 Douglasville, Ga.-1/31/1904
Clarence Aubrey Keaten 1/5/1905 Douglasville, Ga.
John Coburn Keaten 12/17/1906 Douglasville, Ga.
Lettie Kathryn Keaten 4/10/1912 Douglasville, Ga.
Keader Carlton Keaten 1/10/1917 Douglasville, Ga.
Wayne Holland Keaten 4/29/1909 Douglasville, Ga.

Marriages
Clarence Aubrey Keaten to Nettie Winn 10/8/1927
John Coburn Keaten to Elon McCullough 2/9/1929
Lettie Kathryn Keaten to Fred E. Rowden 11/17/1931
Keader CarltonKeaton 1st to Margaret Hudson, 2nd to Kathryn
   Griffin 3/9/1946
Wayne Holland Keaton 1st to Ruby Jenkins, 2nd to Edna Wiley

GEORGE WASHINGTON LANE BIBLE
Owner: Tom Lane, 2091 Ben Hill Rd.,
East Point, Georgia

George Washington Lane 5/14/1854 Dallas, Ga.-12/21/1934, son of
James C. Lane and wife, Nancy Williams Lane, m. Martha Josephine
Hawkins, 1/29/1863 Dallas, Ga.-11/1/1945 Dallas, Ga., on
11/18/1880. Their Children:

Births
Hattie Cora Lane 9/21/1881 Dallas, Ga.-8/6/1882
Hanna Alena Lane 2/6/1883 Dallas, Ga.-11/15/1884
James Tilman Lane 8/5/1885 Dallas, Ga.-8/18/1960
John Williams Lane 3/15/1888 Dallas, Ga.-6/15/1888
Mauddy Beatrice Lane 6/23/1889 Dallas, Ga.-9/6/1889
Thomas Theodore Lane 7/14/1891 Dallas, Ga.
Jesse Andrew Lane 7/29/1897 Dallas, Ga.-6/4/1964
Lillian Irene Lane 8/18/1902 Dallas, Ga.

Marriages
James Tilman Lane to Devie Motes
Thomas Theodore Lane to Myrtle Buford 8/26/1917
Jesse Andrew Lane to Ella Wills
Lillian Irene Lane to William Dewey Thomason

JAMES C. LANE BIBLE OF MADISON-PAULDING CO.´S
Owner: Tom Lane
2092 Ben Hill Road
East Point, Ga.

James C. Lane 4/26/1818 (Madison Co.)-6/20/1896 Dallas, Ga.,
m. 12/27/1839 Madison Co., Nancy Williams 5/19/1818 Madison Co.
-6/27/1905 Dallas, Ga. Their Children:

Births
Permelia Elizabeth Lane 10/1/1840 Dallas, Ga.-2/16/1920
Berry Tilman Lane 7/6/1843 Danielsville, Ga.-8/13/1928
John W. Lane 5/25/1846 Dallas, Ga.
Sarah Frances Lane 12/27/1848 Dallas, Ga.-8/26/1921
Eliza J. Lane 2/25/1850 Dallas, Ga.-6/13/1913
Nancy Carrie Lane 5/4/1851 Dallas, Ga. -10/15/1940
George Washington Lane 5/14/1854 Dallas, Ga.-12/21/1934
Judy Emma Lane 3/26/1859 Dallas, Ga.-1/3/1942
Thomas J. Lane 10/18/1862 Dallas, Ga.-4/18/1864

Marriages
Berry Tilman Lane to Ann Hudson
Sarah Frances Lane to Abe J. landers
Eliza J. Lane to E. A. Davis
Nancy Carrie Lane to Thomas M. Collins
George Washington Lane to Martha Josephine Hawkins 11/18/1880
Judy Emma Lane 1st to Joseph B. Howell, 2nd to J. E. Butler

WILLIAM CASSELS LEE BIBLE
Owner: Mrs. E. G. Stucki
Stone Mountain, Ga.

William Cassels Lee 10/17/1873 Brooklett, Ga.-3/11/1933 Brooklett,
Ga., son of William Baker Lee, m. 1904 Ann Cornelia Groover
9/25/1879 Emmett Grove, Ga.- 2/22/1954 Savannah, Ga., dau. of
James Bulloch Groover and wife, Sarah Ann Wilson Groover.
Their Children:
Sarah Elizabeth Lee b. 7/24/1908 Brooklett, Ga. m. 8/21/1926
 Edwin Gootfried Stucki
William Clifford Lee b. 3/4/1912 Brooklett, Ga. m. 3/16/1939
 Dorothy Bacon

EDWIN GOTTFRIED STUCKI BIBLE
Stone Mountain, Georgia

Edwin Gottfried Stucki b. 7/8/1905 New Glarus, Green Co.,
Wisconsin, son of Gottfried Stucki and wife, Anna Maria Kunz of
Bern, Switzerland, m. 8/21/1926 Brooklett, Ga., Sarah Elizabeth
Lee, b. 7/24/1908 Brooklett, Ga., dau. of William Cassels Lee and
wife, Ann Cornelia Groover Lee.
Their Children:

Births
Edwin Gerald Stucki 8/17/1933 Savannah, Ga.
Sarah Anne Stucki 3/1/1936 Savannah, Ga.
Wilfred Lee Stucki 5/6/1937 Savannah, Ga.
Ronald Lamar Stucki 6/4/1940 Atlanta, Ga.

Marriages
Edwin Gerald Stucki to Willie Jeannette Holland 4/24/1953
Sarah Anne Stucki to Arthur Frank murphy 6/20/1954
Wilfred Lee Stucki to Jacqueline Elizabeth Stokes 8/11/1962
Ronald Lamar Stucki to Norma Harriett Martin 4/26/1964

MONTILLA CLARK BIBLE
Owner: O. F. Payne
1510 Kan. Blvd. E.
Charleston, W. Va.

William D. Clark b. 10/13/1792, son of Joseph Clark, d. 4/9/1865
Va., m. Jane Mary Elhason (Eliason), dau. of Ebenezer.

Births of Their Children:

Montilla Clark 5/1/1836	James William Clark 6/1/1831
Ann Hersey Clark 9/6/1828	Edwin Parsons Clark 3/33/1833
Mary Jane Clark 3/2/1830	Indianna Haynes Clark 11/13/1834

(Montilla Clark Bible, Births, contd....)

Novella Virginia Clark 10/28/1842

Montilla Clark m. 11/10/1846 Bettie Miller Perkins, dau. of Grief
F. and Clars S. Perkins, 4/28/1827-8/22/1888. Their Children:

Jane Beatrice Clark 5/8/1848
Oscar Clark 10/20/1850
Clars S. Clark 10/17/1852
Bathsheba Clark d. 12/28/1869

GOTTFRIED STUCKI BIBLE
Owner: Edwin G. Stucki
Stone Mountain, Georgia

Gottfried Stucki 4/27/1873 Bern, Switzerland-7/6/1946 Elberta,
Ala., son of Samuel Stucki and wife, Anna Marie Hausemann Stucki
of Switzerland, m. 11/25/1899 Anna Marie Kunz, Bern, Switzerland,
1/4/1880 near Zurich-8/1958 Elberta, Ala., dau. of Henreich Kunz
and his wife, Susanna Niffeler Kunz. Their Children:

Births
Martha Stucki 9/20/1900 Switzerland
Olga Stucki 8/21/1901 Lansen, Switzerland
Hilda Stucki 9/20/1902 New Glarus, Wisconsin
Hermina Stucki 6/24/1904 New Glarus, Wisconsin
Edwin Gottfried Stucki 7/8/1905 New Glarus, Wisconsin
Alfred Stucki 8/13/1906 New Glarus, Wisconsin
Otto Stucki 12/9/1907 New Glarus, Wisconsin
Freida Claira Stucki 10/31/1909 New Glarus, Wisconsin
Esther Lydia Stucki 6/3/1911 Elberta, Ala.
Walter Albert Stucki 8/11/1912 Elberta, Ala.
Paul Samuel Stucki 9/18/1913 Elberta, Ala.
Anna Stucki 9/19/1914 Elberta, Ala.
Edna Stucki 9/19/1916 Elberta, Ala.
Frederick Stucki 12/24/1918 Elberta, Ala.
Flora Stucki 1920 Elberta, Ala.-d. infant
Louise Stucki 5/28/1921 Elberta, Ala.-d. 1932

Marriages
Martha Stucki 1st to Theodore Pferrer, 2nd to Eric Erikson
Olga Stucki to Fred H. Woerner 10/14/1943
Hilda Stucki to Lewis H. Boynton 3/6/1924
Hermina Stucki to Henry W. Gebert
Edwin Gottfried Stucki to Sarah Elizabeth Lee 8/1/1926
Alfred Stucki to Hilda Heinkleman 3/1/1943
Otto Stucki to Ella Benson
Esther Lydia Stucki to Walter Hacker 1/8/1935
Walter Albert Stucki to Mary Adeline Futrell 7/25/1933
Paul Samuel Stucki to Esther McCann 8/5/1936
Anna Stucki to James Kimos
Edna Stucki to Charles Besserer 10/12/1935
Frederick Stucki to Dorothy Brown

211

GRIEF G. PERKINS BIBLE
Owner: O. F. Payne
1510 Kan. Blvd. E.
Charleston, W. Va.

Grief G. Perkins m.
Clara S. Perkins 3/19/1804-10/11/1865   Their Children:

Births
Bettie Perkins 4/28/1827
Archelaus Perkins 9/17/1829
James William Perkins 5/6/1831

JOSEPH D. MORGAN BIBLE*
Owner: Hugh Watts Randall
Cedartown, Ga.

Births
Joseph D. Morgan 6/15/1818   Orvin B. Morgan 12/16/1862
Martha A. Payne 10/10/1824   Robert J. Morgan 10/25/1864
E. Crabbe 4/14/1837   Emery A. Morgan 9/24/1866
Isaac C. Morgan 1/8/1839   Lena D. Morgan 10/9/1868
Nancy E. Morgan 3/22/1840   Cora L. Morgan 10/24/1870
Martha L. Morgan 6/3/1841   Della D. Morgan 3/8/1873
Anslem L. Morgan 12/10/1842   Ida O. Davis 9/16/1872
Mary Park Morgan 5/31/1844   Lena D. Morgan 8/7/1890
Joseph L. Morgan 1/9/1846   Hugh Dean Morgan 9/20/1892
Josephine S. Morgan 9/30/1851   Lonnie L. Morgan 12/16/1894
Cynthia S. Morgan 7/1/1853   Elma Jo. Morgan 4/14/1899
Lellea A. Morgan 10/14/1855   Emery C. Morgan 8/2/1902
Burton E. Morgan 7/19/1859   Hugh D. Morgan Jr. 7/24/1916
Newton H. Morgan 4/1/1861   Vera J. Morgan 4/27/1919

Marriages
Burton E. Morgan 12/20/1882   Lena D. Morgan 6/7/1908
Newton A. Morgan 4/1/1881   Hugh D. Morgan 10/27/1915
Robert J. Morgan 4/8/1883   Lonnie L. Morgan 9/23/1916
Emery A. Morgan 10/6/1889   Emery C. Morgan 11/8/1927
Cora L. Morgan 10/6/1889   Elma J. Morgan 6/7/1936

Deaths
Virginia C. Morgan 11/11/1850
Diatha E. Morgan 7/15/1853
Martha P. Morgan 3/1/1858
Orvin B. Morgan 8/25/1866
Joseph D. Morgan 3/12/1874
Newton H. Morgan 8/4/1881
Emery C. Morgan 1/9/1971

*See also p. 426.   212

LEWIS STANTON BIBLE Of Columbus, Ga.

Lewis Stanton b. 10/13/1916 m. 5/14/1937 Ella Mae Calhoun
  b. 5/17/1917

Births
Lewis Stanton Jr. 3/9/1939   Ella Jane Stanton 2/11/1945
Sarah Elizabeth Stanton 10/25/1943

Janie Glenn Norman 11/17/1896 m. 11/20/1913 Edgar Roy Calhoun
  b. 4/11/1899

HENRY T. DUKE BIBLE Of Columbus, Ga.

Henry T. Duke b. 6/21/1919 m. 7/7/1940 Annie Norman Maupin
  b. 4/28/1918

Charles Norman Duke b. 8/16/1944

HENRY RENEW BIBLE
Owner: Mrs. C. W. Renew
Americus, Ga. 31709

Births
Henry William Joseph Renew 3/10/1842-10/23/1921
Eliza Ann Pilcher Renew 4/1850-9/21/1920
Lula Geneva Renew Young Hart 10/1/1869 m. Wheeler Hart 1918
Leola Ann Renew 6/1890
Ruthie Ann Renew 1871-11/17/1888
Timothy N. Renew 6/30/1876-7/1/1889
John Renew Jr. 6/1/1879-1881
Charles Winn Renew 3/10/1881-1961

Marriages
C. W. Renew to Emily Powell 11/16/1906
Leola Ann Renew to John Kenemore 2/17/1899
Lula Renew to William Young 1890
Lula Renew to John H. Young 1899 (2nd)
Jula Renew to Wheeler Hart 1918 (3rd)

213

MRS. JOHN ELLIS POPE BIBLE *
Jackson, Georgia

Dorothy Alexander Pope b. 7/10/1919 m. 8/29/1936 John Ellis Pope
b. 2/13/1916 d. 10/7/1944

John Ronald Pope b. 11/1/1938
Dorothy Marilyn Pope b. 11/5/1940

GROVER C. BARFIELD, JR. BIBLE
Columbus, Georgia

Grover C. Barfield Jr. b. 6/28/1918 m. 9/6/1939 Sara Frances
Glenn b. 9/26/1922

Grover Cleveland Barfield III b. 5/18/1944

Parents of Grover Cleveland Barfield, Jr.:

Grover Cleveland Barfield Sr. b. 7/1885 m. 7/3/1915 Louise
Calhoun b. 11/8/1895

B. M. BARNES BIBLE
Jackson, Georgia

Bertie Mitchell Barnes b. 10/14/1884 m. 7/29/1908 Cory Beatrice
Nelson b. 10/9/1886

William Herschel Barnes b. 8/30/1909 m. Louise Bankston 6/20/1936
Dorothy Louise Barnes b. 2/10/1919 m. Woodrow Tingle 10/27/1940

MATTHEW GARDNER CULPEPPER BIBLE
Owner: Mrs. Brooks Culpepper
Talbotton, Georgia

Births
Julian R. Culpepper 5/6/1860   Julia Culpepper 3/17/1887
Nathan G. Culpepper 3/8/1852   Brooks Culpepper 11/8/1889
Mattie Lou Culpepper 1/10/1882   Janie Culpepper 8/21/1898
Norah Culpepper 5/27/1884
N. G. Culpepper m. Julia R. Brooks 12/14/1880

*See also p. 200.   214

ROBERT ARVESTER BRASWELL BIBLE
Owner: C. W. Renew, Americus, Ga.

Robert Briant Arvester Braswell b. 5/12/1872 Brunswick Co., Va.,
    d. 2/16/1934
Minnie Lea Collum 5/18/1875-10/17/1946 m. 2/22/1891
James C. Collum 1845-12/11/1916

Children:

Eugene Douglas Braswell b. 3/24/1894
James Arther Braswell 7/31/1897-9/1/1897
Leon Braswell 3/23/1900-3/23/1900
Rosa Lee Braswell b. 6/16/1902
Lillie May Braswell b. 6/16/1905
Nellie Ree Braswell b. 11/11/1913
Mary Ruth Braswell 9/17/1918-9/17/1918

George Briant Braswell 1879-1953
Martha J. Braswell 1891-1931

G. H. JORDAN BIBLE
Owner: Frank J. Jordan
Talbotton, Georgia

G. H. Jordan of Butler, Taylor Co., Ga. m. C. F. Weaver of
Talbot Co., Ga. 5/11/1875 at Mrs. Millers, Rev. John S. Searcy of
Missionary Baptist Church. Wit: H. D. McCrary and J. W. Hough.

C. C. WINFREE BIBLE
Owner: Mrs. Frances Winfree Henry
Ashville, Alabama

Marriages
C. C. Winfree to M. B. Miller 2/12/1879
C. C. infree to Miss M. S. Irvin 3/25/1885

Births
W. C. Winfree 4/3/1880   Irvin Winfree 8/26/1891
Carey C. Winfree 6/1/1886   Mattie B. Winfree 8/26/1891
Bonner Winfree 6/13/1808

Mattie B. Winfree d. 8/11/1881

215

VIRGINIA SARAH BRYAN BIBLE Of Chatham Co.

Gift of her Beloved Mother in 1823. "We were married at Dr. Screven's house in Savannah 2/10/1835...I was born in Savannah, Ga. 3/27/1804 and my dear wife, Virginia Sarah, was born on Wilmington Island 9/22/1810.

Debra Bryan Mackay b. at my mother's in Savannah 11/26/1835 William Mackay born at my mother's in Savannah 11/3/1837

My beloved wife and children lost at sea in steamer `Pulaski' 6/14/1838...going north in search of her health...."

F. K. BURFORD BIBLE Of Butts Co.
Owner: Mrs. Eslyn Jinks, Jackson, Ga. 30233

Marriages
F. K. Burford to R. E. Hunt 5/31/1859
J. D. Burford to L. E. Curry 12/10/1882
W. T. Burford to Fannie Kimbell 10/19/1884

Births
F. K. Burford 11/9/1830   Z. Z. Burford 3/3/1866 (Zacoma Zane)
R. E. Burford 3/1841   J. A. Burford 4/9/1868
W. T. Burford 6/11/1861   L. M. Burford 3/5/1870
J. D. Burford 6/11/1861   A. C. Burford 6/23/1875
F. K. Burford 1/4/1864   A. G. Burford 2/18/1878

JOSEPH S. GARRETT BIBLE

Marriages
Joseph S. Garrett to Virginia E. Heard 5/11/1858
Robert Young Garrett to Ann Hanson 1895
Charles L. Pierce to Josephine Garrett 4/18/1895
George J. Garrett to Matilda Blanton 5/19/1915
Louise Harrington Peirce to Alfred Williams Porter 7/27/1976

J. H. O'NEAL BIBLE
Jackson, Georgia

J. Horace O'Neal b. 3/16/1895
Mrs. J. H. O'Neal b. 1/17/1895

J. Horace O'Neal m. Inez Tompkins 4/24/1917. Their Children:
Dorothy Ann b. 2/17/1918 m. 6/12/1943 to Carl B. Waldrop
Barbara O'Neal b. 5/11/1921 m. 9/30/1945 to Henry F. Grady

ROBERT WHITE BIBLE Of Newton Co.
Owner: Julia Aiken, Covington, Ga.

Robert White b. Ireland 4/1/1776 m. Elizabeth More b. 6/6/1772

Births
John White 8/12/1799   James White 11/29/1810
Margaret White 11/8/1801   Thomas White 11/4/1812, twin
William White 9/26/1803   Adams White 11/4/1812, twin
Robert White 10/27/1805   Hugh White 3/5/1816
David White 4/10/1808   Elizabeth White 5/25/1820

All b. in Ireland, they emigrated to Charleston, S. C. and went
to Savannah, Ga. for a time before removing to Newton Co., Ga.,
near Covington. They came from Ireland in 1829, when hugh White
was 13 years old. (From Mr. George Edwin Aiken)

          CHARLES HARDMAN WHITE BIBLE Of Newton Co.

Charles Hardman White 6/18/1885-3/24/1925 m. Leila Stephenson,
mother of Ackie, Annie, James, Charles, etc., grandmother of
Sarah White Callaway and Thomas Green Callaway, Jean Lee
Moore....

                HALL-CLINKSCALES BIBLE
                Owner: Ophelia C. Harris
                     Hartwell, Ga.

Marriages
Mathew Hall 11/27/1804 7/14/1890 m. 3/27/1828 Polly Fellars
   1/25/1813-7/14/1894
John Lawson Hall 5/22/1833-11/22/1859 m. 4/27/1854 Mary Elizabeth
   Long
Rueben Pyles Clinkscales 1/26/1846-6/25/1908 m. 10/29/1872 Mary
   Cornelia Hall 1/23/1856-6/19/1921

Births
Female twins 1/3/1829-1/3/1829
Leonora Trengivilla Hall 3/27/1858-1/12/1859
Lawson Ophelia Hall 12/16/1859
Reuben Pringle Clinkscales 10/19/1876

Deaths
Thomas Jefferson Fellars Hall 2/20/1832, age 1 yr., 6 mos., 5
   days
Mary Eutts 12/4/1857, aged over 90 yrs.
James Lawson Clinkscales 4/5/1875

                        217

ELISHA ROBERTS BIBLE
Owner: Mrs. J. G. Johnson
College Park, Georgia

Elisha Roberts b. Wilkes Co., Ga. 11/17/1827 d. Conyers, Ga.
   3/28/1894
Ada Amerson b. Wilkes Co., Ga. 1/7/1872 d. Jackson, Ga.
   12/25/1903

Elisha Roberts and Ada Amerson whose mother was Ada Calloway m.
   in Rockdale Co., Ga. 7/16/1854

Joe Samuel Johnson b. Walton Co., Ga. 11/2/1859, d. Atlanta, Ga.
   4/6/1926
Mary Bell Roberts b. Thomson, Ga. 1/4/1863

Joe Samuel Johnson and Mary Bell Roberts m. Conyers, Ga.
   10/9/1881

JAMES THOMPSON STEWART BIBLE
Owner: Mrs. H. J. Maddox
Jackson, Georgia

James Thompson Stewart b. 3/16/1832
Nanet Jane Deason b. 12/1834   Their Children:

Births
John William Stewart 9/29/1857   Joseph H. Stewart 3/19/1868
Mary Jane Stewart 8/29/1859   Sara Margaret Stewart
James Rufus Stewart 9/16/1861   12/11/1869
Robert Jackson Stewart 5/29/1866   Annie Laurie Stewart 10/29/1871
Benjamin Henderson Stewart 6/31/1878

Deaths
Mary Jane Stewart 9/11/1867   James Rufus Stewart 7/11/1872
Joseph H. Stewart 3/19/1868
Benjamin Henderson Stewart 3/3/1879

THOMAS B. HIGGINBOTHAM BIBLE
Owner: Mrs. Sue Higginbotham
Lavonia, Georgia

Marriages
Thomas B. Higginbotham b. 4/21/1855 m. 11/17/1874 by Rev. W. T.
   Norman, Sue N. J. Ledbetter b. 5/24/1854
Arnetta Higginbotham b. 12/22/1875 m. 12/22/1896 E. R. McMurray
   by Rev. M. A. Simmons

CARWELL HESTER BIBLE
Owner: Mrs. Ella Hester Tribble
Lavonia, Georgia

Marriages
Carwell Hester 1796-3/15/1863 m. 12/25/1819 by Canceler, Esq.,
  Elizabeth Whitmire 3/22/1798-2/5/1896
Malinda Hester 11/9/1828-7/1852 m. 7/16/1847 by Rev. Eady,
  Aaron Robberson
Abraham Hester 12/8/1819-4/22/1862 m. 6/20/1849 Emily Dean
Henry W. Hester b. 7/10/1821 m. 4/5/1851 by O. E. Barton, Esq.,
  Malinda Clayton
Elizabeth Capehart m. 5/28/1862 Waddy Thompson Hester 7/7/1839-
  5/13/1864
James Fisher b. 2/7/1828 m. 11/17/1868 Mary E. Robberson b.
  6/15/1853

Births

Children of Carwell Hester and Elizabeth Whitmire:

Abraham Hester 12/8/1819   Samuel R. Hester 9/11/1830
Henry W. Hester 7/10/1821   Carwell Hester Jr. 9/19/1832
Jeptha N. Hester 2/17/1823   Mary Elizabeth Hester 9/29/1834
Louisa Hester 12/29/1825   Waddy Thompson Hester 7/7/1839
Malinda Hester 11/9/1828

Children of Malinda Hester and Aaron Robberson:

H. T. Robberson 9/12/1848   Mary E. Robberson 6/15/1853

Children of James Fisher and Mary E. Robberson:

B. T. Fisher 4/22/1854   W. T. Fisher 8/23/1859
Jeptha Fisher 12/20/1857

Deaths
Louisa Hester 4/5/1823   S. R. Hester 9/20/1862
Jeptha Hester 3/20/1850   Carwell Hester Jr. 1/21/1863
M. E. Fisher 10/11/1860

ALBERT HENRY JONES BIBLE
Owner: Mrs. Henry J. Lawhon
Jackson, Georgia

Births
Albert Henry Jones 6/5/1910   Tom Daniel Jones 5/18/1932
Myrtle Young Jones 12/6/1910   Myrna Loy Jones 10/28/1937
Luther Murray Jones 5/11/1928

Henry J. Hawhon 7/1/1904
Henry Franklin 6/10/1944

JOHN G. HIGGINBOTHAM BIBLE
Owner: Mrs. Will Turner
Greenville, S. C.

Marriages

John G. Higgenbotham b. 3/3/1807 m. Eliza Jane Baxter 8/25/1872, who was b. 9/11/1836
Jane Elizabeth Higgenbotham b. 2/14/1834 m. Dickerson; Ray and Scott.

Births

Hester Lorene Melving Higgenbotham 8/23/1873
Bailey Joseph Dearly Higgenbotham 2/1/1875
Lola Julia Caroline Stanton Higgenbotham 1/2/1878
Sarah S. Higgenbotham 1811
Sarah Ann Higgenbotham 11/5/1828
Benjamine Thomas Higgenbotham 6/6/1830
John Thornton Higgenbotham 6/16/1832
Mary London Higgenbotham 11/20/1835
Elijah Benson Higgenbotham 12/16/1838
Dosia James Higgenbotham 3/28/1841
Prissiler Frances Higgenbotham 7/2/1843
William Green Higgenbotham 1/14/1845
Reuben Crumley Higgenbotham 3/16/1846
Jeptha B. Higgenbotham 10/26/1847

ALBERT CRAWLEY FINLEY BIBLE
Owner: Albert Finley, Jackson, Ga.

Husband - Albert Crawley Finley b. 8/5/1883
Wife - Katie Ann Finley b. 9/15/1883
Married - 11/27/1912   Their Children:

Annie Elizabeth Finley b. 10/25/1913
James Danielly Finley b. 7/14/1916

James Danielly Finley m. Nancy Butler 6/7/1941

Kate Danielly (Katie Ann) Finley d. 2/20/1937

JOSEPH CARTER YOUNG BIBLE
Owner: Mrs. J. C. Young, Jackson, Ga.

Births

Joseph Carter Young 8/5/1894   Myrtle Cluie Young 12/6/1910
Ella Wilkins Young 10/14/1888   Oscar Young 9/2/1914
J. C. Young, Jr. 3/9/1909

OSCAR YOUNG BIBLE
Jackson, Georgia

Oscar Young b. 9/2/1914
Marguerite Durden Young b. 4/1/1920
Edward Lee Young b. 12/10/1937

BENJAMINE T. HIGGINBOTHAM BIBLE
Owner: Mrs. William B. Higginbotham
Royston, Georgia

Marriages
Benjamine T. Higginbotham 6/6/1830-1/7/1864 m. 12/13/1849
  Frances E. Cook 5/24/1831-2/20/1915
William Carlisle Agnew m. 2/15/1866 Mary Jane Higginbotham
  b. 2/17/1851
William Bowers Higginbotham b. 3/9/1858 m. 1/20/1881 Mary M.
  Glover
Coda McDonald m. 2/23/1893 John C. Higginbotham 5/4/1864

Births
Martha E. Higgenbotham 6/24/1853
Thomas B. Higgenbotham 4/21/1855
Sarah Thornton Higgenbotham 10/27/1860

Deaths
Marthie E. Higginbotham Phillips 10/4/1899
Sallie T. Higginbotham Ridgway 3/31/1898

J. D. THOMAS BIBLE
Owner: Mrs. A. E. Hardy
Jackson, Georgia

J. D. Thomas b. 1/18/1865 m. 11/29/1885 Mary E. L. Jones
  b. 10/19/1867. Their Children:

Annie Lee Thomas b. 2/2/1887 m. J. J. Hardy
Eddie Thomas b. 4/14/1889 m. Lucy Thompson
Nora Thomas b. 5/19/1892
Joel Thomas b. 2/19/1896
Ezra Thomas b. 6/17/1900 m. Nannie Coleman
Louie Thomas b. 11/17/1902 m. Azzie E. Hardy
Alonzo Thomas b. 10/16/1907 m. Ruth Thompson

Deaths
Nora Thomas 6/25/1893   Joel Thomas 6/12/1897

G. TERRELL WILLARD BIBLE
Owner: Mrs. A. E. Hardy, Jackson, Ga.

Dorothy Hardy Willard b. 9/15/1926 m. 1/10/1942 G. Terrell
Willard b. 11/2/1924

Child: Cecil Gerald Willard b. 12/14/1942

FRANCIS JENKINS BIBLE
Owner:Russell Jenkins
Madison, Georgia

Marriages
Francis Jenkins b. 2/5/1735 m. 3/7/1760 Cassandra Grafton
b. 6/2/1745
Francis Jenkins b. 12/15/1764 m. 8/4/1800 Dorothy Henrietta
Marie Edmondson Orm b. 10/15/1782

Births
        Children of Francis Jenkins and Cassandra Grafton:
William Jenkins 2/19/1762   Mary Jenkins 6/24/1771
Francis Jenkins 12/15/1764   Jesse Jenkins 5/2/1773
Phebe Jenkins 1/13/1767   Priscilla Jenkins 4/5/1775
Thomas Jenkins 7/9/1769

        Children of Francis Jenkins and Dorothy Orm:
Cynthia Jenkins 6/19/1801   Jesse Jenkins 3/26/1811
Andrew Jenkins 6/14/1804   Eliza Jenkins 3/1/1813
William Jenkins 12/12/1805   John Milton Jenkins 12/11/1814
Francis Jenkins 10/29/1807-10/31/1809
Thomas Jenkins 5/27/1809   Alvin Jenkins 9/26/1818
Nancy Jenkins 4/17/1823   Archibald E. Jenkins 4/29/1820
Lorenzo Clark Jenkins 12/24/1816
Francis Jones Jenkins 2/10/1826

W. M. THAXTON BIBLE
Owner: Mrs. W. M. Thaxton
Jackson, Georgia

Births
W. M. Thaxton 3/14/1893   Thoren Thaxton 3/29/1923
Clyde Gray Thaxton 8/23/1902   Riley Thaxton 6/23/1927
Annie Mervyn Thaxton 6/23/1927

Marriages
W. M. Thaxton to Mary Clyde Gray 9/12/1930 Conyers, Ga.
Annie Mervyn Thaxton to Walter D. Pope Jr. 6/24/1937
One Child: Cheryl Ann Pope b. 2/7/1944

222

```
                    JOHN HARDY BIBLE
                 Owner: Mrs. A. E. Hardy
                    Jackson, Georgia


John Hardy, Grandfather          Elizabeth Hardy, Grandmother
John David Thomas, Grandfather   Mary E. L. Thomas, Grandmother

Azzie Elton Hardy b. 11/2/1894 Jackson, Ga. m. 3/10/1923 at
Indian Springs, Ga. Louie Thomas Hardy b. 11/17/1902 Jackson, Ga.

Children:

John Elton Hardy 12/19/1923-12/19/1923
Lamar Shirley Hardy 4/26/1925-6/3/1944
Dorothy Ann Hardy 9/15/1926
Merlene Hardy 9/9/1931
Bernard Franklin Hardy 9/17/1934



                    J. W. L. DANIEL BIBLE



Births
J. W. L. Daniel 12/14/1794     Jinny's child, Mary, 5/30/1832
Sarah Ann Daniel 6/16/1805     Wm. Thomas Daniel 1/7/1836
James Alexander Daniel 3/9/1824  Susanah Frances Daniel 6/1/1839
Elizabeth Jane Daniel 3/30/1826  Mary Elizabeth Daniel 11/23/1840
John Calvin Daniel 7/19/1829   Wm. Lewis Daniel 12/4/1845

Deaths
J. W. L. Daniel 2/1/1870
Daniel, consort of J. W. L. Daniel, 2/16/1833
Missouri Daniel, consort of J. W. L. Daniel, 9/29/1867
William Thomas Daniel 7/18/1837, aged 18 mos.
Mary E. Lumpkin 5/30/1862, aged 21 yrs.
William Lewis Daniel 6/15/1860, aged 16 yrs. Died at Richmond,
    Va. while engated in defense of Southern Confederate States.
    He was a member of the Baldwin Blues, a volunteer company
    from Milledgeville, Ga.
John C. Daniel 4/30/1866. Came to death by a short fired by
    Ransom Godwin in self defense. Aged 37 yrs.

Marriages
J. W. L. Daniel to Sarah Ann Graham 3/8/1823
J. W. Daniel to Missouri Clary Hutcherson Powell, wid. of
    Andrew Cumings 8/7/1835.
George Robert Lumpkin to Mary Elizabeth Daniel 11/23/1861
Elizabeth Jane Godwin to Nicholas H. Wyse 6/24/1869
```

GEORGE M. LEDBETTER BIBLE
Owner: Mrs. Addie Clodfelter Ledbetter
Tallulah Falls, Georgia

Marriages
George M. Ledbetter 3/26/1825-4/17/1904 m. 4/27/1848
  Sarah J. martin 9/23/1829-2/4/1903
Celeb M. ledbetter 3/4/1849-3/31/1924 m. 11/16/1871 Mary
  E. Parker
Sue N. J. Ledbetter b. 5/24/1854 m. 11/17/1874 Thomas B.
  Higginbotham
W. F. Ledbetter b. 10/4/1857 m. Lizzie Black
George R. Ledbetter 6/22/1868-3/4/1908 m. 12/8/1892 Addie
  L. Clodfelter b. 3/24/1866

Births
David A. G. Ledbetter 6/13/1852-8/19/1852
John M. Ledbetter 7/11/1861-8/31/1864

Children of George R. Ledbetter and Addie Clodfelter:

Allice C. Ledbetter 9/18/1893
George F. Ledbetter 3/25/1895
David T. Henry Baxter 5/22/1896
Wallas Smith 10/10/1905

                WILLIAM GORDON BARNES BIBLE
                 Owner: Mrs. W. G. Barnes
                    Jackson, Georgia

Husband - William Gordon Barnes b. 11/6/1886
Wife - Nina Garr Barnes b.4/19/1890
Married - 5/7/1913   Their Children:

Esta Elise Barnes b. 4/13/1914
Gordon harold Barnes b. 1/31/1916
Homer Wayne Barnes b. 7/31/1918

Marriages
Esta Elise Barnes to Joseph Allen Suddeth 6/13/1943
Gordon Harold Barnes to Elizabeth Sitten 2/28/1942
Homer Wayne Barnes to Addie Jean Shoemaker 9/25/1942

                    JESSE CLAY BIBLE
                   Monticello, Georgia

Joseph Early Clay b. 5/17/1900
Linton Hargrove Clay b. 6/23/1912
Jessie Clay b. 7/2/1879
Sallie Wilson Clay b. 9/16/1884 m. 5/1906
Jessie Clay Jr. b. 4/14/1924

                         224

W. B. BLIZZARD BIBLE

Births

W. B. Blizzard 12/7/1861
Emmer Cate Blizzard 11/25/1886
W. T. Blizzard 4/2/1889
Cary Lizzie Blizzard 7/10/1890

Susie Belle Blizzard 10/13/1891
Ruby Ione Blizzard 8/17/1913

W. D. Blizzard m. 1st Francis F. Freeman d. 4/24/1911, dau. of
Floyd Freeman on 12/23/1883 and 2nd Hattie Freeman on 3/11/1912

LEDBETTER-VERNER BIBLE
Owner: Mrs. Sue J. Higgenbotham
Lavonia, Georgia

Marriages

Mary Verner, dau. of David Verner, d. 9/24/1860, age 77 yrs.,
  m. 4/15/1803 John Ledbetter d. 1/25/1831, age 54 yrs.
Henry Ledbetter b. 5/10/1805 m. 6/11/1825 Charity Shockley
James Verner Ledbetter b. 2/21/1807 m. 7/14/1829 Martha Sisk
John Ledbetter 2/7/1809-8/2/1856 m. 12/30/1830 Susan Williams
Joel Ledbetter 7/27/1811-10/25/1873 m. 2/27/1834 Mary Parker
Esther Ledbetter 6/3/1816-11/23/1885 m. 3/13/1845 John Martin
David T. Ledbetter b. 2/4/1819 m. 11/5/1840 Nancy Tilly
George Montgomery Ledbetter b. 3/26/1825 m. 4/27/1848
  Sarah Jane Martin
George Richardson Ledbetter 10/16/1864-3/6/1908 m. 12/8/1892
  Addy L. Clodfelter
Caleb Martin Ledbetter b. 3/4/1849 m. 11/16/1871 Mary Elizabeth
  Parker
Susan Nancy Jane Ledbetter b. 5/24/1854 m. 11/17/1874 Thomas
  Benjamine Higginbotham
William Franks Ledbetter b. 10/4/1857 m. 11/24/1891 Lizzie Black

Births

Children of John Ledbetter Sr. and Mary Verner:

Henry Ledbetter 5/10/1805
James Verner Ledbetter
  2/21/1807-4/25/1863
John Ledbetter 2/7/1809-
  8/2/1856
Joel Ledbetter 7/27/1811-
  10/25/873

Esther Ledbetter 6/3/1816-11/23/1885
David T. Ledbetter 2/4/1819
Mary Carline Ledbetter 2/2/1821-
  6/19/1881
Daniel Lewis Ledbetter 4/1/1823-
  8/28/1844, 21 yrs., 4 mos.,28 days

Catharine Ledbetter 12/24/1813-3/15/1875
 Children of George Montgomery Ledbetter and Sarah Jane Martin:
Caleb Martin Ledbetter 3/4/1849
Susannah N. J. Ledbetter 5/24/1854
William Franks Ledbetter 10/4/1857
George R. Ledbetter 10/16/1864-3/6/1908
David A. G. Ledbetter 6/13/1852-8/19/1852
John M. Ledbetter 7/11/1861-8/31/1861
James Ledbetter 6/22/1868-9/27/1868

DR. J. H. BULLARD BIBLE Of Jasper Co.
Owner: Mrs. Alice Bullard Hearn
Eatonton, Georgia

Marie Corine Bullard b. 11/21/1878
William Howard Bullard b. 9/9/1881
Legree Swann Bullard b. 1/18/1882
Frank Leverett Bullard b. 4/7/1886
Edwin Baldwin Bullard 3/11/1880-9/1/1921

J. H Bullard m. A. E. Leverett 6/6/1877

J. H. Bullard d. 2/26/1928

JOHN M. CURRY BIBLE

John M. Curry m. Emma L. Garland 2/1/1860
Sarah L. Curry b. 9/6/1829
John Marshall Curry b. 9/21/1841
Emma Louise Garland b. 11/29/1841
Sarah Jane Curry b. 2/20/1862
William Edward Curry 11/7/1865-8/3/1871
Mary Alice Curry b. 8/8/1868
Mary Frances Curry 6/20/1871-9/18/1871
John Edward Curry b. 8/23/1874

M. M. McMURRAY BIBLE Of Franklin Co.
Owner: R. A. McMurray, Atlanta, Georgia

M. M. McMurray of Franklin Co., Ga. 10/2/1836-7/10/1905 m.
   1/28/1864 Elizabeth Yow of Franklin Co. b. 2/1/1848

Births
Richard A. McMurray 1/19/1865   Charlie E. McMurray 4/21/1879
Sallie C. McMurray 6/4/1867   Pearl M. McMurray 12/10/1880
William T. McMurray 7/20/1868   John B. McMurray 3/18/1883
Edward R. McMurray 7/20/1868   Grover C. McMurray 5/15/1885-
Frederic A. McMurray 9/9/1872   7/12/1886
Mary C. McMurray 3/9/1875   Ross C. McMurray 1/1887
Vennie S. McMurray 7/31/1877   Guy M. McMurray 6/16/1891

ABEL FARRAR BIBLE Of Jasper Co.*

Abel Farrar b. 11/13/1850 m. M. J. Turk 11/22/1876
Mary Jane Turk Farrar 12/16/1849-5/4/1915, age 65 yrs., 4 mos.
Otis Farrar b. 10/30/1877   Mary Farrar b. 3/4/1880

*See also p. 150.   226

JAMES PERSON FAULKNER BIBLE
Owner: Mrs. Hattie Faulkner

James Person Faulkner 2/12/1855-1/17/1915
Hattie Lewis Faulkner b. 10/27/1854
Jones Person Faulkner m. Hattie Lewis 11/16/1876

BLEDSOE-SHIELDS BIBLE
Owner: James C. Bledsoe
Jackson, Georgia

James C. Bledsoe 12/7/1892-4/8/1893
Baker Fleetwood Bledsoe b. 10/31/1910
W. H. Bledsoe b. 1/16/1869 m. 1st Ella McClure 12/13/1871
   m. 2d Mrs. Mattie Hodges 12/16/1909, m. 3rd Mrs. Carrie
   Gordon 12/5/1928
Mrs. Kattie Bledsoe b. 9/15/1873
Mary Alburia Bledsoe b. 9/9/1913

Mrs. Ella Bledsoe d. 10/7/1907
Mrs. Mattie Bledsoe d. 6/3/1928

RICHARD A. W. GOODMAN BIBLE Of Jasper Co.

Births
Mary Ann Goodman 6/7/1825   John Wiley Goodman 7/25/1849
William C. Goodman 11/8/1843   Joseph Goodman 8/14/1854
Stephen Goodman 7/27/1845   Richard A. Goodman 3/29/1856
James Taylor Goodman 11/2/1847 Richard A.W. Goodman 3/29/1755

JAMES L. HEAD BIBLE
Owner: Mrs. John White Garland
Barnesville, Georgia

Births
James L. Head 1/30/1808   Elizabeth V. Head 1/8/1837
Beneta A. Callaway 2/11/1819   James J. Head 3/16/1839
Mary Milner 2/25/1795   Pitt M. Head 5/28/1841
Polly M. Head 12/13/1834   Apsyllah T. head 11/16/1842

RANDOLPH SPALDING BIBLE

Randolph Spalding d. Savannah, Ga. 3/25/1862
Mary Bass Spalding, his wife, d. Sapelo Island 9/19/1898
Sarah McKinley Wylly, wife of William C. Wylly, d. Athens, Ga.
5/1897
Clara Lucy, dau. of Bourke and Ella B. Spalding, b. Riverside,
Sapelo Island, Ga. 5/27/1881 d. 9/3/1881 Athens, Ga.

Marriages
Archibald Carlisle McKinley to Sarah Elizabeth Spalding at
The Ridge near Darien, Ga.
Thomas Spalding to Sarah B. McKinley 1/2/1871 Milledgeville, Ga.
Bourke Spalding to Ella P. Barrow 11/3/1874 Athens, Ga., by
Rev. Josiah lewis
William C. Wylly to Sarah McKinley Spalding 3/188- Milledgeville
William McKinley, son of Archibald C. and Sarah E. Spalding
b. & d. 186-
Randolph Spalding, son of Bourke and Ella Barrow Spalding
b. 9/30/1879
Clara Lucy Spalding b. 3/27/1881 Riverside d. 9/3/1881 Athens
T. Bourke Spalding, son of Randolph and Mary Bass Spalding,
d. 9/5/1884 Sapelo Island, Ga.
Thomas Spalding,on of Randolph and Mary Bass Spalding, d.
Macon, Ga. 1/27/1885

THOMAS SPALDING BIBLE

Marriages
James Spalding, native of City of Edinburgh m. Margery McIntosh
of Town of Darien, Ga. 11/5/1772 and had one only child -Thomas
Spalding b. 3/25/1774. Thomas m. at Bellville, McIntosh Co.,
11/5/1795 and had issue.

Richard Leake, native of City of Cork, Ireland, m. Jane Martin of
Island of St. Christopher, Carribean Sea, 1775 and had only one
child - Sarah Leake b. 1778

Hester Margery Spalding m. William Cooke 1/30/1821 at Darien, Ga.
Jane M. L. Spalding m. Daniel Heyward Brailsford 6/13/1821 at
Darien, Ga.
Charles Spalding m. Evelyn Hall 3/7/1832 at Darien, Ga.

Births
Jane Martin Leake Spalding 10/8/1796 Savannah, Ga.
James Spalding 12/12/1797 St. Simons Island, Ga.
Son b. & d. 1/13/1798 St. Simons Island, Ga.
Margaret Spalding 5/10/1800 at Lancaster, England
Hester Margery Spalding 4/23/1801 Cityh of London, Gr. Britain
Mary Ann Elizabeth Spalding 5/11/1803 Bellville, Ga.
Margery Spalding 12/8/1804 Bellville, Ga.
Elizabeth Sarah Spalding 6/23/1806 Sapelo Island, Ga.
Charles Harris Spalding 1/17/1808 Sapelo Island, Ga.
Catherine Spalding 10/13/1810 Sapelo Island, Ga.

Bible of Thomas Spalding, Births, contd....)

Thomas Spalding 2/13/1813 Sapelo Island, Ga.
Two Sons b. & d. between 1813 and 1817
Emily Screven Spalding 2/28/1817 Darien, Ga.
Dau. b. & d. 1818 Darien, Ga.
Randolph Spalding 12/22/1822 Darien, Ga.

Deaths
Died at Lancaster 3 wks. old, Margaret
My dear Father d. Savannah 3/7/1802
Margaret Spalding 11/6/1806 Sapelo Island, less than 2 yrs. old
Mary Ann Spalding 2/18/1818 near Darien, Ga., age 14 yrs., 9 mos.
Mrs. Margery Spalding, Mother of my dear husband, 3/30/1818,
   65 yrs. old., near Darien, Ga.
Thomas Spalding 5/22/1819 near Darien, Ga., 6 yrs., 3 mos. old
My dear Mother, Mrs. Jane Leake, 10/9/1820, Sapelo Island, age
   75 yrs. (as we supposed)
James Spalding, our son, 11/24/1820, Milledgeville, Ga. in the
   discharge of his duty as representative of the people of
   McIntosh Co. in the St. Legislature of Ga....
Emily Spalding 4/10/1824 Darien, Ga.

Above death entries signed by Sarah Spalding

Died near Darien at Ashtilly at res. of her son, Charles Spalding,
   5/17/1849, Mrs. Sarah Spalding, age 65 yrs.
Died at Ashtilly near Darien, at res. of his son, Charles
   Spalding, 1/4/1851, Thomas Spalding, aged 76 yrs., 10 mos.
Dau., Elizabeth, 3/30/1876, Darien, Ga., aged 69. (or 1896)
Above entries signed by Charles Spalding

Sarah Morris d. 12/24/1857
Mrs. Jane Brailsford d. 5/23/1861
Mrs. Cooke d. 10;17/1861
Randolph Spalding d. 3/1862
Thomas Spalding, son of Randolph Spalding, b. 9/16/1849
Thomas Bourke Spalding b. 2/23/1851
Sarah E. Spalding b. 9/16/1844

Charles Harris Spalding, last surviving child of Thomas and Sarah
Spalding d. at The Nook 2/4/1887, Spalding Co., age 79 yrs.

O. B. KNOWLES BIBLE
Owner: Mrs. W. D. Pope
Jackson, Georgia

Births
O. B. Knowles 3/16/1861   Robert C. Knowles 3/7/1889
L. A. Knowles 6/9/1860   Grover B. Knowles 9/20/1891
O. A. Knowles 3/4/1883   Derner T. Knowles 3/22/1893
J. B. Knowles 7/13/1885   Eva B. Knowles 2/18/1895
Rebecca L. Knowles 9/3/1867

Marriages
O. B. Knowles to Lanie Adaline Maddex 12/28/1881
James Bellow Knowles 4/24/1855
David Maddex to Rebecca Hunt 8/7/1881

(O. B. Knowles Bible contd....)

Deaths

Nathan C. Williamson 9/18/1880	J. C. Maddex 5/20/1905
James Edgar Knowles 6/20/1885	James Bellow Knowles 9/26/1865
Grover B. Knowles 12/24/1891	Olin A. Knowles 9/11/1870
H. A. Garat 12/9/1901	Oscar B. Knowles 6/26/1942

WALTER DARDEN POPE BIBLE
Owner: Mrs. W. D. Pope, Jackson, Ga.

Births

Walter Darden Pope 3/20/1880	Walter Darden Pope Jr. 6/2/1914
Rebecca Lavenia Pope 9/3/1887	Eva Ruth Pope 2/11/1913
Fannie Boyt Pope 4/5/1905	Harris Miller Pope 3/9/1900
John Dozier Pope 9/6/1905	Rebecca Lounette Pope 6/5/1922
Oscar Bryan Pope 3/31/1910	Sam Foster Pope 9/9/1925
Lawrence Crawford Pope 4/19/1912	

CHARLES HUGH WHITE BIBLE

Ada White, dau. of Hugh White, m. Wood Aiken. Ada White b. 6/29/1871. She is the mother of Julia Aiken, lives on Monticello Street, Covington, Ga.

Mother of William Aiken, Medical Doctor, m. 1st Allie Louise Travis, dau. of Dr. William Darricot Travis, Covington physician. Issue: Twins, one lived to adulthood, married & lives Lyons, Ga.

Dr. William Aiken m. 2nd Peripa Travis, wid. of his wife's (1) bro., William Travis. No issue. He d. 1971.
Peripa and William Travis had 3 sons - Robert, William, John. William is married, has one dau., Julia Travis.

JAMES ANDREW KIMBELL BIBLE
Owner: Mrs. J. A. Kimbell, Jackson, Ga.

Marriages
Allie J. Crumbley to James Andrew Kimbell 5/20/1894 at H. A. Crumbley's. Signed J. A. Jackson

Births

J. A. Kimbell 7/10/1875	Gladys Jane Kimbell 7/5/1898
Allie J. Kimbell 6/6/1877	Lillah May Kimbell 6/4/1900
Paul Kimbell 5/13/1895	Dollie Missie Kimbell 7;24/1904
Vanie Allen Kimbell 8/28/1896	

Deaths
Paul Kimbell 9/12/1896

JESSE G. B. GRAYBILL BIBLE
Of Baldwin Co., Ga.

Jesse G. B. Graybill of Baldwin Co., Ga. and Mary Francis Dickson
of Hancock Co., ga., m. 1/14/1841 at Sparta, Hancock Co. by Rev.
E. C. B. Thomas, Baptist Minister. Wit: AM E. Dickson, --Michael-
Lawrence. (Jesse Goodwin Butts Graybill)

Births
Jesse G. B. Graybill, son of Michael & Judith Graybill, b.
10/9/1817
Mary F. Grayvill, dau. of William and Lucy Dickson, b. 12/19/181-
Leonidas Josephus Graybill, son of Mary F. and Jesse G. B.
Graybill, b. 4/13/1843
William Graybill, son of Mary F. & Jesse G. B. Graybill, b.
4/20/1846
Mary Jopetra Graybill, dau. of Mary F. and Jesse G. B. Graybill,
b. 10/8/1848
George Washington Graybill, son of Mary F. and Jesse G. B.
Graybill, b. 11/16/1850
Francis Graybill, dau. of Mary F. and Jesse G. B. Graybill, b.
11/20/1853
Michael Hamilton Graybill, son of Mary F. and Jesse G. B.
Graybill, b. 1/28/1856
Henry Thomas Graybill, son of Mary F. and Jesse G. B. Graybill,
b. 3/20/1858
Jessie Julia Graybill, dau. of Mary F. and J. G. B. Graybill, b.
12/31/1860

Deaths
Leonidas Josephus Graybill, son of Mary F. and J. G. B. Graybill,
d. 5/9/1853
William Graybill, son of Mary F. and J. G. B. Graybill, d.
9/16/1852, aged 6 yrs., 5 mos., 26 days.
Mary Jopetra Graybill, dau. of Mary F. and J. G. B. Graybill, d.
12/21/1849, aged 1 yr., 2 mos., 13 days.
George Washington Graybill, son of Mary F. and J. G. B. Graybill,
d. 7/30/1854, aged 4 yrs., 6 mos., 13 days.
Jesse G. B. Graybill d. 10/19/1894, aged 77 yrs., 10 days. (bur.
Danville Cemetery, Gregg Co.)
Mary F. Graybill, wife of J. G. B. Graybill, d. 7/2/1907 (bur.
Danville Cemtery, Gregg Co.)
Francis Graybill, dau. of J. G. B. Graybill and Mary F. Graybill,
d. 12/16/1907, bur. Danville Cemetery, Gregg Co.
Henry Thomas Graybill d. 11/24/1932, bur. Danville Cemetery.
Jessie Julia Graybill Cunyus d. 12/19/1944, bur. Peatown
Cemetery, Gregg Co.
William and Waty Cunyus m. 12/29/1812 (Tattnall Co., Ga.), D.
Brinson officiating.
William Cunyus b. 10/26/1789
Waty (Guilford) Cunyus, wife of William Cunyus, b. 6/21/1793
            Children of William and Waty Cunyus:
Mary Ann b. 7/9/1813 (Ga.)
William Cunyus, Jr. b. 2/3/1815, d. infancy
John Floyd Cunyus b. 4/24/1816 (Ga.)
William Henry Cunyus b. 12/6/1830 (Ga.)
(Mary Ann Cunyus m. William Federick in Ga.) Children: William
Willis b. 1/18/1834
William Henry Cunyus m. Mary Cordelia Prothro 7/1/1855 at Camden,
Rusk Co., Texas. Mary Cordelia b. 3/15/1838. Children:
Mary Cordelia 6/16/1857-4/11/1893

231

(Jesse G. B. Graybille Bible contd.....)

Walter 2/2/1859-11/23/1856
James Prothro 4/20/1861-

William Henry Cunyus m. 2d 1866? Laura Beatrice Dyer. Children:
Sophronia Louise, Amanda, Georgia Oliver

Deaths
William Cunyus d. 1/4/1864, bur. Peatown Cemetery, Gregg Co., Tx.
Waty Cunyus d. 7/30/1873, bur. above.
Walter Cunyus, d. 11/23/1956, bur. above.

Walter Cunyus and Sallie M. Morgan m. 9/9/1886, had 13 children,
8 still living.

JAMES THOMAS COMER BIBLE
Owner: Mrs. Mary Brockman, Charlotte, N. C.

James Thomas Comer b. Athens, Ga. 3/7/1849, d. 7/25/1911 Comer,
Ga., m. at Maysville, Ga. 7/5/1886 to Margaret Bowen (Alexander)
Comer, b. Maysville, Ga., 12/16/1867, d. Charlotte, N. C.
5/14/1926. Children:

Blanche Comer b. and d. Athens, Ga. 11/18/1887
Charlie Alexander Comer b. 5/4/1890, d. 11/10/1893 Maysville, Ga.
George Duval Comer b. 4/23/1892 Maysville, Ga., d. 1/21/1927
Mimie Comer b. & d. 8/15/1894
Mary Olivia Comer b. 8/7/1896 Maysville, Ga. m. Charles Raven
  Brockman 11/28/1918. Children:
  Marvin Comer Brockman (foster son) b. Guilford Co., N. C.
  6/29/1925. William Adams Brockman b. 12/16/1929, Mt. Vernon,
  N.Y.
Margaret Comer b. 4/14/1900 Comer, Ga. m. Walter Cavin 7/6/1926
Children: Margaret Ann Cavin (Peggy)
Mary Rutherford, dau. of above, d. 10/30/1840
James W. Simmons (Husband) d. 11/11/1867
Catharine LeGay (Wife) d. 8/21/1889
Ann Elizabeth Berry nee Devereaux nee Simmons, dau., d.--

BENJAMIN SIMMONS BIBLE
Owner: A. I. Butts, Sr.

Benjamin Simmons m. Elizabeth Spratling 5/23/1738. Their
children:

John b. 2/23/1740	Martha b. 4/23/1756
Benjamin b. 4/25/1742	Spratley b. 7/23/1759
Mary Lucy (third) b. 6/24/1744	Henry b. 4/18/1763
Mary (4th) b. 8/12/1746	
Lucy b. 1/13/1749	
Sarah b. 2/19/1751	
Kezia b. 3/27/1754	

BENJAMIN & SARAH SIMMONS BIBLE
Owner: Joseph Paul Thorp, Chatfield, Tx.

Benjamin Simmons m. Sarah Butts 2/2/1772
Sarah, wife of Benjamin, d. 2/28/1821
Children:

James Simmons b. 1/1/1773   Patsy b. 10/20/1782
Sarah b. 1/1777   Elley b. 5/20/1786
Benjamin b. 10/1778   John B. b. 2/11/1789
Jess b. 5/31/1780   Catharine L. b. 1/1791
(The above b. Greenville Co.,Va.)

JESSE SANFORD THOMAS BIBLE

Jesse Sanford Thomas b. 1/22/1816
Mary Ann Daniel, dau. of Young Daniel, b. 9/25/1825. They m.
10/28/1841. Children:

Mary Catherine b. 11/21/1842   Deaths
Mary Elizabeth Minerva b. 7/28/1844   Martha C. 12/23/1843
David Young b. 5/17/1846   John Simms 5/17/1851
William Sandford b. 11/29/1848   David Young 8/27/1866
John Simms b. 6/9/1850   Jesse Sanford ---
Sarah Georgia Missouri b. 10/10/1852
Mark Blandford b. 11/21/1854

Sallie G. M. Thomas, dau. of Jesse S. and Mary Daniel Thomas, m.
Arthur C. Myrick 12/16/1873. Children:

William Fletcher Myrick b. 10/16/1876
Mary E. Myrick b. 9/13/1879
Charles Arthur Myrick b. 3/25/1881
Thomas Howell Myrick b. 9/30/1882

WILLIAM FLETCHER MYRICK BIBLE

William Fletcher Myrick b. 10/16/1876
Henrietta Hinton b. 3/11/1881 m. 10/22/1896. Children:

Mary b. 12/6/1879
Julia Thomas b. 7/13/1900
Jesse Lucile b. 11/14/1902

John A. Smith m. Mary E. Myrick, b. 9/13/1879, on 3/1899. Their
children:

Charles Arthur Smith b. 1/1900
William Buie Thomas b. 2/22/--, m., Lucie Franks Bennett, b.
10/6/1877, on 1/3/1897. Children:

Guy Bynum Thomas b. 6/26/1898
Sallie May Thomas b. 5/30/1900

CHRISTOPHER WHITE BIBLE of Jackson Co., Ga.
Owner: Grady H. White, Hapeville, Ga.

Births
Christopher White 1/31/1802
Jane Lee 1/30/1810
Elizabeth Wells White 6/1/1830
William Canady White 10/21/1831
Tilmon Davis Oxford White 9/16/1833
Susan? Christopher? Mary? White 8/28/1847
Eliza Jane White 6/10/1835
Jesse Marion White 1/1/1837
Clarissa Amanda White 4/26/1839
Sarah Ann Lilis White 4/21/1841
Alcy Carolina Lee White 3/14/1843
Lee Andrew White 3/11/1845

Nancy Ann Elizabeth Borders b. 8/15/1853 Wisc.?
Canada Moriss? Borders? b. 2/23/1855
Dilmus Millard Jackson Borders b. 9/23/1856
Eliza Jane Juriah Borders b. 3/20/1859
Lafayette Henry Davis Borders b. 1/25/1863
William Jesse Marion Christopher Jackson Harris b. 7/27/1862
Nancy Ann Clarissa White b. 10/8/1862
Jesse M. Harris b. 7/30/1837
Georgia Lieugenia Kansus Borders b. 9/13/1860
William Lea Andrew White b. 11/25/1864
Jessie Borders Johns White b. 6/1/1867

Christopher White, son of Jesse White and Elizabeth White and
Jane Lee, dau. of Henry Lee and Lilis Lee, was m. 7/9/1829
Lafayette H. Borders, son of Michael A. Borders and Nancy Borders
and Elizabeth W. White, dau. of Christopher White and Jane White,
was m. 11/14/1852
Jessie M. Harris and Sarah Ann L. White m. 2/5/1860
James A. Estes and Eliza Ann Whitemire m. 11/5/1861
William C. White and Amanda E. Baxter m. 12/29/1861
David D. Murray and Clarrissa A. White m. 7/21/1873
A. J. Gunnels? and Susan H. White m. 11/15/1868
George May and Susan M. Gunnels m. 11/5/1878

Deaths
Christopher White 3/30/1847   Jesse M. White 6/15/1880
Jesse M. harris 4/16/1862   Jane White, consort of
William J. M.C. J. Harris 7/7/1863   Christopher, 4/19/1885
Lee A. White 7/6/1864   James L. Morris 4/22/1887
Delania   Estes 5/5/1864   Amanda Elizabeth White
Ailsey C. L. White 10/21/1868   7/15/1907
William C. White 11/2/1918

Births
Arie C. C. Gunnels 7/21/1869?   James C. May 3/29/1887
Luten? D. Murray 4/3/1874   James H. Morris 9/24/1857
Ladie P. Murray 2/14/1876   John C. May 1/4/1881
Lucy Jane Murray 1/17/1877
Elizabeth A. May 10/3/1877

James L. Morris m. 12/26/188-   Lola G. Terrell b. 4/30/188-
J. F. Borders m. 11/18/18--   Parks Terrell b. 10/2/18--
Lola G. Terrell b. 4/30/188-   John D. Donahough b. 7/24/1878
R. P. Terrell and N. E. B. Donahough m. -/18/18--

Marriages

Miss Isabella A. Bivins of Milledgeville, Ga. and Henry E. Hendrix of Lexington, S. C., 7/21/1859 by Rev. Mr. Flynn.
Miss Annie V. Hendrix of Milledgeville, Ga. and Henry Emersin McCombs of Milledgeville, Ga., 10/14/1883, by Rev. D. McQueen

Births

Henry E. Hendrix 12/3/1833
Isabella A. Hendrix 2/15/1842

Charlie Bivins Hendrix 6/20/1860	Bernard Herty Hendrix 5/14/1874
Anna Victoria Hendrix 11/2/1862	Corrinne Belle Hendrix 6/29/1876
Hattie Rogers Hendrix 9/27/1865	Ernest Manry Hendrix 10/23/1878
Edwin Hendrix 10/9/1868	Claude Foster Hendrix 3/31/1880
Maurice Heyward Hendrix 8/5/1871	Mattie Lucile Hendrix 10/5/1882

Deaths

Maurice Heyward Hendrix 7/30/1873
Bernard Herty Hendrix 5/29/1876
Ernest Manry Hendrix 7/30/1879
Mattie Lucille Hendrix 9/22/1863
Isabella A. Hendrix 5/30/1897
Henry E. Hendricks 5/25/1903

Marriages

Gus Ped Harper and Beulah Kathleen Harper 2/5/1905
Precious Lillian Harper, dau. of Gus and Beulah Harper, and Raymond Lester Adams 2/2/1926
Selma May, dau. of Gus and Beulah Harper and Calfrey Clinton Clark 11/22/1938 at Baptist Tabernacle in Atlanta, Ga.

Births

Gus Ped Harper 8/10/1825
Beulah Kathleen Brown 12/12/1886
Precious Lillian Harper 10/30/1905
Selma May Harper 8/7/1907
Raymond Lester Adams, son of Raymond and Precious Adams, 11/15/1926
Douglas Tyre, son of Ray and Precious Adams, 11/20/1927
Constance Joan, dau. of Calfrey and Selma Harper Clark 1/15/1933

WILLIAM FRANKLIN JENKINS, JR.
Owner: Miss Caroline Virginia Jenkins
Eatonton, Ga.

Susie May Thomas b. 6/22/1877 (wife of W. F. Jenkins, Jr.)
Children:
Leila May Jenkins b. 10/26/1900
George Thomas Jenkins b. 10/24/1903

Leila May Jenkins and Joseph Head Owen m. 6/11/1924

Joseph head Owen b. 11/15/1899

Caroline Virginia b. 6/29/1925
Susan harriett b. 5/4/1929

JAMES HENDERSON BIBLE

Betsy Henderson, wife of James Henderson, b. 5/19/1774
Polly Henderson b. 10/13/1792
William Henderson b. 4/14/1794
James G. Henderson b. 5/14/1796
Sally Henderson b. 1/15/1799
Matilda Henderson b. 10/25/1801
Betsy (Elizabeth C.) Henderson b. 3/3/1804
Cynthia Henderson b. 3/25/1807
Nancy A. Henderson b. 8/27/1809
John Henderson b. 4/16/1812
Polly A. Henderson b. 3/25/1814

Polly A. Henderson m. William Garner 3/6/1810
William Henderson m. Cata Thornton 2/7/1815
Sara Henderson m. John A. Cogburn 12/15/1818
Matilda Henderson m. Jerry Clarke 11/27/1820

Polly Garner d. 12/15/1810
James Henderson d. 8/15/1814
Nancy A. Henderson d. 9/8/1814
Betsy Henderson d. 4/14/1816
James Guy Henderson d. 8/18/1816
Cynthia Henderson d. 10/15/1819
Matilda Clarke, dau. of James and Betsy Henderson, d. 4/29/1829
William Henderson d. 2/19/1832

236

WILLIAM THOMAS WYNN BIBLE
Owner: Dr. William T. Wynn, Milledgeville, Ga.

William Thomas Wynn b. Henry Co., Ga. 10/30/1874 m. 2/13/1902
Mary Ellison (Floyd) Wynn b. Clayton, Ala. 7/18/1880. Children:

William Thomas Wynn, Jr., b. Abberville, Ala. 9/21/1903 m. 1st
    5/29/1924, 2d, 2/23/1929
Winfrey Irvin Wynn b. Enterprise, Ala. 3/6/1908 m. 9/16/1931
Ellison Floyd Wynn b. Pulaski, Tenn. 8/29/1910
Mary Mildred Wynn b. Pulaski, Tenn. 1/23/1913
Lawrence Wynn b. Pulaski, Tenn. 11/9/1915

WINFREY LOCKET WYNN BIBLE Of Chattahoochee Co.
Owner: Dr. William T. Wynn, Milledgeville, Ga.

Winfrey Locket Wynn b. Chattahoochee Co., Ga. 2/17/1844 d.
    2/2/1917, m. 10/19/1871
Ema (McCarty) Wynn b. Macon Co., Ga. 9/15/1850 d. 1/4/1930.
    Children:
James Edgar Wynn b. Russell Co., Ala. 10/10/1873
William Thomas Wynn b. Henry Co., Ga. 10/30/1874 m. 2/13/1902
Charles Ross Wynn b. Talbot Co., Ga. 8/11/1881

ROBERT & PATIENCE JENKINS BIBLE
Owner: Rev. J. W. R. Jenkins
Eatonton, Ga.

(Parts of this record have been lost)

Robert Jenkins and Patience Saunders m. 12/11/1811 Their
    Children:
Augustus M. Jenkins b. 1/11/1813   Thomas Jefferson b. 5/27/1823
Emily Ann b. 9/15/1814   Joshua Williams b. 5/20/1825
Quintillian Washington b. 3/29/1816 Sarah Jane Rebecca
Robert Carter b. 11/15/1817   b. 11/5/1826
Nancy b. 3/20/1819   Patience b. 1/17/1829
Franklin Sanders b. 10/27/1821

EDWARD EZEKIEL BASS BIBLE Of Milledgeville

Edward Ezekiel Bass and Bessie Ione Bass m. 1/4/1899

Births
Edward Ezekiel, son of John Archie and Sarah Robinson Bass, 3/7/1869
Bessie Ione, dau. of Wesley Arnold and Martha Ellen Bass, 4/28/1878

Their Children:

Sara Ione Bass b. 2/22/1900
Wesley Edward Bass b. 8/1/1902
Martha Bass b. 10/21/1910

Ellis Garfield Dean b. 10/17/1891
Florence Cole, dau. of Wallace Norton and Bessie Arline Cole, b. 9/27/1906

Edward Bass Dean b. 7/15/1923
Florence Elizabeth Bass b. 11/26/1929
Wesley Edward Bass, Jr. b. 8/21/1931

Marriages
Bessie Ione Bass and Ellis Garfield Dean 3/22/1917
Wesley Edward Bass and Florence Cole 1/22/1929

W. A. N. BASS BIBLE
Owner: Mrs. L. C. Wall, Milledgeville, Ga.

Marriages
W. A. N. Bass and Mollie R. Jones 11/25/1874
Pearl Bass and W. S. Edwards 2/3/1897
Emmie Bass and L. C. Wall 12/3/1902
Carrie Bass and W. H. Leonard 9/29/1903
Benjamin Bass and Lillian Pittman 9/18/1909
Ruby Bass and J. N. Atkinson 6/24/1909
Marilu Bass and E. J. Lee 9/26/1917
Carrie Bass Leonard and T. J. Wall 8/14/1924

Births
W. A. N. Bass 4/16/1854	Emily Bass 4/24/1883
MOllie R. Bass 9/26/1853	Carrie Bass 5/28/1885
Pearl Bass 9/24/1875	Ruby Bass 3/28/1887
Benjamin Bass 2/9/1876	Marilu Bass 7/1/1897
Charlie Bass 7/23/1881	

Deaths
Charlie Bass 7/20/1883	Benjamin Bass 1/28/1928
Mollie R. Bass 6/6/1923	W. A. N. Bass 10/26/1931

WESLEY ARNOLD BASS BIBLE
Owner: Mrs. E. E. Bass, Milledgeville, Ga.

Wesley Arnold Bass, son of Milton and Elizabeth Ann Culver Bass,
b. 12/23/1847, d. 1/25/1931
Mattie Ellen Bass, dau. of John and Eliza Harper Amoss, b.
1/29/1851 d. 8/19/1927
Wesley Arnold Bass and Mattie Ellen Amoss m. 11/27/1873
Bessie Ione Bass, dau. of Wesley Arnold and Mattie Ellen Bass,
b. 4/28/1878
Frank Hall Bass, son of above, b. 11/6/1883 d. 3/3/1887
Bessie Ione, dau. of above, m. Edward Ezekiel, son of John Archie
and Sara Bass 1/4/1899
Milton Bass, son of Edmund Bass, b. 3/24/1816 d. 2/11/1883
Elizabeth Ann Culver, dau. of George and Eliza Culver,
b. 10/11/1812, d. 1/26/1868

MARSHALL HALL BLAND BIBLE
Milledgeville, Ga.

Marshall Hall Bland m. Ruby Garnett Taylor 12/19/1894 at
Knoxville in Diocese of Tenn. according to form of solemnization
of Matrimony of Protestant Episcopal Church...12/19/1894. /s
Samuel L. Ringgold, Rector, St. John's Church.

Marshall H. Bland b. 10/11/1862 m. Ruby G. Taylor 12/19/1894 d.
1/20/1936
Ruby G. Taylor b. 11/24/1874
Elizabeth (Bess) Bland b. 9/18/1895
Frances Nylic Bland b. 2/26/1898 m. Harold T. Moore 2/1918
Joe M. Moore b. 10/29/1918
Marshall Bland Moore b. 2/28/1920

Lucie Graham Bland b. 3/29/1900 m. Robert S. Rodenberry, Jr.
7/1/1920 Thaddeus Hall Rodenberry b. 6/19/1921

Marshall Hall Bland, Jr. b. 6/28/1902 m. Stella McConnel
6/30/1932 who was b. 2/4/1910

DAVID J. BUSH BIBLE
Owner: Mrs. L. C. Wall
Milledgeville, Ga.

Marriages
Daniel J. Bush of Hancock Co., Ga. to Margaret E. Ezell of
Hancock Co., Ga. 12/26/1867 at res. of H. Cummings by Rev. John
J. Hymen. Wit: W. S. Lattimore, Harris Cummings
W. D. McJunkin and Mary Lizzie Bush 7/25/1895
D. J. Bush and Martha E. James 1/14/1897, Rev. B. N. Ivey
officiating

(David J. Bush Bible contd....)

Births
David J. Bush 2/27/1844   Mary Lizzie Bush 6/13/1872
Martha E. Ezell 6/15/1830   George Daniel Bush 4/8/1875
David Lee Bush 2/7/1871   Mary Ann Ezell 4/30/1819

Deaths
Martha E. Bush, wife of D. J. Bush, 12/12/1891
Mary Lizzie McJunkin, wife of W. D. McJunkin and dau. of D. J.
    and Martha E. Bush, 7/14/1896
D. J. Bush 4/18/1911

ROBERT FRANCIS CRUTCHFIELD BIBLE
Owner: Mrs. Albert Crutchfield, Conyers, Ga.

Marriages
Robert Francis Crutchfield and Martha Jane Tunnell 9/28/1856
    by Isaac R. Williams, J. P.
Albert Alonzo Crutchfield and Anna Herrin 12/15/1885 at Social
    Circle, Ga.
John Henry Crutchfield and Mattie Willie 8/20/1888 by Rev.
    P. A. Jesup, Eastman, Ga.
Roberta Francis Crutchfield and O. W. Bush 6/20/1889, at
    Eastman, Ga.

Births
Robert Francis Crutchfield 5/28/1836
Martha Jane Tunnell 11/18/1839

William Edward 6/19/1857   John Henry 11/28/1861
Albert Alonzo 10/19/1858   Roberta Francis 2/5/1865
Mary Francis 10/2/1860

Deaths
William Edward Crutchfield 6/19/1857
Robert Francis Crutchfield killed in Battle in Virginia 2/1865
John Henry Crutchfield 10/5/1889
Roberta Francis Crutchfield 7/22/1890
Martha Jane Crutchfield 8/8/1905
Albert Alonzo Crutchfield 3/10/1920

WARREN EDWARDS BIBLE
Owner: Mrs. Warren Edwards
Milledgeville, Ga.

Warren Edwards and Mary Miller, eldest child of A. J. and L. E.
Miller were m. at home of bride's parents in Wilkinson Co., Ga.
6/25/1878, George F. Goetchius, of the Presbyterian Church at
Milledgeville, Ga. officiating.

Warren Edwards b. 10/22/1857 d. 4/26/1921
Mary Miller b. 1/19/1860

(Warren Edwards Bible contd....)

Essie Evaline, eldest child of Warren and Mary Edwards, b. in
  Wilkinson Co., Ga. 6/21/1879
Annie Charlotte b. Baldwin Co., Ga. 8/12/1881
Andrew Martin, third child of Warren and Mary Edwards, was
  b. Baldwin Co., Ga. 7/11/1883
Lucile b. 6/21/1885
Talmadge, Will Miller, and Lucille d. in infancy aged
  respectively, 10 mos., 10 days, 13 mos.
Eugene Jackson, seventh child of Warren and Mary Edwards,
  b. 7/29/1891
Sarah Frances, eighth child of above, b. 10/21/1893
Fannie, ninth child, b. & d. summer 1899

Essie m. Samuel C. Patterson 9/25/1903 and d. 6/29/1905, leaving
  an infant son, Rienzi Baker Patterson, b. 6/15/1905
Annie Charlotte m. Leroy Brown 9/1903
Andrew Martin m. Irene McCreary 6/1911
Sarah Frances m. Samuel Patterson 6/26/1913
Eugene Jackson m. Florence Allison 8/1917

JAMES MONROE GRIMES BIBLE
Owner: Miss Mattie Grimes
Milledgeville, Ga.

Marriages
James Monroe Grimes and Mary West Jackson 12/8/1869
Benjamin Franklin Grimes and Emma Lee Grimes 12/21/1902
Tip Camel Goodwyn and Pearle Belle Grimes 11/13/1907
John Rivers Grimes and Minnie Goolby 6/23/1909
James Carlos Grimes and Frances Louella Harper 11/30/1910
John Rivers Grimes and Maud Harper 3/22/1919

Births
James Monroe Grimes 10/18/1841
Mary West Jackson 10/14/1841

Emma Lee Grimes 10/13/1870   Pearl Belle Grimes 10/8/1876
Lena Rivers Grimes 8/10/1872   Martha Davis Grimes 12/15/1878
James Carlos Grimes 7/12/1874   John Rivers Grimes 3/3/1881

Deaths
James Monroe Grimes 5/21/1913
Mary W. Grimes 2/11/1926   Tip Camel Goodwyn 10/18/1932
Benjamin Franklin Grimes 1/14/1933

241

JAMES WALLER BIBLE Of Hancock Co.
Owner: John W. Waller, Culverton, Ga.

James Waller b. 12/15/1768 d. 1/0/1817
Elizabeth Waller b. 5/7/1772, wife of James Waller, d. 2/6/1845
Martha Waller b. 1/27/1790
Martha Waller Newsom d. 5/16/1833
Ellis M. Waller b. 8/28/1796 (d. unmd.)
Elizabeth K. Waller b. 5/28/1799
James B. Waller b. 2/5/1802 d. 6/16/1839
Fillis E. Waller b. 6/5/1804
Ibby C. Waller b. 5/1/1807
Ibby Waller Ransom d. 4/22/1863
Irwin N. Waller b. 10/8/1809 d. 3/1/1879

WILLIAM WALLER BIBLE Of Siloam, Ga.
Owner: Mrs. J. A. Reynolds, Atlanta, Ga.

William N. Waller and Sidney Winfield Tunnell m. 4/9/1867

Births
William N. Waller 11/2/1841   Clarence Sidney Waller 2/7/1874
Sidney W. Tunnell 7/27/1847   Pauline Waller 4/26/1875
Claude Wingfield Waller 8/28/--   Mable Harris 6/17/1877
Annie Lou Waller 5/31/1870   Lamar Waller b. 5/12/1881
                                   Willis Waller 2/20/1883

Marriages
J. A. Reynolds to Annie Lou Waller 4/9/1890
Paul B. Diver and Pauline Waller 10/19/1895

Deaths
Lamar Waller 6/7/1881   Willis Waller 3/3/1890
Mable Harris Waller 12/4/1881   William N. Waller 11/4/1882
Clarence Sidney Waller 7/12/1874   Sidney W. Tunnell Waller
                                   7/1910 at Griffin, Ga.

LEE EDWARD OXLEY BIBLE

Lee Edward Oxley m. Hatti McPherson 12/22/1896 at Parents home by
J. E. Mosely, N. P.

Births
Lee Edward Oxley 3/25/1876 Pulaski Co.
Harriett Anna McPherson 9/5/1879 Bibb Co.
Orrie May Oxley 10/28/1897 Bibb Co.
John Doris Oxley 12/14/1900 Bibb Co.
Lee Edward Oxley, Jr. 10/15/1905 Bibb Co.
William Henry Oxley 11/25/1906 Bibb Co.
Lewis Carlyle Oxley 7/19/1909 Bibb Co.
Georgia Ellen Oxley 9/18/1915 Bibb Co.

(Lee Edward Oxley Bible contd....)

Marriages
Orrie May Oxley to Roman H. Raby 4/4/1928, G. Wright. P. B.
John Doris Oxley to Vivian Arnold 1921
Lee Edward Oxley, jr. to Laurine Everidge 11/1/1922, Gorden
  Wright, P.B.
William Oxley to Mildred Opal Ferrel 3/3/1926, Rev. Taylor
Ellen Oxley to Alvin Herring 7/24/1937. J. E. Sammond V.P.M.

Deaths
John Timothy Daniel McPherson, son of Ennels and Susan Fatima
  Erwin McPherson, b. 12/13/1853 d. 1/15/1935
Georgia Caroline Tucker, dau. of George Churchill and Amyrinthia
  Tapley Tucker b. 9/2/1850, d. 5/6/1942
George Ennels McPherson, son of John Ennels McPherson and Georgia
  McPherson b. 11/8/1877 d. 2/12/1955
Lillian Esther McPherson (Tidwell Strozier), dau. of John T. D.
  and Georgia McPherson, b. 7/1/1892, d. 7/7/1956
John Henry McPherson, son of John T. D. and Georgia McPherson,
  b. 1/24/1882 d. 7/3/1957
William Malcolm McPherson, son of John T. D. and Georgia
McPherson, b. 8/15/1888, d. 6/30/1963
Charlotte Brown, wife of Romas Edward Raby, 2/22/1960, Riverside
  Cemetery, Macon, Ga.
Romas Edward Raby, son of R. H. and Orrie May Raby, 11/22/1966,
  Riverside Cemetery, Macon, Ga.
Lewis Carlyle Oxby, son of Lee Edward Oxby, Sr. and Hatti
McPherson Oxley 6/4/1967 Bromville, N. Y., bur. Doles Cemetery,
Bibb Co., Macon, Ga. (burned)
R. H. Raby, Husband of Orie May Oxley 5/8/1939, heart attack,
  bur. Shiloh, Macon, Ga.
Lee Edward Osley Sr., husband of Hatti McPherson, 4/4/1948, heart
  attack, bur. Mt. Zion Cemetery, Macon, Ga.
John Doris Oxley, Husband of Vivian Arnold, 12/30/1951, heart
  attack, bur. Richmond, Va.
Laurine E. Oxley, wife of L. E. Oxley, Jr., dau. of Eugene and
  May Bryant Everidge, 1/8/1960, cancer, bur. Memorial Park
  Cemetery

William Henry Oxley b. 11/25/06 d. 6/82 m. Opel Mildred Ferrel
3/2/25. Three Children:
Ellen Elizabeth 8/5/27 (Married)
Mary Kathleen 9/16/28 (married)
William Henry II 9/8/29 (not married)

Ellen Elizabeth m. Charles Lee Judd
Divorced Charles Lee and remarried William Thomas Smith 5/1950
Two children:
Linda Lee Hudd Thompson (William Cato), has two children-Kristie
  and Kari
William Thomas Smith (June), has two children: Cindy, Joey

SAMUEL PENNINGTON BIBLE
Owner: Mrs. Mollie Hillsman
Eatonton, Ga.

Samuel b. 1800, son of Ephraim Pennington, d. 1872
Eliza Jane Shi b. 1800, dau. of Samuel and Jane Shi
Samuel Pennington b. 7/15/1765 d. 12/14/1835

Children of Samuel and Eliza Jane Pennington:

James m.---Crawford
William m. Nancy Maddox
Samuel m. Sarah Howard
Mary Jane m. Francis S. Hearn

Note added: Samuel, son of Thomas of Va. and Warren Co., Ga.

SAMUEL CRATUS PATTERSON BIBLE
Owner: S. C. Patterson, Milledgeville, Ga.

Marriage
Samuel Cratus Patterson to Essie Evaline Edwards 9/25/1903
Samuel Cratus Patterson to Sarah Frances Edwards 6/26/1913
(Samuel Cratus Patterson Bible contd....)

Births
Samuel Cratus Patterson 3/1/1874
Essie Evaline Edwards 6/21/1879 d. 6/29/1905
Rienz Baker Patterson 6/15/1905
Sarah Frances Edwards 20/21/1893

     Children of Samuel Cratus Patterson and Sarah:

Jane 10/26/1914   Lydia Allen 8/5/1920
Warren Calvin 5/10/1918   Rosemary 7/23/1922
Samuel Cratus, Jr. 6/14/1926

NICHOLAS POWERS BIBLE

Marriages
Lilly Ann Lynn Powers to R. O. Beavers 6/4/1863 by Rev. James
     Rainwater
Elizabeth Caroline Powers to Dr. O. T. Dozier 4/30/1874 by Rev.
     Hamilton
Stella Marks Powers to Willie A. Shannon 11/23/1875 by Rev.
     Saxton, Rome, Ga.
George Thomas Powers to Mattie J. Rogers 12/6/1879 by Rev.
     J. W. Burke, Macon, Ga.

JAMES QUILLIAN BIBLE
Owner: David Turner Quillian

James Quillian 3/1757-1838
Sarah Waggoner d. 1805 m. 11/9/1779
James Milton Quillian 5/10/1793-1869
Sarah Pritchett 3/25/1794-12/26/1944
Wiley Hargrove Quillian 12/8/1820-3/30/1893
Nancy Lou Meadows 5/5/1832-6/30/1889
James Christopher 7/3/1849 m. Levice Pierce 3/17/1872

ALEXANDER REID BIBLE

Notes: Son of Samuel Reid, Rev. War Soldier, bur. Putnam, Ga.,
Capt. during war. Tombstone reads: Major Alexander Reid d.
3/26/1832, age 64 yrs. Elizabeth, his wife, d. 1/23/1860, age 87.

Children:
John Brewer Reid m. Sarah Blanton
Samue Reid m. nancy Moreland
Edmund Reid m. Elizabeth Bulloch Terrell
Nancy Reid m. 1st Nathan Lyons, 2d William Briscoe
Alexander Sidney Reid m. Louisa Jordan
Andrew Reid m. 1st White, 2d Mary A. Clopton
Rebecca Reid m. Thadeus Reece
William Reid m. Martha Wingfield
James Lewis Reid m. Martha Trippe
David Henry Reid m. Sarah Adams

JAMES THOMAS BIBLE
Owner: Martha G. Thomas

James Thomas. His wife, Martha Walker b. 4/2/1747
Son, John Sherrod Thomas, b. 10/13/1779

GREEN B. THOMAS BIBLE
Owner: Mrs. D. W. Brannen

Green B. Thomas d. -/13/1832

245

```
                   HENRY PERCIVAL THOMAS, JR. BIBLE
                       Owner: Mrs. D. W. Brannen



Henry Percival Thomas, Jr. b. 4/23/1883
Wife, Mary Ellen Curry b. 2/1880



                   WILLIAM CAMPBELL THOMAS BIBLE
                       Owner: Mrs. D. W. Brannen



William Campbell Thomas b. 9/4/1876
Wife, Frances Dunlap



                   HENRY PERCIVAL THOMAS BIBLE
                       Owner: Mrs. D. W. Brannen



Henry Percival Thomas b. 7/7/1838
Wife, Sarah Florence Campbell b. 7/8/1849
   Children:
Eliza Neyle Thomas b. 5/2/1874
William Campbell Thomas b. 11/4/1876
Elizabeth Lewis Thomas b. 8/7/1879
Henry Pervical, Jr. b. 4/27/1882



                   JOHN SHERROD THOMAS BIBLE
                       Owner: Mrs. D. W. Brannen



John Sherrod Thomas b. 10/13/1779 m. 2d Eliza Hester Neyle
   b. 9/13/1779
Son, Henry Pervical Thomas, b. 7/7/1838



              JOHN HOWARD UNDERWOOD BIBLE Of Baldwin Co.
                       Owner: J. H. Underwood



Births
John Howard Underwood b. Baldwin Co. 6/8/1892
Ida Louise Powers b. Jasper Co. 6/27/1891

                               246
```

(John Howard Underwood Bible, Births, contd....)

George Powers Underwood b. 11/26/1915 Baldwin Co.
Howard Burke Underwood b. 12/24/1919 Baldwin Co.
Carolyn Louise Underwood b. 1/13/1931 Baldwin Co.

Marriages
John Howard Underwood to Ida Louise Powers 6/16/1914 Monticello,
Ga.

RICHARD L. BUTT BIBLE
Owner: Mrs. Jessie Whitaker Ansley
Ft. Myers, Fla.

Frances Precello Butt, dau. of Elizabeth C. and Richard L.
Precello b. 9/23/1847
Mary Virginia Butt b. 6/16/1849
Jenette Leonard Butt b. 3/5/1852
Sarah Elizabeth Butt b. 4/1/1854
Richard Lamar Butt b. 11/17/1856
John H. Butt b. 1859

Deaths
John H. Butt 7/19/1860   Elizabeth C. Butt 11/15/1861

E. J. WILLIAMS BIBLE
Owner: Mrs. Carrie Mobley Penuel
Thomson, Ga.

E. J. Williams 7/8/1806-4/26/1877
K. M. Williams 9/1808-12/31/1864
John M. Williams 4/15/1830-7/4/1847
Elizabeth B. Williams 8/2/1832-10/31/1833
Helen V. Williams 8/26/1834-7/27/1855
Carrie A. Williams 9/21/1837-1/27/1892
George Williams 3/3/1842-7/7/1861
Ezekiel Williams 9/23/1846-3/6/1854
Kissire Williams 7/11/1850-
William S. Mobley 11/20/1866-
Helen Mills 9/1868-6/4/1899
John Williams Mobley 12/1/1870-8/15/1932
Carrie Mobley 9/27/1894-
Hodges T. Mobley 7/30/1896-
Caroline Mobley Penn 3/19/1926-
Lucretia Ann Penuel 12/2/1927-
Jane R. Mobley 3/13/1927-

WILLIAMS-MOBLEY-PENUEL BIBLE
Owner: Mrs. Carrie Mobley Penuel
Thomson, Ga.

Carrie A. Williams m. Dr. Samuel Goode Mobley 1864
William Simkin Mobley m. Meilie Lucretia Timmerman 5/25/1893
Carrie Mobley m. Furman Penuel 3/11/1922
Hodges T. Mobley m. Margie Hill 7/1925

ALICE ATWOOD WILLIAMS BIBLE

James Brantley Williams m. Alice Atwood 5/5/1910, Presbyterian
  Church, Milledgeville, Ga.
James Brantley Williams b. 12/22/1878
Sara Alice, dau. of James Alfred Williams and Anna Langston
Bayard Atwood b. 4/2/1886
James Bayard, son of J. B. and Alice Williams b. 10/6/1912
  Providence, R. I.
Robert Hackney, son of above, b. 1/2/1915

LAMAR HAM BIBLE

Births
Lamar Ham 7/7/1885   Annie Bell Ham 1/14/1918
Annie Bell Sanford 5/29/1887   Jones Ham 2/15/1922
Henrietta Ham 8/3/1907   Lamar Ham Jr. 9/28/1924
Mary Ham 12/3/1928

Marriages
Lamar Ham to Annie Bell Sanford 9/5/1906

JAMES CARLOS GRIMES BIBLE

James Carlos Grimes m. Frances Louella Harper 11/30/1910

Births
James Carlos Grimes 7/12/1874   Oscar Harper Grimes 6/11/1914
Frances Louella Harper 8/14/1888 Velma Louise Grimes 4/28/1916
Margaret Lee Grimes 9/7/1911

WILLIAM B. & NANCY TALLANT HOLBROOK BIBLE
Owner: Homer Cox

Marriages
John W. Holbrook and Sarah Jane Haddin 10/6/1855

Charles W. Cox b. 3/29/1852
Thomas C. Holbrook b. 12/22/1856
Ida A. Cox b. 7/14/1876
William A. Cox b. 3/5/1878
John L. Cox b. 11/23/1880
Charles H. Cox b. 12/17/1874

Births
Sarah J. Holbrook 9/26/1837   Cenia Lovine Holbrook
John W. Holbrook 5/8/1839   6/18/1848
Annie Elizabeth Holbrook 2/11/1841 Hannah Caledonia Holbrook
Samuel Asberry Holbrook 5/2/1843   12/22/1856
Nancy Mahuldah Holbrook 7/12/1859
William B. Holbrook 2/24/1813-2/2/1858, age 44 yrs., 11 mos.,
   22 days

Deaths
Samuel Asbury Holbrook---

ALFRED JOINER BIBLE

Births
Alfred J. Joiner 10/14/1827
Priscilla Frances, wife, 4/14/1830
Martha Ann Celia, dau., 9/18/1858
Mary Elizabeth Wright Joiner 10/20/1850
Asa Brient Joiner 6/23/1853
Priscilla and Pherriba Joiner 1/23/1856
Alfred Glover Joiner 10/12/1859
Charles Joiner 9/4/1861
Emer Frances Joiner 10/25/1865
Lafayett Joiner 11/1/1868
C. Claudy Joiner 12/30/1871

Marriages
Alfred Joiner to Priscilla Collins 11/20/1847
George C. Smith to H. C. Joiner 2/6/1868

WILLIAM HUGH DICKSON BIBLE

William Hugh Dickson, son of David, grandson of William, great-
   grandson of Michael and gg-grandson of Simeon, b. 9/14/1785
Sarah, his wife, b. 5/16/1791. Their Children:

249

(William Hugh Dickson Bible contd...)

Births
James Otterson Dickson 8/10/1811
Elizabeth Caroline Dickson 11/13/1813
David Monroe Dickson 9/15/1815
Sarah Ann Otterson Dickson 10/14/1817
Elizabeth Ann Riley DIckson 10/14/1819
William Hugh Crawford Dickson 11/26/1821
Christopher Columbus Dickson 10/17/1824
John Sanders Dickson 5/13/1828
Martha Jane Dickson 5/21/1830
Thadeus Holt Dickson 6/18/1818

Deaths
Elizabeth Caroline Dickson 7/18/1815
Thadeus Holt Dickson, son of James C., d. 8/23/1823
Gen. David Dickson 5/3/1830
Sarah, wife of William H. Dickson, 8/3/1835
William H. Dickson 10/8/1803, age 78 yrs.
John S. Dickson 7/16/1853
David Monroe Dickson 5/21/1888 Morgan Co.

JESSE HAMILTON DICKSON BIBLE

Births
Jesse Hamilton Dickson 8/26/1847   Henrietta Helena Dickson
  Martha Marinda Dickson 3/16/1853   11/5/1855
Mary Tululah Dickson 2/20/1872   Annie Evans Dickson
David Albert Dickson 1/19/1874   8/25/1861
Martha Perl Dickson 2/3/1876   Jesse Lafayette Dickson
Annie Evans Dickson 1/1/1895   9/20/1887 Pine Level, Ala.
  Pine Level, Ala.   James Charles Dickson
                                       11/18/1903 Lamfasas, Tx

Marriages
Jesse H. DIckson of Pine Level, Ala. to Henrietta Helena Townsend
  of Montgomery Co., Ala. 9/16/1897 by Rev. S. L. Townsend
Jesse H. Dickson of Pine Level to Anne Elizabeth Evans of
  Montgomery Co., Ala. 2/17/1886 by Rev. J. S. Williams
Jesse H. Dickson of Pine Level, Ala. to Martha M. Townsend of
  Montgomery Co., Ala. 2/5/1871, res. of H. W. Townsend by Elder
  Thomas J. Miles of Pine Level, Ala., wit. H. H. Talbot and
  Henry Townsend

Deaths
Martha M. Dickson 9/12/1876
Henrietta Helena (Evie) DIckson 7/13/1886
Jesse Hamilton Dickson 5/1/1920 Houston, Tx.
Annie Evans Dickson 8/1931 Houston, Tx.
Evie Dickson Pratt 11/22/1932 Houston, Tx.

DAVID DICKSON BIBLE

David Dickson, son of William and grandson of Michael, b.
7/23/1750, old style
Sarah, his wife, b. 2/14/1750, old style
Martha, his second wife, b. 3/22/1764
Anne Allen Dickson, his third wife, b. 3/21/17--

Births

W. Hugh Dickson 9/14/1785   Nancy Campbell Dickson 12/2/1801
Michael Dickson 12/9/1788   Charles Allen Dickson 3/22/1804
William Dickson 3/20/1790   Patsey Ealse Dickson 11/30/1805
Elizabeth Dickson 2/16/1791   John Orr Dickson 6/1/1808
David Dickson Jr. 3/22/1792   Robert David Dickson 1/2/1810
James Dickson 7/1794   Martha Dickson Smith 12/8/1827
Thornton Smith Dickson 8/21/1801

David Manson Dckson 8/19/1835 (or 1825)
Thomas Hyde Dickson, son of David, 2/1/1812
Nancy Eliza Dickson 3/28/1813
Martha Letitia Dickson 9/10/1814
David Harris Dickson 10/1816
Julia Maria Dickson 3/1818
Zebulon Montgomery Pike Dickson 7/1819

David Dickson Smith, son of Jepthey Smith and Nancy Smith
b. 3/6/1825
William Hugh Smith b. 4/9/1820
Elizabeth Posy Dickson b. 3/10/1814

Deaths

Sarah, wife of David Dickson 9/17/1785, 35 yrs., 7 mos., 3 days
Martha, 2d wife of David Dickson, 9/9/1796, 32 yrs., 5 mos., 18
days
Elizabeth, dau. of David Dickson, 11/16/1792, 1 yr., 9 mos.
Elizabeth Echols 9/20/182- age 58 yrs., 7 moms., 6 days
Patsey 1/23/1828 --

Births

Christopher Columbus Dickson 10/17/1825
John Sanders Dickson 5/13/1828
Martha Jane Dickson 5/20/1830
Jonathan H. Glass 5/5/1779
Mary Dickson, wife of John --
Michael Dickson -/9/--
William Dickson -/20/--

Deaths

Nancy Eliza, 1st dau. of David Dickson 9/14/1813
David Dickson 5/23/1830
Anna Dickson 1/30/1840
Mary, wife of John Dickson, 5/8/1847, age 28 yrs.
Thornton S. Dickson 10/28/1867
Charles A. Dickson 9/1873
John O. Dickson 1/23/1883

Births

Robert D. Dickson 1/2/1810   Sherman Glass Dickson 9/8/1848
Matheny Dickson 8/14/1813   William Wyatt Dickson 6/25/1843

(David Dickson Bible, Births, contd....)

Manson Dickson 8/15/1833   David Sumpter Dickson 4/15/1841
Mary Ann Dickson 2/14/1835   Annie Allen Dickson 12/31/1838
Elisabeth C. Dickson 9/27/1836

Deaths
Robert David Dickson 3/25/1859
Matheny, wife of Robert Dickson 8/30/1891
Manson Dickson 9/26/1833
Mary Ann Dickson 10/10/1835
Annie Allen Dickson 3/22/1847
David Sumpter Dickson 5/14/1842
Sherman Glass Dickson 2/25/1865

JAMES ALSTON CLARK BIBLE

James Alston Clark m.   Sarah Margaret Biggart 5/13/1877, dau. of
Martha M. Hammond and William Alexander Biggard. "This was found
in my grandfather's papers. M. C. Womack."

JOHN MABEN EVANS BIBLE
Owner: Mrs. C. F. Mobley
1196 Tuckawanna Dr., S. W.
Atlanta, Ga.

John Maben Evans b. 7/29/1820   William R. 1/24/1859
Martha M. H. Evans b. 4/27/1827   Gold G. 7/29/1861
Emma C., 1st dau., b. 12/24/1849   M. J. 2/21/1864
Joseph P. b. 3/14/1854   Jasper Whitfield E.
Mary L. 11/1/1854   8/25/1869
Sarah M. 7/17/1857   Martha Isabella 8/16/1873

Deaths
Sarah M. Evans, dau. of John M. and M. M. H. Evans, 9/1858

WILLIAM DAVID CARRINGTON BIBLE
Owner: Anna Carrington

Births
William David Carrington 12/24/1849
Amanda Paralee Bennett 3/22/1850   Their Children:

Anna Clara 11/22/1831   Martha May 5/7/1879

(William David Carrington Bible contd.....)

Clyde Belle 7/7/1874   Hal Cleveland 8/13/1882

Marriages
William David Carrington to Amanda Paralee Bennett 12/14/1870
  in Madison Co., Ga.
Anna Clara Carrington to Edward Fisher McGowan 12/21/1892
  in Danielsville, Ga. by J. A. Shank, M. G.
Clyde Belle Carrington to Benny Thomas Moseley 11/29/1893
  Danielsville, Ga. by Y. G. Adams, M. G.
Hal Cleveland Carrington to Mattie Herring, Commerce, Ga.---

Deaths
William David Carrington 1/10/1913 Commerce, Ga.
Amanda Parlee Carrington 10/25/1938 at home of her granddau.,
  Ruby McGowen Hartman, Athens, Ga.
Ed. Fisher McGown 6/18/1912 Decatur, Ala.
Clyde Belle Carrington Moseley 9/26/1896 Danielsville, Ga.
Berry Thomas Moseley 12/19/1839 Danielsville, Ga.
Lula Inez Moseley, dau., d. infancy
Jane Lee Moseley Boggs, Danielsville, Ga. ---
Mattie Herring Carrington 2/18/1954 Commerce, Ga.

A. L. KING BIBLE

A. L. King of Clarke Co. m. Lula E. Ritch of Jackson Co.
12/20/1876 by Rev. W. W. Oslin

Births
Jimmie Leona King 11/26/1877   Janet Ritch King 9/26/1884
Annie Louise King 12/13/1879   Alexander Lee King 1/24/1888
Rubie King 7/17/1882   Scott King 8/12/1890

H. D. MOORE BIBLE

H. D. Moore and Jessamine Evans m. 1/27/1889

Births
John William Moore 12/25/1889   Infant 4/17/1896
James Mell Moore 2/5/1891   Mary Elizabeth Moore 5/25/1897
Henry lee Moore 5/8/1892   Magnolia Jane Moore 4/25/1899
Alexander Stephens Moore 9/29/1893 Jessamine Moore 3/5/1871
Brantley Hersekel Moore 12/22/1894 Henry Newton Moore 5/8/1868

Deaths
Infant boy 4/23/1896   John William Moore 2/28/1933
Henry Newton Moore 6/12/1900

253

JOHN THADDUS FLOYD BIBLE
Owner: Mrs. William T. Wynn
Milledgeville, Ga.

John Thaddus Floyd b. Chattahoochee Co., Ga. 11/11/1847,
    d. 3/12/1874
Regina (Ellison)Floyd b. Macon, Wesleyan, 1/18/1845, d. 9/1/1917
Their Children:

William Ellison Floyd b. Clayton, Ala. 3/30/1875 d. 10/29/1935
    m. 6/6/1900 Alice Floyd b. Clayton, Ala. 5/21/1878 m. 4/7/1898,
    d. 5/26/1910
Mary Ellison Floyd b. 7/18/1880 m. 2/13/1902
Julia Capers Floyd b. 11/25/1883 m. 12/3/1913
John Thaddus Floyd Jr. b. 8/15/1886 m. 12/30/1909
Florence Gertrude Floyd b. 4/5/1889 m. 5/3/1917

E. C. ROBISON BIBLE
Owner: Mrs. E. C. Robison, Jackson, Ga.

William F. Robison (bro. of E. C.) b. 1839 m. 1st Savannah
Stillwood, 2d Trudie Stone, d. 9/17/1905

E. C. Robison b. Washington Co., Ga. 5/5/1850 d. 3/26/1909
John, bro. of E. C. Robison (Dr.) m. 1904, d. 1/1895
Winfield Robert Robison d. 3/1904 m. Sally Shinholster, b. 1842,
    on 10/30/1867
Mary Elizabeth Robison -

(William Robison had bro., Gen. Samuel, father of above children)

S. J. SMITH BIBLE

S. J. Smith b. 3/3/1853 m. Mary Jane 8/14/1855

Births
S. J. Smith 5/15/1880   Emma Florida Smith 12/10/1891
W. F. Smith 9/27/1881   Annie May Smith 4/2/1893
P. A. Smith 5/21/1883   Mary Alice Smith 10/20/1895
Sallie Ophelia Smith 7/25/1885   Robert Lee Smith 12/6/1897
C. H. Smith 2/7/1887   Ethel Minus Smith 12/29/1907
L. B. Smith 12/27/1888   Mildred Sandifer Smith
                                         4/20/1910
Deaths
Mary Jane Smith 1/21/1904
Stephen Jackson Smith 5/22/1921
Stephen Jackson Smith of Butts Co., Ga. m. Mary J. Hale of Butts
Co. 1/2/1879, at res. of Joseph Hale, Rev. J. T. Kimble

GEORGE REED BIBLE
Owner: Judge L. B. Moon

George Reed m. Kathrine Chambers 6/1767

Births
Margaret Reed 4/15/1768   Henry Reed 2/3/1773
Jennet Reed 12/15/1769   George Reed 11/27/1774
Alexander Reed 8/19/1773   Hannah Reed 12/17/1776

4/15/1778 one dau. dead
Robert Reed 4/20/1779-4/24/1813   Elizabeth Reed 9/13/1786
Kathrina Reed 8/19/1781   Fanney Reed 9/18/1787
Samuel Reed 11/12/1783   George Reed Sr. 5/1746

E. T. MULLIS, SR. BIBLE Of Bleckley Co.

E. T. Mullis Sr. 11/10/1874-4/7/1936
Noral T. Mullis 3/1/1878-7/10/1951
Effie G. Mullis 3/5/1898-1/5/1899
Fisher Mullis 10/13/1900-10/18/1950

MADDOX BIBLE
Owner: Miss Mattie Maddox
Jackson, Ga.

Nancy Jane McCallum b. 7/13/1853
Charley Luther Maddox b. 8/14/1875
Lewis Nathaniel Maddox b. 7/14/1877
Walter Ellis Maddox 7/24/1880-9/18/1880
Benjamin Franklin Maddox b. 10/27/1878
Mattie Jane Maddox 8/29/1881
Jefferson Few Maddox b. 5/5/1884
Robert Wright Maddox b. 7/20/1886
J. B. Maddox b. 2/10/1890
Dulane Cleveland Maddox b. 10/29/1892
Mary Lucile Maddox b. 4/16/1896

Newton Nathaniel Maddox d. 10/27/1876, age 73 yrs.

EMMA VIRGINIA WEAVER MORGAN BIBLE
Owner: Mrs. Wallace Harris, Cochran, Ga.

Marriages
Dr. Y. H. (Young Hiram) Morgan of Cochran to Miss E. V. Weaver
of Cochran, 1/18/1871, by Rev. D. N. Fann. Wit: W. H. Morgan,
B. F. Ryle

Births
Emma V. Weaver 8/6/1850   Henrietta Morgan 4/27/1878
Dr. Y. H. Morgan 4/28/1847   India Morgan 8/13/1880
Allie Deborah Morgan 12/29/1871   Ruby Morgan 4/26/1883
Anna Belle Morgan 1/26/1873   Watts Morgan 4/24/1889
Leola Young Morgan 1/28/1874   Y. H. Morgan 11/13/1892
Ella Morgan 2/27/1876

Deaths
Little Anna Belle 9/28/1873   India 9/19/1880
Little Allie 10/25/1873   Emma Virginia 11/28/1892
Little Ella 6/14*1878

BENJAMIN AIKEN COOK BIBLE
Owner: Mrs. Albert Jones, Cochran, Ga.

Benjamin Aiken Cook 4/30/1855-2/22/1943 m. Margaret A. Weaver
12/16/1880. She was b. 2/22/1855 d. 11/17/1924 Children:

James Marcelus Cook b. 3/1/1883 m. Lizzie Bell Sawyer
Mamie Estelle Cook b. 1/1/1855 m. Albert A. Jones
Willie Cook b. 6/12/1886
Maggie Lena Cook b. 10/29/1882 m. William C. Jones
Benjamin Franklin Cook b. 6/6/1891 m. Gertrude Floyd
Clyde Romanier Cook b. 3/11/1894 m. Allen Dempsey Cain

THOMAS JEFFERSON COOK BIBLE
Owner B. F. Cook, Cochran, Ga.

Thomas Jefferson Cook 12/30/1826-11/1904
Rebecca Elizabeth Howe 7/8/1830-11/3/1922
Meridah Albinus Cook 10/3/1851-3/21/1914
Arelius Cicero Cook 7/23/1853-
Benjamin Akin Cook 4/30/1855-2/21/1943
Martha Ann Swan Cook 8/10/1858
Thomas Marion Cook 10/5/1861-6/1939

T. J. Cook m. Elizabeth Rebecca Howe 12/25/1850

256

RICHARD FREDERICK CROOMS BIBLE
Owner: Mrs. John Newton Crooms, Cochran, Ga.

Richard Frederick Crooms b. 3/19/1833 m. 12/8/1854
Fann D., his wife, b. 5/30/1838

Richard F. Brown Crooms   John E. Crooms b. 2/3/1863
  b. 12/28/1869
Elen Crooms b. 3/7/1855   Marion Chaphaman Crooms b.
Thomas B. Crooms b. 3/22/1857   9/27/1865
Margaret V. Crooms b. 7/13/1859 Robert H. Crooms b. 9/27/1865

STEPHEN WILLIS THORNTON, SR. BIBLE

Stephen Willis Thornton, Sr. b. LaGrange 1874, m. 9/17/1906 by
  Rev. J. J. Lanier, St. Stephens Episcopal Church, Milledgeville,
  Ga.
Ann Florence Turk, his wife, b. 2/8/1882   Their Children:

Stephen Willis Thornton, Jr., 1st son, b. LaGrange 4/6/1914
John Pope Thornton b. 9/8/1917 LaGrange

JACOB P. WELCH BIBLE

Jacob P. Welch m. Martha Susan Whitaker, dau. of W. W. Whitaker
7/14/1840 by Rev. Walter Branham

Births
Mary Cantey Welch 11/12/1842   Jacob Warren Welch 8/21/1855
Warren Perry Welch 4/16/1845   Martha Whitaker Welch 10/22/1857
William Thomas Welch 4/16/1847   Samuel Riley Welch 11/5/1859
George Washington Welch   Eugene Almeda Welch 4/23/1862
  10/30/1849   James Madison Welch 1/22/1866
Sarah Crowell Welch 9/3/1853

J. T. BERRYHILL BIBLE
Owner: Mrs. Kanawah Smith
Cochran, Ga.

Births
Lilla Bell Berryhill 10/2/1889   Valeria Berryhill 5/4/1904
Nettie Kanawah Berryhill 4/13/1891 Mildred Louise Berryhill
Bulah Lee Berryhill 12/15/1892   12/12/1906
James Samuel Berryhill 3/7/1894 Infant son 1/30/1910
Lucien Osmon Berryhill 2/28/1896

(J. T. Berryhill Bible contd.....)

Ruthie Viola Berryhill 3/5/1898
Linden Rhinalder Berryhill 2/5/1900

Deaths
Bulah Lee Berryhill 1/19/1893
Valeria Berryhill 3/7/1905
Infant son 1/31/1910

HERSCHEL V. SANFORD BIBLE Of Baldwin Co.
Owner: Mrs. Lamar Ham, Milledgeville, Ga.

Herschel V. Sanford m. Mary M. Martin 9/17/1876 Gwinnett Co.

Herschel V. Sanford b. 10/8/1847
Mary M. Martin, his wife, b. 4/9/1852
Virgil Sanford b. 11/7/1878
Mollie Sanford b. 9/6/1881
Etta Sanford b. 5/3/1884
Annie Bell b. 5/29/1887

Marriages
Annie Bell to Lamar Ham 9/5/1906
Mollie Sanford to Franklin Rush 1930
Etta Sanford to S. E. Centerfit 1913

Deaths
Herschel V. Sanford 1/7/1928
Mary Martin Sanford 6/15/1930

JOHN C. THOMAS BIBLE
Owner: Martha G. Thomas

Mary Bryan Neyle, gr-granddau. of the Patriot, Jonathan Bryan,
and John S. Thomas m. 6/24/1830 Christ Church, Savannah, by Rev.
Mr. Nevich. Children:

Mary Neyle Thomas b. 5/10/1831 at Clifton, near Milledgeville
John Greenberry Thomas b. 3/28/1833 Milledgeville
Eliza Neyle Thomas b. 8/7/1834 at Clifton
Bryan Morel Thomas b. 5/8/1836 at Clifton
Mrs. John S. Thomas d. at this time

G. P. SAUNDERS BIBLE
Owner: G. P. Saunders, Jackson, Ga.

G. P. Saunders m. Willie McKinley 2/22/1899

(G. P. Saunders Bible contd....)

Births
G. P. Saunders 5/15/1867   Hue Morris Saunders 3/14/1901
Willie Saunders 7/9/1873   Katie Sue Saunders 5/27/1905
Mary Lee Saunders 1/8/1901   George Ray Saunders 3/24/1908
Annie Mae Saunders 10/15/1902

Deaths
Hue Morris Saunders 1/9/1904
Katie Sue Saunders 10/3/1905
Willie Mae Saunders 6/15/1904

                ROBERT C. GARDNER BIBLE
                Owner: Mrs. Nelle G. Johnson
                       Flovilla, Ga.

Robert C. Gardner 11/11/1850-4/25/1914
Kate B. Gardner b. 6/21/1854
Eva Atwood Gardner b. 12/19/1874
Maggie Vinella Gardner b. 8/21/1877
Robert Clarence Gardner b. 10/8/1880
Kate Pearl Gardner b. 9/19/1883
Leo Edwin Gardner b. 9/6/1886
Nellie Ira Gardner b. 10/21/1889

Frances Kathleen Maddux b. 10/11/1903
Marguerite Aline Maddux b. 10/11/1906
Hugo Leclare Maddux b. 2/11/1911
John Atticus Maddux 2/20/1917=4/20/1918

Robert Clement Gardner d. 4/7/1930
Maggie Gardner Maddux d. 7/3/1926

         H. B. WHITAKER BIBLE Of Flovilla, Ga.

Robert Judson Whitaker b. 8/6/1813 d. 1887
Fannie Teal 1820-1877

                JOSEPH ANSLEY BIBLE
                Owner: Miss Ethel Jackson
                       Forsyth, Ga.

Marriages
Joseph Ansley to Mary Simpson 12/6/1798
Joseph Ansley to Amasa Adkins 7/17/1823

                        259

(Joseph Ansley Bible, Marriages, contd....)

Joshua Lazenby to Maria Ansley 4/29/1815
Marlin Ansley to Zeruah Johnson 9/8/1825
George W. Ray to Mary Ansley 11/1823
Rebecca Ansley to Adam Grenade 8/19/1839
Franklin Green to Mary Winifred Ansley 6/8/1846
A. G. Andrews to M. W. Green 12/22/1852
Thomas W. Barrow to Eliza A. Ansley 2/5/1856
Daniel Scribner to Sarah J. Ansley 2/5/1856
William A. Ansley to Sarah A. Cheves 5/11/1857
G. A. Ansley to M. E. Harris 1/18/1866
John E. Pye to Julia E. Ansley 11/12/1867
Robert Lemuel Fort to Zeruah Ethleen Ansley 9/6/1900

Births
Joseph A. Ansley 3/5/1775
Mary Simpson 1/19/1778
Amasa Adkins 3/3/1796

Mariah Ansley 10/22/1799	Martha Ann Ansley 7/17/1826
Marlin Ansley 3/15/1802	Elizabeth Ansley 7/6/1828
Mary Ansley 7/30/1804	Elvira Ansley 4/26/1830
Sarah Ansley 10/22/1806	Penelope Ansley 3/1/1832
Rebecca Ansley 6/28/1809	Joseph Adkins Ansley 5/9/1834
Harriet Ansley 9/12/1812	Amasa Matilda Ansley 9/15/1836

Jane Eliza Ansley 3/19/1817
Lucinda Ansley 11/1/1818
   Children of Marlin Ansley and Zeruah Johnson, b. 12/31/1801:
Mary Winifred Ansley b. 6/29/1826
Elizabeth Ann Rebecca Ansley b. 1/22/1828
Joseph Russell Ansley b. 2/16/1830
William Augustus Ansley b. 3/7/1832
Fred Adolphus Ansley b. 4/7/1834
Sarah Jane Ansley b. 2/16/1836
John Green Ansley b. 2/16/1838
Julia Emma Ansley b. 2/7/1842

Children of William Ansley and Sallie Cheves:

William Augustus Ansley 3/7/1832-3/31/1915
Sallie Anne Ansley 10/28/1835-5/19/1914
Warren Landrum (Lummie) Ansley 4/6/1858-2/18/1860
Zeruah Ethleen (Ettie) Ansley b. 11/16/1859
Arlette Ansley b. 3/30/1862
William Augustus, Jr. 6/6/1864-8/20/1868
Roma Ansley 6/29/1866-10/9/1866

Deaths
Mary (Simpson) Ansley 8/13/1820	Bobbie Ansley Barrow 7/12/1872
Amasa (Adkins) Ansley 9/2/1838	John E. Ansley 3/8/1875
Joseph Ansley 9/21/1838	Eula W. Barrow 10/15/1875
Harriet Ansley 9/1820	D. D. Scribner 4/23/1863
Marlin Ansley 8/4/1850	Mary Winifred Green Andrews
Franklin Green Ansley 12/5/1849	7/31/1882
A. G. Andrews 7/12/1862	Sarah Jane Scribner 8/9/1883
Jos. Russell Ansley 5/17/1856	Thos. Warren Barrow 4/25/1899
F. A. Ansley 1/16/1862	Eliza Ann Ansley Barrow
Julia E. Ansley Pye 7/3/1872	5/2/1899
Wimberly Pye 7/18/1869	Sarah Anne, wife of W. A.
Eula Pye 7/16/1872	Ansley, 5/18/1914
John E. Pye 10/18/1872	William A. Ansley 5/31/1915

Marriages

John L. Brooking and Matilda Low 12/15/1819
John L. King and Rebecca Brooking 2/1/1844
Jasper Henry and Lucy S. Brooking 4/7/1846
Isaac H. Brooking and Cenith A. Petiscord 7/28/1846
James C. Brooking and Sarah Ann Pedacord 10/18/1848

Births

John L. Brooking 2/13/1796
Matilda Brooking 2/3/1805
Sarah Ann King, dau. of John and Rebecca King, 4/26/1845
Henry Thomas King, son of above, 4/15/1847
John Thomas Henry, son of Jasper and Lucy Henry, 1/30/1847
Isaac Henry Brooking, son of John and Matilda Brooking, 11/4/1821
Elizabeth Rebeckah Brooking, dau. of above, 10/11/1823
Lucy Sarah Brooking, dau. of above, 12/22/1825
Martha Ann Henry, dau. of Jasper and Lucy Henry, 1/18/1849
Louisa Brooking, dau. of James and Sarah Ann Brooking, 9/2/1849
Mariah Mennyfee King, dau. of John and Rebecca King, 10/8/1849
Louisiana T. Brooking, dau. of Cenith and Henry Brooking,
    4/16/1850
George W. Henry, son of Lucy and Jasper Henry, 1/16/1851
Robert E. Brooking, son of James and Sarah Ann Brooking,
    9/11/1851
George W. King, son of John and Rebecca King, 11/14/1851
Elizabeth Henry, dau. of Sarah and James Brooking, 11/15/1853
Matilda Jane Henry, sau. of Lucy and Jasper Henry, 11/24/1856
Louisa Frances Henry, dau. of Lucy and Jasper Henry, 11/24/1856
Susan Jane Brooking, dau. of James and Sarah A. Brooking,
    10/23/1854
James Curtis Brooking, son of John and Matilda Brooking,
    4/15/1828
Thomas Sparks Brooking, son of above, 9/10/1831
James Harrison Brooking, son of Henry and Cenith Ann Brooking,
    5/11/1847
Elizabeth Ellin Brooking, dau., of Henry and Cenith Ann Brooking,
    9/17/1848

Deaths

Isaac Henry Brooking 9/10/1816
Thomas Sparks Brooking 9/26/1839
John L. Brooking 8/14/1876
Matilda Jane Brooking 3/8/1882
James Curtis Brooking 1/26/1820
Susan Jane Brooking Lane 9/1915
Nancy H. Brooking, wife of James Curtis Brooking, 2/14/1924

Elizabeth R. Brooking baptised 9/21/1826 by Benjamin Gordin

JOHN EDMONSON BIBLE
Owner: Ida Brown Perry
Americus, Ga.

John Edmonson and Rebecca Braswell m. 4/15/1829
Nancy Ann Rebecca Edmonson b. 10/23/1859
Seala An Edmonson b. 10/23/1862
John Edmonson and Nancy Macker m. 9/15/1824
Mary Thomis Edmonson b. 1/31/1864
Junius C. Brown b. 11/24/1859
Robert Collins b. 9/15/1809
Jane Edmonson b. 8/23/1792
John Edmonson b. 4/26/1794
Joseph Edmonson b. 12/25/1795
Thomas Edmonson b. 3/8/1798
Rebecca Edmonson b. 5/22/1798
Rebecca Collins b. 12/4/1815
Lemandy Collins b. 10/13/1839
Green Collins b. 10/3/1841
Sarah Elizabeth An Collins b. 7/25/1844

Joseph Edmonson d. 2/17/1827
Thomas Edmonson d. 10/4/1833
Rebecca Edmonson d. 7/24/1843
Rebecca Collins d. 9/26/1863
Robert Collins d. 6/8/1870
Lemandy Collins d. 9/2/1872
---Braswell d. 12/1/1834
Rebecca Braswell d. 11/8/1826
James Braswell d. 6/29/1853
Rebecca Edmonson d. 12/27/1857
Hiram Allen d. 2/24/1876
Mary Ann Edmonson d. 3/31/1908

JOHN BARNES BIBLE
Owner: Ida Brown Perry
Americus, Ga.

John Barnes b. 11/4/1816
Nancy Barnes b. 10/20/1830
John T. Parks b. 8/12/1832
Zachariah J. parks b. 8/17/1834
Sarah Ann Parks b. 8/22/1836
Johnathon M. Parks b. 11/2/1838
---H. Parks b. 5/10/1841
David Cicero Parks b. 7/21/1843
Hiram Alen Parks b. 8/18/1845

John Barnes d. 1852
John Parks d. 6/4/1872
John and Nancy Barnes m. 11/5/1846
John W. Barnes b. 2/28/1848, son of John and Nancy Barnes
Henry Thomas Barnes b. 5/27/1851

(John Barnes Bible contd....)

Zachariah Parks b. 8/17/1854
Joseph Marion Barnes b. 7/11/1849
Hannah M. M. Wishiam b. 9/9/1855
Zachariah J. Wishiam b. 2/21/1858
John Park b. 2/25/1805
Elizabeth Allen b. 3/9/1813
Job Allen d. 12/28/1861
John T. Parks d. 1857
H. M. M. Parks d. 10/28/1857
J. M. Parks d. 3/25/1862

BENJAMIN ADAMS, SR. BIBLE
Owner: Forrest Prather, Dearing, Ga.

Benjamin Adams Sr. b. 12/19/1814
Wife, Elizabeth Evans, dau. of Jesse Evans and Elizabeth Smith
of Warren Co., Ga., b. 1/16/1821. Their Children:

Jesse Adams b. 1/10/1838   Sarah E. Adams b. 8/13/1841
Celia C. Adams b. 9/11/1851
Benjamin Adams, Jr. b. 9/9/1849 m. Susan Bynum b. 10/28/1846,
   dau. of John Bynum

Children of Benjamin Adams, Jr. and Susan Bynum:

Oscar T. b. 10/11/1867   Harvey T. b. 2/16/1878
Ada A. b. 4/27/1869 d. 1/10/1945   Emmie b. 8/30/1880
John B. b. 11/29/1870   Jessie L. b. 1/28/1883
Mary A. E. b. 9/25/1872   Alex P. b. 12/19/1885
Edgar F. b. 9/21/1874   Lillie E. b. 2/14/1887
George D. b. 8/18/1876   Esther Rubie b. 10/25/1889

Marriages
Benjamin Adams Jr. to Susan W. Bynum 1/6/1867
Ada M. Adams to John Quincy Prather (12/1/1850-7/31/1920) on
   7/25/1886 (Parents of Forrest Prather)
Annie E. Adams to W. A. Stapleton 5/22/1892
Edgar F. Adams to Mary Alice Guy 4/25/1894 (son, Lucius Whitley,
   b. 1904)
George M. Adams to Addie Culpepper 11/29/1900
Oscar T. Adams to Minnie L. Story 1/16/1901
Ruby E. Adams to Alex B. Huff 1/11/1905

Deaths
Benjamin Adams, Jr. 4/3/1910, wife, Susan, d. 10/1912
John B. Adams 11/25/1872
Harvey T. Adams 9/19/1880
Alec B. Huff, son of Ruby and Alec Huff b. 10/5/1907 d.
   12/10/1909

JOSEPH WOLF BIBLE
Owner: Miss Ruby Mathews
Gadsden, Ala.

Marriages
Joseph Wolf and Hannah Doster 12/8/1825
J. C. Wolf and M. L. Hunt 12/26/1867

Births
Richard H. Hunt 9/7/1813   Robert Turman Hunt 7/19/1842
Rhoda Ann Hunt 1/22/1818   Eugeneous Beamon Hunt 6/3/1846
Martha Ann Malissa Hunt 3/27/1840   Mary Laurah Hunt 6/17/1850
                                           Rhoda Luvenia Hunt 3/10/1853

Rachel C. Wolf 9/15/1826   Mary Jane Wolf 1/20/1836
Elizer Catherine Wolf 5/22/1828   Phillip Tally Wolf 11/20/1838
Jacob Hill Wolf 2/16/1830   Joseph H. Wolf 2/8/1840
Permelia Emeline Wolf 12/26/1831   Hannah Elizabeth Wolf 4/17/1843
William Goren Wolf 10/20/1833   John C. Wolf 3/18/1845

M. L. Wolf 6/17/1850   Gervitus Alvie Wolf 7/21/1878
Theodosia E. Wolf 8/3/1869   Nonie Ora Wolf 2/15/1882
Adolphus C. Wolf 9/13/1874

Deaths
William G. Wolf 12/19/1861 Evins Port, Va.
Jacob Hill Wolf 1831
Rachel C. Summerlin 12/6/1860
William D. Gordon was killed at Battle of Chickamauga 9/20/1863
Joseph Wolf 7/24/1877
Hannah E. Wolf 11/29/1881

MARY MARTIN GREEN BIBLE

Mary Martin Green b. 8/31/1813 m. 1/20/1831, d. 10/11/1873
James Jefferson Green b. 10/25/1831
Charles Green b. 2/21/1833
Lucy Ann Elizabeth Green b. 6/20/1834
George Washington Green b. 10/30/1836
Nancy Adaline Green b. 6/4/1839
Mary Matilda Green b. 1/20/1842
John E. B. Green b. 5/11/1844
Armenda Jane Green b. 6/15/1846
Josiah Franklin Green b. 9/16/1849
Charlotte Rebecca Green b. 11/21/1854

ISAAC MEADOWS BIBLE Of Madison Co.
Owner: Ana Adams, Ohio

Isaac Meadows b. 2/1/1779 m. Nancy Bridges 12/12/1805. Children:

Births
John Bennet Davis Meadows 10/1/1808
Berry Jones Madows 10/27/1809
Martha Gordon Meadows 9/23/1811
James Williamson Meadows 9/13/1813
Isaac Terrell Meadows 4/15/1815
Esther Davis Meadows 4/2/1817
Julia Melitia Meadows 10/12/1819
David Bridges Meadows 5/24/1823

Second Marriage of Isaac Meadows to Mary Perry 3/20/1845

ISAAC HENRY BENTLEY BIBLE

Isaac Henry Bentley 5/26/1840 - 7/15/1908
Frances Caroline Bentley 4/16/1841-10/8/1923
William Isaac Henry Bentley 8/15/1863-12/30/1936
Frances Louise Jane Bentley b. 5/19/1865
Charlie Richard Elias Bentley 3/15/1867-9/16/1923
James Robert Udolphus Bentley 9/8/1868-12/3/1951
Wilaby John Calvin Bentley b. 11/4/1869
Martha Emily Amanda Bentley 12/9/1870
Mentie Bessie May Bentley b. 11/25/1872
Asa Melvin Lavonia Bentley b. 2/1/1874
Homer Luther Cornelius Bentley b. 4/23/1875
Alice Estelle Mansalynn Bentley 5/13/1877-3/20/1952
Verney Elmer Choice Bentley 3/18/1884

ALFRED B. DAVIES BIBLE
Owner: Mrs. J. M. Murphy
402 W. French St., Temple, Tx.
(dau. of Richard Cole)

"A present from Mrs. Rachel Blalock, Alice Coles Bible, 1/10/1893"

Alfred B. Davies and Alice, his wife, m. 12/3/1823
James R. Davies 1/10/1826-2/12/1905
Elizabeth C. Davies b. 11/6/1827
John W. Davies 1/15/1830-7/27/1884
Susan E. Davis b. 6/20/1833

(Alfred B. Davies Bible contd.....)

Bartilda J. Davies b. 11/22/1835
Margaret M. Davies b. 4/16/1841

William T. Cole and his wife, Alice m. 4/1847

William Isaac Cole b. 1/5/1848
Richard Moses Cole b. 10/10/1849
Alice Cole d. 7/27/1894

WILLIAM BROOKS BIBLE Of Walton Co.
Owner: Mrs. Emmett Langley, Walton Co., Ga.

William Brooks b. 12/1/1782
His companion, Jain (Jane) Brooks b. 12/2/1782. Children:

Births
Hamilton Brooks 10/18/1802   Jeckmeah W. Brooks 1/1/1818
Sinderella Brooks 12/27/1803   Amdmiles Brooks 8/3/1820
Larkin Brooks 1/12/1805   James W. Brooks 11/29/1822
John Brooks 1/12/1807   Othenial H.(Husky) Brooks 4/18/1825
Bradford Brooks 4/1810   Phinnath Brooks 10/1812
William Brooks 1/6/1814

William Brooks and Jane Weaver m. 1/31/1802

CORNELIUS P. HUNTER BIBLE
Owner: Cornelius Peeples Hunter
Lafayette, Ala.

Cornelius P. Hunter b. 4/24/1827 d. 1/18/1902, age 74 yrs., 8
mos., 24 days

Deaths
Malissa Sousan Hunter b. 2/14/1835 d. 4/15/1900, age 65 yrs., one
mo., one day

Births
William Lucious Hunter 8/30/1870   John Richard Hunter 8/21/1877
Dora Elvira Hunter 10/10/1872

Grandparents:
Elisha Hunter b. 8/2/1766 d. 10/20/1826
Rebecca Hunter b. 5/15/1780

Cornelius Peeples Hunter b. 4/24/1827
Eleaser Elisha Hunger b. 10/19/1828 d. 10/25/1828
Columbus Vespacius Hunter b. 8/4/1830
Mary Ann Sophrone Hunter b. 2/22/1836
William Gustavous Hunter b. 5/11/1838

UEL HARPER BIBLE
Owner: Miss Alverto McKelvy
Cartersville, Ga.

Births
Uel Harper 8/17/1801   William N. McKelvy 11/8/1818
Anna Harper 12/4/1808   Mildred A. Harper 1/17/1831
Edward Johnson 5/18/1829   George P. McKelvy 12/30/1846
Milley Angeline Harper 1/17/1831   Frances A. McKelvy 12/17/1848
Frances Hannah Harper 2/21/1833
John Thomas Harper 9/9/1839
Rodrick Harper 6/29/1845

William N. McKelvy and Mildred Angeline Harper m. 2/11/1849
Uel Harper and Anna Fargason m. 4/10/1828
Anna Harper d. 9/1/1874
Edward Johnson d. 11/9/1836
Mildred Angeline Harper d. 6/11/1919
William N. McKelvy d. 8/24/1889
John Thomas Harper d. 12/11/1854
Nancy E. McKelvy d. 1/8/1851
Kezeah Alice McKelvy d. 2/6/1853
Elizabeth W. McKelvy d. 2/14/1855
Uel H. McKelvy d. 12/21/1857
John N. McKelvy d. 12/16/1859
Thomas R. McKelvy d. 1/6/1862
Katie McKelvy d. 4/3/1864
Mildred Mary McKelvy d. 5/26/1866
Alverda Lane d. 1/10/1869
Mattie McKelvy d. 4/10/1871
Charles S. McKelvy d. 7/6/1875
Uel Harper McKelvy d. 11/17/1881
Kezeah Alice McKelvy d. 8/8/1924   Jessie Mary Harper b. 7/6/1878
Rodrick Harper b. 6/29/1845   Rodrick Harper b. 6/29/1886
Mary Ann Neal b. 7/25/1846   Frank Kennedy Harper b.9/5/1888
Anna Avelene Harper b. 5/17/1870   Clarice Harper b. 9/18/1890
Pleasant Marvin Harper b. 6/6/1875

THOMAS J. FARISS BIBLE
Owner: Mrs. George Washington Fariss
Camp Hill, Ala.

Thomas J. Fariss b. 6/24/1828 d. 2/7/1905 m. Troup Co., Ga.,
   Sarah Anne Murry, b. 11/17/1834, d. 11/6/1904

James Thomas Fariss b. 6/27/1854
George Washington Fariss b. 8/15/1859
Henry J. Callaway (Callie) Fariss b. 2/8/1865
Mary Frances Fariss b. 11/7/1851 d. 9/4/1869, age 18 yrs.

George W. Fariss m. 10/20/1881 Tommie Ola Fargason b. 8/21/1860

267

(Thomas J. Fariss Bible contd....)

James T. m. 1st Mary Elizabeth Henderson b. 8/18/1852 d. 9/1885,
   2nd, Belle Wyatt
Henry J. Callaway (Callie) Farris m. Dixon Henderson b. 8/25/1867
   d. 8/30/1935 (m. 12/3/1881 by F. Henderson, J. P., bond E. N.
   Henderson)

Father - John Johns Fariss b. 11/1801 d. 4/29/1898, age 96 yrs.,
   7 mos.
Mother - Julia Fitzpatrick
Brothers and Sisters - Nancy Cornelia Farris m. John Butler;
Martha Ann Fariss m. William Mitchell Butler; Mary (Mollie) Julia
Farris m. Green Moss; Billie (d. young).

                    JAMES DISMUKES BIBLE
           Owner: Mrs. Florence Williams Scott
                 Oakland Farm, Eatonton, Ga.

James Dismukes b. 2/28/1784
Gillian Cooper Dismukes, wife of James Dismukes, b. 6/25/1785,
   m. 8/29/1808.

Their Children:

Frances Perry Dismukes b. 6/14/1809
Permelia T. Dismukes b. 12/23/1810
Benjamin Davis Dismukes b. 8/29/1812

Garland Terry Dismukes b. 8/20/1813
William henry Dismukes b. 10/6/1815
Samantha Edna Dismukes b. 8/2/1817
Sarah Williams Dismukes b. 1/7/1819
James Cooper Dismukes b. 1/7/1821

James Cooper Dismukes and Benjamin Davis Dismukes d. in young
manhood.

AUGUSTUS C. SMITH BIBLE
Owner: E. L. Smith, Jackson, Ga.

Augustus C. Smith of Monroe Co. m. Sarah Jane Phinazee of Monroe
Co. 12/16/1852 at res. of H. Phinazee by Rev. Absolom Ogletree.

Births
Augustus C. Smith 3/5/1830
Jane Phinazee Smith 9/15/1835
Fannie A. Smith 10/30/1853
Asa H. Smith 11/18/1855
J. Harris Smith 10/13/1857
Lizzie Smith 12/23/1859
Kittie Smith 4/21/1862
James M. Smith 8/24/1885

Wissie F. Smith 6/16/1868
Edward Lee Smith 8/19/1870
Ernest Smith 1/7/1873
Rufus Smith 7/19/1875
Thomas Olin Smith 2/8/1879
Harold McGriggin 7/20/1874
Elmer Griffin 2/22/1886
Milton Smith 7/12/1904

Marriages
Fannie A. Smith to W. B. Griffin 12/19/1872
Kittie Smith to W. B. Griffin 6/1/1880
Asa H. Smith to Zollie Morrison 4/15/1880
J. Harris Smith to Addie Askin 12/2/1880
Lizzie Smith to E. P. Hunt 8/28/1887
Milton Smith -

Deaths
Augustus C. Smith 4/20/1907
Jane P. Smith 12/31/1919
Fannie A. Griffin 3/7/1879
John Harris Smith 4/6/1890
Asa Hiram Smith 5/14/1917

Rufus Smith 2/1909
James M. Smith 1/17/1917
Kittie Smith Griffin 2/6/1931
Ernest M. Smith 4/12/1931
Thomas Olin Smith 4/24/1935

Asa Smith 1801-10/1/1850
Sarah Elizabeth, wife of Asa Smith, d. 11/12/1858
Milton J. Smith --
Mary Smith 10/8/1838-9/1/1880
Green T. Smith 8/12/1840-12/13/1861
James P. Smith 2/1842-7/1/1862
Sarah E. Smith, wife of John Gray, b. 2/1845
J. G. Phinazee 1/5/1828-5/6/1895
Hiram Phinasee 11/3/1802-1/11/1883
Elizabeth B., wife of Hiram Phinasee, 11/3/1803-4/14/1884
John H. Phinazee 3/20/1842-6/8/1863
Mary E. Todd 1/19/1832-2/1864
A. J. Phinazee b. 5/10/1830
Arra Collier 11/30/1837-2/4/1889
C. O. Darden 7/11/1826-12/26/1893
John H. Darden 10/27/1847-12/16/1894
Little Julia, dau. of Asa and Zollie Smith, d. 9/27/1894, 3 1/2
   yrs. old
Matt F. Phinazee d. 9/28/1894
Little Vera, dau. of W. B. and Kittie Griffin 6/4/1884-9/1/1885,
   age 15 mos.
Little John Harris, son of E. P. and Lizzie Hunt, 9/16/1895-
   1/21/1896, 4 mos.
Little Clayton Buttrill, son of Lee and mamie Smith 1/16/1897-
   6/16/1897, 5 mos.
Infant son of W. B. and Kittie Griffin d. 10/1881
Mrs. Joe Sutton 3/14/1840-9/30/1900
Little Asa Smith Griffin 7/6/1900-9/21/1901

ISAAC W. SMITH BIBLE
Owner: Mrs. Mitchell Bond
Jackson, Ga.

Births

Isaac W. Smith 1/9/1787
Edy Smith 10/23/1783
Richard Smith, son of Richard and
    Adaline Smith, 9/20/1837, 10 days
    after death of his father
Senisy Smith 11/22/1807
George W. Smith 2/27/1809
James R. Smith 11/22/1810
Richard Smith 8/28/1812
Jeptha Smith 6/14/1815
William J. Smith 4/9/1817
Francis Asbury Smith 8/7/1821
Martha A. Smith 7/11/1825

Mary C. Smith 5/16/1828
Elizbeth child 10/9/1849
Marthy
Reny's child Sam 12/30/1849
Ezebelleh, her child,
    7/7/1851, Mary
Charles 1/1853
Scroferd 1/1853
Tempy 1/15/1856
William M. Penn 5/6/1803

Marriages

James R. Smith to Mary A. Hunt 11/10/1839
Archibald Bigby to Martha A. Smith 12/11/1839
James M. Shields to Mary C. Smith 12/31/1841
Francis A. Smith to Mary A. Brady 9/16/1842
George W. Smith to Frances M. Roan 11/24/1829
William M. Penn to Louisa Smith 1/27/1824
Jeptha Smith to Seney? M. Pennington 1/6/1835
Richard Smith to Adlie E. Watkins 4/16/1835
William J. Smith to Harriet H. Smith 2/28/1839
Lemuel N. O'Neal to Martha Ann (Shields) O'Neal 1/20/1861
William J. Bledsoe to Mary F. Shields 11/23/1865
William J. Shields to Martha J. McMichael 12/15/1867
George W. McMichael to Laura O. Shields 12/23/1869
Isaac W. Smith to Edy Smith 8/1806
    Note: After death of Edy Smith, Isaac m. Lucy Bond, wid. of
        J. M. D. Bond I.

DAVID FRANCIS BOURQUIN BIBLE

David Francis Bourquin m. Elizabeth Fox 7/3/1783   Children:

Anna Sophia Bourquin b. 6/30/1784
Edward Bourquin b. 8/24/1786
Elizabeth Bourquin, wife of David F. Bourquin, d. 3/11/1788
David F. Bourquin, son of David F. and Ann Bourquin, d. 4/9/1794
Margaret L., dau. of Ann Bourquin, d. 10/6/1796
Benjamin Fox, Jr., son of Benjamin Fox the elder, d. 3/13/1787
David F. Bourquin and Margaret Thornton m. 7/20/1794, Savannah,
    Ga. Their Children:
Benedict Bourquin b. 6/11/1795
Eliza Ann Bourquin, b. 4/23/1797
Charlotte M. Bourquin b. 3/23/1801
Robert H. Bourquin b. 3/12/1806
Ann Sophia Bourquin and Stephen G. Williams m. 3/24/1801
Ann Sophia Bourquin, consort of Stephen Williams, d. 6/19/1811

JOSEPH G. MILES BIBLE

Joseph G. Miles m. Sallie I. Johnson 6/13/1875
Sallie I. Miles b. 11/18/1854
Joseph G. Miles b. 9/30/1850
Mary R. T. Johnson b. 2/7/1860

Children:
Ada E. Miles b. 3/19/1876   Verna E. Miles b. 1/19/1882
Loomis C. Miles b. 4/12/1878   Homer I. Miles b. 12/14/1885
Jabez E. Miles b. 5/12/--

Deaths
Joseph G. Miles 2/3/1911
Sallie Inez Johnson Miles 6/15/1893

ANDREW J. MUNDY BIBLE Of Fayette Co., Ga.
Owner: John Ellis Mundy

Andrew J. Mundy of Fayette Co., Ga. m. Nancy Wallis of Fayette
Co., Ga., 9/10/1840 at res. of D. R. Wallis by Elijah P. Allen,
Judge, Inferior Court.

Birth
Reuben Mundy 4/11/1777   Patsy Mundy 1/21/1820
Mrs. Mary Andrews Mundy 5/9/1790   Reubin T. Mundy 8/9/1821
Julia Ann Mundy 1/24/1805   George W. Mundy 7/10/1823
Mandy Malvina Mundy 3/9/1800   Mary Ann Mundy 7/6/1826
Hilory C. Mundy 1/26/1811   Leroy Mundy 8/11/1828
Andrew J. Mundy 12/8/1814   Emily Mundy 12/21/1830
Elizabeth Mundy 10/4/1816
Kisiah Mundy 4/20/1818

Andrew Jackson Mundy 12/8/1814
Nancy Wallis Mundy 5/15/1820

Reubin W. Mundy 6/7/1841   Margarett E. Mundy 10/11/1851
Mary M. Mundy 6/29/1842   Patsey L. Mundy 6/11/1853
Robert S. Mundy 11/29/1843   John Marshall Mundy 3/12/1855
William M. Mundy 11/2/1845   Julia F. Mundy 1/23/1857
Andrew J. Mundy 3/8/1849   Erasmus T. Mundy 10/16/1861

Mrs. Mariah E. Whatey Mundy 6/3/1862
James Munday 2/11/1882
Andrew J. Munday 7/1/1885
E. T. Munday 7/12/1903

Deaths
Reubin Mundy 2/28/1856   Mrs. Nancy Mundy 11/11/1886
Mrs. Mary Mundy 1/21/1876   A. J. Mundy 5/--
Julia F. Mundy 3/6/1870   E. T. Mundy Jr. 2/7/1927

J. P. S. NASH BIBLE

Births
J. P. S. Nash 5/11/1841
Mary J. Nash 8/30/1850
Sarah Lula Victoria 12/27/1869

Oscar & Arthur b. 4/20/1872

John Quincy b. 1/16/1875
Minnie A. Nash b. 6/17/1876
Emmett Nash b. 7/-/1879
James Pleasant Walter b. 2/3/1882

Deaths
J. P. S. Nash 5/15/1924
Mary J. Nash 12/28/1928

Arthur d. 9/28/1873
Oscar d. 10/12/1873
Emmett Nash 1/5/1881
Sarah Lula Delany
    7/19/1886
J. Walter Nash 12/2/1897
J. P. Nash---

Marriages
J. P. S. Nash and Mary J. McCullough Nash m. 12/32/1868
Carl L. Nash and Mattie Lee Foster m. 11/2/1912
John Quincy Nash and Arie Ferguson m. 10/15/1901
Carrie Bird Nash and James B. Raven m. 4/9/1911

Children of J. P. S. and Mary J. Nash:

Sarah Lula Victoria 12/27/1869
Oscar & Arthur 4/20/1872
John Quincy 1/16/1875
Minnie H. 6/19/1876

Emmett 7/13/1879
James Pleasant Walter 2/3/1882
Carrie Byrd 11/7/1885
Pearl Gertrude 7/10/1888
Carl Lemuel 9/23/1889

Carrie Bird b. 11/7/1885
Pearl Gertrude b. 7/10/1888
Carl Lemuel b. 9/23/1889

Carrie Bird Nash Raven
    d. 5/31/1954
Carl Lemuel Nash d. 11/30/1937
John Quincy Nash d. 2/1/1856

WALTON L. INGLETT BIBLE
Owner: Randolyn Friedlander
233 Fairfield Dr., Ellenwood, Ga. 30049

George C. Inglett b. 4/2/1865
Joanna Rhoda b. 8/20/1852
Willey, May. Inglet b. 1/20/1887
Rozey. Lee. Inglet b. 9/9/1888
Wiley Washington Inglet b. 5/20/1891
Loney Barnes Inglet b. 6/3/1893
Walton L. Inglet b. 12/25/1837
Mary A. E. Inglet b. 5/8/1840

Juley An Persiler Inglet
    b. 4/26/1862
George C. Inglet b. 4/2/1865
Sary Frans Inglet
    b. 10/19/1868
Henry E. Inglet b. 5/14/1872
Rutha Sophrona Jane Inglet
    b. 4/23/1875
Alfurd P. Inglet b.
    8/20/1877
Jeney Melisey Inglet b.
    1/12/1880
Mintey Elisebeth Inglet
    b. 8/22/1883

George C. Inglet d. 10/7/1897

JAMES SPURLIN BIBLE *
Owner: Mrs. John C. Henderson
3770 Peachtree Road, N. E.
Atlanta, Ga. 30319

James Spurlin Book bought of William V. White in Pike Co., the
505th Dist. Ga. 7/4/1836.

Marriages
James Spurlin and Nancy his wife m. 12/10/1829
Columbus G. Coggin and Frances M. Spurlin m. 12/24/1854
William J. Newell and Frances M. Coggin m. 2/14/1866
William G. Spurlin and Lydia Coats m. 12/29/1859
Joseph M. Scott and Rhoda Obedience Spurlin m. 1/28/1866

Children of Joseph M. Scott and Rhoda Spurlin Scott:
Ida Inez Scott 9/12/1868
Zachery Lumpkin Scott 9/26/1871
Jessie James Scott 6/23/1876
Lucy Kate Scott 6/6/1879
Eugene Fred Scott 2/4/1889

WILLIAM SPURLIN BIBLE *
Owner: Mrs. John C. Henderson
3770 Peachtree Road, N. E.
Atlanta, Ga. 30319

James Spurlin, son of William Spurlin b. 6/20/1802
Nancy Michel, but now Spurlin, dau. of Starling Michel,
b. 8/18/1808
William Spurlin, son of John Spurlin and Myally, his mother,
b. 1/12/1769
William Spurlin, son of above, d. 4/30/1835
Nancy Spurlin d. 9/13/1875
William G. Spurlin d. 7/15/1864, prisoner of war at Ft. Delaware
James A. Spurlin killed in battle of Malvern Hill, Va. 7/1/1862
Amanda S. Spurlin d. 8/23/1863
Columbus Coggin d. in Va. Army 6/25/1862
James S. Coggin, son of C. G. and Frances M. Coggin, d. 6/25/1866
James Spurlin, son of William Spurlin, d. 11/18/1887
Frances M. Spurlin, dau. of James Spurlin and Nancy her mother b.
3/1/1831
Wilson L. Spurlin, son of James Spurlin and Nancy his mother b.
5/14/1832
William G. Spurlin, son of James Spurlin and Nancy his mother b.
1/28/1836
Claudy H. Spurlin, dau. of William G. Spurlin and Lydia her
mother d. 10/25/1863
William Charles Spurlin, son of William Spurlin and Liddie his
mother d. 9/17/1887
Sarah Spurlin, wife of William Spurlin d. age 92 11/4/1859
Martha Ann Spurlin, dau. of James Spurlin and Nancy her mother
d. 7/22/1894
James A. Spurlin, son of James Spurlin and Nancy his mother b.
9/8/1838

*See also p. 319.   273

(William Spurlin Bible contd....)

Amandah Samaria Spurlin, dau. of James Spurlin and Nancy her
    mother b. 1/28/1841
James Silas Coggin, son of C. G. and Frances M. Coggin, b.
    11/25/1855
Daniel W. Coggin b. 9/29/1857
Varina Davis Coggin 7/2/1860
William Charles Spurlin, son of William C. and Lydia Spurlin,
    b. 2/1/1864
Lydia Spurlin b. 2/29/1835
Martha Ann Spurlin, dau. of James Spurlin and Nancy her mother
    b. 12/28/1843
Rodah Obedience Spurlin, dau. of James Spurlin and Nancy her
    mother b. 7/2/1846
Claudy H. Spurlin b. 11/7/1860
Sarah F. Newell b. 6/20/1867
Nancy D. Newell b. 3/25/1869

JOHN BRUNT BIBLE

Births
Martha A. Brunt, dau. of John and Patience Brunt, b. 6/18/1827
Frances Brunt, dau. of John and Patience, b. 8/13/1829
John T. Riley b. 1/25/1844
James Robert Riley b. 1/20/1847
John Brunt b. 5/25/1804
Patience Brunt b. 4/10/1809

Marriages
James G. Riley and Mary F. Riley 6/8/1843
John Brunt 12/27/1825

Deaths
Mary F. Riley 3/25/1847   Patience Brunt 10/4/1883
John Brunt 12/28/1855

HENRY B. HECKLE BIBLE *

Births
Martha Heckle 8/13/1844   James A. Heckle 8/11/1853
John E. Heckle 1/20/1847   Anna M. Heckle 9/18/1855
George J. Heckle 2/7/1849

Deaths
Anna M. Calhoun 6/17/1878
Anna J. Heckle 4/13/1924, Palm Sunday, age 100 yrs., 4 mos., 29
days

*See also p. 423.   274

LUCY ANN STOVALL BIBLE
Owner: Mrs. Dyra Stovall Campbell
105 Orchard N. W., Fairburn, Ga.

Bible presented to Lucy Ann Stovall by J. R. B. Stovall 8/15/1907

Bonds Holy Matrimony - This certifies that J. R. B. Stovall of
Forsyth Co., Ga. and Lucy Ann Morgan of Forsyth Co., Ga. were
joined together by me in the bonds of Holy Matrimony at 9 o'clock
A. M. on the 14th day of Nov. in 1880. /s/ D. S. Mc?Cresy,
Minister of the Gospel. Wit: A. J. Morgan. G. B. H. Stovall

Deaths
Jesse Stovall 9/20/1893   James L. Stovall 1/16/1940
Essie Stovall 10/20/1893   Marvin Rudloph Campbell 5/1/1956
Miner Lugen Robert Stovall 8/13/1898
Laura Eveline Spear 2/6/1917   Allie Bradshaw 5/7/1949
Lucy Ann Stovall 1/19/1940   Paul Speer 1929
John R. B. Stovall 4/25/1943   Louella Bradshaw 12/7/1964

J. R. B. Stovall b. 12/11/1862   Jessie Stovall b. 8/1/1893
Lucy Ann Morgan b. 12/16/1861   Essie Stovall b. 8/1/1893
Thadius M. Stovall b. 10/21/1881   Minor E. R. Stovall b.
Louella Stovall b. 8/19/1884   3/3/1898
Lowea Evelyn Stovall b. 8/14/1887 Dyra Doshia Stovall
                                       b. 8/11/1901

Marriages
Paul A. Speer m. Laura E. Stovall 9/27/1903
Allie C. Bradshaw m. Louella Stovall 2/18/1906
James L. Stovall m. Lorene Lassetter 11/10/1912
Marvin Rudolph Campbell m. Dyra Doshia Stovall 10/6/1922

          JAMES DILLARD BIBLE Of Elbert Co., Ga.*
               With Rev. War Pension W7020

Elizabeth Emaly Dillard b. 10/14/1786 James Dillard b. 7/13/1799
Nancy Dillard b. 7/28/1793   Sarah Joice Dillard b.
Mary Varnon Dillard b. 10/3/1795   3/22/1801
Jense (Jane) Dillard b. 8/25/1797

          JAMES LANGHAM BIBLE Of Jasper Co., Ga.
               From Rev. War Pension Application

Births
James Washington Langham, son of James & Elizabeth, b. 6/1/1810
John Madison Langham b. 4/15/1815
Marshal Jackson Langham b. 2/10/1818
Samuel Hamond Langham b. 2/22/1820
Jane Aaleseann Syrene Langham b. 5/18/1822
Martha Ann Elizabeth Langham b. 10/14/1824
Thomas T. Langham b. 4/15/1829
*See also p. 440.   275

JONATHAN JOYNER BIBLE
From Rev. War Pension W300

Births
Poley Joyner, dau. of Jonathan Joyner and Elizabeth, his wife,
   b. 9/11/1792
Sally Joyner, dau. of same, b. 6/25/1791
Thomas Johner b. 1/18/1796
Jonathan Joyner b. 8/4/1799
Henry Joyner b. 3/15/1802
Jonathan Joyner d. 9/15/1804

THOMAS DAUGHERTY BIBLE
From War of 1812 Claim WC 96939

John Daugherty b. 6/6/1817
Jacob Daugherty b. 5/1/1819
Anderson Daugherty b. 6/12/1821
Elizabeth Amanda Daugherty b. 2/25/1824
Thomas Daugherty b. 3/22/1826
Joel Scott Daugherty b. 3/16/1828
Sarah Emily Daugherty b. 4/15/1830
William Edmond Daugherty, son of Thomas Daugherty and Sarah, his
   wife, b. 10/15/1832

EVAN HAINES BIBLE
From Rev. War Pension

Births
Evan Haines 7/17/1756
Charity Haines 4/25/1770
Ellis Haines (brother) 3/9/1765

Children of Evan and Charity Haines:

Elizabeth Haines 10/8/1789	David Haines 3/1/1802
Ellis Haines 6/10/1791	Katherine Haines 11/9/1807
Jonathan Haines 12/21/1795	Nathan Haines 7/8/1810

ISAAC STEELE, SR. BIBLE Of DeKalb Co., Ga.
From Rev. War Pension #R10094

Births

Isaac Steele 10/23/1732	John Steele 2/27/1780
Grissel Dixon 6/10/1750	Ruth Steele 3/13/1782
James Steele 4/4/1771	Isaac Steele Jr. 7/18/1786
Michael Steele 4/2/1773	Moses Steele 5/18/1788
Margret Steele 6/28/1775	Jane Steele 9/22/1790
William Steele 1/9/1778	

IRA M. STEELE BIBLE

Births

Isaac Steele 7/18/1786
Cynthia Cox 7/18/1792
William A. J. Steele 3/26/1815
Mary I. Steele 5/16/1817
John D. Steele 6/7/1819

Rhoda H. Steele 4/1/1823
Michael A. Steele 3/17/1821
Ira M. Steele 4/29/1825
Isaac Steele 8/7/1827
Moses F. Steele 8/3/1829

Deaths

Cynthia Steele d. 5/16/1865
Isaac Steele d. 4/16/1865

JAMES SANDERS, JR. BIBLE
From Rev. War Pension R9179

Births

James Sanders 3/18/1762
Elizabeth Sanders, his wife 2/18/1754
Tabitha Sanders 11/14/1786
Elizabeth Sanders 9/2/1789

Sally Sanders 5/16/1791
Malinda Sanders 6/2/1793
Malintha Sanders 6/2/1793
Eleanor Riley Sanders
4/11/1795

JOHN CAULDER BIBLE Of McIntosh Co., Ga.
From Rev. War Pension W8578

Births

Allen P. Caulder 6/25/1822
Seraphina Caulder 12/8/1824
George W. 5/2/1821
Eugene M. 9/9/1830

Deaths

Robert Patrick Caulder
1/13/1818
Zeriphena Ann 11/12/1831
Hugh P. 9/14/1822
John M. 1/12/1834
James K. 4/1837
William M. 8/1/1839
Phebe 5/7/1803
John 1/24/1845
Winewood F. 1/22/1851

COLLENS-EATON BIBLE

Marriages

James W. Eaton and Margaret Collins 10/15/1838
James Eaton and Saray An Elender Jordan 2/9/1866
J. L. H. Woodman and Margaret Ann Ellender Eaton 2/8/1900
Randolph Co., Ga.
Buyan Jordan and Susan B. Livingston 10/31/1900 Terrell Co., Ga.

(Collens-Eaton Bible contd....)

Births

Elender Collens 3/1/1787	John Collens 12/20/1815
Susan Collens 1/2/1809	Margaret Eaton 10/20/1815
Margaret Collens 10/20/1810	James Collens 6/6/1817
James W. Eaton 3/2/1813	Elizabeth Collens
Isaac Collens 6/12/1813	Rebecca Collens 6/4/1822
	Elender Collens 11/10/1824

Amanda Ann Eaton 7/1/1839 Randolph Co., Ga.
James Eaton 8/17/1841 Randolph Co., Ga.
Ellender Eaton 4/17/1844 Early Co., Ga.
Rebecca Eaton 9/28/1846 Early Co., Ga.
Daniel Eaton 1/9/1849 Early Co., Ga.
Stafford Eaton 5/2/1851 Early Co., Ga.
Margaret Eaton 2/18/1853 Early Co., Ga.
A. B. Right Eaton 6/4/1856 Calhoun Co., Ga.
William Eaton 1/18/1860 Dawson, Ga.
Elizabeth Cariean Eaton 12/17/1866 Terrell Co., Ga.
Frances Demarias Jordan 9/6/1867 Terrell Co., Ga.
James L. Eaton, son of J. H. and G. E. Eaton, 11/29/1868
James Lewis Harvey Woodman 1/29/1876
Samuel Wesley Eaton 10/25/1877
Margaret Ann Ellen Eaton 12/13/1880
Joe Jordan 6/27/1904
Iren Jordan 6/17/1916

Deaths

Rebecca Eaton 2/16/1847	J. W. Eaton 4/12/1889
Elender Eaton 12/16/1859	Virner Jordan 4/24/1889
William Eaton 11/13/1867	Margret Eaton 8/5/1904
Ellender Collins 11/25/1873	Margaret Eaton 1/22/1906
Fanny Jordan 5/1/1874	Dan Eaton 4/29/1918
Salley Jordan 7/1/1884	

S. J. HAMMETT BIBLE

Births

S. J. Hammett 2/27/1838	James Samuel Hammett 9/16/1872
S. J. Cooper 11/2/1840	Virgil Al Stewart Hammett 1/3/1875
Versenay Virginia Hammett 5/7/1870	

Marriages
S. J. Hammett and S. J. Cooper 12/17/1867
Sydney J. Hammett and Sarah J. Cooper 12/17/1867

Deaths
Sarah J. Hammett 11/14/1876
Sydney J. Hammett 4/3/1876
James Samuel Hammett 6/27/1875

JEPTHA MITCHAM BIBLE

Jeptha Mitcham of Ala. and Eliza Williams of Ga. m. 9/7/1871
at J. H. Williams' by Rev. John McGhee. Wit: T. J. Williams,
W. J. Key
Jesse Mitcham m. Sarah Mullins 11/5/1894
Henrietta Mitcham m. Tilten or Tilden Bryant -/10/1895
Tom Foster m. Lilliam Mitcham 11/10/1901
Charley Beck m. Pearl Mitcham 11/10/1901
Ira Mitcham m. Sandra Hill 2/4/ or 2/11/1901
Ira Mitcham m. Ethel Mitcham Cooper Funderburk 9/12/1909
Mamie Mitcham m. Baker Stewart 11/7/1909
Raymond Mitcham m. Berter Granger 11/3/1907
Jeptha Mitcham b. 10/18/1848 d. 7/4/1901
Eliza Williams b. 11/3/1853
? E. A. Mitcham d. 4/29/1902
Jesse Mitcham b. 10/10/1872 d. 9/12/1904
Lilian Mitcham Raymond b. 4/16/1875
Henrietta Mitcham b. 5/3/1876
Ira Mitcham b. 4/11/1878 d. 8/1910
Pearley Mitcham b. 3/20/1880 d. 1909
Raymond Mitcham b. 2/14/1882
Evie Mitcham b. 6/28/1884 D. 4/13/1899
Jeffie Mitcham b. 5/26/1886
Mamie Mitcham b. 2/19/1888
Ethel Mitcham b. 5/3/1890
Bertha Mitcham b. 5/6/1892
Watson Mitcham b. 5/16/1895 d. 4/9/1896
Springer Foster b. 9/30/1901 or 1904
Rufus Foster b. 7/20/190-
Herman Foster b. 11/19/1908 d. 5/5/1909
Watson Mitcham b. d/9/1896, 10 mos., 25 days
Evie Mitcham d. 4/13/1899, 15 yrs., 9 mos., 15 days
Jeptha Mitcham d. 7/4/1901, 52 yrs., 8 mos., 14 days
E. A. Mitcham d. 4/29/1902
Jesse Mitcham d. 9/12/1904
Pearlie Beck d. 1909
Ira Mitcham d. 8/1910

JOHN NEWTON BIBLE
Owner: Mrs. Margaret Newton Miller, Athens, Ga.

John Newton b. in Pa. 2/20/1759 m. in N. C. 11/6/1786 (or 1783)
Catherine Lowance, b. in E. Jersey 8/26/1756. He d. Lexington
Ga., Oglethorpe Co., Ga., bur. under the pulpit of the
Presbyterian Church. She d. Athens, Ga. 10/12/1846.

Elizur Lowrance Newton, son of John Newton, b. Oglethorpe Co.,
Ga. 2/10/1796 m. Greene Co., Ga. 5/14/1822 Eliza Taylor Callier,
b. in Warren Co., N. C. 11/5/1802

William Henry Newton, eldest son of Elizur Newton, b. 7/11/1823
in Athens, Ga., m. 4/26/1846 in Madison, Ga. Miriam Keturah
Walker, b. 4/11/1826 Morgan Co., Ga. He d. 4/18/1893 Maysville,
Ga., and she d. 12/6/1903 Madison, Ga.
James T. Newton, son of William H. Newton, b. 7/17/1860 in
Morgan Co., Ga. m. 3/16/1882 in Cuthbert, Ga., Lucie T.
Flewellen, b. 1/10/1861 in Randolph Co., Ga.

WILLIAM CRAIG ORR BIBLE
Owner: Judge R. C. Orr, Athens, Ga.

Marriages
William Craig Orr b. 7/7/1814, d. 7/18/1859 m. 9/8/1840 Cynthia
Ann Montgomery, b. 7/27/1818, d. 8/1/1888

Mary Cornelia Orr b. 10/3/1845 m. 7/2/1868 Cyrus R. Smith
Robert Craig Orr b. 6/28/1859 m. 7/15/1890 Florida Agnes Carr

Births Grandfather and Grandmother Orr:
William Orr b. 8/22/1771 in Mecklenburg, N. C., d. 7/2/1861 in
Talladega, Ala.

J. F. WALKER BIBLE
Owner: Mrs. James M. Bonner, Covington, Ga.

Births
Nannie S. Walker 5/23/1860	Fred Moore Walker 10/4/1886
Albert S. Walker 2/8/1862	Nina May Walker 12/20/1886
William H. Walker 10/20/1863	J. H. Edwards 10/1806
Robert L. Walker 1/20/1865	Nancy Stevens 2/26/1814
Charlie W. Walker 3/4/1868	L. N. Edwards 3/29/1832
Hampton C. Walker 4/2/1871	W. H. Edwards 7/7/1833
John F. Walker 12/13/1873	M. R. Edwards 4/6/1835
Nathaniel P. Walker 3/21/1876	M. A. Edwards 2/16/1838
Annie W. Martin 10/4/1881	A. S. Walker 8/11/1830
Florence M. Walker 1/11/1882	Laura A. Walker 12/19/1854
	Edward Y. Walker 2/15/1857
	Adda F. Walker 11/14/1858

Marriages
J. H. Edwards and Nancy Stevens 12/15/1829
N. S. Walker and Maria E. Edwards 10/12/1853
W. B. Martin and Lona Walker 12/25/1877
Dr. N. P. Walker and Miss Alice Cross--
Mozelle Walker and T. F. Athon 1/1/1908
J. F. Walker and Adda F. Walker 3/24/1880
Dr. E. Y. Walker and Annie Lee Moore 12/10/1886
A. S. Walker and Minnie Henderson 2/21/1889
W. H. Walker and Estelle Adams 12/26/1894
Charles W. Walker and Mamie E. Anderson 3/1/1897
H. C. Walker and Clara Anderson---
James Felix Walker b. 2/26/1847 d. 9/4/1935
Nina M. Walker to Pascal Bryan McElheny 7/14/1910
                    Their Children:
Frances Olivia McElheny b. 2/5/1912
Walker Terrell McElheny b. 2/27/1921
Frances Olivia McElheny and Franklin Greer, Jr. m. 8/16, d.
11/5/1943 in Service
Walker McElheny and Joan Agnes Hoehner m. 12/19/1948
John Terrell McElheny b. 8/4/1953
Adda Frances Walker b. 11/14/1858
Frances M. Greer m. James M. Bonner 9/17/1946
Brenda Walker Bonner b. 12/14/1947
Janet McElheny, dau. of Walker and Joan Hoehner

(J. D. Walker Bible contd....)

Deaths

M. A. Edwards 2/12/1844
J. H. Edwards 3/6/1889
Nancy S. Edwards 6/23/1892
L. M. Edwards 7/8/1895
Robert L. Walker 12/22/1895
Dr. N. S. Walker 1/24/1902
Mrs. A. S. Walker 4/4/1905

Charles Wesley Walker 7/6/1905
W. H. Walker 4/18/1912
Mrs. M. R. Walker 12/28/1911
James Felix Walker 9/2/1905
H. C. (Cape) Walker 2/17/1942
Adda F. Walker 7/26/1946
Mozelle W. Athon 1/17/1947

WILLIAM B. MARTIN BIBLE
Owner: Mrs. Hartley Davis
3092 Ridge Ave., Macon, Ga.

Births

Nathaniel Sadler Walker 8/11/1830
Mariah Rebecca Edwards 4/6/1835
William B. Martin 4/9/1854
Laura Avlona Walker 12/19/1854
Annie Walker Martin 10/4/1880
Riddie Stevens Martin 1/13/1882
Eunice Barney Martin 3/1/1886
Mary Jessie Martin 3/26/1888
Fannie Ruth Martin 9/2/1893
Evelyn Athon 10/28/1905

Marjorie Athon 11/17/1907
Dorothy Athon 1/25/1910
Avlona Athon 12/2/1913
Virginia Black 7/27/1909
William Frederick Black
   4/1/1911
Otho Bruce Andrews 7/12/1916
Barney Ruth Andrews 9/1918
Claudia Ann Veal 10/25/1926

Deaths

Jesse H. Edwards 3/16/1889
Nancy Edwards 6/23/1892
W. J. Martin 5/22/1886
L. N. Edwards 7/8/1895
N. S. Walker 1/24/1902
Robert L. Walker 12/22/1895
Charles W. Walker 7/6/1905
Minnie H. Walker 4/4/1905

Mariah R. Walker 12/28/1911
William H. Walker 4/1913
W. B. Martin 5/30/1927
Riddie Stevens Martin
   1/28/1929
Avlona Walker Martin
   7/10/1936
William Frederick Black
   12/20/1940

Marriages

Nathaniel S. Walker to Mariah R. Edwards 10/12/1853
William B. Martin to Laura A. Walker 12/25/1877
Joseph D. Athon to Annie W. Martin 5/19/1901
W. F. Black to Mary Jessie Martin 12/26/1906
O. B. Andrews to Eunice Barney Martin 12/31/1912
Fannie Ruth Martin to J. Wright Veal 12/21/1924

JOHN GOODMAN BIBLE
Owner: Mrs. Montague Tuttle
691 Peeples St., Atlanta, Ga.

John Goodman b. 10/31/1772
Sarah Goodman b. 9/29/1778
Mary Goodman b. 2/9/1800

Betsy Goodman b. 12/12/1806
John Tharp Goodman b. 3/22/1810
Kiziah Goodman b. 5/10/1812

(John Goodman Bible contd....)

Sarah Goodman b. 4/5/1779
Nancy Goodman b. 3/3/1815
Robert Hope Goodman b. 2/21/1819
Susannah Goodman b. 2/11/1823

Stephen Goodman b. 3/19/1777

John Goodman, his Book, this 8/13/1815
Sally Goodman, her hand and pen, this 8/13/1815
Polly Goodman

THOMAS C. WYCHE BIBLE
Owner: Mrs. Thomas Fitzgerald Green, Sr.
Athens, Ga. 30601

Marriages
Thomas C. Wyche and Catharine Wyche 3/5/1826
Remer Young and Mary Wyche 5/7/1846
Charles Thomas Irvine and Martha Susan Wyche 11/21/1848
James L. Wyche and Elizabeth Hannah Wyche 11/26/1851
John G. Pettus and Caroline C. Wyche 12/16/1857
John L. Linton and Alice M. Wyche 10/23/1860

Births
Thomas C. Wyche 3/25/1801
Catharine Wyche, his wife, 1/11/1809
Mary Wyche 3/27/1827
Martha Susan Wyche 4/28/1829
Elizabeth Hannah Wyche 8/26/1831
George Archibald Wyche 8/4/1833
Catharine Caroline Wyche 5/11/1836
Thomas Lawson Wyche 11/13/1838
Alice Maude Wyche 10/29/1840
John Thomas Irvine, son of C. T. and Martha L. Irvine
   b. 12/8/1849
Catharine MacIntyre Wyche, dau. of T. L. and E. H. Wyche,
   b. 4/12/1855
Elizabeth M. Wyche 6/14/1857

Deaths
Catharine Wyche 12/27/1864   Elizabeth Hannah Wyche 12/10/1858
Thomas C. Wyche 7/5/1870   George Archibald Wyche 11/26/1834
Mary Young 5/14/1861   Catherine Caroline Wyche Pettus
Martha S. Irvine 11/17/1864   Thomas 12/31/1929

Marriages
John Linton Green and Margaret Louise Bickerstaff 11/2/1942
Hope Linton and Thomas Fitzgerald Green III of Athens, Ga.,
   10/22/1902
Alice M. Wyche and Jon. L. Linton 10/23/1860

John Lanier Linton d. 5/3/1908 Thomasville, Ga., bur. Laurel Hill
Cemetery. Their Children: Ctherine McIntyre and J. Lawson Linton
bur. in family cemetery at "Mill Pond" plantation, the old Wyche
estate (Thomas Co., Ga.

282

(Thomas C. Wyche Bible contd....)

Births
Thomas Wyche Young, 1st child of Mary & Remer Young, b. 7/7/1847
Susannah Elizabeth Young 12/2/1848
Henry Michael Young 3/21/1850
Mariah Lawson Young 9/27/1851
Sarah Hannah Young 9/10/1853
Catharine Margaret Young 1/25/1855
John Remer Young 4/7/1856
Lanier Wyche Linton, son of L. L. and A. M. Linton, b. 10/6/1861
Catherine McIntyre Linton 10/27/1865
Margaret Josephine Linton 7/4/1863
Lucy Alice Linton 12/23/1867
Lawson lanier Linton7/31/1870
Hope Cally Linton 10/22/1874
Archibald Thomson McIntyre Linton 12/10/1878

Deaths
Thomas W. Young 7/13/1870
Thomas Fitzgerald Green 12/27/1934 Athens, Ga.
John Linton Green 9/30/1959
Lucile Alice Linton 5/22/1960

John Linton Green II b. 11/14/1947
Thomas Fitzgerald Green, Jr. b. 8/6/1903

                    Sheets inserted in Bible:

Littleton Wyche b. 2/28/1772
Susanna Mitchell b. 9/20/1780
The above were m. 5/8/1798
Nancy Rains Wyche, their dau., b. 2/27/1799
Thomas Clark Wyche b. 3/25/1801
Rebecca Taylor Wyche b. 5/11/1803
Martha Wyche b. 8/10/1805
Mariah Wyche b. 11/7/1807
Elizabeth Wyche b. 12/2/1809
Henry Wyche b. 4/30/1812
Margaret Bryan Wyche b. 7/14/1815
William Wyche b. 1/12/1818

John Alston and nancy Rains Wyche m. 3/4/1813
Leonard T. Warner and Rebecca Taylor Wyche m. 12/7/1819
Hardy Bryan and Martha Wyche m. 10/15/1823
Hardy Bryan and Mariah Wyche m. 8/5/1824
Loverd Bryan and Elizabeth Wyche m. 1/31/1826
Thomas C. Wyche and Catharine MacIntyre m. 3/5/1826
Robert Raiford and Margaret B. Wyche m. 5/8/1834
Henry Wyche and Elizabeth G. Coulson m. 8/13/1835
Malachi Rayford and Patience Wyche m. 11/10/1834
William Wyche and Louisa M. Thomas m. 8/15/1838
Littleton Wyche and Mary Elizabeth Coalson m. 4/14/1850

Patience Wyche b. 8/7/1820
Littleton Wyche, Jr. b. 2/8/1823

Thomas Mitchell Alston, son of John D. and Nancy R. Alston b.
   12/30/1814
James Alston b. 1/22/1817
Eliza Alston b. 5/30/1819
Philip Alston b. 12/4/1821

                        283

(Thomas C. Wyche Bible contd....)

Deaths
George Wyche 2/15/1809, age 76
Littleton Wyche Sr. 3/15/1834 age 62 yrs., 13 days
Susanna Wyche 7/39/1850, age 70
Martha Bryan, wife of Hardy Bryan, d. 6/30/1824
Nancy Rains Alston--
Martha Ann Warner---
Henry Beaty Wyche 8/17/1839

Births
Littleton Wyche Warner, son of Leonard T. and Rebecca T. Warner,
    b. 1/20/1821
Susan W. Waner b. 2/14/1823
Martha Ann Wanrer b. 8/8/1825
Virginia Spingler b. 4/26/1833
Nathaniel R. M. Spengler b. 9/5/1835
Charlotte McGee Spengler b. 3/7/1839
Elizabeth S. Spengler b. 12/17/1840
(Thomas C. Wyche Bible contd....)

Caroline Bryan, dau. of Hardy and Maria Bruan, b. 8/12/1825
Leon Bryan b. 6/19/1827
Magnolia Bryan b. 8/11/1829
Iredell Edward Wyche Bryan b. 8/10/1831

Henry Beaty Wyche, son of William and Louisa M. Wyche,
    b. 6/26/1939
Mary Olive Wyche b. 7/9/1840

Births
John Thomas Irvin, son of Charles T. and Martha Irvine,
    b. 12/8/1849

The following is a "Penmanship practice of Susan" -

Received of Thomas C. Wyche, Administrator of the estate of
Littleten Wyche late of Thomas County Deceased the sum of three
hundred Dollars in full of all demands against him this 10th day
of January 1848. Susan Wyche.

A list of ages and names-

Thomas C. Wyche age 25 March 1801
Catharine Wyche was b. 1/11/1807 and m. 3/5/1826
Mary Wyche b. 3/27/1827
Martha Susan Wyche b. 4/28/1829
Elizabeth Hannah Wyche b. 8/26/1831
George Archibald Wyche b. 8/4/1833
George d. 11/26/1834
Catharine Caroline Wyche b. 5/11/1836
Thomas Lawson Wyche b. 11/13/1838
Alice Maude Wyche b. 10/29/1840

MOSES WADDELL LINTON BIBLE
Owner: Mrs. T. F. Green, Sr., Athens, Ga. 30601

Deaths
Moses W. Linton 8/6/1885
Lucy A. Linton 8/13/1885
Margaret Stubbs 11/3/185
Benj. F. Linton 1/16/1883
Thomas Fitzgerald Green
  12/27/1934
John Linton Green 9/30/1959

John Lanier Linton 5/3/1908
Thomas C. Wyche 7/5/1870
Catherine Wyche 12/27/1864
Alice M. Wyche Linton 9/14/1890
Lucy (Lucile) Alice Linton
  5/22/1960
Margaret Josephine Linton Wade
  3/26/1931 Thomasville, Ga.

Births
Maud Ella Linton b. 2/27/1888 d. 7/1/1892
Wyche Waddell Linton b. 6/8/1889 d. 7/30/1894
William A. Linton b. 2/8/1891 d. 1960
Callie Ann Linton b. 10/31/1892 d. 8/6/1902
Fitzgerald Linton b. 4/29/1913
Mary Alice Linton b. 1/19/1915
Thomas Fitzgerald Green Jr. b. 8/6/1903
John linton Green b. 5/13/1906
Lucile Linton Green b. 2/28/1809
John Linton Green Jr. b. 11/14/1947

Marriages
Wyche Waddell Linton and Amanda P. Alderman m. 9/28/1886
Wyche Waddell Linton m. 2d Sarah Campbell 6/4/1908
Margaret Josephine Linton m. Philip Alston Wade 1/16/1884,
  Presbyterian Church, Thomasville, Ga.
Philip Alston Wade b. 10/7/1857 d. 6/24/1898
Moses Waddell Linton and Lucy Ann Lanier m. 4/30/1829
Benjamin F. Linton b   /1830
James A. Linton b. 10/25/1831
Margaret J. Linton b. 2/27/1834
John Lanier Linton b. 1/5/1836
Linton W. Stubbs, son of F. P. Stubbs and M. J. Linton b.
  10/4/1855
Thomas C. Wyche and Catherine MacIntyre m. 3/5/1826
B. F. Linton and Rebecca Mountree m. 12/5/1849
James A. Linton and Sallie Young m. 1/6/1858
Frank P. Stubbs and Mag Linton m. 1/9/1855
John L. Linton and Alice M. Wyche m. 10/23/1860
Linton W. Stubbs and Phena Budd m. 4/12/1882
Hope Linton and Thomas Fitzgerald Green m. 10/22/1902 in
  Thomasville, Thomas Co., Ga. at home of her arents, John Lanier
  Linton (d. 5/2/1908) and Alice M. Wyche, decd, 9/14/1890

Births
Moses Waddell Linton 12/15/1807
Lucy A. Lanier b. 9/7/1812
Thomas C. Wyche 3/25/1801
Catherine MacIntyre 1/11/1809
Thomas C. Wyche and Catherine MacIntyre m. 3/5/1826
Mary, dau. of T. C. W. and C. W., 3/27/1827
Martha Wyche 4/28/1829
Elizabeth H. Wyche 8/26/1831
George Archibald Wyche 8/4/1833
Catherine Caroline Wyche 5/11/1836

285

(Moses Waddell Linton Bible, Births, contd....)

Thomas Lawson Wyche 11/13/1838
Alice Maude Wyche 10/29/1840
John Lanier Linton and Alice M. Wyche m. 10/23/1860
Wyche Waddell Linton, son of J. L. L. and A. M. Linton, 10/6/1861
Margaret Josephine Linton 7/4/1863
Catherine MacIntyre Linton 10/27/1865
Lucile Alice Linton 12/23/1867
Lawson Lanier Linton 7/31/1870
Hope Callie Linton 10/22/1874
Archibald Thompson MacIntyre Linton 12/10/1878

Catherine MacIntyre Linton d. 10/14/1869
Lawson Lanier Linton d. 12/8/1877
Rebecca Taylor Wyche m. Warner 12/7/1819 & Spengler & James
Newman

THOMAS CROWDER BIBLE
Owner: Mrs. T. F. Green, Sr.
Athens, Ga. 30601

Thomas Crowder m. Eliza Dick, wid. of John Dick, 12/26/1804
Frances Maria Crowder m. Ezra B. Jones 11/3/1825
Adeline E. A. Crowder m. Thomas F. Green 12/4/1828
Mary H. Green m. Lucian Bowdre 3/1/1838
William Gustavus Crowder m. Martha Smith
Arabella M. Crowder m. R. L. Nash 1/1844
Maria H. Dick m. William D. Lucas 1814

Thomas Crowder, son of Mark Crowder and Anne, his wife, b.
1/22/1774
Eliza Crowder, dau. of John Hawkins and Mary, his wife, b.
9/22/1774
Maria H. Dick, dau. of John Dick and Eliza, his wife, b.
2/28/1794
Frances Maria Crowder b. 11/24/1805
Adeline Eliza Ann Crwoder b. 1/22/1808
Mark Thomas Crowder b. 9/11/1809
Martha Hawkins Crowder b. 1/12/1812
Louisa Matilda Crowder b. 6/19/1813
William Gustavus Crowder b. 1/24/1815

Matilda Crowder b. 8/5/1817
Arabella Matilda Crowder b. 8/5/1817
Thomas Crwoder Jones b. 6/17/1827
Joseph John Jones b. 3/4/1829
Thomas Fitzgerald Green b. 9/4/1829, d. infancy
Frances Elizabeth Jones b. 2/25/1831
Adeline Eliza Ann Green b. 9/23/1831
Mary Elizabeth Hawkins Green b. 8/9/1833
Martha Crowder Green b. 11/20/1836
William John Green b. 1/23/1839
Thomas Fitzgerald Green Jr. b. 3/3/1843 m. 9/18/1868 Ella Bibb
   Lipscomb
Thomas Fitzgerald Green b. 7/26/1869 m. 10/22/1902 Hope Linton,
   Thomasville, Ga.

(Thomas Crowder Bible contd....)

Thomas Fitzgerald Green Jr. b. 8/6/1903 m. 12/8/1955 (Jane
   Oliver)
John Linton Green b. 5/13/1906 d. 9/30/1959 m. 11/7/1942
   Margaret Louise Bickerstaff
John Linton Green Jr. b. 11/14/1947
Lucile Linton Green b. 2/1908 Athens, Ga.

Deaths

Louisa Matilda Crowder 9/23/1815   Mark Thomas Crowder 5/17/1829
John   Hawkins 12/19/1786   Thomas Fitzgerald Green
Mary Hawkins 10/27/1800   11/8/1830
                                      Maria H. Lucas 10/9/1831
                                      Adelia M. Lucas 10/4/1831
                                      Georgianna Adeline Lucas
                                         10/8/1831
                                      Caroline Eliza Lucas
                                         10/15/1831

                     MARTHA HAWKINS BROOKS' SCRAPBOOK
                          Dau. of Thomas Crowder

"....She was daughter of Thomas Crowder and his wife Elizabeth
Hawkins widow of John Dick. She was granddaughter of John Hawkins
and his wife Mary Waller, widow of Webley. 1st Gen. John Hawkins
(my grandfather) was born Sept. 14, 1733 in Baltimore, Maryland.
Mary his wife, daughter of Capt. John Waller, was born in King &
Queen Virginia June 20,1734. She was the widow of Mr. Webley. He
died leaving one child named Benjamin Waller Webley in Halifax
Co., N. C. She removed from there to Hillsboro and then married
John Hawkins second of April 1768."

Hardrus Hawkins b. 11/8/1769 Elizabeth Hawkins b. 9/22/1774
Mary Hawkins b. 9/9/1771   Frances Mariah Hawkins b. 10/10/1779
John Hawkins b. 3/6/1773

John Hawkins Sr. d. 12/19/1786
Mary Hawkins, my grandmother, d. 10/27/1800
Thomas Crowder, son of W. G. C., 9/15/1842
Thomas F. Green, son of A. E. A. Green, 7/26/1869
William Henry, son of M. L. 1/7/1845
John R. Crowder, son of W. G. C. 3/3/1844
Elizabeth G., dau. of W. G. C.
Lady Mary, dau. of M. H. J. 1/5/1848
Fannie Joseph, dau. of A. E. A. G.
Clarence Julian S. of Elizabeth Jones, Nov.--
Fannie Dorris, dau. of Elizabeth Jones, 1/6/1854
Adie Green Houston, dau. of Mary H. Green
James Garnett S. of Mary Jackson 2/15/1852
Minnie O. Houston, dau. of Mary H. Green Houston, 2/18/1855
Eugene Crawford, son of Mary H. Green Houston, b. 7/24/1857
Thomas Fitzgerald, son of Mary H. Green, 12/31/1858
Thomas Green, son of Mattie C. Green Bass, 8/15/1859
David Eugene b. 2/1850
Adie Green, dau. of Mattie
Mary Rabun, dau. of Mattie Bass
Mattie Crowder

(Martha Hawkins Brooks' Bible, Births, contd...)

Hamlin H. and Willie R., twins, 4/23/1867
Charles Larkin Bass 4/3/1869
Julia Louise Bass 8/11/1869
Adie Green Cook 5/29/1871

Marriages
Mary Lucas m. Bowdrie 3/1/1838
W. G. Crowder m. Martha Smith
F. Elizabeth Jones m. Dr. J. O. Owens 10/2/1849
Mary Hawkins Green m. Adlai Osborn Houston 11/18/1857
George J. Lucas m. Emeline Edwards
Martha (Mattie) C. Green m. Dr. Charles Henry Bass 8/10/1858
Adeline E. A. Green m. W. A. Hall 7/1860
Thomas F. Green, Jr. m. Ella Lipscomb 10/18/1868
Anna Maria Green m. Samuel Austen Cook 4/8/1869
Fannie J. Green m. Dr. James Phillips 11/1871
Minnie O. Houston 2/1874
Prescius Minnie d. today, 4/17/1875
Thomas Crowder d.--
Elizabeth Hawkins Crowder d.---
Willie J. Green
William Gustavus Crowder
Thomas Crowder Nash
Mary Hawkins Green Houston d. 2/25/1860
David Eugene Houston 3/17/1860
Adeline E. A. Crowder Green d.---
Adeline E. A. Green Hall
Lieut. Lucian Bowdrie killed Battle of Atlanta
Arabella M. Crowder Nash d. 9/23---
Joseph John Jones killed at taking of Columbus by the yankees

MRS. FRANCES KINNEBREW BIBLE
Owner: Mrs. Billups Buder
2110 Spring Creek Road, Decatur, Ga.

Marriages
Rev. J. H. Kinnebrew and Miss F. C. Billups m. 12/24/1868
Annie Ruth Kinnebrew to Frank Resler m. Columbus, Miss. no issue.
Laura Welsh Kennebrew to John Q. Hayes (Little Rock) Ark. m.
  Columbus, miss.
Jessie Norton Kinnebrew to Edward E. Buder m. Columbus, Miss.

Births
J. H. Kinnebrew b. 8/9/1842 Oglethorpe Co., Ga. near Bairdstown
Fannie C. Billups alias Mrs. F. C. Kinnebrew b. 11/2/1843 in
  Coosa Co., Ala.
Mary Augusta Kinnebrew b. 9/3/1870 at Barnwell C. H. in Barnwell
  Co., S. C.
Annie Ruth Kinnebrew b. at Covington, Ga. 7/6/1873
Mollie Grace Kinnebrew b. at Madison, Ga. 12/13/1875
Laura Welch Kinnebrew b. Gadsden, Ala. 3/25/1878
Jessie Norton Kinnebrew b. Gadsden, Ala. 9/3/1883
Elizabeth Billups Kinnebrew b. Gadsden, Ala. 2/20/1885 "Bibber"

(Mrs. Frances Kinnebrew Bible contd....)

Deaths
Mary Augusta Kinnebrew d. Covington, Ga. 6/3/1873, age 2 yrs.,
    9 mos.
Jennie Billups d. Columbus, Miss. 4/20/1898, age 48 yrs.
Mrs. M. A. Billups d. Worth Co., Ga. 8/8/1885

Obituary: "Little Mary, only daughter of Rev. J. H. Kinnebrew,
died in Covington, on Tuesday last. She was about two and a half
years of age, and a very bright child...."

JOSEPH BILLUPS BIBLE

Births
Joseph Billups, son o f Richard and Elizabeth Billups,
    b.3/29/1797
Mary Ann Billups, formerly Mary Ann Daniel, b. 3/9/1817
Thomas A., son of Richard and Elizabeth Billups, b. 8/2/1792
Ann L., dau. of Richard and Elizabeth Billups, b. 1/16/1795
Billups Kinnebrew Buder b. 9/13/1914, son of Jessie Kinnebrew
    and Edward E. Buder
Diana, dau. of Billups K. and Imogene McAfee Buder 3/27/1942

Deaths
Elizabeth Billups 6/8/1830   Joseph Billups 5/17/1849
Richard Billups 9/8/1812

Births
Ann Elizabeth Billups, dau. of Joseph and Mary Ann Billups,
    b. 4/9/1837
John Richard, son of J. and M. A. Billups, b. 1/26/1839
Mary Jane, dau. of J. and M. A. Billups, b. 10/14/1840
Francis Cunningham, dau. of J. and M. A. Billups, b. 11/2/1843
Joseph Alexander Early, son of J. and M. A. Billups, b. 7/7/1845
Virginia, dau. of J. and M. A. Billups, b. 11/20/1847

Marriages
Joseph and Mary Ann Billups m. 12/15/1835

JOHN T. DANIEL BIBLE

Inside Bible of Mrs. Frances Kinnebrew, with note: "Account of
ages and deaths of J. T. Daniel Family drawn off from old record
24th Dec. 1845"

John T. Daniel b. Va. 1/29/1773
Ann T. Daniel b. Va. 7/31/1777
James Andrew Daniel b. 8/22/1804
William Hannah Daniel b. 12/14/1808
Elizabeth Ann Daniel b. 9/14/1810
Jane Cunningham Daniel b. 1/13/1813, wife of J. B. Lennard
Mary Ann Daniel, wife of J. Billups b. 3/9/1817
Mrs. Ann T. Daniel, wife of J. T. Daniel, d. 7/15/1837

(John T. Daniel Bible contd....)

William H. Daniel, son of J. T. and Ann Daniel, d. 8/19/1837
Eliza A. King, wife of Thomas B. King and dau. of J. T. and
   Ann T. Daniel, d. 8/1836
Jane C. Lennard, wife of John B. Lennard and dau. of J. T. Daniel
   and Ann T. Daniel d. 10/14/1845

John T. Daniel and Ann T. Hannah m. 6/16/1803
Martha Ann, dau. of William H. and A. E. Daniel, b. 9/25/1828
John Webster, son of W. H. and A. E. Daniel, b. 12/29/1829
Oscar Adolphas Moore, son of W. H. and A. E. Daniel, b. 1/7/1834
William Hugh, son of W. H. and Eliza Adeline Daniel, b. 3/23/1836
Martha A. Daniel m. John Scott 11/14/1845
John T. Daniel d. 3/9/1845

Notes written on blank page in Bible:

"John T. Daniel had a sister Betsy or Eliza Ann Daniel who m.
William Redd. She lived in Prince Edward Co., Va. He was from
Buckingham Co. Children given in "History Redd Family" was mother
of cousin Morgan Smith, Birmingham, and mother of Wm. Redd of
Birmingham and his twin brother James of Columbus, Ga.

Another one of his sisters married Mr. Ellington of Washington,
Ga., they both died early and left two boys, Simeon and Bruce,
whom their uncle John T. Daniel reared. Simeon married Mary (I
think) Venable. Their children were Ike and Charlie and two
girls. Bruce married his own cousin Jane Daniel, daughter of
James Kelsie Daniel of near Greensboro, Ga. Bruce and Jane had
two daughters. Bell and Euphrasia. These girls both died
(unmarried) in Europe while studying there.

John T. Daniel had another sister who married Mr. Cunningham. She
died early and left one son Joseph whom John T. Daniel reared.
Joseph married Emily (I think) Alford. Their children, George,
John Daniel, Joe, Emily, Jane, Sally.

George was educated West Point, N. Y. married young lady of
Augusta, >Ga. John David Cunningham, a prominent lawyer of
Atlanta, Ga., married his cousin Cornelia Dobbins. Their oldest
son John married his own cousin Miss Shaw. Ruth died. There were
others, George, etc. John T. Daniel´s brothers were James Kelsie,
Cunningham, William (I think). James Kelsie Daniels children were
Jane, who married Bruce Ellington, Oliver Porter m. (1) Miss
Clark of Augusta, Ga. (II) m. Miss Victoria Cone only dau. of
Judge Cone of Greensboro. She afterwards married Joel Abbot
Billups of Madison, Ga. Joel Abbot Billups was son of John
Billups of Athens, Ga. and brother of Thomas Billups of Columbus,
Miss.

BENJAMIN F. PACE BIBLE

Marriages
Abraham J. Humphrys and Amanda C. Meadow 9/19/1851
Benjamin F. Pace and Amanda C. Humphreys 12/4/1856
John P. Jacoway and Carrie Lee Pace 10/2/1879
Joseph A. Bennett and Mary C. Pace 12/26/1880

(Benjamin F. Pace Bible, Marriages, contd....)

Robert S. Rodgers and Susie E. Pace 9/8/1886
Thomas Cumming and Leonorah H. Pace 6/26/1888
William P. Pace and Julia A. Street 6/14/1893
Ben L. Pace and Delia Able---
Robert H. Tatum and Sallie B. Pace 6/28/1899

Births
Mary C. Pace 3/25/1857   Walter Wood Pace 8/22/1864
Leonorah H. Pace 10/23/1858   Susie E. Pace 4/8/1867
William Peyton Pace 7/26/1860   Benjamin Long Pace 5/21/1871
Carrie Lee Pace 8/24/1862   Sallie Boys Pace 9/7/1874

Deaths
Dr. A. J. Humphrey 1/6/1856   May Asbury 7/3/1853
Martha Meadow 10/19/1874   Benjamin F. Pace 7/5/1892
Matilda Gordenhire? 11/2/1877   Amanda C. Pace 9/27/1911
James Meador 5/21/1831   William Peyton Pace 9/30/1921
                                  Walter Wood Pace 7/5/1926 at
                                    Oklahoma City

LEVI ABBET BIBLE

Levi Abbet b. 2/1/1812, d. 6/18/1885
Dosha Abbet b. 10/17/1811 d. 6/14/1888
Levi Abbet and Dosha Henderson m. 6/6/1888?
James D. Lafayette Abbet b. 3/8/1833 d. 12/1863
James Abbet b. 9/29/1862 d. 7/1863
Talitha Caroline Abbet b. 8/30/1835
William Pinckney Abbet b. 1/7/1838
Greenberry Abbet b. 2/7/1840 d. 7/29/1862 in the hospital in
   Petersburg, Va. (C.S.A.)
Starling Shadric Abbet b. 8/31/1842
Nancy Naomany ? Jane Abbet b. 1/24/1844
Jarvus? Marion Abbet b. 3/31/1847 d. 5/1865
Justen Kimsey Abbet b. 4/20/1849
William henderson b. 12/24/1824
Lyda Henderson b. 9/2/1812
William and Lyda Henderson m. -29/1843
Jared Henderson b. 12/24/1821
Elizabeth (Henderson) Parkson d. 1/18/1840
Elizabeth Henderson and Marcus Parkson m. 12/5/1830
Sarah Frances Henderson b. 7/26/1829
G. W. Henderson d. 9/21/1887
Elizabeth Henderson d. 11/2/1887
Nancy Henderson b. 4/17/1816
Henry Bugg b. 7/22/1816
Henry Bugg and Nancy Henderson m. 9/15/1837 or 1839
N. J. Satterfield d. 4/17/1887
Barbery Satterfield d. 4/13/1887
Jasper Henderson b. 5/31/1844
William Draton Bugg b. 4/6/1847 d. 8/31/1847
L. N. Smathers b. 11/16/1849

(Levi Abbet Bible contd....)

Sarah Henderson d. 7/21/1841
Sarah Henderson d. 9/6/1858
Thomas Henderson d. 9/2/1859
Henry Henderson b. 5/25/1864
Sarah Jane Williams b. 7/15/1861
Buemey? Williams b. 1/3/1865
Nancy F. Williams b. 7/15/1861

TIMOTHY BRICE BIBLE
Owner: Mrs. J. P. Bondurant, Athens, Ga.

Timothy Brice of Brooks Co., Ga. and Mary S. Fall of Coweta Co.,
Ga. m. 12/15/1866 at Senoia, Ga.

Sallie E. Brice and J. D. Butler--
Lucy Brice and J. M. Burnett--
J. M. Brannon and Jennie E. Brice 1/9/1901
R. J. Clower and Willie M. Brice 6/18/1901
George L. Bunch and Eliza Brice 5/1900
Frank C. Brice and Florine Faith 6/3/1908
J. T. Brice and Malta Matthews 12/28/1912
J. Sam Brice and Amy Peterson 3/25/1913
M. Louetta Brice and B. J. Spear--

Timothy Brice b. 10/4/1838	Timothy Brice 4/11/1910
Mary S. Fall 11/12/1847	Mary S. Brice 9/6/1904
Sallie E. Brice 1/15/1868	Sallie Brice 7/24/1906
Lucy Brice 11/16/1869	Eliza Brice 3/26/1904
Jennie E. Brice 9/10/1870	Henry M. Brice 9/24/1879
Willie M. Brice 5/18/1873	Charley Brice 6/4/1881
Eliza J. Brice 1/5/1875	Stella E. Brice 12/9/1887
Frank C. Brice 11/3/1876	James Burnett 10/11/1940
Henry M. Brice 12/13/1878	Lucy Brice Burnett 9/1/1941
Charley Price 7/20/1880	Dr. R. J. Clower 1/12/1942
J. Tom Price 8/30/1882	Florine Faith Brice 12/9/1942
Milton F. Brice 7/28/1884	Dr. J. M. Brannon 7/22/1942
Stella E. Brice 10/27/1886	Milton Fall Brice 11/1/1944
J. Sam Brice 10/16/1889	John Thomas Brice 3/13/1949
M. Louette Brice 10/27/1890	Frank Calvin Brice Jr. 4/22/1945
	Jennie Brice Brannon 5/18/1953

Francis S. Brice Sr. b. 3/4/1804 d. 1/26/1878
Elizabeth Annie Brice d. 9/14/1880
Calvin J. Fall b. 3/18/1815 d. 4/10/1879
Sarah B. Fall b. 9/21/1818 d. 1/10/1890

WILLIAM DICKINSON LUCKIE BIBLE
Owner: Dr. James Buckner, Birmingham, Ala.

"Judge William Dickinson Luckie b. Oglethorpe Co., Ga. and made
his home in Newton Co., Covington, Ga., during his adulthood. His
home stood on the site of the present Covington Post Office.
Judge Luckie, his wife, Eliza, and two sons, Charles Alexander
and Lorenzo Foster Luckie are buried in family plot, old section
Covington City Cemetery, in marked graves."

Marriages
William Dickinson Luckie and Eliza Buckner m. 6/23/1829
Alfred Tilghman Luckie and Lizzie Augusta Alexander m. in Athens,
    Ga. 4/30/1874, by Rev. Charles W. Lane
James Buckner Luckie and Eliza Imogene Fielder m. 2/15/1859 by
    Rev. James McKee
James Buckner Luckie and Susan Oliver Dillard m. 11/27/1866 by
    Rev. James McKee
William Dickinson Luckie and Mary Alice Rushton m. 2/5/1868 by
    Rev. Rufus K. Porter

Births
William Dickinson Luckie, son of James Luckie and Rebekah Lane,
    his wife, b. 9/2/1800 in Oglethorpe Co., Ga.
Eliza Buckner, dau. of Tilghman Buckner and Elizabeth Freeny,
    his wife, b. 10/13/1807
Children of William Dickinson Luckie and Eliza Buckner, his wife:

Elizabeth Luckie b. 8/27/1831
James Buckner Luckie 7/16/1833 in Newton Co., Ga.
Rebecca Luckie b. 11/13/1834
Lorenzo Foster Luckie b. 5/27/1838
William Dickinson Luckie, Jr. b. 8/14/1842
Alfred Tilghman Luckie b. 6/16/1847
Eliza Urania Luckie b. 12/28/1850
Charles Alexander Luckie b. 10/23/1844

Children of Alfred Tilghman Luckie and Lizzie Augusta Alexander:
Lizzie Alexander Luckie b. Athens, Ga. 2/1/1875

Deaths
Charles Alexander Luckie 8/6/1845
Eliza Buckner, wife of William D. Luckie, 5/11/1856
Lorenzo Foster Luckie d. from wounds recd in battle of
    Petersburgh, Va. 7/30/1864
William Dickinson Luckie 1/3/1870
Eliza Urania Luckie 11/27/1872, bur. in Atlanta, Ga.
Alfred Tilghman Luckie 2/8/1879
James Buckner Luckie 12/12/1908

ROBERT HENRY BIBLE

Robert and Celia Henry's marriage and children's ages:
Robert Henry and Celia Fields m. 4/24/1785.
Ages of our children:
Mary Henry b. 5/12/1786   Temperance Henry b. 4/16/1798

(Robert Henry Bible contd...)

Lydia Henry b. 2/5/1788   Liza Henry b. 4/22/1800
Loucey Henry b. 11/26/1789   Robert Henry b. 9/2/1803
Nancey Henry b. 12/24/1791   Jane Henry b. 10/31/1806
Joel Henry b. 11/27/1793   Celia Henry b. 11/30/1809
William Henry b. 4/22/1796   Dau. Mutual b. 5/8/1813
                                 Theophilus Henry b. 7/31/1816

BUTLER WILLIAMS BIBLE

Butler Williams b. 4/23/1799 d. 2/15/1854 m. 8/19/1824 Sarah
Williams, b. 5/28/1809. d. 2/12/189-. Their dau., Luticia
Williams b. 2/23/1833 d. 11/19/1851 m. 8/31/1848 Crayton Dickson.
Their dau., Luna Arramenta Dickson b. 8/1/1849 d. 12/20/1879
Arlington, Tarrant Co., Tx. m. 4/4/1867 James Daniel Cooper.

Marriages
Butler Williams and Sarah Williams 8/19/1824
Martha A. Williams and W. J. Jeter 6/26/1844
Luticia Williams and Crayton Dickson 8/31/1849
S. G. Williams and R. J. Haden 11/8/1849
Benjamin F. Williams and Terecia Haden 12/13/185-
Nathaniel Black and Sarah Williams 7/30/1855
James D. Cooper and Luna A. Dickson 4/4/1867
James D. Cooper and Mary F. Thomas 1/20/1881
James N. Cooper and Laura Boulware 12/13/1896
Nathaniel Black and Sarah Williams 7/30/1855

Births
James D. Cooper 10/12/1841
Luna A. Dickson 8/1/1849
Daniel Dickson Cooper, son of J. D. and L. A. Cooper 4/3/1868
James N. Cooper, son of J. D. and L. A. Cooper, 2/8/1870
William David Cooper, son of J. D. and L. A. Cooper 4/10/1872
Martha Luticia, dau. of J. D. and L. A. Cooper 1/28/1874
John Marvin Cooper, son of J. D. and L. A. Cooper 7/17/1878
Oscar Thomas Cooper, son of J. D. and Mary Cooper, 3/26/1882
Horace Wyatt Cooper, son of J. D. and Mary Cooper, 3/19/1883
Luke W. Jeter 9/19/1845
Luna Arramenta Dickson 8/1/1849
Benjamin R. Williams, son of S. G. and R. J. Williams 11/12/1850
Sherman O. Williams 2/25/1852
Sarah B. Williams, dau. of S. G. and R. J. Williams, 11/15/1852
James D. Cooper 10/12/1884
James Newton Cooper 2/8/1870

Deaths
Martha Luticia, dau. of J. D. and L. A. Cooper, 6/3/1875, age
  16 mos., 6 days
Luna A. Cooper, wife of J. D. Cooper, 12/20/1879, age 30 yrs, 4
  mos., 20 days
Daniel D. Cooper, son of J. D. and L. A. Cooper, 8/15/1891, age
  23 yrs., 4 mos., 12 days
Martha A. Williams 8/9/1846
Lydia Williams 5/1831
Sarrah G. Williams 2/12/1846
Butler Williams, Jr. 5/28/1849

294

(Butler Williams Bible contd....)

Luticia Dickson, dau. of Butler and Sarah Williams, 11/19/1851, age 19 yrs., 9 mos., 29 days
Luke W. Jeter a "solger" of the Confederate States 6/10/1862 at the Hospital in Columbus, Miss.
Butler Williams 2/15/1854, age 54 yrs., 9 mos., 23 days

JONAS SHIVERS BIBLE
Owner: Martha Milner, Barnesville, Ga.

Marriages
Jonas Shivers and Martha M. Denson 2/1/1821
John W. Coppage and Eliza Tucker 7/15/1834
Jonathan J. Milner and Sarah M. D. Shivers 9/18/1839
Jonas Silvers and Sarah M. Tucker, wid. of John Tucker, decd, 10/28/1824
Christopher C. Shivers and Sarah A. E. Turner 11/18/1849
Jonas Cowin Shivers and Sarah C. Smith 5/5/1853
Barnaby Shivers and Mary Elizabeth Sappington 10/27/1853
Arthur W. Smith and Eunice Shivers 11/2/1854
Barnaby Shivers and Dorothy Hardaman 7/5/1855

Births
Jonas Shivers, son of Jonas and Patience, his wife, b. 10/14/1750 in Isle of Wight Co., Ga.
Lilory Shivers, dau. of Barnaby Godwin and Wilkinora, his wife, b. 12/22/1750
Barnaby Shivers, son of Jonas Shivers and Lilory, his wife, b. 7/29/177- in Va.
Rachel Cowen, dau. of George Cowen and Mary, his wife, b. 9/15/1780 in N. C.
Jonas Shivers, son of Barnaby Shivers and Rachel his wife, b. 8/9/1801
Martha M. Denson, dau. of John E. Denson and Sarah his wife, b. 8/9/1801
Sarah W. Milner, dau. of John H. Milner and Eunice his wife, b. 11/13/1801
Eliza Tucker, dau. of John Tucker and Srah W. Milner his wife, b. 6/10/1820
Sarah M. D. Shivers, dau. of Jonas Shivers and Martha M. Denson, his wife, b. 11/12/1821
Christopher C. Shivers, son of Jonas Shivers and Sarah W. Milner, his wife, b. 3/29/1828
Barnaby Shivers, son of Jonas Shivers and Sarah W. Milner, his wife, b. 7/19/1829
Jonas Cowin Shivers, son of Jonas Shivers and Sarah W. Milner, his wife, b. 3/27/1831
Lilory Rachel Shivers, dau. of Jonas Shivers and Sarah W. Milner, his wife, b. 10/23/1832
Eunice Shivers, dau. of Jonas Shivers and his wife, Sarah W. Milner, b. 1/25/1836
Jabez S. Shivers, son of above, b. 9/3/1837
Washington L. Shivers, son of Jonas Shivers and Sarah R. Kendrick, his wife, b. 1/11/1841
Francis M. Shivers, son of above, b. 10/3/1842
Zachary T. Shivers, son of above, b. 6/24/1845

(Jonas Shivers Bible contd....)

William Thomas Shivers, son of above, b. 1/22/1849
Cornelia R. Randolph, dau. of above, b. 10/22/1851

Deaths

Martha M. Shivers 11/12/1821	Rachel Shivers 11/29/1830
Lilory Shivers 8/28/1825	Sarah W. Shivers 9/16/1837
Jonas Shivers 11/12/1826	Barnaby Shivers 12/31/1851
William Thomas Shivers 8/16/1850	

John Kendrick 2/17/1843, aged abt 82 yrs.
Cornelia Rebecca Randolph Shivers 7/7/1854
Mary W. Shivers 12/23/1854
Jonas Shivers 7/28/1861
Francis Marion Shivers 8/4/1861
Washington Lafayet Shivers 7/4/1862 in the hospital at
   Washington, Ark. in defense of his country
Jabez T. Shivers 12/19/--in Pike Co., in his 18th yr. while in
   defense of his country
Sarah R. Shivers 5/19/1867
Eliza Coppage 10/24/1893

Paper included in Bible:
Barnaby Shivers, son of Jonas Shivers and Lilory, his wife, b.
   7/29/1775 in Va., Isle of Wight Co.
Rachel Cowin, dau. of George Cowin and Mary his wife, was b. in
   Rowan Co., N. C. 9/15/1780
D. 11/9/1830 Mrs. Rachel Shivers, consort of Barnaby Shivers,
   aged 50 yrs., 2 mos., 4 days, a member of the Baptist Church.

JOSEPH M. STAMPS BIBLE of Carroll Co., Ga.
Owner: Mrs. Carrie McDonald, Campbell, Texas

Births

J. M. Stamps 7/20/1850	James Olin Stamps 9/13/1889
Z. B. Stamps 1/22/1856	Mattie Lou Stamps 10/5/1892
R. G. T. Stamps 6/10/1882	Joseph David Stamps 8/22/1893
Carrie E. Stamps 12/17/1884	Bessie Novela Stamps 12/20/1901
Savannah Estelle 9/17/1887	Manuel Lee Stamps 4/26/1903

Marriages

Dutch Stamps and Tabbie Hendrix 12/28/1875
Carrie Stamps and Keake Johnson 10/18/1901
Rogert G. T. Stamps and Mollie Bell 12/25/ 1904
Mattie Stamps and Henry Johnson 7/10/1910
J. O. Stamps and Lillian Kirk 11/3/1918
Bessie Stamps and Walter Johnson 10/12/1919

Deaths

J. M. Stamps 8/7/1908
Z. B. Stamps 11/24/1918
Estelle Stamps 11/25/1918

```
                WHORTON FLETCHER BALLARD BIBLE
          Owner: Grace Nations, Centralhatchie, Ga.


Whorton Fletcher Ballard b. 3/5/1822 d. 12/25/1860 m. Sarah Ann
  Stamps Ballard, b. 1/15/1823, d. 11/27/1879. Their Children:

Mary Frances Ballard b. 3/22/1850
James Madison Ballard b. 8/3/1852
Thomas Parks Ballard b. 11/2/1853
Martha Adaline Ballard b. 2/2/1855

Isom m. Lula 5/17/1905
Thomas Ballard m. Mary E. McCaw 11/9/1876. Their Children:
William Fletcher b. 2/6/1878        Magie b. b. 9/10/1886
Robert L. b. 1/26/1880              Jessie Owen b. 1/24/1889
Thomas Isom b. 12/5/1881            Josie A. b. 1/20/1893
Howard Volly b. 4/14/1884          M. Hubert b. 8/29/1901
                                    Emma Lou b. 12/28/1906


                    JAMES BALLARD BIBLE
          Owner: Mrs. C. A. Goodman, Navasota, Texas


James Ballard b. 7/13/1804
Mary Ballard b. 5/15/1804  Their Children:

Reubin Ballard b. 10/16/1823     Samuel Ballard b. 8/4/1830
Ellinder M. Ballard b. 12/4/1826  Elizabeth Ballard b. 7/25/1835
Harriett Ballard b. 10/24/1828   William K. Ballard b. 8/28/1838

Harriet Ballard m. James Lee 9/26/1847. James Lee b. 12/16/1809.
Their children:
Robert E. Lee b. 6/27/1848       Mary Etta Lee b. 1/25/1855
James Lee b. 4/11/1850           William Lee b. 8/22/1858

Elizabeth Ballard m. Greenberry A. Lee b. in 1819. Their
  Children:
Richard B. Lee b. 5/14/1858      Robert E. Lee b. 2/2/1865
James Henry Lee b. 5/2/1860      Ellen Lee b. 4/7/1871
Mary Josephine Lee b. 6/11/1862


                    JOHN BALLARD BIBLE
          Owner: Mrs. John L. Askew, West Point, Ga.


John Ballard and Mary Continent of Virginia
Joseph Ballard b. 4/17/1735
Jesse Ballard b. 11/18/1737
Rebecca Ballard b. 8/19/1738, d. 5/15/1818 m. Francis Shackleford
Anne Ballard b. 4/10/1740
Benjamin Ballard b. 2/27/1743, d. 6/16/1832
Joshua Ballard b. 12/25/1745, d. 1/19/1832, m. 1st Suffish Moor
  11/27/1787, m. 2nd Susannah Barkesdale 7/15/1795
Susannah Ballard b. 3/23/1750


                         297
```

(John Ballard Bible contd...)

Mary Ballard b. 11/17/1753

Rebecca Ballard m. Francis Shackleford
Willoughby Shackleford 12/30/1765
Francis Shackleford b. 9/23/1773 d. 7/21/1805 at Sullivan's
    Island, S. C., age 31
Sarah Shackleford 9/11/1775
George Shackleford 6/17/1779 Onslow Co., N. C., d. 1/31/1852
    Pintala, Ala., m. in Montgomery Co., N. C. 5/23/1824 to Annette
    Jeter
Daniel Shackleford 9/9/1781
Mary Shackleford 6/17/1784 d. 4/13/1874 m. William Bethea

JOHN WESLEY BALLARD BIBLE
Owner: I. N. Ballard, Carrollton, Ga.

John Wesley Ballard's father, Wesley Ballard, son of Whorton and
    Saloma Ballard
Saloma Ballard nee Saloma Redwine, a German
Winnie Ballard, nee Winnie Floyd, dau. of Eli Floyd, 3rd son of
William Floyd of N. Y., signed Declaration of Independence
7/4/1776. Eli Floyd's wife was Sarah King, dau. of Richard
Bradford and Martha Bradford, nee Threadpeth.
J. W. Ballard's father, Wesley Ballard, son of Whorton and Saloma
Ballard, nee Saloma Redwine. His mother, Winney Ballard nee
Winnie Floyd.

Wesley Ballard b. 5/10/1803   William L. b. 8/20/1834
Winny Ballard b. 2/27/1811   John W. b. 12/7/1845
Owen R. b.7/10/1832   Benjamin O. b. 9/9/1847

Millie A., (wife of John W. Ballard above), b. 8/24/1855
John Wesley b. 12/23/1875
Isaac Newton b. 9/26/1889
Cora (wife of John Wesley above) b. 7/10/1874

Marriages
John W. Ballard and Mildred A. Ingram 4/12/1871 by David Moore,
    M. G.
J. W. Ballard and Laura Cora Price 7/11/1901 by H. Ashmore, Esq.
Isaac Newton and F. Virginia Young 6/30/1912
son, William N. and Minnie Robinson, 7/1/1933
Woodrow Ballard and Margaret Bradley 7/15/1947
J. Wesley Ballard and Carrie Lancaster 1/15/1905 by Rev. E. E.
    Robinson

Deaths
O. R. Ballard 12/14/1857   Carrie Ballard 11/23/1954
William L. Ballard 5/26/1860 Carrie Mae Ballard 4/4/1920
Wesley Ballard 7/30/1872   Mildred Ann Ballard 6/1/1900
Winnie Ballard 3/28/1890   John W. Ballard 8/25/1932

THOMAS MCKOY BIBLE
Owner: Mrs. Lillie Stewart, Atlanta, Ga.

Catharine b. 1/27/1772
Thomas McKoy 10/15/1770
Polly Anna d. 8/23/1826
Martha McKoy d. 3/3/1826
John McKoy d. 8/23/1830
Thomas McKoy Sr. d. 9/27/1846
Elizabeth b. 1792
Marthy McKoy b. 1/5/1790

John McKoy b. 3/22/1797
Benjamin McKoy b. 1/26/1801
Sary McKoy b. & d. 6/4/1802
Thomas McKoy b. 3/18/1804
Polly McKoy b. 11/22/1806
T. James McKoy b. 8/7/1811-
    d. 1/19/1842
Catherine McKoy b. 11/29/1814
Elizabeth McKoy b. 4/22/1792

WILLIAM HENRY HUDSON BIBLE
Owner: Mrs. Evie Hudson, Douglasville, Ga.

Married 2/24/1870 Lucy Rebecca McKoy Hudson b. 11/23/1851,
    d. 6/8/1928 and
William henry Hudson b. 1/23/1845 d. 8/24/1926 Children:
Henry Still Hudson b. 12/20/1870 d. 1/26/1923
Mary Elizabeth Hudson Duncan b. 8/21/1872, d. 11/3/1931
Susan Polina Hudson b. 3/15/1874 d. 9/29/1874
Lucy Newman Hudson Richards b. 9/18/1875 d. 6/26/1911
Benjamin Franklin Hudson b. 12/1/1877 d. 4/1/1957
Albert Sidney Hudson b. 10/11/1879 d. 11/23/1944
Robert Lafayette Hudson b. 3/16/1881 d. 12/7/1938
Laura Weston Hudson Eidson b. 3/31/1883 d. 2/27/1920
William Homer Hudson b. 2/5/1885
Effie Lou Hudson Truett b. 8/21/1886, d. 2/14/1959
Martha Talala Hudson b. 5/7/1888, d.--
Frances Allan Hudson Brannon b. 10/9/1890, d. 7/22/1961
Ruby Lee Hudson Gary b. 9/17/1893 d.--
Clifford McKoy Hudson b. 1/17/1897 d. 1/27/1966

CULLEN A. J. POPE BIBLE
Owner: Mrs. Herman J. Amos, Butler, Ga.

Births
Cullen A. J. Pope 3/7/1836
Laura Pope 1/23/1847
James M. Pope 2/3/1871
Herbert J. Pope 4/6/1876
William P. Pope 11/7/1879
Mintie Louise Adams b. Reynolds, Ga. 6/3/1880
Laura Wynelle Pope b. Butler, Ga. 11/6/1898
Ralph Jackson Pope b. Butler Ga. 2/24/1902
Louise Adams Pope b. Butler, Ga. 12/16/1906
Horace James Pope b. 5/21/1916 Butler, Ga.
Alicenel Amos b. Butler, Ga. 7/30/1922
Lewise Carol Amos b. Butler, Ga. 9/26/1925
Kathryn Pope Amos b. 4/21/1927 Butler, Ga.
Mary Joan Pope 4/2/1935 Atlanta, Ga.

(Cullen A. J. Pope Bible, Births, contd.....)

Richard Jackson Pope 10/14/1936 Atlanta, Ga.
James Chandler Pope 10/19/1944 Gainesville, Ga.
Joe David Pope 11/14/1949 Gainesville, Ga.
Pattie Jane Pope 7/20/1955 Carrollton, Ga.
Henry Dawson Moore IIII 11/8/1947 Washington, Ga.
Carol Paige Mercer 3/6/1954 Florida
Stephen Harvey Mercer 10/22/1955 Brunswick, Ga.
Richard Michael Williams 1/26/1957 Gainesville, Ga.
Mary Kathleen Williams 9/17/1958 Mannhem-Kaefectal, Germany
Allison Marie Williams 1/12/1969 Dalton, Ga.
Kathryn Angela Pope 9/14/1958 Atlanta, Ga.
Richard Mark Pope 7/27/1959 Gainesville, Ga.
Jennifer Anne Pope 3/16/1961 Gainesville, Ga.
William Ralph Pope 5/14/1969 Gainesville, Ga.
Kerrie Heather Moore 10/12/1970 Brunswick, Ga.
William Marcus Williams 11/12/1959 Ft. Riley, Kansas

Marriages
Cullen A. J. Pope and Laura Beeland 10/22/1868 Taylor Co., Ga.
Herbert J. Pope and Mintie Louise Adams 4/11/1897 Columbus, Ga.
James Herman Amos and Laura Wynelle Pope 9/8/1921 Butler, Ga.
Ralph Jackson Pope and Mary Ocie Rich 8/3/1929 Atlanta, Ga.
Lewise Adams Pope and John Alen 7/13/1940 Atlanta, Ga.
Horace James Pope and Jessie Evelyn Chandler 12/25/1941 at
  Fayetteville, Ga.
Alicenel Amos and Henry Dawson Moore 11/24/1945 Atlanta, Ga.
Kathryn Pope Amos and Joseph Burford Mercer 11/23/1949 Butler
Mary Joan Pope and William Rogers Williams 5/5/1956 Gainesville
Richard Jackson Pope and Janet Adams McGarrity 10/12/1957
  Elberton, Ga.
James Chandler Pope and Susan Douglas May 8/10/1968 Valdosta, Ga.
Henry Dawson Moore III and Mary Beth Land 1/2/1970 Jacksonville,
  Fla.

Deaths
C. A. J. Pope 2/8/1896 Butler, Ga.
Laura Beeland Pope 4/20/1911 Butler, Ga.
James M. Pope 6/23/1871
William T. Pope 8/31/1880
Herbert Jackson Pope 9/24/1915 Macon, Ga.
John D. Allen 6/21/1950 Atlanta, Ga.
Lewise Pope Allen 7/30/1954 Bremen, Ga.
Lewise Carol Amos 10/30/1929 Butler, Ga.
James Herman Amos 8/22/1958 Butler, Ga.
Joe David Pope 2/26/1952 Atlanta, Ga.
Joseph B. Mercer 12/12/1964 Brunswick, Ga.
Mintie Louise Adams Pope 1/21/1967 Gainesville, Ga.
Horace James Pope 11/27/1970 Gainesville, Ga.

JAMES ANTHONY ADAMS BIBLE
Owner: Mrs. James Herman Amos, Butler, Ga.

Births
James Anthony Adams 3/3/1842 Talbot Co., Ga.
Martha An Elizabeth Johnson 9/23/1843 Macon Co., Ga.
Enoch Stephen Adams 8/26/1866 Taylor Co., Ga.
Dora Elizabeth Adams 1/12/1868 Taylor Co., Ga.
James Madison Adams 5/26/1873 Reynolds, Ga.
Mintie Louise Adams 6/3/1880 Reynolds, Ga.
Sarah Rebecca Adams 9/27/1870 Taylor Co., Ga.
Vandeline Judson Adams 2/15/1883 Reynolds, Ga.
Herbert Jackson Pope b. 4/6/1876 Butler, Ga.

Laura Wynelle Pope 11/6/1898 Butler, Ga.
Ralph Jackson Pope 2/24/1902 Butler, Ga.
Lewise Adams Pope 12/16/1906 Butler, Ga.
Horace James Pope 5/31/1916

Marriages
James A. Adams and Martha A. E. Johnson 10/16/1865 Taylor Co., Ga
William M. Goodwin and Dora E. Adams 10/18/1885 Reynolds, Ga.
William M. Musselwhite and Sarah Rebecca Adams 3/5/1890, Reynolds
J. A. Adams and Sallie H. Lawrence 2/10/1892 Guyton, Ga.
Herbert J. Pope and Mintie L. Adams 4/11/1897 Columbus, Ga.
James M. Adams and Susie Paschal 12/27/1904 Eatonton, Ga.
V. Judson Adams and Annie Cobb Andrews 7/1910 Atlanta, Ga.

Deaths
Martha An Elizabeth Adams, wife of James A. Adams, d. in
   Reynolds, Ga. 7/19/1887
Sallie H. Adams, wife of J. A. Adams, d. Savannah, Ga. 6/20/1892
James A. Adams d. Reynolds, Ga. 12/6/1895
Dora E. Goodwin d. Panhandle 8/24/1898

Mintie Louise Adams Pope, wife of Herbert J. Pope, d. 6/21/1967
   Gainesville, Ga.

V. Judson Adams d. 10/5/1968 Houston, Texas

PARMENAS HAYNES BIBLE
Owner: Mrs. Sarah Jane Haynes LeSueur

Parmenas, son of Parmenas and Delia Haynes, b. 3/11/1783
Jane Haynes, dau. of John and Susannah Phelps b. 2/1789
Parents of:

Polly Eliza Haynes b. 5/27/1808   Lucy Phelps Haynes b. 1/15/1821
John Phelps Haynes b. 1/4/1812   Robert Henry Haynes b.2/17/1823
Delia Ann Haynes b. 6/22/1815   Sarah Jane Haynes b. 6/21/1825
William Glenn Haynes b. 5/1/1818   Richard Parmenas Jasper
                                          Haynes b. 9/3/1827

Parmenas Haynes d. 1849
Jane, his wife, d. 11/2/1844

DAVID HODGES Of Oconee Co.
Owner: Mrs. John W. Cash, Bogart, Ga.

Dave Hodges m. Mrs. Elizabeth A. Henden 3/10/1889 by Rev. J. R.
  Pickens
Joseph Hodges m. Sarah Epps 2/2/1818

Deaths
Sarah Epps Hodges 10/27/1845   S. E. A. Hodges 8/22/1900

William Hodges b. 1/16/1811 d. 3/20/1867 m. 10/18/1836 Mrs.
  Anna W. Tompkins
Nancy Smith Floyd Hodges, wife, b. 11/16/1815 d. 1/14/1871, dau.
  of Silas and Martha Dorsey Floyd. Their Children, b.
Sandersville, Washington Co., Ga.:

James William Hodges 11/16/1837-5/17/1838
Araminta Elizabeth Hodges 9/5/1839-7/30/1859 m. Frederick Tebeau
  6/17/1856
Martha Hodges 10/5/1841-12/10/1917 m. Stephen Benjamin Jones
  8/21/1860

GEORGE WASHINGTON POWELL BIBLE
Owner: Mrs. Aubrey Sanders
991 Magnolia St., Macon, Ga.

Births
George Washington Powell 4/25/1849   George Hendrix Powell
Sara Eliza Kinchen Powell 6/9/1852   12/11/1885
Cora Lee Powell 1/8/1872   Effie Claude Powell 1/12/1889
Lillie May Powell 7/18/1876   Mary Washington Street
Georgia Cornelia Powell 2/14/1878   4/16/1891
Herbert Edgar Powell 9/9/1880   Jimmie Elizabeth Powell
Ozrow Kinchen Powell 7/11/1883   5/13/1893

302

(George Washington Powell Bible contd....)

Deaths
George Washington Powell 12/8/1919
Sara Eliza Kinchen Powell 11/23/1931
Ozrow Kinchen Powell 9/22/1949

JOHN W. HOOPER BIBLE
Owner: Mrs. Julius Y. Talmadge
Athens, Ga.

John W. Hooper b. 12/23/1797
Sarah A. Word, wife, b. 7/17/1809. Their Children:

Eliza E. Hooper b. 5/30/1828   John W. Hooper Jr. b. 10/13/1833
Jane E. Hooper 9/22/1829   Sarah Joyce Hooper b. 6/6/1836
Robert M. Hooper b. 9/18/1831   William Thos. Hooper b. 1/7/1840

WILLIAM JARRETT BIBLE

Marriages
William Jarrett to Martha F. Davis 1/28/1848

Births
William Jarrett 1/14/1812
Martha F. 12/24/1830
Their Children:

William Allen Jarrett b. 12/1/1848
Mary Elizabeth Jarrett b. 8/21/1850
Whitson Perce Jarrett b. 11/14/1852
Frances Nichols Jarrett b. 8/13/1854
Martha Leola Jarrett b. 6/18/18-

Deaths
William Allen Jarrett 12/5/1848
Martha Frances Jarrett 8/24/1854, 24 yrs., 8 mos.
Martha Jarrett 4/4/1857
Nicholas Jarrett 3/7/1815
William Jarrett 4/21/1869
John Streetman 2/4/1874

Marion Howel Streetman m. M. E. Streetman 12/25/1870
M. Leola Streetman b. 6/18/1873

303

ROBERT BENJAMIN TUCK BIBLE
Owner: W. B. Tuck, Athens, Ga.

Robert B. Tuck b. 2/16/1832
Mrs. Mary Tuck b. 10/2/1831
William Boid Tuck, son of above, b. 4/21/1854
James Thomas Duglas Tuck b. 9/31/1855
E. F. Hardman b. 11/30/1835
John Robert Hardman b. 7/30/1868
Mary Rintrow b. 10/20/1831

Robert B. Tuck and Miss Mary Pinson m. 1/15/1852
Robert B. Tuck d. 9/1/1861
E. F. Hardman and Mrs. Mary Tuck m. 10/11/1867
John Robert Hardman, son of above, b. 7/31/1868
Julien Mandier Hardman b. 12/28/1875
(Robert Benjamin Tuck Bible contd....)

Sara Ida Tuck b. 8/21/1857
W. B. Tuck and Sarah Ida Bonds m. 11/14/1874

BOYD AND PRUDENCE TUCK BIBLE
Of Jackson Co., Ga.
Owner: W. B. Tuck, Athens, Ga.

Susannah P. Tuck b. 2/4/1830
Robert Bennett Tuck b. 2/16/1832
Marston Thomas Tuck b. 4/17/1834
Nancy Duberry Tuck b. 5/21/1836
William Boyd Tuck b. 1/1/1839
Mary Virginia Tuck b. 2/19/1841
Joseph Edward Tuck b. 7/4/1843

Victory S.--Tuck b. 12/6/1845
Frances Ann Mericia Tuck b. 3/21/1848
Eliza Anna Tuck b. 5/27/1850
Fransina Elizabeth--Tuck b. 9/12/1853
Emma Thomson Tuck b. 2/3/1856

Annerh Erlizer Tuck b. 4/28/1858
Joseph Edwin Pinson Trible b. 2/15/1846

HENRY JENNINGS BIBLE

Sons of Giles P. Jennings and Sudie Thompson:

Robert M. Jennings b. 9/15/1870 Heirs-Tallie B. Mrs. Grady
   Flanigan, w. (Elenora Todd)
Ben S. Jennings b. 1/30/1873 wife (Mrs. Leana Pledger Hamilton)
W. R. & W. C. Jennings b. 5/15/1875 wife, W. L. heirs, Alva
Mattie T. Jennings b. 10/17/1878 Ewell & Herman Bolton, heirs
E. H. Jennings b. 12/6/1873 Serene, G. H., & Wm. Benajah
Heirs of W. R. Jennings, Gladis, Vera, Pattie, Margaret and
   Walter. Wife, Alma

GEORGE KESLER BIBLE
Owner: Mrs. Oliver Kesler
Ashland, Ga.

Births
George Kesler 6/1/1809
Polly Kesler 9/26/1812
Marthy Emaline Kesler 4/15/1833
Mary Jane Kesler 9/9/1834
James Monroe Kesler 4/19/1836
Sarah S. Kesler 9/20/1837
Nancy H. Kesler 1/8/1839
William H. Kesler 4/2/1840
Rowena Frances Kesler 11/28/1841
Eliza Ann Cordellia Kesler
  8/11/1859
Mary J. Kesler d. 1/9/1835

Barbara Ann Kesler 2/-
Luza Ann Catharine Kesler
  2/14/1845
Julia Ann Clementine Kesler
  9/2/1846
George W. Kesler 9/6/1848
Russel Renoe Kesler 3/27/1850
Oliver Parks Kesler 1/1/1852
C. T. Kesler 10/18/1853
Samuel Jackson Kesler
  12/13/1855

R. R. KESLER BIBLE
Owner: Mrs. R. R. Kesler, Ashland, Ga.

Russel R. Kesler b. 3/27/1850
Annie Hassletine Kesler b. 12/31/1853
Lucy Bernettie Kesler 11/3/1873
Roena Enna David Kesler 10/20/1876
Russell Dawson Kesler 10/24/1878
Baby 11/20/1888

Marriages
R. R. Kesler and A. H. Payne 11/20/1872
Emma D. Kesler and Elbert B. Wells 2/17/1894
Dawson Kesler and Dora Kelly 8/4/1907

JOHN GREEN PITTMAN BIBLE

Births
John Green Pittman 10/3/1782
Polly Moore, his wife, 11/8/1781
John Moore Pittman 4/28/1812
    John's Children:
Robert William Taylor Pittman 12/9/1834

Marriages
John G. Pittman to Polly Moore 1/24/1804 by Hon. Thomas Johnson
John Moore Pittman to Mary Ann Church Jones 1/21/1834 by
  Sterling Mayer.

JOHN PORTERFIELD Of Madison Co., Ga.
Owner: Mrs. Nancy E. Hale, Athens, Ga.

John Porterfield b. 5/4/1815
Biddy Porterfield b. 1/5/1820

Malita Jane b. 11/20/1839   Joice Amanda Arminda b. 2/21/1847
Martha Harriet b. 4/18/1841   James Allen b. 12/15/1848
Tempy Caroline b. 2/26/1843   Nancy Amaline b. 10/12/1850
Tabatha Elizabeth b. 6/14/1845 Mary Frances Parale P.
                                    b. 8/30/1852

MRS. C. F. NOLES BIBLE
Eastman, Ga.

Deaths
William Taylor Noles 10/1843   Jonathan Noles 1/9/1891
Mary Louise Noles 11/5/1843   Mary Frances Noles decd
Wright Noles 4/7/1875   Jerome Charles Burch 2/20/1947
Sara Beatrice Noles 3/14/1882   age 39

JOSHUA HAMMOND RANDOLPH BIBLE
Owner: Annie R. Howard, Athens, Ga.

Joshua H. Randolph b. 8/15/1805 m. Nancy Oliver 10/11/1827,
   d. 12/26/1860
Nancy Oliver b. 3/28/1808, d. 11/13/1877
John W. Randolph b. 6/23/1828 d. 9/25/1847
Nancy A. Randolph b. 5/18/1833
Mary A. Randolph b. 5/18/1833
Joshua W. Randolph b. 9/29/1835 d. 9/16/1858
James E. Randolph b. 10/31/1835
Susan J. Randolph b. 6/17/1839
Hilliard J. Randolph b. 5/10/1841
Susan C. Randolph b. 10/9/1843

Fannie E., youngest child of Joshua H. and Nancy Randolph, m.
   Wiley C. Howard 1/22/1867 and d. 12/13/1925
James E. Randolph m. Elizabeth C. Thompson 2/3/1876
Francis E. Randolph b. 1/22/1849
Nettie V. Howard, dau. of Wiley C. & Fannie E. Hoard b. 2/16/1868
Annie R., dau. of above, b. 10/20/1869
Ida Pauline, dau. of above, b. 9/2/1873
James Frank, son of above, b. 3/6/1878 m. Doyle Hinton 4/1914
Lucy Fannie Howard b. 11/19/1888
Minnie May Randolph b. 12/19/1881
Ida Pauline Howard m. Thomas Fletcher Comer 6/12/1895 and reared
   two daus., Martha Howard Comer and Frances Elizabeth Comer

(Joshua Hammond Randolph Bible contd....)

Joshua Hammond Randolph, son of James E. and E. C. Randolph,
   b. 8/12/1877, d. 2/28/1878
Fannie May Randolph, dau. of James E. and E. C. Randolph,
   b. 5/6/1879, d. 6/15/1880

R. G. SMITH BIBLE
Owner: Mrs. W. M. Saye, Athens, Ga.

R. G. Smith b. 6/13/1842
Martha Ann Seagraves b. 3/22/1844

Mary Elizabeth Smith b. 12/6/1870   Mitchel Smith b. 8/28/1880
Robert Washington Smith b. 7/31/1872   Callie Smith b. 3/27/1882
Annie Susan Smith b. 1/19/1874   Nora Smith b. 11/8/1885
Martha Ella Smith b. 8/4/1875   Newton Anderson Smith
William Loyd Smith b. 7/13/1877   b. 12/28/1878

R. G. Smith d. 6/8/1898   Callie Smith Johnson d. 12/1/1911
Mitchel Smith d. 6/12/1906   William Loyd Smith d. 2/14/1919
Martha Ann Smith d. 2/12/1909

AUGUSTUS E. ROSS BIBLE
Of Eastman, Ga.

Russell Ross b. 2/8/1897
Mary An Amanda Ross b. 6/25/1919 Dodge Co.
John Samuel Bush b. 10/19/1937 Dodge Co.

PAGE WHITE & MARTHA BROWN WHITE BIBLE
Of Madison Co., Ga.
Owner: Mrs. Sarah A. Tolbert, Hull, Ga.

Elizabeth White b. 8/21/1777   Lucy White b. 4/23/1797
Isaiah White b. 11/10/1778   Stephen White b. 5/24/1787

Sarah Ann O'Kelly m. William A. Tolbert

J. E. RITCH BIBLE Of Athens
Owner: Mrs. Lula Ritch King, Athens, Ga.

J. E. Ritch m. N. J. Alexander 12/13/1855
A. L. King m. L. S. Ritch 12/20/1876

Births
J. E. Ritch 12/1827   Edward L. Ritch 6/3/1860
Mrs. W. J. Ritch 1/19/1835   John Lee Ritch 2/10/1866
Tullulah E. Ritch 11/21/1856   Katie Estelle Ritch 3/22/1870
Ida E. Ritch 4/11/1858   Joseph S. Ritch 2/27/1874

Deaths
Edward L. Ritch 11/1/1890 Aberline, Tx.
J. Lee Ritch 2/26/1900 Denver, Colorado
J. E. Ritch 6/17/1904 Athens, Ga.
Joseph S. Ritch 6/12/1908

JOHN B. WEST BIBLE
Of Buncombe Co., N. C. & Whitfield Co., Ga.

John B. West m. Nancy Griggs 1817
John B. West d. 11/1872

Births
Lucinda 9/3/1818   Andrew Jackson 6/15/1832
Celina 1/25/1821   Sophronia Adaline 10/1/1834
John H. 10/18/1822   Margaret Ann 9/6/1836
William W. 9/9/1825   Mirah Miranda 12/18/1839
Phidelia Siler 4/3/1827   Joseph Manson 7/23/1844

HOWELL STREETMAN BIBLE Of Athens

Note: All pages but one torn out

John M. Walker d. 4/25/1850
William Jarrett d. 4/21/1869

BOURKE SPALDING BIBLE Of Sapelo Island, Ga.

Bourke Spalding b. 2/8/1849 at "Avenel" Oglethorpe Co., homeplace
plantation., m. Ella P. Barrow 11/3/1874 in Athens by Rev. Josiah
Lewis, Jr.

Randolph Spalding, 1st son, b. 9/30/1879 on Sapelo Island
Clara Lucy, dau., b. 5/27/1881, Sapelo Island, d. 9/3/1881
Bourke Spalding d. 9/5/1884, at Sapelo

WILLIAM H. PURYEAR BIBLE
Owner: Mrs. J. D. Tribble, Athens, Ga.

William H. Puryer m. Lucy A. Christopher 7/4/1848
J. D. Tribble m. Ida J. Puryear 12/28/1897

Births
William H. Puryer 7/4/1824   Ida J. Puryer 10/28/1869
Lucy A. Puryear 3/9/1828   J. D. Tribble 7/16/1867

Deaths
William H. Puryer 5/28/1870
Lucy Ann Puryer 10/2/1855

GEORGE STOVALL BIBLE Of Greene Co.
Owner: J. Frank Stovall, Madison Co.

George Stovall m. Polly (Mary) Welburn 1/25/1794. Their Children:

William H. Ray and Patsey (Martha) G. Stovall m. 12/10/1811
David C. Culbertson and Sarah Stovall m. 6/15/1819
Littleberry Stovall and Mary Buchanan m. 6/14/1819
Robert Stovall and Eliza McSpa?---
Powhatan W. Stovall (1st) m. Temperance Bishop---
Powhatan W. Stovall (2d) m. Sarah Ann Crawford 11/16/1827
John Stovall m. Martha Bishop 12/22/1830
Ozier Stovall m. Julian Peek---
Columbus Watson m. Elba Stovall---

JOHN WALKER BIBLE Of Wilkes Co.
Owner: Mrs. George S. Mayne, Athens, Ga.

Births
John Walker b. Hampshire Co., Va. 12/7/1766, m. in Va. 1790 to
Martha Smith b. 11/17/1770. Their Children:

William Walker 1/3/1791   George Walker 3/12/1803
John Walker 5/12/1793   Richard Walker 5/13/1805
Taylor Walker 11/14/1795   Robert Walker 10/10/1807
James Walker 8/6/1798   Sophia Walker 8/13/1810
Nancy Walker 2/24/1801   Martha Walker 4/14/1813

Deaths
William Walker 9/25/1823   George Walker 9/11/1824
John Walker 3/1842   Richard Walker 8/1867
Taylor Walker 6/27/1817   Robert Walker 4/1882
James Walker 1876 in Ala.   Sophia Walker 10/1/1857
Nancy Walker 1874 in West Point

GEORGE REID BIBLE
Owner: Judge L. B. Moon, Jefferson, Ga.

George Reid m. Katherine Chambers 6/1767

Births
Margret 4/15/1768   Kathrina 8/19/1781
Jennet 12/11/1769   Samuel 11/12/1783
Alexander 8/19/1771   Elizabeth 9/13/1786
Henry 2/3/1773   Fanny 9/10/1787
George 11/27/1774   George Sr. 5/1746
Hannah 12/17/1776
Dau. b. dead 4/15/1778
Robert 4/24/1779

R. Reid d. 4/24/1813

RUSSELL ROSS BIBLE
Owner: Augustus E. Ross, Eastman, Ga.

Births
Russell Ross (Monroe Co.) 2/22/1834
Mary Ann Amanda Ross Pike Co. 8/8/1841
John Samuel Bush Ross Washington Co. 1/24/1860
Augustus C. Ross Monroe Co. 12/9/1865
Millie Ann Bush Ross Dodge Co. 6/29/1900
Ruby Amanda Ross 3/31/1920
Harold Augustus Ross 5/31/1922
Etta Louise Ross 12/13/1927

CAPT. PARMENAS HAYNES BIBLE
Rev. War Soldier of Bedford Co.,
Va. and Oglethorpe Co., Ga.

Henry Haynes, my father, was b. 12/24/1701, d. 12/2/1784
Parmenas Haynes b. 7/1/1742 m. Elizabeth Baber 12/15/1767 who was
b. 9/21/1749 d. 3/1/1813
          My first marriage was to Elizabeth Baber
Nancy Haynes b. 12/10/1768 m. 12/28/1797 Jesse Eley, her second
   marriage.
Robert Haynes b. 11/2/1770 m. 9/27/1794 to Lucy Phelps
Richard Haynes b. 3/5/1773 m. 7/4/1800 to Abi Ragen, dau. of
   Johnathan Ragen
Elizabeth Haynes d. 11/29/1779
Nancy Haynes m. 1st to James Shackleford 11/25/1797 of Bedford
   Co., Va.

(Parmenas Haynes Bible contd....)

Parmenas Haynes m. Delia Greer 12/2/1781, who was b. 10/31/1758, the second marriage to Delia Greer 12/2/1781, dau. of Aquilla Greer.
Salley Haynes b. 11/7/1785 m. 9/3/1807 Woody Jackson
Delia Haynes b. 2/10/1788 m. William Greer 3/24/1808
Polley Haynes b. 12/2/1794 m. 4/7/1812 John Thorington of Oglethorpe.
Jasper Haynes b. 11/3/1797 m. 5/17/--Lucy Slaten of Oglethorpe Co. who was b. 8/8/--
Henry Haynes b. 7/8/1800 d. 10/16/182-

JEANNETTE HOLLAND AUSTIN BIBLE
2018 Levgard Lane, Riverdale, Ga. 30296

Jeannette Holland b. 7/28/1936, Atlanta, Ga., dau. of Laurel Benjamin Holland and Marguerite Elizabeth Evans
m. 1st 4/25/1953 Edwin Gerald Stucki b. 8/17/1933, Conyers, Rockdale Co., Ga. (div. 6/28/1967) m. 2d Kenneth Milton mcCall 5/25/1975 Sandy Springs, Ga. (div. 5/5/1877) m. 3rd 5/13/1977 Jerry Franklin Austin, Jekyll Island, Glynn Co., Ga., the son of Louis Austin and Ruby Austin of Atlanta, Ga.
Children:
Suzanne Teri Stucki b. 3/27/1960
Christopher Lewis Austin b. 5/19/1978

CHARLES E. LAMBDIN BIBLE Of Pike Co.

Marriages
Charles Edwin Lambdin b. 3/28/1839 Alexandria, Va. d. 3/3/1888 m. 1st 12/25/1860 Martha Middlebrooks b. 9/5/1842 d. 3/24/1866; m. 2nd 9/10/1866 Annie Middlebrooks b. 1/14/1844

William Wallace Lambdin b. 10/25/1861 m. 12/24/1883 Annie Smith
Annie Lambdin b. 4/14/1832 m. 6/1/1904 Pierce Hammond

Births
James Madison Middlebrooks, father of Annie M. Lambdin, Malinda Stroud, mother of Annie M. Lambdin, b. 1809, d. 1894 Yatesville, Upson Co., Ga.
Child of Charles E. Lambdin and Martha Middlebrooks:
William Wallace Lambdin.
Children of Charles E. Lambdin and Annie Middlebrooks:
James Madison Lambdin 1/16/1863   Mary Mabel Gordon Lambdin
Annie Lambdin 4/14/1882   7/21/1877
Children of Annie Lambdin and Pierce Hammond:
Mary Hammond 3/20/1905   Chas. Lambdin Hammond 10/29/1917
Maud Hammond 4/29/1911   Alex. Dudley Hammond 11/3/1922
Pierce Hammond Jr. 3/7/1915

Deaths
Grace Lambdin, dau. of Wallace and Annie, d. 1/1/1885

THOMAS J. BROWN BIBLE
Owner: Emily Brown Edwards
Macon, Ga.

Thomas J. Brown's Book presented to him 6/16/1858 by his Father,
Sam. W. Brown

Marriages
Thomas J. Brown to Susan E. Dickey 5/1/1861

Births
Thomas Jefferson Brown 6/29/1838
Susan Ellen Brown 2/5/1843
Shadrach Willard Brown 3/25/1862

Marriages
Thomas Henry Brown to Martha Emily Crawford 8/1/1893 Dayton,
  Tenn.
Jefferson Crawford Brown to Elizabeth LaMotte 10/8/1921 Columbia,
  S. C.
Emily Louise Brown to Prentiss Stillwell Edwards 9/1/1923 Tampa,
  Fla.

Births
Thomas Henry Brown 8/25/1868 near Thomasville, Ga.
Mary Ellen Brown 1/28/1895, Dayton, Tenn.
Jefferson Crawford Brown 5/2/1896, Dayton, Tenn.
Emily Louise Brown 3/6/1906, Macon, Ga.
Jacqueline LaMotte Brown 5/14/1926, Tampa, Fla.
Mary Lane Edwards 9/20/1924-9/20/1925 Macon, Ga. Lived 8 hrs.
Prentiss Stillwell Edwards Jr. 10/3/1925, Tampa, Fla.
Mary Lane Edwards, 8/17/1927, Macon, Ga.
Crawford Brown Edwards, 6/26/1929, Macon, Ga.

Deaths
Thomas Jefferson Brown 11/25/1877
Susan Dickey Brown 1/5/1875
Thomas Henry Brown 8/28/1928 iN Tampa, Fla., bur. in Myrtle
  Hill Cemetery, Tampa, Fla.

On front page - Samuel Willard Brown 5/1/1811-3/4/1877 (dates
from tombstone in Gwaltney Cemetery)
Elizabeth Brown (2nd wife of S. W. Brown) 12/26/1813-6/1893

JOSEPH BLAIR BIBLE
Owner: Mrs. Regina Smith
Marietta, Ga.

Births
Joseph Blair 3/6/1801   Columbus Blair 11/9/1836
Elisebeth Blair 1/27/1808   James Blair 3/8/1839
Sarah Blair 4/17/1826   Albert Blair 6/4/1842

(Joseph Blair Bible, Births contd....)

Allen Blair 8/1/1828   Washington Blair 4/9/1845
Margaret Blair 5/17/1831   Joseph Alby Blair --/24/1852
-----Blair -/10/1834

Marriages

Joseph Blair to Elizabeth Stockton 12/28/1823
Martin McElwreath to Sarah Blair 10/26/1844
Charles James to Margaret Blair 9/19/1847
Allen Blair to Marindy Newbern 4/11/1850
Columbus Blair to Sarah M. Kidd 1/1/1857
Loyd Blair to Piety S. James 11/7/1855
Loyd Blair to Lell Kidd 8/15/1861
T. R.? Blair to Sara --- 6/3/1866

Deaths

Joseph A. Blair 6/7/1854, age 1 yr., 6 mos., 11 days
Piety S. Blair 9/17/1859
Albert Blair 5/8/1862, age 20 yrs., 4 mos., 2 days
Loyd Blair 12/1/1862, 29 yrs., 10 mos., 21 days
Joseph Blair 4/21/1871, 70 yrs., 1 mo., 15 days
Elisebeth Blair, wife of Joseph Blair, 7/13/1887, age 79 yrs.,
    5 mos., 16 days

WARNER LEE BELL BIBLE
Owner: Mrs. T. A. Lassetter
808 Lakeshore Drive
Lexington, Ky. 40502

Father - Warner Lee Bell, b. Carroll Co., Ga.
Mother - Mary Ella Thompson, b. Heard Co., Ga.

Marriages

Warner L. Bell of Bremen, Ga. to Mary E. Thompson of Bremen, Ga.
    11/25/1902 at Harner, by Rev. Marton Hankam. Wit: C. A. Thompson
    and others.
Emmett L. Bell to Aquer Roberta Cubbedge 8/14/1926
Pearl E. Bell to Chester M. Sharp 3/3/1927
Mary Louise Bell to Richard F. Korte 7/3/1941
Olive Grace Bell to Darling Dell Meadors 8/27/1944

Births

Warner L. Bell 6/7/1881   Lily Mae Bell 9/20/1907
Mary E. Bell 10/10/1882   Louise M. Bell 4/13/1909
Emmette L. Bell 10/4/1903   Ollie G. Bell 8/17/1914
Pearl E. Bell 7/15/1905   Pierce L. Bell 1/18/1918

Deaths

Lily Mae Bell 6/20/1908   Warner L. Bell 3/18/1968
Pierce L. Bell 12/4/1920   Richard F. Korte 4/6/1957
Emmette L. Bell 11/26/1967

313

Births

William Lassetter 3/6/1819
Parthenia L. Lassetter 6/3/1821
Sarah Ann Elizabeth Lassetter
  10/31/1840
Melissa Jane Lassetter 2/6/1842
Eustatia Lassetter 9/15/1843
Tabatha An Lassetter 8/6/1845
Leonora T. Lassetter 1/12/1849
Salina Oregon Lassetter 7/17/1847
Minerva Caroline Lassetter 1/6/1851
Martha Caldonia 12/22/1852
William Benjamin Horton 1/1/1892
Peyton Hewling Horton 10/1/1894

Amanda George Lassetter 9/17/1854
James Rufus Lassetter 7/28/1856
John G. W. Lassetter 7/2/1858
Wm. B. Lassetter 2/5/1860
Cheadle Lassetter 10/10/1861
Divine Lassetter 8/11/1863
Newton Allen Horton 9/14/1857
  in Pike Co., Ga.

Marriages

William Lassetter to Parthenia L. Brown 12/22/1839
Sarah Ann Elizabeth lassetter 1/8/1857
Eustatia Lassetter 12/22/1857 or 1859
Minerva Caroline Lassetter 11/26/1867
Salena Oregon Lassetter 12/17/1868
Tabatha Ann Lassetter 5/6/1869
Caldonia Lassetter 7/27/1871
Amanda G. Lassetter 12/3/1873
J. G. W. Lassetter to Miss Mollie E. Barnett 12/27/1883
E. Divine Lassetter to Newton A. Horton 2/9/1890

Deaths

Eustatia Jones 3/8/1864, 20 yrs., 6 mos., 23 days
Melissa J. Lassetter 9/9/1877, 37 yrs., 7 mos., 3 days
Lenora T. Lassetter 1/9/1880, 30 yrs., 11 mos., 27 days
Parthenia L. Lassetter, wife of William, 11/28/1883, 62 yrs., 5
  mos., 25 days
William Lassetter 2/16/1888, 68 yrs., 11 mos., 10 days
Newton A. Horton 12/29/1916
Mrs. N. A. Horton 6/1/1930
Clifford Almand Horton 5/11/1951
Lt. Col. William Benjamin Horton 1/20/1954

P. Crenshaw of Clark Co., Ala. m. S. McClinton of Clark Co.
9/4/1863 at S. McClinton's by M. E. King, J. P. Wit: John
Harrison; J. M. Perry

(Pleasant Crenshaw Bible contd....)

Births
Pleasant Crenshaw 6/4/1838   John M. Crenshaw 4/15/1871
Susan Crenshaw 3/12/1837   George M. Crenshaw 1/3/1873
Willie C. Crenshaw 6/2/1866   Una M. Crenshaw 1/27/1875
Annie E. Crenshaw 10/22/1867   J. Whit. Crenshaw 4/17/1876
M. Eliza Crenshaw 5/6/1869   Emmit R. Crenshaw 11/30/1877

Annie May Day 6/29/1896

Deaths
Emmitt R. Crenshaw 8/1878   John M. Crenshaw 1/12/1909
Willie Crenshaw Day 3/15/1897   Susan Crenshaw 1/20/1909
Pleasant Crenshaw 5/7/1904

Annie E. Crenshaw 7/14/1947   Una M. Crenshaw 7/14/1962
M. Eliza Crenshaw 8/7/1954   J. Whit. Crenshaw 8/14/1969
George M. Crenshaw 8/9/1964

E. S. HOLTAM BIBLE

E. S. Holtam, son of Specer Holtam and Nancy Holtam, b. 8/3/1783
--------d. 10/8/18-4
Emeline Hedrick, dau. of E. S. Holtam, 12/16/1907, age 77 yrs.,
   10 mos., 29

Births
Dolly James 3/13/1788   Caleb W. Muncrief 8/21/1846
Sarah James 7/13/1790   James Muncrief 11/28/1848
Mary An Muncrief 2/24/1844

Deaths
Spencer Jackson Holtam 1/20/1841
Malinda C. Moncrief, dau. of E. S. Holtam, 3/29/1850
Mary C. Flinn, dau. of E. S. Holtam, 2/9/1851
Sarah A. Holtam 9/27/1867, 77 yrs., 2 mos., 13 days

William J. Merrell b. 11/30/1811
Spencer J. Holtam b. 1/7/1818   Sarah Ann Holtam 12/14/1827
Abner S. Holtam b. 6/27/1820   Emily Jane Holtam 12/14/1827
Thomas J. Holtam b. 1/21/1823   Mary C. Holtam 2/27/1833
Malind C. Holtam 2/3/1826

Elijah S. Holtam d. 8/17/1868, 85 yrs., 14 days

Marriages
Abner S. Holtam 3/2/1843   Malinda C. Holtam 2/17/1842
William J. Merrell 1/9/1833   Sarah Ann Holtam 3/20/1845
Thomas J. Holtam 7/4/1844   Emeline Jane Holtam 1850
Mary Caroline Holtam 4/17/1849

315

IRA B. HOLTAM BIBLE
Owner: Ira Baker Holtam

Ira B. Holtam m. Annie E. Crenshaw at her home near Morvin (Clark Co., Ala.) 1/11/1885.

Ira B. Holtam b. 9/4/1864 Clark Co., Ala. d. 7/1952 m. 1/11/1885
Annie Crenshaw b. 10/22/1867 Clark Co., Ala., d. 7/14/1947
Lenora B. Holtam b. 12/7/1885 Clark Co., Ala. d. 10/31/1970 m. 3/2/1912
Nece Holtam b. 12/24/1887 Clark Co., Ala. d. 10/22/1978 m. 8/3/1923
Minnie E. Holtam b. 10/22/1889 Clark Co., Ala. m. 7/7/1919
Please A. Holtam b. 9/14/1891 Clark Co., Ala. d. 12/10/1972 m. 6/8/1922
Una Ercell Holtam b. 8/23/1894 Clark Co., Ala. d. 11/28/1971 m. 8/11/1919
Ira Clinton Holtam b. 6/18/1896 Clark Co., Ala., d. 12/13/1896
Infant unnamed 2/3/1900 Clark Co., Ala. d. 2/3/1900
Leon Bly Holtam b. 9/26/1902 Clark Co., Ala. d. 11/24/1918
Norman Shelton Holtam b. 9/8/1904 Clark Co., Ala. m. 1/11/1927
Willie Mary Holtam b. 10/22/1906 Clark Co., Ala. m. 10/4/1936

WARREN SAMUEL WATSON BIBLE

This is to certify that Warren Samuel Watson of Brownsville, Paulding Co., Ga. and Martha Jane Taylor of Powder Springs, Cobb Co, Ga., were united by me in the Bonds of Holy Matrimony at Home of Samuel C. Taylor, Father of Martha Jane Taylor, Powder Springs, Cobb Co., Ga. on 27th day of Oct. 1870. In presence of A. L. Bartlette, David McEachern and wife. Married by Rev. William Campbell.

Marriages
Hillyer Horace Kemp to Nora Olive Watson 10/21/1897
Warren Samuel Watson, Jr. to Annie Lou Logan 12/28/1899
Charlie Rogers Watson to Ottie Ozelle Kemp 12/15/1904
Maurice Linton Brooks to Julia Agnes Watson 12/13/1908
William Watson Rutland to Martha Frances Watson 9/23/1909
Colonel Jones Bates to Bertha Alice Watson 11/13/1910
Robert Lee Watson to Nannie Scott 1/1/1916
Judson Fredrick Watson to Lois Day 12/24/1923

Births
Warren Samuel Watson 8/8/1849   Charlie Rogers Watson 12/17/1880
Martha Jane Taylor 1/2/1849   Robert Lee Watson 1/24/1883
Mary Lilla Watson 12/21/1871   Julia Agnes Watson 3/15/1885
Coleman Motley Watson 5/31/1873 Martha Frances Watson 3/10/1887
Nora Olive Watson 12/19/1874   Bertha Alice Watson 8/4/1889
Minnie Odessa Watson 2/18/1877 Judson Frederick Watson 3/9/1892
Warren Samuel Watson Jr. 10/29/1878

(Warren Samuel Watson Bible contd....)

Deaths
Minnie Odessa Watson 8/14/1887   Robert Lee Watson 2/26/1928
Mary Lilla Watson 6/30/1895   Martha Jane Taylor Watson
Coleman Motley Warren 8/4/1895   5/28/1932
(Warren Samuel Watson Bible, Deaths, contd....)

Warren Samuel Watson Sr. 2/15/1908   Nora Olive Watson 2/1/1960

Martha Frances Watson Rutland 3/25/1972
Charlie Rogers Watson 12/1972
Julie Agens Watson Brooks 1/1973
Bertha Alice Watson Bates Jan. or Feb. 1979

JOHN M. DUKE BIBLE

John M. Duke, his Book, N. Y.

Robert Green Duke b. 6/15/1793
Vilett b. 11/27/1798

Martha Jane Duke b. 10/21/1861 m. John Thomas Camp (Sr.)
Robert Green Duke b. 10/30/1866 m. Mentory Stephens (b.
   3/20/1871)
Jane Duke b. 7/27/1820
John M. b. 6/15/1822
Charity P.? Duke b. 1/24/1824 (46 yrs. old, d. Clayton Co., Ga.
   1/1870
James W. Duke b. 5/19/1827
Elizabeth L. Duke b. 7/30/1829
Lucenda R.? Duke b. 4/2/1832
Thomas J. Duke b. 2/28/1835
Lana A. Duke b. 11/29/1838

Mary Elizabeth Duke b. 3/28/1856
Sarah Katherine Duke b. 11/27/1858
Martha Jane Duke b. 10/21/1861
Robert Green Duke b. 10/30/1866

STARLING CAMP BIBLE
Owner: Mrs. Van Rhames, Melda, La.

Prince b. 2/--
Solomon b. 7/182-
Sarah b. 9/--
Jasper b. 5/--
Samuel or Eaphrom b. 12/--

317

(Starling Camp Bible contd....)

Births
Starling Camp 10/22/1793   Claricy Camp 8/5/1824
Polly Camp 8/20/1805   William Jarrell 10/20/1893
Evloin Camp 3/3/1823

Deaths
Claricy Camp 8/5/1824   Abednigo Camp 7/20/1836
Starling Camp 4/2/1830   William Jarrell 12/7/1847
Thomas S. --   Fhoau?
William Jarrell b. 10/20/1893
John B. Menght b. 8/1898

Marriages
Starling Camp to Polly Camp (Mary Fish) 5/24/1822
G. L. Wilkins to S. F. McRight 1/25/1857

Births
John Gray 1/6/1830   Sarah McRight 2/23/1838
G. L. Wilkins 6/30/1828   John Robbest Wilkins 11/23/1859
Willis F. Jarrell 5/7/1841
Maryanie Eveline Wilkins 3/11/1860

Nathan F. Camp 4/3/1820   Thomas T. Jarrell 1/28/1837
James B. Camp 10/30/1832   Willis F. Jarrell 5/7/1841
Abdnigo Camp 2/6/1835   Daniel Fish 12/18/1828

Deaths
Mary Jarrell 5/28/1862, 56 yrs., 10 mos., 23 days
Nathan F. Capte b. 1/7 d. 1/19/1865
Willis Jarrell 6/28/1864
James B. Camp 1874
Thomas Jarrell 11/23/1864

Marriages
John B. McRight to 10/13/1836 Evline Camp
James B. Camp to Mary Ann Dillars 5/8/1850
Nathan Camp to Sarah An Andrews 3/2/1848

William Thrash b. 6/10/1819

Deaths
Daniel Fish
John R. Wilkins 5/19/1869   George L. Wilkins 7/29/1917
John B. McRight 10/15/1899   Sarah Wilkins 7/11/1930
Eveline McRight 10/17/19-3

J. W. BINGHAM BIBLE

J. W. Bingham m. Susan Lackey 10/24/1844

Births
James Wiley Bingham 7/5/1823   Henry Thomas Bingham 7/29/1854
Susan Bingham 5/15/1824   Wm. Lucious Bingham 3/13/1857

(J. W. Bingham Bible contd....)

Calvin Christopher Bingham
  1/12/1846
John Westley Bingham 2/17/1848

Alexander Bingham 9/2/1859
Martha Hane Bingham 4/27/1863
Robert Levi Bingham 1/2/1867

Deaths

Alexander Bingham 12/8/1860
Susan Bingham 6/7/1896
James W. Bingham 2/1/1897
Henry T. Bingham 5/14/1900
Martha J. Bingham 9/2/1935

Wm. S. Bingham 4/7/1904
Joel J. Bingham 2/7/1906
John W. Bingham 10/17/1916
C. C. Bingham 1/23/1926

JAMES SPURLIN BIBLE *
Owner: Mrs. John C. Henderson
3770 Peachtree Rd., N. E.
Atlanta, Ga. 30319

James Spurlin Book bought of William V. White in Pike Co., Ga., 505th Dist., 7/4/1836.....

Marriages

James Spurlin to Nancy 12/10/1829
Columbus G. Coggin to Frances M. Spurlin 12/24/1854
William J. Newell to Frances M. Coggin 2/14/1866
William G. Spurlin to Lydia Coats 12/29/1859
Joseph M. Scott to Rhoda Obedience Spurlin 1/28/1866

Children of Joseph M. Scott and Rhoda Spurlin Scott:

Ida Inez Scott 9/12/1868
Zachery Lumpkin Scott 9/26/1871
Jessie James Scott 6/23/1876

Lucy Kate Scott 6/6/1879
Eugene Fred Scott 2/4/1889

WILLIAM SPURLIN BIBLE *
Owner: Mrs. John C. Henderson
3770 Peachtree Road, N. E.
Atlanta, Ga. 30319

James Spurlin, son of William Spurlin, b. 6/20/1802
Nancy Michel, but now Spurlin, dau. of Starling Michel, b. 8/18/1808
William Spurlin, son of John Spurlin and Myally, b. 1/12/1769
  d. 4/30/1835
Nancy Spurlin d. 9/13/1875
William G. Spurlin d. prisoner of war at Ft. Delaware, U. S., 7/15/1864
James A. Spurlin killed in battle at Malvern Hill, Va. 7/1/1862
Amanda S. Spurlin d. 8/23/1863
Columbus Coggin d. in Va. Army 6/25/1862

*See also p. 273.

(William Spurlin Bible contd....)

James Spurlin, son of William Spurlin, d. 11/18/1887
Frances M. Spurlin, dau. of James Spurlin and Nancy, b. 3/1/1831
Wilson L. Spurlin, son of above, b. 5/14/1832
William G. Spurlin, son of above, b. 1/28/1836
Claudy H. Spurlin, dau. of William G. Spurlin and Lydia, d.
   10/25/1863
William Charles Spurlin, son of above, d. 9/17/1887
Sarah Spurlin, wife of William Spurlin, d. 11/4/1859, age 92 yrs.
Martha Ann Spurlin, dau. of James Spurlin and Nancy, d. 7/22/1894
James A. Spurlin, son of above, b. 9/8/1838
Amandah Samaria Spurlin, dau. of above, b. 1/28/1841
James Silas Coggin, son of C. G. and Frances M. Coggin, b.
   11/25/1855
Daniel W. Coggin b. 9/29/1857
Varina Davis Coggin b. 7/2/1860
William Charles Spurlin, son of William G. and Lydia Spurlin,
   b. 2/1/1864
Lydia Spurlin b. 2/29/1835
Martha Ann Spurlin, dau. of James Spurlin and Nancy, b. 12/28/1843
Rodah Obedience Spurlin, dau. of James Spurlin and Nancy, b.
   7/2/1846
Claudy H. Spurlin b. 11/7/1860
Sarah F. Newell b. 6/20/1867
Nancy D. Newell b. 3/25/1869

GEORGE T. JOHNSON BIBLE
Owner: Jasper J. Johnson

Births

George T. Johnson 11/11/1822
Mary E. (Emaline) Johnson 4/15/1830
Martha Caroline Johnson 1/3/1848
John David Johnson 6/23/1850
William Washington Johnson
   4/18/1853
George Franklin Johnson
   2/25/1856
Sarah Emaline Johnson 8/10/1859
Minie Louanah Johnson 6/16/1872

Mary Ann Johnson 5/25/1861
Susan Anne Johnson 11/8/1863
Nancy Ann Johnson 4/6/186-
Elizabeth Olive Johnson
   3/27/1866
Dora Angaline Johnson
   2/18/1868
James Thomas Johnson
   5/30/1870

Marriages

John D. Johnson of Union Hill, Ga. to Fannie S. Westbrook of
   Union Hill, Ga. 11/8/1874 at home of bride's parents.
Grier Alison Murdock to Mary Emaline Johnson 2/9/1896
Richard Lee Johnson to Leila Janett Martin 12/23/1906
George Benton Miner to Tochie Stella Johnson 12/24/1906
Corace Johnson to Homer Rickerson 2/18/1917
Florence Johnson to Charlie Atkins 8/22/1931

Births

John David Johnson 6/23/1850
Fannie Syrepthia Westbrook
   11/8/1844

Clifton Lamont Murdock 3/1/1897
Turner Lee Murdock 10/21/1900
Eunice Lorena Murdock 6/18/1904

Mary Emaline Johnson 6/22/1876   Stella May Ruth Murdock
Corace Comargo Johnson 8/19/1879   11/28/1907
James Nolen Johnson 7/19/1881   Agnes Gertrude Miner 1/8/1908
Richard Lee Johnson 2/19/1883   Florence Mabel Johnson 2/14/1908
Tochie Stella Johnson 7/2/1884   Grier Alison Murdock 3/21/1876
George Torence Johnson & Georgia   Florence Johnson 6/21/1886
Leila Janett Martin 6/25/1878
George Benton Miner 3/19/1881

Deaths
James Nolen Johnson 11/19/1882   Geo. Torence Johnson 11/20/1886

Marriages
Richard Lee Johnson of Cherokee Co., Ga. to Leila Janett Martin
of Gilmer Co., Ga. 12/23/1906 at Union Hill, Ga. by Rev. W. D.
Stephenson.

Births
Richard Lee Johnson 2/19/1883   Olive Lee Johnson 2/17/1910
Leila Janett Martin 6/25/1878   Alice Vera Johnson 8/25/1913
Mabel Florence Johnson 2/14/1908   John Jasper Johnson 6/17/1917
Verna Adelyn Johnson 8/16/1921

THOMAS AND HANNAH COOKE BIBLE Of Rabun Co.
Owner: Mrs. C. H. Willis, Barnesville, Ga.

Marriages
Thomas Cooke b. 11/1801 N. C. m. 12/11/1832 Hannah Cannon,
  who was b. 10/30/1809 in Franklin Co., Ga., d. 11/15/1888, bur.
  Pleasant Grove, Ga.
Elizabeth Melvina Cooke b. 4/19/1846 Ga., d. 12/9/1906 m.
H. Wimpy, bur. Pleasant Grove, Ga.

SIMEON ALFRED WHATLEY BIBLE
Owner: Mrs. E. T. Whatley
Brunswick, Ga.

Simeon Alfred Whatley 4/16/1811-2/5/1880 m. 11/13/1843 Jane
Caldwell Tolbert 2/2/1824. Their Children:
John Thomas Whatley 9/4/1844-4/15/1865 N.C. Confed. Soldier
Simeon Lenader Whatley b. 5/2/1846
Mary Frances Whatley b. 5/2/1848
Susan Jane Whatley b. 4/23/1850
Valula Puella Whatley b. 4/3/1852
William Alfred Whatley b. 4/14/1854
Payson Sparks Whatley b. 1/8/1856
Ida Enola Whatley b. 3/23/1858
Tolbert Whatley 12/14/1859-7/14/1861
Annie Lizzie Whatley 12/7/1861-7/10/1863
Edgar Tolbert Whatley b. 11/3/1863
John Thomas Whatley 5/9/1856-6/9/1868

DEMPSEY RIGGS BIBLE

Dempsey Riggs b. 1/8/1808
Frances Nevils No Riggs b. 5/2/1815   Their Children:

Births
Oliza G. 1/1/1832   Nicy 2/20/1847
Rachel E. 3/18/1834   Dicy 2/20/1847
John W. 3/22/1836   Joshua 11/1/1849
Nancy 12/28/1837   Jason 9/10/1851
Stephen J. 11/4/1839   Sarah 5/30/1853
Jacob 10/16/1841   Jefferson 5/22/1855
James M. 6/4/1843   Josel 2/2/1857
Jasper 4/15/1845

THOMAS HALL BIBLE
Owner: R. Marvin Hall
Crawford, Ga.

Thomas Hall m. Margaret Ray -as 2/2/1792 by Rev.--Tho--
Their Children:

Births
Elizabeth Hall 11/18/1792   Elenor Hall --/23/1798
John Cunningham Hall 4/12/1794   Margaret Hall 11/16/1802
----Hall 8/1796   Thomas Hall 11/16/1802
Daniel Hall 10/16/1800   Jane Hall ---
Isaac Hall 8/6/---

IRA R. GREER Of Greene Co.
Owner: Dr. Guy W. Greer
Whitesboro, Texas

Ira R. Greer b. 5/6/1813
Martha M. White b. 1/22/1814

Ira R. Greer m. Martha M. White 9/11/1834 Their Children:

Births
Sarah A. Greer 7/29/1845   Bethna Greer 4/20/1845
Mary M. Greer 2/7/1837   Aryan H. Greer 2/22/1847
Martha J. Greer 4/2/1838   Willmirth A. Greer 5/8/1849
Gilbert I. Greer 1/7/1840   Ira J. Greer 6/15/1851
Ann R. Greer 5/29/1841   Henry F. Greer 3/22/1853
John N. Greer 5/12/1843   George T. Greer 6/30/1855

GODLIF DASHER BIBLE Of Effingham Co.*
Owner: Mrs. Fannie Fox Keller
210 W. Bolton St., Savannah, Ga.

Godlif Dasher b. 4/3/1799 Effingham Co., Ga. m. Sarah Smith Bird
on 6/3/1832
Sarah Smith Bird b. 3/7/1807, dau. of Eleanor Giles. Sarah Smith
was from Black Creek, Bryan Co., Ga.
Their Children:

Births
(Dr.) Horace C. Dasher 1/3/1833   Ralphene E. Dasher 7/18/1845
Ellen B. Dasher 11/19/1834   Hortense I. Dasher 12/11/1848
Susan C. Dasher 1/18/1843   John Dasher 12/11/1848
Pembroke Dasher 5/3/1838

Andrew Hamil Bird m. Eleanor Giles, both of S. C. Their son:

Andrew Hamil Bird b. 6/8/1814 d. 1/15/1847 m. Mrs. Frances
(Wilson) Fox in 1842. Their Children:

Andrew Hamil Bird b. 4/1846 d. 1/18/1863. He was Lieutenant in
Bryan Guards, 25th Regt., Ga. Volunteers, Wilson's Brigade,
drowned in Cape Fear River while attempting to reach the wrecked
Steamer, Columbia. His sister, Irene Bird, b. 3/14/1844 m. Robert
Wade.
              Note by Mrs. Frank Fox, New Smyrna, Fla.---
Benjamin Frank Fox b. 1818 d. 1841, age 23 yrs., m. Frances
Wilson of Liberty Co., Ga. and had one son, Dr. Benjamin Franklin
Fox, b. 7/21/1841, several mos. after death of his father.

CLEMENT HALL ASHFORD BIBLE
Owner: Mrs. C. H. Ashford
Atlanta, Ga.

This certifies that Clement Hall Ashford of Watkinsville, Ga. and
Wilhelminia Anderson of Watkinsville, Ga., were joined in Holy
Bonds of matrimony at home of F. Anderson, 11/8/1877. Wit:
Woodson Ashford, John Anderson, Earl Overby and E. E. Anderson.
Rev. Eustus W. Speer officiating.
              Four children were born of this union.
Thomas Booth Ashford b. 2/24/1879 Watkinsville, Ga.
Homer Cloud Ashford b. 10/3/1881 Watkinsville, Ga.
Foster Kirkpatric Ashford b. 1/21/1887 Watkinsville, Ga.
Margaret Louisa Ashford b. 3/12/1891 Watkinsville, Ga.

Margaret Louisa and Arthur Preston Flowers, M. D. m. 11/8/1913 at
St. Mark's M. E. Church, South, Atlanta, Ga., Bishop Warren A.
Candler and Rev. A. M. Reglett officiating.

Arthur Preston Flowers, the second, b. 12/16/1921, at Davis
Fisher Hospital, Dr. J. T. Floyd officating, Atlanta, Ga.

*See also p. 339.
323

SAMUEL ARMISTEAD BIBLE
Owner: Henry Madison, Sr.
Charlotte Co., Va.
(Purchased by him in 1804)

Dr. Samuel Armistead m. Sallie Martin 2/11/1807
Sallie Martin Armistead d. 10/1/1811
Rev. Samuel Armistead m. Nancy Madison 9/24/1812, his second wife

Henry Madison Armistead, son of Samuel and Sallie, b. 12/23/1807
Joseph Martin Armistead, son of Samuel and Sallie, b. 11/7/1809
Samuel Marris Armistead, son of Samuel and Sallie, b. 7/24/1811
Katherin Penn Armistead, dau. of Samuel and Nancy, b. 11/3/1813,
    (m. Ben Wyatt).M.F.B.
Martha Ann Armistead, dau. of Samuel and Nancy, b. 12/11/1815,
    m. Daniel Williamson
Lucy Clayborne Armistead, dau. of Samuel and Nancy, b. 6/1/1818,
    (m. Brice Martin)
Harriett Armistead, dau. of Samuel and Nancy, b. 6/1/1820
Sarah Madison Martin Armistead, dau. of Samuel and Nancy,
    m. 8/13/1822 (m. Hezekiah Ford) M.F.B.
James Madison Armistead, son of Samuel and Nancy, b. 10/23/1824,
    (m. Fannie Steptoe) M.F.B.
Justina Caroline, dau. of Samuel and Nancy, b. 1/8/1827 (m. Rev.
    R. C. Anderson, Presbyterian Minister) M.F.B.
Louis Lee, son of Samuel and Nancy, b. 1/5/1831
Louis Lee Armistead m. Nannie B. Mitchell 12/13/1860

ABNER F. HOLT BIBLE
Owner: Flewellen Holt
Macon, Ga.

Births
Abner F. Holt 6/3/1811   Philip Thurmond Holt 8/20/1840
Eliza Holt 2/12/1815   Abner Thurmond Holt 9/25/1842-
Mary Victoria Holt 9/23/1833   2/24/1909
William Flewellen Holt 8/23/1835   Ella Lane Holt 11/15/1844
Ann Eliza Holt 7/29/1838   Parthenia Raines Holt 7/7/1847
Edgar Holt, son of William F. and Martha C. Holt, b. 9/5/1859
Ida Holt b. 5/29/1861
William Flewellen Holt b. 9/16/1863
Leon Holt b. 6/18/1865
Abner Skelton Holt b. 1/25/1871
Abner Flewellen Holt, son of Abner Thurmond Holt and Fannie Moore
    Searcy b. 10/20/1864
Charles Couch Holt, son of Abner Thurmond Holt and Fannie Moore
    Searcy b. 7/20/1866
James Thweatt Holt, son of Abner Thurmond Holt and Fannie Moore
    Search b. 4/1868
Fannie Holt Thomas, dau. of Abner Thurmond Holt and Fannie Moore
    Search b. 10/7/1871
Daniel Searcy Holt, son of Abner Thurmond Holt and Fannie Moore
    Search b. 6/25/1875
Alberta Holt Smart, dau. of above, b. 8/16/1877

(Abner F. Holt Bible contd....)

Abner Flewellen Holt, Jr., son of Abner Flewellen Holt and Lollie
Wells b. 9/25/1886.

Tarpley Holt b. 3/18/1777
Betsey Lane Flewellen b. 8/24/1793
Ann Lane Holt b..12/8/1816
William Simon Holt b. 12/26/1818
Margaret Eliza Holt b. 1/6/1821
Martha Sarah Hines Holt b. 8/11/1823
Tarpley Lafayette Holt b. 8/21/1827
Phillip Thurmond b. 6/8/1764
Thomas Wells Holt, son of Abner Flewellen Holt and Lollie Wells
b. 11/22/1890
Thomas Wells Holt, Jr., son of Thomas Wells Holt and Estelle
Wright, b. 9/7/1914

Marriages
Abner F. Holt to Eliza Addison 7/31/1832
John B. Ross to Ann L. Holt 5/8/1834
Tarpley Holt to Betsey lane Flewellen 12/21/1809
T. M. Furlow to Margaret E. Holt 11/4/1839
R. H. Ward to Martha S. H. Holt 3/15/1842
William S. Holt to Henrietta Dean 12/18/1844
William F. Holt to Martha C. napier 6/30/1858
Abner F. Holt to Frances M. Search 11/11/1863
Abner Flewellen Holt to lollie G. Wells 10/14/1885
Thomas Wells Holt to Estelle Wright 12/12/1912
Abner Flewellen Holt, Jr. to Aurelia Wray 7/8/1920

Deaths
Fannie M. Search d. 10/15/1906
Abner Skelton Holt, son of Wm. F. and M. C. Holt, 5/30/1871
Leon Kell Holt, son of Wm. F. and M. C. Holt, 3/10/1873
Martha C. Holt, wife of Wm. F. Holt, 5/31/1884
Dr. William Flewellen Holt 9/10/1901
Wm. Flewellen Holt, Jr., son of Martha C. Napier and Dr. Wm. F.
Holt, 3/14/1927
Ida L. Holt, dau. of Martha C. Holt and Dr. Wm. F. Holt, 4/1928
Tarpley holt 5/26/1840
Philip Thurmond 6/9/1841
Philip Thurmond Holt, son of A. F. and E. Holt, 4/30/1842
E. Holt 4/30/1842
Ann Lane Ross 9/29/1844
Ella Lane Holt 8/2/1845
Joseph R. Allison 4/6/1835, age 42 yrs.
Dr. Abner F. Holt 10/25/1848
Eliza Holt 11/25/1847--9
D. in Americus at res. of her Uncle T. M. Furlow, Parthenia R.
Holt, 9/5/1857
Edgar Holt, son of Wm. F. Holt and M. C. Holt 7/22/1865

325

```
                    JOSEPH STILES BIBLE
                 Owner: Mrs. Homer Bivins
                     Baldwin Co., Ga.


Joseph Gill Stiles d. 2/18/1858
Sarah Stiles d. 2/5/1842

Children:

Births
Sarah Stiles 12/22/1799          Mary A. Stiles 1/10/1817
Nancy Stiles 9/9/1801            Joseph Stiles 6/21/1819
Agnis Stiles 6/15/1803           Amanda M. Stiles 1/16/1822
Margret Stiles 7/25/1805         John Stiles 7/9/1825
Elizabeth Stiles 3/31/1808       Louisa M. Stiles 10/31/1843
Cynthia Stiles 1/21/1810         M. H. Stiles 11/19/1846
Margery P. Stiles 8/5/1814

Sarah Stiles Summers d. 8/18/1890
Joseph Stiles d. 1898



                    E. P. GIBSON BIBLE




Annie B. Stiles 9/22/1856-8/10/1922
E. P. Gibson 6/18/1852-10/19/1907

Children:

Ellsworth Marion Gibson 5/9/1880-3/1919
Joseph Snead Gibson 3/18/1884-12/4/1935
Lucy Caro Gibson 5/12/1886-1/22/1916
Mary Elizabeth Gibson 9/20/1888-6/9/1901
Annie Jones Gibson 10/15/1890
Peter Conn Gibson 8/20/1894

E. P. Gibson m. Annie B. Stiles 11/17/1872

Lucy Ann Anderson Gibson 2/5/1829-3/26/1905



                    REID-MORSE BIBLE
                 Owner: Mrs. Lida Reid Morse
                      Eatonton, Ga.



Children of Frank P. Morse and Lida Reid Morse:

Mary Francis Morse b. 11/29/1905    Frank Rogan Morse b. 8/30/1910
Nannie Reid Morse b. 3/15/1907      John Reid Morse b. 8/10/1912
Florence Ellen Morse b. 11/8/1908
```

BENJAMIN HARDY RUSSELL, JR. BIBLE
Owner: Mrs. Wallace Butts
Milledgeville, Ga.

Births
Joseph P. Chambers 10/18/1871   Wm. Henry Russell 1/31/1888
Katy Russell 3/11/1872   Mary Russell 8/18/1886
Mattie Gertrude Russell 12/13/1873   Frederick Russell 2/1/1893
Gus Russell 12/24/1877
Annie Bell Russell 5/9/1881
Benjamin Franklin Russell 7/18/1883
Alice Lavinia Russell 8/18/1889

Marriages
B. H. Russell to Mattie P. Stanley 12/1/1870
L. Burt Chambers to B. A. Davis 1/12/1871
Wm. T. Clay to Mattie Davis 9/14/1871
Mary Russell to C. L. Henderson 3/25/1903

Deaths
Mattie Gertrude Russell 8/12/1871   George Irvin Russell
Mattie P. Russell 7/18/1899   6/11/1879
Benj. Hardy Russell 10/19/1922   C. L. Henderson 6/1/1903
Mary Russell 5/5/1933   Mark Russell 9/10/1933
Mollie Bailey, wife of Charles Gus Russell, 1914

ALEXANDER HUDSON REID BIBLE
Owner: Mrs. Lida Reid Morse, Eatonton, Ga.

Alexander Hudson Reid b. 1840
Mary Ann Rogan b. 6/27/1842
Alexander H. Reid m. Mary Ann Rogan 12/7/1865 Eatonton, Ga.

Births of Children
Mamie Reid 9/25/1866   Eliza Mitchell Reid 1/12/1879
Charles Rogan Reid 1/12/1868   Ruth Reid 1/18/1882
Nancy Cloud Reid 10/8/1871   Stella Reid 8/12/1885
Lilburn Reid 4/14/1874
Margaret Frances Reid 7/4/1876

Marriages
John D. Vaughn to Mamie Reid 6/26/1890 Eatonton, Ga.
Charles R. Reid to Nannie Gurr 7/5/1891 Ft. Valley, Ga.
Nannie C. Reid to Fred J. Poag 4/1909 Lumber City, Ga.
Margaret Reid to S. B. Reese 1908, Birmingham, Ala.
Lida Mitchell (Eliza) Reid to Frank P. Morse 2/1/1905
Ruth Reid to Dr. Lester F. Watson 1906 Lumber City, Ga.
Stella Reid to Joseph S. Turner, Jr. ---

Deaths
Alexander H. Reid 6/14/1899 Eatonton, Ga.
Mary Ann Rogan Reid 10/16/1915
Frank P. Morse 1/16/1912 (dropped dead)

327

PETER ROQUEMORE BIBLE
Owner: A. H. Baker

Births
James M. Roquemore 3/1/1800
Mary Roquemore 3/22/1802
Thomas J. Roquemore 1/28/1804
John H. Roquemore 7/12/1805
Peter Roquemore 1/10/1807
William B. Roquemore 12/28/1808
Josiah Roquemore 10/8/1810
Martha Roquemore 6/16/1812

Eliza Roquemore 9/8/1814
Harriet Roquemore 3/13/1816
Caroline Roquemore 9/7/1817
Nancy Roquemore 6/8/1819
Amanda Roquemore 12/8/1822
Henry G. Roquemore 4/20/1825

Peter Roquemore 3/19/1778-2/17/1852
Katy Murphey 11/19/1783-7/27/1847
Polly (Mary) Garrard d. 5/28/1861

Peter Roquemore b. 1778 and wife, Katy Murphy, b. 1783 were
parents of above listed 15 children. Peter Roquemore was interred
in Walton Cemetery, Carthage, Panola Co., Texas, and his wife as
interred at Seale, Russell Co., Ala. in Howard Cemetery Lot.

ELIJAH ROBINSON BIBLE
Owner: Mrs. W. E. Robinson]
Milledgeville, Ga.

Births
Elijah Robinson 8/22/1840
Matilda Robinson 2/27/1843
James Robinson 1/19/1845
Sara Robinson 1/2/1847

Margaret Robinson 2/18/1849
John A. Robinson 1/22/1852
Linzy J. Robinson 10/18/1853-
    12/18/1854

Deaths
Martha A. Robinson 7/20/1839
Nancy E. Robinson 3/10/1848
Edward Robinson 11/3/1863
Peggy Robinson 12/29/1882

Tabitha Truitt 10/16/1853
Enlow Robinson 9/28/1879
Roscoe Conkling Robinson
    10/30/1881

Marriages
Edward Robinson to Peggy Truitt 10/23/1828
James Robinson to Samantha Odom 4/31/1871
W. E. Robinson b. 1/31/1872
Oscar Robinson b. 10/8/1873
Neal Robinson b. 8/11/1875
Vera Robinson b. 6/10/1877
Mary Anthon Robinson b. 10/10/1882
Bob Robinson b. 3/13/1884
Carl Robinson b. 3/12/1886
Clarence Bascom Robinson b. 6/20/1889

P. G. PURSER BIBLE
Owner: Mrs. C. B. Wright
Cochran, Ga.

Births

P. G. Purser 5/21/1828
Mrs. E. J. Holland Purser 1/31/1859
Sarah Drucilla Purser 3/1/1877
J. J. Purser 12/10/1878
A. C. Purser 3/27/1881

J. D. Purser 9/4/1883
Q. E. Purser 11/18/1886
P. R. Purser 5/10/1889
Vera Purser 4/24/1896

Marriages

P. G. Purser to E. J. Holland 4/31/1876
Sarah Drucilla Purser m. 1890
A. C. Purser m. 1903
P. R. Purser m. 1907

Deaths

P. G. Purser 5/6/1910   J. D. Purser 1905

ELIJAH COOK BIBLE

Births

Elijah Cook 9/4/1844
Samantha J. Cook 2/20/1845
Minnie B. Cook 10/27/1868
Thomas Cook 1/1/1870

Elijah Cook 1/27/1872
Eva L. Cook 2/15/1880
James E. Cook 9/19/1884

Deaths

Elijah Cook, Sr. 6/28/1915
Samantha J. Cook 6/9/1923
Eva L. Stocks 9/22/1941

James E. Cook 6/24/1955
Minnie B. Cook 8/8/1956
Thomas Cook 2/26/1958

Marriages

Elijah Cook, Sr. to Samantha J. Powell 10/20/1867 at Starling
    Tracks
Minnie B. Cook to John R. Taylor 10/3/1888
Thomas Cook to Mariah Watkins 11/22/1896
Elijah Cook (Jr.) to Lila M. Hendricks 12/29/1895
Eva L. Cook to W. C. Stocks 2/5/1902
James E. Cook to Lottie Taylor 4/10/1907

R. H. OGLESBY BIBLE

Births

William G. Oglesby 12/18/1873
B. G. Oglesby 2/24/1876

Annie Sue Oglesby 5/18/1884
Georgia P. Oglesby 5/12/1887

(R. H. Oglesby Bible, Births, contd....)

C. W. Oglesby 11/23/1878   Lucy Oglesby 10/8/1890
Claudia May Oglesby 5/4/1881
R. H. Oglesby d. 11/1922
W. J. (Bud) Green m. Roxie White of Texas. She d. 12/29/1936

JOHN BRANAN BIBLE
Owner: Mrs. Evie Cranford
Cochran, Ga.

John Branan 11/12/1776-1859   Nancy Branan 1/11/1785-1862
Westley Branan b. 2/12/1812   Mary A. Branan b. 12/19/1814

Westley Branan m. Mary Adline Griffin 4/28/1831

Births
Louisa Francis Branan 7/9/1832   Nancy Isebella Branan 12/4/1847
Alfred Fletcher Branan 5/23/1834   Willis Frankling Branan
Mary Wilmoth Branan 2/8/1837   2/15/1849
Sarah Elizabeth Branan 11/5/1839   Thos. Caswell Branan 12/3/1851
Georgia A. Branan 7/15/1843   Lemeon Parks Branan 2/25/1854-
John Westley Branan 7/12/1845   9/9/1864
                                    Lambert H. Branan 12/6/1856
                                    Gilbert L. E. Branan 5/2/1859
                                    Arazona Texas Branan 6/10/1862

My mother, Roberta Francis Holland b. 8/22/1861. Roberta Holland
Willingham d. 12/4/1943

W. G. GREEN BIBLE
Owner: Miss Georgia Oglesby
McDonough, Ga.

W. G. Green m. Frances E. Gleaton 12/18/1851
R. H. Oglesby m. L. J. Green 1/16/1873

Births
William G. Green 2/9/1829   W. J. Green 12/1/1855
Frances E. Green 2/3/1835   Frances Amelia Palistine Green
Lucinda (Jones) J. Green 3/13/1853   10/18/1858
                                    James M. Green 5/14/1861

Deaths
William G. Green killed 9/19/1862   Palice Green 10/25/1940
Frances E. Green 9/15/1904   Lucinda J. Oglesby 3/17/1904

JOHN C. GUNN BIBLE
Owner: Mrs. Lucy J. Edwards
Jackson, Ga.

John C. Gunn 5/25/1852-1/2/1928   Ollia A. Gunn b. 3/4/1858
Lucy E. Gunn b. 8/26/1854   Lucy J. Barnes Gunn b. 7/3/1838

Deaths
Lucy J. Gunn 11/15/1904   Oliver H. Gunn 12/20/1923
Carrie E. Pulliam 6/16/1881   John C. Gunn 1/2/1928

STEPHEN WHITE BIBLE

A copy of the Records from "A Serman" by The Rev. and Learned Mr.
William Wilson 1738. Owned by Stephen White, Lucy White, Martha
White, Rhoda White.

Births
Elizabeth White 8/21/1777   Stephen White 5/24/1787
Sarah White 11/10/1778   Lucy White 4/23/1797

JOHN B. WINTER BIBLE
Winterville, Ga.
Owner: Mrs. John B. Winter
143 Grady Ave., Athens, Ga.

John B. Winter m. Julia E. Lowe by Rev. John Calvin Johnson
11/27/1884

John Harold Winter b. 12/24/1885

NATHANIEL JACKSON WILLIAMSON BIBLE Of Jackson Co.
Owner: Mrs. A. S. Hardy
2003 Jefferson Rd., Athens, Ga.

Nathaniel J. Williamson m. Mary J. Thomas 4/2/1871

Births
N. J. Williamson 6/11/1844   Charles F. Williamson 10/18/1879
Mary J. Williamson 11/22/1854   Mary Jane Williamson 3/29/1882

331

(Nathaniel Jackson Williamson Bible, Births, contd....)

Willie B. Williamson 11/10/1871   Allen G. Williamson 9/6/1884
James W. Williamson 11/10/1871   Junius S. Williamson 10/4/1886
Nannie G. Williamson 4/27/1873   Ada Belle Williamson 5/2/1889
Sallie E. Williamson 4/15/1875
Howel N. Williamson 6/23/1877

Deaths
James Wilbur Williamson 11/14/1871
Sallie Eudorah Williamson 10/20/1876
Charles Frank Williamson 7/18/1880
Nathaniel Jackson Williamson 4/6/1906
Mary J. Williamson 4/1940

JOHN GRAHAM BIBLE Of Oglethorpe Co.
Owner: Mrs. R. F. Brooks
Lexington, Ga.

John Graham b. 8/29/1778
Mary Taylor, relative to Pres. Zachary Taylor, 1/9/1780-12/1872

Children:

Armistead Graham b. 5/12/1801
Josiah Graham b. 4/12/1804
Serena Graham b. 12/8/1805
Mary Graham b. 10/7/1807 m. Eli Carter
William Graham b. 9/21/1809 m. Mary Simmons
David Graham b. 1/9/1815 m. Susan Pinkney Simmons. Children:

Mary Jane Graham b. 12/16/1838 m. Pleasant Lafayette Wheless
John William Graham b. 5/13/1840 m. 1st Queen Noel, 2nd,
    Sara Tiller
Sara F. Graham b. 3/4/1842 m. David Holloman
Serena E. Graham b. 11/9/1843 m. Richard B. Mathews
Susan Pinkney Graham b. 12/5/1845 m. J. C. G. Sevens
George T. Graham b. 3/30/1848 m. Sarah Cunningham
Annie T. Graham b. 8/9/1850 d. childhood
Lucy C. Graham b. 9/12/1853 m. Frank Hill
Rhoda T. Graham b. 11/25/1856 m. William Cunningham
David F. Graham b. 3/25/1859 m. 1st Jessie Thornton, 2nd,
    Nancy Bray Patman
Martha B. Graham b. 9/15/1861 m. Joseph M. Harris

JAMES EDWARD WHITEHEAD BIBLE Of Oconee Co.
Owner: James Fred Whitehead
Milledge Ave., Athens, Ga.

James Edward Whitehead b. 11/24/1841 m. 1/5/1871
Sarah Ann Susan Southerland b. 8/13/1843

332

(James Edward Whitehead Bible contd....)

Births
Asa H. Whitehead 11/18/1872   George P. Whitehead 8/1/1880
William Walker Whitehead 11/1/1874   James Fred Whitehead 7/7/1882
Maude Elizabeth Whitehead 10/24/1876
Annie Estelle Whitehead 10/31/1885

Deaths
George P. Whitehead 6/1881   Mrs. Anna Whitehead 6/18/1928
James Edward Whitehead 6/19/1890   Sara Henson 1947
Maude Elizabeth Whitehead 12/28/1911
Estelle Whitehead Harrison 6/23/1927

                CALVIN TAYLOR STOREY BIBLE Of Jackson Co.
                     Owner: Mrs. W. H. Williamson
                              Toccoa, Ga.

Calvin Taylor Storey b. 3/16/1848 m. 11/21/1875 Martha Jane
   Maxwell b. 9/8/1854

Births
James Maxwell Storey 4/4/1877   Clifford Taylor Storey 9/10/1884
Hugh Hampton Storey 9/28/1878   Jos. Brantly Storey 2/10/1889
Annie Clyde Storey 9/5/1880   Jessie Frances Storey 2/10/1889
George Wynn Storey 8/30/1882   Hattie Lucile Storey 6/12/1893

                ROYAL STOKELY BIBLE Of Oglethorpe Co.
                Owner: Mrs. Claire Martin, Crawford, Ga.

Royal Stokely b. 4/10/1784   Jane b. 7/21/1785

Births of Children:

Mary 10/10/1806   Rhoda 3/5/1819
Joseph 10/22/1808   Charles 6/19/1821
John H. 12/1/1810   Stephen H. 1/27/1824
Sarah 4/11/1813   Royal 5/27/1826
Nathan H. 3/5/1816   Dave V. 11/13/1828

Royal Stokely d. 11/17/1893, he m. Elizabeth D. Farr 2/3/1859
She d. 1/1929

MARY LITTLE BIBLE
Owner: Mrs. J. E. Wright
324 College St., Macon, Ga.

Births
Sarah B. Little 10/27/1814-9/9/1828   Anderson Little 11/9/1822
Micajah Little 1/14/1817   Saphrona A. Little
George G. Little 5/7/1819   6/15/1828

Deaths
William B. Little 6/14/1855   George G. Little 8/1864
Cagee Little 12/30/1837   Micajah Little 9/17/1862
Mary Little Sr. 10/27/1838

HENRY GREER BIBLE
Owner: Mrs. Susie Calahan Morton
Pickens, Miss. (dau. of Mary Eugenia Greer)

Marriages
Henry F. Greer to Anne A. Ragan 12/9/1830
James H. Greer to Jane H. Ragan 5/29/1833
A. D. Greer to Rebecca A. Crow 10/8/1837
Henry O. Beasley to Lucy S. Ragan 10/15/1840
Benjamin F. Miller to D. J. Greer 12/13/1854
Henry F. Greer to Mary E. A. Foote 12/9/1847
D. H. Cahran to M. E. A. Greer 2/13/1866

Births
William Greer 9/22/1787   Delila Greer 2/10/1788

Henry Franklin Greer 4/24/1809   James H. Greer 2/24/1811
Abraham Dinet Greer 10/22/1813   Wm. Amariah Greer 6/9/1818
Martial Ragan Greer 12/10/1820   John Jasper Greer 2/24/1825
Wm. Caloway Greer 6/20/1827   Delila Jane Greer 12/23/1832

Jeremiah Ragan 2/8/1788   Mary Greer 9/21/1790
Jane Haynes Ragan 4/1/1813   Ann Atkins Ragan 2/26/1816
Lucy Sophronia Ragan 12/6/1820   James Ragan Greer 12/20/1831
Wm. Franklin Greer, son of Henry and Ann Greer, 4/1/1834
Richard Foote Greer 10/9/1856
Jane Foote Cahran 2/12/1868
Delila Jane Greer 6/23/1846
Erasmus Jeremiah Greer 1/13/1839
Ann Sophronia Greer 12/29/1841
Henry Marshall Greer 5/26/1846
Mary Elizabeth Alexander Foote 8/31/1825
Gerard Martial Greer 11/4/1845
Henry Foote Greer 2/27/1851
Mary Eugenia Greer 3/27/1852
Sarah Mildred Greer 9/13/1854

(Henry Greer Bible contd....)

Deaths
William Greer 3/23/1848, 60 yrs., 6 mos., 8 days
Delila Greer 2/11/1845, 57 yrs., 1 day
Henry F. Greer 6/13/1858, 48 yrs., 1 mo., 17 days
James H. Greer 3/23/1846, 35 yrs., lacking one day
Jeremiah Ragan 1/31/1827
Mary Ragan 10/6/1826, age 36 yrs.
Ann Atkins Greer 12/24/1846, 30 yrs., 8 mos., 21 days
William Franklin Greer 5/28/185, 8 yrs., 27 days
Henry Marshall Greer 6/20/1847, age 1 yr., 26 days
Henry Foote Greer 4/10/1852, 1 yr., 1 mo., 14 days
Sarah Mildred Greer 3/25/1859, 4 yrs., 6 mos., 12 days

WILLIAM A. EVANS BIBLE
Owner: Mrs. W. A. Evans
798 Baxter St., Athens, Ga.

Parents - William A. Evans b. 10/3/1879, son of J. A. Evans and
    G. V. Evans
Lulie E. Evans b. 3/11/1886, dau. of R. H. Hawks and C. E. Hawks

Marriages
Lulie E. Hawks to W. A. Evans 5/15/1904
James Robert Evans, son of William A. Evans and Lulie E. Evans, to
    Annie May Kyles 12/25/1906
James Robert Evans to Annie Mae Mixon 4/17/1943
Henry Raiford Evans to Frances George 4/8/1944
George William Evans to Mary Fredonia Geddings 10/6/1944

Births
James R. Evans 10/27/1907   Henry Raiford Evans 2/20/1916
George W. Evans 1/9/1911   Eddie Warren Evans 12/11/1919
Cynthia S. Evans 5/28/1913   Elinor Louise Evans 6/16/1922

Deaths
Elinor Louise Evans 1/9/1927   William A. Evans 8/11/1943
Mamie Lou Evans 6/11/1942   John Coleman Evans 12/27/1943

J. DAWSON ELDER BIBLE Of Oglethorpe Co.
Owner: Cortney B. Elder
Arnoldsville, Ga.

J. Dawson Elder of Clarke Co. m. Mattie P. Aycock of Oglethorpe
Co., Ga. 12/20/1865 at Seaborn R. Aycock´s, by Rev. John Calvin
Johnson of Watkinsville, Clarke Co., Ga.

Our Father, J. D. Elder, b. 5/8/1842
Our Mother, Mattie P. Elder, b. 1/25/1847

(J. Dawson Elder Bible contd....)

Births

Eddie D. Elder 10/19/1866	Seaborn Allie Elder 9/1/1883
Charlie E. Elder 10/25/1868	Preston Elder 9/4/1884
Minnie L. Elder 2/12/1876	Courtney B. E.der 2/7/1886
Anna Rubie Elder 5/27/1877	Mary Janette Elder 5/8/1887
Emory A. Elder 12/16/1881	Eula Clyde Elder 3/29/1893

Deaths

Eddie Dawson Elder 8/20/1868   J. D. Elder 5/1/1917
Mrs. Mattie Aycock Elder 2/3/1930

DUKE ATLAS DANIELL BIBLE Of Clarke Co.
Owner: George C. Daniell
Bogart, Georgia

Births

D. A. Daniell 1/20/1841	M. N. Daniell 5/31/1873
S. E. Daniell 9/6/1843	G. B. Daniell 9/29/1876
P. F. Daniell 9/28/1854	G. C. Daniell 6/24/1879
Parilee Wages 7/3/1868	J. E. Daniell 11/23/1883
William L. Daniell 5/17/1871	

Marriages

D. A. Daniell to S. E. Daniell 9/15/1867
Parilee Wages 1/8/1885
D. A. Daniell to P. F. Daniell 3/24/1898

ARTHUR COX BIBLE
Owner: Mrs. Arthur Cox
330 Hampton Ct.
Athens, Georgia

Arthur Cox b. 1/2/1873 m. Annie Preston Hodgson b. 2/14/1872, on
1/17/1895

Births

William Cox 11/1/1895-d. same day	Joseph M. Cox 7/29/1903
Henry Cox 12/13/1896-d. same day	Lila Wingfield Cox 12/12/1905
Arthur Hodgson Cox 4/1/1898	Hallie Wingfield Cox
Elisha Carson Cox 10/7/1900	7/12/1908
	Nathan Preston Cox 7/6/1911

Deaths

Joseph M. Cox 3/21/1906   Arthur Carson Cox 12/1/1939

JAMES HARDY BIBLE

James and Mary Hardy m. 1/15/1801
John F. Sadler m. Eliza Hardy 3/1/1827
Garrison Linn m. Maria Hardy 4/3/1827
Thomas W. Teasley m. Elizabeth Teasley 2/6/1879

Births
James Hardy 3/10/1770   Eliza Hardy 10/28/1810
Mary Wilson Hardy 6/1/1773   Richard B. Hardy 10/20/1812
Miles Hardy 11/27/1803   John Hardy 11/24/1814
Maria Hardy 12/4/1805   Western Hardy 3/2/1817
James W. Hardy 3/23/1808   James Hardy ---

Deaths
James Hardy 2/9/1865
Mary Hardy, wife of James Hardy, 7/19/1849
Miles Hardy, son of James and Mary Hardy, 6/6/1843
Maria Linn (formerly Maria Hardy) 5/20/1847 at Cassville, Ga.
Eliza Hardy Sadler 5/3/1889
William M. Teasley 3/11/1907
Thomas W. Teasley 9/12/1911
Ethel, dau. of Thomas W. and Elizabeth Teasley,   12/6/1881-
    7/13/1883
Mary Sadler Jones 4/3/1913
Elsie Sadler Maybin spring, 1911
James Benson Teasley 1/1925, son of Loyd and Grace Benson Teasley

THOMAS ADAMS BIBLE
Owner: Mrs. B. C. Teasley
Hartwell, Ga.

Thomas Adams m. Sallie Ford 10/4/1786
            Births of Their Children:
Elizabeth 7/13/1787   Richard 6/24/1798
Thomas F. 6/5/1791   Abner 3/16/1800
Mourning 2/8/1793   John 3/30/1801
James B. 3/25/1795   Nichols 7/29/1804
Culvie 3/9/1797

J. O. MASON BIBLE
Owner: Wiley Mason, Machen, Ga.

Marriages
J. O. Mason 1/18/1838-8/6/1915 m. 8/12/186- Mary J. Mooneyham
    7/13/1847-12/13/1897
Mary Anna Louisa Mason b. 10/13/1867 m. 11/9/1886 Jim Knowles

(J. O. Mason Bible contd....)

Wiley Mason b. 1/30/1876 m. 11/24/1898 Matty Mooneyham b.
12/1/1879
I. N. Mason b. 11/25/1877 m. 12/18/1900 Juley Mooneyham
James Mason b. 8/4/1873 m. 11/18/1903 Mary Hunnicut

Births
Josephus Mason 3/15/1870   Sidney Wilson Mason 9/22/1882
Elen Mason 3/25/1872   John Marshall Mason 3/22/1886
H. D. Mason 3/27/1880   Lillie Teril Mason 11/1888

Leila Knowles 9/26/1887   Geo. Washington Mason 10/24/1902
Charlie Shaw Mason 9/4/1899   Thomas B. Mooneyham 10/14/1916

Deaths
Elen Mason 9/17/1873   Charlie Shaw Mason 11/21/1918
John Marshall Mason

ISAAC DAVIS ADERHOLD BIBLE *
Owner: Mrs. Carlton Thomas
Lavonia, Ga.

Isaac Davis Aderhold, C. N., 6/26/1834-5/26/1880, age 45 yrs.,
11 mos.
Elizabeth Jacobs 3/12/1837-6/5/1915 m. in Gwinnett Co. 9/23/1858
at Joseph Jacobs by Jack Nunley, J. P.

S. K. CANNON BIBLE
Of Lavonia, Georgia

John W. Cannon b. 7/12/1841   J. M. Cannon b. 11/26/1843
S. K. Cannon b. 6/4/1846

JACOB HAYS BIBLE Of Hart Co.

Jacob Hays 4/2/1818-5/27/1874   S. L. Hays 1/20/1852
Nancy Hays 2/28/1816   J. B. Hays 1/11/1853
William F. Hays 6/16/1844   Mary E. White 10/2/1859
J. R. Hays 2/13/1846   Edward B. Hays 5/12/1896-
J. S. Hays 12/6/1849   7/2/1899

*See also p. 162.   338

CLAYTON HERNDON BIBLE
Owner: Mrs. Bessie Herndon

Clayton Herndon b. 9/2/1871 m. 12/8/1896 Elizabeth Webb, b.
12/7/1871

Infant son 9/3/1897-9/3/1897
John Walker Herndon b. 1/10/1899

GODLIF DASHER BIBLE Of Effingham Co.*
Owner: Mrs. Fannie Fox Keller
210 West Bolton St., Savannah, Ga.

Godlif Dasher b. 4/3/1799 in Effingham Co. m. Sarah Smith Bird
6/3/1832, b. 3/7/1807, dau. of Eleanor Giles. Sarah Smith Bird
was from Black Creek, Bryan Co. Their Children:

(Dr.) Horace C. Dasher b. 1/3/1833
Ellen B. Dasher b. 11/19/1834
Susan C. Dasher b. 1/18/1843
Ralphene E. Dasher b. 7/18/1845
Hortense I. and John Dasher b. 12/11/1848
Pembroke Dasher b. 5/3/1838

Andrew Hamil Bird m. Eleanor Giles, both of S. C., their son:

Andrew Hamil Bird 6/8/1814-1/15/1847, m. Mrs. Frances (Wilson)
Fox in 1842. Their Children:

Andrew Hamil Bird 4/1846-1/18/1863. He was Lieutenant in Bryan
Guards, 25th Regt., Ga. Vols., Wilson's Brigade, drowned in Cape
Fear River while attempting to reach the wrecked Steamer,
"Columbia". His sister, Irene Bird, b. 3/14/1844 m. Robert Wade.

CLARENCE AUGUSTUS BURN BIBLE
Owner: Mrs. J. E. Condon
Grove & Twelfth Sts.
Charleston, S. C.

Henrietta Maria Seyle 3/12/1848-7/18/1926 m. Clarence Augustus
Burn 12/23/1869
Clarence Augustus Burn 6/18/1849-2/21/1880. Their Children:
Clarence Augustus Burn 12/30/1870-5/15/1929 m. Birtie Riley
Anna Idonia Burn 11/15/1872-7/22/1908 m. William Aldrich Carson
6/14/1891
John Paul Burn 9/1/1877-11/17/1928 m. Angel Nolte 9/8/1904
Eliza Anice Burn 5/17/1875-6/12/1876
Clarence Burn 4/2/1880-9/28/1911 m. Eddie Quinley

*See also p. 323.

SHIRLEY BIBLE

Births
Matilda Shirley 7/20/1817   Susan Finch Shirley 11/1/1848
Benjamin Franklin Ballard 1835   Mary Shirley 7/22/1851
James Shirley 5/20/1842   Joseph Shirley 7/22/1851
William Briant Shirley 4/2/1844   Wilson M. Golden 12/27/1852

Wilson Golden m. Susan Finch Shirley 10/5/1871
Alexarine Golden b. 1/2/1873

SAMUEL RUTHERFORD BIBLE
Owner: Mrs. T. G. Rutherford
Roberta, Ga.

Samuel Rutherford b. 2/5/1813
Elizabeth, his wife, b. 12/27/1818 Their Children:

Births
William Rutherford 7/20/1839   Susan Rutherford 9/6/1843
Eliza Bersheebee Rutherford 8/24/1841 Robt. Rutherford 7/29/1845
Mollie Rutherford 10/4/1847
Elizabeth Rutherford 12/31/1853

SAUNDERS BIBLE

Deaths
Merry Arthur Saunders 1/23/1822 Jasper Co.
Mrs. Elizabeth Saunders 11/14/1850
Susan Lucinda Saunders 8/29/1841
Billington M. Saunders 7/21/1843
Elizabeth Miller 2/12/1845
Samuel Hunter Saunders 12/9/1845
Seaborn J. Saunders 7/8/1854
Dr. Henry Saunders 4/16/1859
William R. Miller 7/29/1860
Margaret E. Saunders Barksdale 8/20/1903

ALEXANDER SINCLAIR BIBLE
Owner: Miss Willie Allbritton
Quitman, Ga.

Alexander Sinclair m. Catherine Waters 9/12/1806

Births
David Waters Sinclair 8/13/1807   Alexander Sinclair 6/20/1815
William Waters Sinclair 7/5/1809   James Waters Sinclair 6/26/1816
Jean Sinclair 12/5/1810   Henrietta Gordon Sinclair
Benjamin Waters Sinclair   9/10/1818
   9/12/1812   Elizabeth Anne Sinclair
Catherine Sinclair 3/27/1814   2/15/1820
                                   Margaret Sinclair 7/8/1821

Deaths
David Waters Sinclair 8/3/1848 at Bangulpore East India
William Waters Sinclair 7/26/1853 at Goanally East India
James Waters Sinclair 2/8/1819

JOHN J. SIMPSON BIBLE
Owner: J. J. Simpson
19 Brookwood Dr., Atlanta, Ga.

Marriages
John J. Simpson to Mary E. Blanchard 7/10/1857
Kathrine P. A. Simpson to John B. Roberts 11/17/1870 Terrell Co.
John J. Simpson to Frances A. Smith 1/18/1855

Births
Kathrine Priscilla Ann Simpson 8/2/1852
William Appleton Simpson 11/18/1855
George Parks Simpson 11/16/1858
Edward Hawkins Simpson 12/13/1801
John James Simpson Jr. 8/10/1864
John J. Simpson 10/26/1820
Frances Ann Smith Simpson 10/23/1837

MICAJAH PAULK BIBLE

Marriages
Micajah Paulk 3/4/1810 to Charlotty Ogburn
Micajah Paulk 3/19/1823 to Kiziah Harvel
Micajah Paulk 8/7/1828 to Nancy Ross (3rd wife)
John Paulk Sr. 6/2/1818 to Malissa Ann Harvel
Sophia Paulk 1/21/1836 to Oran Nash

341

(Micajah Paulk Bible, Marriages, contd....)

Anderson Hall 1/20/1836 to Edney Paulk
Francis Metilda Paulk 10/30/1845
Anderson Williams 8/18/1858 to Martha Ann Amanda Paulk
William Hooks 3/1/1860 to Nancy Missouriann Paulk
James R. paul 12/3/1872 to Lugenia E. Collins

Deaths
Charlotty Paulk 9/13/1822
John Paulk Jr. 7/7/1823
Jonathan Paulk 11/29/1833
John Paulk Sr. 9/14/1824
William Ross Paulk 2/25/1842
Micajah Paulk Jr. 6/4/1842
Nancy Ross Paulk 9/30/1843
Sophia Nash Paulk 7/8/1845
Francis Willis Paulk 1/7/1846
James Ogburn Paulk 7/13/1846

William Joseph Paulk 1/25/1848
T. Patkman Beall 7/11/1850
Elias Lawhorn 8/22/1855
Micajah Paulk Sr. 12/19/1855
Mary Jane Williams 9/8/1872
Nancy Missouriann Collins
    6/12/1911
John Paulk 7/4/1851
Mary Ann Paulk 6/21/1851
Ella Lugenia Paulk 7/13/1890
Amanda Collins 2/27/1896

Births
Eurias Paulk 10/14/1780
John Paulk 12/13/1791
Jonathan Paulk 12/25/1793
Charlotty Paulk 2/26/1795
Priscilla Paulk 3/12/1811
Sophia Paulk 10/17/1813
Andey Paulk 1/1/1816
Mary Ann Paulk 4/18/1817
Susan Paulk 1/1/1819
Jacob Paulk 11/28/1820
Francis Matilda Paulk 7/14/1829
Martha Amanda Paulk 1/29/1831
Dorkes Paulk 9/12/1816
William Paulk 12/16/1819
Micajah Paulk Sr. 5/8/1822
William Joseph Paulk 3/6/1833

Nancy Mazuary Ann Paulk 3/24/1835
Micajah Paulk Jr. 1/1/1842
James Ross Paulk 6/6/1843
Manda Hooks 2/19/1861
Lugenia E. Paulk 8/15/1849
John Paulk 10/22/1805
Mary Ann Paulk 6/20/1807
Cincinattus Collins 1/4/1868
James Franklin Williams 8/1/1859
Nancy M. Ann Williams 7/23/1861
Fanny Cemetta Williams 10/1/1863
Laura Beann Williams 10/28/1865
Mary Jane Williams 1/17/1870

CRAWFORD TUCKER BIBLE
Owner: Mrs. Annie H. Swann

Crawford Tucker m. Elizabeth S. Reid 8/17/1828
Crawford Tucker m. Margaret L. Reid 11/22/1830
E. C. Harris m. Margaret L. Tucker 4/1865
Charles A. Hawkins m. Harriet V. Tucker 4/18/1866

Births
Crawford Tucker 9/18/1787
Elizabeth S. Tucker 10/21/1805
Margaret Lockhart Tucker 3/12/1813
Mary Elizabeth Augustin Tucker, dau. of Crawford and Elizabeth S.
    Tucker, 5/13/1829
Joseph Ruffin Tucker, son of Crawford and Margaret L. Tucker,
    4/13/1832

(Crawford Tucker Bible contd....)

William Horace Tucker, son of above, 12/5/1833
John Edmond A. Tucker, son of above, 7/7/1835
Junious Cornelia Tucker, dau. of above, 4/29/1837
Washington Franklin Tucker, son of above, 7/8/1838
Crawford Tucker, son of above, 10/16/1839
Benjamin Vestal, son of above, 5/23/1841
Julia Colson Tucker, dau. of above, 7/12/1842
Margaret Isabella Tucker, dau. of above, 11/23/1844
Harriet Virginia Tucker, dau. of above, 2/28/1846
Georgia Carolina, dau. of above, 1/25/1849
Charles Puryear Tucker, son of above, 6/10/1851

Deaths
Crawford Tucker 1/24/1852
Margaret L. Harris 7/23/1877
Elizabeth S. Tucker 11/12/1829
Washington Franklin Tucker 9/11/1838
Benjamin Vestal Tucker 8/24/1841
Julia Colson Tucker 9/27/1842
Margaret Isabella Tucker 4/18/1845
Georgia Carolina Tucker 10/2/1849
Charles Puryear Tucker 6/1/1852
Crawford Tucker killed in 2nd Battle of Manassas 8/30/1862. He
   was Lieut. in 1st Ga. Regular
John E. A. Tucker 3/25/1877
William Horace Tucker 4/4/1878
Crawford Tucker, son of J. E. A. Tucker and grandson of Crawford
   and Margaret Tucker, was killed on G. P. R. R. in a
   wreck 8/2/1887
William Horace Tucker, son of W. H. Tucker, 2/27/1896, grandson
   of Crawford and Margaret Tucker.

ELIZABETH G. MILLS BIBLE
Owner: Mrs. Charles Gardner Mills
Griffin, Ga.

Births
Thomas R. Mills 10/27/1807
Elizabeth G. Tufts 7/31/1821
Charles G. Mills 6/20/1842
Thomas R. Mills 4/6/1844
Thomas R. Mills 6/8/1845
Louisiana Tufts Mills 3/26/1848
William Martin Mills 2/23/1849
Mary E. Mills 6/26/1851
John M. Mills 2/26/1855
James M. Mills 6/19/1857
Mary C. Cope 8/8/1850

Mary E. Reid 3/4/1849
Lavonia Hammond 1/18/1859
Sallie G. Banks ---
Maria Ann Mills 10/9/1803
Martin Tufts 8/24/1824
Charles Gardner Mills 5/3/1887
Blanton Winslop Mills
   12/18/1923
Wallace Wooten Mills 8/27/1920
Rosalind Blakely Mills
   4/23/1915
Chas. Gardner Mills III 3/1914

Marriages
James Mills to Anna Harris of England
William Mills to Catherine, native of Willsboro, Sussex, England
William Mills (2nd wife) to Mary Ann McIntosh in St. Augustine,

(Elizabeth G. Mills Bible contd....)

Fla. 2/17/1797 in Cathedral. She was dau. of Roderick McIntosh
of Inverness, Scotland, and Christina Matheson
Thomas Roderick Mills of Savannah and Elizabeth G. Tufts of
Savannah, 10/1/1840, by Rev. Joseph Binney
Thomas R. Mills to Mary Ansley Cope in Savannah, 11/13/1869 by
Rev. Mr. Landrum
Charles G. Mills to Mary E. Reid, Macon, Ga. 4/19/1870 by Rev.
Mr. Bass
John B. Mills to Lavonia Hammond, Griffin. 2/26/1879 by Rev.
Mr. Pinkerton
James M. Mills to Sallie G. Banks, Griffin, 5/14/1878, by Rev.
Mr. Pinkerton
Charles G. Mills to Rosalind Blakely 4/2/1913, Griffin, Ga.,
by Rev. Mr. King
Charles G. Mills Jr. to Claire Wooten 11/20/1919 Dawson, Ga.
by Rev. Mr. Stafford

Deaths
Louisiana A. Tufts 2/22/1845   J. M. Mills ---
Thomas R. Mills 8/27/1845   J. M. Mills 3/23/1911
Louisiana Tufts Mills 2/23/1848   William M. Mills 8/14/1912
J. M. Tufts 1/20/1851   Chas. Gardner Mills 3/17/1914
Mary E. Mills 7/2/--   Rosalind Blakely Mills
Mary Martin Tufts 2/6/1871   12/18/1917
Maria Ann Mills 6/1/1879   Wallace Wooten Mills 1/1/1923
Thomas R. Mills 2/27/1881   Chas. Gardner Mills II
                                    12/30/1925

JAMES ALFORD ROGERS BIBLE
Owner: Mrs. J. M. Arthur, Eastman, Ga.

James Alford Rogers 2/21/1786-7/3/1854 m. 4/3/1812
Susan P. Ashley Rogers 8/8/1795-10/18/1840
Martha E. Rogers 2/27/1813
John L. A. Rogers 2/20/1815-8/16/1817
William H. Rogers 4/16/1817-8/7/1855
Susan Ann Rogers 10/18/1819
James Collins Rogers 8/6/1822
Josiah Sherward Rogers 2/24/1825-9/24/1840
Wiley Alford Rogers 7/24/1827-10/30/1827
Albert Jones Rogers 12/6/1829-9/22/1839
Mary Kesiah Rogers 4/6/1832
Baby 1/31/1835-5/7/1835
Helen Josephine Rogers 5/3/1836
Tabitha Gertrude Rogers 2/18/1839
Lutitia Wineyford Rogers 10/18/1840

JAMES HUDSON ROWE BIBLE
Owner: James Hudson Rowe, Pell City, Ala.

Shadrack Rowe, Rev. Soldier, b. 1762 d. 9/1853, father of James
Hudson Rowe.

James Hudson Rowe b. 6/4/1801 m. Kathryn Moss McKloney 1823 (she
was b. 4/19/1802). Their Children:

Births
James E. Rowe 12/8/1825-2/28/1905
Amanda Rowe 12/10/1927
William Hughes Alexander Rowe 8/4/1829-6/1/1882
Elizabeth Jane Rowe 6/18/1831
Sarah Frances Rowe 3/11/1833
Martha Susan Rowe 7/14/1835-7/31/1837
Nancy Emily Rowe 2/16/1837
Elizabeth Ann Rowe 2/5/1838
Cynthia B. Lear Rowe 4/4/1840
Virginia Josephine Rowe 9/15/1843
Olga Ann Caroline Rowe 1/13/1840

Lydia Cathrine Dunnigan, dau. of Amanda Rowe, 1/6/1851

Alexander Morse, father of Cathrine Elizabeth Rowe,
2/24/1771-5/20/1857

Grandchildren of James Hudson Rowe:

James Hudson Rowe 3/27/1882
Luther A. Rowe 2/27/1889-6/1/1889
Samuel Oren Rose 1/11/1893

JOHN ROBINSON BIBLE Of Baldwin Co.
Rev. War Pension W5747

John Robinson b. 5/6/1756   Jeriah Robinson b. 8/19/1769
    m. 3/27/1788   Their Children:

Solomon Robinson 4/1/1789   Luke Robinson 3/20/1797
John Robinson 8/4/1792   William Robinson 2/9/1798
Salley Robinson 8/3/1794   Mariah Robinson 4/3/1801

345

DANIEL McNEIL BIBLE
Owner: Mrs. Sarah McNeil Biggs
Talbot Co., Ga.

Daniel McNeil 4/7/1778-1/1847 m. 4/19/1798

Births of Children:

Samuel McNeil 11/24/1800   Margaret McNeil 3/15/1811
Sarah McNeil 10/10/1802   Jemima McNeil 12/6/1812
Mary McNeil 8/5/1804   D. U. (Ulyses) McNeil 3/9/1815
William McNeil 10/7/1807   Henry McNeil 10/18/1817
Jane McNeil 5/17/1809   Mildred McNeil 1/2/1820

WILLIAM McKINLEY BIBLE
Owner: Guy McKinley
Milledgeville, Ga.

William McKinley 8/10/1744-4/22/1798
Mary Beatty 6/25/1756-12/14/1806

Children:

Ester Barksdale McKinley 10/13/1772-2/28/1808
Elizabeth Montgomery McKinley 1/16/1775-3/3/--
John Wilson McKinley 9/1/1777-
Archibald Carlisle McKinley 9/9/1779-
James Beatty McKinley 2/22/1782-
Mary Ansley McKinley 12/26/1784-10/1828
William Harris McKinley 6/23/1787-10/10/1793
Robert Mecklin McKinley 8/25/1790-
Jane Moseley McKinley 9/9/1792-

BENJAMIN HODGES BIBLE
owner: Mrs. Walter Powers
1726 Barnard St., Savannah, Ga.

Births
Benjamin Hodges 1755   Julia Ann Rolls 7/12/1817
Jane Phelps 1/23/1763   Helen Jane Hodges 5/3/1838
Josiah J. Hodges 5/16/1813

Deaths
Benjamin Hodges 6/4/1818   Julia Abb Hodges 7/19/1863
Jane Hodges 7/19/1863   Josiah J. Hodges 1890

346

```
                        THOMAS HEARD BIBLE
                   Owner: George Heard Tunnell



Thomas Heard m. Ann Richards 1/8/1830

Births
Thomas Heard 2/20/1803           Ann Richards 10/21/1808

    Their Children:

Benjamin Pope Heard 12/10/1830     George Heard 2/11/1840
Martha Angeline Heard 3/29/1832    Henry Heard 3/1/1842
Columbus Heard 12/18/1833          James Willis Heard 7/8/1844
Franklin Heard 3/3/1836            Margaret Delaney Heard 2/5/1847
Elizabeth Emily Heard 2/8/1838     Francis Ann Heard 3/14/1849

Marriages
Martha Angeline Heard to Jesse William Tunnell 9/6/1857
Elizabeth Emily Heard to Benjamin LeRebour 11/20/1853
Margaret Delaney Heard to Milus A. Oliver 12/3/1874
James Willis Heard to Lizzie Otto in Baltimore, Md.
Francis Ann Heard to Joseph L. Lane 1/5/1871

Deaths
Benjamin Pope Heard 6/21/1833
George Heard 7/21/1861 on Battlefield in Va.
Franklin Heard 5/23/1862 in Hospital, Richmond, Va.
Elizabeth Emily Heard Le Rebour 5/12/1912
Martha Angeline Heard Tunnell 9/14/1904
Thomas Heard 5/28/1863
Ann Richards Heard 1892
Columbus Heard 10/22/1912
Margaret Delaney Heard Oliver 2/5/1917
Francis Ann Heard Lane 8/30/1913
Henry Heard 2/28/1919
James Willis Heard d. Brooklyn, N. Y.


                     SAMUEL GEORGE WYNN BIBLE
                  Owner: Mrs. Edith Wynne Hunter
                          Ocalla, Fla.



Births of Children of S. G. and S. E. Wynn:

Mary Elizabeth Wynn 10/29/1854
Laura Catherine 78/23/1856-9/3/1857
Samuel G. Wynne 2/7/1869 m. Sarah Catherine Woodall 12/27/1853
Edith Wynne 3/25/1864 m. Albert Sam Hunter 3/8/1882

Albert Sam Hunter d. 11/10/1922
```

WILLIAM M. WINTERS BIBLE
Owner: L. P. Suddath
530 Luckie St., Atlanta, Ga.

William M. Winters m. Angelina Bowen 12/25/1845

Births
William M. Winters 6/15/1816   Helen Mar. Winters 2/15/1847
Angelina Bowen Winters 11/13/1822   Eugenia Arabella Winters
                                          5/14/1849

William M. Winters d. 5/3/1851

W. H. WILKINSON BIBLE

W. H. Wilkinson m. Nancy Elizabeth Davison 1/1/1871

W. W. Wilkinson b. 5/19/1839
Mrs. N. E. Wilkinson b. 4/10/1849
Vickie V. Wilkinson b. 10/14/1871

THOMAS WILCOX BIBLE

Julia Wilcox Bozeman, wife of Henry Marsh Bozeman, dau. of Thomas
  Wilcox and Abigail McDuffie Wilcox.
Thomas Wilcox 2/17/1812-4/1897 m. Abigail McDuffie 11/25/1830
Abigail McDuffie b. 2/22/1816
Thomas Wilcox, was son of John Wilcox and Mary Lea, who m. 8/2/1778
John Wilcox 11/19/1777-1/2/1852
Mary Lea Wilcox d. 7/27/1848
John Wilcox, was son of John Wilcox and-----Butler.
John Wilcox 6/21/1728-1793

JOSIAH WHITEHURST BIBLE
Owner: Julian Bloodworth

Josiah Whitehurst m. Thuly Ann Wilkinson 8/5/1824

Births
Josiah Whitehurst 10/17/1802
Thuly Ann Whitehurst 10/15/1806
Morgan L. Whitehurst 6/18/1825

(Josiah Whitehurst Bible, Births, contd....)

Wilkinson M. Whitehurst 7/27/1827
John L. Whitehurst 12/17/1829
Georgiann Whitehurst 4/13/1832
Missouri A. Whitehurst 2/.22/1834
Thomas C. Whitehurst 3/20/1836
Christiana E. Whitehurst 12/1/1837
Louisa J. Whitehurst 11/4/1840
Charles L. Whitehurst 7/12/1845
Laura Whitehurst 10/11/1848
Josiah I. Whitehurst 4/16/1850

Deaths
John L. Whitehurst 10/14/1857   Thomas C. Whitehurst 3/23/1890
Laura E. Whitehurst 12/5/1864   Morgan L. Whitehurst ---
Josiah   Whitehurst 8/21/1875   Charles L. Whitehurst 5/2/1925
Wilkinson M. Whitehurst 7/23/1873 Thulia A. Whitehurst 2/23/1881
Louisa J. Whitehurst, wife of E. F. M. Calloway, 3/3/1881
Christiana E. Smith, nee Whitehurst, 4/16/1896
Missouri A. Whitehurst 12/3/1906

MILLARD WHITEHEAD BIBLE
Owner: Mrs. L. N. Betts, Athens, Ga.

Millard F. Whitehead m. Nancy Malcom 1/15/1873

Births
M. F. Whitehead 10/21/1850   Lilla T. Whitehead 2/2/1881
Nancy A. Whitehead 11/8/1855   Daisy V. Whitehead 3/4/1883
Minie E. Whitehead 12/12/1873   William Malcom 8/13/1813
Alver E. Whitehead 1/24/1875   Luise Malcom 5/4/1817
Valie Whitehead 9/6/1878

Deaths
M. F. Whitehead 2/21/1918   William Malcom 1/6/1899
Nancy A. Whitehead 11/30/1927   Luise Malcom 5/2/1898

HENRY WHITE BIBLE Of Jasper Co.
Owner: Mrs. Sadie White Malone
Monticello, Ga.

Henry White 4/24/1724-6/17/1802
Celia White, wife of Henry White, 9/18/1731-3/31/1799
John White, son of Henry and Celia White, 10/20/1749-10/8/1823
William Page White, son of John and Barsheba White, b. 12/1/1815
Elizabeth Hardy White, wife of William P. White,
  6/20/1827-12/31/1892

Deaths
Barsheba White, wife of John White, 12/27/1837
Barsheba White 3/11/1905

BENJAMIN B. WHITE BIBLE
Owner: Martha Stamps, Upson Co.

Benjamin B. White 10/20/1811-11/25/1887, b. in Elbert Co., m.
1st Louisa A. Burton 5/30/1839. She d. 2/1/1844, age 22 yrs.
She was a dau. of William B. Burton. She had one son, Tom White.

Benjamin B. White m. 2d Mary O. Richardson 12/8/1846. She d.
6/14/1854

Benjamin B. White m. 3rd Sarah O. Stamps 10/1/1868. She d.
12/24/1923

Amos W. White 8/21/1848-1/23/1914 m. 1st Laura Cauthern.

JACOB W. WHEELER BIBLE
Owner: Jacob W. Wheeler, Hollywood, Ga.

Jacob W. Wheeler m. Elizabeth Mariah Wheeler 1/28/1869

Jacob W. Wheeler b. 6/16/1848
Elizabeth Mariah Wheeler b. 5/5/1848

GREEN B. TURNER BIBLE
Owner: Mrs. A. C. McCall

Green B. Turner b. 4/4/1787 m. Rebeckah Mosely 7/24/1811, dau.
of Henry Mosely b. 10/23/1796

Births of Children:

Anderson Lee Turner 12/15/1812   Lenezer T. Turner, dau.,
Polley Spratlen Turner 1/29/1815   12/15/1825
James Henry Turner 12/8/1822   Green Berry Turner 1/21/1831

REBECCA VALLENTINE BIBLE

Silas Leslie 1780-4/25/1856 m. on 1801 Bethany Tison 1785-1832

Rebecca Leslie, dau. of Silas and Bethany Leslie b. Wilkinson
   Co. near Gordon, Ga., d. 2/18/1873
Thomas Vallentine d. 12/8/1857

(Bible of Rebecca Vallentine contd....)

Children of Rebecca and Thomas Vallentine:

Andrew Vallentine d. 1/27/1837
Sarah Vallentine b. 6/6/-- m. Robert Taylor 12/25/1838
Levi Vallentine b. 10/5/1822
James Vallentine b. 11/1825
Elizabeth Vallentine b. 6/20/-- m. John King 8/17/1845
(Rebecca Vallentine Bible contd....)

Thomas Vallentine b. 4/---d. 3/10/1852
William (Rick) Vallentine b. 1833 m. Sarah Jane Hardy 3/4/1858
Bethany Vallentine b. 4/3/1855 m. Daniel Stinson
Nancy Ann Vallentine b. 4/13/1833 m. 1st Green 2d Carroll. She
   d. 9/24/19--
Easter Ann Sibby Vallentine 5/6/1839-11/11/-- m. John Sheffield
Silas Washington Vallentine b. -/24/184- m. Lucinda Day
John F. Vallentine 1843-6/13/--
Joel Jackson Vallentine b. 6/18/1845 m. Nancy Vandiver

Sarah Ann Rebecca Sheffield d. 11/13/186-
John M. Sheffield d. 9/---

                JAMES OGLETHORPE VARNEDOE BIBLE

Bartholomew Austin Busby 8/10/1788 S. C.-12/1/1862 m. Mary
   Elizabeth Mallard 11/14/1839
Rebecca Ann Busby b. 12/21/1840 m. James Madison Bacon
Harriet Louise Busby 12/21/1842-11/8/1896 m. James Oglethorpe
   Varnedoe 5/9/1860
Anne Elizabeth Busby b. 4/27/1844 m. Willie Winn 12/15/1860
Mary Austin Busby 7/23/1845-8/15/1845
James Oglethorpe Varnedoe b. 6/24/1842
Willie Winn b. 4/15/1843

James Madison Bacon d. 8/24/1862
Anne Elizabeth Busby Winn d. 1901
James Oglethorpe Varnedoe d. 1/3/1927

                    GEORGE WALKER BIBLE

George Walker b. 11/14/1763   Betsey Walker b. 3/15/1767
                 Births of Their Children:
Joel Walker 1/12/1788   David Walker 5/1/1798
George Walker 1st 5/1789   Charles Walker 10/16/1800
Polly Walker 4/29/1790   Betsey Walker 3/18/1803
George Walker 8/13/1793   Rebecca Walker 5/6/1806
Thomas Walker 9/4/1795   Thomas D. Walker 5/9/1808
                                 Sarah H. Walker 8/9/1/1810

                        351

DAVID J. WALLER BIBLE

David J. Waller b. 5/19/1866 m. 12/11/1890 Mary Elizabeth Dye b.
6/15/1869 Births of Their Children:

Sallie Lee Waller 11/3/1891   Albert Waller 6/31/1899
James Thomas Waller 1/4/1893   Wardlow Waller 10/6/1901
Willie Daniel Waller 1/17/1895   Mary Willard Waller 5/18/1905
Nina Waller 5/12/1896   Joe Waller 3/17/1903
Clem Waller 10/18/1897   Doretha Waller 10/21/1906
                                   Louise Waller 4/15/1908

JULIA ANN WARTHER BIBLE
Owner: Mrs. A. B. Griffin
Bainbridge, Ga.

Mrs. Julia Ann Warther 12/23/1848-2/24/1826
Joseph Warther 5/11/1865-7/13/1931
J. H. Derrick 11/15/1890-
Mrs. John H. Derrick 12/23/1848-
Mary Ann Derrick 6/17/1855-

ABNER WEBSTER BIBLE *
Owner: Mrs. M. L. Kelley
Thomaston, Ga.

Abner Webster b. 12/25/1761
Elizabeth, his wife, b. 2/14/1766
                    Births of Their Children:
William Webster 9/21/1784   Martin Webster 11/10/1794
Ann Webster 1/13/1786   Seborn Webster 8/10/1796
Pherebea Webster 12/24/1788   Labon & Elbom Webster 7/25/179
Mariah Webster 1/20/1793   Reuben Webster 12/17/1800
John Webster 12/15/1790   Samuel Webster 6/24/1802

MOSES GUYTON SR. BIBLE
Owner: Helen Bishop, Eastman, Ga.

Moses Guyton 10/27/1758-6/21/1807   Mary Guyton 4/4/1791
Tabithia Guyton 12/10/1764-2/10/1811 Charles Guyton 9/6/1793
John Guyton 2/5/1784   Joseph Guyton 9/12/1795
Judith Guyton 3/22/1786   Sarah Guyton 8/24/1797
Hannah Guyton 6/22/1788   Moses Guyton 9/4/1799
Elizabeth Guyton 11/25/1803   Tabithia Guyton 8/11/1801

*See also p. 103.   352

MOSES GUYTON, JR. BIBLE
Of Buckeye, Laurens Co.

Moses Guyton 9/4/1799
Mary Ann, nee Lane, 2/18/1811
Tabitha Jane Guyton 12/6/1830
Mary Elizabeth Guyton 7/7/1833
Sarah Caroline Guyton 5/4/1836
Margaret Lane Guyton 2/7/1839

Augusta Helena Guyton 5/7/1841
Emma Saxon Guyton 8/24/1843
Moses Guyton 8/30/1846
Julia Elmira Guyton 10/17/1849
Amos Charles Guyton 9/3/1852
Charles Guyton 3/31/1855

LAZARUS SOLOMON BIBLE
Owner: Mrs. A. J. Toole, Dublin, Ga.

Children of Lazarus Solomon and wife, Elizabeth Bedgood:

Delilah Solomon 9/12/1789-2/23/1815
Henry Solomon 3/22/1791
William Solomon 12/7/1792
Mary Solomon 1/13/1795
John Solomon 1/3/1797
Dicey Solomon 1/25/1799
James   Solomon   10/17/1800
Elizabeth Solomon 3/11/1814

Sarah Solomon 10/10/1802
Fannie Solomon 9/17/1804
Peter Solomon 8/4/1806
Hardy Solomon 5/17/1808
Carol Solomon 9/30/1810
Lewis Solomon 10/4/1812

HENRY FELDER BIBLE

Henry Felder b. 7/9/1794
Harriett Felder b. 10/1/1795
Samuel Felder b. 11/24/1796
Ann L. Felder b. 4/20/1799 (m. 1821 David Houser)
Lewis Felder b. 4/5/1801
Rebecca L. Felder b. 4/30/1803
Henry Felder, b. 1748, son of John Henry Felder and Mary Eliza-
beth Shaumloffel
Margaret Standmeyer b. 1773, dau. of Martin and Margaret.

N. H. LEVERETT BIBLE Of Jasper Co.

Births
Nathan Hillery Leverett 5/7/1832
L. E. M. Leverett 6/22/1834
A. J. Leverett 9/5/1850
M. J. Leverett 12/8/1851
T. J. Leverett 3/27/1853
J. H. Leverett 1/14/1855
Hillery Elizabeth L. (Lumsden) Leverett 11/23/1863

D. Leverett 4/10/1856-
     8/8/1859
M. M. Leverett 5/17/1858
W. L. Leverett 3/31/1866
L. S. Leverett 4/26/1868
N. O. Leverett 6/21/1872

MARY ELIZABETH GOOLSBY WOOLFOLK BIBLE
Owner: Mrs. G. C. Barfield, Columbus, Ga.

Mary Elizabeth Goolsby b. 5/1/1832 m. Sowell C. Woolfolk
 (4/6/1830-11/25/1885) on 10/12/1852

Katie Eolins Woolfolk b. 7/29/1853
Mary Sowell Woolfolk b. 8/14/1858
Lula Woolfolk b. 4/13/1861
Mary E. Woolfolk b. 7/9/1870
Katy E. Woolfolk b. 8/4/1871
Lula Woolfolk b. 11/4/1877

JOSEPH ALEXANDER BIBLE
Owner: Mrs. Lula Ritch King
Athens, Ga.

Joseph Alexander m. Lucinda 5/3/1832
John J. Alexander b. 2/16/1833
Nancy J. Alexander b. 1/19/1835
Samuel L. Alexander b. 2/28/1837

J. J. Alexander d. 10/11/1863 Gordensville, Va.

J. W. WEBB BIBLE

J. W. Webb b. 11/22/1853 m. Sarah J. Cook 3/12/1871

S. J. Webb b. 4/29/1854   W. T. Webb b. 6/28/1872
Martha A. Webb b. 6/29/1874

VINSON R. PORTER BIBLE
Owner: Mrs. M. J. Gorrie
3224 Brookwood Rd., Birmingham, Ala. 35223

Vinson R. Porter b. 8/19/1792
Amelia B. (Beall) Porter b. 1/3/1792, Their Children:
Eleanor Catherine Porter b. 11/28/1813
Ann Caroline Porter b. 3/15/1816
Mary Adeline Porter b. 2/17/1819
Elizabeth Eveline Porter 4/1822
Oliver A. J. (Anthony Josiah Rees) Porter b. 4/9/1823
Ann Eliza Porter b. 9/5/1830

Deaths
Vinson R. Porter 12/18/1851   Elizabeth Eveline Porter 6/10/1822
Amelia B. Porter 2/4/1869   Oliver A. J. Porter 8/7/1832 (1872?)
Ann Carolina Porter 10/9/1825 Ann Eliza Porter 8/7/1834

Marriages
Vinson R. Porter and Amelia B. Rees 9/22/1812
Eleanor Catherine Porter and Joseph Dan Lyon 12/20/1832
Mary Adeline Porter and Pleasant Davis 12/24/1837
William Rees, our grandfather, was b. 8/27/1769. Eleanor Beall,
wife of William Rees, was b. 5/18/1769. Children:
Leathy B. Rees m. David Lawson
Amelia B. Rees m. Vinson R. Porter
Elizabeth F. Rees m. 1st Charles Hudson, 2d,----Moreland
Thaddeus B. Rees m. 1st Rebecca Ried, 2d Martha Floyd
John Rees m. Ann Bracken
Abraham F. Rees m. Sallie Mathews
Nancy Walter Rees m. Daniel Hightower
Josiah B. Rees m. Elizabeth Pitts
Polly Allen Rees m. Henry Pruitt
Mary Dent Rees m. William Park
Eliza Green Rees m. Elisha Bastion
Epsy Barton Rees m. Green Stephens
William Rees m. Luvany Evens

ALFRED McSWAIN BIBLE
Owner: Mrs. Preston Nixon, Rt 3, Box 154
Carrollton, Ga. 30117

Alfred McSwain m. Lucinda Rebecca Evans 12/29/1819
Alfred McSwain b. 12/22/1798
Lucinda Rebecca McSwain b. 7/2/1805
D. C. McSwain b. 10/25/1820
Mary Ann McSwain b. 2/16/1822
Eliza Matilda McSwain b. 2/29/1824
Wilson Croghan McSwain b. 11/5/1825
Margaret Emily McSwain b. 8/11/1827
Babe b. 4/5/1829
Lucinda Jane McSwain b. 5/25/1830
Sarah Frances McSwain b. 1/5/1832
John Evans McSwain b. 5/21/1834
Augustus Alfred McSwain b. 4/16/1836
Nancy Sims? McSwain b. 2/7/1838
Titus Hiram McSwain b. 12/1/1840
Charlotte Calista (Cynthia) McSwain b. 11/26/1842

355

(Alfred McSwain Bible contd....)

Deaths

Mary Ann McSwain d. 10/20/1825   Babe d. 5/7/1830
Margaret Emily d. 4/16/1839
Wilson Crogham McSwain d. 11/12/1861 in Williamsburg, Va. pf
chronic diarrhia
Augustus Alfred McSwain d. 5/18/1862 in Richmond, Va. of chronic
diarrhia
John Evans McSwain d. 4/14/1865 at Elmira Prison, N. Y. of
typhoid and pneumonia
Eliza M. McSwain d. 2/3/1878
Alfred McSwain d. 11/28/1879
Dennis McSwain b. 11/2/1768   Nancy McSwain d. 10/4/1826
Edmund McSwain b. 4/6/1771   Elizabeth McSwain d.9/19/1826
Sarah McSwain b. 8/28/1813   Willis D. McSwain b. 10/28/1818
Margot McSwain, wife of Dennis   Martha McSwain b. 10/30/1816
  McSwain 5/24/1821
Joanna McSwain d. 7/5/1826

ANNA and PINKNEY W. PILSON BIBLE

Births

Cleton Hilson 3/18/1833   Hetty Hilson 11/5/1842
Hilrey Hilson 10/21/1834   Aaron Henche 6/7/1844
Rutha Hilson 6/5/1836   Lency Hilson 11/25/1845
Martha Ann Hilson 10/13/1837   H. Hilson 9/10/1847
Laborn Hilson 4/15/1839   Lucenda Hilson 3/25/1849
Pinkney W. Hilson 5/10/1841   Sarah Nancy Adelia 10/27/1850
  Anna Odom Hilson d. 10/5/1887

Marriages

P. W. Hilson and A. E. Odom 2/7/1832
G. W. Vickry and Rutha Hilson 7/27/1854
T. J. Seale and Martha Hilson 2/29/1860
A. H. Hilson and J. E. Johnson 10/11/1865
H. T. Seale and Lucinda Hilson 1/29/1871
A. T. Sims and N. A. Hilson 12/10/1868

THEOPHILUS STERLING LUCKIE BIBLE
Owner: Glenn B. Ray, Rt.1, Box 548, Oxford, Ga. 30267

This certifies that the rite of Holy Matrimony was celebrated
between Theophilus Sterling Luckie of Atlanta, Ga. and Lucie Lola
Benton of 19th District, Decatur Co., Ga. on 10/11/1855 at James
Tinsley Benton´s by Joseph Bradford, Methodist Minister. WItness:
John J. Cooper and William Nelson Benton.

Marriages

Emma Louisa Luckie and Edward M. Nash 11/3/1878, 18th District,
DeKalb Co., Ga. by Rev. Simmons, Methodist Minister.
Lulia Lucie Luckie and R. P. Nesbit 1/17/1884 by Rev. McClelland,
Presbyterian Minister of Stone Mountain, Ga.
Dollie Isabella Luckie and Richard Newman Pounds by Elijah Wood,
1/15/1885
Lane Lowry Luckie and Alice McDonald by M. T. Ellis, Presbyterian
Minister, Doraville, Ga. 1/1/1919

(Theophilus Sterling Luckie Bible contd....)

Births
Rebecca Frances Luckie, 19th Dist., Decatur Co., Ga. 7/12/1856
Emma Louisa Luckie, 19th Dist., Decatur Co., Ga. 6/16/1857
Lulu Lucie Luckie, Gadsden Co., Fla. 10/12/1858
Dollie Isabella Luckie, Atlanta, Ga. 11/10/1860
Lane Lowry Luckie, 18th Dist., DeKalb Co., Ga. 5/16/1876
Infant son, 18th Dist., DeKalb Co., Ga. 6/4/1879
Ella May Luckie, 18th Dist., DeKalb Co., Ga. 5/3/1882

Deaths
Infant son, 18th Dist., DeKalb Co., Ga., 6/4/1879
Ella May Luckie, 18th Dist., DeKalb Co., Ga., 3/19/1885
Rebecca Francis Luckie, Dakulla, Fla., 6/6/1883
T. S. Luckie, 2/17/1902
Lucie L. Luckie, 4/10/1910
Mrs. Dollie Pounds, 5/5/1921
Mrs. Emma L. Nash, 1/14/1923
Lane L. Luckie, 12/1/1946

Memoranda
T. S. Luckie b. Covington, Newton Co., Ga. 8/27/1829 and m. in
Decatur Co., Ga., 10/11/1855, being then 26 yrs. 1 mo. 14 days
old, Lucie L. Benton, b. in Lawrenceville, Gwinnett Co., Ga.,
1/24/1837 and m. in Decatur Co., Ga., 10/11/1855, being then 18
yrs. 8 mos. 17 days old. Difference in age, 7 yrs., 4 mos., 27
days. T. S. Luckie and Lucie and their son, Lane L. Luckie,
baptized into the Methodist Church South on 5th Sun. in Aug.,
being the 30th, 1885; Rev. Morgan.
                    (Loose Sheet in Bible)
James T. Benton b. 11/26/1808, d. 12/3/1860
Caroline Melissa Ponder b. 8/5/1809 and date of her death is not
known.
James T. Benton and Caroline Melissa Ponder m. 2/18/1829
Children of James and Caroline Benton:--
William Nelson Benton b. 11/31/1829
Parmelia Francis Benton b. 6/21/1831
Nathan Benton b. 3/24/1833
Louisa Loyd Benton b. 11/22/1834
Lucie Lola Benton b. 1/24/1837
Zalemma Benton b. 3/31/1839
Emma Benton b. 1/13/1842
James Tinsley Benton b. 11/20/1842
Susan Caroline Benton b. 10/12/1844
Mary Elizabeth Benton b. 12/29/1846
Augustus Loytte (LaFayette)?) Benton b. 10/26/1848
George Washington Benton b. 10/25/1850
Nancie Lowia Benton b. 1/2/1853

Deaths
Emma Benton 1/21/1842
Zalemma Benton 1/21/1860
                    (Loose Sheet in Bible)
Mr. T. H. Luckie d. 10/16/1873 with consumption
Mr. N. F. Luckie took the consumption in 1874
Miss L. L. Luckie merited for good lessons 5/30/1874, C. F.
CHeek, Instructuress.
Frances Luckie: Final Report. Number of recitations 275. Number
required 275. Studies pursued History, Geography, Grammar,
Philosophy, Spelling. Number of Absences- none. Number of lessons
lost - none. Conduct in the session good. Grade of Scholarship-80
(Maximum 100)

JESSE AND SARAH AKINS VEAZEY BIBLE
Owner: Camille Veazey, dau. of of Eli A. Veazey, Siloam, Ga.

Jesse Veazey and Sarah Akins m. 2/13/1823

Births
Jesse Veazey 7/10/1799   Sarah Akins b. 1/9/1806
Their Children:--
Nancy Akins Veazey 11/19/1823   Martha Veazey 7/20/1832
Elizabeth Lee Veazey 4/29/1825   Eli Akins Veazey 5/16/1834
Emmaline Veazey 1/12/1827   Mary Ann Veazey 10/19/1836
Sarah Ann Veazey 11/15/1828   William Dawson Veazey
Asenath Akins Veazey 8/24/1830   11/24/1838
Francis Marion Cone Veazey 11/15/1840

Deaths
Asenath Akins Veazey d. 8/13/1832, age 1 yr., 11 mos., 20 days
Jesse Veazey 10/11/1842
Martha Veazey 10/12/1842
Emmaline Jones 9/4/1850
Francis Marion Cone Veazey 7/28/1862. Death caused by a wound
received in battle near Richmond, Va. on 1st day of July 1862,
age 21 yrs., 8 mos., 15 days.
William Dwson Veazey 2/2/1876
Mrs. Sallie (Sarah Veazey) A. Brown 6/27/1891
Elishia L. Veasey (son of Eli A. Veazey and Mary Frances Jackson
Veazey) was killed by a train in Atlanta, Ga. 5/16/1891.
Elizabeth Lee Underwood d. 12/22/1901, dau. of Jesse and Sarah
Veazey.

SAMPSON F. BARFIELD BIBLE
Owner: Richard and Epsy Barfield, Bibb Co., Ga.

Sampson F. Barfield and Rebecca Woodson m. 1/24/1856
Sampson F. Barfield and Lucy E. Sanders m. in Bibb Co., Ga.
12/26/1875

Births
Richard Barfield b. Jones Co., Ga. 9/18/1809
Epsy Barnett b. Washington Co., Ga. 11/29/1809 (or 1807)
John T. Barfield b. Jones Co., Ga. 10/27/1829
Georgia A. Barfield b. Wilkinson Co., Ga. 7/12/1831
Sampson F. Barfield and Salla A. Barfield b. Wilkinson Co., Ga.
9/23/1833
Richard H. S. Barfield b. in Bibb Co., Ga. 8/4/1835
George W. Barfield b. in Bibb Co., Ga. 1/31/1837
Benjamin F. Barfield b. in Bibb Co., Ga. 9/27/1838
Cathrin Emmer Barfield b. in Bibb Co., Ga. 9/26/1876
Effie Hallena? Barfield b. in Bibb Co., Ga. 1/1/1878
Thomas Washington Barfield b. 0/19/1879 Bibb Co., Ga.
John Heard Barfield b. 3/31/1881 Bibb Co., Ga.
Rebecca Woodson b. Bibb Co., Ga. 4/2/1836
Silvester E. Barfield b. 2/28/1855? Bibb Co., Ga.
Narcissia M. Barfield b. 12/3/1858 Bibb Co., Ga.
Benjamin B. Barfield b. 2/3/1860 Crawford Co., Ga.
Frederic M. Barfield b. 4/2/1862 Crawford Co., Ga.
Fannie R. Barfield b. 10/25/1864 Bibb Co., Ga.
James R. Barfield b. Crawford Co., Ga. 4/17/1867

(Barfield Bible contd....)

William Edgar Barfield b. in Pulaskey (Pulaski) Co., Ga. 8/10/1870
S. F. Barfield b. Wilkinson Co., Ga. 9/22/1833
Lucy E. Barfield was received and baptised into ? by Elder F. M.
Sikes? 10/19/1886?

Deaths
Micheal G. Barfield d. of wound received in battle 7/31/1864
Benjamin B. Barfield d. in Pulaskey (Pulaski) Co., Ga. 7/21/1868,
age 8 yrs., 5 mos., ·18 days of congestive fever
Narcissia M. Barfield d. Pulaskey (Pulaski) Co. Ga. 4/20/1870,
age 12 yrs., 4 mos., 17 days of Dropsey of the Heart
Fannia B. Barfield d. from congestion of lungs in Pulaskey
(Pulaski) Co., Ga. 7/10/1871, age 6 yrs. 7 mos.? 15 days.
Rebecca Barfield d. of congestion of lungs in Pulaskey (Pulaski)
Co., Ga., 3/19/1872?, age 36 yrs., 3 mos., 8 days.

WILLIAM REED BIBLE
Owner: Laura McClain Mallon

William Reed b. 5/8/1756, d. 7/9/1840
Frances Reed, his wife, b. 9/12/1760, d. 6/7/1836
Joel Reed b. 11/26/1777
Rebecca Reed b. 11/7/1781, d. 2/15/1830
Daniel Reed b. 6/10/1783, d. 1/22/1865
Mary Reed b. 1/3/1785
Charlotte Reed b. 4/4/1787
Matilda Reed b. 3/30/1789
Jesse Reed b. 1/25/1791
Asa Reed b. 1/14/1793
Susannah Reed b. 2/3/1795
Rebecca Reed b. 2/11/1796, d. 10/24/1869
Francis Reed b. 12/14/1815. Dead.
Tilford Reed b. 7/30/1817, d. 7/25/1818
John L. Reed b. 9/24/1818, d. 7/27/1877
Kezziah Reed b. 12/15/1819, d. 4/1895
William B. Reed b. 4/24/1821, d. 2/5/1894
Sarah Reed b. 1/24/1823, d. 4/1/1863
Nancy O. Reed b. 2/23/1824, d. 3/15/1908
Joshua Reed b. 10/30/1825, d. 9/25/1906
Jesse Reed b. 7/19/1827 d. 9/20/1862
Leasy Reed b. 3/4/1829
Rebecca Reed b. 1/7/1831
Lorrah Reed b. 3/28/1833, d. 8/20/1856
Silas Reed b. 3/28/1836, d. 10/29/1861
Daniel R. Reed b. 11/18/1838

Levi Reed b. 2/9/1797   Keziah Reed b. 1/29/1799
Francis Reed b. 2/6/1801   William Reed b. 3/8/1804

JOHN AND MARY MOON BIBLE
Owner: Mrs. Louanna Kirkpatrick, Franklin, Tenn.

Thomas Moon, the son of John Moon and Mary, his wife, b. 10/25/1742

James Moon b. 10/5/1745	John Moon b. 11/4/1755
Elizabeth Moon b. 3/23/1748	Johnney Moon b. 5/26/1759
Joseph Moon b. 3/20/1750	Rachel Moon b. 1/26/176--
Jemmy Moon b. 10/4/1752	

Joseph Moon and Ann, wife, m. 4/13/1772

Daniel Moon b. 4/27/1773	Samuel Moon b. 4/17/1781
Mary Moon b. 1/30/1775	Joseph Moon b. 7/19/1783
William Moon b. 1/25/1777	John Moon b. 11/4/1785
Grace Moon b. 1/26/1779	Jesse Moon b. 1/30/1788

John Moon and Sary, wife, m. 8/22/1780

Lawrence Moon b. 10/28/1781	John Moon b. 1/18/1788
Elizabeth Moon b. 10/20/1783	Joseph Moon b. 12/15/1789
William Moon b. 9/29/1785	

Thomas and Leucrecher Moon m. 12/26/1769

Sarah Moon b. 7/7/1772	Thomas Moon b. 10/5/1779
John Moon b. 2/19/1774	Elizeabeath Moon b. 10/17/1780
Jasse Moon b. 2/24/1776	Edom Moon b. 12/26/1782
Maray Moon b. 3/7/1778	Leucrecher Moon b. 4/18/1785

BACON BIBLE, Lexington, Ga.
Owner: Mrs. William Booth, Rt. 2, Commerce, Ga. 30529

Marriages
John W. Bacon and Mary Elizabeth Jordan, 4/21/1846
John W. Bacon and Mrs. Caroline Thompson, in Oxford, Ga., 10/15/1874, by Rev. William Florence
Sarah Elizabeth Bacon and Rev. James B. Hunnicutt, 7/13/1892 in Lexington, Ga., by Rev. E. A. Gray
Charles Thomas Bacon and Mary Lula Moore, 12/4/1884, near Marysville, Ga., by Rev. J. R. Parker

Births
John W. Bacon b. 11/22/1824, d. 12/25/1899
Mary E. Bacon b. 7/4/1825, d. 7/21/1872
Their children--
Richard Lewis Bacon b. 4/16/1847, d. 8/12/1849
John Henry Bacon b. 4/23/1849, d. 7/24/1850
Charles Thomas Bacon b. 8/20/1853, d. 4/22/1934
Lilla Mary Bacon, b. 9/29/1856, d. 10/26/1857
Mary Applewhite Bacon b. 11/3/1858
Annie Birdie Bacon b. 7/18/1868, d. 7/4/1888

Thomas Hall, son of Elizabeth and Henry Jordan, b. 9/12/1823
Their children--
Mary Elizabeth b. 7/4/1825
Lucy Jane, b. 8/14/1827
John Julius b. 11/30/1829
Temperance Louisa Jordan b. 10/4/1832
Sarah Celestia b. 10/7/1834
William Applewhite b. 10/1836

360

(Bacon Bible contd....)

Laura Victoria Jordan b. 6/16/1839, d. in Marietta.
Rosa Dinatia Jordan b. 1842, d. in childhood.

Deaths
Richard L. Bacon d. 8/12/1849, aged 2 yrs., 3 mos., 26 days.
John Henry Bacon d. 7/20/1850, 1 yr., 2 mos., 27 days.
Lilla Mary Bacon d. 10/26/1857, 1 yr., 27 days.
Parents of above children, Mary E. Bacon, d. 7/21/1872. John W.
Bacon, d. 12/25/1899.

Sarah Elizabeth, eldest dau. of John W. and Mary E. Bacon, and
wife of Rev. J. B. Hunnicutt, d. Athens, Ga., 7/17/1894.
Charles Thomas Bacon, son of John W. and Mary E. Bacon, d. in
Maysville, Ga. 4/22/1934, aged 80 yrs., 8 mos., 2 days.
Annie Birdie Bacon, youngest dau. of John W. and Mary E. Bacon d.
Athens, Ga. 7/4/1888, aged 1 yrs. Her short life was given to the
service of those she loved. The blessed Savior filled her life
with gladness and its close with peace.
Sarah Elizabeth, eldest dau. of J. W. and M. E. Bacon, and wife
of Rev. J. B. Hunnicutt, d. in Athens, Ga. 7/17/1894. All
beautiful traits of character were hers. Her sweet and useful
life closed on earth to begin in larger service and fuller
happiness in the Kingdom of Heaven.   43-3-23
Caroline E. Parks Bacon d. 7/11/1898. As Mrs. Caroline Thompson
she m. John W. Bacon 11/14/1874. A true wife and mother and a
faithful follower of our Lord Jesus Christ.

Obituaries in Bible:

From the obituary of John Warren Bacon, born Jefferson, Jackson
Co., Ga. 11/22/1824, to Charles Bacon. Charles came from South
Hadley, MA in the early part of the 1800´s "and gave promise of a
very successful business career but died young, leaving a widow
and three minor children—John W. Bacon, a sister, and our worthy
Ordinary Hon. Joel J. Bacon. Soon after his death, the widow,
Sarah Deupree Bacon, sister of Judge Lewis Deupree, removed to
Lexington with her children. In early manhood he fell in love
with Mary E. Jordan, daughter of Hon. Henry Jordan, Judge of the
Inferior Court of Oglethorpe County...and they were married. The
issue of this marriage were several children, all of whom care
now dead excepting Mr. Charles Bacon, a prominent and successful
merchant of Maysville, Ga. and Miss Mamie (Mary A.) Bacon, who is
widely known through the state as a prominent educator and
author. After the death of his wife...he married Mrs. Caroline
Thompson, by whom he had no children....The most successful part
of his business career was spent in Marietta, Ga. where he won
the esteem of all for accurate, conscientious and honest business
methods. When a mere boy, John Bacon joined the Methodist Church
and he was a member of the first temperance organization in the
state. On Friday afternoon, December 22nd the pbulic school at
Maysville closed for the holidays. There were sixty children
pupils of the school. He purchased sixty little Christmas gifts
and went to the school and presented each child with a gift
making to them a short speech in which he spoke of the importance
to children of early fixing their hearts and minds upon pure
purposes and honorable ambition. Heis remains were brought to
Lexington and after memorial services were held in the Methodist
Church on the 26th of December, were laid to rest in the cemetery
at the Presbyterian Church in the afternoon of that day."

(Bacon Bible contd....)

"Lilla Mary Bacon died in Marietta, Ga. Mrs. Mary Elizabeth Bacon died in Lexington, Ga., and Lizzie Bacon, who attended the Georgia Normal and Industrial College at Athens, joined the Presbyterian Church in Lexington under Rev. Mr. Green. Her married life was brief but blest with the sincere affection of her husband and step children...."

GEORGE HUMPHRIES BIBLE
Owner: Mrs. Thomas J. Shackelford, Athens, Ga.

George Humphries b. 8/9/1779
Abigail McDonald b. 10/20/1778 (1769 written over)
The said George and Abigail m. 4/26/1792
Nancy Humphries b. 12/15/1794
Joseph? Humphries b. 4/17?/1797
Elisabeth Humphries b. 2/17/1799
Allin Humphries b. 10/20/1800?
? Humphries b. 5/12/1802 (1801 crossed out)

JOHN T. COVEY BIBLE
Owner: Mrs. Mary Alice Duncan
Rt. 3, 3 Box 266, Connelly Springs, N. C. 28612

John T. Covey b. 5/6/1805, d. 11/3/1858
Nancy Fisher Covey b. 2/15/1813
John and Nancy m. 8/8/1830. Their children:--
Harriet L. Covey b. 8/14/1831   Virginia H. Covey b. 9/1/1841
Meranda W. Covey b. 8/20/1834   Alice B. Covey b. 3/6/1847
Charles Fisher Covey b. 1/25/1837   John W. Covey b. 5/19/1839
Emery Fletcher Covey b. 3/30/1850
Benjamin Franklin Covey b. 2/20/1854

EDWARD LEE BIBLE
Owner: Varney Graves, Fayetteville, Ga. 30214

Husband's Father: Needham Lee
Husband's Mother: Nancy Whorten
Wife's Father: Awther Stripling
Wife's Mother: Lockie Bawyhm (Bougham) Stripling
Husband: Edward Fields Lee   Birthplace: (Helena) Shelby Co.,
Ala., Date: 2/21/1831 Wife: Susan Stripling Lee. Birthplace:
midway,   Barber Co.   Date: 12/29/1848   Place of Marriage:
Tallapoosa, Ga.   Date of Marriage: 11/25/1860   Witnesses:
Mother, Father, Bro. Frank, Sally Stripling, S. W. Lee, P. R. V.
William Westbrook.

Marriages
Karen Lee to Fred Averett at Episcopal Church, Birmingham,
6/4/1884

(Edward Lee Bible, Marriages, contd....)

Ruth M. Lee to J. W. Davidson at C. P. Church, Birmingham, 12/26/1893
Wessie B. Lee to Arlie Barber at home, Birmingham, 8/16/1894
Maisie E. Lee to J. L. Austin at home, Helena, 6/6/1906
Nan (Nannie) P. Lee to H. J. Posner, Birmingham, at home, 8/15/1907
Sue A. Lee to P. Y. Whitman, at C. P. Church, Birmingham, 10/18/1908
Gertrude A. Lee to Rev. Fanious Josephus Tyler at Birmingham 1/23/1922

Deaths

William Westbrook Lee 1862   Needham Lee Austin 3/6/1941
Sue Stripling Lee 4/30/1893   Ruth Lee Davidson 3/25/1942
Edward F. (Fields) Lee 8/13/1912   Gertrude Lee Tyler 11/23/1944
Julius W. (Wesley) Davidson 11/5/1916
Fred Averett (Uncle) 10/12/1917
Flanious Josephus Tyler 7/6/1929
Sue Lee Whitman 12/1/1931
Wilkins Averett 6/13/1932
Nanie (Nannie) Lee Posner 7/6/1944
Karen Lee July - 11 years ago
Joseph L. Austin, Sr. 8/20/1949
Wessie Lee Barber 3/31/1950

Names of Children:

William Westbrook Lee b. 9/1861   Sue Alley Lee 7/14/1887
Gertrude A. (Amanda) Lee 6/24/1967 Joseph LaFayette Austin b.
Kareen H. Lee 10/17/1869   1875
Ruth M. Lee 9/23/1873   Nannie P. (Pauline) Lee 4/28/1881
Wessie B. Lee 3/31/1876
Maisye E. (Esther) Lee 8/22/1879

ANTHONY R. CHEATHAM BIBLE

Births

Anthony R. Cheatham 2/11/1794, Father
Mary W. Cheatham 6/6/1794, Mother
James L. Cheatham 1/31/1814   John L. Cheatham 5/2/1823
Catharine L. Cheatham 2/5/1816   Mary E. Cheatham 6/21/1825
Ann M. Cheatham 2/5/1816   Amelia J. Cheatham 3/5/1828

James Anthony Thompson 12/25/1836   Louisa Jane Archber 3/20/1836
Mary Louisa Nabers 6/6/1836

Marriages

Anthony R. Cheatham and Mary W. Collins 11/24/1812
Catharine L. Cheatham, one of eldest daus. of A. R. and M. W.
    Cheatham to George M. Archer, 3/6/1832
Ann M. Cheatham, one of eldest daus. of A. R. and M. W. Cheatham
    to Asbury Thompson, 1/28/1834
Sarah H. Cheatham, third dau. of A. R. & M. W. Cheatham, to W.
    Nabors 3/24/1835?
James L. Cheatham, eldest son of Anthony R. Cheatham to Martha
    Mathews 11/2/1837

363

(Anthony Cheatham Bible, Marriages, contd....)

Adaline M. Cheatham, 4th dau. of A. R. & M. W. Cheatham, to H. N.
    Langford, 12/1838
Elizabeth B. Cheatham to F. Carlton Brown, 11/10/1841
John L. Cheatham to Adaline M. Patterson 9/26/1843
Jane A. Cheatham, youngest dau. of A. R. & M. W. Cheatham to H.
    G. Brooks, 12/26/1843

Deaths
Anthony R. Cheatham 4/10/1832   Annie T. Patillo 11/1/1861
Ann M. Thompson 5/27/1880   Asbury Thompson 9/2/1882
Joseph E. Thompson 2/28/1884   Anna J. Thompson 9/23/1889
Louisa C. Archer, consort of G. M. Archer and dau. of A. R. and
M. W. Cheatham, d. 3/22/1836
James A. Thompson, son of Ann and Asbury Thompson, d. 1/20/1838?
Mary W. Cheatham d. 6/21/1840. aged 46 yrs., 15 days
William J. Thompson d. 12/16/1840

JOHN ABERCROMBIE BIBLE *
Owner: Edith Barlow, Gainesville, Ga.

Marriages
John Abercrombie and Catharine Peck 10/8/1846

Births
John Abercrombie 12/22/1822   John Abercrombie 6/5/1853
Catharine Abercrombie 1/14/1827   James Abercrombie 5/29/1857
Eliza & Fanny Abercrombie 7/17/1847
Elizabeth Abercrombie 6/13/1849
Joseph Abercrombie 3/6/1851
Rebecca J. Abercrombie b. 6/23/1855
Next Page: Isabel Caroline Abercrombie b. 7/11/1859
Harriett Lovey Abercrombie b. 11/13/1861

Deaths
John Abercrombie 8/9/1854   John Abercrombie 9/30/1864
Catharine Abercrombie 5/25/1864   Martha Elizabeth Abercrombie
                                        5/18/1896

WILLIAM STEVENS BIBLE
Owner: Mrs. Annie Mirian Hearn
Box 367, Riceboro, Ga.

William Stevens, the son of John Stevens and Mary, his wife, b.
4/20/1789
Mary Stevens, wife of William Stevens, b. 8/2/1795
Their children:--
John Stevens b. 5/27/1816   William Stevens b. 6/28/1824
Mary Ann Stevens b. 2/23/1818   Sabary Stevens b. 3/12/1827
James Stevens b. 4/22/1820   Eventon Stevens b. 4/17/1833
Elizabeth Ann Stevens b. 5/20/1822

*See also p. 90.   364

(William Stevens Bible contd....)

Deaths

John Stevens 7/19/1837	Cynthia Pierce 2/21/1871
Evington Stevens 8/9/1841	Elizabeth A. Stevens 6/15/1882
William Stevens 11/8/1854	William Stevens 3/17/1899
Mary Stevens 10/14/1867	

Nancy M. Durden, w. of William Stevens, d. 5/25/1913

ASA PRIOR BIBLE
Owner: Mrs. L. G. Harp
5184 Oxbow Rd., Stone Mtn, Ga. 30087

Births

Ephraigm Prior 10/3/1806	Asa Alfred Prior 6/5/1822
Middleton Prior 11/6/1808	W. H. C. Prior 2/2/1825
Matilda Prior 5/24/1810	L. A. Prior 12/10/1826
Haden Prior 1/4/1812	S. A. A. Thatcher Prior 10/2/1828
Allen Prior 1/20/1814	Angelina A. Prior 7/28/1831
Jackson Prior 7/12/1815	

Marriages

Deaths

Matilda G. Prior 11/4/1830	Allen Prior 3/1/1815
H. N. Prior 11/3/1836	Mary Prior 1822
A. J. Prior 3/15/1836	Asa Alfred 1/2/1839
Minerva E. Prior 8/8/1839	Martha Prior 1863
W. H. C. Prior 4/20/1847	Dr. W. H. C. Prior 3/18/1873
	Ephraigm Prior 2/14/1877
	Middleton Prior 4/27/1882

Family Record
W. H. C. and Ann C. Prior:

Henry Clay Prior b. 8/15/1848	Mary Prior b. 8/10/1854
Hellen Prior b. 4/27/1850	Edwin Prior b. 11/6/1855
Ella Prior b. 5/16/1851	Willie Walter Prior b. 12/5/1865

Marriages
Ella Prior to William E. Ware, 4/13/1871
Mollie E. Prior to Allen T. Murchison 8/9/1881
William W. Prior and Ellie Jones 4/21/1892

Deaths
Edwin Prior 10/20/1857, age 2 yrs.
Helen Prior, oldest dau. of William H. C. and Ann C. Prior d.
   4/21/1862, age 12 yrs.
H. C. Prior 8/23/1885
James P. hughes 1/1/1901
My mother (Ann C. Prior) E. R. Hughes 10/15/1891 in her 87th yr.
Ann C. Prior 1/26/1914, age 83
Willie Walter Prior 10/15/1916
Ellie Jones Prior 1/1/1957

THOMAS JACKSON HANCOCK BIBLE
Owner: Merlyn Holloman Whiting
103-B Westcliff Center, Warner Robins, Ga. 31093

Marriages
Emelin Hollomon and Thomas J. Handcok m. 7/28/1857
Thomas J. Hancock d. 9/18/1873
William A. Hollomon b. 5/26/1847?
Mary A. Hollomon b. 2/25/1850
Addie? J.? Hollomon b. 1/12/1880?
John H. W. Hollomon b. 7/2/1882
Edger S. Hollomon b. 4/18/1884?

Births
Jackson Hancock 2/2/1837
Emelin Hollomon 6/12/1847
Sarah Hancock 1861
-------?
Leah? Hancock 3/31/1841

George Wilson Aulthinn? and Addie Lee Hollomon m. 6/20/1886

Deaths
John Hollomon 10/5/1857   G. W. Hollomon 1/6/1897
Miram E. Hollomon 1/26/1897   Elizabeth J. Hollomon 6/20/1840
Thomas Hancock 9/18/1878   William A. Hollomon 9/26/1882
T. J. Hancock 12/3/1864   Mary A. Hollomon 2/6/1877
Mary S. Hollomon 12/5/1864   Larrie Hancock 10/5/1928, age 67
                                 yrs., 6 mos., 4 days
Sarah C. Stembridge d. 7/16/1889
William A. Hollomon married Mary Hancock 8/22/1869
Henretta Emeline Hancock d. 8/3/1800, age 60 yrs, 6 mos., 21 days
   (lined paper inserted in Bible)---

Marriages
T. J. Hancock and Heneretta E. Hollomon 7/28/1859
Sarah E. Hollomon (entry lined out)
Seaborn E. Hollomon and Josephine Long 1/8/1874
Artemus Stembridge to Sarah Hollomon 11/19/1874
John J. Hollomon to Elizabeth E. Hancock 12/13/1855
T. J. Hollomon and M. E. Hancock 9/1/1867
William Hollomon to Mary Hancock 8/22/1869
James A. Hollomon to Elizabeth Jinnings 1/4/1872

Births
George W. Hollomon 12/17/1833   Seaborn E. Hollomon 4/29/1849
John J. Hollomon 12/7/1835   Mary E. Hollomon 4/25/1851
Elizabeth J. Hollomon 11/25/1837   Sarah C. Hollomon 6/5/1853
Heneretta Emeline Hollomon 6/12/1840 Addie L. Hollomon 6/12/1870
Thomas J. Hollomon 12/6/1842   John H. Hollomon 7/2/1872
James A. Hollomon 5/9/1845   Wilborn Hollomon 4/13/1871
William Hollomon 5/26/1847   Carrie M. Hollomon 2/17/1875

Deaths
Elizebeth J. Hollomon 6/20/1840   Mary I. Hollomon 12/5/1878
John Hollomon 10/5/1857   T. J. Hancock 12/3/1864
John J. Hollomon 9/5/1864   Sarah C. Stembridge 7/16/1889
Tommy Hancock 9/18/1873
Addie L. Hollomon (name crossed out)

GEORGE GRAY BIBLE
Owner: Mrs. Evelyn F. Booth
281 North Ave., Athens, Ga. 30601

Betsy Gray, dau. of George Gray and Ann, his wife, b. 9/18/1775
William Gray b. 1/7/1777
Nancy Guttrely? Gray b. 5/17/1780
Jeremiah Griffon Gray b. 7/28/1801

Jeremiah G. Gray b. 7/28/1801, d. 12/28/1822

George Gray, husband of Anna Gray, d. 12/15/1806 at his
plantation in Clark Co.
Jeremiah G. Gray was b. the 28 ?
Ann Gray, wife of George Gray, d. 12/26/1821, at her plantation
in Clark Co., aged 73 yrs.
Elizabeth Gray b. 7/11/1825
Evaline Gray b. 7/13/1827
William Gray b. 10/11?/1829
Susannah Caroline Gray b. 12/2/1830
Jeremiah Griffin Gray b. 12/20/1838
Francis Ann Gray b. 10/3/1842

Jeremiah G. Gray b. 7/28/1801
12/1822 ??
Naomi Gray, wife of Jeremiah G. Gray, b. 3/8/1799
Elizabeth Gray b. 7/11/1825
Evaline Gray b. 7/13?/1827
William Gray b. 10/16/1829
Susannah Gray b. 12/2/1830
Jeremiah Griffin Gray b. 12/20/1838
Frances Ann Gray b. 10/3/1842
Evaline Gray d. 7/28/1834
Frances Ann Gray d. 7/20/1865?

Evaline Gray d. 7/28/1834

Robert Barber d. 9/18/1850
Sarah Barber d. 1/6/1853
Hon. Charles Daughrety d. 11/26/1853
Richard Wilson d. 4/22/1857
Mr. and Mrs. Barber, infant baby, d. 10/1/1857
Mary Barber d. 10/5/1857
Joseph Barber d. 11/6/1857
William Mathews d. 1/24/1858
Rachel Gray d. 5/26/1858
Sebourn Simons d. 8/16/1858
Frances Ann Gray d. 7/20/1865
Asbury Hull d. 1/25/1866

THOMAS FLEMING BIBLE
Owner: Denver O'Barr, Hart Co., Ga.

Thomas Fleming b. 1/24/1811   George Fleming 4/15/1853
Faney Fleming, w. of Thomas Fleming, 7/4/1813

367

(Fleming Bible contd....)

Leonard Fleming, son of Thomas, 1/4/1834
John Fleming 9/23/1836   Avery Fleming 10/7/1885
Daniel Fleminb 1/22/1838   Lu Ida Fleming 5/29/1868
Thomas Fleming 3/12/1840   Craton O'Barr 8/20/1884
Elizabeth Fleming 5/15/1842   Michael O'Barr 8/19/1886
Rebecca Fleming 11/29/1844   Fanny O'Barr 1/26/1889
Winny Fleming 7/8/1847   Walter O'Barr 4/8/1892
Peter Fleming 12/28/1849   Lawson O'Barr 11/10/1894
George Fleming 4/15/1853   Avis Louise O'Barr 12/22/1910
Frances Fleming 11/27/1855   Denver Brown O'Barr 1/4/1902
T. J. Fleming, son of W. D. Fleming, b. 3/29/1882

WILL MINOR BIBLE
Owner: Mrs. Alice Smith Ennis, Milledgeville, Ga.

Will Minor m. Nancy Smith 3/23/1820
Francis Minor b. 2/11/1821   Julia Minor b. 4/2/1827
Evaline Minor b. 3/24/1823   Nancy Minor b. 3/6/1799
Sharlotte Minor b. 3/23/1825   Will Minor b. 11/22/1827

Francis Smith d. 8/29/1821   Elizabeth Smith d. 4/16/1816
Margaret Smith d. 6/22/1800   Catherine Smith d. 10/18/1800
Sallie Simpson b. 7/25/1849
C. W. Ennis b. 9/28/1845   R. E. Ennis b. 9/12/1806
E. F. Ennis b. 9/15/1847   R. M. Ennis b. 7/14/1855
E. A. Ennis b. 6/16/1850   Annie P. M. Ennis b. 8/28/1890
P. T. Ennis b. 2/18/1853   H. J. Simpson b. 8/15/1878

Evaline, w. of Pleasant M. Ennis, d. 6/14/1881
Scharlotte, w. of Pleasant M. Ennis d. 6/9/1887
Mr. P. M. Ennis d. 1/31/1891
H. J. Simpson d. 12/24/1913

TATE BIBLE
Owner: Erick J. Moran
Marietta, Ga. 30060

Marriages
William Andrew Tate and Mary Rebecca Bryant, 3/3/1918 by Rev. J.
T. Hornsby of East Point, Ga.
Lawrence Jefferson Webb and Annie Mae Tate 1/30/1909 by a
Methodist Minister.
Robert Pierce Hill and Annie Mae Tate 8/15/1915 by Rev.
Brinsfield

Births
Alice Tate, 1st dau. of Jeremiah Thomas Tate and his wife, Amanda
Louisa Tate, b. Clayton Co., Ga. 11/21/1883
John Thomas Tate b. 9/3/1885
Samuel Alston Tate b. Fulton Co. 1/1/1889
Annie Mae Tate b. 11/4/1894, Fulton Co.

(Tate Bible contd....)

William Andrew Tate b. 5/9/1897, Fulton Co.
J. T. Tate, Sr., b. 10/12/1856, Father
Amanda Tate, Mother, b. 5/24/1859
Babe, inf. of J. T. and Amanda Tate, d. East Point, Ga. 11/5/1892
Jeremiah Thomas Tate d. East Point, Ga. 6/26/1826
Amanda Louise Tate d. East Point, Ga. 8/28/1826
Both deaths at old home place on Washington St., East Point, Ga.

Samuel A. Tate d. 12/5/1950
Annie Mae Tate Hill d. 8/5/1961
Alice Key Tate Speir d. 4/17/1967 in Little Rock, Ark.
William Andrew Tate d. 12/4/1967
John Thomas Tate d. 2/13/1970

Jeremiah Thomas Tate b. 10/12/1856
Amanda Luisa Dyer b. 5/24/1859

Births

Willis Tate 5/14/1808   James G. Tate 3/4/1842
Malinda Ware 6/1/1813   John C. Tate 2/14/1845
William Jasper Tate 9/19/1835   Benjamin S. Tate 5/14/1848
Lucinda W. Tate 9/9/1837   Martha Ann Susan Tate and Mary
Margaret L. Tate 12/28/1839   Ann Elizabeth Tate 9/17/1851
Jeremiah Thomas Tate 10/12/1856

Deaths

Willis Tate d. 1/15/1877, b. 5/14/1808
Malinda Tate d. 6/28/1887
Margaret Tate Head d. 10/1917
Thomas Tate d. 6/26/1926

Births

Lou Ella Webb, 1st dau. of Annie Mae Tate Webb and Lawrence
Jefferson Webb, b. 11/30/1909 at home of Jeremiah Thomas Tate,
East Point, Ga.

JAMES WILSON BIBLE
Owner: Mrs. Nina N. Usher
11800 Abercorn St., Savannah, Ga. 31406

James Wilson b. 12/8/1795
Sarah S. Wilson, wife of James Wilson, b. 3/7/1804
James Wilson and Sarah S. Langley m. 12/19/1820
Mary E. Wilson b. 8/29/1822
Rebecca C. Wilson b. 1/8/1825--The little Boy was b. 9/6/1826 and
d. 9/14/1826
Sarah S. Wilson b. 9/7/1828, d. 7/31/1829
Sarah S. Wilson, w. of James Wilson, d. 9/2/1829
James Wilson and Eliza Bourquin m. 5/6/1830
Margaret Frances Wilson b. 7/21/1831
Eliza Ann Wilson b. 5/11/1833
Louisa Caroline Wilson b. 10/26/1835
Henrietta H. Wilson b. 6/1/1838
Mary E. Wilson and M. H. Powers m. 4/20/1841
Rebecca C. Wilson and H. Y. Oliver m. 12/19/1844

JAMES A. HUNTER BIBLE
Owner: Sally Hunter,
431 Green St., N. W.
Gainesville, Ga,

William Marion Hunter b. 9/1/1867 (called "Uncle Rap")
John A. Hunter b. 3/31/1873, d. 1/6/1875
James V. Hunter b. 3/28/1875, his children were: 1st Fanny b.
5/25/1899; 2d Minnie Irene b. 9/21/1902
Mary M. Hunter b. 1/24/1876
Frances J. Hunter b. 6/4/1879

JACOB PURCELL BIBLE
Owner: Lois Burnette DuVall

Jacob Purcell b. 10/13/1773   Mary King, his w., b. 12/18/1777

Joshua Purcell, son, b. 7/30/1802 Darius E. Purcell b. 12/10/1810
John Purcell b. 1/21/1804   Abraham Purcell b. 4/23/1812
Jacob Purcell, Jr., b. 5/4/1805   E. V. (Elijah) Purcell
Elisha W. Purcell b. 5/20/1807   b. 8/6/1814
Jarrett M. Purcell b. 5/5/1809   Martha Ann Purcell b. 3/27/1817
                                 Mary Ann Purcell b. 7/27/1823

JAMES BIBLE

Mary James b. 2/10/1799   William James b. 1/9/1818
Nancy James b. 10/10/1801   H. G. James b. 1/9/1818
Rebecca James b. 8/30/1802   Joseph F. James b. 9/6/1830
John James b. 5/11/1804   in Union Dist., S. C.
Sarah James b. 4/14/1806   Sarah C. James b. 4/1832
Druary James b. 11/6/1808   L. A. James b. 8/1827
Martha James b. 12/31/1810   Mary E. james b. 8/1828
Thomas James b. 12/6/1812   Lucianda James b. 1829
Elizabeth James b. 5/31/1815   Eula A. James, dau. of J. F. James
Susannah James b. 6/26/1817   and George A. James b. 2/24/1877
Edgar Hoyt James b. 9/22/1878 in Pennington, Trinity Co., Texas

MICHAEL LEONARD SHOCKLY BIBLE
Rev. Pensions #W5190 & W4212

Michael L. Shockly b. 1/11/1784   Mary Ann Shockly b. 9/11/1820
Friend O. Shockly b. 11/17/1809   Francis Shockly b. 1/17/1823
John Shockly b. 11/5/1811   James M. Shockly b. 9/26/1826
Elizabeth Shockly b. 2/23/1814   Harriet S. Shockly b. 2/4/183
Susan Shockly b. 1/23/1816   Andrew J. Shockly b. 1/20/183
Benjamin S. Shockly b. 2/18/1818   Jonathan N. Shockly b. 8/2/18

HARDY LEONARD WHEELUS BIBLE
Owner: John Melvin Wheelus
2805 Zane Grey Dr., S. E., Atlanta, Ga. 30316

Husband: Hardy Leonard Wheelus b. 10/19/1890, at Wellston,
Houston Co., Ga., son of S. T. Wheelus and Harriett M. Barker.
Wife, Mary Emmie Tucker, b. 10/8/1891, at Byron, Houston Co.,
Ga., dau. of Thomas James Tucker and Mattie Etherdige

Births
Sheron Thomas Wheelus 11/16/1914   Hardy Leonard Wheelus, Jr.
Herman Evan Wheelus 2/12/1916   3/19/1922
Buford Earl Wheelus 3/24/1919   Mary Virginia Wheelus 8/1/1923
Infant (stillborn) 10/8/1920   Bailey Mazo Wheelus 5/1/1925
Johnny Melvin Wheelus 4/20/1934

Marriages
Hardy Leonard Wheelus and Mary Emmie Tucker 1/4/1914
Sheron Thomas Wheelus and Flora Cates 1/9/1934
Herman Evans Wheelus and Margaret Brightwell 6/4/1939
Buford Earl Wheelus and Helen Ruth Elrod 4/25/1941
Hardy Leonard Wheelus, jr. and Myrtle Borders 8/26/1942
John Melvin Wheelus and Mable Claire Veal 1/15/1956
Sheron Thomas Wheelus

Deaths
Infant, 10/8/1920
Mary Virginia Wheelus 8/2/1923
Bailey Mazo Wheelus 5/22/1925
Mary Emmie Tucker Wheelus 3/23/1964
Hardy Leonard Wheelus, Jr. 9/19/1968
Herman Evans Wheelus 11/27/1969
Hardy Leonard Wheelus, Sr. 2/27/1974

ASA WARE MORGAN BIBLE
Owner: Melvin Morgan, Woodbury, Ga.

Asa Ware Morgan b. 10/27/1827, d. 8/18/1900
Elizabeth Ann Jane Brown b. 11/3/1840, d. 1/4/1936
Their Children:--
Mary Ann Deborah Morgan b. 5/26/1859, d. 10/29/1859
William Augustus Morgan b. 9/19/1861
James Asa Morgan b. 9/22/1863, d. 1/12/1919
Sarah Elizabeth Morgan b. 6/22/1869, d. 3/17/1960
Thomas Jefferson Morgan b. 8/22/1869, d. 1/8/1937
Martha Ann Elisa Jane Morgan b. 10/8/1872, d. 3/7/1916
Young Frederick Allen Morgan b. 2/21/1875, d. 6/3/1935
Annah Lee Morgan b. 5/14/1877, d. 2/12/1900
Caludia Sophronia Morgan b. 6/19/1880, d. 6/24/1952

Father of Asa W. Morgan was Hiram Morgan;
Mother of Asa W. Morgan was Elizabeth Haisten.
Father of Elizabeth Ann Jane Brown was Allen Brown;
Mother of Elizabeth Ann Jane Brown was Elizabeth Ann Routon.

ASA BENNETT BIBLE
Owner: Mrs. Era Lowen
1179 Goldsmith Rd., Stone Mtn, Ga. 30083

Marriages
Asa Bennett and Pheba 4/4/1838
Joseph Bennett and Mary Wilson 12/23/1860
Joseph Bennett and Sally Wilson 11/27?/1860
Joseph Bennett and Mildrid Howard 9/27/1882
Jesse Bennett and Bessie Stringer 1/10/1912

Births
Asa Bennett 2/21/1805   Francis Elisebeth Bennett 1/20/1884
Pheba Malinda Bennett 8/9/1823   Amy Lular? Bennett 7/12/1887
Joseph Milton Bennett 6/21/1839   Mary Bennett 2/7/1839
James Jackson Bennett 1/1/1843   Sarah Bennett 4/5/1841
William Earley Bennett 5/9/1846 Mildred Parthena Bennett 6/9/1841
Frances McDonal Bennett 10/19/1849   Era Jesse Bennett 3/25/1913
Andrew Jackson Bennett 9/5/1852   Farra Bessis----?
Sarah Ann Elizabeth Bennett
8/20/1854   Altas Bennett 11/5/1914
General Green Bennett 5/11/1857   Sallie Loretta Bennett 8/25/1916
Josephine Easter Candis Bennett   William Tomas Jack Bennett
  1/24/1862   1/9/1920
Joseph Milton Bennett 2/18/1872   Anna Estelle Bennett 3/24/1922
Mary Lowduskey Bennett 11/11/1873 Sylvia Louise Bennett 6/28/1923
Jesse Dillard Bennett 6/15/1877   Carl Tate Bennett 9/9/1925
Infant Bennett, stillborn, 12/1927

Deaths
James Jackson Bennett 6/28/1845   Sally Bennett 1/15/1882
Josephine Bennett 7/31/1862   Joseph Milton Bennett
Mary Bennett 6/11/1862   5/22/1905
Olivia Savage 1/5/1906   Parthenia Mildred Bennett
                                       3/30/1906
The first heir of Joseph and Sally Bennett d. 10/14?/1870

JOHN DORTCH MOSS BIBLE
Cherokee Corner, Oglethorpe Co., Ga.
Owner: Sarah Hunter Moss, Athens, Ga.

Marriages
John D. Moss to Miss Martha Strong 3/18/1824
Rufus L. Moss to Miss Mary Anthony 8/8/1848, d. in Rome, N. Y.
  State, 9/4/1848
Rufus L. Moss to Miss Elizabeth Freeny Luckie 4/6/1854 in her
  father and mother's home, Covington, Ga.
John C. Moss to Miss Catherine Echols 7/1858
John D. Moss to Miss Byrd Lee Hill of Richmond, Va., 4/14/1891,
  First Baptist Church, Dr. George W. Cooper officiating.
Birdie Strong Moss to Emmet J. Bondurant 10/13/1892, First
  Methodist Church, Athens, Ga.
Rufus LaFayette Moss, Jr. to Miss Leila Pope Strong of
  Mississippi, 2/7/1898

(John Dortch Moss Bible, Marriages, contd....)

William Lorenzo Moss to Miss Marguerite Eleanor Widle 6/1/1925,
in Norwood, Pa.
Sallie A. Moss to Thomas C. Newton, 2/5/1880
Rufus LaFayette Moss III to Miss Anne Cubbedge 9/8/1917 in Macon,
Ga., Episcopal Church, Rev. Lee officiating.
Mary Valentine (Minnie) Moss to John William Firor at the Church
of Our Savior, Brookline, Mass., 6/15/1920, Rev. Henry Knox
Sherrill officiating.
John Hill Moss and Catherine Russell at Putnam, Conn. 10/12/1920,
Rev. Boynton Merrill officating.
Judith Elizabeth Jay Moss to Ralph Volney Harlow 6/21/1921 at
Rufus LaFayette Moss residence, 479 (formerly 919) Cobb St.,
Athens, Ga., Rev. Walter Anthony officiating.
Thomas Strong Moss to Sarah Jane Lesley 5/25/1924 at the home of
her mother, Mrs. C. C. Martin, 804 1/2 Platt Ave., Tampa, Fla.
Elizabeth Luckie Moss to Henry Herman Harris 4/18/1925, at 626
Hill St., Athens, Ga., Rev. Cyprian P. Wilcox officiating.
Elizabeth Moss Bondurant to Dwight Warren Ryther, Jr., 8/20/1926,
First Methodist Church, Athens, Ga.
William Byrd Moss to Marion Theresa Eppes at Episcopal Church,
Athens, Ga., 5/16/1928, Dr. A. G. Richards, Rector.
John Parnell Bondurant to Mary Claire Brannon, 12/24/1928,
Tallahassee, Fla. (Secretly 9/17/1928, Greer, S. C.)
Frank Alexander Pope to Mary Elizabeth Ward 10/23/1893, Aberdeen,
Miss. Died 2/22?/1910.
Charles Strong, Sr. to Sarah Thompson 11/29/1785.
Obadiah Echols to Elizabeth Strong 8/7/1804
Genl. Bur. Pope and S. K. Strong 12/12/1815
Capt. Thomas W. Goulding and Miss Susan Strong 2/5/1818
Ebenezer Newton to Ann T. Strong 12/1/1819
Col. Elisha Strong to Ann S. hill 9/18/1821

Births

John D. Moss 2/10/1792	Alexander Hamilton Moss 9/8/1830
Martha M. Moss 11/7/1805	John C. Moss 12/22/1833
Rufus L. Moss 1/13/1825	Susan M. Moss 6/30/1839
Georgia Anna Virginia Moss 5/22/1826	
James Oglethorpe Moss 10/2/1828	Sarah A. Moss 9/12/1840
	Julia Pope Moss 3/22/1842

Rufus L. Moss 1/13/1825	John D. Moss 2/1/1866
Elizabeth Luckie 8/27/1831	Elizabeth Luckie Moss 3/10/1864
Mary Alice Moss 1/21/1836	Martha Strong Moss 12/21/1866
Rufus LaFayette Moss 8/26/1858	Sarah Hunter Moss 9/26/1871
Eliza Buckner Moss 4/12/1861	William Lorenzo Moss 8/23/1876

John Hill Moss b. 9/2/1893 at 919 Cobb St. (R. L. Moss
residence), Athens, Ga., son of John D. Moss and Byrd Lee Hill.
Rufus LaFayette Moss b. 1/18/1895 at 919 Cobb St., Athens, Ga.,
son of John D. Moss and Byrd Lee Hill.
Minnie Valentine (Mary) Moss b. 9/23/1896 at 325 Pulaski St.
(John D. Moss residence), Athens, Ga., dau. of John D. Moss and
Byrd Lee Hill.
Judith Elizabeth Moss b. 5/26/1898, 325 Pulaski St., Athens, Ga.,
dau. of John D. Moss and Byrd Lee Hill.
William Byrd Moss b. 4/15/1904, 325 Pulaski St., Athens, Ga.
John Dortch Moss III b. 8/30/1819, 255 Bond St., Macon, Ga.,
while his father, Rufus LaFayette Moss III was with the American
Expeditionary Forces in France.

(Moss Bible contd.....)

William Lee Moss, son of William Byrd Moss and Marian Eppes Moss,
    b. 2/14/1929 at Athens Gen. Hospital, Athens, Ga.
Mary Catharene Moss, dau. of William Byrd Moss and Marian Eppes
    Moss, b. 6/3/1931, Athens Gen. Hospital, Athens, Ga.
Elizabeth Harlow,   dau.   of Ralph Volney Harlow and Judith
    Elizabeth Moss Harlow b. 8/17/1931, Syracuse, N. Y.

Rufus Moss Bondurant b. 11/29/1893 in Danville, Va.
Elizabeth Moss Bondurant b. 11/4/1902, Hancock Ave., Athens, Ga.
Mary Jopling Bondurant b. 12/18/1905, Cobb St., home of Mr. and
    Mrs. E. J. Bondurant, Athens, Ga.
John Parnell Bondurant, b. 8/21/1907 at 725 Cobb St., Athens, Ga.
Birdie Moss Bondurant b. 11/30/1909 at 725 Cobb St., Athens, Ga.
Mary Claire Bondurant, dau. of John Parnell and Mary Claire
    Brannon Bondurant, b. 2/5/1930, St. Marys Hospital, Athens,
    Ga., m. James R. Warren 11/27/1953, First Meth. Church, Athens.
Elizabeth Luckie Moss Jr. b. 11/23/1898 at 919 Cobb St. (R. L.
    Moss residence), Athens, Ga.
Thomas Strong Moss b. 10/19/1900 at 919 Cobb St., Athens, Ga.
Rufus LaFayette Moss IV b. 12/24/1902 at Hill St. (residence of
    R. L. Moss Jr.), Athens, Ga.
Susan Strong Moss b. 12/3/1904, Hill St., Athens, Ga.
Sara Jane Moss, dau. of Thomas Strong Moss and Sara Lesley,
    b. 7/16/1926 at Bayside Hospital, Tampa, Fla.
Mary Emily Harris, dau. of Henry Herman Harris and Elizabeth
    Luckie Moss, b. 9/30/1926 at Mission Hospital, Asheville, N.C.
Henry Moss Harris, son of Henry Herman Harris and Elizabeth
    Luckie, b. 8/13/1929 at Mission Hospital, Asheville, N. C.
Anne Byrd Firor,   dau.   of John William Firor and Mary Valentine
    Moss b. 4/24/1921, Montezuma, Ga.
Nancy Moss, dau. of John Hill Moss and Catherine Russell, b.
    9/23/1921, Putnam, Conn.
Judith Mary Harlow, dau. of Ralph Volney Harlow and Judith
    Elizabeth Joy Moss, b. New England Baptist Hospital 11/29/1922.
David Leonard Firor, second, b. of John William Firor and Mary V.
    Moss 11/4/1923, Athens General Hospital, Athens, Ga.
John Russell Moss, son of John Hill Moss and Catherine Russell,
    b. 6/21/1924, Putnam, Conn.
Cope Cubbedge Moss, son of Rufus LaFayette Moss III and Anne
    Cubbedge Moss, b. 3/18/1925, St. Marys Hospital, Athens, Ga.
Janet Mabel Harlow, dau. of Ralph Volney Harlow and Judith E.
    Moss, b. 10/18/1925, New England Baptist Hospital, Boston, Mass.
John William Firor, son of John William Firor and Mary Valentine
    Moss, b. at St. Marys Hospital, Athens, Ga., 10/18/1927.
Hugh Valentine Firor, third son of John William Firor and Mary
    Valentine Moss Firor at St. Marys Hospital, Athens, Ga.,
    3/24/1929.

Marguerite Eleanor Moss, dau. of William Lorenzo Moss and
Marguerite Widle Moss b. Boston, mass. 6/21/1930.

Charles Strong, Sr. b. 1/18/1764
Sarah Thompson, his wife, b. 7/25/1764.
Elizabeth Strong b. 1/1/1787
William Strong b. 9/1788
Elisha Strong b. 2/11/1792. (Marginal note: Father of Thomas
    H. C. Strong)
Sarah K. Strong b. 7/15/1795 (Marginal note: Mother of Julia Pope
    Stanley)

374

(Moss Bible contd....)

Ann T. Strong b. 12/1/1797 (Marginal note: Mother of Henry Newton)
Susan Strong b. 10/16/1799 (Marginal note: Grandmother of Sue Gerdine)
Charles Strong b. 12/21/1801
Martha Strong b. 11/7/1805 (Marginal note: Mother of Rufus L. Moss)

Deaths
Charles Strong, Sr. 6/19/1827
Alex H. Moss 9/4/1831
Susan M. Moss 9/24/1840
James O. Moss 10/10/1852, his remains deposited in Athens.
Mary L. Moss, wife of R. L. Moss, 9/4/1848
Nathl. A. Moss, son of David Moss, 1/7/1839 at Cherokee Corner.
John D. Moss 4/23/1864
Elizabeth Luckie, infant dau. of Rufus L. and E. L. Moss, 2/28/1865, aged 11 mos., 18 days.
Martha Strong Moss 9/14/1877
Mary Alice (Anthony) Moss 1/5/1892
Sallie A. Moss, wife of Thomas C. Newton, 9/29/1900, 109 Hancock Ave., Athens, Ga.
Rufus Moss Bondurant 1/12/1896 at 109 Hancock Ave., Athens, Ga.
Susan A. Strong, wife of Thomas Strong, 9/26/1911, 626 Hill St., Athens, Ga.
Thomas Strong 3/22/1898, Washington, D. C.
Rufus LaFayette Moss, Sr. 10/24/1912, at his home on Cobb St.
Eliza Buckner (Lily) Moss 8/7/1921 in Baltimore, Md.
Elizabeth Luckie Moss, wife of Rufus LaFayette Moss), 4/22/1922, at 479 (formerly 919) Cobb St., Athens, Ga.
Mary Joplin Bondurant 7/20/1923, Cobb St., Athens, Ga.
Nancy Moss, dau. of John Hill Moss and Catherine Russell Moss, 9/23/1925, on her 4th birthday, Putnam, Conn.
Emmet J. Bondurant 3/17/1926, in Atlanta, Ga.
Byrd Lee Hill Moss, wife of John D. Moss, 11/28/1926, Athens, Ga.
Elizabeth Moss Bondurant Ryther, wife of Dwight Ryther, Jr., 9/14/1929, Athens, Ga.
Julia Pope Moss 5/11/1931, Athens, Ga.

MARY ANN ELIZABETH CAMPBELL BIBLE
Owner: Mrs. Albert J. Souther, Rt. 1, Murrayville, Ga. 30564

James N.? Campbell b. 6/11?/1808
Emely Campbell b. 10/?/1820
Mary Ann Elisabeth Campbell b. 9/26/1835
John Graham Campbell b. 12/4/1836
David Anderson Campbell b. 5/24/1838
Benjmin (sp?) Hableton Campbell b. 4/30/1840
Nancy Aveline Campbell b. 1/18/1842
William Henry Clay Campbell b. 1/23/1845
Thomas Asbary Campbell b. 6/26/184--
Margelte Emely Elsabeth Campbell b. 7/7/1857
David Benjamin Campbell b. 1/21/1863
David Benjamin Campbell d. 5/5/1863

HENRY ENGLISH BIBLE of Greene Co., Ga.
Owner: Miss Pauline Stokely, Pelham, Ga.

Marriages
Nancy English to William Beasley 6/1805
Lucy English to V. Haralson 1/10/1809
Hanah English to William Edmondson 2/20/1817
Polly English to David Browning 2/27/1817

Births
Augustus P. Edmondson 12/31/1817
Elisabeth Edmondson 4/2/1820
Lucy English 2/20/1785
Nancy English 4/5/1787
Salley English 9/13/1789
Stephen English 11/1/1791
Dinah English 7/12/1794
Henry English 8/25/1796
Polley English 4/1/1799
Gene English 7/27/1801
Nancy E. Browning 12/16/1817
Henry English Haralson 1/15/1810

Sally Greer b. the 16th Sept.1814
Betsey Ann Greer 3/13/1818

Elisabeth Haralson 3/23/1812
Jane Haralson 12/21/1813
Jonathan Crawford Haralson
   2/9/1816
Mary Ann Haralson 9/11/1818
William Greer 4/6/1768
Henry Greer 1/3/1796
Aquila Greer 8/11/1799
Nancy Greer 1/12/1801
Lucy Greer 9/8/1803
Elisha Greer 9/27/1806 (dead)
Jesse Greer 9/16/1808
Ebenezer Greer 5/7/1811.

Deaths
Betsey English 8/29/1806, age 42. "Oh that I may be ready to meet
the call of God when it shall come as I believe she was. Henry
English."
Nancy English, second wife of Henry English, Sr., 9/10/1814, age
51. "O may I when I quit the state of action be as well prepared
to meet the Prince of Peace as I have reason to hope she was.
Henry English, Sr."
Stephen English 8/16/1816
Gene English 1/7/1817
Polly Browning 10/8/1819

WILLIAM READ BIBLE
Owner: Rev. B. E. L. Timmons
Atlanta, Ga.

Saraan Read b. 6/4/1811
William Read b. 3/10/1806
James Read b. 9/20/1803
Elizabeth Thetford, dau. of William Thetford and Margaret, his
wife, b. 4/3/1798
Catherine Thetford b. 12/23/1775
Walter Thetford b. 1/5/1787

Agnes Lockhart Thetford b.10/4/1794
Rebekah Thetford b. 3/25/1784
Sarah Thetford b. 12/15/1786

MIDDLETON POPE BIBLE
Oglethorpe Co., Ga.

Middleton Pope b. 5/2/1794, d. 11/20/1850 in Oglethorpe Co., Ga.,
"Home Place"
Lucy H. Lumpkin Pope b. 2/28/1803, d. 8/1888.
Middleton Pope and Lucy Lumpkin m. 11/27/1820
Sarah Pope, only child of Middleton and Lucy Pope, b. 10/17/1821
Henry Aug. Pope b. 8/6/1760
Clara Hill, his first wife and mother of Middleton Pope, b.
  8/9/1763

DANIEL POPE BIBLE *

Births
Daniel Pope 11/21/1805   Alston B. Pope 4/10/1839
Rebecca Pope 2/13/1805   Sarah D. Rebecca Pope 11/19/1840
Mary Ann Pope and Martha Ann
Pope, daus. of Daniel and Rebecca Pope, 1/10/1827. And residue of
their children: Henry G. W. Funderburke 12/1/1844
Comforte Eliza Pope 2/10/1829 Zachariah Daniel Booth 7/27/1845
William Wiley Pope 10/7/1830   Sarah Elizabeth Booth 2/17/1847
John Allen Pope 6/9/1832   Laura Booth 9/29/1848
Simon Daniel Pope 1/23/1834   James H. Funderburke 6/17/1846
Andrew Jackson Pope 6/26/1836 Mary E. Funderburke 7/27/1848
                               Rufus H. Jenkins 11/6/1858
                               L. S. Jenkins 4/25/1862

Marriages
Daniel Pope and Rebecca Pope 4/9/1826
Martha Ann Pope and David H. Funderburke 3/7/1844
Mary Ann Pope and James A. Booth 10/14/1844
Sarah R. Pope and Louis S. Jenkins 2/4/1858
Simon D. Pope and Minerva A. Davy 7/25/1860
Mary Alice Pope, dau. of A. J. and F. M. Pope, b. 7/3/1862
Andrew J. Pope and Fannie M. Cason m. 2/11/1861

Deaths
Comforte Eliza Pope 8/13/1835, age 6 yrs, 6 mos., 3 days.
Daniel Pope 11/13/1840, age 34 yrs, 11 mos., 11 days
L. S. Jenkins 5/3/1862
Lewis S. Jenkins, dau. of Lewis S. and Sarah R. Jenkins,
  5/17/1863, age 1 yr., 22 days.
Rebecca Pope 1/3/1895, age 89 yrs., 10 mos., 20 days.
Simon Daniel Pope 5/3/1907
Minerva Ann Pope 3/22/1911

Births
Mary Allice Pope 7/3/1862   Thomas Austin Funderburk
Lewis Alston Pope 10/16/1864   12/9/1861
Martha Susan Funderburk 3/28/1850 Julie Funderburk 9/29/1864
Sarah Rebecca 4/12/1852
William Daniel Funderburk 6/23/1856
John A. J. Funderburk 4/12/1859

*See also p. 80.   377

GENERAL BURWELL POPE BIBLE
Oglethorpe Co., Ga., Owner: Mrs. T. P. Stanley, Athens, Ga.

Marriages
Burwell Pope, son of Henry Pope and Priscilla Wooten, m. 9/8/1772
Burwell Pope, son of above Burwell Pope and Priscilla, his wife,
m. Sarah Key Strong, dau. of Charles Strong and Sarah Strong, his
wife, 12/12/1815.
John H. Pope, son of Burwell Pope and Sarah, his wife, m. Damaris
C. Hubbard, dau. of Robert Hubbard 10/15/1850
Julliann Tabitha Pope, dau. of Burwell Pope and Sarah, his wife,
m. 11/8/1854 Marcellus Stanley.
J. H. Pope, son of Burwell Pope and Sarah, his wife, m.
1/10/1855, Mary Frances Caldwell, dau. of John and Lucinda
Caldwell of Texas.
A. F. Pope, son of Burwell and Sarah K. Pope m. Mary E. Ward of
Aberdeen, Miss. 10/18/1893.
Thomas Pope Stanley, son of Marcellus and Julia Pope Stanley m.
to Margaret Laura Morton 10/5/1898.

Births
Burwell Pope, son of Burwell Pope and Priscilla, his wife, b.
9/7/1790.
Sarah K. Pope, dau. of Charles Strong and Sarah, his wife, b.
7/15/1795. (Their children-)
1st son, Edwin Elisha Pope, b. 10/14/1820.
2d son, Charles Burwell Pope b. 3/7/1822.
3rd son, John Hardeman Pope b. 8/26/1827.
4th son, Alexander Franklin Pope b. 6/5/1829.
5th son, Benjamin Henry Pope b. 12/19/1830.
1st dau., Juliann Tabitha Pope, b. 1/23/1825.
Charles H. Sanders b. 2/27/1798.
William Alonzo Pope b. 12/13/1833.
William Edwin Pope b. 7/8/1836.
Robert Pope, son of Burwell and Priscilla, his wife, b.
9/28/1775, d. 10/7/1831, aged 56.
Tabitha Pope, dau. of Burwell Pope & Priscilla, b. 1/11/1778
Nancy Pope, dau. of Burwell Pope & Priscilla, b. 4/28/1780
Martha Pope, dau. as above, b. 4/18/1782.
Willie Pope, son as above, b. 12/14/1784.
Sarah Pope, dau. as above, b. 11/24/1787.

Deaths
Edwin Elisha Pope, 1st son of B. Pope and Sarah, his wife, d.
6/3/1822, aged 19 mos., 9 days.
William Alonzo Pope d. 7/12/1835, aged 19 mos.
Charles Burwell Pope d. 10/23/1839.
Burwell Pope, son of Henry Pope, d. 1/9/1800, age 49, b. 1752.
Priscilla Pope, wife of above, d.-18--in the fifty--yr. of her age
Ann Hill, dau. of above, d. on --18 in year of her age.
Gen. Burwell Pope d. 5/11/1840, age 50.
Damaris Carter Pope, wife of John H. Pope, d. 8/3/1851.
Sarah K. Strong, wife of Burwell Pope, d. 7/28/1877.
Julia Tabitha Pope, wife of Marcellus Stanley, d. 10/1/1894.
Marcellus Stanley d. 5/2--th/1890.
Benjamin H. Pope, son of Burwell and Sarah Pope d. 11/27/1898.
Alexander F. Pope, son of Burwell and Sarah Pope, d.---
William E. Pope, son of Burwell and Sarah Pope, d. 4/22/1914.
Sarah Pope Stanley d. 4/17/1920, age 71. Never married.

(Children of Bryant Page and Judy C. Wall)
William Matthew Page b. 4/15/1867 (m. Georgia Watson Stone)
James Henry Page b. 4/7/1868
Syon Alvaro Page b. 7/17/1869
Joseph Ezekiel Page b. 5/18/1870
Jonathan Euriah Page b. 3/8/1873
Pollie Luella Page b. 4/15/1875 (m. C. B. Nevels 1/10/1897 in
Terrell Co., Ga.)
Rachel Ann Sylvester Page b. 8/11/1877 (m. R. J. Nevels 12/2/1900
Terrell Co., Ga.)
Anna Estella Page b. 10/3/1880 (m. John T. Layton 1/19/1902
Terrell Co., Ga.)
Henry Thomas Page b. 12/17/1882
Judy C. Wall and Bryant Page m. 9/10/1865
J. C. Wall was 26 yrs. of age.
Bryant Page was 24 yrs. old.
J. C. Wall b. 4/18/1840.
Bryant Page b. 2/11/1842, d. 1/25/1911.
J. C. (Wall) Page d. 3/23/1917
Georgia Watson Jernigan b. 6/8/1864.
William Page and Georgia Jernigan m. 11/20/1886.
Mamie Caroline Page b. 8/9/1890.
Lucious Lavaughn Page b. 9/21/1893.
Clara Sylvester Page b. 10/26/1898.
Julia Thelma Page b. 1/17/1904.
Georgia Page d. 1/30/1929.
William Page d. 10/16/1932.

JOSHUA MARBUT & JOHN PRESSLEY MARBUT BIBLE

Marriages
2/18/1808 Joshua Marbut and Sarah Longshore.
10/31/1833 John P. Marbut and Susannah Boozer.

Births
3/26/1788 Joshua Marbut   11/12/1790 Sarah Longshore
(Their children):
1/20/1809 John P. Marbut   Young Joshua Marbut 3/22/1823
4/27/1811 Kezia Marbut   Emaly Demasius Marbut 8/22/1825
10/13/1814 Elizabeth Marbut   Robert Longshore Marbut 5/24/1828
12/12/1817 Euclidas Marbut   Mary Jane Marbut 1/27/1831
6/30/1820 Sarah Marbut   Burr Johnston Marbut 2/24/1834

1/7/1816 Susannah Boozer, wife of John P. Marbut.
Children of John P. and Susannah Boozer Marbut:

5/12/1835 George Frederick Marbut   Deaths
2/19/1837 Job Joshua Marbut   Sarah Marbut 5/12/1856
10/5/1839 Sarah Elizabeth Marbut   Joshua Marbut 2/27/1863
4/25/1842 John Ivy Boozer Marbut
10/31/1845 Samuel Pearce Marbut
1/8/1851 Susannah Kerrene Marbut
2/7/1854 Mary Icedare Marbut

NEEDHAM LEE BIBLE
Owner: Mrs. Andrew Mumford
1065 Country Lane, Atlanta, Ga. 30324

Husband's Father: Needham Lee
Husband's Mother: Nancy Whorten Lee
Wife's Father: Awthur Stripling
Wife's Mother: Lockie Bougham Stripling
Husband: Edward Fields Lee
Birthplace: Helena, Shelby Co., Ala.   Date: 2/21/1831
Wife: Susan Stripling Lee
Birthplace: Midway, Barber Co.   Date: 12/29/1848
Place of Marriage: Tallapoosa, Ga.
Date of Marriage: 11/25/1860
Witnesses: Mother, Father, Brother Frank, Sallie Stripling, S. W.
Lee P. R. V. William Westbrook.

Births
William Westbrook Lee 9/1861   Wessie B. Lee 3/31/1876
Gertrude Amanda Lee 6/24/1867   Maisy Esther Lee 8/22/1879
Kareen H. Lee 10/17/1869   Nannie Pauline Lee 4/28/1881
Ruth M. Lee 9/23/1873   Sue Alley Lee 7/14/1887

Marriages
Kareen Lee to Fred Averett, Episcopal Church, Birmingham 6/4/1889
Ruth M. Lee to J. W. Davidson, C.P. Church, Birmingham 12/26/1893
Wessie B. Lee to Arlie Barber, Home Birmingham 8/16/1894
Maisie E. Lee to J. L. Austin, Home Helena 6/6/1906
Nan P. Lee to H. J. Posner, Home Birmingham 8/15/1907
Sue A. Lee to P. Y. Whitman, C.P. Church, Birmingham 10/18/1908
Gertrude A. Lee to Flavious Josephus Tyler, Birmingham, 1/23/1922

Deaths
William Westbrook Lee 1862   Needham Lee Austin 3/6/1941
Sue Stripling Lee 4/30/1893   Ruth Lee Davidson 3/25/1942
Edward Fields Lee 8/13/1912   Nanie Lee Posner 7/6/1944
Julius Wesley Davidson 11/5/1916 Gertrude Lee Tyler 11/23/1944
Fred Averett 10/12/1917   Karen Lee, July, 11 yrs. ago
Flavious Josephus Tyler 7/6/1929
Sue Lee Whitman 12/1/1931
Wilkins Averett 6/13/1932
Joseph L. Austin, Sr. 8/20/1949
Wessie Lee Barber 3/31/1950

BONNELL-LOVETT BIBLE
Owner: Miss Belle Lovett

Births
John Bonnell b. 10/19/1750, d. 8/21/1809
Winifred Bonnell, wife, b. 7/2/1754
Elizabeth, dau. of John and Winifred Bonnell, b. 5/30/1775 m.
John Faubus Lovett.
Martha Bonnell b. 10/8/1778, d. 1811 (m. Hughes--Owen)
Thomas Cuyler Lovett, son of Elizabeth and John F. lovett, b.
1795.

(Bonnell-Lovett Bible contd...)

Robert Watkins Lovett, Sr. b. 1797, d. (1878) m. Lucy Roberts, dau. of Emily Williamson and James Roberts.
Their son, Robert Watkins Lovett, Jr. (Dr.) m. 1st Elizabeth Andrews, dau. of Bishop Andrews and 2d Marietta Smith and 3rd Sarah Isabella Price.
Eliza Maria Hughs b. 7/22/1803
Rosamond Hughes b. 12/29/1806, d. 1811

Alabama Eliza Greening b. 1/29/1839
Susan Reece Greening b. 2/16/1841

H. M. OSGOOD BIBLE
Owner: Alexander K. Leonard
Talbotton, Ga.

Harrison M. Osgood b. 11/29/1809
Susan Ann Leonard b. 10/18/1818
Marcus Mortimer, son of Harrison M. and Susan Ann Osgood, b. 5/24/1836
Alexander K. Leonard b. 9/1/1809
Sarah F. Cox b. 10/22/1813 (33 struck through)
James Van Leonard, son of Alexander K. and Sarah F. Leonard, b. 4/19/1833 and----
John Porter Leonard, son of Alexander K. and Sarah F. Leonard, b. 9/23/1834
Susan Osgood Leonard, dau. of Alexander K. and Sarah F. Leonard, b. 9/15/1837
Susan Cox Leonard, dau. of A. K. and Sarah F. Leonard b. 10/8/1840
Harrison M. Osgood and Susan Ann Leonard m. 3/24/1835
Alexander K. Leonard and Sarah F. Cox m. 1/19/1832 by Rev. Lovic Pierce (Methodist)
Alexander K. Leonard and Elizabeth Harvey m. 6/1/1843
Marcus Mortimer, son of Harrison M. and Susan Ann Osgood, d. 6/12/1836, aged 18 days, 17 hrs.
Susan Ann Osgood, consort of H. M. Osgood, d. 8/12/1836, aged 17 yrs., 9 mos., 25 days.
Harrison M. Osgood d. 1837 at the Island of St. Croix.
James Van Leonard, son f A. K. and Sarah F. Leonard d. 7/2/1833
Susan Osgood Leonard, dau. of A. K. & Sarah Leonard, d. 9/7/1838
Sarah F. Leonard, consort of A. K. Leonard, d. 10/13/1841, aged 27 yrs., 11 mos., 14 days.
Family Record of Jonathan Osgood:
Jonathan Osgood b. 9/21/1761 and his wife, Orange Osgood, b. 7/11/1766. Children:
Amelia Lewis Feen Osgood b. 9/5/1794
Eliza Orange Wadsworth Osgood b. 12/9/1799
Jonathan Walter Dandolo Osgood b. 7/29/1802
Amanda Almira Osgood b. 4/1/1806
Harrison Mortim*er Osgood b. 11/29/1809

Deaths
Jonathan Osgood d. 5/21/1822, aged 60 yrs., 8 mos.
Orange Osgood d. 4/12/1837, aged 70 yrs., 9 mos., 1 day.
Eliza Orange Wadsworth O. Whitcomb d. 9/12/1827, aged 27 yrs., 9 mos., 3 days.

WALLACE BIBLE
Owner: Mrs. J. R. Asbury, Crawfordville, Ga.

Sarah Wallace b. 11/15/1776   Espy Wallace b. 7/20/1786
John Wallace b. 4/8/1781 d. 10/19/1817
Benjamin Wallace b. 10/1/1788
Mary Anne Wallace b. 2/23/1815 (dau. of John Wallace and his
    wife, Fanny)
Martha Frances Wallace b. 11/7/1817
    Children of Benjamin Wallace and his wife, Catherine:
William Leveritt Wallace b. 2/11/1812, d. 10/17/1843
John Baldwin Wallace b. 9/13/1813, d. 10/17/1843
Charnal Jasper Wallace b. 9/20/1815, d. 7/9/1849
James Jefferson Wallace b. 10/26/1817, d. 9/20/1880
Florinda Wallace b. 8/16/1819, d. 9/15/1852
Newton W. Wallace b. 6/8/1821, d. 3/4/1857
Celia Ann Morgan Wallace b. 4/17/1823, d. 9/6/1863
Marion DeKalb Wallace b. 3/8/1826, d. 9/20/1901

Benjamin Wallace d. 6/20/1862
Catherine Wallace d. 4/14/1860, b. 12/25/1786

Florinda Wallace m.--Wall 7/4--
Celia Ann M. Wallace m. E. C. Hixon 7/4/1850, d. 8/25/1863
Marion D. Wallace m. Elizabeth Moore 1/17/1850

William M. Wallace b. 10/23/1871, d. 10/2/1881
Ann William Wallace b. 1/19/1844, d. 4/5/1911, dau. of William S.
Wallace and his wife, Lethe, m. Ship)
Cornelia C. Wallace b. 2/15/1841, dau. of Charnal J. Wallace and
    his wife, Sarah)
Alexander Hamilton Wallace b. 10/18/1847
Mary Ellin Wallace b. 12/11/1849

            MARION D. AND ELIZABETH WALLACE BIBLE
            Owner: Mrs. J. R. Asbury, Crawfordville, Ga.

Marion D. Wallace b. 3/8/1826 d. 9/20/1901
Elizabeth Wallace b. 2/8/1828 d. 1/28/1901
m. 1/17/1850 by E. S. Hunter, Esq.
            Children of M. D. and Elizabeth Wallace:
Emma C. Wallace b. 3/17/1851, d. 3/8/1855
Frank P. Wallace b. 7/1/1852, d. 3/10/1855
McHenry S. Wallace b. 6/10/1854, d. 3/18/1855
Ella E. Wallace b. 6/34/1856, 11/19/1909
Newton W. Wallace b. 11/24/1858
Mary M. Wallace b. 8/30/1860, d. 2/2/1907
Celia M. Wallace b. 6/30/1863
Tacitus C. Wallace b. 9/5/1865
Louisa C. Wallace b. 12/8/1867, d. 5/6/1909

Marriages
Ella E. Wallace to Webb Thaxton
Mary M. Wallace to Carlisle Darden
Celia M. Wallace to J. R. Asbury
Louisa C. Wallace to--Hall

                        382

ANDREW BIBLE
Owner: Mrs. Fremon Dixon, Dewey Rose, Ga.

Benjamin Andrew b. 10/23/1788, d. 8/22/1882
Lucy Tate Andrew, his wife, b. 3/5/1792, d. 1871
Their Children:
William Tate Andrew b. 10/18/1818
Elizabeth Elenor Andrew b. 6/10/182-, d. 1870
Lucy Mildred Hodges b. 12/22/1823
John Benjamin Andrew b. 2/20/1825, d. 1894
Amanda Elizabeth Andrew b. 7/20/1827, d. 1850
Robert Sampford Andrew b. 2/11/1830, d. 1862
Alfred Parks Andrew b. 7/17/1832, d. 1869
James Asbury Andrew b. 12/17/1834, d. 1900

John Benjamin Andrew Family:

John Benjamin Andrew b. 2/20/1825, d. 1894
Rhoda Harriet Andrew, wife, b. 8/11/1822, d. 1883
Their Children:
Lucy Jane Andrew b. 11/25/1853
Albert Benjamin Andrew (twin) b. 4/19/1855
Alford Thomas Andrew (twin) b. 4/19/1855, d. 1930
Sarah Elizabeth Andrew b. 1/16/1858
James Asbery Andrew b. 2/25/1860, d. 1900
John Fremon Andrew b. 9/21/1862, d. 1925
Eliza Elenor Andrew b. 4/7/1865

Family of Alford Thomas Andrew:

Alford Thomas Andrew b. 4/17/1858, d. 6/24/1930
Lettie Jordan Andrew, wife, b. 12/21/1871, d. 9/18/1940
Their Children:
Jasper Robert Andrew b. 10/27/1895, d. 5/14/1952
Frazier Alford Andrew b. 11/5/1897, d. 1950
Harriet Elizabeth Andrew Berry b. 3/12/1903, d. 1957
Nancy Andrew Dixon b. 9/16/1909

ELI SHANKLE BIBLE
Owner: Mrs. A. M. Shankle, Commerce, Ga.

Eli Shankle b. 8/5/1784, d. 4/15/1852, age 68
Rebecah Shankle b. 12/4/1786, d. 12/4/1866, age 80
Seabarn McHendree Shankle b. 7/8/1825
Ophelia Amanda Shankle b. 9/11/1830, d/ 6/21/1857, age 27
Polly Shankle b. 3/5/1811
James W. Shankle b. 10/18/1812, d. 2/12/1847, age 35
Levi M. Shankle b. 2/9/1815
Elisabeth Shankle b. 5/20/1819
Eritha Shankle b. 6/1/1821
Martha An Shankle b. 1/29/1823

Cornelia Amanda Hood, only child of Ophelia A. Hood (decd) b.
2/6/1856, d. 8/28/1862

383

CLAYBROCK WILLIAMSON

Births
Claybrock Williamson 5/11/1769
m. 12/24/1799 Polly Callaway b. 6/1/1780
Elizabeth Williamson 1/4/1802
Jabez D. Poyner 12/24/1825

David Poyner m. Elizabeth Williamson 1/27/1825

Claybrook Williamson d. 2/13/1824, 54 yrs., 9 mos.

SILAS WEEKS BIBLE
Owner: Mrs. Elsie Sparkman
Hampton, Fla.

Silas Weeks 12/23/1811-1/20/1880
Kiziah Thigpen 8/21/1847-7/17/1881, 2nd wife of Silas Weeks, m.
7/4/1850. Their Children:

Births
Aisa (Elisie) Weeks 2/14/1852   Charles J. Weeks 5/6/1864
Faraba Weeks 9/14/1853   William T. Weeks 3/21/1866
Hester Weeks 10/16/1855   Emma A. C. Weeks 2/25/1869
Cary (Kate) Weeks 7/6/1860   Lila McM. Weeks 2/8/1871
Silas N. Weeks 7/6/1860   George W. Weeks 8/10/1873
Mary Weeks 3/17/1862   Trumon D. Weeks 2/29/1876

Hester Weeks d. 2/13/1886 (m. Wyley Tillis abt 1883)

MICHALL SMITH BIBLE
Owner: Mrs. D. B. Dowling
963 Heard Ave., Augusta, Ga.

Morria Smith, son of Michall Smith and Milly, his wife, b.
1/15/1784
Susannah Smith, dau. of above, b. 2/15/1787
Sarah Smith, dau. of above, b. 9/18/1789
John Smith, son of above, b. 10/29/1792
David Smith, son of above, b. 3/23/1794
Henry Leroy Smith, son of above, b. 1/23/1797
Annie Smith, dau. of above, b. 9/20/1799
Milly Elizabeth Miller, dau. of Stephens Miller and Susannah, his
wife, b. 3/29/1822
Stephens Miller d. 2/16/1822, aged 39

CHARLES RYALL BIBLE
Owner: Pearl R. Gnann

Charles Ryall m. Christina Smith 5/5/1808   Their Children:
                        Births of Children:
William Arthur 2/8/1809   Edna Preventia 5/2/1817
Isaiah Benjamin 8/1/1810   Rebecca T. 7/20/1819
Ann Elizabeth 10/6/1812   Mary Massie 7/10/1826
Sarah Dorothy 11/5/1814

JOSHUA PITTS BIBLE Of Effingham Co.
Owner: Alphonso Cassidy Edwards
Effingham Co., Ga.

Joshua Pitts b. 2/27/1805   James N. Pitts b. 3/29/1837
Ann, his wife, b. 5/18/1799

THOMAS PENGREE BIBLE

Thomas Pengree m. Catharine Waters 5/14/1806
              Births of Their Children:
Elizabeth 3/6/1807   Catharine 10/20/1817
Mary 10/30/1809   Martha 5/18/1820
Sarah 3/19/1811   Caroline 4/28/1822
Nancy 1/17/1813   Louise 2/26/1825
James Marion 9/24/1815

MILLER BIBLE
Owner: Mrs. Essie Daniel Dowling
963 Heard Ave., Augusta, Ga.

Births
John F. Miller 1/4/1837   Alexandria H. Miller 12/20/1848
Leroy J. Miller 12/20/1839   Frederick M. Miller 6/12/1850
W. Henry Miller 2/6/1841   James F. Miller 2/20/1852
Josiah Miller 11/19/1842   Stephen S. Miller 9/13/1855
Thomas J. Miller 12/19/1845   Sarah Miller 6/15/1857
Elizabeth J. Miller 5/1/1847   Susie Miller 3/5/1865
                                 Randy Miller 10/28/1828

385

WILLIS A. MANGHAM BIBLE
Owner: Charles R. Gwyn, Sr.
Zebulon, Ga.

Births
Willis A. Mangham
Temperance Brewer Mangham
James C. Holmes b. Wilkes Co. 4/24/1785
Rebecca Holmes b. Wilkes Co. 1/29/1788
Wiley E. Mangham b. Putnam Co. 1/9/1805
Malinda Holmes Mangham b. 4/18/1810 Wilkes Co.
Dr. Charles Frederick Redding b. 8/27/1825 Monroe Co.
Mary J. Mangham Redding b. 9/5/1831 Pike Co.
Dozier Redding Gwyn b. 11/20/1850 Pike Co.
Wiley Mangham Redding b. 8/19/1853 Pike Co.
Charles Redding Gwyn b. 4/2/1874 Pike Co.
Wiley Orin Gwyn b. 8/18/1871 Pike Co.

Deaths
Wiley E. Mangham 6/1891 Zebulon, Pike Co., Ga.
Malinda M. Holmes Mangham 5/30/1888 Zebulon, Pike Co., Ga.

WILLIAM A. MILLER BIBLE

William A. Miller 12/23/1840-3/26/1913
Lucinda Snelson Miller 8/16/1836-3/18/1914
Emma Lorah Miller, dau. of above, 11/1/1861-5/9/1921
John William T. Miller b. 7/3/1863
Mary H. Miller b. 12/15/1866
Ida Belle Miller 10/10/1868
Curtis Miller 7/13/1870
Etta Lee Miller 5/2/1872-3/17/1933
Henry B. Miller b. 7/4/1874
Dumpy Miller 2/16/1876-12/13/1879
Laura Miller 3/21/1879-2/14/1889

William A. Miller m. Lucinda Snelson 11/29/1860

GEORGE HENDERSON MITCHELL BIBLE

George Henderson Mitchell m. Sallie Beatrice Rosse 12/19/1889
Susie A. Mitchell m. John Reeve Roberts 6/22/1919
            Children of George H. Mitchell:
William Thomas Mitchell b. 10/22/1890
Susie Aldora Mitchell b. 10/16/1892
James Corbet Mitchell b. 1/24/1894

JOHN McDONALD BIBLE

Births
John McDonald 1766
Margret McDonald 1773
Mary McDonald 1/12/1793
Flora McDonald 2/13/1795
Nancy mcdonald 1/2/1799
Hugh McDonald 6/2/1801
Donald McDonald 10/22/1803
Angus McDonald 2/1/1806
John McDonald 4/26/1808
L. McDonald 10/3/1810
Floris McDonald 1/26/1813
Margaret McDonald 1/18/1816
Roderick McDonald 11/18/1819

Floris McDonald 1/26/1813
Margaret McDonald 1/18/1816
Roderick McDonald 11/18/1819
Margaret C. McDonald 1/29/1833
Flora C. McDonald 4/19/1834
John A. McDonald 1/9/1836
Nancy Ann McDonald 9/26/1837
Robert Bruce McDonald 10/26/1839
William W. McDonald 10/12/1841
Helen M. McDonald 3/4/1844
Charles J. McDonald 10/12/1846

Births of Charles J. McDonald, Sr.'s Children:
William W. McDonald 10/9/1872
Alma McDonald 6/17/1874
Mary McDonald 7/11/1876
Etta McDonald 6/18/1878

Donald McDonald 4/9/1880
J. B. McDonald 7/4/1883
C. J. McDonald Jr. 6/18/1885
Florrie McDonald 7/2/1887

Marriages
A. F. Lester to M. C. McDonald 11/23/1871
C. J. McDonald to L. F. Jackson 12/11/1871
A. J. Yates to M. A. McDonald 12/10/1882
E. U. Ethridge to Mary McDonald 10/9/1898
M. A. Dixon to Alma McDonald 2/27/1901
J. B. McDonald to Etta Mae Burnside 6/19/1907
C. J. McDonald, jr. to Etta Graddick 3/24/1917
Donald McDonald to Mary M. Johnson 12/8/1831
Asbury F. lester to Flora C. McDonald 4/27/1856
William McCampbell to Margret McDonald 11/26/1840

Deaths
W. M. McDonald 4/10/1862
John A. McDonald 1/31/1862
Robert B. McDonald 2/8/1862
Flora C. Lester 6/17/1870
Donald McDonald 3/3/1874
William W. McDonald 2/7/1882
Mary C. Hamlen 10/9/1887
Mary M. McDonald 12/20/1891
John Anna Lester 5/23/1897
John F. Lester 6/24/1897

M. C. Lester 8/24/1898
Florrie Ann McDonald 9/13/1907
Kathren Louise Dixon 2/28/1908
Mary J. Mathews 4/15/1914
A. F. Lester 5/25/1914
Lillian Lester 12/27/1911
Lilliam Mathews 11/27/1916
Louise F. McDonald 4/7/1924
C. J. McDonald 4/7/1924
N. A. Yates 6/24/1925
John B. McDonald 9/3/1933
Helen M. McDonald 1/28/1935

Births of Etta McDonald's Grandchildren:
A. J. Dixon 1/31/1902
Kathrine Dixon 6/14/1906
Erwin Dixon 2/15/1909
Charles Dixon 11/21/1914
Jack McDonald 3/18/1908
Eugenia McDonald 12/24/1910

Henry McDonald 6/14/1912
Richard M. McDonald 4/22/1914
Mary McDonald 12/16/1917
W. R. McDonald 5/4/1924
James McDonald 7/27/1920
Sallie Lou McDonald 6/21/1926

Births of Great Grandchildren:
Barbara Nanette Dixon 3/9/1933   Jaculyn Annitte Dixon 3/9/1933

387

JAMES M. NEWTON BIBLE
Owner: George W. Newton
Monticello, Ga.

James M. Newton, father of Aristarchus, b. 1740, m. Miss Fischer
Wood iN Va. and moved to Greene Co., Ga. Brothers of Aristarchus
Newton: Ezekiel Newton, Charley Newton, Willis Newton

Deaths
Oliver H. P. Newton 4/17/1846
Angellina Newton 7u/18/1858
James M. Newton, husband of Jane Elvira Gieger and father of
    George W. Newton was killed in battle at Sharpsburg 9/17/1862
Marcus D. Lafayette Newton 3/15/1848
Aristarchus Newton 9/5/1896
Richard Newton 3/27/1898
Willis Newton 4/27/1896
George W. Newton 8/1/1851 m. Mollie Bogan 11/20/1870

WILLIAM H. P. NICHOLS BIBLE
Clarkesville, Ga.

Births
William H. P. Hichols 3/31/1854   James M. Nichols 1/22/18--
Martha E. P. Nichols 12/7/1848   Georgia Ett Nichols 11/1/18-4

STOKELY MORGAN, SR. BIBLE
Lowndes Co., Ga.

Births
Stokely Morgan Sr. 9/6/1775   William Joseph Morgan 11/19/1819
William Louis Morgan 9/8/1812   Henry James Morgan 5/26/1823
Hannah Louise Morgan 2/8/1811   Sarah Frances Morgan 7/15/1824
Luke John Morgan 4/6/1821   Mary Ann Morgan 7/15/1826
Elizabeth Jane Morgan 8/9/1820   Asa H. Morgan 9/6/1803

Marriages
Stokely Morgan Sr. to Miss Mary Evans 4/22/1800
William Louis Morgan to Mary Ann Mogan 1/5/1835 (cousins)
Hannah Louise Morgan to John Louis Calhoun 2/5/1835
Luke John Morgan to Sarah E. Flemister 11/14/1845
Elizabeth Jane Morgan to A. P. Wilson 1/2/1845
Sarah Jane Morgan to W. C. Robinson 7/6/1846

Deaths
Stokely Morgan Sr. 2/10/1833   William Jessie Morgan -/13/1836
Luke John Morgan 5/29/1864   Henry James Morgan 2/12/1827

388

Births

Stokely Morgan 9/6/1775	Mary Ann Morgan 9/8/1812
Luke John Morgan 12/1777	Henry Joseph Morgan 11/13/1846
William Louis Morgan 8/13/1842	Mary Ann Morgan 11/28/1848
Luke John Morgan 6/28/1840	Sarah Corinthia Morgan 6/22/1852
William Louis Morgan 11/6/1811	
Charley Stokely Morgan 12/13/1835	

Deaths

Luke John Morgan 5/1841	Mary Ann Morgan 4/29/1888
William Louis Morgan 4/13/1913	Henry Joseph Morgan 5/1/1871
Luke John Morgan 1841	Mary Ann Morgan 3/4/1929
William Louis Morgan -/10/1861	Charlie Stokely Morgan 6/13/1927

SHATTEN C. MITCHELL BIBLE

Shatten C. Mitchell b. 7/31/1802
Mahallah Mitchell, wife of S. C. Mitchell, d. 4/2/1852
William P. Mitchell b. 1834
George Washington mitchell b. 12/20/1846
Mahallah jane Mitchell b. 1/10/1845
Josephine A. Mitchell b. 2/1/1848
Mary Ann Mitchell b. 5/27/1849

Mary Ann Mitchell m. Thomas Russell Cook 1/16/1872 Griffin, Ga.

Mariah Jane Mitchell d. 4/15/1843
Sarah Elizabeth Mitchell d. 10/16/1843
George Washington Mitchell d. 9/16/1847
William P. Mitchell d. 8/21/1861, 21 yrs., 30 mos., 27 days
    Part of this record has been torn out of Bible

BRYDIE MITCHELL BIBLE
Owner: D. B. Mitchell
Columbus, Ga.

David Brydie Mitchell m. Rebecca Thweatt 1822
David Brydie Mitchell b. 3/10/1824
David Brydie Mitchell m. Caroline Owens 4/25/1861
David Brydie Mitchell b. 6/21/1862
Louisa Owens Mitchell b. 9/24/1865
Thacker Howard Mitchell b. 4/12/1869
James Owens Mitchell b. 3/20/1877
J. H. Mitchell b. 10/6/1878
John Whitaker Mitchell b. 10/22/1881

(Brydie Mitchell contd....)

Rebecca Thweatt Mitchell d. 3/18/1824
David Brydie Mitchell 4/4/1824
Louisa Mitchell d. 10/13/1871
J. H. Mitchell d. 10/25/1892
James Whitaker d. 10/16/1907
Carolyn Owens Mitchell d. 5/18/1825

DAVID BRYDIE MITCHELL BIBLE
Owner: D. B. Mitchell
Columbus, Ga.

Births
David B. Mitchell 6/21/1862   Emmie Mitchell 11/27/1896
Jennie Berry Thomas 11/11/1869   Brydie Mitchell 7/2/1898
Lilliam Mitchell 2/28/1890   Thos.Howard Mitchell 1/10/1902
Brady Mitchell 10/1/1892   Jennie Nell Mitchell 5/28/1904

Deaths
Emmie Mitchell Humber 10/18/1918
Jennie Nell Mitchell 9/5/1905

Marriages
David B. Mitchell to Jennie Berry Thomas 12/21/1888
Emmie Mitchell to W. Thomas Humber 9/12/1916
Brady Mitchell to Mabel Howard 4/29/1919
Thomas Howard Mitchell to Harriet Leak 10/1/1930
Harriet Turner Mitchell b. 1/31/1933

ANDREW H. METTS BIBLE

Andrew H. Metts m. Martha V. Holder 10/7/1857 Hawkinsville, Ga.
Andrew Hiram Metts b. 4/2/1832 Washington Co., Ga.
Martha V. holder b. 6/22/1832 Pulaski Co., Ga.
George Clark Metts b. 8/9/1858 Pulaski Co., Ga.
Mary Lowry Metts b. 12/31/1859 Daugherty Co., Ga.
John Allen Metts b. 8/23/1861 Pulaski Co., Ga.

BRINSON BIBLE
Owner: Mrs. Hannah Edwards
Effingham Co., Ga.

Ruby Mae Brinson b. 8/1/1914
Nellie Brinson b. 11/5/1916

ELIJAH GREGORY BIBLE

Elijah Gregory m. Emeline Perry, dau. of Job Perry 6/20/1826

Deaths
Inscription on his tomb"....He(Elijah Gregory) died 8/18/1821,
   54 years old."
Sarah, wid. of Job Perry and Mother of Emeline P. Perry, d. at
Danbury 1/20/1852, age 84 yrs.

FRANCIS MERIWETHER BIBLE *
Owner: J. B. Jenkins, Albany, Ga.

Francis Meriwether b. 10/31/1737 m. Martha Jameson abt. 1765. Ten
                              Children:
Thomas b. 1766 m. Rebecca Matthews
Valentine b. 1768 m. Barbara Crosby
Mary b. 1770 m. William Barnett
Elizabeth b. 1772 m. William Matthews
Mildred b. 1774 m. Joel Barnett
Margaret (Peggy) b. 9/1/1776 m. Dr. John A. Bradley
D. Nancy b. 1778 m. William Glenn
Lucy b. 1780 m. Grover Howard
Sarah b. 1782 m. James Olive
Nicholas b. 1784

Deaths
Francis Meriwether 1/2/1803
Martha Jameson Meriwether, wife of Francis Meriwether, 5/29/1818
Margaret J. Meriwether Bradley, wife of Dr. John A. Bradley,
   3/14/1819

SAMUEL MEREDITH BIBLE
Owner: Wyatt Meredith Allen, Allentown, Ga.

Samuel Meredith 10/30/1810-8/27/1895
Elizabeth Meredith, his wife, 8/27/1813-8/30/1897
Sarah Rebecca Meredith 11/16/1838-7/5/1926
John Meredith 9/22/1840-8/3/1862
Susanna Meredith b. 7/17/1846
Wyatt Meredith 3/27/1847-6/23/1857
Daniel Morgan Meredith 9/23/1849-1916
Samuel Jackson Meredith 11/13/1851-5/30/1881
James Franklin Meredith 2/20/1854-11/12/1881
Virgil Meredith 6/5/1859
Samuel Meredith m. Elizabeth 2/18/1838
Virgil Ovid Meredith m. Elizabeth King 3/10/1885
Clara Lucile Meredith b. 1/5/1886

*See also p. 135.   391

FRANCIS MAULDIN BIBLE
Owner: Mrs. Thomas Mauldin
Thomaston, Ga.

Births
Francis Mauldin 5/30/1836   Annie F. Mauldin 2/15/1869
Sarah A. Hunt Mauldin 7/11/1837   Thomas H. Mauldin 6/9/1872
James R. Mauldin 2/14/1865   Carrie J. Mauldin 10/21/1875
Mattie A. Mauldin 4/28/1866   Bessie Lou Mauldin 10/11/1906
Mary E. Mauldin 7/7/1867   Tommie Byrd Mauldin 5/29/1908

Marriages
Francis Mauldin to Sarah A. Hunt 2/24/1864
Thomas H. Mauldin to Birdie Thompson 2/1/1898

Deaths
Annie F. Mauldin 9/8/1886   Carrie J. Adams 6/6/1906
Sarah A. Mauldin 1/16/1898   Mattie A. Thompson 1/10/1914
Francis Mauldin 5/16/1903   James R. mauldin 5/1925

W. A. MANRY BIBLE

Births
W. A. Manry 6/3/1868   Claud S. Manry 7/31/1897
Florence O. Manry 9/12/1870   Florrie Belle Manry 9/5/1899
Irwin A. Manry 1/6/1889   Mary Luelle Manry 8/28/1902
Allen E. Manry 12/1/1890   William C. Manry 10/1/1904
Willard E. Manry 2/11/1893   Mary C. Manry 7/20/1884
Robert F. Manry 2/21/1895   Lillie W. Manry 7/7/1899

Deaths
Robert F. Manry 5/28/1896
Florence A. Manry 8/8/1906

Marriages
W. A. Manry to Florence A. Wagner 12/25/1887
W. A. Manry to Mary C. Boike 9/18/1910
Allen Eugene Manry to Lillie Wilkinson 11/18/1916

OWEN REGISTER BIBLE
Owner Mrs. L. O. Hooper

Owen Register b. abt 1783 d. 1826 m. Hannah Green d. 6/22/1857
                    Births of Their Children:
William K. Register 10/5/1808   Mary Register 11/27/1818
Susannah Register 3/17/1810   Ann Register 3/5/1819
Sarah Register 1/27/1812   Jemima Register 8/22/1822
Daniel Register 10/14/1814   Lucy Green Register 11/12/1825

392

SAMUEL J. POWELL BIBLE
Owner: Arthur C. Powell
Quitman, Ga.

Samuel J. Powell 1/20/1820-7/9/1885
Rachel Elizabeth French 8/9/1824-3/2/1897, age 72 yrs.
Elizabeth French d. 3/1/1875
Samuel J. Powell m. Rachel E. French 11/29/1842
William J. Powell m. Lula Harrell 12/18/1882

DAVID MATTOX BIBLE

Births
David Mattox 4/9/1783
Sarah Mattox 7/14/1788
Nathan Mattox 11/2/1807   Mary V. Mattox 3/12/1819
John W. Mattox 11/1/1809   Sarah P. Mattox 3/28/1822
Henry P. Mattox 10/22/1811   Michael G. W. Mattox 4/13/1825
Elizabeth N. Mattox 12/15/1813   Lucy Jane Mattox 1/22/1828
William D. Mattox 8/28/1816   James Clark Mattox 8/26/1830

JOHN JUSTUS GROVENSTINE BIBLE

John Justus Grovenstine m. Mary Reisser, dau. of Israel Reisser

Births
Hannah Catherine Grovenstine   Susannah Grovenstine 9/27/1810
  8/7/1803   Naomi Grovenstine 1/11/1812
Mary Grovenstine 8/30/1809
Salome Grovenstine 2/21/1805   Lydia Grovenstine 8/23/1807
John Justus Grovenstine d. 12/12/1812
Mary Reisser Grovenstine d. 6/24/1857

BENJAMIN SMITH BIBLE

William Gainer b. 1758 m. 1778   Benjamin Smith d. 1799
Martha Williams Gainer b. 1762   Mary Thomas Smith d. 1794
Jordan Smith 1777-1835
His wife, Mary Gainer Smith, b. 1779
William Smith 1802-1867 m. 1824 Elizabeth Tarver Smith 1806-1878

DR. GEORGE FRANKLIN SMITH BIBLE
Owner: J. J. Simpson
19 Brookwood Dr., Atlanta, Ga.

Dr. George Franklin Smith b. 8/16/1832 m. 4/15/1858
Nancy Elizabeth Rains b. 11/25/1842

RICHARD STROTHER BIBLE
Owner: Mrs. J. N. Boyer
Sparta, Ga.

Richard Strother b. 4/10/1768 m. 2/23/1832 by James Dickson,
  Mary Black b. 1/10/1801

Richard Strother d. 7/10/1838

ANDREW JACKSON SMARR BIBLE

Births
Andrew Jackson Smarr 7/10/1828
Mary Pearson Smarr 2/2/1831
John Briton Smarr 8/1/1847-1903
Emma Josephine Smarr 12/16/1849-1914
William Jefferson Smarr 4/18/1851
Mary Jane Smarr 3/6/1853-2/28/1870, age 17 yrs.
Nannie Victoria Smarr 10/9/1854 m. George Washington Calloway
George WashingtoN Calloway 6/1/1846-7/8/1918
James Pierson Smarr 7/2/1857

DANIEL DAVIS BIBLE

Daniel Davis of Lumpkin Co., Ga. m. Rachel Martin of Albemarle
  Co., Va. 11/1/1808 by Rev. Littleton Meaks
Mrs. Davis d. 9/23/1843   Loremza Down Davis b. 7/25/1817
Daniel Davis d. 6/10/1868   Coalman Dvis 8/13/1819-8/27/1887
Martain Davis b. 8/27/1809   Geter Lynch Davis 8/24/1821-
William Davis b. 1/24/1811   11/17/1844
John Davis 4/16/1813   Delilah Davis d. 3/23/1885
Delilah Davis b. 8/8/1815   C. J. Davis d. 3/23/1885
                                 Armand Davis d. 6/26/1901

WILLIAM OGLETREE BIBLE

William Ogletree 1764-1835 m. 1785 Mary Bird 1766-1830

Children:

Philemon Ogletree b. 1792 m. 1st Miss Harper 2d Miss Harper
3d Mrs. Eliza Crawford Glynn (Tigner)
James Ogletree
John Ogletree
William Ogletree
David Ogletree m. Frances Fletcher
Absalom Ogletree b. 1811 m. Matilda Stewart
Fannie Ogletree
Elizabeth Bird Ogletree b. 1803 m. Hiram Phinazee
Mary B. Ogletree m. Harris Phinazee

OLIVE BIBLE
Owner: Mrs. T. G. Bethel

Births
Polly Olive 12/5/1798   Elizabeth Olive 10/15/1790
Hendon Olive 11/21/1780   Sally Olive 3/5/1793
John Olive 10/11/1782   Nancy Olive 10/24/1796
James Oliver 3/13/1785
Heziah Olive 9/22/1787

Heziah Olive d. 8/4/1802

William Cliff m. Happy Olive 10/20/1799

Patsey Parrish Clift 2/7/1801-6/25/1819
George Olive 6/22/1807
Jane Olive 7/1810
Kerrenhappuch Clift b. 3/24/1761

RICHARD W. PEEPLES BIBLE
Social Circle, Ga.

Richard W. Peeples b. 11/5/1860 m. 2/26/1882 Mary J. b. 2/25/1859
Claude W. Peeples b. 5/2/1884
Carrie L. Peeples b. 9/19/1889
Carrie L. Peeples m. Harry M. Carr 2/17/1917
Mary E. Carr b. 1/13/1918

ISAAC JAMES RICKS BIBLE Of Taylor Co.

Isaac James Ricks b. 5/8/1827 m. 1/26/1862 Taylor Co. Sarah
Montgomery Ricks b. 11/24/1837 Taylor Co., Ga.

Isaac James Ricks d. 4/14/1895 Taylor Co., Ga.
Sarah Montgomery Ricks d. 8/11/1920 in Reynolds Co., Taylor Co.
  Both bur. Reynolds Cemetery, Reynolds, Ga.

ROBERT RODDENBERY BIBLE
Owner: Robert S. Roddenbery
Moultrie, Ga.

Births
Robert Roddenbery 10/7/1805
Vicy Roddenbery 5/16/1808
Lewiza Roddenbery 9/15/1828
Mary Ann Roddenbery 9/15/1830
John K. Roddenbery 3/24/1832
Sarah Roddenbery 3/21/1834
Seabern A. Roddenbery 2/18/1836

Frances Roddenbery 6/2/1838
Margaret Roddenbery 10/2/1840
Nancy Roddenbery 1/2/1843
Elizabeth I. Roddenbery
  11/16/1844
Georgia Ann Roddenbery
  11/10/1847

Matthew Brinson 9/16/1763
Daniel Melson Hall Parker 6/10/1845
William Albert Parker 3/7/1848
Louise Ann Parker 2/23/1839

Stephen P. Parker 2/17/1843

Sampson Roddenbery 3/22/1836
Archibal Roddenbery 3/24/1842
Henry Roddenbery 8/14/1843
George Roddenbery 3/21/1846
Susan F. Roddenbery 5/16/1848

Mary Roddenbery 1/13/1850
Martha Roddenbery 12/28/1852
Richard Roddenbery 8/18/1854
Elizabeth Roddenbery 1/13/1839

Josiah T. Carter 7/8/1850
Charlotty S. Carter 3/26/1854

Matthew S. Brinson 12/8/1821
Lavenea C. Brinson 9/1/1823

Malindy Roddenbery 7/5/1853
Martha A. Roddenbery 1/29/1857

William Roddenbery 7/18/1860

Robert Roddenbery m. Vicey Anderson in N. C.

Deaths
Frances Roddenbery 5/6/1853
Mary Ann Carter 11/26/1855
Elizabeth Jane Roddenbery 8/29/1864
Josiah T. Carter 11/5/1869

Dottie L. Hambleton 9/7/1873
Sarough Smith 2/21/1875
Robert Roddenbery 12/18/1877
Louisa Davis 7/22/1829

SAMUEL BECKHAM BIBLE*
Owner: Miss Pensacola Musgrove
Atlanta, Ga.

Marriages
Samuel Beckham to Elizabeth Houghton 2/18/1790
William Rogers to Elizabeth C. Mitchell 12/24/1829

Births
Samuel Beckham, son of Simon and Susan Beckham, 11/24/1760
Elizabeth Houghton, dau. of Joshua and Nancy Houghton, 12/18/1769
Nancy F. Beckham, dau. of Samuel and Elizabeth Beckham, 6/18/1792
Mary B. Beckham, dau. of above, 10/11/1794
Elizabeth H. Beck, dau. of above, 11/24/1796
Erasmus G. Beckham, son of above, 4/3/1798
Susan C. Beckham, dau. of above, 4/13/1800
Albert G. Beckham, son of above, 6/18/1802

Deaths
Elizabeth Beckham, wife of Samuel, 1/31/1805, age 35 yrs., one
  mo., 13 days
Samuel D. B. Mitchell 7/25/1807, 4 yrs., 11 mos., 17 days
Erasmus G. Beckham 1/11/1820, 21 yrs., 9 mos., 8 days
Andrew A. E. McMitchell 8/14/1825, 6 yrs., 4 mos.
Samuel Beckham 11/2/1825, 65 yrs., wanting 22 days

MICHAEL W. PERRY BIBLE
Owner: Miss Edwina Holt
Columbus, Ga.

Births
Augustus B. Perry 5/2/1817-9/20/1822, age 5 yrs., 4 mos., 20 days
Louise Jelene Perry 1/2/1819-7/6/1819, 6 mos., 4 days
Michael W. Perry 3/10/1795
Martha E. Perry 11/5/1793
Henry F. Wimberley 12/5/1812
Augustus B. Perry 5/2/1817
Louisa Jelene Perry 1/2/1819
Sarah Ann Charlotte Perry 10/8/1820
John W. Perry 3/14/1823
Jared Banks Beckom 12/24/1803
Alfred Renfrow 9/11/1806

*See also p. 149.

WILLIAM DAVID GAULDING BIBLE
Owner: Mrs. William Mattox
Elberton, Ga.

Births
William David Gaulding 6/1/1836
Sarah Jane Gaulding 10/16/1838
John Tyler Gaulding 4/15/1841
Mary Gaulding, dau. of Richard and Mary V. Gaulding, 8/15/1843
David Mattox, son of Richard and Mary V. Gaulding, 3/4/1846
Edward G. Gaulding, son of above, 5/10/1848
Lucy Frances Gaulding, dau. of above, 11/4/1851

EXLEY BIBLE
Owner: Mrs. T. A. Ward
Savannah, Ga.

Births
Elvira E. Exley 12/26/1857
Mary Martha Exley 1/29/1825
Susannah Emailer Exley 12/25/1836
Benjamin F. Exley 12/24/1853
Amanda Elizabeth Exley 10/27/1838
Mary Elvira Seckinger 2/4/1839

Luke A. E. Exley 10/29/1840
Mary E. Rahn 12/2/1857
Sarah A. Rahn 10/29/1859
William E. Rahn 11/14/1862
Nola M. Rahn 3/6/1864
James Marion Dasher 9/4/1846

JOHN CRAWFORD EDWARDS BIBLE

Births
John Crawford Edwards 11/10/1833
Cinderella Ann Edwards (nee Hanson) 6/23/1838
Charles Henry Francis Marion Edwards 6/3/1855-1/11/1910
Martha Cinderella Edwards 1/22/1857
James Byrd Edwards 9/27/1858
John Crawford Edwards 6/12/1860
Duncan McCowan Edwards 4/20/1862
Mary Elizabeth Ida Edwards 2/17/1866
Edward Lee Edwards 12/20/1857
Acrean Mahala Edwards 7/23/1870 (Aunt Dooly died)
Eugene Esther Edwards 12/20/1874
Alonzo Norval Edwards 5/27/1876
Telulah Ellen Edwards 1/17/1878
Gordon Lowe Edwards 3/2/1880
Isabella Ann Edwards 11/13/1883

Mrs. J. C. Edwards d. 10/30/1922

EDMUND AND CLARA HARRIS JACKSON BIBLE
Owner: Mrs. Martha W. Blalock, Jonesboro, Ga.

Edmund Jackson, Sr. and Clara, his wife, m. 2/4/1808.

Edmund H. Jackson d. 2/18/1861
Clara, wife of Edmund Jackson Sr. d. 11/21/1861
Edmund d. 3/25/1864
Clara Banks d. 5/24/1855?
Permelia H. Jackson d. 8/30/1809
Algernon S. Jackson d. 10/4/1826

HARTWELL JACKSON BIBLE

Births
Andrew B. Jackson b. 8/7/1819, d. 4/28/1892 m. 1/3/1836 Elizabeth A.
  Thomas, b. 3/24/1818
Lovely A. Jackson b. 10/4/1820 d. 9/29/1889
Hillman Jackson b. 12/1/1821 d. 12/5/1873
Lorena L. Jackson b. 4/1/1824 d. 6/9/1874
Drewry W. Jackson b. 7/7/1825 d. 2/24/1909
Almeda P. Jackson b. 12/2/1827 d. 9/18/1893
Zarephath Jackson b. 8/5/1829 d. 5/11/1883
Elizabeth Ann Jackson b. 1/27/1835 d. 4/14/1897
Sarah C. Jackson -
Amelia D. Jackson b. 11/13/1837 -

JOHN CHAMBLESS BIBLE
Owner: Mrs. C. J. Zellner, Forsyth, Ga.

Marriages
John Chambless b. 4/13/1797 m. Elizabeth Jordan 8/22/1798
Thomas E. Chambless, son of John and Elizabeth, b. 2/27/1824 m.
  Mary Cleveland 7/27/1833
Elizabeth Jordan Chambless b. 11/27/1855 m. Frank Roquemore
Edan Armstrong Chambless b. 9/3/1857 m. Wiley E. Zellner
Zachariah Cromwell Chambless b. 5/24/1863 m. Sallie Inman
Mary Ellen Chambless b. 12/1/1867 m. 8/27/1885 Charles J.
  Zellner, b. 6/7/1860
Fannie C. Chambless b. 7/13/1871 m. Robert H. Holmes
William Cromwell Cleveland b. 5/20/1803 m. Edna Cleveland
  b. 9/13/1803

Births
Children of Thomas E. Chambless and Mary Cleveland:
Elizabeth Jordan, Edna Armstrong, Zachariah Cromwell, Mary Ellen,
  Fannie C.
Children of William C. and Edna Chambless:
Mary b. 7/27/1833
Wiley

HENRY CHAMBLESS BIBLE

Marriages
Henry Chambless to Rachel Danielly 10/12/1809
Lawson G. Chambless to Martha E. (Elizabeth) Russell 9/6/1834
Mary G. Chambless to G. L. Davis 6/17/1838
J. B. Chambless and Adeline Hobbs 5/16/1858
Sarah Ann Chambless to John Pye 12/8/1853

Births
Lawson Green Chambless 8/24/1810
Jane Chambless 5/22/1812
Mary Chambless 2/14/1814
Christopher Chambless 3/2/1817
Lovicy Chambless 8/10/1819

Andrew D. Chambless 7/4/1822
William Henry 10/4/1824
Joseph B. Chambless 1/6/1827
John F. Chambless 3/14/1829
Sara Ann Chambless 5/30/1832

Deaths
Henry Chambless 8/31/1834
Christopher Chambless 12/22/1830
Lovicy Chambless 8/10/1822

William Henry Chambless 1/23/1885
Martha Pye Chambless 3/30/1878
Sara Ann Chambless Pye
    11/10/1894

LITTLETON CHAMBLESS BIBLE of Jones Co.

Littleton Chambless b. 2/9/1764
Cynthia Chambless, his wife, b. 8/23/1764

John D., son, b. 1/23/1785
Obedience, his wife, b. 10/27/1788. Their Children:

Mary b. 7/31/1810
G. Zachariah L. b. 7/31/1814
William H. b. 9/3/1814
Thomas G. b. 12/18/1816

Littleton C. b. 7/2/1820
Nancy M. b. 9/13/1823
John T. b. 8/21/1826
Henry B. b. 2/21/1826

Children of G. Zachariah L. Chambless:
Thomas Taylor b. 4/15/1847
Elizabeth b. 3/27/1847
Marietta Stroud b. 1/2/1851
Littleton b. 6/13/1852

Theordoxica Lenorah 10/6/1856
Alonza Jackson b. 7/21/1854
James Graves b. 4/26/1859
Rena Augusta b. 3/15/1863

Deaths
Mary Chambless, wid. 9/15/1853
Littleton Chambless 1/17/1833
Mary Chambless 9/15/1812
Elizabeth Ledbetter, wid.,
    8/7/1823
Cynthia Chambless, wid.,
    4/27/1827
William H. Chambless 8/29/1826
Obedience   Chambless 1/5/1857
John D. Chambless 3/14/1857
Sara Jane, wife of G. Zachariah L. Chambless 8/2/1839

John W. Chambless 2/1/1836
William D. Chambless 8/12/1839
Sara Jane Chambless 8/21/1803
Thomas Taylor Chambless 1/12/-
Marietta Stroud Chambless 8/11/-

Henry Littleton Chambless
    10/6/1858
Sarah Elizabeth Chambless
    1/2/1860

JEPTHA AND SUSAN CHAMBLESS BIBLE

Jeptha, son of Christopher and Mary, m. 3/2/1819 Susan Jones,
   dau. of Adam Jones and Susan.
Christopher m. Amanda Edwards 11/16/1841
Hiram P. Picmore m. Lovicy Chambless 11/17/1851
Thomas J. Baldwin, son of Anderson Baldwin, m. Martha Ann
   Chambless, dau. of Jeptha Chambless, 10/10/1842
John H. Mattock m. Mary Chambless 11/30/1849

Births
Jeptha 3/12/1798
Susan, dau. of Adam Jones and Susan, 4/2/1820
Christopher, son of Jeptha and Susan, 2/11/1820
Susan M., dau. of Jeptha and Susan, 2/7/1822
Jeptha C., son of above, 7/8/1823
Lovicy, dau. of above, 12/30/1824
Harriett, dau. of above, 5/22/1826
Artean, dau. of above, 5/24/1828
Seaborn, son of above, 8/25/1829
Nathan, son of above, 2/13/1831
Martha Ann, dau. of above, 1/7/1833
Katherine 3/17/1834
Josephus 1/30/1835
Francis M. 7/20/1837
Mary 4/13/1839
George W. 2/23/1842
Eleanor--
Frank--
Augusta--

Deaths
Harriett, dau. of Jeptha and Susan, 9/1827
Nathan, son of above, 1/13/1832
Josephus, son of above, 1/30/1842
Jeptha, son of Christopher, 1/14/1846
Augusta, dau. of Jeptha and Susan, 1859
Susan, wife of Jeptha, 8/4/1862
Mrs. Susan M. Young 1/6/1910

WILLIAM JORDAN BIBLE
Owner: John W. Slappey, Sylvesta, Ga.

Lieut. William Jordan b. 3/31/1744, d. 9/23/1826 m. Anne Medlock
in 1786 who was b. 1759, d. 1817. Parents of Elizabeth Jordan.

Deaths
Israel Sneed Jordan 7/8/1829   William Medlock Jordan 1/17/1834

FREDERICK ASHMORE BIBLE Of Lincoln Co., Ga.
Owner: Mrs. Otis Ashmore
909 Whitaker St., Savannah, Ga.

Frederick Ashmore and wife, Bridget, m. 2/8/1759.

Births
John Ashmore 1/22/1760   William Ashmore 11/17/1765
Elizabeth Ashmore 12/29/1761   Pointon Ashmore 1/12/1768
Sarah Ashmore 8/3/1763   Peter Ashmore 12/28/1770
                                Mary Ashmore 2/5/1773

JOHN DANIELLY BIBLE

John Danielly's Bible, 2/9/1839.

Births
James Cody 10/5/1793   Mary Hodo Cody 11/23/1823
Mary Cody, his wife, 1/12/1800 Sina A. Cody 12/10/1825
Sarah Ann Cody 8/28/1818   Michael Cody 2/6/1827
Abner McCormick Cody 6/12/1820 Emily Moore Cody 3/30/1829
Green W. Cody 3/23/1822

Births
John Danielly 4/1/1803
Martha Danielly, his wife, 11/6/1805
Catharine Baker Daniely 3/21/1829
Francis McDade Danielly 7/10/1830
Mary Jane Danielly 8/31/1833
Sann Danielly 1/26/1836
Sarah Ann Danielly 5/17/1838
Rody Danielly 7/25/1840

Births
Martha Caroline Danielly 12/6/1842   Charity Malinda Danielly
Susannah Frances Danielly 7/6/1845   4/13/1857
John Andrew Danielly 7/6/1845   Nancy Aldora Danielly
Penelope Elizabeth Danielly 10/25/1846   12/3/1859
Malinda Danielly, his wife, 1/5/1828 Jackson Danielly 10/3/1862
Eliza Ann Rebecca Danielly 10/16/1849 Levisa W. Danielly
Allen Cleaveland Danielly 8/29/1851   11/18/1865
Josephene America Danielly 6/12/1853 Allie Osa Huckabee
Mahala B. Danielly 5/25/1855   5/17/1897
                                      Cornelius Perry Huckabee
                                          11/15/1902
                                      Dora Huggins 3/28/1888
Marriages   Euda Huggins 8/24/1889
James Cody and Mary Cody 9/11/1817
John Danielly and Martha Danielly 3/11/1828
Jepthah Castleberry and Susannah Frances Castlberry 5/16/1837
John Danielly and Malindy Danielly 9/23/1845

Deaths
Abner M. Cody 9/19/1829
John and Malinda Danielly Family moved to Clay Co. 11/26 or the
    27th, 1868

(John Danielly Bible, Deaths, contd.....)

Mrs. P. E. Norman d. 6/9/1897   J. H. Huckabee d. 4/11/1917
A. C. Danielly d. 11/22/1900   C. P. Huckabee d. 7/6/1834
Mrs. Malinda Danielly d. 11/22/1900

Catharine B. Danielly d. 6/6/1829
Martha Danielly, wife of John, d. 7/6/1845
Charity Malinda Danielly d. 9/30/1862
Eliza A. Hearn, wife of Henry M. Hearn d. in Eastland, Texas
7/28/1872
Jackson Danielly d. 11/13/1881
John Danielly d. 4/8/1870

            SAMUEL ADAMS BIBLE of Twiggs Co., Ga.
      Owner: Dr. William E. Chappell, Va. Polytechnic Inst.
                    Blacksburg, Va.

Marriages
Samuel Adams and Eliza Oliver m. 1/22/1829
Samuel J. Adams and Alabama Hearne m. in Robertson Co., Texas,
    10/16/1867
Thomas E. Baker and Nancy T. Adams m. in Stewart Co., Ga.,
    3/3/1857
Daniel P. Adams and Net Graham m. Fannin Co., Texas 3/10/1878
Jack D. Adams and Mary Richardson m. 10/1889, Fannin Co., Texas
D. P. Adams and Sallie Nobles m. Kemp, Texas, 1/6/1884?

Births
Samuel Adams 10/30/1802   Job K. Adams 4/8/1840
Eliza Oliver 9/10/1812   Ann E. Adams 6/14/1842
William F. Adams 12/30/1829   John E. Adams 5/14/1844
Frances C. Adams 9/3/1831   Willis A. Adams 3/22/1847
Nannie T. Adams 2/10/1834   Daniel P. Adams 11/24/1848
Oliver H. Adams 11/8/1835   Jack D. Adams 8/3/1850
Samuel J. Adams 4/14/1837   Lizzie C. Adams 1/4/1852
Bryant B. Adams 4/8/1840   George W. Adams 11/30/1854

Deaths
Frances C. Adams 6/20/1845   D. P. Adams 4/29/1918
Oliver H. Adams 5/17/1836   J. D. Adams 11/12/1927 Lufkin, Tx
Ann E. Adams 1/9/1850   Samuel Adams 5/9/1872
Lizzie C. Adams 4/19/1857   Samuel J. Adams 2/19/1889
George W. Adams 4/7/1857   Eliza Adams 6/3/1899
Job K. Adams 5/22/1859   Willis A. Adams 10/19/1900
J. E. Adams 3/12/1863   B. B. Adams 7/4/1909
Children of W. T. Baker:
Inf. dau. 8/15/1860
Eva Baker 10/1/1874
Clare Baker 7/21/1883

T. C. Baker 10/9/1893
A. Fannie Baker Cobb 3/31/1911
T. E. Baker 7/2/1909

                         403

SIMEON BANKS BIBLE Of Bulloch Co., Ga.
Owner: Mrs. Charles S. Mann, East Point, Ga.

Simeon Banks, son of Elisha Banks, b. 12/6/1789, and Mary, his
wife, b. 12/26/1789, and was m. 12/21/1809
Matilda Banks, second wife of Simeon Banks, b. 9/18/1800, and m.
8/4/1850
Children:

Cuyler Banks b. 10/7/1811   Amos Banks b. 4/5/1827
Ekisha? Banks b. 11/6/1815   Polly Ann Banks b. 2/7/1829
Ira L. Banks b. 10/31/1816?   Betsy Ann Banks b. 9/12/1831
Clarissa Banks b. 1/19/1819   Belinda S. Banks b. 2/2/1834
Simeon C. Banks b. 7/18/1821   Robert Cone, grandson of Simeon
Thomas F. Banks b. 8/17/1823   Banks, b. 12/10/1837

EDWARD P. LUCAS BIBLE
Owner: Mrs. R. H. Wilder, Orlando, Fla.

Births
Emmie V. Lucas, dau. of Edward P. and Sarah J. Lucas b.
12/27/1865
Eddie R. Lucas, dau. of Edward P. and Sarah J. Lucas b. 8/25/1869
Emmie V. Bass, dau. of Dr. J. L. and Emmie V. Bass, b. at
Willacoochee, Ga. 5/4/1888
Emmie Inez Bass, dau. of W. L. and E. R. Bass, b. at Kingstree,
3/23/1887
Natalie Bass, dau. of W. L. and E. R. Bass, b. at Lake City,
S.C., 11/27/1890
Sallie G. Bass, dau. of W. L. and E. R. Bass, b. at Lake City,
S. C., 3/8/1892
Gretchen Bass, dau. of W. L. and E. R. Bass, b. at Lake City,
S. C. 3/3/1896

Marriages
Edward P. Lucas to Sarah J. Brown, Charleston, S. C. 10/23/1863
Eddie R. Lucas to W. L. Bass 6/16/1886, Kingstree, S. C.
Emmie V. Lucas to Dr. J. L. Bass, Kingstree, S. C., 5/23/1887

REV. WILSON CONNER BIBLE
Owner: Mrs. Gladys McCallister Poe, Mt. Vernon, Ga.

Wilson Conner and Mary Cook m. 10/8/1789
George Cooper and Nancy Conner m. 12/20/1810
John Griffin and Harriet Conner m. 5/25/1813
James C. Conner and Penelope Rials m. 10/1/1818
Joseph Ryals and Lucy Ann Conner m. 3/31/1822

William Dewitt Clinton Conner b. 9/23/1819
George Washington Cooper b. 4/31/1821
Ghomas Benton Conner, son of James Conner, b. 8/29/1821
Joseph Rials and Lucy Ann Conner m. 3/31/1822

(Rev. Wilson Conner Bible, Births, contd....)

Harriet Griffin-----b.---
Wilson Conner b. 7/7/1768
Mary Conner b. 8/1/1774
James Gassoway Conner b. 8/28/1790
Nancy Conner b. 4/20/1792
Harriet Elizabeth Conner b. --, 1793

Mary Ann Sullivant b. 11/10/1825
Thomas Benton Conner b. 10/21/1798
Betsy Conner b. 3/9/1801
Polly Goldwin Conner b. 1/25/1804
Eliza Tarpley Conner b. 7/29/1807
Mariah McDonald Conner b. 6/13/1810

Wilson Conner Cooper, son of George and Nancy Cooper,
    b. 9/16/1812
Wilson Walker Conner b. 4/19/1813
Mary Ann Elizabeth Cooper b. 12/4/1813
Samuel Conner Griffin, son of John and Harriet Griffin,
    b. 9/23/1814
Panellopy Lucreacy? Cooper b. 6/14/1815
Elizabeth Griffin b. 10/19/1815

Thomas B. C. Cooper b. 12/26/1824 Samuel C. Griffin d. 10/21/1814
Louisa Ann Conner b. 10/25/1815   James C. Griffin b. 2/18/1818
Ellenor Cook Cooper b. 2/10/1817   Penelope Ryals b. 9/11/1799
Martha Lewis Conner b. 3/30/1818   Lurany Cooper b. 2/16/1819

Thomas Conner Sr. d. 8/4/1768, age 90 yrs.
Margret, his wife, d.---age 60 yrs.
John Beverly d. 1786, age 80 yrs.
Ann Beverly d. 1787, age 81 yrs.
Elinor Cook d. 9/15/1793, age 50 yrs.
Ann Conner d. 9/1791, age 60 yrs.
Lewis Conner d. 8/30/1793, age 37 yrs.
William Conner d. 7/1797, age 32 yrs.
William Conner d. 7/1797, age 32 yrs.
Bellis? Conner d. 1820, age 5 yrs.
James Conner was unfortunately killed by a fall from his horse
    1805 in the 51st years of his age.
Thomas Conner, Jr. d. 9/12/1802, age 75 yrs.
Ananias Long d. 7/32/1807
Patsy Conner d. 2/4/1809, age 7 yrs., 10 mos., 25 days precisely.
Elizabeth Long, wid. of Ananias Long, d. 5/10/1809.

            ACTON NASH BIBLE Of Wilkes Co., Ga.
        Owner: James Roy Smith, Jr., College Park, Ga.

Acton Nash and Margaret Nash, his wife, m. 8/12/1799
Rubin Nash b. 2/4/1801   Anton nash b. 5/1/1806
Elizabeth Nash b. 6/3/1802   Thomas Nash b. 7/9/1807
Jacob Brozey Nash b. 10/17/1803 Barbary Nash b. 5/2/1809
Theodosey Nash b. 2/4/1805   Sary Damaskus Nash b.
                                    11/25/1810

```
                    JOEL COLLEY DAVIS BIBLE Of Morgan Co., Ga.
                    Owner: Wade H. Davis, Rutledge, Ga.


Joel Colley Davis,  son of John M.  Davis and Mary Malcom  Davis,
and Emma Johnson Day, dau. of Benson Day and N. F. Henderson Gay,
were m. 12/5/1867

Births                                        Deaths
Joel Colley Davis 9/11/1847                       12/20/1914
Emma Johnson Day 7/3/1851                         8/3/1932
Johnnie T. Davis 1/29/1869                        3/29/1934
Julian A. Davis 7/1/1870                          10/1/1949
Lena Dempsey Davis 1/19/1872                      1/27/1954
Benson Davis 11/3/1873                            4/28/1952
Elisha J. Davis 8/27/1875                         8/30/1876
Freddie B. Davis 1/20/1878                        9/21/1885
Wade Hampton Davis 12/2/1879
James Joel Davis 12/24/1882
Jessie Lilla Davis 9/23/1884                      12/24/1887
Rabon B. Davis 6/28/1886                          12/30/1887
Emory Davis 4/11/1889                             6/6/1962
Day Davis 8/21/1896

Marriages
John T. Davis to Clara A. Hollis 12/14/1890
Julian A. Davis to Katie Lee Hanner 10/8/1892
Julian A. Davis to Mrs. O. C. (Malcom) Cowan 12/25/1912
Lena D. Davis to George S. Oxford 12/9/1888
Benson Davis to Kate O. Powell 2/15/1896
Wade H. Davis to Leila Estes 12/23/1900
James J. Davis to Gussie Haile 8/6/1905
Emory Davis to Clyde Knight 6/4/1914
Day Davis to Clyde Haile---



                              LEWIS HALL BIBLE
                    Owner: Mrs. Sarah Hall Cannon, Monticello, Ga.



Lewis Hall b. 6/25/1753, d. 4/22/1821
              Children of Lewis Hall by 1st wife:
Bridget b. 6/27/1776 m. 1st Sion Hall, 2nd, A. D. Smith
Thomas b. 6/27/1778 m. Permelia Swilley, dau. of John Swilley
Enoch b. 3/3/1780 m. Elizabeth
Lewis b. 2/12/1782 m. Rebecca
Alston b. 9/23/1785
Isaac b. 1/5/1788
John b. 4/15/1793
              Children of Lewis Hall by 2nd wife:
Flora b. 2/12/1796 m. James Kemp
Instance b. 4/28/1800 m. Drucilla Sellers
Piety b. 1/9/1803 m. Henry Cook, 1820
Priscilla b. 12/11/1805 m. B. H. Smith
Seaborn b. 3/3/1807 m. 1st Ann Gainey, 2d, Crecy Quinn
James b. 2/22/1809 m. 1st Rebecca Bell 2d, Ava Mann
Rebecca b. 12/28/1810 m. Daniel D. Davis
Jehu b. 5/20/1813 m. Catherine Johnson
```

(Lewis Hall Bible contd....)

Elphens b. 10/21/1814
Nancy b. 1/1/1817 m. George Wilcox
William L. b. 3/7/1819, d. age 3

JOHN DEASON SR. BIBLE Of Jasper Co.
Ownèr: Mrs. Helen Womack
3461 Manana Drive, Dallas, Texas 75220

Births

John Deason Sr. 8/25/1816	R. C. Deason & A. H. Deason 1/8/1840
Nancy Deason 4/1/1810	Mary E. Deason 12/18/1842
Mary Jane Deason 2/24/1830	W. F. Deason 6/22/1848
J. C. Deason 8/7/1836	Jeremiah Deason 2/2/1850
Walter Deason 2/7/1838	Tabitha G. Deason---
John Deason 2/8/1838	G. T. Deason 3/16/1852

Timothy Deason 6/27/1856	Jessa Deason 1/16/1868
James Deason 12/5/1863	T. J. Deason 2/22/1853
Emmer A. Deason 1/7/1866	Jones, step-son of John Deason b.1816

Marriages
John Deason and Nancy Barclay 12/23/1835
John Deason and Selenah (Selena) Bridges 10/9/1845
John Deason and Mary Janes Jones 8/17/1854 "Mother of Jesse
  Deason"

Deaths

James C. Jones 6/4/1854	Della Deason 4/7/1961
J. C. Deason 8/8/1836	Mary Etta Deason 2/23/1894
Nancy Deason 12/18/1842	Robert Jefferson Deason 2/23/1947
Mary E. Deason 9/27/1846	Jerry T. Deason 6/17/1949
Anderson H. Deason 9/16/1849	Beacher Ward Deason 6/8/1951
Selenah Deason 2/12/1854	Della Deason 4/7/1961
R. C. Deason 5/1862	J. Calvin Deason 11/18/1966
Walter Deason 7/1863	Chester 3/12/1971
James Deason 7/2/1865	Jessie Mae 11/3/1973 at Nursing
Home	

Memoranda
Jesse Deason and Della Ann Nelson m. 7/31/1886
Minnie Beatrice Deason b. 7/2/1887
Jessie Mae and Josie Lee Deason b. 5/9/1890
Mary Etta Deason b. 9/21/1892
John William Deason b. 12/21/1894
Jeremiah Timothy Deason b. 12/5/1896
Robert Jefferson Deason b. 12/5/1896
Henry Ward Beecher Deason b. 2/3/1900
Genetta Odella Deason b. 4/9/1902
Della Ann Nelson b. 2/3/1865
Minnie Charlsey Deason b. 9/16/1906
Horace Chester Deason b. 5/9/1904
James Calvin Deason b. 11/26/1909
John William Deason and Hester Hillin m. Henderson, Tx.
  10/25/1913
Jesse James Deason b. 7/29/1917

JAMES SAUL BIBLE
Owner: Stan Crowley
110 A Longwood Dr., Charlottesville, Va. 22903

Births
James Saul b. 10/1832 in Walker Co.   Julia Pink Saul b. 8/12/1865
Hannah Randolph b. 3/13/1835 (Ala.)   Nancy Elizzie Saul
Mary Francis Saul b. 12/31/1853   b. 11/28/1867
Ulysses Tyley Saul b. 11/29/1855   John Perry Saul b. 7/16/1870

Sarah Jane Crawford b. 4/3/1876

Charles Mancil Saul b. 1/14/1857   Merida Saul b. 1/18/1861
Dicy Scynora Saul b. 4/14/1859   James Green Saul b. 3/12/1863

Deaths
John Saul 9/10/1864 "Baps grandpa, wife, Dicy Netherland"
Dicy Saul 1/1/1861
Mary Francis 10/29/1862
Dicy Synora Barnette 2/4/1882
Ulysses Tyley Saul 10/6/1895

Marriages
James Saul to Hannah Randolph 9/30/1852

WILLIAM FRANCIS MEDCALF BIBLE
Owner: Mrs. Margaret Barrow
4320 Glenhaven Dr., Decatur, Ga.

Births
William Francis Medcalf 6/23/1824
Martha Eviline Medcalf 11/12/1823
Children of W. F. and M. E. Medcalf:
Mary Elizabeth Medcalf 7/19/1846   William Bartlett Medcalf
John Thomas Medcalf 8/7/1848   6/20/1857
Jehu Alexander Medcalf 9/8/1850   Nancy Ann Medcalf 1/19/1860
James Henry Medcalf 1/19/1853   Martin Tilmon Medcalf
William Barnett Medcalf 6/20/-   4/6/1863
Edithia? Jane Medcalf 4/17/1855   Ebbey Neeza Medcalf 3/3/1866

James Martin Thompson 4/17/1836
John Robert Thompson 7/19/1840

Deaths
James Martin Thompson 12/27/1862   Martha Evelene Metcalf (sp?)
Edithia Jane Medcalf 8/21/1880   1/13/1917
Martin Tilmon Medcalf 9/12/1882   William Francis Metcalf (sp?)
John Robbert Thompson 10/20/1882   7/20/1917
James Henry Medcalf 10/30/1882   Evelene Metcalf (sp?)1/13/1917

HILLIARD JUDGE DEASON BIBLE
Owner: Mrs. Myrtle Bartlett Jones
Colorado City, Texas

Births
Hilliard Judge Deason 11/27/1812
Hannah Posey Deason 3/16/1824 Nee Blackstock, dau. of Richard
  Blackstock and Cassandra Wright
James Henrey Deason 9/5/1840
Joseph Richedd Deason 11/28/1841
John Collinsworth Deason 3/21/1843
Daniel Marion 9/14/1844
Elizabeth Deason 3/26/1846

Jeremiah Deason 9/28/1847
Pleasant Pearse Martain 2/9/1851
Emerintha Caroline 12/24/1852
Martha Zeller Deason 7/2/1857
Joseph Sterling Deason 5/24/1864
Danil Marion Deason 10/24/1865
Jeams Frankling Deason 2/22/1868
Sarah Ann Deason 11/3/1869
Georgia Deason 4/22/1879
Matty Flora Deason 4/26/1874

Evie Arnold 10/9/1870	George Washington Bartlett-----
John Arnold 4/24/1874	(b. 10/28/1875-4/18/1960)
James Arnold 4/24/1874	William---12/17/1877
	Hannah Eldora Bartlett 5/10/1880

Marriages
H. J. Deason and H. P. Blackstock 3/10/1839
James Henrey Deason, son of H. J. and H. P. Deason, m. Martha
  Lewis 8/6/1863
J. F. Bartlett and M. Z. Deason 11/12/1874

Deaths
Elizabeth Deason, dau. of H. J. and Hannah P. Deason 9/1846,
  aged 5 mos.,--days
Joseph Richard Deason, son of H. J. and Hannah P. Deason
  4/3/1862
James Henry Deason, son of H. J. and Hannah P. Deason,
  -/10/1874
---Franklin and
---nel Marion

DANIEL ARINGTON BIBLE

This certifies that rite of Holy Marriage was celebrated between
J. A. Arington of the one part and N. A. Johnson of the other
part on 19th day of Sept. 1876 at bride´s residence by S. M.
Lipscomb, J. P. Wit: David Johnson, Sarah A. F. Johnson

(Daniel Arington Bible contd....)

Marriages
Daniel Arington b. 1/10/1830
P. J. (Jane) Arington b. 6/14/1828
Daniel Arington and P. J. Vowell m. 10/3/1854
Marvin E. Arington m. 8/12/1902
M. L. Arington m. S. G. Nichols 11/12/1905
Pearly J. Arington m. R. J. Breed 6/20/1909
Anna P. F. Arington m. Truit Rowe 1/8/1911
Willie B. Arington m. John Rice 4/23/1911
Dora I. Arington m. S. T. Barfield 11/6/1917

Births
Madorah I. Arington 12/20/1877   Pearlly J. Arington 1/10/1891
Anner P. F. Arington 3/17/1880   Willie Bell Arington 6/16/1893
Marvin E. Arington 10/22/1882   J. A. Arington 11/17/1855
Mary L. Arington 7/11/1886   Nancy A. Jonston Arington
                                        10/19/1850

Deaths
Parmealy J. Arington 7/10/1892, age 64   Marvin Arington 4/27/1942
Daniel Arington 12/7/1891, age 62   Dora I. Arington Barfield
Ollie May Arington 11/7/1889,   6/2/1953
   age 5 mos., 22 days   M. Lula Arington 6/8/1953
John A. Arington 5/9/1924, age   James Truit Rowe 4/8/1955
   68, 5 mos., 22 days   R. J. Breed 7/29/1956
Nancy A. Arington 1/6/1925, age   Sam G. Nichols 10/4/1958
   67 yrs., 2 mos., 17 days
Pearley J. Breed Arington 9/6/1933   Marvin Arington 4/2/1942
S. G. Barfield 8/10/1934, age
   75 yrs., 6 mos., 7 days

WILLIAM JACKSON MARTIN BIBLE Of Putnam Co.
Owner: Doc Martin, Shady Dale, Georgia

Marriages
William Jackson Martin 3/18/1824-5/22/1886 m. 10/1/1850 Mary Ann
   Lynch, d. 5/16/1908
Martha Sophia Martin, dau. of William J. and Mary Ann, m.
   11/17/1869 William E. Cosby
William B. Martin m. Lona Walker
Fannie Martin m. 11/24/18--Rev. M. J. Cofer
John B. Martin m. 12/20/188--Sallie Caswell
Carrie Martin m. 11/27/1890 m. J. T. Prather
Steve A. martin m. 10/19/1892 Eliza Buckner
Walker I. Martin m. 3/31/1895 Lizzie Black 2/15/1877-12/11/1915
R. L. Martin m. 2/14/1899 Victorine Kergosiene

Births
Sidney Smith Cosby -/6/1870   Mary Elizabeth Cosby 6/31/1877
Winnona Cosby 10/18/1872   Wm. Stephens Cosby 10/5/1879
Emma Lavenia Cosby 11/28/1874   Sidney Smith 11/6/1870
Tressie True Martin 12/31/1895   James J. Martin 4/22/1908
Clarence Curtis Martin 7/26/1897 Fannie Lee Martin 1/5/1911
Janie Victorine Martin 3/5/1899 Andrew Barnett Martin 7/15/--
Wm. Walker Martin 9/22/1900   Gladys Frankie Martin 8/10/1922

(William Jackson Martin Bible, Births, contd.....)

M. M. Martin 6/10/1902   Mable Elizabeth Martin 5/31/1914
Sara Martin 11/17/1904   Evelyn Juanita Martin 3/26/1924
Mary Martin 7/17/1906   Nathaniel W. Martin 7/18/1870

Deaths
W. B. Martin 5/30/1927   G. W. Dennis 4/19/1926
M. L. Martin 6/24/1927
Mrs. Carrie Eugenia Pearson Dennis 8/27/1826

                    JEREMIAH B. HATCHER BIBLE
                      Owner: Lizzie Hancock
                 3896 Columbus Rd., Macon, Ga. 31204

Marriages
Maryann Hatcher m.--
Sallie A. E. Hatcher m. 9/31/1870
John W. Hatcher m. 11/29/1872
Caroline F. C. Hatcher m. 3/11/1875
Charity A. S. Hatcher m. 8/-/1880
Nannie S. E. Hatcher m. 2/27/1881
Anice Virginia Hatcher m. 8/10/1887

Births
Reubin S. Hatcher 11/16/1843   Cicero Hatcher 4/28/1827
Margaret Cosel 7/16/1791   Elizabeth Hatcher 7/23/1829
Jeremiah B. Hatcher 2/26/1813   Francis Narcisa Hatcher 5/1/1831
Nancy T. Hatcher 8/13/1814   Obedience B. Hatcher 1/11/1833?
Reuben T. Hatcher 9/11/1816   James Hatcher 10/19/1835
Robert Hatcher 11/20/1818   William G. Hatcher 9/5/1842
Polly Hatcher 2/20/1820   Margaret A. Hatcher 1/14/1844
John Hatcher 12/3/1821   Mary H. Hancock 10/1/1836
Amanda Hatcher 6/13/1823   John H. Hancock 4/9/1838
Henry Hatcher 4/11/1825

Robert H. Hatcher 5/8/1858
Charity A. S. Hatcher 4/16/1860
Josephine Sarah Hatcher -/26/1862, d. 8/4/1950
Reubin S. Hatcher 10/16/1844
Patience M. A. Hatcher 5/4/1846
Samuel B. Hatcher 5/11/1848
Sarah A. E. Hatcher 2/23/1849
John T. Hatcher 4/7/1850
Nancy E. Hatcher 1/29/1852
James C. Hatcher 4/21/1858
Martha O. Hatcher 10/16/1854
Caroline Amanda Hatcher 5/10/1856

Deaths
Francis Narcisa Hatcher 5/5/1841
John Hatcher, Sr., b. 3/7/1757   John Hatcher b. 5/7/1786
Mary Hatcher b. 1763   Margaret Hatcher b. 7/17/1791
Marryed 12/30/1779   d. 1/25/1854
Jeremiah B. Hatcher b. 9/20/1780 Robert Hatcher d. 1/25/1854
Nancy Hatcher b. 11/4/1782   Benjamin L. Hatcher
Mary Hatcher b. 10/26/1784   d. 12/30/1870
Reubin Sanders Hatcher d. 9/13/1846

                            411

WILLIAM SYLVESTER LUNGER BIBLE
Owner: Mrs. J. W. T. Armacost
Spruce Hill Farm, Hampstead, Md. 21074

William Sylvester Lunger m. Miss Sallie Underwood 7/4/1888,
Siloam, Ga.

William Sylvester Lunger b. Waldo, Ohio 4/7/1862
Sallie U. Lunger b. Siloam, Ga. 11/2/1862
Stillborn baby boy b. Atlanta, Ga. 6/1/1889
Maurice Lafayette Lunger b. Atlanta, Ga. 6/7/1890
Mable K. Lunger b. Atlanta, Ga. 9/22/1892
Willie May Lunger b. Atlanta, Ga. 8/10/1895
John Carter Lunger b. Atlanta, Ga. 6/5/1897
William S. Lunger, Jr. b. Atlanta, Ga. 10/20/1899
Mable K. Lunger d. Atlanta, Ga. 8/8/1895
William S. Lunger Sr., d. Atlanta, Ga. 6/1/1928
Sallie U. Lunger d. Atlanta, Ga. 2/16/1935
Maurice L. Lunger d. Atlanta, Ga. 3/14/1952
John Carter Lunger d. Chatt. Tenn. 3/7/1966

John Carter Lunger m. Eunelle Simms, Atlanta, Ga.
John Carter Lunger, Jr., b. Atlanta, Ga. 12/30/1920
John Carter Lunger, Jr. d. Atlanta, Ga. 6/1/1923
John Carter Lunger, Sr. m. Alma Johnson, Chatt. Tenn.
Alma Johnson Lunger d. Chatt. Tenn. 9/17/1963

William S. Lunger, Jr. m. Inez Imogene Hicks, Atlanta, Ga.
8/12/1920
Muriel Christine Lunger b. 9/30/1922, Atlanta, Ga.
M. C. Lunger m. Daniel Fred. Caldemeyer, 11/4/1944, Baltimore,
Md.
Daniel Dawson Caldemeyer b. 6/16/1946 Evansville, Ind.
M. C. Lunger Caldemeyer m. John William Tracey Armacost 3/5/1955,
Alex., Va.
Suzy Underwood Armacost b. 9/30/1959, Baltimore, Md.

JAMES S. ROBERTS BIBLE
Of Lowndes Co., Ga. and Polk Co., Fla.
Owner: Mrs. W. L. Guthrie, Punta Gorda, Fla.

James S. Roberts, son of Reubin and Elizabeth, b. 7/22/1838
Mary Cone Knight, dau. of William Cone Knight and Rachel,
his wife, b. 6/25/1843
James S. Roberts and Mary Cone Knight m. 9/12/1865
Their children:

Charles L. Roberts b. 7/7/1866, d. single
Albert Sidney Roberts b. 10/31/1867 m. Rebecca J. Peters
10/9/1895
Augustus E. Roberts b. 2/22/1869, d. infancy
John Q. Roberts b. 6/24/1870 m. Leola L. Gresham 7/26/1900
Mitchell S. Roberts b. 10/4/1872 m. Frances Hancock 7/10/1898
William R. Roberts b. 4/5/1875, d. single
Mineola Roberts b. 11/7/1877 m. Willoby H. Stephens 4/18/1896

(James S. Roberts Bible contd....)

Mary Cone Roberts b. 9/6/1879 m. James W. Wilson 2/16/1898
Julian B. Roberts b. 12/29/1881 m. Effie E. Blackburn 5/25/1904
Linton Stephens Roberts b. 7/6/1884 m. Mrs. Everal Skinner 7/1915
Rachel E. Roberts b. 1/17/1887 m. Walter J. Quick 3/1909
Claudia P. Roberts b. 8/25/1888, d. single

Deaths
Augustus E. Roberts 5/26/1870
Leola L. Roberts 2/21/1901 (wife of John J. Roberts)
Mary C. Wilson 11/6/1902
Mary Cone Roberts 9/5/1904 (wife of James S. Roberts)
John Q. Roberts 9/28/1924
Charles L. Roberts 11/21/1917
James S. Roberts 4/20/1922
Claudia P. Roberts 4/14/1923
Rachel E. Roberts Quick 1/27/1928 (wife of Walter J. Quick)
Linton Stephens Roberts 4/6/1931
Albert S. Roberts 10/9/1936
Mitchell Sherod Roberts 12/20/1942
William R. Roberts 11/11/1947
Mary Frances Roberts 9/23/1949 (wife of M. S. Roberts)

Reubin Roberts, son of John and Phoebe O'Steen Roberts, b. in
    Wayne Co., Ga. 4/17/1807
Elizabeth, his wife, dau. of William and Elizabeth Clements,
    b. Wayne Co., Ga. 10/25/1805
Reubin Roberts and Elizabeth Clements m. 3/31/1835

Children of Reubin Roberts and Elizabeth, his wife:

Sherod E. Roberts b. 3/26/1837 m. Keziah Knight
James S. Roberts b. 7/22/1838 m. Mary Cone Knight
Ezekiel W. Roberts b. 2/13/1840, killed in war, never married
Amanda A. Roberts b. 11/6/1843 m. John W. Hagan
Thomas Jefferson Roberts b. 1845, killed in war, never married

                        JOHN STOCKS BIBLE
            Owner: H. R. Philpot, Cedartown, Ga.

Births   Deaths
John (Jack) Stocks 8/5/1789
Caroline Stocks 11/14/1800
Thomas Franklin Stocks 4/3/1820
Martha Ann Stocks 7/12/1822
Charity Hunter Stocks 9/26/1824
Elizabeth Jane Stocks 6/22/1826
William Abraham Stocks 4/15/1828   8/17/1829
Sara Antionette Stocks 12/1833 (grandmother)
Caroline Matilda Stocks 2/1834
Julia Catherine Stocks 4/4/1837
John Thomas Stocks 8/23/1842   1/22/1870

Caroline I. Stocks, dau. of F. F. and M. E. Stocks, b. 5/5/1844
John Stocks m. Matilda Hunter 7/3/1817
Thomas F. Stocks m. Mary E. Casey 1/7/1841

                            413

Births
James R. Henry 6/17/1810
Permelier F. Henry 10/10/1822
Robert Vanbunn 7/21/1840
Sarah Jane Henry 11/3/1841
Andrew Lafayette Henry 11/1/1843

Mary Eliza Henry 10/-/-
Martha Josephine Henry 11/1847
William Milton Henry 3/1/1850
James Mathew Henry 10/17/1853

(Great grandfather James R. Henry b. S. C. 1810; Grandfather
William Milton Henry b. Gwinnett Co. year 1850)

Marriages
J. R. P. F. Henry m. 10/1/1839
James L. David b. 12/15/1859

Births
John P. Henry 7/18/1876
Mary Francis Henry 1/18/1878
James Archy Henry 5/30/1879

William Edward Young Henry
    11/20/1882
Manda Eugenia Henry 3/14/1884

Bessie L. Henry 7/18/1885
Nita Josephine Henry 11/27/1886
(My Mother borned Commerce, Ga. 11/27/1886)
Mamie Gertrude Henry 11/27/1886

W. M. Henry 3/1/1850
M. C. Henry 9/2/1849

Deaths
John P. Henry 10/7/1887

Marriages
W. M. and M. C. Henry m. 10/3/1875
J. F. Henry and E. W. S-----m. 8/7/1898

JOSEPH PARKER BIBLE
Owner: Mrs. Rom B. Parker, Sr., Enfield, N. C.

Temperance Holt b. 1780, d. 1/27/1852
James Harvey Parker, son of Joe and Temperance (Holt) Parker,
    b. 1/10/1823, d. 6/16/1899
Joseph Parker b. 5/8/1822
Joseph Parker b. 1/18/1761
James Harvey Parker m. Mary C. Scott 12/21/1841
Mary C. Scott b. 1/26/1819 d. 8/13/1902. Their children:
James William Fletcher Parker b. 11/6/1842 m. Bettie J. Herring
    1/3/1865
Cornelia Ann Mitchell b. 10/20/1843 m. J. H. Godwin 6/27/1867 and
    Dr. M. Garrett 2/7/1872. She d. 4/6/1878
M. Garrett b. 2/7/1872. She d. 4/6/1878
Joseph John Parker b. 12/24/184 d. 6/4/1845
Sam Watts Parker b. 5/3/1847 m. Mary V. Hunt 4/16/1873
Mary Jane Parker b. 10/29/1849 m. A. S. Barber 5/24/1875
William Rebecca Parker b. 9/26/1852 m. R. R. Bullock 11/3/1875
Infant son 12/13/1850-4/29/1851
Mary C. Scott, dau. of Mrs. Rebecca M. Scott, d. 6/11/1863,
    aged 65 yrs.

JONES HICKS BIBLE Of Habersham Co., Ga.

Jones Hicks b. 12/5/1803 m. Elizabeth Howe, b. 4/11/1815, d.
4/14/1897. He d. 4/14/1875. Children:
Catherine Hicks b. 2/4/1834 d. 10/23/1903
Aretus William Hicks b. 3/2/1836 d. 11/5/1914 m. Mary Carson
Daniel Hicks b. 12/26/1838 d. Chimborazo Hospital, Va., 4/20/1863
Emma Hicks b. 7/10/1840 d. 3/15/1871 m. Mr. Hudson, Americus, Ga.
William Rufus Hicks b. 7/12/1847 d. 7/12/1908 m. Kate McMichael
Edward Hicks d. 4/30/1892 m. Julia Arringtn
Susan S. Hicks b. 1/13/1851 d. 2/15/1852
Milton jones Hicks b. 3/11/1849 d. 1922 m. Lula Hinton
Lewis Beck Hicks b. 5/20/1853 d. 8/7/1916 m. Mattie Carson

Buried Hicks Family Cemetery, Macon, Ga., 6 miles south of
Reynolds, Ga.

BEVERLY D. EVANS BIBLE
Owner: Mrs. A. L. Evans
302 S. Harris St., Sandersville, Ga.

Beverly D. Evans m. Sarah P. Smith 10/24/1861 in Sandersville
Beverley Daniel Evans, 4th son of Thomas Evans and Jane Beverly
Daniel b. 2/6/1826
Sarah Patience Smith, 4th child of William Smith and Elizabeth
Jordan Tarver, b. 1/21/1841
Beverly D. Evans m. 5/6/1856 Isabella Charlotte Smith. She d.
Marion C. H., S. C. 6/30/1856

SIDNEY DEFOOR BIBLE
Owner: Mrs. Geneva Holden DeFoor
108 W. St., Ringgold, Ga. 30736

Father: Sidney DeFoor b. 10/7/1816 d. 5/11/1878
Mother: Annie Thurman DeFoor b. 9/10/1828 d. 9/24/1902

Children:
James Martin b. 8/7/1845 d. 12/9/1927 m. 11/16/1870 or 1869 Marie
A. Huie
Susan L. b. 6/27/1847 d. 1/18/1921 m. 1/10/1866 Gustavus T. Fite
Martha Elizabeth b. 3/31/1851 d. 8/1851
David Thomas b. 5/29/1853 d. 8/3/1882 m. 1/9/1879 Arminda
McBrayer
Mary Jane b. 5/12/1856 d. 5/5/1928 m. 8/13/1891 Howell Cobb Green
John Leander b. 1/10/1859 d. 8/9/1931 m. 8/14/1881 Savannah
Clementine Jones
Lucy S. b. 8/23/1861 d. 1935 m. 1/10/1904 W. A. Bagley
Albert Edward b. 5/8/1864 d. 1918 m. 9/6/1885 Belle Jones
Sarah F. b. 8/3/1867 d. 6/11/1928 m. 8/28/1912 Robert A. Sloan

415

(Sidney DeFoor Bible contd.....)

Julia Ann b. 1/12/1871 d. 6/27/1911 m. 8/22/1899, 1st wife of
    Robert A. Sloan

(Most of this record is also in an old DeFoor diary. Most of
these DeFoors are buried in Gordon Co., Ga., except James Martin
DeFoot and Mary A. Huie DeFoor are buried in Clayton Co., Ga.)

GEORGE DAVIS MEDLOCK BIBLE
Owner: Bertha Medlock Wingette

Marriages
G. D. Medlock and C. O. Hamilton 12/13/1888

Births
George Davis Medlock 1/3/1863
Caroline Ophelia Medlock 8/17/1870
Winnie Davis Medlock 3/11/1907

Flora Nettie Medlock 11/24/1890   Clara May Medlock 1/15/1899
George Clark Medlock 4/18/1892   Janie Irene Medlock 8/5/1900
Claud Hamilton Medlock 1/1/1894   Bertha Pauline Medlock
Emmett Poole Medlock 10/29/1895   6/3/1902
                                     Allie Bird Medlock 3/10/1905

Clara and Jack Cameron McArthur m. 2/29/19-
Janie and Paul Earnest Bleir m. 2/18/193-
Winnie and Frank Casmor Brown m. 1/30/1926
Allie and Jim Hoyt Langley m. 5/10/192-
Nettie and Wesley Leon Hanson m. 2/7/191-
Fay Chapman and Emmett m. 6/10/193-
Ellie J. Stargel? and Claude Medlock m. 8/19/39
Bertha and Norman Eugene Wingette m. 4/11/194-
Ollie Medlock Langly m. Roland S. Brown 9/20/1940

Deaths
G. D. Medlock 8/14/1947, bur. 8/16/1947
Caroline Ophelia Hamilton Medlock 9/8/1961, bur. 9/10/1961
Jack Cameron McArthur 5/8/1956
Jack Cameron McArthur, Jr. 10/8/1944
Clara Medlock McArthur 8/17/1976
George C. Medlock 12/23/1973, bur. 12/26/1973
Roland S. Brown 12/3/1973
Fay Chapman Medlock 12/27/1976
Emmett Pool Medlock 2/2/1976

THOMAS JEFFERSON GREENE BIBLE
Owner: Gerda McKown

Marriages
Thomas Jefferson Greene and Mary H. Heronton m. by S. Malone,
   Esq., 1/14/1838
S. A. Tidwell and A. L. Greene m. by Rev. S. Harvey 9/18/1859
S. H. Lindsay and M. Ella Greene m. by Rev. S. Dodd 9/9/1866
T. J. McKown and L. C. Greene m. 12/16/1866 by Rev. S. Harvey
F. S. Williams and A. A. A. Greene m.--
G. T. Stephens and Arabella L. Greene m.---
John H. Greene and Callie Landrum m. by Dr. Stacy 5/6/1880

Births
Eliza Jane Greene 11/4/1858   Willie P. Tidwell 5/31/1861
Amanda Lucretia Greene 9/24/1840   M. M. Tidwell 7/26/1863
Lucy Ann Lavonia Greene 3/18/1842   Charlie W. Tidwell 8/27/1865
Malissa N. A. Greene 6/2/1843   Sallie Annie Tidwell 3/23/1869
Martha Ellen Greene 1/31/1845   Carrie Crawford 11/14/1867
William T. Greene 8/29/1846   Maggie L. Crawford 4/20/1870
Leonora C. Greene 1/18/1849   Mamie Lou Crawford 3/18/1872
John H. Greene 11/27/1851   Virgil McKown 10/18/1867
William J. Greene 2/18/1854   Mattie L. McKown 9/4/1870
Avy Ann A. Greene 10/9/1855   Robert Bruce Crawford
Arabella Loretta Greene 7/18/185-   10/28/1874
Lillian M. Landrum 12/7/186-   William Wallace Crawford
                                        2/21/1877
                                     Lillian L. Crawford 3/5/1880

Deaths
William T. Greene 11/10/1847   M. Callie Greene 7/27/1884
Malissa N. A. Greene 3/6/1850   Nelly Greene 4/1884
Eliza Landrum 12/5/1862   Mary H. Greene 9/2/1887
William J. Greene -/1885   Martha Ella Lindsay 10/27/1895
Leonora C. Greene McKown 2/13/1908

ZACKARIA AUSTON MANN BIBLE
Owner: Wynette Mann Brown, Hapeville, Ga.

Births
Zackaria Auston Mann, son of J. W. Mann and Elizabeth, his wife,
   b. 8/27/1854 (or 1853)
Malinda Almeda Mann, dau. of Young L. Wootten and Tarrissa, his
   wife, b. 1/4/1856
Luther Eugeneous Mann, son of Zackaria Auston Mann and Mittie,
   his wife, b. 10/30/1877
Eva Inez Mann, dau. of above, b. 7/15/1879
Lowal Mason Mann, son of above, b. 7/14/1881
Otis Mann, son of above, b. 7/23/1884
Emma Claudine Mann, dau. of above, b. 11/21/1886

Marriages
Zackaria Auston Mann and Mittie Wootton m. 2/3/1876
Jarrell Berriman and Mary Mann m. 9/2/1916

(Zakaria Auston Mann Bible contd....)

Otis Mann and Beatrice Mundy m. 7/8/1906
Howell E. Smith and Janie Mann m. 7/18/1914
Luther E. Mann and Bertha Wooster m. 12/28/1913

Births
Ora Elizabeth Mann, dau. of Z. A. and M. A. Mann, b. 7/25/1889
Janie Wynette Mann, dau. of above, b. 8/3/1893
Mary Zeomy Mann, dau. of above, b. 9/20/1898

Deaths
Lowal Mason Mann 8/10/1886   Otis Ashmore Mann 5/1/1932
Eva Inez Mann 12/30/1906   Emma Claudine Mann 12/26/1952
Ora Elizabeth Mann 5/16/1930   Luther E. Mann 12/26/1943

H. E. Smith, Jr., b. 9/26/1915

BRYANT JACKSON BIBLE
Of Fayette and Campbell Co.´s

Births
Aba 2/15/1856   Violea L. 10/7/1876
Nancy R. 1/17/1856   M. A. F. 1/13/1880
Needham 11/18/1819   Claudia I. 4/14/1886
Martha Jane 2/8/1822   Ollie Lee 10/17/1890
Matthew 6/12/1812   Lular Miranda 8/14/1894
                                   Dewey 5/4/1898

Marriages
Bryant Jackson to N. R. Jones 10/31/1875
I. C. Jones to Ollie Lee Jackson 9/19/1909
Vergle Gosette to Claudia Ila Jackson 11/28/1912
Oscar West to Viola Jackson 12/27/1919

FLORENCE M. DUDLEY AND WALTER F. McKENZIE BIBLE
Owner: Pearl H. Davis
Jonesboro, Georgia

Marriages
David Dudley to Martha Morrison 1/25/1817
Alexis Dudley to Frances M. Dudley 1/19/1856
Walter F. McKenzie to Florence A. Dudley 8/23/1884

Births
Daniel Dudley 11/6/1792
Martha Morrison 4/1/1793

418

(Dudley Bible contd....)

Children of Daniel and Martha Dudley:

Mary A. Dudley 4/12/1818   Autas L. Dudley 2/21/1830
David E. Dudley 5/6/1820   Alexis Dudley 3/30/1819
Joseph B. Dudley 8/1/1823   Frances M. Dudley 3/10/1825

Deaths
Daniel Dudley 12/12/1880, aged 88 yrs., 1 mo., 6 days
Martha Morrison Dudley 2/19/1865, 71 yrs., 10 mos., 18 days
Joseph B. Dudley 12/16/1825, 2 yrs., 4 mos., 15 days
Autas L. Dudley 3/12/1834, 4 yrs., 15 days
Alexis Dudley 5/20/1901, 82 yrs., 1 mo., 20 days
Florence A. Dudley b. 1/29/1861

Issue of Walter F. McKenzie b.12/12/1857 & Florence A. Dudley:

    Edna F. McKenzie b. 6/27/1887
    Helen E. McKenzie b. 5/19/1894
    Beulah A. McKenzie b. 3/1/1899

                TIDENCE LANE, JR. BIBLE
        Rev. War Pension appl. dtd 9/30/1833
                Jefferson Co., Tenn.

                    Wife: Mary

Births
Lydia Lane 1/6/1786   Noah Lane 10/18/1798
Isaac Lane 8/8/1788   Mary Lane 11/20/1800
Nancy Lane 7/4 or 24/1791   Right Lane 6/7/1803
Esther Lane 11/6/1793   James Madison Lane 11/3/1803
John Lane 6/4/1796

WILLIAM DAVID PHILLIPS BIBLE

Children of William David Phillips and Ellen Virginia Wright, his wife:

Robert Clifford Phillips 9/9/1884-1/9/1957 m. 9/24/1905 Louvella Josephine Young b. 9/30/1889, dau. of James A. and Elizabeth Jennings Young

Myrtle Irene Phillips b. 9/16/1886 m. S. E. Wilson

Charles Wesley Phillip 9/101888-4/14/1958 m. Nora Pearl Duke b. 2/11/1898, dau. of Eugene and Hattie Nelms Duke

Isaac Raymond Phillips 8/25/1891-5/5/1952 m. Nettie Boatright 6/26/1895-5/9/1840, dau. of Willie C. & Laura Lasseter Boatright

Thomas Monroe Phillips 2/14/1894-3/30/1977 m. 2/15/1914 Jennie Beatrice Tate 9/26/1895-1/28/1929, dau. of William Samuel Tate 6/12/1869-3/11/1950 and Lucy Cole Tate 10/21/1877-7/18/1909

Rachel Gordie Phillips 7/17/1897-4/6/1949 m. C. C. Duke, son of Eugene and Hattie Nelms Duke

Infant b. 8/24/1899

Clark Phillips b. 12/23/1900 m. Aileen

Sylvia Gladys Phillips 3/8/1904-2/1/1972 m. Thomas Grady Crews b. 10/14/1898, son of Joseph Thomas and Louvie Huff Crews

ISAAC P. GAY BIBLE *
Owner: Mrs. Carolynne Gay Sumner
P. O. Box 236, Hartsville, S. C.

Births

Isaac P. Gay 12/14/1804	Elizabeth Gay 11/14/1805
Winston W. Gay 9/30/1825	Thomas G. Gay 10/25/1827
Robert Gay 11/21/1829	Sanford Gay 8/18/1840
Mary Elizabeth Gay 10/27/1831	Isaac Walter Gay 12/14/1861
Edwin Gay 12/8/1833	Beulah Elizabeth Gay 3/3/1864
Zarado Gay 12/26/1835	Susan Gay 9/26/1866
William Judson Gay 5/6/1843	Maud H. Gay 11/5/1869
John Henry Gay 7/10/1838	John R. Gay 9/22/1872
	Emily Gay 7/18/1875
	Thomas Richard Gay 7/1877
	Mary Blanche Gay 8/23/1880

Everette Moore Gay 1/14/1908, son of Thomas Richard Gay
Alice Carolyn Gay 1/27/1910, dau. of Thomas Richard Gay
Mary Gay Sumner 7/27/1947, dau. of William A. and Carolynne Gay Sumner, Hartsville, S. C.

*See also p. 57.   420

(Isaac P. Gay Bible contd....)

Nina Caroline Taylor 12/26/1974, dau. of Mary Gay Sumner Taylor
and E. Reginald Taylor, Camden, S. C.

Deaths

Edwin Gay 8/13/1836
Sarah Frances Gay 7/13/1843
Robert Gay 1/5/1854
Elizabeth Gay 4/17/1857

John H. Gay 10/18/1862
Zorada North 3/12/1876
Isaac P. Gay 3/20/1877
Sanford Gay 1/11/1911
Carrie P. Gay 10/22/1924
Everette Moore Gay 7/4/1920

Thomas Richard Gay, son of Sanford Gay, 9/13/1939
John Robert Gay, son of Sanford Gay, 10/22/1947
Mary Blanche Gay Redwine, dau. of Sanford Gay, 10/30/1952
Beulah Elizabeth Gay Carmichael, dau. of Sanford Gay, 1/29/1953
Pearly Murphy Gay 7/5/1961, wife of Thomas Richard Gay

Marriages

Isaac P. Gay to Elizabeth Shepherd 12/19/1824
Zorado Gay to Benjamin W. North 7/2/1850
Thomas G. Gay to Harriet Lynch 2/14/1854 or 1856
Winston W. Gay to Martha Glass 3/7/1835
Sanford Gay to Caroline S. Cole 10/18/1860
William J. Gay to Georgia Jones 2/6/1860
Thomas Richard Gay to Pearl Adelia Murphy 10/18/1905
A. P. Carmichael to Beulah Elizabeth Gay 11/18/1883
Alice Carolynne Gay to William Arthur Sumner 6/26/1943, dau. of
    Thomas Richard and Pearl Adelia Gay
May Gay Sumner to Edgar Reginald Taylor 6/21/1969, dau. of
    Carolynne and William Sumner
Sibyl Elizabeth Sumner to George Barry Cauthen 5/22/1971, dau. of
    Carolynne and William Sumner

From an old paper inside Bible:

Richard Cole m. Susan Vance 7/1/1827   Their Children:

James Madison Cole b. 4/11/1828
John Newton Cole b. 2/27/1830
Elizabeth Jane Cole b. 7/8/1833

Emily Carr Cole b. 12/8/1835
Mary Louvenia Cole b. 2/7/1838
Pelina Caroline Cole
        b. 2/2/1840

William M. Cole m. Mary L. Cole 5/1/1856   Their Children:

William E. Cole b. 5/8/1857
Lula Cole b. 6/2/1859
Mary Susan b. 7/22/1861
Edmund Daniel Shadrick b. 9/11/1866

William M. Cole b. 12/2/1832
Richard Cole d. 10/25/1842

Deaths

Richard Cole 10/25/1842
James M. Cole 12/16/1862
John N. Cole 10/20/1862
Emily Carr Shell 4/6/1867
Perlina Vance 7/21/1854
Joseph Vance 7/12/1837

John Hunter 11/20/1871
Susan Overton Hunter 3/12/1890
William M. Cole 8/16/1862
Isaac Walter Gay 11/18/1862
Sudie Gay 1/1/1868

421

Alston Bailey 10/30/1815-8/4/1902
Jane C. Nichols 5/6/1824-7/22/1904
Sarah Frances Bailey b. 3/4/1840
Dicy Bailey 11/4/1841-12/30/1892
William Foster Bailey 12/22/1843-4/8/1862
John Henry Bailey 10/28/1845-1/1/1863
Mary Elizabeth Bailey 3/28/1848-1/13/1895
Matilda Jane Bailey 4/20/1850-5/12/1899
Juliann Bailey 7/3/1852-5/16/1891
Matilda Susann Bailey b. 7/18/1856
Luther Clark Bailey b. 8/29/1859
James Wesley Bailey b. 8/12/1862
Nancy Carolyn Bailey b. 7/24/1864
Alston Bailey m. Jane Nichels 6/6/1859

DAVID LAY BIBLE
Owner: Mrs. Ollie J. Adams

Marriages
David Lay to Epsey Landrum 8/27/1823
David Lay to Tabitha Ellison 12/4/1838
George T. Johnson to Mary E. Lay 9/24/1846
George T. Johnson to Nancy A. Daniel 5/6/1858
George W. Daniel to Martha C. Johnson 8/12/1866

Births
David Lay 3/3/1804   Mary Emaline Lay 4/15/1830
Epsey Lay 8/23/1801   Martha Jane Leonora Lay 8/18/1832
Samuel Nolan Lay 6/5/1824   David Dupree Lay 6/7/1834
Joseph William Lay 5/23/1826   Larkin Randolph Lay 6/23/1836
Elijah Washington Lay 4/10/1828   Epsey Tabitha Lay 8/28/1838

Deaths
David Dupree Lay, son of David and Epsey Lay, 8/25/1835
Eprsey Lay, consort of David Lay, 9/8/1838
Epsey Tabitha, dau. of David and Epsey Lay, 10/14/1838
David Lay 11/4/1839
Joseph William Lay 10/4/1850
Mary E. Johnson, consort of George T. Johnson 2/8/1858
James Thomas Johnson 12/11/1871
George Torance Johnson 1/27/1875

J. R. B. STOVALL BIBLE
Owner: Mrs. Dyra Stovall Campbell
105 Orchard, N. W., Fairburn, Ga.

This Bible presented to Lucy Ann Stovall by J. R. B. Stovall 8/15/1907
J. R. B. Stovall of Forsyth Co., Ga. m. Lucy Ann Morgan of Forsyth Co., Ga. 11/14/1880. Wit: A. J. Morgan; G. B. H. Stovall

Deaths
Jessie Stovall 9/20/1893   James L. Stovall 1/16/1940
Essie Stovall 10/20/1893   Marvin Rudolph Campbell
Miner Eugen Robert Stovall 8/13/1898   5/1/1956
Laura Eveline Spear 2/6/1917   Allie Bradshaw 5/7/1949
Lucy Ann Stovall 1/19/1940   Paul Speer 1929
John R. B. Stovall 4/25/1943   Louella Bradshaw
                                     12/7/1964

Births
J. R. B. Stovall 12/11/1862   Jessie Stovall 8/1/1893
Lucy Ann Morgan 12/16/1861   Essie Stovall 8/1/1893
Thadius M. Stovall 10/21/1881   Minor E. R. Stovall 3/3/1898
Louella Stovall 8/19/1884   Dyra Doshia Stovall 8/11/1901
Lowea Evelyn Stovall 8/14/1887   James L. Stovall 12/13/1889

Marriages
Paul A. Speer to Laura E. Stovall 9/27/1903
Allie C. Bradshaw to Louella Stovall 2/18/1906
James L. Stovall to Lorene Lassetter 11/10/1912
Marvin Rudolph Campbell to Dyra Doshia Stovall 10/6/1922

HENRY B. HECKLE BIBLE *
Owner: Joseph M. Lee III
1444 Iroquois Path, N. E.
Atlanta, Ga. 30319

Births
Martha Heckle 8/13/1844   James A. Heckle 8/11/1853
John E. Heckle 1/20/1847   Anna M. Heckle 9/18/1855
                                     George J. Heckle 2/7/1849

Deaths
Anna M. Calhoun 6/17/1878
Anna J. Heckle 4/13/1924, age 100 yrs., 4 mos., 29 days

*See also p. 274.   423

SAMUEL DUNLAP BIBLE
Owner: J. W. Abercrombie

Births
Samuel Dunlap 2/16/1777
Elizabeth Jones 8/13/1778
Susannah Dunlap 9/10/1799
Mary Dunlap 12/5/1801
John Dunlap 6/10/1802
James Dunlap 3/18/1804

Nancy Dunlap 10/25/1805
Esther Dunlap 10/23/1807
Enoch Dunlap 4/23/1809
Cathy Dunlap 9/26/1811
Samuel Dunlap 10/5/1812

JOHN BAREFIELD BIBLE
Owner: Mrs. T. D. Wilson
Rt. 1, Box 207, Palmetto, Ga. 30268

John Barefield b. 3/22/1788
Annie Parker b. 9/30/1806 m. 1/8/1826 Their Children:

Births
William Barefield 2/10/1815
Richard Barefield 12/9/1816
Alexander Barefield 4/7/1818
Nancy Barefield 12/1/1819
John Barefield 4/29/1821
Solomon Barefield 4/22/1822
Elizabeth Barefield 1/18/1825
Marion Barefield 12/26/1846

Louise Barefield 12/26/1827
Benjamin Barefield 12/1/1829
Mitchell Barefield 10/15/1831
Jefferson Barefield 3/9/1834
Mary Barefield 2/15/1837
Lewis Barefield 12/1/1839
Henry Barefield 8/26/1842
Marion Barefield 12/26/1846
Mazy Barefield 9/8/1848

The first born and decd was b. 10/22/1813

JAMES E. COOK BIBLE

James C. Cook of Coweta Co. m. Sallie H. Brown of Coweta Co.,
12/18/1872 at W. F. S. Powell's by Rev. W. F. S. Powell. Wit: W.
B. Berry; M. L. Farmer

John F. Cook m. Martha S. Parks 12/8/1842
E. W. Glass m. Martha E. Cook 2/3/1875

Births
John F. Cook 7/30/1819
Martha S. Parks, his wife, 2/24/1826
James C. Cook 7/23/1850
Sallie H. Brown, wife of J. C. Cook 9/25/1854
William B. Cook 1/12/1874

(James E. Cook Bible, Births, contd....)

Stella May Cook 5/23/1876
John F. Cook 6/18/1878
Millard C. Cook 11/2/1880
Martha Bessie Cook 5/17/1885

Mellie Cook, dau. of J. C. and Sallie H. Cook, 11/6/1889

Deaths
Millard C. Cook, son of J. C. and Sallie H. Cook, 4/12/1883
Millie Cook, dau. of J. C. and Sallie H. Cook, 7/20/1891, age
  1 yr., 8 mos., 14 days
Sallie H. Cook, wife of J. C. Cook, 3/4/1899
James Caleb Cook 4/15/1939
Lewis M. Cook 2/5/1920
Julian Cook d. early in 1904 (Bird's son)
William Bird Cook 10/5/1955

JOHN COOK BIBLE
Owner: Mrs. J. D. Lambert, Jr.

Marriages
John Cook to Mary Cook 11/14/1786
Caleb and Sarah Cook 1816
Bird Parks to Martha 3/1/1803
John F. Cook to Martha S. Parks 12/8/1842
Calvin L. Holland to Mary T. Cook, dau. of Caleb and Sarah Cook,
  12/16/1845
James C. Cook to Sallie H. Brown 12/18/1872
E. W. Glass to M. E. Cook 2/3/1875

Births
Katie Cook Glass 10/2/1879
Martha Bessie Cook 5/17/1885
Mel Cook, dau. of J. C. and Sallie H. Cook, 11/6/1889
Sallie H. Cook 9/25/1854

Bird Parks 6/11/1779
Martha, his wife, 5/5/1784

Their Children:

Polly Parks 1/9/1804   James Parks 8/9/1815
Thomas Harrison Parks 11/28/1805   Sandal?Ann Parks 1/11/1818
Eliza Emily Parks 7/3/1808   Bird Parks 12/1/1820
John Isham Parks 9/26/1810   Welcom Parks 1/13/1824
William Bird Parks 3/24/1813   Martha Page Parks 2/24/1826

John F. Cook 7/30/1819   John Hill Cook 6/1/1855
Calvin L. Holland 9/26/1815   Thomas Lee Cook 8/20/1862
Perkins Fitch Cook 8/30/1843   William Bird Cook 1/12/1874
Bird Parks Cook 1/10/1849?   Stella May Cook 5/23/1876
James Caleb Cook 7/23/1850   John F. Cook Jr. 6/18/1878
Martha Emily Cook 10/5/1852   Millard C. Cook 11/2/1880
Martha S. Parks, consort of J. F. Cook 2/24/1826
Mary P. Cook consort of C. L. Holland, 11/12/1821

425

(John Cook Bible contd....)

Deaths

William Bird Parks 1/18/1818
John Isham Parks 6/28/1826
Welcome Parks 1/23/1828
Bird Parks Sr. 12/27/1849?
Martha Parks, his wife, 10/28/1852
Sallie H. Cook wife of J. C. Cook, 3/4/1899

J. C. Cook 4/15/1939
Millard C. Cook 4/12/1883
son of J. C. Cook & Sallie
Mellie Cook 7/20/1891 age
1 yr. 8 mos., 14 days

JOSEPH D. MORGAN BIBLE *
Owner: Hugh Watts Randall
Cedartown, Ga.

Births

Joseph D. (Dossett) Morgan 6/15/1818
Martha A. Payne 10/10/1824
E. Crabbe 4/14/1837
Isaac C. Morgan 1/8/1839
Nancy E. Morgan 3/22/1840
Martha L. Morgan 6/3/1841
Anslem L. Morgan 12/10/1842
Mary Park Morgan 5/31/1844
Joseph L. Morgan 1/9/1846
Josephine S. Morgan 9/30/1851
Cynthia S. Morgan 7/1/1853
Lellea A. Morgan 10/14/1855
Burton E. Morgan 7/19/1859
Newton H. Morgan 4/10/1861

Orvin B. Morgan 12/16/1862
Robert J. Morgan 10/25/1864
Emery A. Morgan 9/24/1866
Lena D. Morgan 10/9/1868
Cora L. Morgan 10/24/1870
Della D. Morgan 3/8/1873
Ida O. Davis 9/16/1872
Lena D. Morgan 8/7/1890
Hugh Dean Morgan 9/20/1892
Lonnie L. Morgan 12/16/1894
Elma Jo. Morgan 4/14/1899
Emery C. Morgan 8/2/1902
Hugh D. Morgan Jr 7/24/1916
Vera J. Morgan 4/27/1919

Marriages

Burton E. Morgan 12/20/1882
Newton A. Morgan 4/1/1881
Robert J. Morgan 4/8/1883
Emery A. Morgan 10/6/1889
Cora L. Morgan 10/6/1889

Lena D. Morgan 6/7/1908
Hugh D. Morgan 10/27/1915
Lonnie L. Morgan 9/23/1916
Emery C. Morgan 11/8/1927
Elma J. Morgan 6/7/1936

Deaths

Virginia C. Morgan 11/11/1850
Diatha E. Morgan 7/15/1853
Martha P. Morgan 3/1/1858
Orvin B. Morgan 8/25/1866

Joseph D. Morgan 3/12/1874
Newton H. Morgan 8/4/1881
Emery C. Morgan 1/9/1971

*See also p. 212.

JAMES M. SCOTT II BIBLE
Owner: Mrs. Edward Pason Scott, Summerville, Ga.

James M. Scott II b. 3/3/1790, d. 1/20/1872
Rebecca Scott b. 1/2/1792, d. 12/3/1857
Children:
Jackson O. Scott b. 12/22/1816, d. 4/20/1868
William C. Scott b. 3/17/1818, d. 1/6/1865
James M. Scott III b. 2/17/1821, d. 3/3/1854
Amanda Scott b. 4/4/1824, d. 1866
Rebecca Jane Scott b. 2/26/1827
Mary Elizabeth (Betty) b. 12/4/1828
Dunlap Scott b. 6/20/1831

ADAMS BIBLE
Owner: Harve N. Adams, Murrayville, Ga.

Marriages
Charlie Priest m. 4/20/1913 Anner Adams
Harve Adams to Sarah Jane Grizzle 12/15/1912
J. R Rail b. 2/24/1880
W. B. Rail b. 9/3/1881

Births
David P. Adams 12/10/1841   Harvie N. Adams 6/23/1894
Emley E. Adams 7/7/1857   Anner May Adams 3/30/1896
Henry F. Adams 10/29/1887   Mary Lular Adams 7/11/1898
Laufa J. Adams 3/31/1889   Callie G. Adams 12/8/1902
Charlie G. Adams 7/24/1892

Deaths
Henry F. Adams 12/25/1906   Maggie Adams Wilson 7/14/1935
David P. Adams 11/26/1922   Anna May Adams Priest 9/27/1937
John F. Adams 7/8/1926   James R. Rail 1/9/1949
Margret Emly Adams 8/15/1934   W. B. Rail 1/15/1957
Callie Lenora Adams 10/26/1935

JOHN RANDOLPH BIBLE
Owner: Mrs. T. F. Comer, Athens, Ga.

John Randolph b. 11/16/1773   Nancy Hinton b. 2/15/1776
They were married 12/18/1793. Children:

Frances Randolph b. 3/12/1795   Susan Randolph b.---1802
Wood Lee Randolph b. 2/11/1796   H. T. Randolph b. 5/3/1813
Nancy Ann Randolph b. 1/7/1798   Tandy K. Randolph b.1/6/1815
William Randolph b. 2/4/1800
John H. Randolph b. 2/10/1804
Joshua H. Randolph b. 9/15/1805
W. R. Randolph b. 8/15/1807
Thomas J. Randolph b. 5/3/1809
H. J. Randolph b. 9/15/1811, d. 1887

George M. Lanier b. 2/9/1789
William McCarty Lanier b. 9/4/1850
Thomas Nevel Lumpkin Lanier b. 11/22/1853
Lizzie Harden Lanier b. 5/28/1856
Samuel P. Lanier b. 1/16/1859
Mary Talulah Lanier b. 7/19/1862
George Myrick Lanier b. 9/29/1866
Polly Langford, Lanier's wife, b. 2/22/1800
James N. Lanier b. 11/7/1817
Walter and William Lanier b. 4/9/1819
Caroline Lanier b. 5/17/1821
Katharine C. Lanier b. 4/29/1823
Angeline Lanier b. 3/16/1825
Bazleel Langford Lanier b. 4/11/1827
Martha Warren Lanier b. 8/28/1829

Deaths
William McCarty Lanier d. 9/16/1859
George M. lanier d. 7/22/1854
James N. Lanier and William Lanier killed Bat. Wilderness
George M. lanier in Virginia
Calvin P. Lanier, Charleston, d. during rebellion of 1861-2-3-4-5
Caroline Lanier d. 9/12/1827
Katharine Lanier d. 7/15/1852
Polly Langford Lanier d. 9/1881

F. SHACKLEFORD, SR. BIBLE
Owner: Mrs. Fletcher W. Griffin
6357 Vernon Woods Drive, Atlanta, Ga. 30329

F. Shackelford, Sr. b. 5/8/1746 (d. 10/12/1827) m. Judeth, his wife, b. 10/26/1759.
Births of Their Children:

Phillip Shackelford 9/22/1779   Judeth Shackelford 11/20/1794
F. Shackelford 6/7/1781   Mary Shackelford 1/15/1796
John Shackelford 8/28/1783   Sarah Shackelford 3/1/1797
Charles Shackelford 8/5/1785   Sarah Shackelford 11/9/1800
Nancy A. Shackelford 11/20/1787   Jefferson Shackelford
Reuben F. Shackelford 4/19/1790   2/23/1805
Elizabeth Shackelford 7/10/1792

Sarah Shackelford d. 4/1/1797
F. Shackelford, Sr. d. 10/12/1827

BENNET HILSMAN BIBLE
Owner: Mrs. H. A. Gorham, White Plains, Ga.

Births
Bennet Hilsman 4/30/1776   Jasper Hilsman 4/20/1828
Mary Hilsman 3/3/1787   Minerva Hilsman 11/23/1830

(Bennett Hilsman Bible, Births, contd....)

James Hilsman 11/14/1805   Martha Ada Hilsman 12/26/1853
John R. Hilsman, Sr. 12/21/1809 Mary Hilsman 12/4/1855
Jeffrey Hilsman 6/28/1813   Maria Hilsman 10/21/1857
Josiah Hilsman 5/19/1816   Mildred & Minerva Hilsman
Jeremiah Hilsman 4/25/1818   10/17/1859
Judge Hilsman 5/29/1820   Myrtie Hilsman 12/17/1852
Mary Hilsman 5/30/1822   Maud Hilsman 6/11/1864
Martha Hilsman 9/27/1824   Margret Hilsman 11/25/1868
Mariah Hilsman 12/26/1826   John R. Hilsman 4/2/1871

Deaths
Bennet Hilsman 4/4/1855   Josiah Hilsman 6/3/1872
Mary Hilsman 10/9/1854   Jeremiah Hilsman 10/24/1868
Jasper Hilsman 8/31/1888   Judge Hilsman 9/6/1899
Rebecca Hilsman 4/2/1906   Mary Hilsman 3/25/1865
Mattie Hilsman 5/26/1890   Martha Hilsman 4/23/1884
James Hilsman 12/14/1854   Mariah Hilsman 9/7/1869
John R. Hilsman 6/2/1883   Minerva Hilsman 2/23/1886
Jeffrey Hilsman 9/13/1851

Marriages
Bennett Hilsman to Mary Harvey 10/30/1804
J. L. B. Hilsman to Rebecca A. Mapp 2/19/1853
James Hilsman to Emerline Hudson 10/28/1828
Jeffrey Hilsman to Martha Alexander 9/12/1881
Josiah Hilsman to Josephine Gray 3/8/1843
Jeremiah Hilsman to Martha Ann Janes 5/28/1924
Judge Hilsman to Bermah Howell 10/18/1857
Mary Hilsman to L. B. Mercer 9/20/1890
Martha Hilsman to Sterling Evans 1/1/1861

                    WILLIS M. DOWNS BIBLE
                    Owner: Martha E. L. Downs
                    Oak Hill, Newton Co., Ga.

Births
Willis M. Downs 11/17/1817 Louisa Guffin Downs 12/26/1816
   And They married 9/15/1840.
George W. Downs b. 9/27/1841, d. 7/1846 (Jan. inserted)
Isabella F. T. Downs b. 10/28/1843, d. 2/6/1844
John H. Downs b. 11/21/1845
Tinzy Ann W. Downs b. 11/3/1847
Willis S. Downs b. 8/5/1851, d. 8/23/1852
Willis Milligan Florence Downs b. 7/5/1853 "my granddaddy"
Willis M. Downs d. 8/8/1854

                    GLENN BIBLE *

Marriages
William Glenn and Elizabeth m. 9/3/1798
Asa J. Howard and Elizabeth Gilmer Glenn m. 11/21/1822
Robert Howard and Polly Glenn m. 12/19/1822

*See also p. 141.   429

(Glenn Bible, Births, contd....)

John A. Glenn and Matilda Graham m. 1/22/1829
Minor U. Stephens and Mildred L. Glenn m. 8/3/1852

Births
William Glenn 3/8/1766
John Allen Glenn, son of William and Elizabeth, 12/19/1800
Elizabeth Gilmer Glenn 8/2/1802
Polley Glenn 6/22/1805
Mildred Louisa Glenn 9/3/1807
Rebecca Glenn 12/3/1810
William Hamilton Glenn, son of John and Matilda, 10/22/1829

Deaths
Polley Howard 7/24/1827, aged 22 yrs, 22 days
Mary Elizabeth Howard 7/18/1827, aged 5 mos., 6 days
John A. Glenn 10/2/1853, aged 53 yrs., 10 mos., 11 days
Mildred L. Stephens 10/11/1855, aged 48 yrs., 1 mo., 8 days
Rebecca Glenn Butler 1/25/1894
Elizabeth Gilmer Howard 1/6/1883
Elizabeth Glenn, wife of William Glenn, Sr., 12/22/1850, aged 83
William Glenn Sr. 9/2/1857, aged 91 yrs., 5 mos., 24 days

WHITTEN BIBLE
Owner: Miss Gena Neely, Sharpsburg, Ga.

Phillip Whitten b. 9/13/1776   Johnathan Whitten b. 12/6/1805
Delilah Whitten b. 2/9/1777   Rachel A. Whitten b. 9/4/1808
Robert Whitten b. 10/1/1800   Lucinda H. Whitten b. 6/4/1814
Littleton Whitten b. 3/7/1802   Elizabeth E. M. Whitten
Rebecca Whitten b. 12/16/1803   b. 12/31/1817

John H. Neely b. 2/4/1796   David M. C. Neely b. 4/5/1832
Rebecca P. Neely b. 12/16/1803   Robert L. Neely b. 6/25/1835
William A. B. Neely b. 9/2/1823 Betsy A. Neely b. 3/9/1838
Craten Alonzo Neely b. 7/6/1825 Lutetia S. Neely b. 8/18/1841
Jonathen P. Neely b. 5/24/1827   Nancy Caroline Neely b. 11/8/1843
Adaline D. Neely b. 7/26/1829   John H. Neely b. 11/15/1847

John H. Neely and Rebecca P. Whitten m. 11/12/1822
John Hill (written over) Hubbard Neely d. 7/12/1934, age 86 yrs.,
7 mos., 27 days.

Delilah Whitten d. 1/19/1835   Elizabeth A. Graves 3/21/1902
Rachel Olman d. 10/20/1837   Robert L. Neely 11/8/--
Philip Whitten d. 11/3/1858   William A. B. Neely 2/7/1863
Augustus R. Graves d. 5/25/1863   John H. Neely 3/3/1864
Rebecca P. Neely 12/8/1880

CLARKSON BIBLE
Owner: Mrs. A. L. Clarkson, Chickamauga, Ga.

John Clarkson b. 5/26/1765, d. 2/9/1832 m. Sally, b. 6/20/1770,
d. 8/22/1831. Children:

(Clarkson Bible, Births of Children, contd....)

Polly b. 1/15/1791 m. 12/16/1809
Joseph b. 8/13/1792 d. 1/1845
Parmeley b. 5/27/1794 m. 8/6/1819
Keziah b. 6/17/1796
David b. 10/20/1799 m. 2/16/1826
Betty b. 6/20/1802 m. 8/3/1827
Nancy b. 10/18/1804 m. 2/15/1821
Sallie b. 12/25/1808
Tiney (or Jincy) b. 1/26/1811

Joseph Clarkson b. 8/13/1792 d. 1/1845 m. Nancy b. 1794, d. --
-/28/1855 m. 10/31/1816. Children:
William Clarkson b. 9/5/1817 d. 12/22/1851
James H. Clarkson b. 8/8/1819
John Clarkson b. 10/4/1821, d. 184--
Joseph Clarkson b. 11/21/1823, d. 3/21/1831
Martha Clarkson b. 9/2/1826
Mary Clarkson b. 2/19/1828
Wesley Clarkson b. 1/16/1830
Daniel B. Clarkson b. 12/17/1831
Hurit Clarkson b. 2/18/1834
Nancy Clarkson b. 8/13/1836
Green(berry) Clarkson b. 8/5/1838
James H. Clarkson b. 8/8/1819, d. 6/17/1884 m. Jane Hammonds, b.
5/1/1821, d. 5/21/1883. Son: John M. Clarkson, b. 5/29/1842 m. to
Amanda B. Lawrence, d. 11/29/1927.

NORRIS BIBLE
Owner: Mrs. Merlyn Holloman Whiting, Warner Robins, Ga.

Marriages
W. N. Norris and E. C. Watts 10/6/1888
Lula Belle Norris and Charlie Corbin Young 12/31/1912

Births
W. N. Norris 12/10/1868   Miles Lee Norris 4/25/1898
E. C. Norris 2/22/1863   Jimie Norris 2/--/1902
B. G. Grady 3/10/1891   James Arden Young 9/25/1913
Annie Maud Norris 9/10/1892   Charlie Rogers Young 11/1/1914
Lula Belle Norris 4/29/1896

Deaths
Annie Maud Norris 11/12/1892   W. N. Norris 4/1941
Miles Lee Norris 10/15/1902   Charlie Corbin Young 10/31/1914
E. C. Norris 6/4/1904   Ben Grady Norris 4/23/1972
James N. Norris 11/25/1933

JESSE BLACKWELL BIBLE
Owner: Mrs. Clarence Jackson, Athens, Ga.

Jesse Blackwell and Elmina Bowen m. 3/17/1846
Charles W. Meaders and Nancy A. Blackwell m. 10/12/1869
Charles W. Meaders and Georgia Blackwell m. 8/1873
Fletcher F. Meaders and Mary Blackwell m. 11/1/1874
Horton J. Blackwell and Addie McWhorter m. 12/17/1874

(Jesse Blackwell Bible contd....)

William A. Miller and Leila Blackwell m. 11/28/1889

Births
Jesse Blackwell 5/8/1821   Horton Jeddiah Blackwell 5/10/1854
Elmina Blackwell 11/13/1825   Mary Palmira Blackwell 6/23/1857
Nancy Angeline Blackwell 5/6/1847 Thomas M. Blackwell 3/21/1864
Georgia Blackwell 3/29/1849   Lela Viola Blackwell 4/18/1870
Lavenia Clementine Blackwell 1/15/1852

Deaths
Lavenia C. Blackwell 12/9/1854   Leila Miller 12/20/1892
Thomas M. Blackwell 9/9/1864   Elmina Blackwell 10/4/1912
Nancy Angeline Meaders 8/26/1871 Mary Meaders 10/11/1933
Jesse Blackwell 2/26/1882   Ed Meaders 11/11/1932
Georgia Meaders 2/23/1883   F. F. Meaders 1935

JESSE R. ATKINSON BIBLE
Owner: Mrs. Avice Leynes, Tampa, Fla.

Jesse R. Atkinson b. 5/13/1811
Martha Ann Brewer, his wife, b. 6/29/1810. They m. 11/10/1831

Alvanu (or Alvanee) Atkinson b. 9/3/1832
Arrena Atkinson b. 1/3/1834
Craven Atkinson b. 9/3/1835
Mary Susan Atkinson b. 1/3/1838
Sarah Atkinson b. 12/28/1839
Jesse B. Atkinson b. 6/17/1842
Linly Atkinson b. 10/26/1844
Martha R. Atkinson b. 3/3/1847
Charles A. Atkinson b. 5/8/1849
Phelanthropy Atkinson b. 11/23/1850
Lovey Jane Atkinson b. 12/5/1853
Jacob Atkinson b. 4/12/1776 our G Pa

Deaths
Linley Atkinson 9/28/1848
Jesse B. Atkinson 7/26/1862
Craven Atkinson was killed Bravely Standing at his post in the
Battle of Old Luster (Olustee) Florida 2/20/1864
Martha Ann Atkinson 8/9/1876
Jesse R. Atkinson 11/19/1882
Arrenia Atkinson 1902, Abna Lynns wife

JOSIAH ELI BRADBURY* BIBLE
Owner: Mary Ellen Bradberry, Athens, Ga.

Certificate of Marriage - This certifies that Josiah E. Bradberry
and Mary E. Wier were united by me in Holy Bands of Matrimony at
John N. Wier´s on the 28th day of November in the year of our
Lord 1877. In Presence of: John L. Bradberry, John W. Wier.
Signed: John Calvin Johnson, Local Elder of the M. E. Church
South.

(Josiah E. Bradbury* Bible contd....)

Marriages
Josiah E. Bradberry and Mary E. Wier m. 11/28/1877
Lonnie E. Whelchel and Susie N. Bradbury m. 12/24/1905
Charlie C. Sanders and Ida L. Bradbury m. 4/28/1910
James W. O'Kelley and Effie L. Bradbury m. 12/18/1912
Harvey L. Archer and Belle Bradbury m. 1/20/1921
L. J. Bradbury and Ruby Jane Lancaster m. 10/23/1921

Births
Josiah E. Bradberry 7/22/1855   Annie F. Bradberry 9/24/1878
Mary E. Wier 9/28/1853   John Walter Bradberry 12/4/1880
Susie Naomi Bradbury 9/16/1882   Lillie Belle Bradbury 4/10/1891
Ida Leora Bradbury 7/2/1884   Leonard Josiah Bradbury 3/20/1894
Mary Ellen Bradbury 10/15/1886   Albert Lamar Bradbury 9/19/1896
Effie Lee Bradbury 10/1/1889   Mattie Lou Bradbury 5/31/1899

Deaths
Annie F. Bradbury 11/8/1881   Mrs. Mary E. Bradbury 10/3/1932
John Walter Bradbury 4/3/1885   Josiah Eli Bradbury 3/27/1934
Albert Lamar Bradbury 8/13/1897

*Note: The spelling "Bradbury" and "Bradberry" appears in this
Bible exactly as written. The Census records show "Bradberry".

REV. JESSE MERCER BIBLE
(For whom Mercer University was named)

10/20/1839 Mary Ann, servant girl, aged 14, died.

Jesse Mercer and Sabrina Chivers m. 1/31/1788
Jesse Mercer and (Mrs.) Nancy Simons m. 12/11/1827
Miriam Mercer, 1st dau. of Jesse and Sabrina Mercer, b. 12/1/1798
Jesse Mercer, son of Silas Mercer and Dorcas, his wife, b.
12/16/1769
Sabrina Mercer, wife of Jesse Mercer and dau. of Joel and Sarah
H. Chivers, b. 5/16/1772
Nancy Mercer, 2d wife of J. M. (Jesse Mercer) b. 10/20/1772, dau.
of John and Inez Mills and late wid. of Abraham Simons.
Charlot b. 1/8/1810   These are slaves' births
Wylie b. 3/31/1827
Susan b. 5/19/1825
Henry b. 7/7/1831
Caroline b. 3/1/1833
Alfred to John Laurence b. 5/27/1834
William b. 3/22/1835
Catharine Burma b. 1838   of Servants
Spencer b. 4/18/1802
Claray b. 2/24/1804
Winny b. 6/24/1808
David b. 10/17/1812
Matt b. 10/12/1817
Ellick b. 7/2/1820
Peggy b. 9/19/1819
Mick b. 3/27/1822
Salley b. 8/31/1827
William b. 4/26/1829

(Rev. Jesse Mercer Bible contd....)

Deaths
Miriam Mercer, the first, d. 1799, aged 9 mos., 21 days.
Niriam Mercer, the second, went to her long home on Thurs. 6
o'clock P. M. 12/15/1814, aged 9 yrs., 8 mos., 2 days. The day of
the month on which she left us was 9/21st.
Died at Andersonville, S. C. on the 23rd of Sept. 1826 Sabrina
Mercer, wife of Jesse M., aged 55.

Note: From Mercer Univ., Macon, Ga. Rev. Jesse Mercer was Baptist
Minister.

GEORGE ROMLUS BURTON, SR. BIBLE
Owner: Mrs. G. R. Burton, White Plains, Ga.

Births
George Romlus Burton Sr. 5/20/1870
Annie May Burton 9/15/1873
Jasper Williamson Burton 3/19/1900
Grace Burton Johnson 7/17/1901
Martha Louise Burton Winn 6/4/1903
George Romlus Burton Jr. 7/10/1904
Eldridge Numally Burton 3/3/1907

Martha Louise Burton Winn d. 9/23/1945

LIZZIE E. MORRIS BIBLE
Carroll Co., Ga.

B. A. Morris b. 6/23/1819
Jane Arraminta Morris 3/9/1820
(Benjamin Aron Morris m. Jane A. Terry in 1839)
George Glenn Morris b. 9/20/1840
William F. Morris b. 6/7/1843
Benjamin J. Morris b. 6/17/1846
Lizzie E. Morris b. 7/15/1848
Martha Jane Morris b. 7/14/1852
Celestia Justina Morris b. 7/27/1854
Georgia C. Morris b. 9/16/1856
Minnie Henrietta Morris b. 4/23/1862

Walter T. Hicks b. 5/30/1871   Lillian R. Hicks b. 8/8/1872

B. A. Morris d. 5/19/1863
B. J. Morris was killed near Marietta, Ga. 6/22/1864
Jane A. Morris d. 7/26/1877
G. G. Morris d. 10/2/1906
M. L. Hicks d. 4/10/1917

DAVID MITCHELL BURNS BIBLE
Owner: Mrs. W. B. Burns, Commerce, Ga.

David Mitchell Burns and Sarah Hay m. Jackson Co., Ga. 1/22/1818
David Mitchell Burns d. Jackson Co., Ga. 12/11/1864
Sarah Hay Burns b. 9/16/1801, d.---. They are bur. at Thiatyra
Presbyterian Church in Jackson Co., Ga. Their Children:
William Brantley Burns b. 11/7/1818, d. Banks Co., Ga. 7/6/1867
   (father of David Mitchell and James Crawford Burns)
Samuel Hay Burns b. 2/6/1821, d. 5/2/1857.
James Harvey Burns b. 10/21/1823 m. Louisa Harriet Neal, Franklin
   Co., Ga. 7/1/1847. (Parents of Mrs. Tom Stapler)
David Mitchell Burns b. 10/21/1825 m. Sarah Randolph of
   Jefferson, Ga. 4/20/1855.
Esther Eveline Burns b. 3/9/1828, m. J. Mac Potts.
Andrew Jackson Burns, b. 12/24/1830, d. 3/6/1852.
John Milton Burns (M.D.) b. 12/12/1833 m. 1st Sarah Harriet Long,
niece of Dr. Crawford W. Long, noted discoverer of anaesthesia.
Three children: William m. Bessie Jackson, d. in Fla. 4/26/1943.
Lula m. David Milford, Alice, second wife of Lucas N. Tuck,
Homer, Ga. John Milton Burns m. 2d Julia Caroline Telford, second
dau. of George Brown Telford and Cynthia Isabella Wilson Telford.
Their two sons are Egbert Telford Burns and Alonzo Hay Burns of
Athens, Ga. Both have families. Dr. John Milton Burns
d. 11/21/1908.
Margaret Elizabeth Burns b. 12/28/1837 m. John T. Carithers
   3/12/1857
Sarah Priscilla Burns b. 10/15/1841 m. John B. Davis, lived
   Newnan, Ga.
Alonzo Waddle Burns b. 8/27/1845, d. at Camp Morton, Indiana,
   10/24/1863.

JOHN R. HANCOCK BIBLE
Owner: Elizabeth Shelton, Athens, Ga.

John R. Hancock and Rebecca A. Lyle m. 12/31/1834
John R. Hancock b. 2/16/1811
Rebecca A. Hancock b. 1/28/1818
Silas Smith Hancock b. 12/1/1835, d. 3/11/1839
Robert Jackson Hancock b. 2/9/1839
Elizabeth Jane Hancock b. 10/15/1841
William Parks Hancock b. 6/28/1844, d. 11/13?/1863?
David Lane Hancock b. 7/19/1846
Hugh Harelson Hancock b. 11/19/1849
John Boring Hancock b. 9/24/1852
Martha Frances Hancock b. 1/20/1855
Emily Adaline Hancock b. 8/16/1858

William Lyle Sr. b. 12/21/1770, d. 10/24/1860
Elizabeth Lyle b. 10/29/1784, d. 10/17/1863
Dilmus J. Lyle b. 1/4/1804
Charles B. Lyle b. 6/4/1807
James B. Lyle b. 11/10/1811
John B. Lyle b. 10/29/1813
Elizabeth G. Lyle b. 1/17/1816
Rebecca A. Lyle b. 1/2/1818

435

(John R. Hancock Bible contd....)

Jane Hancock b. 3/19/1776, d. 4/21/1849
William C. Lyle b. 11/25/1819
David S. Lyle b. 9/19/1821

R. T. COMER BIBLE
Owner: Towns Comer, Comer, Ga.

R. T. Comer b. 2/8/817, joined Church 1835
Sarah Comer b. 12/16/1817, joined Church 1839
Joseph Fletcher Comer b. 3/23/1844, joined Church
Austin Fulcher Comer b. 8/26/1845, joined Church
William J. Comer b. 3/14/1847
James T. Comer b. 3/7/1849
Henry Towns Comer b. 11/26/1851

W. T. BURT BIBLE
Owner: Mrs. Wade Harris, Oglethorpe Co., Ga.

W. T. Burt and Mrs. M. J. Tiller m. 11/27/1866
W. C. Haynie and E. F. Burt m. 12/16/1890
J. L. Burt and J. L. Harris m. 11/29/1896
T. H. Burt and W. M. harris m. 8/4/1903

Ella F. Burt b. 5/27/1872   M. J. Burt b. 11/27/1843
William Haynie b. 6/11/1868   J. Mark Burt b. 10/16/1867
Ella F. b. 5/27/1872   J. Linton Burt b. 9/27/1874
Ladie L. Burt b. 7/16/1878   Tom Henry Burt b. 2/14/1883

Ella Frances Burt Haynie d. 3/3/1938

W. T. Burt and Mrs. M. J. Tiller m. 11/27/1866
W. C. Haynie and Ella F. Burt m. 12/16/1890
Linton Burt m. Jessie Harris 11/29/1896

THOMAS BUSH BIBLE
Owner: Mrs. Pearl Shankle, Commerce, Ga.

Thomas Bush and Elizabeth Neal m. 8/26/1819
Thomas Sisson and Louisa Bush m. 9/14/1843
Albert Wymer Henley and Frances Julia Tabitha Bush m. 12/1/1858
Daniel Thomas Bush and Eliza Devereaux Jarrett m. 12/7/1870
Addie E. Bush d. 5/28/1892

Deaths
Louisa A. Sisson d. 8/24/1855, age 33 yrs., 10 mos., 1 day
Peayton Emmet Bush d. 3/12/1867
Mary Louisa Bush, dau.

(Thomas Bush Bible contd....)

Miriam and W. M. G. Bush b. 12/7/1865, d. 8/2/1868
Thomas Bush d. 7/21/1869
Daniel Thomas Bush, son of Thomas and Elizabeth Bush, d. 1/9/1886

Elizabeth Bush b. 12/16/1755
Elizabeth Bush Slayton b. 5/1/1814
Thomas Bush b. 8/31/1793
Elizabeth Neal b. 4/1/1800
Daniel Bush Headen b. 11/9/1801
Armindia Emeline Bush b. 6/1/1820
Lieueasey (Louisa) Averline Bush b. 10/25/1821
William Green Bush b. 10/21/1823
Daniel Thomas Bush b. 4/7/1826
Robert Neal Bush b. 9/16/1827
John Lafayett Bush b. 3/22/1829
Mary Elizabeth Bush b. 1/18/1831
Milton Jackson Bush b. 2/15/1833
Peayton Emmet Bush b. 7/6/1834
Frances Julia Tabitha Bush b. 6/18/1836
Harriett Adeliza Elen Bush b. 10/14/1838
Armindia Emeline Bush d. 1/19/1821
Augustus Floyd Bush b. 3/18/1842
Albert Franklin Bush b. 1/11/1844, d. 10/18/1853, age 9 yrs.,
  9 mos., 7 days
Milton Jackson Bush d. 10/14/1853, aged 20 yrs., 7 mos., 29 days
Lydia Headen b. 6/10/1780, d. 10/22/1812
Daniel Bush d. 2/26/1801
Elizabeth Bush d. 8/29/1829, age 74 yrs.
Augustus F. Bush d. 1/26/1844
Elizabeth Bush, wife of Thomas Bush, d. 2/27/1847, aged nearly
  47 yrs.
Mary Elizabeth Bush d. 10/2/1853, aged 22 yrs., 8 mos., 13 days.
Robert N. Bush d. 10/15/1853, aged 26 yrs., 0 mos., 29 days.

                    HENRY MELVIN KESLER BIBLE
              Owner: Elizabeth Shelton, Athens, Ga.

This is to certify that Henry Melvin Kesler and Francis Mary
Purcell were united by me in the bonds of Holy Matrimony at Mary
Purcell on the 15th day of Aug. in year of ouyr Lord 1863?

Marriages
James Anderson Jarrett and Harit Z. D. L. Kesler m. 5/3/1894
Jhon Pledger Kesler and Eda Josiefine Maddox m.--/22/1893
David Derias Kesler and Mollie Suddath m. --/22/1893
Lam Hugh Kesler and Sarah Frances Hancock m. 12/6/1911
Frances Olivia Kesler and Ernest Dewey Wright m. 2/8/1936
Emily Elizabeth Kesler and Milton Bruce Skelton m. 6/24/1937
Johnnie Hue Kesler and Wilburn Newton Smith m. 7/15/1943

Births
Henry Melvin Kesler 10/15/1847   Isaac Terrell Kesler 1/5/1880
Francis Mary Kesler 6/7/1847   Phillip Jones Kesler 1/4/1882
Hariet Z.?D.S. Kesler 8/28/1868   James Watson Kesler 8/28/1884

                         .

                        437

(Henry Melvin Kesler Bible contd....)

John Pledger Kesler 3/14/1870   Zamie Hen. Kesler 5/7/1888
David Derias Kesler 12/23/1871
William Melvin Kesler 2/21/1874
Doctor Bobie Kesler 10/24/1876
Cornelia Elizebeth Kesler 4/28/1878

Death of Mother. She departed this life 9/24/1910.
Lam Hugh Kesler d. 10/17/1954

JOSEPH FLETCHER COMER BIBLE *
Owner: Mrs. Thomas F. Comer, Athens, Ga.

On Flyleaf: J. P. Comer. A Present from his Father R. T. Comer in
the year of our Lord Mch 20, 1857.

J. F. Comer b. 3/23/1844
Martha H. Comer b. 11/7/1840
J. F. Comer and Martha H. Johnson m. 5/13/1869

Henry T. D. Comer b. 3/21/1870
Joseph Singleton Comer b. 10/16/1871
Thomas F. J. Comer b. 10/16/1871

Thomas F. and Pauline Howard Comer m. 6/12/1895. Children of
Thomas F. and Pauline Comer:
Martha Howard Comer b. 4/10/1898
Frances Elizabeth Comer b. 5/27/1903

Deaths
Joseph Singleton Comer 10/22/1873, age 2 yrs., 6 days. bur. at
    homeplace.
Martha H. Comer 1/14/1895, age 54 yrs., 2 mos., 5 days. bur. at
    homeplace.
Joseph Fletcher Comer d. 8/5/1917, 74 yrs., 4 mos., 22 days. bur.
    at homeplace.
Henry T. D. Comer Sr. 4/18/1944 in Greenwood, S. C., age 74 yrs.,
    18 days. bur. Athens, Ga. cemetery.
Thomas Fletcher Johnson Comer, age 73 yrs., 18 days, d. in Athens
    General Hospital, 11/4/1944. The funeral rites were held at the
    First Methodist Church 11/6 and he was bur. Oconee Hill
    cemetery, Athens, Ga.
R. T Comer 9/6/1893, age 76 yrs., 6 mos., 28 days. Joined
Methodist Church, Athens, Ga. 2/15/1846
Sallie Comer 3/17/1905., age 87 yrs. b. 12/16/1817.
Alsie Fulcher b. 3/18/1819, d. 2/18/1901. Joined 1st M.E. Church
    1876. Sister of Sallie Comer.

David Hill Johnson b. 1/9/1809
Sallie A. (Dowdy) Johnson b. 10/2/1818
Robert T. Johnson b. 11/1/1834
Mary A. S. Johnson b. 1/9/1836
Nancy E. Johnson b. 10/11/1838
Martha Hannah Johnson b. 11/9/1840
Catherine J. Johnson b. 5/28/1842
R. G. Johnson b. 1/9/1844

*See also p. 48.

(Joseph Fletcher Comer Bible contd....)

S. J. Johnson b. 12/31/1846
James N. Johnson bo 9/12/1852
J. G. Johnson b. 8/20/1800
Luke Johnson b. 12/20/1806
J. E. Johnson b. 4/5/1812
M. A. D. Johnson b. 1/13/1817

David H. Johnson d. 8/5/1886   R. G. Johnson d. 6/25/1862
Sallie A. Johnson d. 8/22/1853   S. J. Johnson (Thompson)
R. T. Johnson d. 11/15/1840   d. 12/17/1874
J. N. Johnson d. 10/22/1853   C. J. Johnson (Chistain)
M. A. S. Johnson (Arnold)   d. 7/26/1882
   d. 8/2/1885
Mattie M. Johnson (Comer) d. 1/14/1895
Nancy E. Johnson (Arnold) d. 6/8/1912

M. H. Arnold and M. A. S. Johnson m. 1/10/1854
O. H. Arnold and N. E. Johnson m. 4/10/1856
J. S. Chistain and C. J. Johnson m. 11/13/1866
E. M. Thompson and S. J. Johnson m. 1/14/1869
J. F. Comer and M. H. Johnson m. 5/13/1869

JAMES DOZIER BIBLE
Owner: W. T. Watters

Marriages
James Dozier and Elizabeth Staples m. 4/4/1794
Martin Webster and Lucretia Dozier m. 12/15/1816
William Gresham and Jincy Dozier m. 5/27/1817
John Clark and Sarah Dozier m. 12/20/1821
Isaac MacCrary (McCrary) and Amanda F. Dozier m. 4/24/1823
Thomas Dyer and Nancy Dozier m. 12/2/1831
Tillman F. Dozier and Catherine Patman m. 2/11/1840
T. F. Dozier and M. S. Pinson m. 3/23/1843

Births
James Dozier 3/8/1770
Elizabeth Dozier, wife of James Dozier, 4/8/1779
Mary Dozier, dau. of James and Elizabeth, 2/19/1795
Jincy Dozier 5/30/1797   Rebecca Dozier 2/9/1816
Lucretia Dozier 12/14/1799   Patsey Dozier 1/22/1820
Sarah Dozier 2/10/1802   Eliza Dozier 7/10/1821
Amanda F. Dozier 1/30/1804   Catherine Dozier, dau. of T. F.
Nancy Dozier 7/11/1806   and Catherine Dozier, --/9/1841
Frances Dozier 9/21/1810   Ann Elizabeth Dozier 1/18/1844
Ezekiel Dozier 10/7/1812   Sarah Jane Virginia Dozier
Tillman Dozier 7/29/1814   10/3/1845
                                James Thomas Dozier 11/29/1847
                                Mildred Susan Dozier 4/19/1855

Miriam Susan Pinson b. 11/13/1821, d. 5/29/1855
Mildred Susan Dozier, dau. of T. F. and M. S. Dozier, d. 8/7/1855
Sarah Jane Virginia Dozier d. 1/6/1856
James Thomas Dozier d. 5/28/1882
T. F. Dozier d. 9/22/1888

439

(James Dozier Bible contd....)

Deaths
James Dozier 2/24/1839
Elizabeth Dozier, wife of James Dozier, 6/1/1847
Eliza Dozier, dau. of James and Elizabeth Dozier, 9/10/1846
Mary Dozier, dau. of James and Elizabeth Dozier, 6/10/1795
Sarah Clark, dau. of James and Elizabeth Dozier, 5/4/1838
Francis Clark, dau. of James and Elizabeth Dozier, 2/27/1837
Catherine Dozier 8/17/1841, wife of T. F. Dozier
Catherine Dozier, dau. of T. F. and Catherine, 12/16/1855

$100.00 Claiborn Parish, La. Jany 1st 1861
On day after date I promise to pay Joseph Watters or bearer the
sum of one hundred dollars. Money Loaned. B. A. Watters.

The Company of Capt. James Dozier and family is requested at the
house of R. Harris' on friday 9th January to dine with me.
Robert Harris. January 7th 1824

Children of Tillman Dozier:

Catherine, dau. of T. F. and Catherine Patman Dozier, b.
8/9/1841, d. 1855
Mother of Catherine d. 8/17/1841

Tillman F. Dozier and Miriam S. Pinson m. 3/23/1843
Children of T. F. and M. S. Pinson Dozier:
Mildred Susan Dozier, Ann Elizabeth Dozier

JAMES DILLARD BIBLE*
Rev. War Pension W7020

Pens. appl. of James Dillard dtd 1819 Elbert Co., Ga. states he
had wife and 7 children. Wid., Sarah, appl. 1851, states husband
d. 4/4/1839 Elbert Co., Ga., attaches Bible record-

Births
Elizabeth Dillard 10/14/1786   Sarah Joice Dillard 3/22/1801
Nancy Dillard 7/28/1793   Jane Dillard 8/25/1797
Mary Varnon Dillard 10/3/1795 James Dillard 7/13/1799
Sindy Dillard 9/23/1802   Nehemiah Dillard 9/4/1805
Isaac Dillard 3/27/1807   Marcha Dillard 10/27/1808
Thomas Dillard 5/30/1811

CHARLES WILLIAM ENNIS BIBLE
Owner: Mrs. Cora Ennis Holt, Milledgeville, Ga.

Births
Charles William Ennis, son of Pleasant M. and Evelyn Minor Ennis,
b. 2/27/1845, d. 2/25/1904
Eliza Florelle Barnes, dau. of George Washington and Abigale
Lewis Barnes b. 4/8/1847, d. 1/15/1912

*See also p. 275.

(Charles Ennis Bible contd....)

O'Nora Ennis b. 10/11/1867
Charles Pleasant Ennis b. 6/19/1870
Cora Ennis b. 1/29/1871

James Howard Ennis b. 2/25/1873   Marriages
Erasmus Jordan Ennis b. 10/24/1875   Charles William Ennis and
William Richardson Ennis b. 5/17/1877 Eliza Florelle Barnes m.
Farish Furman Ennis b. 6/6/1879   11/18/1866
Ernest Sanford Ennis b. 7/15/1880   William Romalace Ennis and
William Romalace Ennis b. 2/21/1885   Imogene Dalton m. 6/18/1907
                                       Eleanor Gray Ennis and
                                       Sidney Gustavus Kennedy, Jr.
                                           m. 6/10/1928

HENRY CRAWFORD BIBLE
Oglethorpe Co., Ga.

Henry Crawford b. 1798   Charlotte Crawford b. 10/1/1796
Charles G. Crawford, son of Henry and Charlotte, b. 5/25/1822
Nancy W. Crawford b. 2/17/1827
John McI Crawford b. 1/28/1829
Elizabeth M. Crawford b. 1/1/1831, d. 11/19/1831
Nancy Crawford d. 9/18/1831

WILLIAM BURNS BIBLE
Owner:Mrs. Clara Mays Boone, Maysville, Ga.

William Burns b. Ireland 2/12/1752
Margaret Mitchell, b. Maryland 1/30/1752
William Burns and Margaret Mitchell m. in N. C. and lived in
Orange Co., N. C. for several years until the winter of 1781-1782
when they moved to Georgia, settling where Maysville now stands.
Their graves are on land owned by Mr. Stig Morris. Their
children:
Andrew Burns b. 2/6/1775   Mary Burns b. 5/30/1784
James Burns b. 4/30/1777   John Burns b. 10/11/1788
William Burns b. 10/19/1779   David Mitchell Burns b. 8/30/1790
Sally Burns b. 1/9/1782   Samuel Burns b. 9/1/1795

William Burns, Sr. d. 7/22/1827, aged 75 yrs.
His wife, Margaret Mitchell Burns, d. 1/10/1836, aged 84 yrs.
They are buried at Maysville, Ga. in an old pasture belonging to
Mr. Stig Morris.

441

MICHAEL ELEY BIBLE
Owner: Mrs. Paul Brown, Sandersville, Ga.

Births
Michael Eley b. 11/1/1773   Martha Eley b. 5/12/1773
James J. Eley, son of Michael and Martha Eley, b. 4/1/1797
Hannah Parrott, dau. of Benjamin & Rachael Parrott, b. 7/12/1800
Mary M. Eley, dau. of James and Hannah Eley b. 11/15/1821
John H. Eley, son of James and Hannah Eley b. 12/14/1822
Priscilla N. Eley, dau. of James J. and Hannah Eley b. 5/20/1824
Abner B. Eley b. 12/22/1825

Deaths
Hannah M. Eley d. 5/2/1841, wife of James J. Eley, age 41
James M. Eley d. 9/1/1847, youngest son of James Eley, age 60
Rachel Eley d. 8/2/1853, dau. of James and Hannah, age 24.
Martha Eley d. 11/22/1863, dau. of James and Hannah, age 22.
Elizabeth C. Eley d. 1/21/1869, wife of J. J. Eley, age 70.

HUGH McCRAINEY CLARK BIBLE

Marriages
Hugh Clark b. 10/23/1809 Cumberland Co., N. C.
Cinthia M. Clark b. 3/15/1818 Jackson Co., Ga.

Births
David Alexander Clark 9/7/1840   Marthy Jane Clark 5/12/1850
Joel Erwin Clark 9/7/1842   James Crawford Clark 6/13/1853
Sarah Anne Margaret Clark 5/27/1844 Catherine Mc. Clark 4/11/1856
Mary Stuart Clark 7/21/1846   Didamiah B. Clark 9/23/1858

Deaths
Joel E. Clark 2/20/1843   Mis Morning Clark 5/28/1928
D. Alexander Clark 7/27/1850   D. A. Clark 4/21/1952
James Crofferd Clark 3/23/1910

HARDY PACE BIBLE
Owner: Mrs. Carry Pace Becker
175 Pulaski St., Athens, Ga.

Hardy Pace d. 11/17/1836
Joshua Hopkins d. 6/12/1815, age 50
Susan Hopkins d. 7/29/1822
Columbus Augustus, son of Kennedy Bullard and Susan, his wife,
   d. 12/10/1850.
Louisa A. Tharp b. 10/11/1821
Louisa A. Pace, wife of Thomas B. Pace, d. 3/18/1848
Ceabelle Holder, dau. of H. Pace and Fanny, his wife, d.
   10/4/1853
Hardy Pace, son of Thomas Pace and Ceabelle, his wife, b.
   5/11/1784

(Hardy Pace Bible contd....)

Susan Turner, his first wife, was dau. of James Turner and Alley,
    his wife, b. 4/14/1790
Fannie Hopkins, dau. of Joshua Hopkins and Susan, his wife, b.
    4/22/1793
Thomas Pace, son of Hardy Pace and Fannie, his wife, b. 3/9/1813
Catherine McCrea Pace, wife of Thomas Pace, b. 1/10/1837
Rebeccah Pace b. 9/25/1814
Nancy Pace b. 11/23/1816
Francis C. Pace b. 1/9/1819
Martha Emily Pace b. 9/6/1829
Ceabelle F. Pace b. 4/21/1827
Susan pace b. 2/3/1824
James P. Pace b. 1/14/1821
Ceabelle Florila, dau. of Kennedy Bullard and Susan Hennilu, his
    wife, b. 10/15/1877
Susan Victory b. 10/15/1876
Columbus Augustus b. 5/20/1850
William H. Pace m. Victoria I. Haddock 1/30/1866
Thomas B. Pace m. Catherine McCrea 10/13/1864
James T. Pace m. Laura V. moore 10/11/1849
Thomas B. Pace m. Louisa A. Tharp 1/21/1840
Fanny Hopkins m. Hardy Pace 5/2/1812
Francis E. Cracker, dau. of Hardy Pace and Fanny, d. 1/3/1850
Mary Francis Cracker, dau. of Early Cracker and Francis, his
    wife, d. 3/23/1873
Martha Emily Pace d. 3/17/1848
William H. Pace b. 4/4/1843
Francis L. pace b. 9/5/1845
Louisa Martha Pace b. 12/5/1847
Three, Louisa, Martha, Francis L. and William H. by Thomas B.
Pace and Louisa, his wife.
William Hardy Cracker, son of Farley D. Cracker and Francis, his
    wife, b. 8/17/1840
Thomas Early Cracker b. 9/23/1842
Susan Turner, my first wife, d. 3/15/1810. (wife of Hardy Pace)
Nancy Pace, dau. of Hardy Pace and Fanny, his wife, d. 7/29/1817
William H. Pace d. 5/22/1834
Rebeckah Barton, dau. of Hardy and Fanny Pace, d. 10/29/1836

                        JACKSON WALLACE BIBLE

Marriages
Jackson Wallace and Emily Alice Harris 9/19/1875
Clifford F. Wallace and Alberta Boyd Stratton 9/1/1929

Births
Father- Jackson Wallace 11/18/1849
Mother- Emily Alice Wallace 7/26/1851
Mary Ella Wallace 7/10/1876
Clara May Wallace 2/1/1878
James Henry Wallace 2/26/1880
Sarah Ann Wallace 10/16/1882
Adie Agness Wallace 7/27/1885
Effie Eithel Wallace 1/22/1888

                            443

(Jackson Wallace Bible, Births, contd....)

John William Wallace 5/4/1889
Clifford Franklin Wallace 6/25/1895

Deaths
Emily Alice Wallace 5/24/1927   Adie Agness Wallace 5/7/1886
Clara May Wallace 7/24/1896

MARVIN HAMMONS WESLEY BIBLE

Marvin Hammons Wesley to Mary McClung 12/19/1839

Births
Marvin Hammons Wesley 3/24/1813   Mary Jane Wesley 5/22/1851
Mary Wesley 1/20/1820   Charles Josiah Wesley 5/24/1853
Elizabeth Mandy Wesley 10/18/1840   Franklin Fair Wesley 6/11/1855
John William Wesley 9/28/1842   Samson Wesley 4/16/1860
Pulaska Judge Wesley 5/9/1845   Andrew Jackson Wesley 6/25/1862
Marvin Hammons Wesley 6/7/1847
James Henry lee Wesley 6/4/1849
Robert McClung Wesley 12/26/1864

Marriages
Emma Laura Wesley, dau. of Paul, to John Vernon Yost, Atlanta,
    10/8/1924
Thomas Wesley Spurlock, son of Daisy, to Marguerite Burroughs,
    in Jacksonville, Fla. 11/28/1926
Samuel Eric Braswell, son of Nan, to William Henry Hardie in
    Hopkinsville, Ky. 1-1-1925
Ida Susan Medlock, dau. of Myrtis, to Edward K. Lindorme, in
    Chattanooga, Tenn., 6/17/1928
Mary Elizabeth Wesley, dau. of Paul, to Kenneth O. Weatherwax,
    988 Spring Street, Atlanta, 7/3/1928
Thomas D. Crowley, son of Ida, to Ora Inez Gladden, Atlanta,
    10-28-1928
John Wendell Wesley, son of Terrell Co., Sr. to Lavina Orpha
    Sewell, in Anniston, Ala., 5/5/1929
Verna Pritchard, dau. of Ina to G. C. Slaughter, Decatur,
    5/24/1929
Marvin William Wesley, son of George, to Lorena Mae Pharr, in
    Austin, Texas, 6/8/1929
Josephine Louisa Marbut, dau. of Keturah, to Wilkins McCall
    Stanley, 955 West Peachtree Street, Atlanta, 8/20/1929
Pulaski Henry Spurlock, son of Daisy, to Helen Lea, Macon,
    10/17/1931
Marion Elijah Braswell, son of Nan, to Helen Crossett, Cocoanut
    Grove, Miami, Fla., 10/22/1931
John Wesley Marbut, son of Keturah, to Dorothy Davis, Atlanta,
    Westminster Presbyterian Church, 12/12/1931
Harry Leslie Wesley, son of Terrell C., Sr., to Ruby McMahon,
    Atlanta, 8/1932
Nina Elizabeth Braswell, dau. of Nan, to Clinton Raymond Miller,
    Cocoanut Grove, Miami, Fla., 6/25/1933
Margarete Wesley, dau. of George, to Carl A. Johnson in Austin
    Texas 8/1933

(Marvin H. Wesley Bible contd....)

Terrell Constantine Wesley, Jr., son of Terrell Co., Sr. to
   Katherine Dreese Cooper, First Presbyterian Church, Atlanta,
   4/4/1934
Ottis Hawthorn Wesley, son of Pulaski Judge, to Cecil Cobb,
   Washington, D. C., 11/23/1934
Ina Ernestine Wilson, dau. of John, to Fred Theodore Greer,
   Decatur, 12/23/1934
Louise Wilson, dau. of John, to Lester Buioe, Decatur, 5/11/1935
Benjamin Hill Spurlock, Jr., son of Daisy, to Betty Roberts, Los
   Angeles, Calif. 6/22/1935
James W. Medlock, son of Myrtis, to Hazel Jones, 6/8/1935
Eva Florence Wilson, dau. of William, to Charles Lee Parker,
   8/15/1932
Betty Medlock, dau. of Myrtis, to J. T. McDonald, Heflin, Ala.,
   9/29/1935
Terrell Clifford Marbut, son of Keturah, to Katharine Lott, First
   Methodist Church, Waycross, 8/31/1931
Ora Belle Crowley, dau. of Ida, to Jack L. Shellnutt, Atlanta,
   10/11/1935
Mary Ann Wesley, dau. of Carl, to Osman Prouse Lyman, Jr., 995
   West Peachtree Street, Atlanta, 1/18/1936
Ray Wesley, son of Rupert, to Addie Sorrow, Lithonia, 3/1936
Louise Elizabeth Wesley, dau. of Terrell C., Sr. to Nelson
   Robinson, First Presbyterian Church, Atlanta, 5/9/1936

Births (Children of Pulaski Judge Wesley):
Barbara Ann, dau. of Emma Laura Wesley and John Vernon Yost,
   Miami, Fla., 12/6/1926
John Wendell, Jr., son of Lavina Sewell and John Wendell Wesley,
   Sr., Piedmont Sanitarium, Atlanta, 1/30/1932
John Wesley, Jr., son f Dorothy Davis and John Wesley Marbut,
   Sr.,, Piedmont Sanitarium, Atlanta, 7/10/1934
Elizabeth Jane, dau. of Emma Laura Wesley and John Vernon
   Yost, Emory Hospital, Emory Univ., Ga., 8/4/1934
Mary Jane, dau. of Louisa Josephine Marbut and Wilkins McCall
   Stanley, Emory Hospital, Emory Univ., Ga. 10/10/1934
Janet Ozmer, dau. of Ruby McMahon and Harry Leslie Wesley,
   Winston-Salem, N. C., 10/12/1934
Terrell Constantine III, son of Terrell C. II and Katherine
   Dreese Cooper Wesley, Atlanta, 1/3/1935
Ottis Hawthorn, Jr., son of Cecil Cobb and Ottis Hawthorn Wesley,
   Sr., Washington, D. C., 7/8/1935
Helen Leann, dau. of Pulaski Henry and Helen Lea Spurlock,
   Metter,
   Ga., 10/28/1935

Children of Amanda Elizabeth Wesley Wilson:

Amos Theodore, son of Montine Wellborn and John Wilson, Tucker,
   Ga., 6/29/1929
Doris Lorene, dau. of Lillian Wilson and Russell W. Harris,
   Atlanta, 7/8/1929
Charles, son of Eva Florence Wilson and Charles Lee Parker,
   Atlanta, 7/30/1934
James Oscar, son of Agnes Delores Attaway and Woodrow Theodore
   Wilson, Decatur, 12/23/1934
Betty Anne, dau. of Nina Elizabeth Braswell and Clinton Raymond
   Miller, Cocoanut Grove, Miami, Fla., 9/7/1934
Jo Ann, dau. of Eva Florence Wilson and Charles Lee Parker,
   Atlanta, 5/1/1933

(Marvin H. Wesley Bible contd....)

Doris Payne, dau. of Gladys Medlock and E. R. Payne, Atlanta,
1/18/1926
Ray Payne, son of Gladys Medlock and E. R. Payne, Atlanta,
4/4/1934
Edward K. Lindorme, Jr., son of Ida Susan Medlock and Edward K.
Lindorme, Sr., Atlanta, 12/25/1930
Wade Medlock Lindorme, son of Ida Susan Medlock and Edward K.
Lindorme, Sr., Atlanta, 6/9/1936
Bobby Blackburn, son of Sarah Medlock and B. B. Blackburn,
Atlanta, 2/14/1927
Douglas Blackburn, son of Sarah Medlock and B. B. Blackburn,
Atlanta, 2/14/1927
Jean Wilson, dau. of Cletus Connell and Marvin Wilson, Decatur,
12/3/1931
George Wilson, son of Cletus Connell and Marvin Wilson, Decatur,
2/17/1933
Richard Ferrell Wilson, son of Evelyn Corley and Ferrell Wilson,
Decatur, 3/3/1935
Mary Ruth, dau. of Montine Wellborn and John Wilson, Tucker,
4/5/1931
William David, son of Montine W. and John Wilson, Tucker,
11/29/1933

JOSEPH G. BATES BIBLE
of Atlanta, Ga.

Joseph G. Bates of London, England m. Elizabeth A. Macey of
London, England 12/25/1881 at St. Luke´s Church by Isaac Hawker,

Vicar, Plymouth. Wit: Edward T. Slackets and Anerci Pengsley

Marriages
Eva Jane Bates to William Franklin Methoin 6/6/1906
Howard Edward to Mattie Yammel 8/29/1908
Ruth Elizabeth to Robert Ware Sistrewk 12/19/1917
Louise Macy to Agnew Andrews 1/11/1922

Births
Eva J. Bates 6/2/1885 Montreal, Canada
Howard E. G. Bates 6/18/1887 Concord, N. H.
Annie Maude Bates 10/31/1889 Warner, N. H.
Ruth Elizabeth Bates 7/26/1895 Atlanta, Ga.
Louise Macy Bates 10/31/1897 Atlanta, Ga.
Annie Maude d. 7/19/1891

GEORGE LYON, SR. BIBLE
DeKalb Co., Ga.

Births
George Lyon 12/1/1787 and m. Elizabeth Howard 10/10/1806
Sterling Lyon 7/10/1808
Mary Lyon 5/2/1810 m. Nathan Owen Howard 1830, d. 1839
Niecy Lyon 10/8/1811

(George Lyon Sr. Bible, Births, contd....)

Carter Lyon 4/15/1813
Nancy Lyon 9/12/1814
Johnson Lyon 5/4/1816 m. Elizabeth Blunt 12/28/1837
Elizabeth Lyon 1/8/1818
Sally Lyon 4/18/1820
George Lyon 2/14/1822 m. Helen Mar Wallace Gathright 12/3/1848
Margaret Lyon 10/14/1824
Harriet Lyon 8/13/1825
Thomas Jefferson Lyon 4/13/1827 m. Martha Ann Robertson
Ligivinia Lyon 3/7/1829 m. John H. Morris 5/1/1845
Nancy Emeline Howard 10/30/1835?

George Lyon, Jr. d. 73 yrs. 5/14/1895
Nancy A. L. Dupree d. at 77 yrs. m. Osborne Gathright, then
   Thomas Cook

Children of George Lyon, Jr. and Helen M. W. Lyon (Helen b.
   8/13/1833):
Sara Jane Elizabeth Lyon b. 11/4/1850, d. 8/7/1860
Martha Gathright Ann Tate Lyon b. 8/29/1853
Charles Thomas Lyon b. 8/25/1855, d. 6/10/1856
Lucy Mariah Lyon b. 10/1/1858
Joseph Emanuel Lyon b. 11/9/1867
Wallace A. Lyon b. 10/2/1870

Mrs. Harriett Lyon b. 8/13 S. C.
Thomas B. Robertson b. 10/20/1848
Sarian E. Robertson b. 10/19/1851
George Judson Robertson b. 2/6/1855
William Jackson Robertson b. 9/2/1858
James Washington Robertson b. 9/2/1858
Benjamin Bennit Robertson b. 7/18/1869
Hariett Malipie Patterson b. 8/10/1873
Marthyann Elizabeth Patterson b. 10/14/1874
Arlene Adaline 8/17/1873
John James Robertson b. 6/1877
Ben Thomas Alexander Robertson b. 5/1886
Miss Nora Robertson b. 3/14/1887

Thomas Jefferson Lyon b. 4/13/1827 S. C.
Mrs. Martha Ann Lyon, wid. of Thomas J. Lyon 12th child of
   George and Eliz Howard
Sarah Arminda Lyon b. 10/9/1849
Mary Francis Lyon b. 10/21/1851
James Bedford Lyon bo. 8/1853
Minerva Ann Lyon b. 8/16/1856
Marthann Emma Lyon b. 12/17/1858
William Marian Lyon b. 5/14/1862 dead

          (From letter inside Bible, dtd 9/12/1887):
"Dear Brother and Sister, this is the age of old Great
grandfather's family:
Joseph Lyon b. 2/13/1754
Maryann Marchbanks b. 10/7/1758

Elizabeth Lyon b. 11/13/1734
George Lyon b. 1732
William b. the 24, 1789

(George Lyon, Sr. Bible contd....)

Sarah Lyon b. 12/23/1793
Nancy Lyon b. 3/13/1797
Emanuel Lyon b. 1/3/1803
Next is ages of the Johnson Lyon family,
Johnson Lyon b. 5/4/1816
Elizabeth Lyon b.- /31/1817
George W. Lyon b. 8/12/1838
Nancy M. Lyon b. 9/9/1840
Elizabeth F. Lyon b. 10/2/1842
William M. Lyon b. 12/22/1844
Joseph A. Lyon b. 5/13/1847
John Alonzo Lyon b. 1/14/1850
Eady L. F. Lyon b. 9/9/1852
Rebecca A. Lyon b. 4/6/1855
James A. Lyon b. 9/3/1858
I will send the rest as soon as I can." (letter unsigned)

ALLEN CARVER BIBLE
Coffee Co., Ga.

Allen Carver b. 4/4/1845 (son of James Carver and Sarah
  Ricketson)
Beady Carver b. 2/17/1847 (dau. of Youngie Vickers and Fannie
  Peterson).
Allen Carver of Coffee Co. and Beady Vickers m. 9/14/1865 by Rev.
J. G. Taylor. Children:

Sarah Carver b. 5/25/1866	Fanney Carver b. 12/8/1875
Eliz.th Carver b. 12/21/1867	Jessie Carver b. 12/23/1877
Delila Carver b. 2/28/1870	Margaret Carver b. 3/2/1880
Vincent Carver b. 4/19/1872	Boysey Carver b. 1/9/1882
Wiley Carver b. 12/30/1873	James Y. Carver b. 3/10/1884

Susan Carver b. 4/29/1886
Youngey Carver, son of Vincent, b. 2/18/1897, d. 3/16/1898
Christie Ann Carber b. 10/11/1901

JOHN COLLEY BIBLE *
Owner: Anne Watkins, Atlanta, Ga.

Births
Gabriel Colley 6/17/1809
Elizabeth Colley 5/19/1808

Marriages
Elizabeth Tindall to John Peetett 2/12/1811
Nancy Colley to Kirby Goolsbe 7/25/1813
Mary Colley to James V. Brown 9/26/1816
Francis Colley to F. L. Owens 12/24/1818
Louisa Colley to Welcome Fanning 3/23/1820

Births
John Colley 9/14/1752
Sarah Colley, dau. of Hen'y France, Jr., b. 6/4/1763

*See also p. 178.

(John Colley Bible contd....)

Children:

Gabriel Colley 2/23/1782	Nancy Colley 1/2/1792
Francis Colley 2/20/1785	Spain Colley 1/22/1794
Eliza. Colley 5/12/1788	Louisa Colley 9/23/1801

Mary Colley 5/26/1790
Lieusinday E. Tindall b. 4/26/1809
Demaris Goolsbe 4/25/1814

John C. Fanning 1/19/1821	Sabrina Ellen Fanning 7/13/1835
Sarah F. Fanning 9/11/1822	Charles Ann Fanning 9/23/1838
Mary Fanning 7/5/1824	Victoria A. Fanning 11/16/1840
Nancy Fanning 3/9/1827	Bryan Fanning 10/18/1842
Martha Fanning 2/1/1829	Frances Fanning 1/6/1845
Webster Fanning 3/25/1831	Samuel D. Fanning 7/4/1862
Parks Fanning 3/9/1833	Alace Estelle Fanning 4/23/1864

Deaths
Nimrod Colley
Lieusenday Colley
Lewis Colley
John Colley d. 6/9/1815
Sarah Colley d. 12/21/1833
Thomas B. Tindall d. 11/20th (or 27th)/1809
Parks Fanning d. 8/4/1835
Frances Fanning d. 10/1/1846
Albina Victoria Fanning d. 12/24/1846
Charles Ann Fanning d. 12/28/1850
Mrs. Louisa Fanning d. 10/1/1853
Welcome Fanning b. 7/14/1799, d. 10/3/1873
William S. Brown d. 2/16/1855?
Rev. A. J. Orr d. 7/12/1860
John C. Fanning d. 4/19/1870
Sarah F. Fanning d. 11/30/1869
Webster Fanning d. 4/24/1903
J. A. Brown d. 1/10/1903
Mary P. Johnson d. 3/29/1904
Sabrina Ellen Fanning Brown d. 6/23/1905

NIMMONS BIBLE
Newnan, Ga.

William Nimmons b. 1/1/1799	Laura Ann Nimmons b. 9/13/1834
Susannah Nimmons b. 10/13/1805	Susan Anzonetta Nimmons
Ormon T. M. Himmons b. 8/9/1827	b. 9/17/1839

William Potts Nimmons b. 5/2/1829
William Edward Nimmons, son of O. T. M. and Georgia A. Nimmons,
  b. 4/12/1850
Mary Anzonetta, dau. of O. T. M. and George A. Nimmons, b.
  4/20/1855

Marriages
William Nimmons and Susannah Potts m. 5/4/1826
O. T. M. Nimmons and Georgia A. Story m. 3/22/1849 (Newnan, Ga.)
W. J. Ransom and Laura A. Nimmons m. 12/20/1855
W. P. Nimmons and M. J. Corkin m. 1/19/1860
W. E. Nimmons and Jennie Wilkininson m. 2/6/1889
T. H. Nimmons and Nell Callaway m. 12/10/1902

449

(Nimmons Bible contd....)

Deaths
William Nimmons 3/22/1852   Susannah Potts Nimmons 7/11/1873
Susan Anzonetta Nimmons 3/30/1855 William Potts Nimmons 4/11/1909
O. T. M. Nimmons 2/27/1838 or 58
Laura A. Ransom 5/28/1864

Edwin Ransom, son of W. J. and L. A. Ransom, 4/1859 or 1889
Jennie Wilkinson Nimmons 12/17/1915
Mary J. Corkin Nimmons 9/15/1918
William Edward Nimmons 4/5/1921

W. J. RANSOM BIBLE
of Coweta Co., Ga.

William James Ransom and Laura A. Nimmons m. 12/20/1855
William Nimmons and Susannah Potts m. 5/4/1826
Ormon Thomas Mortimer Nimmons and Georgia Ann Story m. 3/22/1849
William Potts Nimmons and Mary Jane Corbin m. 1/19/1861

Births
William J. Ransom b. 3/14/1828
Laura A. Ransom b. 9/13/1834
Edwin F. (Flowers) Ransom b. 9/24/1856
Willie A. (Anzonetta) Ransom b. 5/1/1859
James T. (Thomas) Ransom b. 5/24/1866

William Nimmons b. 1/1/1799   Susan Annonetta Nimmons b.
Susannah Nimmons b. 10/13/1805   9/17/1839
William Potts Nimmons b. 5/2/1829   Madison Storey Ransom b.
Orman T. M. Nimmons b. 8/19/1827   3/3/1867
                                     Mrs. Georgia A. Ransom
Deaths   10/10/1830
Edwin F. Ransom 4/17/1859   Arthur McBride Ransom
Mrs. Laura A. Ransom 5/28/1864   7/9/1874

JEREMIAH TUCKER BIBLE of Wilkes-Troup Co.'s Ga.
Owner: Harry Nelms, Concord, Tenn.

Jeremiah Tucker b. 2/1/1785   Elizabeth P. Tucker b. 10/13/1819
Milly Tucker b. 5/5/1790   ? Tucker b. 6/29/1821
Matildy Tucker b. 7/28/1809   George P. Tucker b. 1/3/1824
Thomas Tucker b. 8/13/1810   B.? Ann Tucker b. 5/13/1825
Nancy Tucker b. 8/19/1811   George P. Tucker b. 1/3/1824
John Tucker b. 11/1/1812   ? Tucker b. 6/29/1821
Jeremiah Scot Tucker b. 3/24/1814
Polly Tucker b. 8/27/1815   Amos C. Tucker (twin) b.5/13/1825
Daniel Jackson Tucker b. 1/4/1817
William P. Tucker b. 3/24/1818
Elizabeth P. Tucker b. 10/13/1819
Simeon Tucker b. 8/6/1827
James H. Tucker b. 3/1829

(Jeremiah Tucker Bible contd....)

Milly Christine b. 5/4/1833
Nancy E. (Elizabeth) Jackson b. 5/25/1844
G. A. Jackson b. 9/5/1852
M. T. Jackson b. 4/5/1859
M. S. (Martha Sue) Jackson b. 4/5/1860 (or 1858)

HERREN BIBLE, Beulah, Ga. (Wilkes Co.)

Elish Ford Herren b. 8/16/1837
Sarah Helen Herren b. 2/4/1845
Lewis Oswell, son of E. F. and S. H. Herren, b. 11/4/1866
William Ellis, son of E. F. and S. H. Herren, b. 3/2/1868
Lillie Lou, dau. of E. F. and S. H. Herren, b/ 9/29/1869
John Walter Herren, son of E. F. and S. H. Herren, b. 10/23/1871
Bedford Forest, son of E. F. and S. H. Herren, b. 2/6/1873
Bessie Matilda, dau. of E. F. and S. H. Herren, b. 4/13/1874
Robert Lee Herren, son of E. F. and S. H. Herren, b. 4/18/1876
James W. Elisha, son of E. F. and S. H. herren, b. 4/24/1881
Lila Lowe Willis Herren b. 4/13/1875
Willie Joe, son of W. E. and L. L., b. 10/23/1896
Willie Joe, Jr., son of W. Joe and Pansy Herren, b. 12/16/1916
Robert Ford Herren, son of W. Joe and Pansy H., b. 9/22/1918
Pansy Louise Herren b. 5/15/1898
James Ellis Herren b. 7/21/1921
Thelma Carolyn Herren b. 2/22/1924
Nick Willis Herren b. 7/16/1929
Helen Jeanette Herren b. 7/2/1930
Barnie Almond Herren b. 11/23/1936

Deaths
Lewis Oswell, son f E. F. and S. H. Herren, d. 3/26/1867
Bessie Matilda, dau. of E. F. and S. H. Herren, d. 3/9/1876
Elisha F. Herren d. 3/1/1882
Robert Lee Herren d. 9/1881
Lillie Lou Turner d. 4/29/1904
Bedford Forest Herren d. 11/23/1905

STOREY BIBLE

William F. Storey b. 4/16/1800
Edward M. Storey b. 8/25/1832
Mary M. Storey b. 11/20/1801 or 7
Georgianna Storey b. 10/10/1830
William Wallis Storey b. 1/18/1839

BIBLE OF AMBROSE JONES of Columbia Co., Ga.
Owner: Mrs. Glenn Harp, Stone Mountain, Ga.

Births
Ambrose Jones, the father, 1/23/1748
Mary Harris, the mother, 2/4/1763

                    Brothers and Sisters:

Allen Jones 1/25/1778   Ambrose Jones 7/27/1794
Richard Jones 11/13/1780   Charles H. Jones 10/15/1798
Thomas Jones 11/13/1782   Catharine C. Jones 3/7/1800
Sarah H. Jones 8/3/1785   Abraham B. Jones 4/6/1802

John Tyler Allen, the father, b. 5/14/1770
Charlotte Pearre, the mother, b. 12/14/1773

            Brothers and Sisters of Mary H. F. Allen:

Joseph James Allen 5/20/1805   Mercy R. E. Allen 4/27/1809
Alice Avie Allen 11/20/1806   Sarah Louisa Allen 9/12/1813

Gabriel Jones b. Columbia Co., Ga. 4/16/1796
Mary H. F. Allen, b. Columbia Co., Ga. 9/29/1811
William Harris Jones, son of G & M Jones b. 3/1/1834
Mary Alice Jones, dau., 11/20/1835
Gabriel Jones, son, 11/20/1837
Sarah Catharine Jones 3/1/1841
John Ambrose Jones 12/1/1842
Allen Jones 4/30/1846
Charlotte Louisa Jones 7/25/1848
Charles Tyler Jones 10/4/1851
William Harris Jones, son of G & E Jones 4/20/1866
Georgia T. jones, dau. of G. Jones, Jr. b. 6/15/1868
Ellie Gertrude Jones b. 12/6/1870
Mary Jones, dau. of Gabriel and Elizabeth L. Jones b. 11/2/1873
Charles Augustus Jones b. 10/27/1879
Floriede Jones b. 2/4/1883

Marriages
Ambrose Jones and Mary Harris, the father and mother of G. Jones,
on 10/17/1776
Sarah H. Jones, sister of G. Jones, to Archer Avary 10/18/1804
Thomas Jones, a bro., to Sarah N. Marshall 1/1804
Richard Jones, a bro., to Nancy Norment? 12/23/1804
Catharine C. Jones, a sister, to William Yarbrough 12/21/1819
John Lamkin? to Mercy L. R. Allen 11/20/1830
Gabriel Jones to Mary Harriet Francis Allen 3/28/1833
Thomas G. Hight to Mary Alice Jones 5/13/1858
William H. Jones to Mary H. E. Cook 1/4/1863
Gabriel Jones to Elizabeth L. Harrison 4/26/1864
William H. L. Collins to Sarah L. Allen 4/16/1844

Deaths
Ambrose Jones 8/18/1808   Mary Harris Jones 8/28/1820
Allen Jones, b. 1778, d. 10/8/1778 Richard Jones 3/30/1815
Thomas Jones 9/6/1820   Ambrose Jones 9/29/1814

                            452

(Ambrose Jones Bible contd....)

Mary Jones, b. 1788, d. 10/11/1794   Charles H. Jones 8/5/1804
Abraham B. Jones 11/16/1802 or 1812 John Tyler Allen 11/24/1821
Charlotte Pearre Allen 11/16/1816   Joseph James Allen 7/22/1805
Alice Avis Allen 5/27/1855   Sarah Louisa Allen 2/16/1869
Gabriel Jones (b. 1794) 10/31/1859 Mary H. F. Allen 1/18/1874
William Harris Jones killed in Battle of Cold Harbor, Va.
  6/5/1864
Gabriel Jones (b. 1837) accidentially killed 11/11/1889
Sarah Catharine Jones 11/7/1845
John Ambrose Jones 9/9/186-
Allen Jones (b. 1846) d. 3/1/1914
Charlotte Louisa Jones 9/1/1850
Charlotte Tyler Jones 7/12/1852
Thomas G. Hight 2/9/---
Mary M. Scott 2/15/1871
Sarah H. Avery 6/16/1870   Floriede Jones 5/1/1929
Sarah L. Collins 2/1870   Ellie G. Jones Prior 1/1/1953
Mary Jones (b. 1873) 3/5/1952
Charles Augustus Jones (b. 1879) 10/28/1949, Piedmont, Ala.

                    WILLIAM GURLEY BIBLE
          Owner: Jacob Ephraim Gurley, Roscoe, Coweta Co., Ga.

William Gurley b. 6/16/1788, his wife, Rebecca, b. 6/7/1793

Births
Jesse M. 4/11/1817   Jacob Ephraim 1/12/1824
Mary L. 12/11/1819   Joel C. 7/24/1826
Sarah M. 1/5/1822   Matthew P. 4/8/1830

          JACOB E. GURLEY BIBLE of Coweta Co., Ga.

J. E. Gurley b. 1/12/1824. Lydia A. Gurley b. 10/2/1835

Births
William Davis 8/1/1861   Mary E. 1/22/1871
Jacob Thomas 2/22/1863   John Washington 12/29/1872
Richmond Jones 4/7/1866   Lucy Catharine 9/9/1876
Joel Culpepper 9/29/1868

          LEONIDAS A. LANE BIBLE of Jasper Co. Ga.
          Owner: Mrs. Kinda P. Lane, Washington, D. C.

Leonidas A. Lane b. 4/22/1838 m. 9/28/1865 Susan P. Greer (dau.
of Robert and Rhoda) b. 9/24/1847 Jasper Co. Their Children:
Martha Augustus Lane b. 6/21/1866 James D. Lane b. 3/2/1884
Susan Annie Lane b. 9/8/1868   Jordan C. Lane b. 3/10/1881
Lucie Alice Lane b. 12/9/1870   Robert L. Lane b. 2/28/1876
Bertha Estelle Lane b. 5/3/1873   Linda P. Lane b. 8/3/1878
Guy Compton Lane b. 2/23/1887   Ralph N. Lane b. 11/11/1890
                                  Thom A. Lane b. 3/24/1891

453

JOHN MILLER EDGE BIBLE
Owner: Ross Dixon
Hawkinsville, Georgia

Marriages
John Miller Edge b. 8/19/1819 Baldwin Co. m. 11/19/1846 Marietta,
Ga., Clara P. A. Kolb b. 7/25/1824 in Newton Co., Ga., d.
7/26/1886
Mary I. Edge b. 1/21/1852 Marietta, Ga. m. 1/21/1868 in Campbell
Co., Ga. to Frederick Aderhold, Jr.
Peter William Edge b. 7/2/1848 Marietta, Ga. d. 4/9/1889 Twiggs
Co., Ga. m. 12/15/1870 to Harriet S. Miller
John V. Edge b. 6/5/1850 Marietta, Ga. d. 1/9/1901 Douglasville,
Ga. m. R. B. Danforth 3/5/1871
Sarah Octavia Edge b. 6/30/1855 Campbell Co., Ga. m. Dr. J. B.
Bennett of Forsyth Co., Ga. 1/11/1876
Martha Patton Edge b. 6/27/1864 near Fairburn, Ga. d. 5/22/1888
Douglasville, Ga. m. 1/25/1880 Dr. Willis Westmoreland.
James Butt Edge b. 4/16/1861 Cobb Co., Ga. d. 12/14/1905 Cordele,
Ga. m. 12/21/1882 Annie King of Houston Co., Ga.
Jesse K. Edge b. 11/7/1858 Campbell Co., Ga. d. 4/17/1898
Austell, Ga. m. 8/10/1884 Elizabeth May
Clara Kate Edge b. 12/22/1868 Campbell Co., Ga. d. 5/12/1922
Hawkinsville, Ga. m. 2/3/1892 to L. M. Dixon of Macon, Ga.

Births

Children of John Miller Edge and Clara P. A. Kolb:

Peter William, John Valentine, Mary I., Martin Kolb, b. 4/30/1854
in Marietta, Ga., d. 8/22/1857 Sarah Octavia, Jesse K., James
Butt, Martha Patterson, Clara Kate.

WILLIAM JONES BIBLE
Owner: Estelle Jones
Evans, Georgia

Marriages
William Jones (a relative of Owen Jones 1741-1814) b. 1802 in
Carnarvon Co., Wales, d. 10/23/1867 m. 10/8/1835 by Rev. William
Kennedy Mary Isham Keith who d. 6/25/1846

William Henry Harrison Jones 12/27/1840-10/1922 m. Sophie Bell
12/5/1842-1/18/1907

J. B. Griffin to Sarah Jane Jones 7/21/1836-7/16/1917 m.
8/23/1855 by Rev. G. H. Cliett

W. G. Jones to Sophie Ball Main 9/5/1866 by Rev. I. M. Neely

J. M. Jones to Burmah L. Cliett 10/3/1866

(William Jones Bible contd....)

Emory Hugh Cason to Jessie Jones b. 12/24/1868 m. 5/15/1890 by Rev. Lowery.

Arthur W. Jones b. 7/13/1807 m. 10/2/1899 Edith Golden, dau. of Mr. and Mrs. E. S. Golden of Kittanning, Pa.

Births

Children of William Jones and Mary I. Keith:

William Henry Harrison* Jones 12/27/1840
Sarah Jane Jones 7/21/1836
Mary Elizabeth Jones 9/13/1838
John Marshall Jones 8/15/1843
Thomas Isham Jones 7/18/1845

          Children of William H. H. Jones and Sophie Ball:

Arthur Wesley Jones 7/13/1867   William Henry Jones 2/24/1877
Jessie Jones 12/24/1868   Mary Estelle Jones 11/12/1878
Walter Jones 5/18/1874   Douglas Jones 8/31/1880

          Children of E. H. Cason and Jessie Jones:

Junius Augustus Cason 9/2/1891
Hulsey Beall Cason 2/21/1893

          Children of Junius Augustus Cason and Evelyn Collier:

Junius Cason, Jr. 5/10/1921   Evelyn Cason 6/13/1928

Deaths
Thomas Isham Jones 9/27/1846   Mary Elizabeth Jones 7/23/1847
John Marshall Jones 12/25/1884, son of William and Mary Keith
  Jones
Douglas Jones 7/7/1881, son of W. H. H. and Sophie Jones

                    JOHN SWANSON BIBLE
                   Owner: Julia Swanson
                   Covington, Georgia

Marriages
John Swanson to Elizabeth B. Tuggle 5/11/1802
John Swanson to Elizabeth E. Evans 5/21/1829
Robert Kellum to Elizabeth Swanson 6/23/1830

Births
Patrick M. Swanson 1/9/1829   George B. Swanson 10/16/1822
Thomas Jefferson Swanson   James Frank Swanson 1/27/1825
  4/28/1831   Dorothy L. Swanson 6/19/1803
John Swanson 6/6/1779   Mary Swanson 1/8/1810
Emerson Swanson 8/9/1805   Elizabeth Swanson 2/7/1812

                         455

(John Swanson Bible, Births, contd....)

John Swanson 11/17/1807   Nancy Swanson 1/28/1814
William G. Swanson 4/26/1816   Julian Swanson 2/23/1819
                                 Francis M. Swanson 3/25/1827

The last son of John and Elizabeth Swanson 10/1/1821-10/16/1821

          Children of Welden and Dorothy Chisholm:

Elizabeth P. Chisholm 8/3/1821
Weldon G. Chisholm 1/7/1823
Mary Matilda Chisholm 3/5/1825
Dorothy Jane Chisholm 3/24/1827
John E. Chisholm 11/17/1828
W. W. Chisholm 12/6/1830

Deaths
George B. Swanson 11/1/1825   John Swanson 8/12/1847
Emerson Swanson 5/27/1824   Mary Swanson 7/13/1825
Elizabeth B. Swanson 10/30/1843

          IVERSON MIDDLEBROOKS BIBLE Of Monroe Co.
               Owner: Mrs. John Middlebrooks
                  Barnesville, Georgia

Marriages
Iverson Middlebrooks b. 2/16/1844 m. Charlotte Elizabeth
Middlebrooks 12/19/1850-4/10/1925

Sarah Melvina Middlebrooks b. 11/14/1870 m. W. J. Williamson
   1/14/1894
Iverson Middlebrooks m. Miss C. E. Taylor of Pike Co., Ga.
   1/25/1870

Births
John Thomas Middlebrooks 12/15/1872
Alfred Luther Middlebrooks 1/8/1875
Robert Iverson Middlebrooks 3/10/1878
Charlotte Elizabeth Middlebrooks 2/14/1882
Walter Taylor Middlebrooks 8/3/1884
Annie Luther Williamson, dau. of W. J. and Mellie Williamson,
   7/21/1876

Deaths
Alfred Middlebrooks 7/26/1887   Elizabeth Middlebrooks 7/26/1854
Alfred Luther Middlebrooks 1/13/1895, son of Iverson Middlebrooks
who d. 10/1/1914

Charlotte Elizabeth Middlebrooks, dau. of Iverson and Charlotte
Middlebrooks, d. 1/22/1919

A. M. Taylor b. 12/19/1850 m. M. M. McKinley 5/14/1874, d.
4/11/1875

(Iverson Middlebrooks Bible contd....)

Thomas Dumas b. 9/7/1812 m. 2/6/1834 Charlotte Taylor d. 9/13/1893

J. W. J. Taylor 3/23/1824-10/24/1898

ROBERT COLLIER BIBLE of Upson Co.
Owner: Jena Collier, Barnesville, Ga.

Marriages
Robert Collier 11/13/1783-1/6/1850 m. 5/1/1806 Martha Marshall
Booker 1782-5/27/1876 Upson Co., Ga.

Robert Marshall Collier b. 11/9/1814 m. 1st 12/24/1835 Amanda
Fletcher Greene, dau. of Thos. and Patience Greene, b. 4/19/1820
m. 2nd 10/20/1820, Mrs. Susan Jane Whatley of Upson Co., Ga.

Robert Thomas Collier b. 12/7/1837 m. 5/11/1856 Sarah R. Stafford

Births
Edith Louisa Collier 3/16/1807   Mary Booker Collier 3/4/1813
William Vines Collier 6/4/1808   Frances Elizabeth Collier
Sarah Smith Collier 12/28/1809   7/26/1818
Efford   Cobb Collier 5/4/1811   Isaac Cuthbert Collier 9/29/1821

Children of Robert and A. F. Collier:

Robert Thos. Collier 12/7/1837   Obediah Gibson Collier 3/11/1851
Martha P. Collier 7/8/1839   Sarah Eliz. Collier 4/19/1853
Mary Ann Fletcher Collier   Louisa M. Collier 8/1/1855-
    4/27/1842   1/7/1893
Isaac Cuthbert Collier 6/24/1846   Amanda Virginia Collier
William Vines Collier 4/21/1849   6/7/1859-9/12/1890

Deaths
Isaac Cuthbert Collier 5/7/1840 Macon, Ga.
William Vines Vollier 5/11/1877 Columbus, Ga., bur. in Atlanta

457

INDEX

459

Amos (cont.)
301
John Elijah 148
Kathryn Pope 299, 300
Lewise Carol 299, 300
Marianne 148
Wm. Baxter 148
Amoss, John 239
Mattie Ellen 239
Anderson, (?) 168
Clara 280
Cora L. 140
Cyntheann Josephine 40
David C. 38
E. E. 323
Edmond W. 38
Elizabeth 38
F. 323
Frances Cyndonia 40
Harriet 38
Harrison Latimer
(Mrs.) 19
James 38
James Henry 40
Jasper V. 38
Jeptha Manson 40
Jincy W. 38
John 38, 323
John F. 38
John Priar 40, 41
Josiah Eldridge 38
Lucinda Elizabeth 40
Lydia Mae Doner 41
Mamie E. 280
Marion Jefferson 40
Martha 38
Martha Malysa 40
Mattie Viola Noles 45
Melton 38
Moses 38
R. C. (Rev.) 324
Thomas Wesley 40
Vicey 396
Wilhelminia 323
William C. 38
William Gardner 41
Woodson 323
Zachariah Harris 41
Andrew, (?) 383
Albert Benjamin 383
Alford Thomas 383
Alfred Parks 383
Amanda Elizabeth 383
Benjamin 383
Eliza Elenor 383
Elizabeth Elenor 383
Frazier Alford 383
Harriet Elizabeth 383
James Asbery 383
James Asbury 383
Jasper Robert 383
John Benjamin 383
John Fremon 383
Lucy Jane 383
Nancy 383
Rhoda Harriet (Mrs.)
383
Robert Sampford 383
Sarah Elizabeth 383
William Tate 383
Andrews, A. G. 260
Agnes 446
Annie Cobb 301
Barney Ruth 281
Bishop 381
Elizabeth 381
Mary Winifred Green
260

Andrews (cont.)
Matilda 21
O. B. 281
Otho Bruce 281
Sarah An 318
Ansley, Amasa Matilda
260
Arlette 260
Eliza A. 260
Eliza Ann 260
Elizabeth 260
Elizabeth Ann Rebecca
260
Elvira 260
F. A. 260
Franklin Green 260
Fred Adolphus 260
G. A. 260
Harriet 260
Jane Eliza 260
Jessie Whitaker (Mrs.)
247
John E. 260
John Green 260
Jos. Russell 260
Joseph 259, 260
Joseph A. 260
Joseph Adkins 260
Joseph Russell 260
Julia E. 260
Julia Emma 260
Lucinda 148, 260
Maria 260
Mariah 260
Marlin 260
Martha Ann 260
Mary 260
Mary Winifred 260
Penelope 260
Rebecca 260
Roma 260
Sallie Ann 260
Sarah 260
Sarah Anne (Mrs.) 260
Sarah J. 260
Sarah Jane 260
W. A. 260
Warren Landrum 260
Warren Lummie 260
William 260
William A. 260
William Augustus 260
William Augustus (Jr.)
260
Zeruah Ethleen 260
Zeruah Ettie 260
Anthony, Mary 372
Mary Alice 375
Walter (Rev.) 373
Appleby, H. C. 17
Appling, James 118, 179
Lucy 55
Archber, John 153
Louisa Jane 363
Martha 153
Nancy 153
Archer, Aley 153
Ann (Mrs.) 152
Elexander 153
G. M. 364
George M. 363
Harvey L. 433
John 153
Lewis 153
Martha 153
Mary 153
Nancy 153
Thomas 152, 153

Arden, Caroline Matilda
34
Carrie Matilda 37
D. D. 37
D. D. (Sr.) 37
Daniel 35, 37
Daniel D. 36, 37
Daniel D. (II) 37
Daniel D. (III) 37
Daniel D. (Jr.) 36, 37
Daniel D. (Sr.) 37
Daniel Douglas 34, 36
E. E. 37
Eve (Mrs.) 35
Frances Benjamin (III)
35
Frances Benjamin (Jr.)
35
Francis Benjamin 36
Frank Benjamin 36, 37
Franklin Benjamin 35
Inez Rawls 36, 37
Irene 35, 36, 37
Irene (Mrs.) 37
James Edward 36, 37
James Read 36, 37
John 35
Laurence Edward 36
Lydia Ann Caroline 34
M. E. (Mrs.) 37
Mahala Mickler 35
Margaret (Mrs.) 35
Margaret E. (Mrs.) 36,
37
Margaret E. G. 36
Martha 37
Mary Eva 37
Mary Eve 36
Mary Osgood 36, 37
Milton 37
Morgan Rawls 36, 37
Sarah (Mrs.) 35
Sarah E. 34
Sarah Elizabeth 34
Thomas 34, 35, 37
Thomas M. (Sr.) 37
Thomas Milton 36
W. W. 37
William Willey 36
William Wylly 36
Ariail, Joseph (Mrs.)
187
Arington, Anna P. F. 410
Anner P. F. 410
Daniel 409, 410
Dora I. 410
J. A. 409, 410
John A. 410
M. L. 410
M. Lula 410
Madorah I. 410
Marvin 410
Marvin E. 410
Mary L. 410
Nancy A. 410
Nancy A. Jonston 410
Ollie May 410
P. J. 410
P. Jane 410
Parmeley J. 410
Pearley J. Breed 410
Pearlly J. 410
Pearly J. 410
Willie B. 410
Willie Bell 410
Arkinson, Jesse R. 432
Armacost, J. W. T.
(Mrs.) 412

Baker (cont.)
Clare 403
Eliza 168
Elizabeth 168
Emily 168
Eva 403
Frances 168
James R. 168
John Green Duke 168
Jonathan 168
Katherine 92
Katherine M. 92
Lydia 168
Lydia Linea 168
Mary G. 168
Mary W. (Mrs.) 168
N. W. 168
Sarah E. 129
Sarah Frances 167, 168
Seletha 168
Silas 168
T. C. 403
T. E. 403
Thomas E. 403
W. (Mrs.) 76
W. Q. 31
W. T. 403
William 31, 71
Baldree, Catherine 116
Celia 116
Isaac 116
Isaac K. 116
William 116
Baldwin, Anderson 401
Thomas J. 401
Bale, Amanda 166
Caroline Emeline 166
James Alfred 166
John 166
John (Jdg.) 166
Matilda Moore 166
Balinger, Frank Morehead 6
Ball, Sophie 455
Ballard, Anne 297
Benjamin 297
Benjamin Franklin 340
Benjamin O. 298
Carrie 298
Carrie Mae 298
Cora (Mrs.) 298
Elizabeth 297
Ellinder M. 297
Emma Lou 297
Harriett 297
Howard Volly 297
I. N. 298
Isaac Newton 298
Isom 297
J. W. 298
J. Wesley 298
James 297
James Madison 297
Jesse 297
Jessie Owen 297
John 297, 298
John W. 298
John Wesley 298
Joseph 297
Joshua 297
Josie A. 297
Lula (Mrs.) 297
M. Hubert 297
Magie 297
Martha Adaline 297
Mary 164, 298
Mary (Mrs.) 297
Mary Frances 297

Ballard (cont.)
Mildred Ann 298
Millie A. (Mrs.) 298
O. R. 298
Owen R. 298
Rebecca 297, 298
Reubin 297
Robert L. 297
Samuel 297
Susannah 297
Thomas 297
Thomas Isom 297
Thomas Parks 297
Wesley 298
Whorton 298
Whorton Fletcher 297
William K. 297
William L. 298
William N. 298
Winnie 298
Winny 298
Woodrow 298
Ballenger, Achilles 121
Betsy 121
Charity C. 121
Esthan 123
Ethan 121
James 121
Joseph 121, 122, 123
Joseph (Jr.) 121
Milly 121, 122
Peggy H. 121
Phoebe 121
Richard 121
Sarah 123
Sarah (Mrs.) 121, 122
Ballinger, (?) (Jdg.) 6
Florence (Mrs.) 6, 7
Frank 6, 7
Frank Fatio 6
Frank M. 6
Ida Fatio 6
Jane Adams 7
Katherine Fatio 6
Little Mad 7
Little Maddie 7
Madison 7
Madison Adams 6
Mannie (Mrs.) 7
Miriam Pedrick 6
Philip Fatio 6
Webster 7
Bancroft, Edward 59
Elizabeth 59
Emily 59
Irene Ada 59
Lucy Randolph 60
Mary Margaret 59
Matilda R. (Mrs.) 59
Banks, Amos 404
Belinda S. 404
Betsy Ann 404
Clara 399
Clarissa 404
Cuyler 404
Ekisha? 404
Elisha 404
Ira L. 404
Mary (Mrs.) 404
Matilda (Mrs.) 404
Polly Ann 404
Richard (Dr.) 95
Sallie G. 343, 344
Sarah 104
Simeon 404
Simeon C. 404
Bankston, Everitt 166
Louise 214

Barber, (?) 367
A. S. 414
Arlie 363, 380
Joseph 367
Mary 367
Robert 174, 367
Sarah 367
Willie Lee 380
Barclay, Nancy 407
Barefield, Alexander 424
Benjamin 424
Elizabeth 424
Henry 424
Jefferson 424
John 424
Lewis 424
Louise 424
Marion 424
Mary 424
Mazy 424
Mitchell 424
Nancy 424
Richard 424
Solomon 424
William 424
Barfield, (?) 359
Benjamin B. 358, 359
Benjamin F. 358
Cathrin Emmer 358
Effie Hallena? 358
Epsy (Mrs.) 358
Fannia B. 359
Fannie R. 358
Frederic M. 358
G. C. (Mrs.) 354
George W. 358
Georgia A. 358
Grover C. (Jr.) 214
Grover Cleveland (III) 214
Grover Cleveland (Jr.) 214
Grover Cleveland (Sr.) 214
James R. 358
John Head 358
John T. 358
Lucy E. 359
Michael G. 359
Narcissia M. 358, 359
Rebecca 359
Richard 358
Richard H. S. 358
Roxien L. 182
S. F. 359
S. G. 410
S. T. 410
Salla A. (Mrs.) 358
Sampson F. 358
Silvester E. 358
Thomas Washington 358
William Edgar 359
Barker, Harriett M. 371
Barkesdale, Susannah 297
Barkley, Adalaide 197
Adalaide Gertrude 197
Adaliade Gertrude 86
Adalinde 86
Barlett, J. M. 20
Barlow, Edith 90, 364
Barnard, A. F. 40
A. F. (Dr.) 40
Andrew Fuller 40
Ann C. 40
Ann Catherine 40
Bradley G. 40
C. J. 40
Campbell J. 40

Billups (cont.)
Thomas 290
Thomas A. 289
Virginia 289
Bingham, Alexander 319
C. C. 319
Calvin Christopher 319
Henry T. 319
Henry Thomas 318
J. W. 318, 319
James W. 319
James Wiley 318
Joel J. 319
John W. 319
John Westley 319
Martha Hane 319
Martha J. 319
Robert Levi 319
Susan 318, 319
Wm. Lucious 318
Wm. S. 319
Binney, Joseph (Rev.)
344
Bird, Andrew Hamil 323,
339
Andrew Hamil (Lt.)
323, 339
Irene 323, 339
Mary 395
Nancy 173
Permelia A. 173
Sarah Smith 323, 339
Birdsong, Benajah 157
Elizabeth (Mrs.) 157
George L. F. 157
George Lawrence
Forsyth 157
John 157
Parthenope Hamilton
157
Bishop, David L. 20
Elizabeth 20
Enoch D. 20
Helen 165, 352
James 165
James (Jr.) 165
John 165
John E. 20
Leora J. (Mrs.) 4
Margery E. 20
Martha 309
Mary Jane 20
Maxine McC. 17
Nancy J. (Mrs.) 165
Sarah Marget 20
Simeon 165
Stephen 20
Stephen M. 20
Temperance 309
William L. 20
Bivins, (?) 46
Hazel 46
Homer (Mrs.) 46, 326
Hzel 192
Isabella A. 235
Mattie 68
Thomas Ellsworth 46
Black, Lizzie 224, 225,
410
Mary 84
Mary (Mrs.) 394
Nathaniel 294
Samuel N. 85
Virginia 281
W. F. 281
William Frederick 281
Blackburn, B. B. 446
Bobby 446

Blackburn (cont.)
Douglas 446
Effie E. 413
Susannah 11
Blacksheaar, Elijah
Franks 94
Blackshear, (?) 93
A. Laura 93
A. Laura Eve 92
Annie Laura Eve 92
Archibald B. 92
Archie Baker 92
Charles Jefferson 92,
94
Clarence Hamilton 92,
94
David 94
E. F. (Jr.) 92
E. F. (Mrs.) 94
E. F. (Sr.) 92
Elijah F. 92, 94
Elijah Franks 92, 94
Evd. H. 94
Everard H. 94
Everard Hamilton 94
Isabella Powell 92, 94
J. E. 92
James E. 92
James Everard 92, 94
James Everard (Jr.)
(Col.) 93
Joseph W. 92
Joseph William 92, 94
M. L. 92, 94
Marion Floyd 92
Marmaduke David 92, 94
Mary Floyd Hamilton 92
Mary H. 92
Mary Hamilton 92, 94
Sterling Hamilton 92
Walter F. 92
Walter Floyd 92
Zoe E. 95
Zoe Frances 92, 94
Blackstock, H. P. 409
Hannah Posey 409
Richard 409
Blackwell, Elmina 432
Georgia 431, 432
Horton J. 431
Horton Jeddiah 432
Jesse 431, 432
Lavenia C. 432
Lavenia Clementine 432
Leila 432
Lela Viola 432
Mary 431
Mary Palmira 432
Nancy A. 431
Nancy Angeline 432
Samuel H. 104
Thomas M. 432
William F. 104
Blair, (?) 313
A. J. 165
Abegail 39
Albert 312, 313
Allen 313
Benjamin C. 170
Catherine 170
Columbus 312, 313
Edley 170
Elisebeth 312
Elisebeth (Mrs.) 313
Elizabeth 170
Falba N. 168
George H. 170
Georgia Caroline 168

Blair (cont.)
H. F. 165
J. A. (Mrs.) 170
James 170, 312
James M. 170
Jesse M. 168
Joseph 312, 313
Joseph A. 313
Joseph Alby 313
Loyd 313
Lucy 170
Manda Shurley 170
Margaret 313
Martha 168
Mary Etta 168
Powell 170
Regina (Mrs.) 312
Samuel 39
Sara (Mrs.) 313
Sarah 170, 312, 313
Sarah F. 170
T. R.? 313
Washington 313
William D. 170
William Wesley 168
Blakely, Rosalind 344
Blalock, Alonzo L. 136
Ann 138
Coke 163
David 113
Hessie Belle 163
J. L. 113
James 136
Jane Elisabeth 114
John L. 113, 136
Lucy 138
Mamie L. 136
Margaret (Mrs.) 113
Martha W. (Mrs.) 399
Mary L. 136
Mattie Alberta 163
Mattie Talula 163
Nellie Coke 163
Polley 137
Prudence 113, 136
Rachel (Mrs.) 265
T. J. 136
Thomas J. 113, 136
Wm. H. (Jr.) 163
jane 136
Blanchard, Mary E. 341
Bland, Bess 239
Elizabeth 239
Frances Nylic 239
Marshall H. 239
Marshall Hall 239
Marshall Hall (Jr.)
239
Blandford, Mark 233
Blanton, Matilda 216
Sarah 245
Bledsoe, (?) 227
Baker Fleetwood 227
James C. 227
Kattie (Mrs.) 227
Mary Aluria 227
Mattie (Mrs.) 227
W. H. 227
William J. 270
Bleir, Paul Earnest 416
Blewer, Catherine (Mrs.)
34
Frances Eve 34, 35
John 34
Blind, Ellen 110
Ernest 110
Blitch, Georgia Ann 9
Georgia Ann (Mrs.) 9

Bradbury (cont.)
Effie Lee 433
Ida L. 433
Ida Leora 433
John Walter 433
Josiah E. 433
Josiah Eli 432, 433
L. J. 433
Leonard Josiah 433
Lillie Belle 433
Mary Ellen 433
Mattie Lou 433
Susie N. 433
Susie Naomi 433
Bradford, Joseph (Rev.)
356
Richard 298
Sarah King 298
Bradley, (?) (Lt.) 138
Amy 134, 135
Amy Frances 135
Ann Marks 133
B. F. 135
B. Franklin 134
Benjamin Franklin 134
Clary (Mrs.) 134, 135
E. H. 134
Edmund 138
Elizabeth M. 134
Elizabeth Mildred 133
Francis Meriwether 133
George Moss 134
Isaac N. 191
James I. 133
Joe E. 191
John A. 133, 134
John A. (Dr.) 135, 391
Lou 167
Lucy Christian 135
Lucy W. 134
Lucy Winnefred 134
Margaret 298
Martha J. 133, 134
Martha Margaret (Mrs.)
134
Mary Ann Hilley 191
Mary Ardis 133, 134
Nicholas Meriwether
133, 134
Penny 133
Sally 134
Sarah 107, 134, 138
Sarah J. 142
Sarah Winefred 135
Thomas L. 134
Thomas Lutius 133
W. D. 135
William 167
William D. 134
William D. (Sr.) 135
William Drury 134
William Picken 191
William R. 134
William D. 134
Bradly, Margaret Jamison
(Mrs.) 134
Bradshaw, Allie 423
Allie C. 275, 423
Annie 275
Louella 275, 423
Brady, Mary A. 270
Brailsford, Daniel
Heyward 228
Jane (Mrs.) 229
Bramblett, Effie E. 62
Branan, Alfred Fletcher
330
Arazona Texas 330

Branan (cont.)
Georgia A. 330
Gilbert L. E. 330
John 330
John Westley 330
Lambert H. 330
Lemeon Parks 330
Louisa Francis 330
Mary A. 330
Mary Wilmoth 330
Nancy 330
Nancy Isebella 330
Sarah Elizabeth 330
Thos. Caswell 330
Westley 330
Willis Frankling 330
Brane, Katherine V. 205
Branham, Walter (Rev.)
257
Brannen, (?) 47
Allie Gertrude 119
D. W. (Mrs.) 48, 245,
246
Denton Williams 48
Denton Williams (Jr.)
48
E. W. (Mrs.) 47
Eleanor 48
Eugene Bryan 48
Hugh Percival 47, 48
Lewis Alexander 48
Neyle Thomas 48
Sarah Florence 47, 48
Walter Campbell 48
Brannon, J. M. 292
J. M. (Dr.) 292
Mary Claire 373, 374
Branscomb, Albert Leon
177
Clayton Sanford 177
Jackson Ernest 177
John Sanford 176
John Warren 177
Lewis Lightfoot 177
Lucile Elizabeth 177
Brantley, (?) (Gen.) 46
Braselton, Amos 167
Daniel 167
Eizabeth 167
Green 167
Hannah 167
Hannah (Mrs.) 167
Henry 167
Jacob 167
Job 167
John 167
Mary 167
Rebeccah 167
Ruben 167
Sarah 167
William 167
Brasington, Henrietta
Helen 118
James L. 118
Marion Emma 118
Marion Helen 118
Braswell, (?) 262
Eliza 46
Elizabeth 45
Eugene Douglas 215
George Briant 215
James 262
James Arther 215
Leon 215
Lillie May 215
Louisa 25
Marion Elijah 444
Martha J. 215

Braswell (cont.)
Mary A. 98
Mary Ruth 215
Nellie Ree 215
Nina Elizabeth 444,
445
Rebecca 262
Robert Arvester 215
Robert Briant Arvester
215
Rosa Lee 215
Samuel Eric 444
Brawner, Janie 72
Bray, J. W. (Mrs.) 118
Willie Shepperd 118
Breazel, (?) 39
Breckenbridge, E. S. 132
Breckenridge, Amtheana
Vermela 132
Hayns Lewis Gerrard
132
Polina 132
R. J. 132
Breed, R. J. 410
Breedlove, F. L. 64
J. M. 64
Mahala E. 64
Brent, Harry Tindal 144
Howard C. 145
Howard Crumbley 144
Jack Innis 144
Jacquelyn 144
Jane Kate 144
Jennie 144
Jennie Kate 144
Jennie Ruth Newman 144
Lucy Palmer 144, 145
Minnie Lee 144
Minnie Sue 145
Taylor Y. 144
Taylor Young 145
Thomas Y. 144, 145
Thomas Young 144, 145
Wookie 144
Brevard, Mary Martha 149
Brewer, Martha Ann 432
Temperance 386
Brewington, Amelia 146
Sarah Emma 176
Brewster, Mary Dalls 175
Briant, Edward 180
Eliza 180
Nancy (Mrs.) 180
Brice, Charley 292
Eliza 292
Eliza J. 292
Elizabeth Annie 292
Elizar 180
Florine Faith 292
Frances S. (Sr.) 292
Frank C. 292
Frank Calvin (Jr.) 292
Henry M. 292
J. Sam 292
J. T. 292
J. Tom 292
Jennie 292
Jennie E. 292
John Thomas 292
Lucy 292
M. Louetta 292
M. Louette 292
Milton F. 292
Milton Fall 292
Pink Riler 180
Sallie 292
Sallie E. 292
Stella E. 292

Brice (cont.)
Timothy 292
Willie M. 292
Bridges, Nancy 265
Selena 407
Selenah 407
Brightwell, Margaret 371
Mary F. 169
Mary Frances 169
Brinkley, Malinda H. 164
Brinsfield, (?) (Rev.)
368
Brinson, (?) 390
Lavenea C. 396
Matthew 396
Matthew S. 396
Nellie 390
Ruby Mae 390
Briscoe, Elizabeth 50
William 245
Brockman, Charles Raven
232
Marvin Comer 232
Mary (Mrs.) 232
William Adams 232
Brookes, May Belle Clark
131
Brooking, Elizabeth 261
Elizabeth Ellin 261
Elizabeth R. 261
Elizabeth Rebeckah 261
Henry 261
Isaac H. 261
Isaac Henry 261
James 261
James C. 261
James Curtis 261
James Harrison 261
John 261
John L. 261
John Lewis 261
Louisa 261
Louisiana T. 261
Lucy S. 261
Lucy Sarah 261
Matilda 261
Matilda (Mrs.) 261
Matilda Jane 261
Nancy H. (Mrs.) 261
Rebecca 261
Robert E. 261
Ronald 261
Susan Jane 261
Thomas Sparks 261
Brooks, (?) 104
Adeline 129
Amdmiles 266
Bradford 266
Edgar Roland 133
H. G. 364
Hamilton 266
Husky 266
Isham 132, 133
J. D. (Dr.) 133
J. H. 133
Jain 266
James Henry 132, 133
James W. 266
Jane 266
Jeckmeah W. 266
John 266
John St. Claire 129
Joseph Daniel 132, 133
Joseph Wiley 133
Julia R. 214
Larkin 266
Maria (Mrs.) 132
Martha Hawkins 287

Brooks (cont.)
Maurice Linton 316
Noah P. 104
Othenial H. 266
Phinnath 266
R. F. (Mrs.) 332
Robert Augustus 133
Robert Preston 132,
133
Roland Edgar 133
Rosa Clifford 133
Serena (Mrs.) 132, 133
Sinderella 266
T. M. (Mrs.) 133
Teresa (Mrs.) 132
William 266
William Sidney 133
Brown, (?) (Cpt.) 87
Allen 371
Amanda (Mrs.) 175
Amanda M. F. 175
Beulah Kathleen 235
Charlotte 243
Dorothy 211
Elbert Jackson 190
Elizabeth (Mrs.) 312
Elizabeth A. 16
Elizabeth Ann 16
Elizabeth Ann Jane 371
Emily 312
Emily Louise 183, 312
F. Carlton 364
Frank Casmor 416
J. A. 179, 449
Jack 167
Jacqueline LaMotte 312
James V. 178, 448
Jane 52
Jefferson Crawford
183, 312
Jinney 149
John Dozier 190
Joseph 175
Joseph Orr 175
Joseph T. 175
Junius C. 262
Leroy 241
Loyd (Mrs.) 190
Lucy 104
Lucy G. 61
Mamie 95
Martha 307
Mary Ellen 183, 312
Parthenia L. 314
Paul (Mrs.) 442
Roland S. 416
S. W. 312
Sallie H. 424, 425
Sam. W. 312
Samuel Willard 312
Sarah Presley 190
Shadrach Willard 312
Susan Ellen 312
T. H. 183
Thomas Henry 312
Thomas J. 312
Thomas Jefferson 312
William C. (Rev.) 161
William S. 179, 449
Winnie Rebecca 190
Wynette Mann 417
Browne, Honora (Mrs.) 3
Browning, David 376
Elmira 75
Nancy E. 376
Brownjohn, Anna Maira
137
Anna Maria 158

Bruan, Caroline 284
Hardy 284
Maria (Mrs.) 284
Bruce, Mary 13
Brunby, R. T. (Prof.)
149
Richard Trapier 149
Brundage, M. E. 177
Mary E. 176
Brunt, Frances 274
John 274
Martha A. 274
Patience (Mrs.) 274
Bryan, Caroline 284
Hardy 283, 284
Iredell Edward Eyche
284
Jonathan 258
Leon 284
Loverd 283
Magnolia 284
Maria (Mrs.) 284
Martha (Mrs.) 284
Martha W. 183
Pennie 183
Virginia Sarah 216
Bryant, Allie 13
Lucy 62
Mary Rebecca 368
Tilden 279
Tilten 279
Buchanan, Mary 309
Matilda 4
Buchanon, Ann 165
Buckingham, (?) 107
Buckner, Eliza 293, 410
Henry 5
Henry M. 5
Henry Morris 5
James (Dr.) 293
James A. 5
John H. 5
Mary (Mrs.) 5
Rebecca (Mrs.) 5
Tilghman 293
Budd, Phena 285
Buder, Billups (Mrs.)
288
Billups K. 289
Billups Kinnebrew 289
Diana 289
Edward E. 288, 289
Buford, Myrtle 209
Bugg, Elizabeth 55, 164
Henry 291
Priscilla 55
William Draton 291
Buioe, Lester 445
Bullard, Alice 226
Ceabelle Florila 443
Columbus Augustus 442
Edwin Baldwin 226
Frank Leverett 226
J. H. 226
J. H. (Dr.) 226
Kennedy 442, 443
Legree Swann 226
Marie Corine 226
Susan (Mrs.) 442
William Howard 226
Bullock, Amanda Loretta
170
Burton Finly 171
Burton T.? 170
Charles 170, 171
David 37
Edward 37
Elizabeth 37

Bullock (cont.)
Francis Henrietta 170
James 37
John 37
Josephine Amelia 170, 171
Marie Eliza 170
R. 170
R. Freeland 171
R. R. 414
Raymond Bramhill 170
Robert 170, 171
Robert (Sr.) 170
Robert Albert 170, 171
Robert Freeland 171
Sally 37
Shelbey Linwood 171
Shelbey Simwood 171
Sumter Aden 170
Susannah 37
William 37
William O. 37
Willie Simon 170
Winifred 37
Zachariah 37
Bulrice, Francis 15
Bunch, George L. 292
Buntz, Cherry Landslot 204
Elizabeth (Mrs.) 204
Burch, (?) 149
Addie 149
Glorvina Emmeline America 6
Jerome Charles 306
Samuel 6
Susan 149
Susan Maria (Mrs.) 6
Burckhalter, David Lane 66
Hattey Lular 66
John W. W. 66
Mary Elizabeth 66
Minia Arozer 66
Nary Idarlizer 66
Susan Emer 66
Thomas Edgar 66
W. A. 66
Walter Marshal 66
William Andrew 66
Wm. A. 66
Wm. Wiley 66
Burford, A. C. 216
A. G. 216
F. K. 216
J. A. 216
J. D. 216
L. M. 216
R. E. 216
W. T. 216
Z. Z. 216
Burke, J. W. (Rev.) 244
Burma, Catharine 433
Burn, Anna Idonia 339
Clarence 339
Clarence Augustus 339
Eliza Anice 339
John Paul 339
Burnett, J. M. 292
James 292
John William 111
Julia 89, 90
L. B. 90
Mary Ann Susan 111
Sarah Anzaline 111
W. B. 111
Burns, A. H. 66
Alice 435

Burns (cont.)
Alice Isabella 66
Alice J. 67
Alonzo H. 67
Alonzo Hay 67, 435
Alonzo Merrett 67
Alonzo Waddle 435
Andrew 441
Andrew Jackson 435
David Mitchell 435, 441
Egbert Telford 67, 435
Esther Eveline 435
James 441
James Crawford 435
James Elmer 67
James Harvey 435
John 441
John M. 67
John Milton 66, 67, 435
John Milton (Dr.) 435
Joseph Brantley 67
Lula 435
Lula S. 67
Lula Samuel 66
Margaret Elizabeth 435
Mary 441
Sally 441
Samuel 441
Samuel Hay 435
Sarah H. 67
Sarah Priscilla 435
W. B. (Mrs.) 435
William 435, 441
William (Sr.) 441
William Brantley 435
Willie J. 67
Willie Jones 67
Burnside, Etta Mae 387
Burrough, Sarah 90
Burroughs, Marguerite 444
Sarah Ann Owens 90
Burrow, Sarah Ann 111
Burson, B. F. 159
Cynthia Emaline 159
Dickie Angeline Wood 159
George David 159
Isaac E. 159
Isaac Ethreldred 159
James Crossley 159
James Francis Marion 159
Joseph Green 159
Julian Frances 159
Julie Jane 159
Lucinda Aline 159
Martha Ann Elizabeth (Mrs.) 159
Martha Anne America 159
Martha Anne Elizabeth 159
Mary Caroline 159
Nancy Emeline 159
Sarah Eveline 159
Susan Arline 159
Synthia (Mrs.) 159
William Brookfield Newton 159
Burt, E. F. 436
Elizabeth 72
Ella F. 436
Ella Frances 436
Ellia F. 436
J. L. 436

Burt (cont.)
J. Linton 436
J. Mark 436
Ladie L. 436
Linton 436
M. J. 436
T. H. 436
Tom Henry 436
W. T. 436
Burton, Annie May (Mrs.) 434
Eldridge Numally 434
G. R. (Mrs.) 434
George Romlus (Jr.) 434
George Romlus (Sr.) 434
Grace 434
Jasper Williamson 434
Martha Louise 434
Busby, Anne Elizabeth 351
Bartholomew Austin 351
Harriet Louise 351
Mary Austin 351
Rebecca Ann 351
Bush, Addie E. 436
Albert Franklin 437
Armindia Emeline 437
Augustus F. 437
Augustus Floyd 437
D. J. 239, 240
Daniel 437
Daniel S. 66
Daniel Thomas 436, 437
David J. 239, 240
David Lee 240
Elizabeth 437
Elizabeth (Mrs.) 437
Emma M. (Mrs.) 45
Frances Julia Tabitha 436, 437
George Daniel 240
Harriett Adeliza Elen 437
John Lafayett 437
John Samuel 307
Jones Howard 45
Lieueasey Averline 437
Louisa 436
Louisa Averline 437
Martha E. (Mrs.) 240
Mary Elizabeth 437
Mary Lizzie 239, 240
Mary Louisa 436
Milton Jackson 437
Miriam 437
O. W. 240
Peayton Emmet 436, 437
Robert N. 437
Robert Neal 437
Thomas 436, 437
W. M. G. 437
William Green 437
Bussey, David 102
Hezekiah 102
Lucy Ann 102
Nathan 102
Nathan (Sr.) 102
Peter 102
Susanna 102
William Daniel 102
Butcher, Bathsheba 155
Benjamin 155
Edward 155
Ephraira 155
John 155
Kathrine 155

Carter (cont.)
Josiah 106
Josiah T. 396
Josiah W. 106
Josiah Winfield (Dr.)
106
Lucy Ellen 67
M. C. 67
Mary Ann 396
Mary E. 67
McAlphin Calvin 67
Mena OViela 106
Myrtle 16
Nena Violata 106
R. C. 67
R. P. 67
Reuben P. 67
Riley Benson 67
Simeon Josiah 106
Thomas H. 67
Thomas Henry 67
William Gettys 130
Carver, Allen 448
Boysey 448
Christie Ann 448
Delila 448
Eliz.th 448
Fanney 448
James 448
James Y. 448
Jessie 448
Margaret 448
Sarah 448
Susan 448
Vincent 448
Wiley 448
Youngey 448
Case, (?) 48
Annie Otelia 48
Charles Lane 48
Charles Weiderman 48
George Joseph 48
Henrietta Louise 48
Casey, Mary E. 413
Cash, John W. (Mrs.) 302
W. B. 142
Casing, Ella L. 176
Cason, E. H. 455
Emory Hugh 455
Evelyn 455
Fannie M. 80, 377
Hulsey Beall 455
Junius (Jr.) 455
Junius Augustus 455
Castlberry, Jepthah 402
Susannah Frances
(Mrs.) 402
Castleberry, Jepthah 402
Susannah Frances
(Mrs.) 402
Caswell, Benjamin F. 32
Benjamin S. 32
Elizabeth Evans 32
Elizabeth P. 32
Katie C. 32
Lizzie E. 32
Sallie 410
Cater, R. B. 39
Richard Bohun 39
Thomas W. 39
Cates, Flora 371
Catherwood, Lydia Ann 35
S. C. 34
Cato, William 243
Caudell, John 156
Mattie 156
Rebecca M. 156
William W. 156

Caulder, Allen P. 277 277
Eugene M. 277
George W. 277
Hugh P. 277
James K. 277
John 277
John M. 277
Phebe 277
Robert Patrick 277
Seraphina 277
William M. 277
Winewood F. 277
Zeriphena Ann 277
Cauthen, Blanche
Crawford 97
Carolynne Gay (Mrs.)
421
George Barry 421
Nannie 108
Robert Lee 97
Robert Lee (Jr.) 97
Cauthern, Laura 350
Cavin, Margaret Ann 232
Mary Rutherford 232
Peggy 232
Walter 232
Centerfit, S. E. 258
Chaffee, (?) 95
Chaffin, E. F. (Mrs.)
190
Chafin, Martha 104
Chambers, (?) 164
Joseph B. 123
Joseph P. 327
Katherine 310
Kathrine 255
L. Burt 327
Chamblee, George W.
(Jr.) 13
Chambless, Alonza
Jackson 400
Andrew 184
Andrew D. 400
Artean 401
Augusta 401
Aurelius 184
Christopher 400, 401
Cynthia (Mrs.) 400
Edan Armstrong 399
Eleanor 401
Elizabeth 400
Elizabeth Jordan 399
Fannie C. 399
Francis 401
Frank 401
G. Zachariah L. 400
G. Zacharliah L. 400
George W. 401
Harriett 401
Henry 400
Henry B. 400
J. B. 400
James Graves 400
Jane 400
Jeptha 401
Jeptha C. 401
John D. 400
John F. 400
John T. 400
John W. 400
Joseph B. 400
Josephus 401
Katherine 401
Lawson G. 400
Lawson Green 400
Littleton 400
Littleton C. 400
Lovenia Sullivan 184

Chambless (cont.)
Lovicy 400, 401
Marietta Stroud 400
Martha Aann 401
Martha Ann 401
Martha Pye 400
Mary 399, 400, 401
Mary (Mrs.) 401
Mary Brent 206
Mary Ellen 399
Mary G. 400
Mary Lovenia 184
Nancy M. 400
Nathan 401
Obedience (Mrs.) 400
Rena Augusta 400
Sara Ann 400
Sara Jane 400
Sara Jane (Mrs.) 400
Sarah Ann 400
Sarah Elizabeth 400
Seaborn 401
Susan (Mrs.) 401
Susan M. 401
Theordoxica Lenorah
400
Thomas E. 399
Thomas G. 400
Thomas Taylor 400
Wiley 399
William D. 400
William H. 400
William Henry 400
Zachariah Cromwell 399
Chambliss, Mary Brent
207
S. R. 144
Chamlee, Allen K. 13
Alx. S. 13
Emery 13
G. W. 13
G. W. (Jr.) 13
George W. 12, 13
George W. (Jr.) 13
Jerry W. 13
John B. 13
Kindress Light (Mrs.)
13
Malinda (Mrs.) 13
Mary Bruce 13
R. L. 13
Sallie K. (Mrs.) 13
Sallie Katherine 13
Tilman P. 13
Tilmon 13
Tilmon Perkins 13
William 13
Chance, Bishop M. 181
Caccon B. 180
Cannon 180
Charles C. 181
Eliza (Mrs.) 180
Elizabeth E. 180
Elizar Brice 180
George 180
George W. 180
Gr 180
James W. 180, 181
Josifeen 180
Lizzie T. 181
Lucy Ann W. 180
Martha T. 181
Mary J. T. 180
Mary M. 181
Nancy (Mrs.) 180
Nancy A. 180
Nathan T. 180
Noel E. 181

Clay (cont.)
Jessie 224
Jessie (Jr.) 224
Joseph Early 224
Linton Hargrove 224
Sallie Wilson 224
Wm. T. 327
Clayton, George R. 56
Malinda 219
Clement, Julian Deen 131
Clements, (?) 70, 195
Aleph Sikes 195
Alva Edison 195
Ben Harvey 195
Collier Leon 195
Elizabeth 153, 413
Elizabeth (Mrs.) 413
Fred Julian 195
G. M. 195
Gabriel McArrol 195
Henrietta 195
Jennie 144, 145
Leroy Hamilton 195
Mamie Gertrude 195
William 413
Cleveland, Edna 399
Jacob (Sr.) 123
Mary 399
Milly 123
William Cromwell 399
Cliett, Burmah L. 454
G. H. (Rev.) 454
Cliff, William 395
Clift, Kerrenhappuch 395
Cline, Ambrazilla E. 1
Felix 1
Felix C. 1
Felix L. 1
Georgia C. 1
Hirschel E. 1
J. M. 1
John M. 1
John T. 1
Lola M. 1
Lyda Belle 1
Nancy M. E. 1
Sara Sue 1
Walter A. 1
Clinkscales, (?) 217
James Lawson 217
Reuben Pringle 217
Reuben Pyles 217
Clisby, A. W. (Rev.) 202
Clodfelter, Addie 224
Addie L. 224
Addy L. 225
Clopton, Mary A. 245
Clower, R. J. 292
R. J. (Dr.) 292
Coalson, Mary Elizabeth 283
Coats, Lydia 273, 319
Cobb, Cecil 445
Eldridge 68
Elizabeth Craig 68
George Calhoun 68
Harper Bivins 68
Howell 68, 152
Howell (Col.) 152
J. A. 68
J. B. (Maj.) 152
James 14
John A. 68
John Addison 68
L. H. 14
Lamar 68
Lucy Barrow 68
Lucy Middleton 68

Cobb (cont.)
M. B. (Mrs.) 68
Martha J. 14, 122, 129
Martha W. 129
Mary 14
Mary Ann 68
Mary Ann Lamar 68
Mary S. 152
Rebecca (Mrs.) 152
Sarah Pope 68
Wilson Lumpkin 68
Cochran, Frank 207
Martha T. 181
Cockreham, Ruth 22
Cocraham, Ruth 22
Cody, Abner M. 402
Abner McCormick 402
Emily Moore 402
Green W. 402
James 402
Mary (Mrs.) 402
Mary Hodo 402
Michael 402
Sarah Ann 402
Sina A. 402
Cofer, M. J. (Rev.) 410
Coffee, Elisha 122, 126
Elizabeth Francis 126
Eppy F. 126
John Alvin 126
John Morris 126
Milly 126
Polly 124
Sarah Ann 126
Cogburn, John A. 236
Coggin, C. G. 273, 274, 320
Columbus 273, 319
Columbus G. 273, 319
Daniel W. 274, 320
Frances M. (Mrs.) 273, 274, 320
Francis M. 273
James S. 273
James Silas 274, 320
Varina Davis 274, 320
Coker, Martha Mason 181
Cole, Alice (Mrs.) 266
Bessie Arline (Mrs.) 238
Caroline P. 57
Caroline S. 421
Edmund Daniel Shadrick 421
Elizabeth Jane 421
Emily Carr 421
Florence 238
Isaac Walter 421
James M. 421
James Madison 421
John N. 421
John Newton 421
L. P. 26
Lona P. 26
Lucy 420
Lula 421
Martha (Mrs.) 174
Mary L. 421
Mary Louvenia 421
Mary Susan 421
Oscar (Mrs.) 174
Pelina Caroline 421
Richard 265, 421
Richard Moses 266
T. B. 26
Tinie 26
Wallace Norton 238
William E. 421

Cole (cont.)
William Isaac 266
William M. 421
William T. 266
Coleman, Ann Eliza 160
Ann Elizabeth 73, 160
Asbury Richardson 160
Herbert Henry 160
J. C. 73
J. G. 73
Martha Jane 160
Nannie 221
Pleasant P. 160
S. L. 160
Sarah Jane 73
Solon L. 160
Solon Lychurgus 160
Thomas K. 160
Thomas Kennew 160
Coles, Alice 265
Coley, C. (Rev.) 75
Collens, (?) 277, 278
Elender 278
Elizabeth 198, 278
Isaac 278
James 278
John 278
Margaret 278
Rebecca 278
Susan 278
Colley, Eliza 179
Eliza. 449
Elizabeth 179
Elizabeth (Mrs.) 448
Frances 179
Francis 178, 448, 449
Gabriel 178, 179, 448, 449
George 27
John 178, 179, 448, 449
John Thomas 27
Lewis 179, 449
Lieusenday 179, 449
Louisa 178, 179, 448, 449
Mary 27, 178, 179, 448, 449
Mary (Mrs.) 27
Mary Ann Elizabeth 27
Nancy 178, 179, 448, 449
Nimrod 179, 449
Sarah 179, 449
Sebern N. 27
Sebern Newell 27
Spain 179, 449
Susan F. 26
Susan Francis 27
William Franklin 27
Zachariah 27
Collier, Amanda Virginia 457
Arra 269
Edith Louisa 457
Efford Cobb 457
Evelyn 455
Frances Elizabeth 457
Isaac C. 136
Isaac Cuthbert 136, 457
Jena 457
Jena Cuthbert 136
Louisa M. 457
Martha P. 457
Mary Ann Fletcher 457
Mary Booker 457
Obediah G. 136

Creighton (cont.)
Mary A. T. 69
Mary Ann Talula 70
Mattie 69
Mattie King 69
Sarah 70
Sarah Jane 69, 70
William 69, 70
William Alonzo 69, 70
Crenshaw, Annie E. 315, 316
Asa (Rev.) 79
Emmit R. 315
Emmitt R. 315
George M. 315
J. Whit. 315
Jesse 138
John M. 315
M. Eliza 315
Maryan Nancy 138
Miles 138
P. 314
Patience 138
Patience (Mrs.) 138
Pleasant 314, 315
Precious Cain 138
Susan (Mrs.) 315
Una M. 315
William Clinton 138
William Henry 138
Willie C. 315
Crews, Joseph Thomas 420
Thomas Grady 420
Crisson, (?) 204
Cromwell, Charles 202
Charles H. 202
Charles H. (Jr.) 202
Charles Hardeman 202
Marion Moultrie 202
Crooms, Elen 257
Fann D. (Mrs.) 257
John E. 257
John Newton (Mrs.) 257
Margaret V. 257
Marion Chaphaman 257
Richard F. Brown 257
Richard Frederick 257
Robert H. 257
Thomas B. 257
Crosby, Barbara 135, 391
Cross, Alice 280
Crossett, Helen 444
Croucher, Charlotte
Arthur 83
Crougher, Charlotte
Arthur 83
Crow, Elizabeth 185
Jesse 185
Judith Worsham 185
Nancy 185
Rachel 111
Rebecca A. 334
William 185
Crowder, Adeline E. A. 286
Adeline Eliza Ann 286
Anne (Mrs.) 286
Arabella M. 286
Arabella Matilda 286
Elizabeth G. 287
Elizabeth Hawkins 288
Frances Maria 286
John R. 287
Louisa Matilda 286, 287
Mark 286
Mark Thomas 286, 287
Martha 287

Crowder (cont.)
Martha Hawkins 286
Matilda 286
Mattie 287
Thomas 286, 287, 288
W. G. 287, 288
William Gustavus 286, 288
William Henry 287
Crowe, Alphonzo Mason 158
Augustus Haywood 158
Gray 158
John Green 158
Marion Josephine 158
Myry Henson 158
Saraugh Elebeth 158
Crowell, Isabella 22
Crowley, Ora Belle 445
Stan 408
Thomas D. 444
Crumbley, Allie J. 230
H. A. 230
Crutchfield, Albert (Mrs.) 240
Albert Alonzo 240
John Henry 240
Mary Francis 240
Robert Francis 240
Roberta Francis 240
William Edward 240
Cubbedge, Anne 373, 374
Aquer Roberta 313
Culbertson, David C. 309
Cullen, Honora 3
Culler, (?) (Dr.) 152
P. B. (Dr.) 152
P. B. D. H. (Dr.) 152
P. D. 152
Cullers, Celestia
Angeline 114
Culp, Peter H. 62
Culpepper, Absalom 39
Addie 263
Brooks 214
Brooks (Mrs.) 214
Charlie T. 39
Columbus C. 39
Cordealia A. 39
E. A. R. 39
Early G. H. 39
Francis Monroe 39
George W. 39
Henry H. 39
James 39
James M. 39
James Monroe 39
Janie 214
John H. 39
Julia 214
Julian R. 214
Martha A. R. 39
Mary A. 39
Mary F. 39
Matthew Gardner 214
Mattie Lou 214
Mercer 39
N. G. 214
Nancy 39
Nathan G. 214
Norah 214
S. B. 39
Samuel Bartley 39
Sarah Jane 39
William 39
Culver, Bell Louwill 78
Eliza (Mrs.) 239
Elizabeth Ann 239

Culver (cont.)
George 239
John L. 78
Cumings, Andrew 223
Cumming, Thomas 291
Cummings, H. 239
Harris 239
Cummins, Francis (Rev.) 39
Cunninghaam, Sarah 332
Cunningham, (?) 290
Albert 198
Emily 290
George 290
Jane 290
Joe 290
John 290
John Daniel 290
John David 290
Joseph 290
Leon W. (Sr.) (Mrs.) 198
Sally 290
William 332
Cunnington, Addie 21
Addie Lenora 21
Cunyus, Amanda 232
Georgia Oliver 232
James Prothro 232
John Floyd 231
Mary Ann 231
Mary Cordelia 231
Sophronia Louise 232
Walter 232
Waty 232
William 231, 232
William (Jr.) 231
William Henry 231, 232
Curry, John Edward 226
John M. 226
John Marshall 226
L. E. 216
Mary Alice 226
Mary Ellen 246
Mary Frances 226
Sarah Jane 226
Sarah L. 226
William Edward 226
Cush, Samuel 24
Cutts, W. C. 101
DIckson, Evie 250
Henrietta Helena 250
Jesse H. 250
Dabney, A. L. 163
Daisey, Mary Witt 182
Dale, Audie Cantey 41
Dalton, Imogene 441
Ishum 93
Nancy 93
Damas, Isabel 187
Danforth, R. B. 454
Daniel, (?) 71
A. E. (Mrs.) 290
Amanda 42
Ann (Mrs.) 290
Ann T. (Mrs.) 289, 290
Annie Maggie 2
Annie Margaret 2
Betsy 290
C. H. Pattie 2
C. J. 2
Caleb James 1
Cunningham 290
Eliza A. 290
Eliza Adeline (Mrs.) 290
Eliza Ann 290
Elizabeth Ann 289

477

Dickson (cont.)
Anna 251
Anne Allen (Mrs.) 251
Annie Allen 252
Annie Evans 250
Charles A. 251
Charles Allen 251
Christopher Columbus
  250, 251
Clayton 294
Crayton 294
David 249, 251, 252
David (Gen.) 250
David (Jr.) 251
David Albert 250
David Harris 251
David Manson 251
David Monroe 250
David Sumpter 252
Elisabeth C. 252
Elizabeth 251
Elizabeth Ann Riley
  250
Elizabeth Caroline 250
Elizabeth Posy 251
Henrietta Helena 250
James 251, 394
James C. 250
James Charles 250
James Otterson 250
Jesse H. 250
Jesse Hamilton 250
Jesse Lafayette 250
John 251
John O. 251
John Orr 251
John S. 250
John Sanders 250, 251
Julia Maria 251
Lucy (Mrs.) 231
Luna A. 294
Luna Arramenta 294
Manson 252
Martha 251
Martha (Mrs.) 251
Martha Jane 250, 251
Martha Letitia 251
Martha M. 250
Martha Marinda 250
Martha Perl 250
Mary (Mrs.) 251
Mary Ann 252
Mary F. 231
Mary Francis 231
Mary Tululah 250
Matheny 251
Matheny (Mrs.) 252
Michael 249, 251
Nancy Campbell 251
Nancy Eliza 251
Patsey 251
Patsey Ealse 251
Robert 252
Robert D. 251
Robert David 251, 252
Sarah (Mrs.) 249, 250,
  251
Sarah Ann Otterson 250
Sherman Glass 251, 252
Simeon 249
Thadeus Holt 250
Thomas Hyde 251
Thornton S. 251
Thornton Smith 251
W. Hugh 251
William 231, 251
William H. 250
William Hugh 249, 250

Dickson (cont.)
William Hugh Crawford
  250
William Wyatt 251
Zebulon Montgomery
  Pike 251
Dicus, America 44
Elisey Jain 44
Haner 44
Harrison B. 44
Jacob 44
Jacob B. 44
James E. 44
Kayziah 44
Milton 44
Rebecca Ann 44
William C. 44
Winfield 44
Dieffenderfer, Arlene
  Stadden 110
Barbara Ellen 110
Charles Augustus 110
Dora Alma 110
Henrietta Frances 110
M. N. (Mrs.) 107, 110
Maurice Newton 110
Thomas Elmer 110
Diffie, Marie 115
Dill, E. B. (Mrs.) 27
Dillard, Elizabeth 440
Elizabeth Emaly 275
Isaac 440
James 275, 440
Jane 275, 440
Jense 275
Marcha 440
Mary Varnon 275, 440
Nancy 275, 440
Nehemiah 440
Sarah (Mrs.) 440
Sarah Joice 275, 440
Sindy 440
Susan Oliver 293
Thomas 440
Dillars, Mary Ann 318
Dinwiddie, Mary Lee 14
Dirbin, Sarah (Widow) 24
Dismuke, Amanda Pearl
  139
Minnie Lee 139
Rosamond Cooper 139
Susan Maria 139
T. D. 139
William Haynes 139
Dismukes, B. J. (Dr.)
  176, 177
Benjamin Davis 268
Benjamin Ellison 177
Bennie D. 176
Bennie David 176
Camillus 177
David B. 177
Fannie E. 176
Finnie D. 177
Frances Perry 268
Garland Terry 268
Gillian Cooper (Mrs.)
  268
Henry M. 177
Ida 177
Ida J. 177
Ida Josephine 176
Jackey 177
James 268
James Cooper 268
Jimmie H. 176, 177
John C. 177
Joseph Leon 177

Dismukes (cont.)
Leon 177
Lewis Leon 177
Louis L. 177
Louis Leon 176
Lula V. 177
Lula Virginia 176
Martha Elizabeth 177
Mary C. 177
Mary Estelle 177
Mary Gertrude 177
Permelia T. 268
Regina A. 177
Sallie L. 176, 177
Samantha Edna 268
Sarah Williams 268
William henry 268
Diver, Paul B. 242
Dixon, A. J. 387
Barbara Nanette 387
Charles 387
Cora L. 153
E. C. 154
Erwin 387
Fremon (Mrs.) 383
Georgia Ann 153
Grissel 276
J. J. 153, 154
Jaculyn Annitte 387
Kathren Louise 387
Kathrine 387
L. A. 154
L. M. 454
M. A. 387
Marshall Lafayette 153
R. J. 153
R. M. 153, 154
R. T. 153
Robert 72
Robert Marshall 153,
  154
Robert T. 153
Ross 454
Thomas S. 153, 154
W. N. 153
Dobbins, Cornelia 290
Dobbs, Chas. 2
Ilah Maxine 97
Mary 189
Ulah Maxine 96
Dockins, Grovs 154
Hepsy Ann Ellard 154
Lillie V. 154
M. A. (Mrs.) 154
Walter 154
Dodd, S. (Rev.) 417
Dolvin, Jesse Frances 77
Donahough, John D. 234
Dooly, (?) 398
Dorsey, Martha 141, 302
Doster, Hanna 264
J. P. (Jr.) 115
Lucy S. 115
Pauline 115
Dottery, Faney C. 139
J. W. 61
James 139
John 139
John M. 139
John W. 139
M. E. 61, 62
Mary 139
Mary Elizabeth 139
Minia F. 139
R. J. H. 61
Robert J. P. 139
W. G. 61
William Green 139

Doucet, Germaine 191
Douglas, Isabel E. 154
  Isabel Elizabeth 154
  Susan Weakley 154
  Thomas 154
  Thomas (Sr.) 154
Dover, Emly Malinda 154
  Hillary J. 154
  Jason A. 154
  Martha 154
  Mary Caroline 154
Dowdy, Sallie A. 438
  Sarah Ann 56
Downing, D. B. (Mrs.)
  384
Downs, (?) 33
  Cora F. 33
  Cora Florence 33
  Cora Florence O. 33
  David 33
  Elizabeth E. 33
  Elizabeth Ellen 33
  Exa Cleo 33
  George W. 429
  Isabella F. T. 429
  John H. 429
  Leroy 33
  Lula Loretta 33
  M. E. 33
  Martha A. 33
  Martha Agnes 33
  Martha E. 33
  Martha E. L. 429
  Rhoda E. 33
  Rhoda Evie G. 33
  Talmadge L. (Sr.) 33
  Talmage L. 33
  Tinsy Ann 33
  Tinzy Ann W. 429
  W. M. F. 33
  Willis M. 429
  Willis Milligan
    Florence 429
  Willis S. 429
  Willis Shelly 33
Dowse, May W. 56
Doyle, John R. (Jr.)
  (Mrs.) 12
Dozier, Amanda F. 439
  Ann Elizabeth 439, 440
  Catherine 439, 440
  Catherine (Mrs.) 440
  Eliza 439, 440
  Elizabeth (Mrs.) 439,
    440
  Ezekiel 439
  Frances 439
  Francis 440
  James 439, 440
  James (Cpt.) 440
  James Thomas 439
  Jincy 439
  Lucretia 439
  Mary 439, 440
  Mildred Susan 439, 440
  Nancy 439
  O. T. (Dr.) 244
  Patsey 439
  Rebecca 439
  Sarah 439, 440
  Sarah Jane Virginia
    439
  T. F. 439, 440
  Tillman 439, 440
  Tillman F. 439, 440
Driskell, James Thomas
  155
  Joshua 155

Drummer, Tom 41
DuVall, Lois Burnette
  370
Dudley, (?) 419
  Alexis 418, 419
  Autas L. 419
  Daniel 418, 419
  David 418
  David E. 419
  E. J. (Mrs.) 164
  Florence A. 418, 419
  Florence M. 418
  Frances M. 418, 419
  J. T. (Mrs.) 104
  Joseph B. 419
  Martha (Mrs.) 419
  Mary A. 419
Duffie, Daniel (Rev.) 46
Dugan, Elizabeth L.
  (Mrs.) 172
  Lucinda 172
  William 171, 172
  William Rufus 172
Duggan, Arthur Haynes
  194
  Clara Lou 193
  Gladys Eudell 192
  Josee Lou 194
  Miriam 194
  Robert Clay 194
Duke, C. C. 420
  Charity P.? 317
  Charles Norman 213
  Elizabeth L. 317
  Eugene 420
  Henry T. 213
  James W. 317
  Jane 317
  John M. 317
  Lana A. 317
  Lucenda R.? 317
  Martha Jane 317
  Mary Elizabeth 317
  Nora Pearl 420
  Robert Green 317
  Sarah Katherine 317
  Thomas J. 317
  Vilett 317
  W. M. (Dr.) 16
Dumas, Mittie Clark
  (Mrs.) 108
  Thomas 457
Dunbar, Carrie Leola 108
  Daniel Edgar 108
  Daniel Engles 108
  James Andrew 108
  Lizzie Ella 108
  Maggie 108
  Mamie 108
  Mary Hannah Lake 108
  Nettie 108
  Opal May 108
Duncan, Alice Sophronia
  116
  Burwell A. 130
  Catherine 129
  Elizabeth Caroline 116
  Elizabeth D. 155
  Elminia L. 155
  George Alexander 116
  James 155
  James L. 155
  Jessey 155
  John 155
  John C. 116
  John Charles 116
  Louisa Oleva 116
  Maria S. 155

Duncan (cont.)
  Mary A. 14, 15
  Mary Alice (Mrs.) 362
  Mary Ann 116, 122, 155
  Matilda Adaline 116
  Nora K. 14
  O. M. 14
  Phebie A. 155
  Rebecca 155
  Robert 155
  Robert L. 155
  Sarah Mananr? 116
  Thomas Johnson 116
  Thomas M. 155
Dunlap, Cathy 424
  Enoch 424
  Esther 424
  Frances 246
  James 424
  John 424
  Mary 424
  Nancy 424
  Samuel 424
  Susannah 424
Dunn, Drury 117
  F. G. 163
  Martha 117
  Martha (Mrs.) 117
  Rebecca 117
Dunnigan, Lydia Cathrine
  345
Dunson, Lucy Angieline
  114
  Mary Lou 114
Dupree, Nancy A. L. 447
Durbin, Sarah (Mrs.) 28
Durden, Abijah T. 12
  Andrew Jackson 12
  Carolyn Flood (Mrs.)
    30
  David G. 12
  Elisha 12
  Ganaway 12
  George M. 12
  George Washington 12
  James J. 12
  John G. 12
  Katharine 12
  Mahaly (Mrs.) 12
  Mahaly Ebalelah 12
  Mahaly Ebalelah? 12
  Martha 12
  Mary Frances 12
  Mattie 12
  Nancy (Mrs.) 12
  Nancy Ann 12
  Nancy M. 365
  Reubin S. 12
  Warren J. 12
Durham, Ben Young 207
  Caroline 149, 150
  H. 150
  Hardy 149, 150
  Lillie Mae 207
  Lindsey 207
  Mary 150
  S. (Mrs.) 150
  Samuel 149
  Thomas Walton 207, 208
  Tommie Irene 207
  Vera 207
  Willie Ora 207
Durrance, Debbie Iona
  119
Dvis, Coalman 394
Dwight, Richard 18
Dye, Mary Elizabeth 352
Dyer, Amanda Luise 369

Dyer (cont.)
Laura Beatrice 232
Thomas 439
Dykes, Savannah 30
E.der, Courtney B. 336
ENgland, A. R. 18
Eady, (?) (Rev.) 219
Eaton, (?) 277, 278
A. B. Right 278
Amanda Ann 278
Buyan 277
Dan 278
Daniel 278
Elender 278
Elizabeth Cariean 278
Ellender 278
G. E. (Mrs.) 278
J. H. 278
J. W. 278
James 277, 278
James L. 278
James W. 277, 278
Margaret 278
Margaret Ann Ellender 277
Margaret Ann Ellen 278
Margret 278
Rebecca 278
Samuel Wesley 278
Stafford 278
William 278
Eavenson, John M. 128
Mearle 67
Thomas 128
Thomas M. 128
William Allen 128
Eberhart, David 139
E. A. S. 61
George W. 66
J. G. 115
J. M. A. 61
J. T. 61
J. W. 62
J. W. (Mrs.) 61, 139
Jacob 139
John 139
John W. 61
John Woods 61, 62
Joseph 139
M. E. J. 61
Mahala 61
Minia F. 62, 139
N. M. K. 61
R. G. 61
R. J. P. 62
R. P. 61
S. F. S. 61
S. P. 61
Susannah (Mrs.) 139
W. J. 61
Echols, Addie May 129, 130
Ann (Mrs.) 131
Ann Hill 130
Annie E. 205
Catherine 372
Catherine L. 205
Cathleen C. 205
Charles Henry 130
Elizabeth 251
Gaston T. 205
Geralding 205
Hattie L. 205
James Lee 205
John H. 130
John Hill 129, 130, 131
John Hills 131

Echols (cont.)
Katherine V. 205
L. C. 205
Leila Pope 130, 131
Maggie M. 205
Mattie L. 205
Obadiah 373
Oliver C. 205
Sallie Strong 130
Sarah J. (Mrs.) 130
Sarah Jane 131
Sarah Strong 129
Wattro? 131
Willie A. 205
Edge, Albert 101
Albert R. 14, 101
Alberta Rosalyn 101
Artha Lee Della 101
Carry Lela 14, 101
Clara Kate 454
Dora Etta 14, 101
Dora Isabella 101
Henry Tipton 14, 101
Isabella E. 14
James Butt 454
James F. 101
James Filmore 101
James P. 14, 101
James Pomeroy 14, 101
Jesse K. 454
John Miller 454
John V. 454
John Valentine 454
Martha Patterson 454
Martha Patton 454
Martin Kolb 454
Mary I. 454
Nellie 101
Orris E. 14, 101
Orris? Elbert 101
Peter William 454
Robert L. 14, 101
Robert Louis 14, 101
Sarah Octavia 454
Stella L. 101
William Alonzo 101
Edgelly, Mary 38
Edgely, John Thomas 38
Edgerton, M. W. (Rev.) 13
Edmondson, Augustus P. 376
Dora A. (Mrs.) 150
Dora N. 150
Elisabeth 376
Ella N. 150
George W. 150
William 376
Edmonson, Jane 262
John 262
Joseph 262
Mary Ann 262
Mary Thomis 262
Nancy Ann Rebecca 262
Rebecca 262
Seala An 262
Thomas 262
Edward, Charlie 26
Edwards, Amanda 401
Acrean Mahala 398
Alonzo Norval 398
Alphonso Cassidy 385
Andrew Martin 241
Annie 78
Annie Charlotte 241
Bryan 183
Charles Henry Francis Marion 398

Edwards (cont.)
Clark 67
Crawford Brown 312
Dooly 398
Duncan McCowan 398
Edward Lee 398
Elizabeth Corning 183
Elizabeth Winifred 183
Ellen Findley 183
Emeline 288
Emily Brown (Sr.) (Mrs.) 183
Essie 241
Essie Evaline 241, 244
Eugene Esther 398
Eugene Jackson 241
Fannie 241
Gordon Lowe 398
Hannah (Mrs.) 390
Isabella Ann 398
J. H. 280, 281
James Byrd 398
James Wilson 183
James Wilson (Sr.) 183
Jesse H. 281
John Crawford 398
L. M. 281
L. N. 280, 281
Lucile 241
Lucy J. (Mrs.) 331
M. A. 280, 281
M. R. 280
Maria E. 280
Mariah R. 281
Mariah Rebecca 281
Martha Cinderella 398
Mary (Mrs.) 241
Mary Elizabeth Ida 398
Mary Lane 312
Nancy 281
Nancy S. 281
Nellie 183
Prentiss Stillwell 312
Prentiss Stillwell (Jr.) 312
Richard S. 183
Sarah Frances 241, 244
Sarah J. 176
Susan 183
Talmadge 241
Telulah Ellen 398
W. H. 280
W. S. 238
Warren 240, 241
Will Miller 241
William T. 86
Eidson, Arthur W. 140
George P. 140
Hattie L. 140
James Ernest 140
James K. 140
John Deward 140
Mary Blanche 140
Maudie 140
Minnie R. 140
Wilmot K. 140
Elder, Alice (Mrs.) 140
Amanda M. 61
Anna Rubie 336
Aveann 61
Charlie E. 336
Christian B. 61
Clara Lee 140
Cora L. (Mrs.) 140
Cortney B. 335
Courtney B. 336
David 61
David G. 61

Goss (cont.)
Nathaniel H. 44
Nathaniel Harbin 44
Nathaniel Jackson 44
Orpha Louisa 44
Robert Lewis 44
Silas Washington 44
Wilson Lumpkin 44
Goulding, Francis (Rev.)
82
Thomas (Cpt.) 373
Grace, Charles Clay 15
Frank 16
Graddick, Etta 387
Graddy, Ida Nell 191
W. M. 191
William Mercer 191
Grady, Agnes Louisa 57
Annie King 57
B. G. 431
Elizabeth Ann 57
Harriet Matilda 57
Harriet S. 57
Henry 57
Henry C. 57
Henry F. 216
Henry Woodfin 57
Jesse B. 57
John W. 57
Lillia D. 57
Louisa W. 57
Martha Nicholson 57
Sarah M. 57
William G. S. 57
William S. 57
Grafton, Cassandra 222
Graham, Annie T. 332
Armistead 332
David 332
David F. 332
George T. 332
John 332
John William 332
Josiah 332
Lucy C. 332
Martha B. 332
Mary 332
Mary Jane 332
Matilda 141, 430
Net 403
Rhoda T. 332
Sara F. 332
Sarah Ann 223
Serena 332
Serena E. 332
Susan Pinkney 332
William 332
Granade, Thomas Emmett
115
Granger, Berter 279
Graves, Augustus R. 89,
430
Cyrus 4
Elizabeth A. 89, 430
Spencer 4
Varney 362
Gray, Ann (Mrs.) 142,
367
Anna (Mrs.) 142, 367
Betsy 367
E. A. (Rev.) 360
Elizabeth 142, 367
Evaline 142, 367
Frances Ann 142
Francis Ann 367
George 142, 367
Jeremiah G. 142, 367
Jeremiah Griffin 142,

Gray (cont.)
367
Jeremiah Griffon 367
John 269, 318
Josephine 429
Mary Clyde 222
Nancy Guttrely? 367
Naomi (Mrs.) 142, 367
Rachel 367
Susannah 367
Susannah Caroline 142,
367
William 142, 367
Graybill, Francis 231
George Washington 231
Henry Thomas 231
Jesse G. B. 231
Jesse Goodwin Butts
231
Jessie Julia 231
Judith (Mrs.) 231
Leonidas Josephus 231
Mary Jopetra 231
Michael 231
Michael Hamilton 231
William 231
Graybille, Jesse G. B.
232
Green, (?) 70, 351
(?) (Rev.) 362
A. E. A. 287
Adeline E. A. 288
Adeline E. A. Crowder
288
Adeline Eliza Ann 286
Adie 287
Anna Maria 288
Armenda Jane 264
Bud 330
Charles 264
Charlotte Rebecca 264
Dicy 23
Eason 156
Fannie J. 288
Fannie Joseph 287
Franklin 260
George Washington 264
Hannah 392
Howell Cobb 415
James Jefferson 264
James M. 330
John E. B. 264
John Linton 282, 283,
285, 287
John Linton (II) 283
John Linton (Jr.) 285,
287
John linton 285
Josiah Franklin 264
L. J. 330
Lucile Linton 285, 287
Lucy Ann Elizabeth 264
M. W. 260
Martha C. 288
Martha Crowder 286
Mary Ann 135
Mary Elizabeth 45
Mary Elizabeth Hawkins
286
Mary H. 286, 287
Mary H. (Mrs.) 287
Mary Hawkins 288
Mary Martin 264
Mary Matilda 264
Mattie C. 287, 288
Millie Ann 156
Nancy Adaline 264
Palice 330

Green (cont.)
Sarah 93
T. F. (Sr.) (Mrs.)
285, 286
Thomas F. 286, 287
Thomas F. (Jr.) 288
Thomas Fitzgerald 283,
285, 286, 287
Thomas Fitzgerald
(III) 282
Thomas Fitzgerald
(Jr.) 283, 285, 286,
287
Thomas Fitzgerald
(Sr.) (Mrs.) 282
W. G. 330
W. J. 330
William Henry 287
William John 286
Willie J. 288
Greene, A. A. A. 417
A. L. 417
Amanda 136
Amanda Fletcher 457
Amanda Lucretia 417
Arabella L. 417
Arabella Loretta 417
Avy Ann A. 417
Eliza Jane 417
John H. 417
L. C. 417
Leonora C. 417
Lucy Ann Lavonia 417
M. Callie 417
M. Ella 417
Malissa N. A. 417
Martha Ellen 417
Mary H. 417
Nelly 417
Patience (Mrs.) 457
Thomas Jefferson 417
Thos. 457
William J. 417
William T. 417
Greening, Alabama Eliza
381
Susan Reece 381
Greer, A. D. 334
Abraham Dinet 334
Alvin Eugene 106
Ann (Mrs.) 152, 334
Ann Atkins 335
Ann R. 322
Ann Sophronia 334
Aquila 376
Aquilla 311
Aryan H. 322
Bartley 152, 153
Ben 152
Bethna 322
Betsey Ann 376
D. J. 334
Delia 311
Delila 334, 335
Delila Jane 334
Ebenezer 376
Elisha 376
Erasmus Jeremiah 334
Ernest 106
Ernest Willie 106
Frances M. 280
Franklin (Jr.) 280
Fred Theodore 445
George T. 322
Gerard Martial 334
Gilbert I. 322
Guy W. (Dr.) 322
Henry 334, 335, 376

Greer (cont.)
Henry F. 322, 334, 335
Henry Foote 334, 335
Henry Franklin 334
Henry Marshall 334,
335
Howard Jackson 106
Ira J. 322
Ira R. 322
James 106
James H. 334, 335
James Nathl. 106
James Ragan 334
Jerry 152
Jesse 376
Jewel Beatrice 106
John Jasper 334
John N. 322
Lucy 376
Lula Matilda 106
M. E. A. 334
Martha J. 322
Martha Stephens 76
Martial Ragan 334
Mary 334
Mary Eugenia 334
Mary M. 322
Nancy 376
Olin 106
Olin Legree 106
Rhoda (Mrs.) 453
Richard Foote 334
Robert 453
Rubie 106
Rubie Lee 106
Sally 152, 376
Sam 152
Sarah 152
Sarah A. 322
Sarah Mildred 334, 335
Susan 152
Susan P. 453
Susie Calahan 334
Thomas Gill 152
W. O. 106
William 311, 334, 335,
376
William Franklin 335
William Jefferson 106
Willmirth A. 322
Wm. Amariah 334
Wm. Caloway 334
Wm. Franklin 334
Gregory, Caroline
Elizabeth 73
Elijah 391
Ephraim 109
J. G. 73
John C. 73
John C. (Cpt.) 73
Grenade, Adam 260
Gresham, John 189
Leola L. 412
Martha (Mrs.) 189
William 439
Grier, --eth 84
--obert 84
A. M. (Mrs.) 85
Aaron 84, 85
Adaline 85
Adeline 84
Aron 83, 84
Calvin 83
Eliza 84
Elizabeth 83
Elizabeth (Mrs.) 84
H. K. 85
I. D. 85

Grier (cont.)
I. H. 84, 85
I. M. 85
I. O. 85
Isaac 83, 84, 85
Isaac (Rev.) 84
Isaac H. 84
Isabella 85
J. N. 85
James M. 84
James R. 84, 85
Jane 84
Jesse H. 84
Judith 84
Judith E. 85
L. I. 85
M. A. (Mrs.) 85
M. P. 84
M. S. (Mrs.) 84
Margaret 84
Marion 95
Martha Ann (Mrs.) 85
Mary 83, 84
Mary (Mrs.) 84
Melvina B. 84, 85
Polly 83, 84
Polly (Mrs.) 84
R. L. 85
Robert 83, 84, 85
Robert (Jr.) 84
Robert Alexr. 84
Robert L. 84
W. B. 85
William B. 85
William P. 84
Grieve, Calendar
McGregor 95
John 95
John (Jr.) 95
Miller 95
Griffeth, Ann Woods 139
Griffin, (?) 269
A. B. (Mrs.) 352
Amanda Gordon 145
Burten B. 145
Elizabeth 405
Elmer 269
Fanny R. T. 145
Fletcher W. (Mrs.) 428
Gordon B. 145
Harriet 405
Harriet (Mrs.) 405
J. B. 454
James C. 405
John 404, 405
John H. M. 145
Kathryn 208
Laura Armstrong 145
Little Asa Smith 269
Little Vera 269
Margaret A. E. 145
Mary Adline 330
Mary Ann 145
Mary H. 145
Samuel C. 405
Samuel Conner 405
Shepard 145
W. B. 269
Waldon W. 145
Wiley F. 145
William E. 145
Griffith, George E. 61
James Beatty 47
Griggs, Nancy 308
Grimes, Benjamin
Franklin 241
David L. 173
Emma Lee 241

Grimes (cont.)
James 46
James Carlos 241, 248
James Monroe 241
John Rivers 241
Lena Rivers 241
Lilias Amanda 74
Margaret Lee 248
Martha Davis 241
Mary W. (Mrs.) 241
Mattie 241
Oscar Harper 248
Pearl Bell 241
Pearle Belle 241
Velma Louise 248
Grizel, Sarah 28
Grizzle, Sarah Jane 427
Groover, Agnes A. 145
Amanda R. 145
Ann Cornelia 210
C. E. 145
Charles E. 145
Daniel R. 145
James Bulloch 210
Julia E. 145
Samuel E. 145
Saphina R. 145
Sarah R. 145
Sarah R. (Mrs.) 145
Grovenstein, Elizabeth
(Mrs.) 30
Rebecca 30
Grovenstine, Hannah
Catherine 393
John Justus 393
Lydia 393
Mary 393
Mary Reisser 393
Naomi 393
Salome 393
Susannah 393
Grubbs, Florence Matilda
146
Francis E. 146
John R. 146
Guerard, Catherine 40
Norma Frances 97
Guilford, Waty 231
Guise, Prudence 113
Gunn, John C. 331
Lucy E. 331
Oliver H. 331
Ollia A. 331
Susan Douglas 154
Gunnels, Arie C. C. 234
Gunnels?, A. J. 234
Gunter, J. C. 64
J. J. 64
James J. 64
James Weyman (Jr.) 64
Jerusha Caroline 64
John G. 64
John J. 64
M. E. 64
Mahala Emeline 64
Martha B. 64
Martha Bush 64
Mary A. 64
Mary Ann 64
S. F. 64
Sarah Frances 64
Susan Sophia 64
Theophilus H. 64
W. H. 64
Weyman (Dr.) 64
Weyman T. (Dr.) 64
William Henry 64
Wm. Henry 64

Harper (cont.)
Nancy C. 122
P. W. 78
Peterson W. 78
Peterson W. (Dr.) 78,
  79
Pleasant Marvin 267
Precious Lillian 235
Robert Goodloe 79
Rodrick 267
Ruth Berrien 81
Selma May 235
Uel 267
Harrell, Catharine 146
Elizabeth 146
Elizabeth (Mrs.) 146
Elvey 146
Isaac 146
Joanna 146
John W. 146
Levi 146
Levi H. 146
Lovett L. 146
Lula 393
Nancy 146
Needham M. 146
Polley 146
Samuel 146
Sarah 146
William 146
Wright W. 146
Harrington, Jeptha 153
Harris, Ann R. 56
Anna 343
C. W. (Mrs.) 184
Clara 399
Daniel 160
Doris Lorene 445
E. C. 342
Earnest Blake 201
Elizabeth Jane 127
Emily Alice 443
George H. 56
Henry (Mrs.) 129
Henry Herman 373, 374
Henry Moss 374
Isabel 83
J. L. 436
James Arthur 201
James W. 56
Jeptha V. 49, 56
Jesse M. 234
Jessie 436
Jessie M. 234
John Emory 201
John Martin Vincent
  127
Joseph M. 332
Little John 269
Lula Alberta 201
M. E. 260
Mable 242
Margaret L. 343
Martha Emily 127
Mary 452
Mary Emily 374
Ophelia C. 217
R. 440
Rebecca 130
Robert 440
Robert S. 104
Ruben Thomas 127
Russell W. 445
Samuel A. 201
Sarah A. 146
Sarah E. 49, 50, 56
Sarah N. 41
Sarah Naomi 41

Harris (cont.)
Sarah Smith 160
Thomas Marcus (Rev.)
  160
W. M. 436
Wade (Mrs.) 436
Wallace (Mrs.) 256
William 104, 146
William H. 146
William J. M. C. J.
  234
William Jesse Marion
  Christopher Jackson
  234
William L. 56
Harrison, Alfred 196
Earl Dunbar 62
Elizabeth L. 452
Eva Elsie 197
Evelyn Margaret 197
John 314
Letitia 196
Lillie Allen (Mrs.)
  164
Martha I. 2
Moss (Mrs.) 196, 197
Polly 122
Thomas Wesley 196
Wesley Moss 196, 197
Harriss, Benjamin 104
Henry 104
Mary 104
Nancy (Mrs.) 104
Sarah 104
Thomas 104
William 104
Hart, Irma Ragsdale 180
Wheeler 213
Hartley, Daniel 112
Ellen 112
Lewis 112
Hartman, Ruby McGowen
  253
Harvel, Kiziah 341
Malissa Ann 341
Harvey, Elizabeth 381
Mary 429
S. (Rev.) 417
W. D. 201
Harvis, James 65
Hatcher, Amanda 411
Anice Virginia 411
Benjamin L. 411
Caroline Amanda 411
Caroline F. C. 411
Charity A. S. 411
Cicero 411
Elizabeth 411
Francis Narcisa 411
Henry 411
James 411
James C. 411
Jeremiah B. 411
John 411
John (Sr.) 411
John T. 411
John W. 411
Josephine Sarah 411
Margaret 411
Margaret A. 411
Martha O. 411
Mary 411
Maryann 411
Nancy 411
Nancy E. 411
Nancy T. 411
Nannie S. E. 411
Obedience B. 411

Hatcher (cont.)
Patience M. A. 411
Polly 411
Reuben T. 411
Reubin S. 411
Reubin Sanders 411
Robert 411
Robert H. 411
Sallie A. E. 411
Samuel B. 411
Sarah A. E. 411
William G. 411
Hausemann, Anna Marie
  211
Hawker, Isaac 446
Hawkins, Amoretta F. 117
Ann 194
Annie G. 117
Annie Glorianna 117
Benjamin (Col.) 193
Benjamin F. 194
Charles A. 117, 342
Charles Alexander 117
Delia 194
Delia (Mrs.) 193
Eleanor 194
Elinor 193
Eliza Crowder 286
Elizabeth 287
Emily S. 117
Emily Sophia Ann 117
Frances Mariah 287
Frank 194
Geo. Washington 194
Hamlin H. 288
Hardrus 287
John 286, 287
John (Gen.) 287
John (Sr.) 287
John Milner 117
Joseph 194
Lucinda David Ruffin
  194
Lucy 194
Lucy (Mrs.) 194
Martha 288
Martha Josephine 209
Mary 287
Mary (Mrs.) 286
Mildred 194
Peter 36
Philemon 193, 194
Philemon (II) 194
Pilemon 194
Sarah 194
Thomas H. 117
Thomas I. 117
Thomas Ira 117
Thomas P. 194
Vane G. 14
William 194
Willie R. 288
Hawks, C. E. (Mrs.) 335
Lulie 335
R. H. 335
Hay, Sarah 435
Hayes, John Q. 288
Sara Frances 27
Sarah F. 27
Haynes, Anna Sophia 139
Delia 311
Delia (Mrs.) 302
Delia Ann 302
Elizabeth 310
Henry 310, 311
Jasper 311
John Phelps 302
Lucy P. 54

Haynes (cont.)
Lucy Phelps 54, 302
Maria (Mrs.) 139
Nancy 310
Parmenas 302, 310, 311
Parmenas (Cpt.) 310
Polley 311
Polly Eliza 302
Richard 310
Richard Parmenas
  Jasper 302
Robert 310
Robert Henry 302
Salley 311
Sarah Jane 302
William Glenn 302
Wilmer C. 144
Zachariah 137, 139,
  158
Haynie, Addie A. 2
  W. C. 436
  William 436
Hays, (?) 203
  Edward B. 338
  J. B. 338
  J. R. 338
  J. S. 338
  Jacob 338
  Nancy 338
  S. L. 338
  William F. 338
Haywood, Sherwood 193
Head, A. J. 29
  Adline P. 30
  Adline Persiler 29
  Andrew J. 29
  Apsyllah T. 227
  Barnard Carol (Maj.)
    86
  Charles C. W. 30
  Charles J. 87
  Charles P. Mannon 29
  Christer Amanuel 29
  Christopher 29
  Cinthia? 29
  Eizabeth V. 227
  Elizabeth 29
  Elizabeth (Mrs.) 86
  Elizabeth Catherine 29
  Elizabeth Varner 148
  F. M. Beauregard 29
  Flourida Josephine 29
  Frances M. Beauregard
    29
  Georgia Ann Louisa 29
  James A. 29, 30
  James J. 227
  James L. 227
  James W. 197
  John Adams (Gen.) 86
  John H. 29
  John Lanier 86
  John R. 29
  Joseph H. 30
  Joseph Henry 29
  Laura Eleanor 30
  Malinda Ann 29
  Malissa 29
  Maran 29
  Margaret M. 29
  Mary Ann Malissa 29
  Mary Ann S. 29
  Misourie Viola 29
  Pitt M. 227
  Polly M. 227
  Richard 29, 30
  Richard A. 29
  Richard H. 29

Head (cont.)
  Sarah Elizabeth 29
  Shearman 29
  Sherman 29
  Susan Amanda 29
  Susan Amandrill 30
  Susannah 29
  Susannah B. 29
  Susannah Manda 29
  William Layfett 30
Headen, Daniel Bush 437
  Julia F. 58
  Lydia 437
Heaner, Addie Louise 45
Heard, (?) 85, 86
  (?) Coleman 116
  Abraham Faulkner 88
  Ada Gertrude 86, 197
  Almira Ann 88
  Amanda Malvina 87
  Ann (Mrs.) 71
  Annie May? 1
  Barnard 88
  Barnard Carol 86
  Benjamin Pope 347
  Besty 122
  Betsy 122
  Betsy (Mrs.) 86
  Bridge Carol 86
  Caleenah America 88
  Caroline M. 87
  Catherine M. 87
  Charles 85
  Charles C. 87
  Charles F. 86
  Charles Jackson 87
  Charles L. 87
  Charles M. 88, 116
  Charles McHolton 116
  Charles Stewart 114
  Cintha Elizabeth 85
  Cinthia E. 86
  Claudine 86, 197
  Columbus 347
  Cordelia Elizabeth 88
  Daniel Coleman 116
  David Woodson 88
  Delena 86
  Dorah A. 86
  Eleanor E. 87
  Eleanor S. 87
  Eleanor Silverster 87
  Elinor (Mrs.) 87
  Elizabeth 85, 88, 98
  Elizabeth (Mrs.) 88,
    116
  Elizabeth E. 87
  Elizabeth Emily 347
  Ezerbelan? 116
  Frances Ann 71
  Francis Ann 347
  Franklin 347
  George 347
  George C. 98
  George W. 87
  George Washington 86
  Grady T. 1
  Gustavus Peeples 88
  Henry 347
  Hugh H. 87
  Isabella I. 87
  James M. 1
  James Monroe 1
  James W. 86, 87
  James Willis 347
  Jane Lanier 86
  Jesse 85, 86
  Jesse A. 85

Heard (cont.)
  Jesse Anderson 85
  Jesse W. 85
  Job? 1
  John 88
  John Adams 86
  John G. 88
  John Germany 88
  John J. 87
  John Jasper 87
  John M. 1
  John W. C. 87
  John Washington
    Columbus 87
  Joseph 1
  Joseph Collumbus 88
  Joseph Curtis 1
  Joseph Roy 1
  Joseph Sanford 87
  Joseph Stephen 85
  Julyann 87
  Lewis Washington 87
  Lilliam Lee 86
  Lillian lee 197
  Louisa Amanda 87
  M. A. 1
  Margaret Delaney 70,
    347
  Margrett Forgason 88
  Marshall Peeples 88
  Martha 85
  Martha A. 86
  Martha Angeline 347
  Martha J. 86
  Martha Jane 85
  Martha Nobles 87
  Mary 84, 88, 116
  Mary Ann 87
  Mary Elizabeth 114
  Mary Frances 88
  Mary M. 1
  Melissa Ann 1
  Nancy Mary Emeline 1
  Nannie M. E. 1
  Patsy Burch 86
  Patton Alanson 88
  Permelia Darden 86
  Polly (Mrs.) 88
  R. S. (Mrs.) 28
  Rachael E. 1
  Rachel Elisabeth 1
  Richard 116
  Richard (Cpt.) 116
  S. E. 1
  Sabrina Catherine 88
  Sarah 85
  Sarah Hammond 86
  Sophrona M. 89
  Sophronia Massy 88
  Stephen 86
  Stephen (Col.) 86
  Stephen B. 85
  Susan Elisabeth 1
  Susan Elizabeth 1
  Susannah 87
  Thomas 71, 88, 347
  Thomas Amiruns 88
  Thomas Jefferson 86
  Virginia E. 216
  W. D. 1
  Willace A. 1
  William 86
  William Brady 88
  William Charles 85
  William Franklin 1
  William G. 87
  William M. 85
  William S. 1

Henry (cont.)
Robert 293, 294
Sarah Jane 414
Temperance 293
Theophilus 294
W. M. 414
William 294
William Edward Young
414
William Milton 414
Henson, Myry 158
Sara 333
Herndon, (?) 339
Bessie (Mrs.) 339
Catherine 122, 129
Clayton 339
John Walker 339
Larkin 24
Heronton, Mary H. 417
Herren, (?) 451
Barnie Almond 451
Bedford Forest 451
Bessie Matilda 451
E. F. 451
Elish Ford 451
Elisha F. 434
Helen Jeanette 451
James Ellis 451
James W. Elisha 451
John Walter 451
Lewis Oswell 451
Lillie Lou 451
Nick Willis 451
Pansy (Mrs.) 451
Pansy Louise 451
Robert Ford 451
Robert Lee 451
S. H. (Mrs.) 451
Sarah Helen (Mrs.) 451
Thelma Carolyn 451
W. E. 451
W. Joe 451
William Ellis 451
Willie Joe 451
Willie Joe (Jr.) 451
Herrin, Ann 240
H. B. (Mrs.) 151
Martha (Mrs.) 151
Herring, Alvin 243
Bettie J. 414
Billie Frank 207
Elijah E. 200
Elijah J. 200
Elijah Jefferson 200
Henry Bradley 200
J. A. (Mrs.) 200
John Newton 200
Mary A. (Mrs.) 200
Mary Ann 200
Mattie 253
Milton Thomas 200
Susan R. 174, 175
Herron, Albert Burton
190
Newton Rufus 190
Hersey, Ann 60
Isaac 60
Jane (Mrs.) 60
Hess, Emma 176
Hester, Abraham 219
Carwell 219
Carwell (Jr.) 219
Ella 219
Henry W. 219
Jeptha 219
Jeptha N. 219
Julia Ann 151
Louisa 219

Hester (cont.)
Malinda 219
Martha Foster 151
Mary Elizabeth 219
S. R. 219
Samuel R. 219
Steven Cloud 151, 204
Waddy Thompson 219
Hichols, William H. P.
388
Hicks, Aretus William
415
Catherine 415
Daniel 415
Edward 415
Emma 415
Inez Imogene 412
James W. 129
Jones 415
Lewis Beck 415
Lillian R. 434
M. L. 434
Milton jones 415
Rhoda L. 44
Susan S. 415
Walter T. 434
William Rufus 415
Hicky, C. Dan McHenry 95
Louise M. Daniel 95
Higgenbotham, Bailey
Joseph Dearly 220
Benjamine Thomas 220
Dosia James 220
Elijah Benson 220
Hester Lorene Melving
220
Jane Elizabeth 220
Jeptha B. 220
John Thornton 220
Lola Julia Caroline
Stanton 220
Mary London 220
Prissiler Frances 220
Reuben Crumley 220
Sarah Ann 220
Sarah S. 220
William Green 220
Higginbotham, Arnetta
218
Benjamine T. 221
John C. 221
John G. 220
Martha E. 221
Mary Jane 221
Parmelia A. 122
Sallie T. 221
Sarah Thornton 221
Sue J. (Mrs.) 225
Thomas B. 218, 221,
224
Thomas Benjamine 225
William B. (Mrs.) 221
William Bowers 221
Hight, Thomas G. 452,
453
Hightower, Daniel 355
Hiley, (?) 195
Anna Sophia 195
Barbary 195
Cathrina 195
Elizabeth 195
John 195
Mary Magdaline 195
Thomas 195
Hill, Ann S. 373
Ann Scott 129, 130
Byrd Lee 372, 373, 375
Clara 377

Hill (cont.)
E. L. (Rev.) 74
Edwin 66
Frank 332
George 156
Georgia 130
John 430
Margie 248
Mattie 42
Robert Pierce 368
Sandra 279
Sarah 99
Sarah Francis 26
Wutman C. 92
Hillin, Hester 407
Hillsman, Mollie (Mrs.)
244
Hilsman, Bennet 428, 429
Bennett 429
J. L. B. 429
James 429
Jasper 428, 429
Jeffrey 429
Jeremiah 429
John R. 429
John R. (Sr.) 429
Josiah 429
Judge 429
Margaret 429
Maria 429
Mariah 429
Martha 429
Martha Ada 429
Mary 428, 429
Mattie 429
Maud 429
Mildred 429
Minerva 428, 429
Myrtie 429
Rebecca 429
Hilson, A. H. 356
Anna Odom 356
Cleton 356
H. 356
Hetty 356
Hilrey 356
Laborn 356
Lency 356
Lucenda 356
Lucinda 356
Martha Ann 356
N. A. 356
P. W. 356
Pinkney W. 356
Rutha 356
Sarah Nancy Adelia 356
Hines, E. T. (Mrs.) 150
James L. 40
Kennith H. 102
V. R. (Mrs.) 40
Hinton, Amelia 202
Eliza Ritter 202
Fielder Lewis 202
Henrietta 233
James 202
James Whitfield 202
Jesse 202
Leroy 202
Lula 415
Melissa 202
Nancy 427
Polly Ann 202
Sophia (Mrs.) 202
Hixon, E. C. 382
Hoard, Annie R. 306
Fannie E. (Mrs.) 306
Ida Pauline 306
James Frank 306

Hoard (cont.)
Lucy Fannie 306
Nettie V. 306
Wiley C. 306
Hobbs, Adeline 400
Laura Cornelia 201
Hodges, Araminta
Elizabeth 302
Benjamin 346
Dave 302
David 302
Helen Jane 346
James William 302
Joseph 302
Josiah J. 346
Julia Abb 346
Lucy Mildred 383
Martha 302
Mattie (Mrs.) 227
S. A. E. 302
Susie Edna 119
William 25, 302
William Henry (Dr.) 53
Hodgson, Annie Preston
336
Hoehner, Joan 280
Joan Agnes 280
Hofman, David 46
Holbrook, Annie
Elizabeth 249
Cenia Lovine 249
Hannah Caledonia 249
John W. 249
Nancy Mahuldah 249
Samuel Asberry 249
Samuel Asbury 249
Sarah J. 249
Thomas C. 249
William B. 249
Holbrooks, J. E. 67
Holder, Martha V. 390
Holland, (?) 207
Amelia Brewington 147
Archibald 208
Arestus 147
C. L. 425
Calvin L. 425
Charles Hartwell 208
Cynthia 147
Dorothy Elizabeth 207
E. J. 329
Elizabeth M. A. 204
Elmina 147
George Washington 207,
208
Hannah 147
Hetty Cale 147
Isaac 146, 147
James 147
James Tom 206, 207,
208
John 146
Johnny 208
Julia Ann 147
Laurel Benjamin 207
Laurel Benjamin (Sr.)
207
Lula Ann 208
Lydia Camp (Mrs.) 207
Marguerite Evans 207
Maria Louisa 147
Marianne 207
Marie Eleanor 207
Mary 109
Mary Elizabeth 207,
208
Nancy 147
Orlando 147

Holland (cont.)
Roberta Francis 330
Samuel 146
Samuel Marion 208
Silas Casey 208
William 147, 208
Willie Jeannette 207,
210
Hollinshead, (?) (Dr.)
195
Hollis, Clara A. 406
Thomas F. 42
Holloman, David 332
Merlyn 431
Hollomon, Addie L. 366
Addie Lee 336
Addie? J.? 366
Carrie M. 366
Edger S. 366
Elizabeth J. 336, 366
Emelin 366
G. W. 336
George W. 366
Heneretta E. 336
Heneretta Emeline 366
James A. 366
John 336, 366
John H. 366
John H. W. 366
John J. 366
Mary A. 336, 366
Mary E. 366
Mary I. 366
Mary S. 336
Miriam E. 336
Sarah 366
Sarah C. 366
Sarah E. 366
Seaborn E. 366
T. J. 366
Thomas J. 366
Tommy 366
Wilborn 366
William 366
William A. 336, 366
Hollon, Alice 24
Annie Lee 24
Bessie Ophelia 24
C. B. 24
Clifford 24
D. B. 24
J. A. 24
J. H. 24
James 24
James Andrew 24
Lily Mae 24
Mary Eunice 24
Myrtice Mann 24
William 24
Holloway, J. L. (Mrs.)
86, 87, 197
Hollway, James G. 120
James Holl 120
Holmes, Dora V. 7
E. A. 7
Edward A. 7
James C. 386
Malinda 386
Malinda M. 386
N. (Rev.) 46
Rebecca (Mrs.) 386
Robert H. 399
Sarah H. (Mrs.) 7
Holsten, Christina 102
Holt, A. F. 325
Abner F. 324, 325
Abner F. (Dr.) 325
Abner Flewellen 325

Holt (cont.)
Abner Flewellen (Jr.)
325
Abner Skelton 325
Abner Thurmond 324
Alberta 324
Alfred Charles 82
Ann Eliza 324
Ann L. 325
Ann Lane 325
Betsy 138
Charles Couch 324
Daniel Searcy 324
E. (Mrs.) 325
Edgar 324, 325
Edwina 109, 397
Eliza 325
Eliza (Mrs.) 324
Ella Lane 324, 325
Fannie 324
Flewellen 324
Ida 324
Ida L. 325
James Thweatt 324
Leon Kell 325
M. C. (Mrs.) 325
Margaret E. 325
Margaret Eliza 325
Martha C. (Mrs.) 324,
325
Martha Sarah Hines 325
Mary 82
Mary Victoria 324
Parthenia R. 325
Parthenia Raines 324
Philip Thurmond 324,
325
Phillip Thurmond 325
Ruth Lowndes 82, 83
Tarpley 325
Tarpley Lafayette 325
Temperance 414
Thomas Nesbitt 82
Thomas Wells 325
Thomas Wells (Jr.) 325
Virginia 82
William F. 324, 325
William Flewellen 324
William Flewellen
(Dr.) 325
William S. 325
William Simon 325
Wm. F. 325
Wm. F. (Dr.) 325
Wm. Flewellen (Jr.)
325
Holtam, (?) 316
Abner S. 315
E. S. 315
Elijah S. 315
Emeline 315
Emeline Jane 315
Emily Jane 315
Ira B. 316
Ira Clinton 316
Lenora B. 316
Leon Bly 316
Malind C. 315
Malinda C. 315
Mary C. 315
Mary Caroline 315
Minnie E. 316
Nancy (Mrs.) 315
Nece 316
Norman Shelton 316
Please A. 316
Sarah A. 315
Sarah Ann 315

502

Maken, Eliza A. 176
  Eliza Ann 176
Malcom, A. P. 162
  George W. 41
  Luise 349
  Mary 406
  Mary M. 41
  Nancy 349
  O. C. 406
  Susannah Allen (Mrs.)
    41
  William 349
Malcy, Hannah 52
Mallard, Ann Eliza 31
  Florida 32
  Mary Elizabeth 351
Mallon, Laura McClain
  359
Malone, Andrew B. 104
  Benjamin F. 149
  Cader 104
  Charles 71
  Elizabeth 104
  Emma Katie 104
  Eula Clide 104
  Floyd 104
  Francis 104
  Franklin 104
  Isam 104
  Jared 104
  Jeptha 104
  John 104
  Katherine 104
  Martha 104
  Martha C. 104
  Nancy J. 104
  S. 417
  W. F. 104
  Walker 104
  Weyman 104
  William 104
  Wm. Fleetwood Walker
    104
Mangham, Fred (Mrs.) 102
  Mary J. 386
  Wiley E. 386
  Willis A. 386
Mangum, Margaret Rebecca
  53
Mann, Asa 122
  Ava 406
  Betsey 121
  Betsy 123
  Charles S. (Mrs.) 404
  Daniel F. 14, 101
  Elbert 125
  Elizabeth 122, 123
  Elizabeth (Mrs.) 417
  Emma Claudine 417, 418
  Eppy White 125
  Eva Inez 417, 418
  J. W. 417
  James Jackson 125
  Janie 418
  Janie Wynette 418
  Jeptha 122
  Jesse 122
  Jesse Martin 125
  John Washington 125
  Judah John 125
  Lowal Mason 417, 418
  Lucy C. 165
  Luther E. 418
  Luther Eugeneous 417
  M. A. (Mrs.) 418
  Mary 417
  Mary Zeomy 418
  Milly White 125

Mann (cont.)
  Mittie (Mrs.) 417
  Naisai 125
  Nancy 121
  Nancy Kidd 125
  Ora Elizabeth 418
  Otis 417, 418
  Otis Ashmore 418
  Patsy 122
  Sintha Eliza 125
  Z. A. 418
  Zackaria Auston 417,
    418
  nancy (Mrs.) 122
Manning, Benjamin 161
  Nancy 161
  Pharaby (Mrs.) 161
Manry, Allen E. 392
  Allen Eugene 392
  Claud S. 392
  Florence A. 392
  Florence O. (Mrs.) 392
  Florrie Belle 392
  Irwin A. 392
  Lillie W. 392
  Mary C. 392
  Mary Luelle 392
  Robert F. 392
  W. A. 392
  Willard E. 392
  William C. 392
Manson, Joseph 308
  Phidelia Siler 308
Mapp, Rebecca A. 429
Marbut, Burr Johnston
  379
  Elizabeth 379
  Emaly Demasius 379
  Euclidas 379
  George Frederick 379
  Job Joshua 379
  John Ivy Boozer 379
  John P. 379
  John Pressley 379
  John Wesley 444
  John Wesley (Jr.) 445
  John Wesley (Sr.) 445
  Josephine Louisa 444
  Joshua 379
  Kezia 379
  Louisa Josephine 445
  Mary Icedare 379
  Mary Jane 379
  Robert Longshore 379
  Samuel Peace 379
  Sarah 379
  Sarah Ellizabeth 379
  Susannah Kerrene 379
  Terrell Clifford 445
  Young Joshua 379
Marchbanks, (?) 18
  Maryann 447
Marchman, Birdie 70
Marks, Ann 133
Marshall, (?) 71, 72
  Ann 71
  Ave 61
  Caroline M. 72
  Charles E. 62
  Elizabeth 72
  Elizabeth H. 72
  Harriet 72
  James 71
  James Franklin 72
  James Y. 25
  Jane 71
  Katie 71
  Lucy 71

Marshall (cont.)
  Lucy B. 72
  Margaret 73
  Margaret Ellen 72
  Martha 72
  Mary 71
  Mary Jane 72
  Nancy 72
  Rebecca 25
  Sarah 72
  Sarah N. 452
  Soucyann? 25
  Stephen 72
  Stephens 71, 72
  Sueky 71
  William 71
  William B. 72
  William H. 61
Marten, Thomas 106
Martin, (?) (Dr.) 107,
  410
  Alexander Sevens 107
  Andrew Barnett 410
  Annie W. 280, 281
  Annie Walker 281
  Asa 107
  Asa LaFayette 107
  Avlona Walker 281
  Brice 324
  C. C. (Mrs.) 373
  Carrie 410
  Carrie Lou 107
  Charlotte 178
  Claire (Mrs.) 333
  Clarence Curtis 410
  Doc 107, 410
  Elizabeth Ann 107
  Eunice Barney 281
  Evelyn Juanita 411
  Fannie 410
  Fannie Lee 410
  Fannie Ruth 281
  Gladys Frankie 410
  James J. 410
  Jane 228
  Janie Victorine 410
  John 225
  John B. 410
  John B. Wardlaw 107
  John Clark 107
  Joshua Franklin 107
  Laura Brawner 187
  Leila Janett 320, 321
  M. L. 411
  M. M. 411
  Mable Elizabeth 411
  Martha Ann 107
  Martha Sophia 107
  Mary 121, 411
  Mary Ann 107
  Mary Cornelia 97
  Mary Jessie 281
  Mary King 107
  Mary Louisa 107
  Mary M. 258
  Nathaniel W. 411
  Nathaniel Walker 107
  Norma Harriett 210
  R. L. 410
  Rachel 394
  Riddie Stevens 281
  Robert 120
  Robert (Rev.) 3
  Robert E. lee 107
  Ruby May 17
  Sallie 324
  Sara 411
  Sara Elizabeth 107

Mitchell (cont.)
Lilliam 390
Louisa 390
Louisa Owens 389
Mahallah (Mrs.) 389
Mahallah jane 389
Margaret 441
Mariah Jane 389
Mary Ann 389
Nannie B. 324
Oliver E. 59
Rebecca Thweatt 390
Rhoda E. (Mrs.) 189
S. C. 389
Samuel D. B. 149, 397
Sarah Elizabeth 389
Shatten C. 389
Susanna 283
Susie A. 386
Susie Aldora 386
Thacker Howard 389
Thomas Howard 390
Thos. Howard 390
Tirzah 140
William B. 189
William P. 389
William Thomas 386
Mixon, Annie Mae 335
Mobley, (?) 248
C. F. (Mrs.) 252
Carrie 247, 248
Hodges T. 247, 248
Jane R. 247
John Williams 247
Samuel Goode (Dr.) 248
William S. 247
William Simkin 248
Mogan, Mary Ann 388
Moncrief, (?) 1
A. A. (Mrs.) 2
Alethia 2
Annie Burchett 1
Caleb 1, 2
Caleb James 1
D. W. 2
Daniel Washington 1
David W. 2
Drury 1
Franklin 1
John Murray 1
Marion I. 1, 2
Marion Independence 1
Martha (Mrs.) 2
Martha Amanda 2
Preston Caleb 1
Robert 2
Robert M. 2
Robert Marshal 1
Virginia E. 2
Virginia Martha 1
Walter Ivey 2
William M. 2
William Manoah 1
Moncrow, Juler Cesar 153
Montgomery, Ann 74
Cynthia Ann 280
Sarah 396
Moon, A. 51
Almon R. 51
Ann (Mrs.) 360
Archibald 51
Camila 51
Daniel 360
Edom 360
Elizabeth 360
Elizeabeath 360
Grace 360
James 360

Moon (cont.)
Jemmy 360
Jesse 360
John 360
John E. 51
Johnney 360
Joseph 360
Joseph A. A. 51
L. B. (Jdg.) 255, 310
Lawrence 360
Leucrecher 360
Leucrecher (Mrs.) 360
Maray 360
Mary 360
Mary (Mrs.) 360
Mary A. E. 51
Maryann Elizabeth 51
Nicy (Mrs.) 51
P. W. 51
Philip W. 51
Rachel 360
Samuel 360
Sarah 360
Sary (Mrs.) 360
Susan C. 51
Thomas 360
Vicki 208
William 360
William M. 51
Mooneyham, Juley 338
Mary J. 337
Matty 338
Thomas B. 338
Moor, Elizabeth 91
Robert 91
Sarah (Mrs.) 91
Suffish 297
Moore, (?) 253
Alexander Stephens 253
Alice 147
Anna M. 133
Annie Lee 280
Brantley Hersekel 253
Buhl (Mrs.) 6
David 298
Elijah 122
Elizabeth 91, 382
Fannie 97
Fannie T. 96
Fannie Thweatt 96
Frances 96
George 96
H. D. 253
Harold T. 239
Henry Dawson 300
Henry Dawson (III) 300
Henry Newton 253
Henry lee 253
James Mell 253
Jane H. 86, 197
Jean Lee 217
Jessamine 253
Joe M. 239
John B. 95
John William 253
Kerrie Heather 300
L. M. 133
Laura V. 443
Lucie Graham 239
M. G. (Mrs.) 133
Magnolia Jane 253
Marshall Bland 239
Mary Elizabeth 253
Mary Lula 360
Nancy 65
Polly 305
Robert 91
S. V. 16

Moore (cont.)
Sara V. 16
Sarah (Mrs.) 91
Sarah Eliza 194
Thomas 96
Moran, Erick J. 368
More, Elizabeth 217
Moreland, (?) 355
Hannah R. 193
Joseph 193
Joseph F. 193
Mary R. 193
Mildred A. 193
Sarah H. 193
Susan T. 193
Thomas 193
nancy 245
Morgan, (?) (Rev.) 357
A. J. 275, 423
Allie Deborah 256
Amelia Ann 51
Andrew Jackson 51
Anna Belle 256
Annah Lee 371
Anslem L. 212, 426
Armelia A. 51
Asa H. 388
Asa W. 371
Asa Ware 371
Benjamin Franklin 51
Bessie Lorrine 24
Blake B. 51
Blake Brantley 51
Burton E. 212, 426
Caludia Sophronia 371
Charles Stokely 389
Christopher Columbus 51
Cora L. 212, 426
Cynthia S. 212, 426
Daniel M. 51
Daniel Moseley 51
Della D. 212, 426
Diatha E. 212, 426
Dilmus Marshall Jarrett 51
Easther Caroline 51
Elizabeth Jane 388
Ella 256
Elma J. 212, 426
Elma Jo. 212, 426
Emery A. 212, 426
Emery C. 212, 426
Emma Virginia 256
Emma Virginia Weaver 256
Esther Caroline 51
George Dales 51
Hannah Louise 388
Henrietta 256
Henry James 388
Henry Joseph 389
Hiram 371
Hugh D. 212, 426
Hugh D. (Jr.) 212, 426
Hugh Dean 212, 426
India 256
Isaac C. 212, 426
James Asa 371
James Polk 51
Jesse Cleveland 51
John Franklin 44
Joice Josephine 51
Joseph D. 212, 426
Joseph Dossett 426
Joseph L. 212, 426
Josephine S. 212, 426
Joyce Josephine 51

Morgan (cont.)
Kizziah 199
Lellea A. 212, 426
Lena D. 212, 426
Leola Young 256
Little Allie 256
Little Anna Belle 256
Little Ella 256
Lonnie L. 212, 426
Louisa Cass 51
Lucy Ann 275, 423
Luke John 388, 389
Martha Ann Elisa Jane 371
Martha L. 212, 426
Martha P. 212, 426
Mary Ann 388, 389
Mary Ann Deborah 371
Mary Park 212, 426
Melvin 371
Merit 132
Nancy E. 212, 426
Newton A. 212, 426
Newton H. 212, 426
Ora 51
Ora Kate 24
Orvin B. 212, 426
Robert J. 212, 426
Ruby 256
Sally M. 232
Sarah Corinthia 389
Sarah Elizabeth 371
Sarah Frances 388
Sarah Jane 388
Sarah Lucinda 51
Stokely 389
Stokely (Sr.) 388
Thomas Jefferson 51, 371
Thos. Jefferson 51
Vera J. 212, 426
Virginia C. 212, 426
W. H. 256
Watts 256
William 51
William (Sr.) 51
William Augustus 371
William Jessie 388
William Joseph 388
William Kesley 51
William Louis 388, 389
William Marcellus 51
William W. 51
William Wesley 51
Y. H. 256
Y. H. (Dr.) 256
Young Frederick Allen 371
Young Hiram (Dr.) 256
Moris, Patsy W. 124
Morrell, Abram 178
Morris, (?) 123, 128
  B. A. 434
  B. J. 434
  Benjamin Aron 434
  Benjamin J. 434
  Bolley 124
  Celestia Justina 434
  Elisabeth (Mrs.) 50
  Elizabeth (Mrs.) 50
  Elizabeth Heard 124
  Eppy W. 124
  Eppy White 124
  Franklin Ballenger 124
  G. G. 434
  George Glenn 434
  Georgia C. 434
  James 50, 122, 124

Morris (cont.)
James H. 234
James L. 234
Jane Arraminta 434
Jemima 50
John 50, 122, 124
John H. 447
John M. 124
Joseph 50
Lizzie E. 434
Lucy 122
Lucy W. 124
Martha Jane 434
Mary 50, 122, 126
Mary (Mrs.) 202
Milly White 124
Minnie Henrietta 434
Nancy 50
Patsy W. 124
Rebecah 50
Rebeckah 50
Richard 50
Salley 121
Sarah 123, 229
Sarah (Mrs.) 124
Stig 441
Susannah 124
Wiley 50
William 50, 122
William F. 434
Morrison, Ada 183
  Martha 418, 419
  Zollie 269
Morse, (?) 326
  Alexander 345
  Cathrine Elizabeth 345
  Florence Ellen 326
  Frank P. 326, 327
  Frank Rogan 326
  John Reid 326
  Mary Francis 326
  Mehitable 157
  Nannie Reid 326
Morton, Henry Clay 184
  John S. A. 184
  Josephine Isabel 184
  Lou 184
  Nell 106
  Nena 106
  William Jones (Col.) 184
  William M. 184
Mosby, Martha Ann 8
Moseley, Amy Augusta 110
  Arthur Jefferson 110
  Benjamine Richard 110
  Benny Thomas 253
  Janie 110
  John Henry 110
  John Wm. 110
  Lula Inez 253
  Malcolm Jos. 110
  Mary Ethel 110
  Robert Smith 110
  Sarah Jane 110
  Thomas Alphonse 110
  Wade Pauline 110
Mosely, Henry 350
  J. E. 242
  Rebeckah 350
Moss, (?) 374, 375
  Alex H. 375
  Alexander Hamilton 373
  Birdie Strong 372
  Cope Cubbedge 374
  David 375
  E. L. (Mrs.) 375
  Eliza Buckner 373, 375

Moss (cont.)
Elizabeth Luckie 373, 374, 375
Elizabeth Luckie (Jr.) 374
Georgia Anna Virginia 373
Green 268
James O. 375
James Oglethorpe 373
Jeremiah 123
John C. 372, 373
John D. 372, 373, 375
John Dortch 372, 373
John Dortch (III) 373
John Hill 373, 374, 375
John Martin 123
John Russell 374
Judith E. 374
Judith Elizabeth 373, 374
Judith Elizabeth Jay 373
Judith Elizabeth Joy 374
Julia Pope 373, 375
Lily 375
Lucinda 123, 129
Lucinda F. 14
Marguerite Eleanor 374
Martha M. (Mrs.) 373
Martha Strong 373, 375
Mary (Mrs.) 123
Mary Alice 373
Mary Catharene 374
Mary L. (Mrs.) 375
Mary V. 374
Mary Valentine 373, 374
Minnie Valentine 373
Nancy 374, 375
Nathl. A. 375
R. L. 373, 374, 375
R. L. (Jr.) 374
Rufus L. 130, 372, 373, 375
Rufus L. (Jr.) 129
Rufus LaFayette 373, 375
Rufus LaFayette (III) 373, 374
Rufus LaFayette (IV) 374
Rufus LaFayette (Jr.) 372
Rufus LaFayette (Sr.) 375
Sallie A. 373, 375
Sara Jane 374
Sarah A. 373
Sarah Hunter 372, 373
Susan M. 373, 375
Susan Strong 374
Thomas Stong 373
Thomas Strong 374
William Byrd 373, 374
William Lee 374
William Lorenzo 373, 374
Motes, Devie 209
  Lurline Muzette 18
  Robert 18
Motley, M. R. 28
Mountree, Rebecca 285
Moye, Agnes 193
  Cecil G. (Dr.) 193
  Duggan 193

Perkins (cont.)
Bettie 212
Bettie Miller 211
Clara S. (Mrs.) 212
Clars S. (Mrs.) 211
Emily Frances 160
Grief F. 211
Grief G. 212
James William 212
Martha Josephine 206
Mary Elizabeth 160
William Columbus 160
Perry, Augustus B. 397
Emeline 109, 391
Emeline P. 391
Evan P. 44
Ida Brown 262
J. M. 314
Job 109, 391
John W. 397
Julia Chisolm 16
Louisa 44
Louisa Jelene 397
Louise Jelene 397
Martha E. 397
Mary 265
Mary N. 191
Mary Nell 191
Michael W. 397
Peter 107
Sarah (Mrs.) 109
Sarah (Widow) 391
Sarah Ann Charlotte 397
W. W. 161
Perryman, (?) 167
Peters, Rebecca J. 412
Peterson, Amy 292
Fannie 448
Petiscord, Cenith A. 261
Pettus, John G. 282
Pferrer, Theodore 211
Pharr, Alexander 49
Camilla Oliver 49
Emma 49
Fannie Williams 49
Lizzie 49
Lorena Mae 444
Marcus A. 49
Marcus Aurelius 49
Permelia A. (Mrs.) 49
Sallie 49
Phelps, Eleanor (Widow) 39
Jane 302, 346
John 302
Lucy 310
Susannah (Mrs.) 302
Phillip, Charles Wesley 420
Phillips, (?) 420
Achibod 98
Aileen (Mrs.) 420
C. 104
Charles Wesley 420
Clark 420
Fel 193
Isaac Raymond 420
James (Dr.) 288
Minnor 193
Myrtle Irene 420
Rachel Gordie 420
Robert Clifford 420
Sylvia Gladys 420
Thomas Monroe 420
William 42
William David 420
Philpot, H. R. 413

Phinasee, Elizabeth B. (Mrs.) 269
Hiram 269
Phinazee, A. J. 269
H. 269
Harris 395
Hiram 269, 395
J. G. 269
Jane 269
John H. 269
Matt F. 269
Sarah Jane 269
Phinazoe, William H. 102
Pickens, J. R. (Rev.) 302
Pickett, (?) 130
Picmore, Hiram P. 401
Pierce, Charles L. 216
Cynthia 365
Levice 245
Lovic (Rev.) 381
Lovick (Rev.) 74
Pilcher, T. J. (Rev.) 7
Pilson, Anna 356
Pinkney W. 356
Pinckard, Jane 95
Thomas (Jr.) 95
Thomas (Sr.) (Cpt.) 95
Pinkerton, (?) (Rev.) 344
Pinkney, (?) (Rev.) 6
Pinson, M. S. 439
Mary 304
Miriam S. 440
Miriam Susan 439
Pittman, James M. 87
John G. 305
John Green 305
John Moore 305
Lillian 238
Lucinda Alama 87
Robert William Taylor 305
Pitts, Ann (Mrs.) 385
Elizabeth 355
James N. 385
Joshua 385
Sarah Jane 190
Plaster, Benj. 178
Pledger, Leana 304
Poag, Fred A. 327
Poe, Alfred 41
Gladys McCallister (Mrs.) 404
Samuel T. 41
Polk, Archibald L. 199
Berry Franklin 199
Charley Ellison 199
Elizabeth Malinda 199
Frances Jane 199
Georgia Ann Elizur Manerva 199
James Knox 199
Jemima Catherine 199
John Edmuns 199
Joshua Alexander 199
Leah Ellender 199
Sarah Ann 199
Pollard, Charles S. 27
Charles Smith 27
Charles William Newell 27
Martha A. 51
Mary Ann (Mrs.) 27
Ponder, Caroline Melissa 357
Pool, Elisha M. (Jr.) 186

Pool (cont.)
Judah Elizabeth 188
Poole, Elisha M. (Jr.) 186
Emma 186
Everag T. 186
Lila 186
Lucy Coffee 186
Minnie 186
Velma Snelson 114
Pope, A. F. 378
A. J. 80, 377
Alexander F. 378
Alexander Franklin 378
Alston B. 80, 377
Andrew J. 377
Andrew Jackson 80, 377
Ann Hill 378
B. 378
Benjamin H. 378
Benjamin Henry 378
Bur. (Gen.) 373
Burwell 378
Burwell (Gen.) 378
C. A. J. 300
Charles Burwell 378
Cheryl Ann 222
Comforte Eliza 80, 377
Cullen A. J. 299, 300
Daniel 80, 377
Dorothy Alexander 214
Dorothy Marilyn 200, 214
Edwin Elisha 378
Eva Ruth 230
F. M. (Mrs.) 80, 377
Fannie Boyt 230
Frank Alexander 373
Harris Miller 230
Henry 378
Henry Aug. 377
Herbert J. 299, 300, 301
Herbert Jackson 300, 301
Horace James 299, 300, 301
J. H. 378
James A. 299
James Chandler 300
James M. 300
Jennifer Anne 300
Joe David 300
John (Mrs.) 200
John Allen 80, 377
John Dozier 230
John Ellis 200, 214
John Ellis (Jr.) 200
John Ellis (Mrs.) 214
John H. 378
John Hardeman 378
John Ronald 200, 214
Julia Tabitha 378
Juliann Tabitha 378
Julliann Tabitha 378
Kathryn Angela 300
Laura 299
Laura Wynell 300
Laura Wynelle 299, 301
Lawrence Crawford 230
Lewis Alston 80, 377
Lewise Adams 300, 301
Louise Adams 299
Lucy (Mrs.) 68
Martha 378
Martha Ann 80, 377
Mary Alice 80, 377
Mary Allice 80, 377

517

See (cont.)
David Tillman 91
Emeline Elizabeth 91
George Winkfeld 91
Hartmell Harris 91
John 91
John Washington 91
Joshua F. 91
Laurenia S. 91
Lavina Bell 91
Levi P.? 91
Mary Ann 91
Mosses W. 91
Sarah Barthella 91
Seebach, Phillips (Mrs.)
  135
Sellars, Jack 4
Sellers, Drucilla 406
Semmes, Francis 56
Sessions, Leah 78
Sevens, J. C. G. 332
Sewell, Barbara Jean 15
  C. B. (Mrs.) 146
  James Charles 15
  John (Mrs.) 14
  John P. 15
  John Payne 15
  Lavina 445
  Lavina Orpha 444
  Peggy Mae 15
  Robert 186
  Sarah Ann 15
Seyle, Henrietta Maria
  339
Seymour, Harvey L.
  (Mrs.) 16
Sgrong, Addie Hill 131
Shackelford, Charles 428
  Elizabeth 428
  F. 428
  Jefferson 428
  John 428
  Judeth 428
  Judeth (Mrs.) 428
  Mary 428
  Nancy A. 428
  Philip 428
  Reuben F. 428
  Sarah 428
  Thomas J. (Mrs.) 362
Shackleford, Daniel 298
  F. (Sr.) 428
  Francis 297, 298
  George 298
  James 310
  Mary 298
  Sarah 298
  Willoughby 298
Shank, J. A. 253
Shankle, A. M. (Mrs.)
  383
  Eli 383
  Elisabeth 383
  Eritha 383
  James W. 383
  Levi M. 383
  Martha An 383
  Ophelia Amanda 383
  Pearl (Mrs.) 436
  Polly 383
  Rebecah (Mrs.) 383
  Seabarn McHendree 383
Shannon, Willie A. 244
Sharp, Chester M. 313
Shaumloffel, Mary
  Elizabeth 353
Shaw, (?) 290
  George Whitley 96

Shaw (cont.)
  James C. 176
Shearouse, Barnard
  Nesbiet 19
  Herman 19
Sheeflett, James 129
Sheffield, John 351
  John M. 351
  Mary H. (Mrs.) 32
  Pliny 32
  Sarah Ann Rebecca 351
  Susan M. 32
  Susan Mitchell 32
Shell, Benj. Allen 172
  Edmond 171, 172
  Emily Carr 421
  Emily E. (Mrs.) 172
  Esther Jane 172
  Hager 172
  Hariett (Mrs.) 172
  Harriet P. S. (Mrs.)
    172
  I. M. 172
  Isham 172
  Isham Abner Fletcher
    172
  Isham M. 171, 172
  Isum M. 172
  Ivery Isham Malone 172
  James G. C. 172
  John Abner Fletcher
    172
  John Abner Zaccheus
    172
  John Isom Columbus 172
  Laura Ann L. 172
  Lucy 172
  Lucy (Mrs.) 172
  Lucy Elizabeth
    Malviney 172
  Martha 172
  Martha Ann Elizabeth
    172
  Mary (Mrs.) 172
  Mary L. E. 172
  Mary Lee 172
  Mary Wright 171, 172
  Moses Andrew 172
  Peter Harvey 172
  R. H. 172
  Rebecca Antonett 172
  Ruffus 172
  Rufus 172
  Z. A. Z. 172
Shellnutt, E. F. 53
  Jack L. 445
Shelnutt, Alice 140
Shelton, Catherine Ellen
  44
  Elizabeth 17, 93, 435,
    437
Sheperd, Elizabeth 57
Shepherd, Elizabeth 421
Sheppard, Sophia S. 64
Sherman, Thomas C. 32
Sherrill, Henry Knox
  (Rev.) 373
Sherrod, Celia A. 4
Sheshire, Homer Mayson
  178
Shi, Eliza Jane 244
  Jane (Mrs.) 244
  Samuel 244
Shields, (?) 227
  I. L. (Mrs.) 194
  James M. 270
  Laura O. 270
  Lawrence 194

Shields (cont.)
  Martha Ann 270
  Mary F. 270
  Reba Jane 194
Shiflet, Mae 67
Shingler, Adele Turner
  131
  George Pinckney 129
Shinholster, Sally 254
Shirley, (?) 340
  James 340
  Joseph 340
  Mary 340
  Matilda 340
  Susan Finch 340
  William Briant 340
Shivers, Barnaby 73,
  295, 296
  Christopher C. 295
  Cornelia Rebecca
    Randolph 296
  Eunice 295
  Francis M. 295
  Francis Marion 296
  Jabez S. 295
  Jabez T. 296
  Jonas 295, 296
  Jonas Cowin 295
  Lilory 296
  Lilory Rachel 295
  Martha M. 296
  Mary W. 296
  Patience (Mrs.) 295
  Rachel 296
  Rachel (Mrs.) 295
  Sarah M. D. 295
  Sarah R. 296
  Sarah W. 296
  Washington L. 295
  Washington Lafayet 296
  William Thomas 296
  Zachary T. 295
Shockley, Charity 225
Shockly, Andrew J. 370
  Benjamin S. 370
  Elizabeth 370
  Francis 370
  Friend O. 370
  Harriet S. 370
  James M. 370
  John 370
  Jonathan N. 370
  Mary Ann 370
  Michael L. 370
  Michael Leonard 370
  Susan 370
Shoemaker, Addie Jean
  224
Short, C. A. 23
  E. P. (Mrs.) 69
  John P. 23
  John R. 22
  Martha A. C. (Mrs.) 23
Showers, Margaret 110
Shropshire, Naomi 166
Shurley, Manda 170
Sibley, James Longstreet
  78
  Leila Lamar (Mrs.) 77,
    78
Sikes, Aleph Thomas 195
  Elizabeth (Mrs.) 132
  John 132
  Sarah Jane 196
  Teresa Maria 132, 133
Sikes?, F. M. 359
Simmons, (?) (Rev.) 356
  Ann Elizabeth Berry

Tate (cont.)
Samuel Alston 368
Thomas 369
William Andrew 368,
369
William Jasper 369
William Samuel 420
Willis 369
Tatum, Robert H. 291
Tawkesley, Polly 63
Tayloe, William 199
Taylor, (?) (Rev.) 243
A. C. 1
A. M. 456
Augustus C. 1
C. E. 456
Charlotte 457
E. Reginald 421
Edgar Reginald 421
J. G. (Rev.) 448
J. W. J. 457
John R. 329
Lottie 329
Malissa 1
Mamie Pauline 1
Martha Jane 316, 317
Mary 156, 332
Nina Caroline 421
Robert 351
Ruby G. 239
Ruby Garnett 239
Samuel C. 316
Stella 81
Stella Louisa 81
Tallulah F. 19
Zachary (Pres.) 332
Tazewell, Henry 199
Teagle, Lucy R. 2
Teal, Fannie 259
Teasley, B. C. (Mrs.)
337
Elizabeth (Mrs.) 337
Ethel 337
James Benson 337
Loyd 337
Lucy 67
Thomas W. 337
William M. 337
Teat, H. O. 200
Robert (Mrs.) 200
Tebeau, Frederick 302
Tedd, Stikepers Eni
Olifen 102
Telford, George Brown
435
Julia C. 67
Julia Caroline 66, 435
Templeton, W. L. 39
Terrell, Elizabeth
Bolloch 245
Lola G. 234
N. E. B. 234
Parks 234
R. P. 234
Terry, Jane A. 434
Jeremiah S. (Dr.) 39
Sarah (Widow) 39
Tharp, Louisa A. 442,
443
Thaxton, Annie Mervyn
222
Clyde Gray 222
Riley 222
Thoren 222
W. M. 222
W. M. (Mrs.) 222
Webb 382
These, John Holt 120

Thetford, Agnes Lockhart
376
Catherine 376
Elizabeth 376
Margaret (Mrs.) 376
Rebekah 376
Sarah 376
Walter 376
William 376
Thigpen, Kiziah 384
Tho---, (?) (Rev.) 322
Thomas, Alonzo 221
Annie Lee 221
Bryan Morel 258
Carlton (Mrs.) 162,
338
David Young 233
E. C. B. (Rev.) 231
Eddie 221
Eliza Neyle 48, 246,
258
Elizabeth A. 399
Elizabeth Lewis 246
Ezra 221
Green B. 245
Guy Bynum 233
Henry 2
Henry Percival 246
Henry Percival (Jr.)
246
J. D. 221
James 245
Jesse S. 233
Jesse Sanford 233
Joel 221
John 2, 75, 98
John C. 258
John David 223
John G. 75
John Greenberry 258
John S. 258
John S. (Mrs.) 258
John Sherrod 245, 246
Louie 221
Louisa M. 283
Martha A. 5
Martha C. 233
Martha G. 245, 258
Mary Bryan 75
Mary Catherine 233
Mary E. L. (Mrs.) 223
Mary Elizabeth Minerva
233
Mary F. 294
Mary J. 331
Mary Neyle 258
Nancy A. M. C. 2
Nealie E. 42
Nora 221
Sallie G. M. 233
Sallie May 233
Sarah Georgia Missouri
233
Sirena D. 5
Susan (Mrs.) 75
Susan Agnes 75
Susie May 236
Thomas C. 98
Wennie Berry 390
William Buie 233
William Campbell 246
William Sandford 233
Thomason, William Dewey
209
Thompson, Ann (Mrs.) 364
Ann M. 364
Anna J. 364
Asbury 363, 364

Thompson (cont.)
Birdie 392
C. A. 313
Caroline (Mrs.) 360,
361
D. W. 132
Dan 66
E. M. 439
Elisha 56
Elizabeth Ann 44
Elizabeth C. 306
Emma H. 16
Finney C. 65
James A. 364
James Anthony 363
James Martin 408
John 29, 129
John Robert 408
Joseph E. 364
Julia Ann Eliza 53
Kari 243
Kristie 243
L. A. 16
Linda Lee Hudd 243
Lucy 221
Mary E. 313
Mary Ella 313
Robert Dismukes 29
Ruth 221
Sarah 29, 129, 373,
374
Sudie 304
Susan 115
Susannah 115
William J. 364
Thomson, Mary Eunice 81,
82
Thorington, John 311
Thornton, Adeline Rivers
5
Betsy White 124
Biddy 28
Bridget 28
Cata 236
Elizabeth 122, 126
Elzabad 124
Elzy B. 122
Eppy 127
Eppy White 124
James A. 127
Jessie 332
John Martin 124
John Pope 257
Lucinda K. 127
Lucy 121, 123
Lucy (Mrs.) 124
Lucy T. 123
Margaret 270
Mark 124
Memorable 122, 124,
127
Parmelia A. (Mrs.) 127
Sally 124
Stephen Willis (Jr.)
257
Stephen Willis (Sr.)
257
Tabitha E. 127
Thomas 122, 124
Thomas B. 127
Wiley 28
William M. 127
Thorp, Joseph Paul 233
Thrash, William 318
Thrasher, (?) 151
Barton 151
David 151
Elizabeth 151

White (cont.)
Elizabeth W. 234
Elizabeth Wells 234
Emma Lauretta 126
Eppe 122
Eppie 127, 203
Eppy 120, 121, 122,
  123, 124, 126, 128,
  129
Eppy H. 14
Eppy Warren 125
Eugenia Herndon 126
Franky 120, 122
George Walton 126
Gertrude 15
Grady H. 234
Helen Ophelia 15
Henry 349
Hugh 217, 230
Isaiah 307
J. C. 41
J. F. 14, 128
J. Tom (Mrs.) 137,
  139, 158
James 217
James F. 14, 122, 123,
  124, 126, 128, 129
James Franklin 14, 122
James M. 125
James Walton 14, 15
James Washington 125
Jennie 110
Jere 120
Jeremiah 120, 121
Jeremiah Franklin 125
Jesse 234
Jesse M. 234
Jesse Marion 234
Jessie Borders Johns
  234
John 120, 121, 123,
  125, 217, 349
John (Jr.) 122
John (Sr.) 122, 123
John A. 14
John D. 123
John Daniel 125
John F. 123
John M. 14, 122, 124,
  126, 128
John M. (Sr.) 121,
  122, 123, 124
John Martin 120, 121,
  122, 123, 125, 126
John Martin (Jr.) 122
John Walton 15
Joseph Ballenger (Sr.)
  123
Lee A. 234
Lee Andrew 234
Lettice 120, 121
Lettie 121
Lettituce 121
Lucy 122, 307, 331
Lucy Ann 125
Lucy Thornton 121
M. M. 203
M. R. 14
Malissa E. 129
Malissa F. 123, 124
Malissa Frances 122
Malissa M. 14
Margaret 217
Martha 331
Martha Ann 127, 129,
  203
Martha C. (Mrs.) 203
Martha Cheeke 123

White (cont.)
Martha J. (Mrs.) 14
Martha M. 124, 129,
  322
Martha R. (Mrs.) 14,
  123
Martin 14, 120, 122,
  123
Mary 120, 122, 188
Mary (Mrs.) 121, 123
Mary A. L. (Mrs.) 126
Mary E. 15, 127, 338
Mary Ella Catherine
  126
Mary F. 122
Mary Frances 123
Mary M. 14, 120, 128
Mary Martin 121
Mary Mildred 123
Mildred 121
Mildred E. 123
Mildred Elizabeth 122
Mildred M. 127, 129
Milley (Mrs.) 121, 122
Millie 120
Milly 120, 123
Milly (Mrs.) 120, 123
Milly Thornton 123
Nancy Ann Clarissa 234
Nancy Kidd 120, 121,
  122, 125
Nancy Mann 121
Neal J. 14, 128
Oliver C. 14
Page 307
Patsey 121
Patsey E. 125
Patsey Gaines 121
Patsy 122
Patsy (Mrs.) 123, 125
Patsy Gaines 120
Polley Tonyhay 121
Polly 188
Polly M. 125
Polly Wade 125
Rachel 121
Rachel E. 122
Reba Johnson 15
Reuben 120, 121
Rhoda 331
Richard Livey 125
Robert 217
Roxie 330
Ruben 121, 122, 123,
  125, 129
Ruben Ballenge 125
Ruben Harrison 122
Ruby Duncan 15
Ruth P. 15
Sabrina Lucinda
  Aseneth 122
Sadie 349
Salley Morris 121
Sally 122
Sarah 121, 122, 331
Sarah Ann L. 234
Sarah Ann Lilis 234
Sarah C. 122, 127,
  128, 203
Sarah Catherine 122,
  129
Sarah F. 120
Sarah K. 14
Stephen 307, 331
Susan H. 234
Susan? Christopher?
  Mary? 234
Thomas 217

White (cont.)
Thomas E. 128
Thomas E. V. 14
Thomas H. 127, 203
Thomas Herndon 122,
  123
Thomas Hernon 122, 123
Thomas Lowndes 126
Thomas M. 125
Tilmon Davis Oxford
  234
Tom 350
W. Sanford 14
Walter Tillman 126
William 217
William Asa 123, 125
William C. 234
William Canady 234
William Lea Andrew 234
William Mayes 15
William P. 349
William Page 349
William V. 273, 319
hugh 217
mary 107
Whitehead, Addie Harper
  81
Alcey 83
Alice 83
Alver E. 349
Amaninthia 83
Amos 83
Amos (Jr.) 83
Anna (Mrs.) 333
Annie Estelle 333
Asa H. 333
Asbury P. 17
Asbury Parks 17
Bithiah 83
C. M. 82
C. M. (Mrs.) 82
C. T. 17
Catherina Matilda 83
Catherine Matilda 81
Charles Pritchard 81
Charles T. 17
Daisy V. 349
David 83
E. H. 17
Edward Bradford 83
Eldridge H. 17
Eldridge M. 17
Eleanor 81
Eleanor Eunice 81
Eliza C. 17
Eliza Matilda 83
Elizebeth 83
Eunice Thomson 81
Francis R. 17
George Arthur 83
George P. 333
George W. M. 17
Henry 81
J. B. 82
James 82, 83
James Edward 83, 332,
  333
James Fred 332, 333
James Troup 82, 83
Jane Pritchard 81
John 83
John B. 83
John Berrien 81, 82,
  83
John Berrien (III) 81
John C. 17
Julia 83
Kate 82

www.ingramcontent.com/pod-product-compliance
Lightning Source LLC
Chambersburg PA
CBHW070621270326
41926CB00011B/1766